D0605727

oyment Law

ew Challenges
siness Environment

an, J.D., M.B.A. Associate Professor
Wagner College

Prentice Hall
Upper Saddle River, New Jersey 07458

Sr. Acquisitions Editor: Donald J. Hull
Assistant Editor: John Larkin
Editorial Assistant: Jim Campbell
Editor-in-Chief: James Boyd
Director of Development: Steve Deitmer
Marketing Manager: Stephanie Johnson
Production Editor: Kelly Warsak
Production Coordinator: Renee Pelletier
Managing Editor: Valerie Q. Lentz
Manufacturing Buyer: Kenneth J. Clinton
Manufacturing Supervisor: Arnold Vila
Manufacturing Manager: Vincent Scelta
Design Director: Patricia Wosczyk
Interior Design: Ann France
Cover Director: Jayne Conte
Cover Illustration: SPG International
Composition: Pine Tree Composition, Inc.

A Simon & Schuster Company
Upper Saddle River, New Jersey 07458

Library of Congress Cataloging-in-Publication Data

Moran, John Jude.
Employment law : new challenges in the business environment / John Jude Moran.
p. cm.
Includes index.
ISBN 0-13-448250-6
1. Labor laws and legislation—United States. I. Title.
KF3455.M67 1997
344.73'01—dc20
[347.3041] 96-34105
CIP

Prentice-Hall International (UK) Limited, *London*
Prentice-Hall of Australia Pty. Limited, *Sydney*
Prentice-Hall Canada, Inc., *Toronto*
Prentice-Hall Hispanoamericana, S.A., *Mexico*
Prentice-Hall of India Private Limited, *New Delhi*
Prentice-Hall of Japan, Inc., *Tokyo*
Simon & Schuster Asia Pte. Ltd., *Singapore*
Editora Prentice-Hall do Brasil, Ltda., *Rio de Janeiro*

Printed in the United States of America

10 9 8 7 6 5 4 3 2

To
Dad
and
Grandmother Katherine Moran

Contents

Preface ix

Foreword xi

About the Author xiii

Part I Employment Relationship and Liability 1

Chapter 1 ***Employment Relationship*** 3

Types of Authority 4 ◆ Duties of Employees and Independent Contractors 6 ◆ Employer's Duties 8 ◆ Review Questions 10

Chapter 2 ***Employment Contract*** 12

Elements of an Employment Contract 12 ◆ Lawful Purpose 13 ◆ Agreement 13 ◆ Legal Capacity 16 ◆ Promise to Perform 16 ◆ Consideration 16 ◆ Execution in Proper Form 17 ◆ Validity of a Contract 19 ◆ Contractual Rights and Duties 19 ◆ Freedom to Contract 19 ◆ Significance of a Written Contract 19 ◆ Proper Application of State Laws 20 ◆ Assignment 22 ◆ Breach of Contract 23 ◆ Remedies 24 ◆ Contractual Defenses 28 ◆ Impossibility 32 ◆ Release 32 ◆ Mistake 32 ◆ Review Questions 33

Chapter 3 ***Employment Liability*** 36

Liability of Employees and Independent Contractors 36 ◆ Liability of Employers 38 ◆ Liability of Third Parties 50 ◆ Review Questions 51

PART II Employment Procedure 55

Chapter 4 ***Selection*** 57

Discrimination in Selection 57 ◆ Discrimination in Promotions 73 ◆ Review Questions 82

Chapter 5 *Testing* 84

Aptitude Tests 84 ◆ Residency Tests 86 ◆ Honesty Tests 88 ◆ Polygraph Test 88 ◆ Drug Testing 95 ◆ Review Questions 103 ◆ Employee Polygraph Protection Act 104

Chapter 6 *Privacy, Theft, and Whistleblowing* 107

Privacy Act of 1974 107 ◆ Omnibus Crime Control and Safe Streets Act 108 ◆ Electronic Communications Act 108 ◆ Fair Credit Reporting Act 108 ◆ Defamation 109 ◆ Invasion of Privacy 111 ◆ Interference with Business Relations 112 ◆ Employee Theft 114 ◆ Surveillance 116 ◆ Security 117 ◆ Company Policy 119 ◆ Whistle-Blowing 119 ◆ Review Questions 126 ◆ A Selective Amendments to the Constitution of the United States of America 128 ◆ Whistleblower Protection Act 129 ◆ Privacy Act of 1974 130

Chapter 7 *Termination* 132

Termination of Employment 132 ◆ Contesting the Termination 141 ◆ Model Employment Termination Act 142 ◆ Model Employment Termination Act 143 ◆ Retaliatory Discharge 147 ◆ Review Questions 154 ◆ Model Employment Termination Act of 1991 156

PART III Employment Discrimination 159

Chapter 8 *Civil Rights Act* 161

Introduction 161 ◆ Disparate Treatment 166 ◆ Disparate Impact 168 ◆ Retaliation 171 ◆ Equal Employment Opportunity Commission 171 ◆ Civil Rights Act of 1991 173 ◆ Exemptions 174 ◆ Advertising 175 ◆ Conclusion 175 ◆ Review Questions 176 ◆ Civil Rights Act of 1964 178 ◆ Civil Rights Act of 1991 196 ◆ Glass Ceiling Act of 1991 198

Chapter 9 *Affirmative Action* 201

Introduction 201 ◆ Title VII Violators 204 ◆ History of Affirmative Action 208 ◆ Equal Employment Opportunity Act 208 ◆ Affirmative Action Plan Guidelines for the Private Sector 210 ◆ Reverse Discrimination 211 ◆ Conclusion 221 ◆ Review Questions 222 ◆ Uniform Guidelines on Employee Selection Procedures (1978) 223

Chapter 10 *Racial Discrimination* 228

Introduction 228 ◆ Racial Harassment 239 ◆ Color Discrimination 241 ◆ Reconstruction Act 242 ◆ U.S. Constitution 242 ◆ Conclusion 244 ◆ Review Questions 244 ◆ Reconstruction Era Act of 1866 246

Chapter 11 *Sex Discrimination* 247

Introduction 247 ◆ Sex Plus Discrimination 254 ◆ Bona Fide Occupational Qualification (BFOQ) 260 ◆ Equal Pay 261 ◆ Comparable Worth 264 ◆ Grooming 265 ◆ Customer Preferences 267 ◆ Conclusion 270 ◆ Review Questions 270

Chapter 12 ***Sexual Harassment*** **272**

Introduction 272 ◆ Quid Pro Quo 287 ◆ Hostile Work Environment 291 ◆ A Model Sexual Harassment Policy 302 ◆ Conclusion 305 ◆ Review Questions 305

Chapter 13 ***Family Leave and Pregnancy Discrimination*** **307**

Family Leave 307 ◆ Pregnancy Discrimination 317 ◆ Fetal Protection Policies 321 ◆ Review Questions 332 ◆ Family and Medical Leave Act, 333

Chapter 14 ***Sexual Orientation*** **337**

Introduction 337 ◆ Conclusion 353 ◆ Review Questions 353

Chapter 15 ***Religious Discrimination*** **355**

Introduction 355 ◆ Accommodating Religious Beliefs 356 ◆ Bona Fide Occupational Qualification 362 ◆ First Amendment Protection 369 ◆ Conclusion 371 ◆ Review Questions 371 ◆ First Amendment to the Constitution of the United States of America 373

Chapter 16 ***National Origin*** **374**

Immigration Reform and Control Act 380 ◆ Conclusion 389 ◆ Review Questions 390 ◆ Immigration Reform and Control Act, 391

Chapter 17 ***Age Discrimination*** **394**

Age Discrimination in Employment Act 394 ◆ Conclusion 424 ◆ Review Questions 425 ◆ Age Discrimination in Employment Act of 1967 426

Chapter 18 ***Disability Discrimination*** **429**

Discriminating Against the Disabled 429 ◆ Reasonable Accommodations 429 ◆ The Future for Disabled Workers 436 ◆ Conclusion 437 ◆ Review Questions 437 ◆ Americans with Disabilities Act of 1990 439

Chapter 19 ***AIDS Discrimination*** **446**

Workers with Contagious Diseases 446 ◆ A Model for a Company Policy on AIDS 455 ◆ Review Questions 456 ◆ Rehabilitation Act of 1973 458

PART IV Employment Regulation **459**

Chapter 20 ***Labor Law*** **461**

History 461 ◆ Unions 462 ◆ National Labor Relations Act 464 ◆ Sherman Act 467 ◆ Railway Labor Act 468 ◆ Norris LaGuardia Act 468 ◆ The Future for Unions 468 ◆ Review Questions 478 ◆ Clayton Antitrust Act of 1914 479 ◆ Norris LaGuardia Act 480 ◆ Sherman Antitrust Act 483

Chapter 21 ***Collective Bargaining*** **484**

Introduction 484 ◆ Review Questions 496 ◆ National Labor Relations Act of 1935 497

Chapter 22 ***Wage and Hour Regulation*** **501**

Fair Labor Standards Act 501 ◆ Child Labor 511 ◆ Review Questions 512 ◆ Fair Labor Standards Act of 1938 514

Chapter 23 ***Occupational Safety and Health Act*** **516**

Introduction 516 ◆ Administrative Agencies 516 ◆ Secretary of Labor 517 ◆ Permanent Standards 517 ◆ Emergency Standards 519 ◆ Partial and Permanent Disability 522 ◆ Review Questions 532 ◆ Occupational Safety and Health Act of 1970 534

Chapter 24 ***Workers' Compensation*** **536**

Purpose 536 ◆ Reporting a Claim 536 ◆ Origination of Workers' Compensation 540 ◆ Workers' Compensation Board 541 ◆ False Representations 542 ◆ Employee Defenses 542 ◆ Review Questions 556

Chapter 25 ***Employment Retirement Income Security Act*** **558**

Introduction 558 ◆ Defined Benefit Plan 558 ◆ Defined Contribution Plan 558 ◆ Purpose 565 ◆ Fiduciary Duties 569 ◆ Inflation 572 ◆ Tax Incentives 580 ◆ Review Questions 580 ◆ Employee Retirement Income Security Act of 1974 581

Case Index **585**

Subject Index **588**

Preface

Employment Law is an area that is constantly changing. Decisions are being rendered that redefine the parameters of selection, discrimination, privacy, and termination. The number of cases involving disability discrimination is growing rapidly. Sexual orientation may soon be considered a suspect classification under gender discrimination. At-will employment may soon be displaced by the Model Termination in Employment Act's termination for cause contracts in lieu of an employee's right to sue. Arbitration will be the method for dispute resolution. The right of privacy advocates will continue to do battle with the proponents of drug and polygraph testing. As companies continue to find ways to improve the bottom line, diminishing employee theft of goods, services, and time will be a likely target. Surveillance will increase through the implementation of subtle methods.

Employment issues used to be handled by personnel departments with a director as the head. Now, a human resources division is often in place with countless more workers and a vice president as its leader. At the other end of the spectrum, NAFTA and GATT will make inroads against unions, labor laws, OSHA, workers' compensation, unemployment insurance, pension and health benefits, minimum and hourly wage laws, child labor laws, and the number of high-paying skilled and office positions through the deployment of jobs to Mexico and overseas where these laws are not in effect. The global business environment will entice companies to seek out the most efficient labor force per dollar of wages and the least expensive manufacturing plants and office space. American workers will have to work longer, harder, and more efficiently while continuously learning skills to keep them competitive.

Employment issues are now high profile. The study of employment law is important because of the impact it will have on businesses, management, and employees. The focus of *Employment Law: New Challenges in the Business Environment* is on discrimination and employment regulation. As with my first book, *Practical Business Law,* I have written this book presenting principles of law in a step-building approach and illustrating those principles with stimulating employment perspectives (there are more than 100 employment perspectives).

Employment Law: New Challenges in the Business Environment is a simple approach to employment law, with a foundation of legal principles explained in the layperson's language. The principles, once learned, can be applied to understand the judges' opinions in the cases presented.

The ultimate task in learning is to apply the principles of law to factual situations. This can be accomplished through the use of cases and chapter review questions to stimulate class discussions. Cases are included in each chapter that focus on the important principles of law to be learned. These cases are extracted from actual cases to enhance class discussions while providing the student with a pragmatic view of the reasoning behind court decisions. There are over 120 cases, most of which are recent cases decided in the 1990s. This provides the student with a text he or she can truly understand and appreciate. At the same time, the test affords the professor the opportunity to discuss the principles more fully by introducing his or her own examples and instances of practical experience.

Part I sets forth the parameters of the relationship between employer and employee and independent contractor. The distinction between an employer and independent contractor is identified. The rights and duties of the parties are spelled out in the employment contract along with the resulting liability should a breach occur.

Part II speaks to the procedure for selecting and testing employees. A considerable problem for employers is employee theft. Balancing the privacy interests of employees with the employer's desire to utilize testing, investigations, inspections, and surveillance is discussed. Finally, the issues of at-will employment, termination for cause and wrongful discharge are explained.

Part III presents the Civil Rights Act, affirmative action and the various forms of discrimination found in employment. Hot issues include sexual harassment, racial discrimination, disability discrimination, and sexual orientation. In particular, a chapter is devoted to AIDS discrimination because of the immense public concern over this disease.

Part IV addresses government regulation of the workplace with regard to unions, collective bargaining, minimum and maximum wage hours, safety, health, compensation for injuries, and pension and health benefits.

Finally, excerpts from the relevant statutes for each of the above topics are included. Instead of being placed in an appendix, these statutes will appear at the end of the chapter to which they are affiliated. This will promote greater use by the student through ease of access.

This book was written because of the timeliness and importance of employment law and its interaction with the business curriculum. It is important that students understand the impact employment law has on both management and employees.

Finally, I wish to express my sincerest gratitude and appreciation to the individuals who made the publication of this book possible: Don Hull, my editor at Prentice Hall, with whom I have now had the pleasure of writing two books; Diane Reinglas for her excellent typing proficiency and whose diligent effort and dedicated assistance were indispensable to me; Valerie Q. Lentz and Patty Sawyer for their efforts in the production of the book; Kelly Warsak for her tireless effort in making this book as perfect as possible; Peter Shedd for his insightful comments in his review of the manuscript; Charles Carbone and Ralph V. Parmegiani for their invaluable research assistance; and Jude Vanden-Heuvel, Michelle Fabozzi, Paul Fabozzi, and Anthony Mescali for their computer technical skills. A special word of thanks is due to my good friend and mentor of twenty years, Professor E. Donald Shapiro for writing a Foreword. Professor Shapiro is a brilliant legal scholar and a kind and compassionate individual. I am also indebted to Dr. Norman R. Smith, the President of Wagner College, for writing a Foreword. Through Dr. Smith's leadership, Wagner College has been transformed into one of the premier small colleges in America.

J. J. Moran, J. D.

Foreword

It is a privilege to write the foreword to this new textbook *Employment Law: New Challenges in the Business Environment.*

Professor John Jude Moran, a well noted authority in the employment field, has written a book which brings this fast-changing area of law up-to-date in a most lucid and perceptive manner.

Not so many years ago, Employment Law was one of the backwaters of the legal system. This is no longer true. The number of cases involving labor law has grown probably more rapidly than any other area of law in the last decade.

Sexual orientation appears to becoming a suspect classification under gender discrimination. This book deals with this challenging area in detail and with great understanding. Even more significant to those of us trained in the common law tradition, is the rapid changes occurring with "at-will employment," which is being changed beyond recognition from what we previously knew to be its parameters. Those of us who are keenly interested in privacy are being faced with the constant barrage of the demand by the government and employers for drug and polygraph testing. All of these subjects are dealt with in this book and dealt with well.

An entire new division in management has grown up in corporate America and that is the human resources division. Indeed, "human resources" is no longer merely a personnel department, but a major concern for most of corporate America. There are so many changes which have occurred in this area that one would almost have to write a book every month to keep the reader informed of the latest developments in labor law. NAFTA, GATT, OSHA, worker's compensation, unemployment insurance, health benefits, pension benefits, and so many more topics are dealt with by Professor Moran in an understandable and comprehensive manner.

What Professor Moran has accomplished is nothing short of a minor miracle. He has taken an extremely difficult subject matter and made it understandable to all of us who are not labor law specialists. This is a book which I know you will not only enjoy reading and from which you will learn, but also a book which will serve as a valuable resource tool in your future undertakings in this field.

There is no question that Professor Moran deserves high praise from all of us in the legal field as well as corporate America for what he has accomplished.

E. Donald Shapiro
The Joseph Solomon Distinguished
Professor of Law and Supernumerary Fellow
of St. Cross College at Oxford University

Foreword

As Professor Moran's latest text correctly observes, employment law is consuming more and more of every senior executive's time as the incidence of litigation launched by employees who believe they have been mistreated is skyrocketing. With the continued growth in the population of lawyers in the United States, it seems inevitable that no matter how careful an employer is, there will be a lawyer there to represent the cause of any employee who is unhappy with the way they have been treated by the employer.

Because of this new reality, a thorough knowledge of employment law has become a must for anyone expecting to manage people in the years to come, not only in corporations, but in virtually any organization hiring and compensating people for work.

As in Professor Moran's *Practical Business Law* text, this new book is easy-to-read and comprehend. The full array of legal considerations facing employers from the many ways in which employees can accuse employers of discrimination to the changes in labor law and employment regulation is presented. The text will better prepare current and future managers for this challenging and omnipresent aspect of their responsibilities.

Dr. Norman R. Smith
President
Wagner College

About the Author

John Jude Moran was born in Bay Ridge Brooklyn on November 17, 1956. After graduating from Xaverian High School at the age of sixteen, John received his Bachelors Degree in Business Administration from St. John's University's Notre Dame College in two years at the age of eighteen. John then attended New York Law School from which he received his Doctor of Law Degree at the age of twenty one. John's first teaching experience was at the City University of New York, which he began while still in law school. John also taught part-time at St. John's University MBA program. After becoming a member of the New York Bar, John worked for a law firm and then a corporation in Manhattan.

In 1982, John moved to Cameron Lake in Staten Island. At this time, John began writing his first book, *Practical Business Law*. This book was published in 1985. It is now in its third edition and has been used in almost 100 colleges in the United States and six foreign countries. John returned to St. John's University to pursue an MBA in Finance, which he received at the age of thirty.

After teaching at St. Peter's College for one year, John became a member of Wagner College's faculty in 1985. He has served as Chairman of the Department of Business Administration and is currently an Associate Professor. John still resides in Grasmere, Staten Island, with his dogs, Muffin, Cuddles, and Honey Bunch.

PART I

Employment Relationship and Liability

CHAPTER 1

Employment Relationship

The word *employment* may be defined as the rendering of personal service by one person on behalf of another in return for compensation. The person requesting the service is the *employer.* The person performing the service may be either the *employee* or an *independent contractor.* Employment law has its roots in the law of agency.

Agency is a contractual relationship, involving an agent and a principal, in which the agent is given the authority to represent the principal in dealings with third parties. The most common example is an employer-employee relationship wherein an *agent* (employee) is given the power by a *principal* (employer) to act on his or her behalf. An agent may be an employee or an independent contractor. A principal is a person who employs an agent to act on his or her behalf.

A principal (employer) has full control over his or her employee. The employee must complete the work assigned by following the instructions of the employer. An independent contractor is an individual hired by an employer to perform a specific task. The employer has no control over the methods used by the independent contractor. The following are among those who act independently of an employer: electricians, carpenters, plumbers, television repairpersons, and automobile mechanics. Independent contractors also include professional agents such as lawyers, physicians, accountants, securities brokers, insurance brokers, real estate brokers, and investment advisors. Independent contractors may also employ others in their field who will be bound to them as employees.

Employment is a contractual relationship wherein the employee or independent contractor is given authority to act on behalf of the employer. All the requirements of contract law are applicable to the creation of employment. Both the employer and the employee or independent contractor must have the capacity to contract.

CASE

Eyerman v. Mary Kay Cosmetics, Inc.

967 F.2d 213 (6th Cir. 1992)

GUY, Circuit Judge.

Debi Eyerman, an independent contractor, was terminated from her position as a National Sales Director for Mary Kay Cosmetics because of her alcoholism. She had a drunk-driving conviction, an accident attributed to alcohol, and behaved poorly at a meeting due to her inebriated condition. Eyerman was informed she could file for disability.

The law provides,

"It shall be an unlawful discriminatory practice: For any employer, because of the race, color, religion, sex, national origin, handicap, age, or ancestry of any person, to discharge without just cause, to refuse to hire, or otherwise to discriminate against that person with respect to hire, tenure, terms, conditions, or privileges of employment, or any matter directly or indirectly related to employment."

Alcoholism is one of the handicaps protected by this provision.

This issue is whether the relationship between an employer and an independent contractor is covered by the above statute.

The court ruled, "We decided that independent contractors would be covered by Title VII if, under an 'economic realities' test, they are susceptible to the types of discrimination Title VII meant to prohibit." Economic realities is determined by ". . . the employer's ability to control the job performance and employment opportunities" of the independent contractor.

The court continued, ". . . there is no indication in the record that Mary Kay Cosmetics controlled Eyerman's work in any significant way.

Judgment for Mary Kay Cosmetics.

An employment contract may be created expressly, through a writing or a verbal conversation, or impliedly, through the actions of the parties. However, if the employee's or independent contractor's duties involve entering into a contract on behalf of the employer, which is required to be in writing under the statute of frauds, then the employment contract must also be in writing. The statute of frauds is a list of those contracts required to be in writing.

TYPES OF AUTHORITY

Actual Authority

The scope of an employee's authority is usually determined by the employer. Actual authority is the express authority conveyed by the employer to the employee, which also includes the implied authority to do whatever is reasonably necessary to complete the task. This implied authority also gives the employee power to act in an emergency. Implied authority is authority which the employee actually has. It comes with the job.

Employment Perspective

Charlie Moore is a garage mechanic at the Seagate Service Station. His actual authority is limited to servicing automobiles. He has no authority to enter into contracts with customers for his services and has no authority to decide on which cars he will work. One day while the gas attendant is out to lunch, a customer pulls up to the gas pump. Does Charlie Moore have the authority to service the customer? Yes! Inherent in the authority delegated to Charlie is the implied authority to perform those routine tasks necessary for the continuation of the business when the other mechanics or gas attendants are out to lunch or otherwise occupied. Is Charlie an employee or an independent contractor? If Charlie works exclusively for Seagate, he would be an employee. For example, if a boy threw a brick through the office window and it had to be repaired before closing, Charlie would have the authority to board up the window or have a glazier replace the glass—assuming that the service station manager could not be notified—because Charlie would be acting in an emergency. ♦

Apparent Authority

Apparent authority is the authority the employee professes to have which induces a reasonable person to believe in the employee. The reliance on apparent authority must be justifiable. With apparent authority, the employee appears to have the authority to act, but he or she actually does not.

Employment Perspective

In the previous example, suppose Charlie is alone at the service station, finishing a tune-up on a Monte Carlo, when Arthur Moriarity drives up in his Rolls-Royce. Charlie had previously been assigned by his manager to perform a brake job on this Rolls six months ago. Moriarity recognizes Charlie and informs him that there is a rumbling sound in the engine. Charlie inspects the engine and informs Arthur Moriarity that the valves are worn and need to be reseated. Moriarity agrees to leave the car overnight. The next morning Charlie has completed the valve job, but the engine's rumbling has become worse. When Moriarity calls for the Rolls-Royce, he threatens to sue the service station for negligence in its attempted repair of his car. Can the service station raise the defense that Charlie Moore acted without authority. No! Although Charlie did not possess the actual authority to bind the Seagate Service Station to a contract, he appeared to have the authority in entering into the contract of repair. Arthur Moriarity was justified because a reasonable person would believe a garage mechanic would possess the authority to decide whether a car could be repaired at the service station for which he or she worked. ♦

Lundberg v. Church Farm, Inc.

502 N.E. 2d 806 (Ill. App. 2 Dist. 1986)

UNVERZAT, Judge.

Church Farm, Inc., purchased a well-bred stallion named Imperial Guard for $700,000 in 1982. Thereafter, Gil Church, owner of Church Farm, Inc., advertised the breeding rights to Imperial Guard. The price was $50,000, and all inquiries were to be directed to Herb Bagley, manager.

Vern Lundberg signed a contract with Herb Bagley entitling Lundberg to three breeding rights to Imperial Guard in the 1982 and 1983 breeding seasons. Upon syndication in 1984, the breeding rights were to be converted into one share of ownership in Imperial Guard. This part of the contract was signed "Herb Bagley" and "Gilbert G. Church by H. Bagley." The contract also provided that the horse would remain at Church Farm in Illinois unless 50 percent of the shareholders voted to move him. This portion of the contract was signed "Church Farm, Inc., H. Bagley, Manager." The contracts were on printed forms.

Between the 1982 and 1983 breeding seasons, Gil Church moved Imperial Guard to Oklahoma without giving notice to the shareholders. Unable to exercise his 1983 breeding rights, Lundberg brought an action for damages. Gil Church argued that Bagley was not authorized to sign the contracts nor was he given the authority to add or amend its terms. Lundberg retorted that he dealt exclusively with Bagley. The issue is whether Bagley had the apparent authority to bind Church Farm, Inc., to the contract with Lundberg.

The court declared that an employee's apparent authority is that authority which the employer holds his employee out as possessing. In view of the employer's actions, it is the authority a reasonable person would naturally presume the employee to have.

The court stated, "Plaintiffs produced evidence at trial that Gil Church approved the Imperial Guard advertisement listing Herb Bagley as Church Farm's manager and directing all inquiries to him. Church also permitted Bagley to live on the farm and to handle its daily operations. Bagley was the only person available to visitors to the farm. Bagley answered Church Farm's phone calls, and there was a preprinted signature line for him on the breeding rights package."

The court concluded, "The conclusion is inescapable that Gil Church affirmatively placed Bagley in a managerial position, giving him complete control of Church Farm and its dealings with the public."

Judgment for Lundberg.

DUTIES OF EMPLOYEES AND INDEPENDENT CONTRACTORS

Duty of Loyalty

The relationship between employers and employees or independent contractors is a fiduciary one, based on trust and confidence. Inherent in this relationship is the employee's or independent contractor's duty of loyalty. An employee has a duty to inform, to obey instructions and to protect confidential information. An employee or independent contractor has a duty to disclose all pertinent information he or she learns of that will affect the employer, the employer's business, or the task at hand. An employee or independent contractor must not take advantage of the employer's prospective business opportunities or enter into contracts on behalf of the employer for personal aggrandizement without the employer's knowledge. An employee, and in some cases an independent contractor (lawyer, investment banker, sports-team scout), may not work for two employers who have competing interests.

Employment Perspective

Peter Stapelton works as a sales clerk and mechanic in South Shore Auto Parts and Repair Shop. One day Stapelton is approached by Malcolm Ripkin, owner of Ripkin's Limousine Service, who informs him that he would like South Shore to maintain his fleet of seventeen limousines. Stapelton takes Ripkin's card, but instead of passing it along to the owners of South Shore, he decides to negotiate with Ripkin on his own behalf. Stapelton reasons that if he can get the contract for the maintenance of the seventeen limousines, it would enable him to establish his own auto repair station. Stapelton enters into a personal service contract with Ripkin and then contracts with South Shore to purchase all the supplies he needs at wholesale prices. Six months later, South Shore learns of Stapelton's disloyalty. What recourse does the company have? South Shore may sue Stapelton for breach of contract because he violated his duty of loyalty in failing to disclose Ripkin's offer and in taking advantage of South Shore's business opportunity. Stapelton also contracted on behalf of South Shore for his own benefit without informing the company of what he was doing. Stapelton will be liable to South Shore for consequential damages—that is, the loss of profits South Shore sustained because of Stapelton's unauthorized contracts made on behalf of South Shore with himself at wholesale prices. South Shore will be able to recover the difference between the wholesale price and the retail price, and may also fire Stapelton for his disloyal actions. ♦

Duty to Act in Good Faith

An employee or independent contractor has an obligation to perform all duties in good faith. He or she must carry out the task assigned by using reasonable skill and care. The employee or independent contractor has a further duty to follow the employer's instructions and not to exceed the authority delegated to him or her.

Employment Perspective

Steve Torrino worked in a Burger King Restaurant for three years. During his employment, he felt that the manager was continually mistreating him by using abusive language, assigning him hours which purposely conflicted with his class studies, and making him perform janitorial services that were not included in his job description. When an opening arose at a nearby McDonald's on a late shift, Torrino accepted the position, but he retained his regular job with Burger King. During the manager's absence one busy Saturday afternoon, Torrino neglected his routine duties and took charge of the cash register. He proceeded to give away three Whoppers free with every purchase of a small soda. He informed the customers that it was an anniversary celebration. Torrino's intent was to repay the Burger King manager for his unkindness by causing him to lose profits. What recourse does the Burger King manager have against

Torrino? Torrino violated his duty of loyalty to Burger King by working for a competing employer, McDonald's, and by purposely causing Burger King to lose profits. Torrino refused to obey instructions to perform his delegated duties. He exceeded his authority through the authorization of a free offer. If Torrino was displeased with his job, he should have left to find another position rather than allowing his resentment to build up for three years. In all respects, Torrino violated his duty to act in good faith. ♦

Duty to Account

An employee or independent contractor has a duty to account for all compensations received, including kickbacks. Upon the employer's request, an employee or independent contractor must make a full disclosure, known as an accounting, of all receipts and expenditures. The employee or independent contractor must not commingle funds but rather must keep the employer's funds in an account separate from his or her own. Furthermore, an employee or independent contractor must not use the employer's funds for his or her own purposes.

Employment Perspective

Ted Murphy is a securities broker at a branch office of Pearlman & Associates, located in Silver City, New Mexico. All of Murphy's clients signed an agreement appointing him as their agent to buy and sell securities. Murphy would often borrow from individual accounts in order to further his own investment opportunities. He did this without informing either the client or the company; Later he would repay the amount borrowed. Since Silver City is not a large city, many clients make deposits in cash. Murphy would stamp the deposit slip but then deposit the cash in his own account, expecting to repay the money at a later date. Finally, Murphy has a streak of bad luck and is unable to repay the money before the monthly statements are sent out. The clients sue Pearlman & Associates and Ted Murphy, for conversion of the funds in their accounts. What recourse does Pearlman & Associates have against Murphy? The company may sue Murphy for breach of contract and for reimbursement of any of the clients' losses. Murphy breached his duty of loyalty, his duty to act in good faith, and his duty to disclose fully all deposits he received. He commingled clients' funds with his own for the purpose of furthering his own investment schemes. ♦

EMPLOYER'S DUTIES

Duty to Compensate

An employer has the duty to compensate the employee or independent contractor for the work performed. An employee or independent contractor will be entitled to the amount agreed upon in the contract; otherwise he or she will be entitled to the reasonable value of the services rendered. Sales representatives are usually paid according to a commission-based pay structure, which incorporates a minimum level of compensation against which the sales representatives are entitled to draw. An employer must also reimburse an employee for the expenses incurred by the employee during the course of conducting the employer's business. For tax purposes, an employer has

a duty to keep a record of the compensation earned by an employee and the reimbursements made for expenditures. Employers are required to withhold payroll taxes from employees' paychecks. This is not so with fees paid to independent contractors.

Duty to Maintain Safe Working Conditions

The maintenance of safe working conditions is another obligation placed on the employer. Any tools or equipment furnished to the employee must be in proper working order; otherwise, the employer may be liable for the harm resulting to an employee under the Occupational Safety and Health Act.

An employer's liability is not always based on strict liability and therefore not always absolute. There are circumstances where an employee's own negligence will bar recovery.

CASE

Plouffe v. Burlington Northern, Inc.

730 P.2d 1148 (Mont. 1986)

SHEEHY, Judge.

Douglas Plouffe sued Burlington Northern for injuries he received while on the job. Plouffe asserts that these injuries resulted from Burlington Northern's failure to abide by the Federal Safety Appliance Act. This statute was enacted to provide railroad employees and the public with protection from defective equipment on railroad cars and locomotives that might cause them injury.

The accident occurred when Plouffe was attempting to free a stuck hand brake on a railroad car. After bleeding the brakes and attempting to turn the hand brake wheel, Plouffe bent down to rattle the chain connected to the brakes under the car. As he did this, the hand brake slipped, knocking him on the head.

The issue is whether Burlington Northern is absolutely liable for the injury sustained where Plouffe may have been contributorily negligent.

Contributory negligence is not a factor in determining whether the Safety Appliance Act (Title 45 U.S.C. 53) has been infringed. The act states that ". . . no such employee who may be injured or killed shall be held to have been guilty of contributory negligence in any case where the violation by such common carrier of any statute enacted for the safety of employees contributed to the injury or death of such employee."

The court stated, "To prove liability as a matter of law, Plouffe need only to have established a 'defect or insufficiency' due to the railroad's negligence."

Judgment for Plouffe.

Employment Perspective

Dolores Wright, an agent of the Green Bay Housing Authority, is in charge of tenant complaints regarding lack of heat and hot water. She is a part-time employee who works only during the winter months. Wright's office is in a three-story building located in the downtown section and owned by the city. In February, the building's oil burner malfunctioned. Dolores Wright made numerous calls to her superiors, but no action was taken. When Dolores called the oil company people, they said the burner needed to be replaced. It was not replaced. Of her own volition, she bought and paid for a heater, insulated her office, and continued to work through the month of February. At that time, she became ill with pneumonia and was hospitalized. Since she was a part-time employee, the city did not pay for her medical plan. She thereupon sued the city for her medical bills, loss of compensation while she was hospitalized, and the expenses she incurred in attempting to make the office habitable during the month of February. Is she entitled to be reimbursed? Yes! The city is liable for her medical expenses because it failed to provide her with a safe and healthy working environment. She is entitled to compensation for the time she lost from work because the lost time was directly caused by the city's negligence. Also she is entitled to reimbursement for the expenses she incurred in attempting to create a healthy environment in the office. If Dolores never reported the burner's malfunction, would the city have been liable? No! Dolores must put the city on notice to cure the defect before it results in harm to an employee. What if Dolores in a fit of rage or frustration threw a chair through a window and became ill eventually from the cold air blowing in. Would the city be responsible for her illness? No! Dolores caused the problem by her own purposeful act. ♦

REVIEW QUESTIONS

1. Define *agency, principal, agent, employment, employer, employee,* and *independent contractor.*
2. What is the difference between express and implied actual authority? Give an example of each.
3. What is apparent authority? Give an example.
4. Define the employee's duty of loyalty, and give an example of a breach of that duty.
5. Define the employee's duty to act in good faith, and give an example of a breach of that duty.
6. Define the employee's duty to account, and give an example of a breach of that duty.
7. Define the employer's duty to compensate.
8. Explain the employer's duty to maintain safe working conditions.
9. What is the main difference between an employee and an independent contractor?
10. Why does employment create a fiduciary relationship?
11. Fortune was a sales representative for National Cash Register for twenty-five years. After a customer in his sales territory placed an order for $5 million, Fortune was terminated. He alleged that the company wanted to avoid paying him a commission in accor-

dance with their employment contract. What was the result? *Fortune v. National Cash Register,* 364 N.E.2d 1251 (Mass. 1977)

12. Lukaszewski was hired as a speech therapist by the Michigan Handicapped Children's Education Board. She was assigned to a school 45 miles from her home. After renewing her contract for another year, she was offered a similar position at a day care center for more money prior to the commencement of the new school year. This position was near her home. The education board refused to accept her resignation. Thereafter, she resigned for health reasons. The education board replaced her with a person commanding a salary of $1,000 more than Lukaszewski had been paid. Is Lukaszewski in breach of contract? *Handicapped Children's Education Board v. Lukaszewski,* 332 N.W.2d 774 (1983)

13. Debi Eyerman worked her way up through the ranks of Mary Kay Cosmetics until she was appointed a national sales director. At that time, she signed a National Sales Director Agreement, which provided that Eyerman would be an independent contractor, not an employee, and that she would earn a commission based on the performance of her sales group. Eyerman was required to maintain an office, provide advice to salespersons, and to attend meetings when necessary. She was given no power to enter into a contract on behalf of Mary Kay Cosmetics, and the company would exercise no control over her as well. Either party could cancel the agreement upon sixty days' notice. Is Eyerman an employee or an independent contractor? *Eyerman v. Mary Kay Cosmetics, Inc.,* 967 F.2d 213 (6th Cir. 1992)

14. Lorentz was hired by Coblentz, who had an appliance-repair business. Lorentz had to provide his own truck and stock his own parts. At 8:00 every morning, Lorentz had to call in to receive his assignments for the day. He was paid a 50 percent commission. Coblentz withheld federal payroll taxes. Is Lorentz an employee or an independent contractor? What was the result? *Lorentz v. Coblentz,* 600 S.2d 1376 (La. App. 1 Cir. 1992)

15. Mrs. Amoroso was injured by a defective crossbar on a sailboat, which she and her husband had rented at the Diplomat Hotel. The sailboats were owned and operated by Sunrise Water Sports. The rental stand was on the hotel's grounds, the rental fee was billed to the hotel room, and the rental service was advertised in the hotel room. Mrs. Amoroso sued the Diplomat on the theory of apparent authority. What was the result? *Amoroso v. Samuel Friedland Family* Ent., 604, So.2d 827 (Fla. App. 4 Dist. 1992)

CHAPTER 2

Employment Contract

This chapter will address the elements of an employment contract, the contractual rights and duties of the parties, the freedom the parties possess to create their own rights and duties, the proper application of state laws and the significance of a written contract. Assignment of employment contracts is discussed next with its impact on both parties.

If either the employer or the employee or independent contractor does not perform as promised, then a breach of contract occurs. This is explained along with the various remedies, which the aggrieved party may sue for. The fact that a party sues for a remedy does not automatically mean that party will win. The other party may have had a justifiable defense for not performing as promised. These defenses are presented in detail.

ELEMENTS OF AN EMPLOYMENT CONTRACT

An *employment contract* is a legally enforcable agreement. For an agreement to be legally enforceable, the following elements must be present: a mutual agreement, executed in proper form, voluntarily made by two or more capable parties wherein each party promises to perform or not to perform a specific legal act for valuable consideration. Each element in this definition must be satisfied by each party for the contract to be valid. The validity of the contract is what gives it legal effect. The elements of an employment contract are:

- Lawful purpose
- Agreement
- Legal capacity
- Promise to perform
- Consideration
- Executed in proper form

LAWFUL PURPOSE

The purpose for which the employment contract was consummated and the acts undertaken to accomplish that purpose must be lawful. *Lawful* means that the purpose and the acts must not contravene any federal statute or any statute of the state which has subject matter jurisdiction over the contract. When both the means employed and the end result are consistent with the law, then the contract will be valid. If the agreement contemplates the performance of an illegal act or the achievement of an illegal purpose, the contract is invalid.

Restrictive Covenants

Contracts not to compete are generally found to be not in the best interests of the public. However, contracts containing a covenant not to compete may be lawful where the contract involves employment. A clause in an employment contract may prevent an employee from working in the same field for a certain length of time. The courts do not look with favor upon such clauses and enforce them only when the employee's knowledge of trade secrets or the future of the business is at issue. The enforcement of employment restrictions usually applies to management.

AGREEMENT

An agreement is arrived at through an offer by an employer, which is accepted voluntarily by the employee or independent contractor. An agreement, in and of itself, is not binding because it has no legal obligation without the other five contractual elements. Often the terms *contract* and *agreement* are used interchangeably. Keep in mind that for the two terms to be synonymous, the other five elements giving rise to a legal obligation must be present.

Death or Incompetency

Death or incompetency of either the employer or the employee or independent contractor terminates the offer. This applies where the employer is an individual or individuals, not a corporation. An offer is personal, and if the offeror dies, the offer dies with that person. This situation is generally true whether or not the other party has been notified. An offer is enforceable only by the person to whom it is made; if the employee dies, no one else has the power to accept it. A contract is not terminated by incompetency or death, because certain legal obligations have been created that must be carried through. Otherwise, physicians and hospitals would hesitate to make contracts with terminal patients for fear of not getting reimbursed. An exception to this rule would be personal service contracts. An individual's services are unique; there is no way to enforce the contract or provide a remedy. Because an offer has no legal obligations offers generally do not survive the people who make them or the people to whom they are made.

CASE

Decker, Berta and Co., Ltd. v. Berta

587 N.E.2d 72 (Ill. App. 4 Dist. 1992)

STEIGMANN, Judge.

Raymond Berta was a partner in the Decker, Berta and Co. Accounting firm. When the business was sold, he remained as an employee and signed the following document:

"RESTRICTIVE COVENANT. For a period of three (3) years from the date of the termination of his employment, the Employee will not, within a thirty-five (35) mile radius of any present places of business of Employer, directly or indirectly own, manage, operate, or control, or be connected in any manner with any business of the type and character of business engaged in by the Employer at the time of such termination."

The contract also contained the following covenant:

"DISCLOSURE OF INFORMATION. The Employees recognize and acknowledge that the list of the Employer's customers, as it may exist from time to time, is a valuable, special, and unique asset of the Employer's business. The Employees will not, during or after the term of their employment, disclose the list to the Employer's customers or any part thereof to any person, firm, corporation, association, or other entity for any reason or purpose whatsoever. In the event of a breach or threatened breach by an Employee of the provisions of this paragraph, the Employer shall be entitled to an injunction restraining said Employee from disclosing, in whole or in part, the list of the Employer's customers. Nothing herein shall be construed as prohibiting the Employer from pursuing any other remedies available to him for such breach."

When the contract expired, Berta joined another accounting firm. He brought his father-in-law's account with him. Berta also phoned several other former clients, asking them to switch firms. Decker, Berta and Co. sought a preliminary injunction alleging Berta violated the restrictive covenant. There are two types of restrictive covenants: employment and sale of business. Employment contracts face a much stricter test with regard to restraints.

The issue is whether this restrictive covenant is part of the employment contract or the sale of the business.

The court concluded that the seller ". . . purchased Decker, Berta and Co., Ltd. upon the premise that the firm would continue to be operated by Charles R. Decker and Raymond Berta. If either one or both of them left to do accounting work on their own or for another accounting firm, it was conceivable that the firm's clientele would be lost to the departing employee or employees. The purchaser would be left with an office lease, some computers, and whatever personal property is needed by an accounting firm. His assumption and payment of $237,200.00 in firm debts and contract to purchase the firm would have been rendered totally illusory. Therefore, the court concluded that the plaintiff had proved the employee's services were indispensable and part of the agreement to purchase the business."

Judgment for Decker.

CASE Central Adjustment Bureau, Inc. v. Ingram

678 S.W.2d 28 (Tenn. 1984)

DROWOTA, Judge.

Henry Ingram was employed by the Central Adjustment Bureau (CAB) on March 1, 1970. One week later he was asked to sign a restrictive covenant which read, "I, /s/, the undersigned, during the term of my employment with Central Adjustment Bureau, Inc., and/or its wholly-owned subsidiaries, and at any time within two years of termination thereof, shall not compete within the United States, either directly or indirectly with the corporation (1) by owning, operating, managing, being employed by, having a proprietary interest of any kind in, or extending financial credit to any person, enterprise, firm or corporation which is engaged in any business in which the corporation is engaged or directly or indirectly competes with the corporation in any manner; (2) by divulging any information pertaining to the business, trade secrets, and/or confidential data of the corporation, or make any use whatsoever of the same; or (3) by contacting any client or customer of the corporation who has been a client or customer of the corporation during the term of employment.

"I fully understand that the corporation will rely on this covenant in employing me, and I agree that in the event of any breach of this covenant that the corporation's damages are irreparable and that the corporation shall be entitled to injunctive relief, in addition to such other and further relief as may be proper."

Ingram signed the restrictive covenant only after threatened with expulsion. By 1977, Ingram had been promoted to manager of the northern region of CAB. Two years later, he resigned. Prior to this resignation, Ingram opened his own collection agency, which solicited CAB customers with whom Ingram had personal contact.

The court set forth the basic rule of law: "As a general rule, restrictive covenants will be enforced if they are reasonable under the particular circumstances. The rule of reasonableness applies to consideration as well as to other matters such as territorial and time limitations."

The issue is whether the restrictions are unreasonable, and if so, whether they can be modified.

The court concluded, ". . . Ingram made plans and took action prior to his resignation to acquire a proprietary interest in a collection agency, which was intended to operate in direct competition with CAB."

The court concluded that although the geographic scope of the restriction was too broad, Ingram was competing with CAB in the very areas in which he worked. The court upheld CAB's claim invoking the rule of reasonableness. The court stated, "The rule provides that unless the circumstances indicate bad faith on the part of the employer, a court will enforce covenants not to compete to the extent that they are reasonably necessary to protect the employer's interest without imposing undue hardship on the employee when the public interest is not adversely affected."

Judgment for CAB.

Employment Perspective

Joseph Fredericks was a vice president at the Bank of America. One spring evening while eating dinner at the home of his friend Stephen Pearson, talk drifted around to Patricia Pearson, who was about to receive her M.B.A. degree. Fredericks, who had always been fond of her, told her parents he would like to offer her a job in the bank's mortgage service department at a starting salary of $30,000, to begin two weeks after she received her degree. Patricia was ecstatic on hearing the news of Fredericks's offer. On returning home from the university, she hurried down to the bank to thank her benefactor, only to learn that he had been killed the night before in an automobile crash. Patricia and her family were in shock. A few days after the funeral services, she informed the bank of Mr. Fredericks's offer to hire her, but she was refused employment. Did Mr. Fredericks's offer die with him? Yes! Patricia's acceptance of the offer was precluded by his death. ◆

LEGAL CAPACITY

For a contract to be valid and enforceable, the parties involved must have the legal capacity to enter into a contract. Since the parties are binding themselves to a legal obligation, each one must be competent to contract. They must be responsible for their actions to assure that the performance of their promises will be completed in accordance with the terms of the contract. The fulfillment of the requirements of legal age and sanity give rise to the presumption that a party is capable of entering into a contractual relationship.

PROMISE TO PERFORM

A promise is a commitment to perform or not to perform a specific act, in the present or in the future. The act must be one that is possible to perform, not something illusory. The parties become legally obligated to perform the act when they make their promise to perform. The performance of the act is the reason why each party entered into the contract.

CONSIDERATION

Consideration is something valuable given in exchange for something valuable received. The promise to perform a certain act or acts is the consideration given by each party. Generally, what is given need not be identical in value to what is received. It is sufficient that the performance of the act has some intrinsic value. In an employment contract, monetary compensation is given by the employer in return for the employee's or independent contractor's personal services.

Prior Legal Obligation

A promise to pay more than the agreed price for the performance of an existing contract, or a promise to accept less than the amount owed, has no valuable consideration unless something additional is given to serve as consideration. When a person promises to perform an act which he or she is legally obligated to perform, this does not constitute valuable consideration. A contract based on a promise of this sort is not valid and cannot be enforced. This rule concerning preexisting legal obligations applies to people's duty to observe the law, to individuals who have responsibilities through public service and public administrative positions, and to parties bound by contract. For example, police officers cannot enter into a contract with a homeowner to keep watch over his or her house while he or she is away. The police officers are already employed to protect the neighborhood by the town or city.

Promissory Estoppel

When a person changes his or her position in reliance on a promise, and that change in position is foreseeable, the person making the promise will be stopped from asserting that there is no consideration to enforce the contract. This is the doctrine of *promissory estoppel.* It is equitable in that enforcement of a promise may be upheld for reasons of fairness and justice even though the recipient of the promise gave no consideration in return. To invoke the doctrine of promissory estoppel, the person making the promise must reasonably expect it to motivate the other person to change his or her position by taking some substantial and justifiable action in reliance on the promise. The person taking the action must be going to suffer a detriment for his or her reliance on that promise if it is not carried out. This is the reason for enforcing the promise—to prevent the person relying on the promise from suffering a loss.

Employment Perspective

It was the middle of a scorching hot summer. Timothy Woodwirth, who worked on the night shift for the Brooklyn D.A.'s office, was out pounding the pavement during the day in his three-piece suit looking for a higher paying position. He entered the reception area of the law firm of Collins, Egbert, and Phillips. He informed the receptionist of his request for an interview and she notified Mr. Phillips. Mr. Phillips spoke to Timothy and then introduced him to Mr. Egbert. After the interviews, Timothy was offered a position with a salary of $25,000. He was to begin work in two weeks. In the interim, Mr. Collins returned from an extended vacation. He strenuously objected to the hiring of Timothy because of his lack of experience in civil litigation. As senior partner in the firm, he won out. Meanwhile, Timothy had resigned from the D.A.'s office and was ready to begin work when he was advised of Mr. Collins's decision. Has Timothy any recourse? Yes! Although Timothy gave no consideration in return for the promise made by Mr. Egbert and Mr. Phillips to hire him, he relied on their promise by resigning from the D.A.'s office to work for their firm and thus suffered a real detriment, loss of a job. Under the doctrine of promissory estoppel, the law firm must compensate Timothy for lost wages until he finds another suitable legal position. ◆

EXECUTION IN PROPER FORM

Certain contracts are required to be executed in writing in order that they be valid. This requirement is referred to as the statute of frauds requirement, the main purpose of which is to prevent fraud. Whenever possible, all contracts, except those of nominal value, should be reduced to writing in order to evidence the existence of a contract. This is to avoid ambiguity and to protect the parties involved. An employment contract which will continue in existence for more than one year must be evidenced by a writing.

Statute of Frauds

Employment contracts with a duration of performance in excess of one year are required to be in writing. This requirement includes contracts in which the duration is either fixed or indefinite. The majority of states also require contracts requiring forbearance for more than one year to be in writing. However, if there is a possibility, no matter how remote, that a contract may be completed within one year, no writing is required. The reason for this rule is that it avoids future problems in long-term contracts difficult to resolve because of witnesses who relocate, lose their memory, or die. The measurement of time generally commences on the day after the contract is entered into—not the day that performance begins—and runs until performance is completed. This arrangement assures the parties that the time limitation will expire on the anniversary of the day the contract is made.

The Writing Requirement

To satisfy the statute of frauds, the writing of a contract must be sufficiently clear and understandable, and capable of being enforced on its face without an oral explanation. This is not to say that certain oral modifications or explanations are not admissible, but to evidence the existence of a contract, the writing must stand alone. The writing must include the following material terms: subject matter, time, identification of the parties, price, number (quantity), and delivery place.

The writing itself may be a formal written contract, a note, or a memorandum. The writing may make reference to other writings or letters as long as there is some continuity between them. The party against whom enforcement is sought, or an agent of that party, must sign the writing. It need not, however, be written and signed at the time the parties exchange promises as long as this requirement is taken care of prior to a lawsuit by one of the parties. Until the promises are put in writing and signed, they are not legally enforceable. Some states require that a party's contract with his or her agent be in writing where the contracts the agent will be entering into are required to be in writing by the statute of frauds. A signature written in pencil, stamped, or typewritten will usually be as valid as one written in ink. Oral contracts may be substantiated when the material terms are set forth by a writing such as a check, an invoice, a sales slip, or a receipt.

Courts try to determine the parties' principal objective and look at everything else in light of that. Words are given their usual meaning except if they have special significance when used in a trade or business. In such cases, the special meaning will be given precedence. The court will assume that the common practices and procedures of the trade or business will be followed unless the parties specifically state otherwise. Contracts are strictly construed against the party who drafted them and in favor of the other party as long as his or her interpretation is reasonable. Written additions to standard-form contracts will take precedence over the printed matter in these types of contracts.

VALIDITY OF A CONTRACT

A valid employment contract, which is created by the presence of the six elements, can be enforced in a court of law should a breach arise. If one or more of the contractual elements are lacking, then the contract is void. A void contract can be carried out by the parties, but it is not a legal contract and cannot be enforced in a court of law.

CONTRACTUAL RIGHTS AND DUTIES

An employment contract is a legal relationship comprising certain rights and duties. A duty arises to perform specifically what is promised. This duty is a legal one that, if breached, gives the aggrieved party a legal cause of action. A cause of action is a right to sue for a legal remedy. The remedy most often awarded is money damages; however, under certain circumstances, the court may grant equitable remedies. In certain instances, the individual committing the breach may have had just cause for doing so. This just cause will be raised as a contractual defense which, if proven, will relieve the individual from liability for the breach of contract.

FREEDOM TO CONTRACT

Our capitalistic system was formed with a reliance on competition; and its purpose is to maintain free, open, and continuing competition. This is to guarantee fair competition, safe working conditions for employees, and equal employment opportunities.

The parties to a contract have the freedom to set up their own rights and duties concerning such things as payment, and time and place of delivery. This freedom facilitates the smooth and efficient operation of business and individual transactions. Freedom to contract is a well-established principle of contract law. The United States Constitution, in Article I, Section 10, prohibits any state from passing a law impairing the obligation of contracts. Although freedom to contract is a fundamental right in this country, it is not absolute. Contracts which unreasonably restrain trade are illegal and unenforceable. Contracts that involve price fixing and discrimination, or that are unconscionable, are invalid because they are unduly harsh or one-sided. Except for certain limitations such as the ones just mentioned, freedom to contract is protected by the Constitution and by the laws of the individual states. The states set up laws for the interpretation of contractual terms and for the enforcement of promises. These form the laws of contracts.

SIGNIFICANCE OF A WRITTEN CONTRACT

Generally, there is no problem with the validity of an oral contract; the difficulty arises in trying to *prove* its existence. Many valid contracts are dismissed by the courts because their terms cannot be proved. In an oral contract, if one party does not fulfill his or her obligation, the other party, without witnesses, will have an arduous task trying to prove the existence of the contract. The old saying "It's my word against yours" is very true and applicable to oral contracts. Even with witnesses, there are still problems. Over a period of time, witnesses tend to forget; their testimony is often conflicting and may even be perjured. For convenience, simple contracts, particularly those of nominal value, tend to be oral; but valuable and important contracts should be in writing to evidence their existence. All states have recognized this principle by adopting a statute of frauds requiring certain contracts to be in writing. The main purpose behind the statute is to prevent fraud by requiring evidence of the contract's existence. This procedure protects the parties involved by avoiding misunderstandings. A contract expressed in oral or written form is referred to as an *express contract.*

Employment contracts are personal service contracts. Personal service contracts are contracts in which one person promises to perform a service for an employer in return for the employer's promise to provide compensation for the services rendered. Personal service contracts include employment contracts, in which an individual is employed on a salary basis, as well as contracts with professionals or independent contractors, in which performance is on an hourly or per case basis.

PROPER APPLICATION OF STATE LAWS

Each state has its own law of contracts. State laws are enacted to interpret and enforce contracts. When terms or phrases are ambiguous, a conflict may develop. The courts interpret the contract to determine the intention of the parties. The language of the contract is construed according to its fair and reasonable meaning. This determination is made by considering the language within the context of the entire transaction. There must be some substantial connection between the state and the contract or the parties to the contract for the state to have jurisdiction. The state must have sufficient interest to interpret the contract and legally enforce the rights and duties of the parties involved. To determine the proper application of state laws, the following rule applies: When a contract is made between two parties of a state and the contract is to be performed in that state, the law of that state will govern. Personal service contracts are generally governed by the state in which substantial performance is to be rendered; however, as stated before, the parties may stipulate otherwise.

Employment Perspective

The Daily Times, located in Idaho, has a contract with Glazer and Globe, a local law firm, to represent them in contract negotiations with the Merlin Printer's Union. When a contract will be performed in a state other than the one where the parties are located, there is a presumption that the law of the state where performance will take place will govern. The Times has a separate contract with Star Delivery to deliver newspapers across the Idaho border into Montana. The presumption is that Montana law will govern. The parties may override this presumption by stipulating in the contract that the law of the state where the contract is made, Idaho, will govern. ◆

Employment Perspective

The Daily Times in Sun Valley, Idaho, buys the *Morning Star* newspaper, which is based in Jupiter, Florida. Mike Marra signs a contract with the Planet to be editor-in-chief of the *Morning Star.* After six months, the Times is suing Mike Marra for non-

CASE
Respect Inc. v. Committee on the Status of Women

781 F.Supp. 1358 (N.D. Ill. 1992)

SHADUR, District Judge.

Must developed a sex education program called Sex Respect. She negotiated with the Committee on the Status of Women to write three books related to the program, which would be published by the United Communications of America. Must claimed that she and the committee entered into a contract to develop both the books and the program and that she would be compensated for this work as well as to retain rights in the publication. The committee maintained that she would be paid a fixed fee for the publications in return for relinquishing her rights to future compensation from the publications. There is nothing in writing to this effect. It is an oral agreement.

The issue is whether an oral agreement for services is enforceable.

The court held, ". . . an oral contract is unenforceable unless by its terms it is capable of full performance within one year, as measured from the date of its making. . . . By Must's admission, the pilot program was to run for more than one year . . . hence the contract is unenforceable."

Judgment for the Committee.

performance of his duties. Which state law governs? Florida's because it is the state where performance is to be rendered. Could this have been altered by contract? Yes, the parties could designate Idaho law if they wish. ◆

The limitations set forth in the contract must be reasonable. The courts will not enforce restrictions upon employees that are unduly harsh and permit employers to derive more protection than that necessary to guard their secrets or to protect their business interests.

Employment Perspective

David Williams bought a liquor store on the South Side of Chicago. He hired Brian Jackson to manage the store for him. A provision in the contract prohibited Brian from opening a liquor store within the city limits for the rest of his natural life. After learning the trade, Brian quit and opened his own place in the downtown section of Chicago known as the Loop. Can David enforce the provision? No! The provision is too broad in its geographical area and much too unreasonable in its time restraints. ◆

Employment Perspective

AT&T hires Francine Pell and Rita Morse to perfect their telephone and telegraph systems by an oral agreement made on January 1. Pell is to begin work on April 1 and to complete the work on January 31, ten months later. Morse, who is eighty-seven years of age, has a lifetime contract. Neither agreement is in writing. Are the contracts enforceable? Pell's contract is not enforceable. To be enforceable, it must be in writing because its duration is thirteen months, commencing at the time the contract is made—January 1. This situation is true even though Pell does not begin to work until April 1. Morse's contract is enforceable. A lifetime contract does not have to be in writing because it is possible that the person may die within one year of making the contract. ◆

ASSIGNMENT

An *assignment* is the transfer of an employer's or employee's rights in a contract to a third person. Parties transfer their contractual rights to a third person: (1) as payment of a debt; (2) in exchange for payment or performance; or (3) as a gift. The party making the assignment is known as an *assignor.* An assignor is one of the original contracting parties, who is seeking to transfer his or her contractual rights, and possibly his or her contractual duties, to a third person. The third person, to whom the assignment is made, is called an *assignee.* The other original contracting party is referred to as an *obligor.* An obligor is one who owes a duty to perform for an assignee because of an assignment. It is also possible that an assignor or an assignee owes a duty to perform for the obligor.

An assignment must be differentiated from a *novation.* A novation is an agreement made by three persons wherein one of the two original contracting parties is released from all contractual liability through the substitution of a third person. A novation is actually a new contract with the third person, assuming all the rights and duties of the party who has been relieved. In an assignment, an assignor is still accountable under the contract even though the assignor's rights and duties have been transferred to a third person. An assignment is not a new contract because there is no agreement to release the assignor from liability.

Employment Perspective

Bob Hill owns a cattle ranch in Texas. Because an irrigation system is needed to maintain fertile grazing areas, Claude Eastman is hired to construct the irrigation system. A short time later, Bob Hill sells the ranch to John Long, a retired justice, who wants to raise cattle for investment purposes. Eastman agrees to release Hill and render performance for John Long, who has assumed the duty to pay. Subsequently, Eastman is offered a much larger irrigation project in the prairie lands. He assigns his rights and duties under the contract to Timothy Scott, who is equally competent. What is the relationship of the parties in the two situations? The first is a novation. Bob Hill, an original contracting party, is released from all responsibility, while John Long steps into his shoes. The second is an assignment. Eastman, the assignor, assigns his rights and duties under the contract to Tim Scott, the assignee. Scott thereby becomes primarily liable for performance; however, Eastman can also be held accountable, if Scott does not perform. ◆

Clause in Contract Forbids Assignments

A contract containing a clause stating that assignments cannot be made without the consent of the obligor is generally not favored. However, a person may be restricted from assigning an employment contract when his or her duties involve special skill, knowledge, expertise, judgment, character, trust, or confidence. In these instances, clauses prohibiting assignments will be enforced as long as consent is not unreasonably withheld.

Employment Perspective

The circus has come to town! The world-renowned trapeze artists, the Gemini Twins, are the main attraction. There is a covenant in the contract restricting the Gemini Twins from assigning their rights and duties under the contract. Is this covenant enforceable? Partially! The Gemini Twins' duty to perform is properly restricted because it involves special skills and experience. Their right to payment may not be limited. Would the restrictive clause be valid if applied to the sellers of popcorn and peanuts? No! Their task is routine and can be performed by almost anyone. ◆

Alteration of Obligor's Duties

An assignment may not be made that will materially alter the obligor's duties either by placing a greater burden on the obligor to perform or by changing the performance altogether. The obligor may be either the employer or the employee or independent contractor, depending on which party made the assignment.

Employment Perspective

Beefhouse Bob, Inc. makes weekly deliveries of beef to Bill Fields, who operates a Steak and Bake Restaurant in Tulsa. This week the restaurant is overstocked, so Fields assigns his contract with Beefhouse Bob, Inc. to a Steak and Bake Restaurant in Oklahoma City. Must Beefhouse Bob, Inc. perform according to the assignment? No! The assignment has substantially altered his duties under the contract by requesting him to perform in another city that is a great distance away. ◆

Risk Increased to Obligor

Assignments that increase the risk an obligor must endure under a contract will not be allowed.

Employment Perspective

Bongo was a clown in the Sells Floto Circus. Subsequently, the circus was sold and the performer's contracts were assigned to the new owner, who requested Bongo to perform in the lion's den. Must Bongo accede? No! Bongo's contract may not be assigned in this case because it increases the risk of physical harm. ◆

BREACH OF CONTRACT

Most employment contracts are completed without significant problems. Parties generally fulfill their promises under the contract. Breach of contract occurs when a party does not fulfill his or her promise to perform. The breach, which is a failure to perform a material contractual obligation, may take the form of renunciation of the contract, restraining the other party's performance, as well as failure to perform. A breach may be either partial or total. It may be material, incidental, or anticipatory.

A material breach is substantial and goes to the heart of the contract. The other party may treat the contract as canceled and terminate performance.

Employment Perspective

Eleanor Hanley, who is eighty-five years old, lives alone. On a Monday afternoon while she is watching "General Hospital," the picture suddenly disappears. Eleanor quickly telephones Artie's Television Repair Shop. Artie comes to her house and after inspecting the set, tells her he can make it work perfectly for $75. He makes the adjustment, and she pays him. Fifteen minutes later, the picture abruptly disappears again. In a state of agitation, she telephones Artie, and he returns to her apartment. This time he tells her he must take the set back to his shop. An hour later, he calls to say he has encountered major complications with her set and the cost to repair it will be $150. Eleanor tells him she does not want to spend that much money on it and asks him to please return the set and refund her $75. He returns the set but refuses to refund the $75. Has Eleanor Hanley any recourse? Yes! Artie promised to repair the set for $75 but failed to make good on it. Because he has materially breached the contract, she is entitled to a return of her $75. ◆

Incidental breaches involving minor defects occur where substantial performance has been rendered. The party for whom performance was rendered still has a duty to perform. However, he or she has a cause of action for damages to remedy the incidental defects.

Employment Perspective

Donna Eastwood brings her 1966 Plymouth Fury to Max's Service Station. The car has 108,000 miles on it. Donna asks Max to inspect the car and inform her of the necessary repairs. Max tells her the car needs a rebuilt transmission, new shock absorbers, new windshield wipers, and replacement of radiator hoses. Donna authorizes the repairs, which total $875. As she drives the car home, it begins to rain, and she notices the windshield wipers have not been replaced. She decides to stop payment on the check. Would she be well advised to do so? No! All the major repairs have been made. This is an incidental breach. Either Donna should return to the service station and demand that they replace the windshield wipers, or she should issue a new check for the cost of all repairs made except the wipers and request the return of her original check. ◆

REMEDIES

Contractual remedies are the means by which a legal right is enforced where there has been a breach of contract. The purpose of a remedy is to restore the party harmed by the breach to as favorable a position as would have been the case had the contract been carried out as promised, or to the same position he or she had been in before the contract came about. This goal may be accomplished either through compensation or through prevention of the breach. There are two categories of remedies: legal and equitable.

Legal remedies are enacted by the federal and state legislatures and are found in statutes. Equitable remedies can also be granted by the courts for reasons of fairness and justice.

Equitable remedies are granted when the legal remedy that is usually provided would result harshly upon the innocent party. In requesting an equitable remedy, the party must have acted in good faith and commenced the lawsuit without unnecessary delay. Equitable remedies are preferable, especially when the breaching party has little or no money to pay for the loss. These remedies also prevent a party who is breaching the contract from becoming unjustly enriched at the expense of the party who is suffering the loss. In many cases, parties may elect the remedies which they prefer. However, where remedies are conflicting, parties are limited to choosing only one. For example, in a breach of contract involving refusal to sell a house, the aggrieved party is not entitled to specific performance as well as money damages.

Injunction

An *injunction* is an equitable remedy that prevents a party breaching a contract from rendering the same performance elsewhere. An injunction is personal in nature and negative in effect in that it precludes a person from performing certain acts. In cases involving personal service contracts, this remedy is used instead of the remedy of specific performance, because specific performance cannot be granted to compel parties to perform services against their will. However, since the breaching party cannot be compelled to perform a certain act, an injunction can prohibit the party from performing the same act elsewhere. An injunction acts as a restraint against the party breaching a personal service contract.

Employment Perspective

Wild Bill Cary is under a five-year contract with the Texas Tornadoes to play quarterback for them for $100,000 per year. After leading his team to successive central division titles, he is offered a four-year contract from the Hawaii Hurricanes for $500,000 per year. There are still three years remaining on Wild Bill's contract with Texas, but he decides to accept Hawaii's offer. Can Texas prevent Wild Bill from quarterbacking for Hawaii? Yes! An injunction can be granted, but Texas cannot legally force Wild Bill to quarterback for them through specific performance. Wild Bill is bound to Texas for the three years remaining on his contract unless they renegotiate his contract or trade him. The terms of Wild Bill's original contract were designed to protect him from being cut from the team while insuring him a substantial yearly salary. After the contract expires, Wild Bill will have free agent status. ◆

Specific Performance

Specific performance is granted where the only way to fulfill the party's reasonable expectations is to force the breaching party to perform the contract and where the remedies of money damages and rescission are inadequate. Specific performance can be obtained

CASE

Madison Square Garden Corporation v. Carnera

52 F.2d 47 (2dCir. 1931)

CHASE, Circuit Judge.

Madison Square Garden asked for an injunction to restrain Carnera from engaging in a boxing match with Sharkey. The Garden alleged that to permit such a match would be a breach of the restrictive covenant, which would cause them irreparable harm.

Primo Carnera was a professional heavyweight boxer. He entered into an exclusive contract with the Garden to fight the winner of the Schmeling-Stribling contest for the heavy weight title of the world. The contract provided that if the fight with either Schmeling or Stribling did not occur within nine months, Carnera would no longer be bound by the contract's terms. The restrictive covenant provides:

> 1. Carnera agrees that he will render services as a boxer in his next contest, which contest shall be with the winner of the proposed Schemling-Stribling contest . . . at such time, not, however, later than midnight of September 30, 1931, as the Garden may direct . . .
>
> 9. Carnera shall not, pending the holding of the First Contest, render services as a boxer in any major boxing contest, without the written permission of the Garden in each case had and obtained. A major contest is understood to be one with Sharkey, Baer, Campole, Godfrey, or like grade heavyweights. . . .

. . . Subsequently Carnera entered into a contract to box Sharkey before the match with either Schmeling or Stribling. Carnera contends that nowhere in the contract is a match with Schmeling or Stribling agreed upon. Carnera is pledging his services to the Garden for nine months with the hope that such a match can be arranged. If the match does not materialize, Carnera receives no compensation.

The issue is whether Carnera is bound by the restrictive covenant and whether an injunction is the appropriate remedy to enforce it.

The court held that the restrictive covenant is enforceable because its terms were reasonable and voluntarily agreed upon by the parties. An injunction is the appropriate remedy because Carnera's services are unique, and because money damages cannot easily be measured. The court also required the Garden to give Carnera a bond for $35,000. This amount is to compensate Carnera for the loss he would sustain because of the injunction, if the heavyweight title contest never materialized.

Judgment for Madison Square Garden.

only in contracts involving something unique. Subject matters which are unique include real estate, art, antiques, other rare items, and stock of a closely held corporation.

The remedy of specific performance does not apply to personal service contracts, including employment and construction contracts. Although these contracts are unique, parties in breach cannot be forced personally to perform them. To do so would relegate a breaching party to involuntary servitude, which is in violation of the United States Constitution. A meaningful performance could not be assured because the courts do not have the capabilities to monitor mandatory personal performance or to judge whether or not it is adequate. The equitable remedy of specific performance will also not be granted where the result would be unconscionable.

Rescission and Restitution

Rescission and restitution can be both legal and equitable remedies, depending upon whether they are provided by statute or invoked equitably by the court's discretion. *Rescission* is the cancellation of the contract; *restitution* is the returning of the parties to the position they were in before the contract came about. Restitution requires each party to give back the consideration they received and return to the status quo. The right to rescind will expire if the party continues to perform under the contract. This right will also expire if not exercised within a reasonable time. The party wishing to rescind must evidence his or her intent by giving prompt notice.

Employment Perspective

Mable Johnson hires Mark McCormick to build a wall surrounding her estate. Johnson pays McCormick $100,000. McCormick agrees to use a strong bonding cement. Upon inspection, Johnson discovers that McCormick is using the cheapest cement available. This cement will crack and can easily be demolished. What recourse does Johnson have against McCormick? Johnson can rescind the contract because of the material breach caused by McCormick's fraud. McCormick must make restitution by returning the $100,000, and he may also be liable for money damages caused by the delay in construction that will result because of his breach. ◆

Compensatory Damages

The parties to a contract have the right to have their reasonable expectations fulfilled in accordance with the contract. *Compensatory damages* have the effect of awarding the injured party the same benefits that he or she would have received had the contract been carried out as promised.

Employment Perspective

Tree Planters, Inc. had a contract with Big Apple Corp. to plant apple trees along the west coast of the state of Washington. Tree Planter's fee was $1000 per mile, but for every mile not covered before the end of the year, it had to repay $100. An early winter caused Tree Planters to abandon its journey in Seattle 50 miles short of its destination. What are the damages recoverable by Big Apple? Five thousand dollars. The damages stipulated in the contract may be recovered because the parties agreed to these damages, and they are reasonable. ◆

Punitive Damages

Punitive damages are awarded to penalize the party who commits a wrong that injures the general public. These damages are assessed in addition to the compensatory damages awarded to the injured party, usually in cases involving fraud. Punitive damages are not actually a contract remedy, because the law does not exact punishment for breach of contract by itself. When the breach of contract also constitutes a tort, then the court may award punitive damages for the tort in addition to the compensatory damages for the breach of contract. The purpose of punitive damages is both to act as a deterrent to future offenses of a similar nature and to compensate the victim for the mental anguish suffered.

Employment Perspective

Daniel Revson, who lives in Forest Hills, Queens, has been working for General Motors in New York for twenty-five years. Revson receives a promotion and is transferred to Detroit to oversee assembly production. He calls a branch office of Find-A-Home real estate and asks them to find him a six-room apartment in Grosse Point. Five days later, the real estate saleswoman telephones Mr. Revson to notify him of such an apartment for $1,200 a month, which is the going rate for a luxury apartment in the heart of Grosse Point. A lease and a letter of explanation arrive two days later. Revson signs the lease and mails it to the Find-A-Home, along with a check for $3,600: one month's rent, one month's security, and the brokerage fee. Two weeks later, Revson moves to Grosse Point, or so he thought. The address on his copy of the lease proves to be a floor in a modest house on the fringe of Grosse Point. Revson sues the brokerage for compensation and asks the court to award punitive damages. Will they be granted? Yes! Revson is entitled to the return of his $3,600, together with any incidental expenses, such as hotel bills, incurred in trying to find another apartment in Grosse Point. Punitive damages may also be awarded to punish Find-A-Home real estate for the fraud committed and to deter them from committing any future harm. ◆

Duty to Mitigate Damages

Upon learning of a breach, an innocent party has a duty to mitigate damages. This means that the innocent party must, in good faith, attempt to keep the damages as low as possible without incurring any undue risk or expense. A party who does not make a reasonable attempt to mitigate damages will be barred from recovery.

Employees under contract who have been terminated without cause have a duty to mitigate damages by making a good faith effort to seek similar employment elsewhere. The employee need not, however, accept a lower position or look for employment beyond the general vicinity.

CONTRACTUAL DEFENSES

The fact that someone sues for a remedy for breach of contract does not automatically mean they will win. The other party may have a valid reason for not performing as promised. What follows is a recitation of a number of justifiable contractual defenses.

Fraud and Misrepresentation

Misrepresentation is a false statement of a material fact which is justifiably relied on by a person to his or her detriment. If the misrepresentation is intentional, then it is fraudulent. Intent to deceive is the characteristic that separates a fraudulent misrepresentation from an innocent one; it is established by proving the falsity of the representation at the time it was made. The knowledge will be imputed to the party making the statement where that party should have known that the statement was false or that party made the statement in reckless disregard of whether it was false or not.

Employment Perspective

Philip Dodger is a con artist who devises a scheme and employs his innocent young friend, Oliver Tubbs, to carry it out for him. Dodger knows that Mr. Bramley, a wealthy gentleman, is interested in purchasing a thoroughbred horse. He tells Oliver to inform Mr. Bramley that for $20,000 they will deliver a fine horse. Mr. Bramley, believing that this is a good deal, gives Oliver a $10,000 down payment. Bramley trusts Oliver's judgment because he has known him since he was a small boy. Oliver believes that his representations are true. The next day, an old mare is delivered to Mr. Bramley, but he refuses to pay for it. In a suit brought by Oliver and Philip Dodger for nonpayment, what defenses could Mr. Bramley raise? Bramley could raise the defense of fraud against Dodger, because Dodger intentionally deceived Bramley through the false representations that he had Oliver make concerning the horse. Bramley's reliance was justified because of his trust in Oliver. Bramley could raise the defense of misrepresentation against Oliver even though Oliver acted innocently. Bramley's remedy against both parties would be rescission and out-of-pocket damages—$10,000 less the value of the horse received. Bramley would probably not be entitled to punitive damages because the fraud was personal and not perpetrated against the general public. If the particular thoroughbred described in this contract existed, Mr. Bramley would be entitled to the benefit of the bargain—the difference in the value of the horse received and the value of the horse he would have received had the representation been true. ◆

CASE

Hayes v. Equine Equities, Inc.

480 N.W.2d 178 (Neb. 1992)

BOSLAUGH, Judge.

David Hayes bought an office condo from John Chudy. At the time, Hayes expressed an interest in horses. Chudy suggested to Hayes that they buy a horse together called Chocolate Marquis from Equine Equities for $50,000. Chudy told Hayes he had someone lined up to purchase the horse for $75,000. Hayes put up 60 percent of the money and was promised the same share of the profits. There turned out to be no buyer after several reassurances and other delay tactics. Unbeknownst to Hayes, Chudy held a 50 percent interest in Equine Equities and later purchased Chocolate Marquis for $1,300. Hayes sued Chudy and Equine Equities for fraud. He asked for rescission and a return of the purchase price. The defendants claimed the representations were mere sales talk.

The issues are whether the statements were fraudulent or mere puffing and whether Hayes did not promptly seek rescission.

The court held, "Chudy's statements were positive representations of fact upon which Hayes could rely, and the statements did not constitute sales talk or puffing in the sense which the law implies." The court concluded, "Hayes' delay in bringing the action was excused by 1) the continued reassurances by Chudy (not disputed) [;] 2) the later discovery of the horse's true cost to Equines."

Judgment for Hayes.

CASE *Vokes v. Arthur Murray, Inc.*

212 So.2d 906 (D.Ct.App. Fla. (1968))

PIERCE, Judge.

Vokes sued the Arthur Murray School of Dancing for rescission of a contract for dance lessons. The plaintiff contends that she entered into the contract because of fraudulent representations made about her dancing ability.

Audrey Vokes, a widow for over fifty years, had no family. She had a yearning to become "an accomplished dancer" and to develop a new interest in life. She was invited to a dance at Davenport's Dance School, a local franchise of Arthur Murray's School of Dancing. She took free dancing lessons with the instructors while constantly being barraged with flattery and compliments about her dancing potential. She was baited with a trial offer of eight half-hour lessons for $14.50.

The come-on worked over a period of time, for the dance school was able to induce her to buy fourteen dance courses, totaling over 2,300 hours of lessons. The cost was over $31,000. The fourteen course enrollments are evidenced by Arthur Murray's School of Dancing Enrollment Agreement.

The inducement used by the dance school included compliments concerning her grace and poise, and about her rapidly improving and developing dancing skill. She was informed that the lessons would "make her a beautiful dancer, capable of dancing with the most accomplished dancers." The plaintiff was even given dance aptitude tests to determine how many additional hours she needed.

She was sold 545 additional hours at one stage, which qualified her for the "Bronze Medal." Thereafter, 926 hours were added for the "Silver Medal," 347 hours for the "Gold Medal," and finally 481 hours for the classification "as a Gold Bar Member, the ultimate achievement of the dancing studio." The defendant also cajoled the widow into buying a life membership which allowed her to take a trip to Miami at her own expense, where she was "given the opportunity to dance with members of the Miami Studio." She was also talked into buying still more hours in order to be eligible for trips to Trinidad and Mexico, again both at her own expense. In reality, Mrs. Vokes had no "dance aptitude" and actually had difficulty in "hearing the musical beat." She was told she was entering into the "spring of her life," but actually there was no spring in her life or in her feet.

The defendants contend that their misrepresentations relate to opinions, not facts.

The issue is whether a contract can be rescinded where it was entered into through reliance on fraudulent opinions.

The court held that the parties were not of equal bargaining strength, and that the dance studio used their greater strength to their advantage. The studio's opinion of the plaintiff's dancing ability is considered to be one of superior knowledge, equivalent to a statement of fact, because of the studio's expertise. The hours of instruction were unjustified, because Mrs. Vokes lacked ability for improvement. If they had told her the truth, she would have realized this. The widow justifiably relied on their opinion to her detriment.

Judgment for Vokes.

Failure of a Condition

A condition occurs when the parties' contractual duties are contingent upon the occurrence of a future event. Parties must expressly agree when making the contract if they are conditioning their obligations on the occurrence of a particular event. Depending on whether the condition is worded positively or negatively, the occurrence of the future event may or may not require the parties to perform their contractual obligations. The condition may be expressed that if the event occurs, contractual obligations exist. Here, failure of the condition would discharge the parties from their obligations. The party who must satisfy the condition has a duty to make a good-faith effort in that direction by taking positive steps. There are two types of conditions: conditions precedent and conditions subsequent.

Conditions precedent require a future event to occur before parties are obligated to perform their contractual duties. The condition must be satisfied before the contract can be performed. If the condition is not satisfied, the contract is unenforceable.

Employment Perspectives

The Jester, a world famous comic actor, had planned a world tour. He entered into a contract with Armond to serve as his bodyguard if the World Tour took place. The tour was subsequently cancelled through no fault of the Jester. In a suit by Armond for breach of contract, the Jester then raised the defense of failure of a condition precedent. Is this a good defense? Yes! This is a good defense because the condition had to be complied with before the Jester would be bound by the contract. ◆

Conditions subsequent involve existing contracts where parties must continue to perform their contractual obligations until the condition is not satisfied. Once the condition is not satisfied, the contract can no longer be enforced and the parties are excused from performing their duties under the contract. The difference in a condition subsequent is that there is an existing contract, and as long as the condition is satisfied, the contract will be enforceable.

Employment Perspective

Michael Caruso hires Susan Wood through a local employment agency to be his all-purpose secretary until Theresa Mackey, his original secretary, returns from an extended illness. When Theresa returns, the condition subsequent will be satisfied, and the employment contract with Susan Wood will terminate. ◆

Conditions may be implied where the circumstances reasonably indicate that the parties assumed the contract would be conditioned on some stipulated event. Conditions may also be implied where the type of contract entered into necessitates implying certain conditions. Courts may likewise imply conditions for reasons of fairness and justice. Where one party has substantially performed, the fact that every detail was not completed may not be raised as a failure of condition.

IMPOSSIBILITY

Impossibility of performance refers to situations in which it is impossible for the contract to be performed either by the party under contract or by anyone else. Impossibility may be of a permanent or a temporary nature. Permanent impossibility will discharge the parties from their contractual obligations. Temporary impossibility will generally suspend the duty to perform until the impossibility diminishes. At that point, the duty to perform is revived. Personal inability to perform, alone, will not release the parties from their contractual obligations.

Employment Perspective

Yellowknife Mining hired Dawson Metals, specialists in metallurgy, to build a machine which would remove impurities from the gold they found through dredging. Although Dawson Metals used various heating procedures and other methods, they were unsuccessful in their attempts. Yellowknife sued them for breach of contract. Dawson Metals claimed the defense of impossibility. Yellowknife hired another firm at greater expense who was successful. Is the defense used by Dawson Metals viable? No! Personal inability to perform is not equivalent to impossibility. ◆

The event causing impossibility must be brought about by an independent intervening cause. Examples of independent intervening causes are a change in a law that makes performance illegal; the destruction of subject matter which is unique, or is specially designated for a particular contract; or the illness, incapacity, or death of one party whose special skills were required in a personal service contract. Under these circumstances, impossibility does not exist at the time the contract is made but arises sometime thereafter.

RELEASE

Parties may *release* each other from their duties to perform by mutual agreement. One party may release the other party from his or her obligation to continue performance after it has been partially or substantially completed. A party's right to release another is part of the freedom to contract. The release must be supported by consideration in writing and be signed by the releasing party. The Uniform Commercial Code (UCC) requires delivery of a signed writing, but it need not be supported by consideration. The form of a release may be as simple as writing "paid in full" on a check.

MISTAKE

Mistake is a belief that is not in accordance with the actual facts. Mistakes must be material, not incidental. This condition means if not for the mistake, the contract would have been entered into. Parties may have a mistaken belief as to the facts or may make a mistake in judgment as to the value of the contract. There is generally no relief afforded to a party who makes a mistake in judgment as to value. Otherwise, contracts would not be binding if every time a person made a bad deal, he or she could rescind the contract by claiming mistake. However, when a factual mistake is made, parties may be allowed to rescind the contract, depending on whether there is a mutual mistake or a mistake made by only one party.

Employment Perspective

Harrison Whitney, a security analyst at Merrill Lynch, is very dedicated to his work. On the morning of May 24, while he is diligently analyzing a new issue on the Big Board, his wife telephones to remind him to leave the office on time because she has a special dinner planned for him. He hangs up and begins to wonder why she would have a special dinner on the twenty-fourth of May. Then he suddenly remembers that it's her birthday. On his lunch hour, he goes to the jeweler just off Wall Street to buy his wife a birthstone ring. There is a discreet sign saying, "All Sales Final." He tells the clerk, who was newly hired, "My wife's birthday is today; I wish to purchase a sapphire birthstone ring." The clerk, believing sapphire to be the correct birthstone, sold Whitney the ring. When Whitney presents the gift to his wife, to his astonishment, she throws it at him, crying, "My birthstone is an emerald! How could you be so thoughtless? I've said I don't like sapphires at all." Whitney attempts to return the ring to the jewelers, who claim it was a final sale. Has he any recourse? Yes! Both Whitney and the clerk made a mutual mistake of fact concerning the proper birthstone for May. The contract may be rescinded. If Whitney had requested the sapphire ring without asking the clerk whether it was the birthstone for May, then it would have been a unilateral mistake, and Whitney would be without recourse. ◆

REVIEW QUESTIONS

1. What are the elements of an employment contract?
2. What state law governs when there is a dispute?
3. When will a restrictive covenant be enforced?
4. When does an employment contract have to be in writing?
5. May an employee assign his or her rights?
6. May an employer assign its rights?
7. When are assignments prohibited?
8. When will an employment contract be in breach?
9. What remedies are available?
10. Are there defenses to those remedies? If so, what are they?
11. Was the case on page 15 decided in an ethical manner?
12. Tovar, in seeking employment as a resident physician with Paxton Hospital in Illinois, fully described his qualifications to the hospital. The hospital hired Tovar with the assurance that the position would be for life. Tovar gave up a position in Kansas and moved to Illinois in reliance on this promise. Two weeks later, Tovar was fired because he did not have a license to practice medicine in Illinois. Based on Tovar's representation, the hospital assumed he had his license. Tovar sued the hospital for breach of con-

tract. What was the result? *Manuel Tovar v. Community Memorial Hospital,* 29 Ill. App. 3rd 218, 330 NE.2d 247 (1975)

13. Fein was thinking of purchasing a Budget Rent-A-Car franchise. Budget required all prospective purchasers to sign an agreement containing a restrictive covenant not to compete in the automotive business for two years in the Western Hemisphere. After signing the agreement, Budget divulged secret information to Fein regarding the way they developed local businesses. Subsequently, Fein discontinued negotiations and bought a franchise from one of Budget's competitors. Budget sued Fein to enforce the restrictive covenant. What was the result? *Budget Rent-A-Car Corporation v. Fein,* 342 F.2d 509 (5th Cir. 1965)

14. Hanan entered into an oral contract with Corning Glass in February to serve as a management consultant for one year commencing May 1. Corning Glass later refused to honor the contract, setting up the statute of frauds as a defense. What was the result? *Hanan v. Corning Glass Works,* 63 Misc.2d 863, 314 N.Y.S.2d 804 (1970)

15. Cunningham entered into a contract to play basketball for the Carolina Cougars for three years. The contract contained a provision that it could not be assigned without Cunningham's consent. Southern Sports Corporation, owner of the Cougars, sold the team to Munchak Corporation. Cunningham's contract was assigned to Munchak. Subsequently, Cunningham refused to play for the new owner. He claimed the assignment was a breach of contract because it was made without his consent. What was the result? *Munchak v. Cunningham,* 457 F.2d 721 (4th Cir. 1972)

16. In 1930, the Wetherall Brothers Company had the exclusive right to sell steel in New England for United States Steel. This contract was indefinite, subject to termination by either party on two years' notice. In 1950, Wetherall Brothers liquidated their corporation and assigned the exclusive right to represent United States Steel to a Pennsylvania corporation that assumed the name Wetherall Brothers. United States Steel was not given notice of the assignment but subsequently learned of it and terminated the contract. The new Wetherall Brothers brought an action for breach of contract. Was the assignment effective? *Wetherall Brothers Co. v. United States Steel Corp.,* 105 F.Supp. 81 (1952)

17. Rixse, an architect, agreed to draw plans for the proposed construction of a new building by Wetzel. Wetzel breached the contract by refusing to perform. At the time of the breach, Rixse had completed only the preliminary drawings. He continued to prepare the remainder of his plans after he had been notified of the breach. Rixse sues Wetzel for nonpayment of the entire contract price. What was the result? *Wetzel v. Rixse,* 93 Okla. 216, 220 P.607 (1923)

18. William Clark had performed legal services for Nellie Ellis for many years. His firm prepared a petition for Mrs. Ellis when she was diagnosed with Alzheimer's. A temporary guardian was appointed for Mrs. Ellis. Mr. Clark refused to release Mrs. Ellis's records and filed a counterpetition claiming Mrs. Ellis had retained him to fight the conservatorship. Was there a conflict of interest? *In Re Ellis,* 822 S.W.2d 602 (Tenn. App.1991)

19. Tommy DeRamus worked as an advertising salesman for Birmingham Television Corp. DeRamus signed an agreement stating that he would not work for any other television or radio station in the Channel 42 broadcast area for six months after his employment terminated. Jack Gunnels, the local sales manager at Channel 6, offered DeRamus a higher-paying job, which he accepted. Birmingham contends that Channel 6 tortiously

interfered with its business by inducing DeRamus to leave Channel 42 and take a job with Channel 6. What was the result? *Birmingham Television Corp. v. DeRamus,* 502 So.2d 761 (Ala. Civ. App. 1986)

20. Dennis Harris was police chief of Plano, Illinois, when Bud Johnson was elected mayor. Harris asked Johnson if Johnson wanted Harris to remain as police chief; otherwise, he would take advantage of other opportunities offering similar pay. Johnson told Harris he would appoint him if he stayed on but later terminated Harris' employment. Harris was forced to take another position with a substantial reduction in pay. Therefore, Harris sued Johnson for breach of promise, asked for the difference in pay as the measure of damages, and cited the promissory estoppel doctrine. What was the result? *Harris v. Johnson*, 578 N.E. 2d 1326 (Ill. App. 2 Dist. 1991)

21. David Duwell left Bobcat Enterprises for Portman Equipment Co., a competitor. This action was in violation of the restrictive covenant Duwell signed while employed with Bobcat. Bobcat sought an injunction. Duwell's current position involves renting industrial forklifts, a business Bobcat does not engage in. What was the result? *Bobcat Enterprises, Inc. v. Duwell,* 587 N.E.2d 905 (Ohio App. 12 Dist. 1990).

22. Gregory Harthcock was hired as a chemist by Zep Manufacturing. He signed a nondisclosure covenant that restricted work in the same field for two years and that did not specify geographic location. Subsequently, he left Zep's employ for a job with its competitor, Panther Industries. Zep sought to enforce the restrictive covenant; Harthcock claimed it was indefinite in its terms. What was the result? *Zep Mfg. Co. v. Harthcock,* 824 S.W.2d 654 (Tex. App.-Dallas 1992)

23. P.M. Palumbo, Jr., M.A., Inc., is a professional corporation providing medical services. Dean Bennett was hired as an independent contractor according to the employment contract. The contract contained a restrictive covenant prohibiting Bennett from competing. Subsequently, Bennett terminated the employment and violated the restrictive covenant. When sued, Bennett argued that the contract is void because the law does not permit a professional corporation to provide services through an independent contractor. The court agreed. Palumbo argued that this technicality should not prevent the court from enforcing the restrictive covenant. What was the result? *P.M. Palumbo, Jr., Inc. v. Bennett,* 409 S.E.2d 152 (Va. 1991)

24. Hardin entered into an employment contract with Lance Roof Inspection on January 1, 1981. The agreement contained a restrictive covenant that prevented Hardin from competing with Lance for a period of 24 months from the date of the agreement. The original contract terminated on December 31, 1982, but the parties extended the term until the end of 1985. Shortly after the extension had expired, Hardin started his own business in competition with Lance. Lance argued that the restrictive covenant went into effect only after Hardin left in 1985. What was the result? *Lance Roof Inspection Service, Inc. v. Hardin,* 653 F.Supp. 1097 (S.D. Tex 1986)

25. D&B Computing Services sold Nomad, a software product, to Must Software. The contract for sale assigned to Must the right to enforce any violation of the employment agreement related to the sale of Nomad. Larry Parcler, a former D&B employee, started Diversified Business Systems to provide consulting services to users of Nomad. Two former D&B employees, who had been at Must, left to join Diversified. The issue is whether the restrictive covenant in an employment contract that is assigned when the business is sold still has validity. What was the result? *U3S Corp. of America v. Parker,* 414 S.E.2d 513 (Ga. App. 1991)

CHAPTER 3 Employment Liability

LIABILITY OF EMPLOYEES AND INDEPENDENT CONTRACTORS

Employees and independent contractors will be liable for breach of contract if they fail to uphold their duties, including duty of loyalty, duty to act in good faith, and duty to account for all receipts and expenses. An employee will be liable for all unauthorized acts or misrepresentations made to third parties in the principal's name.

An employee's and independent contractor's liability extends to situations in which they contract in their own name or on behalf of their employer without authority. To protect themselves against personal liability, they should always sign the employer's name and then their own name as agent.

Employment Perspective

Robert McMillen lists farmland that he owns north of Cheyenne, Wyoming, with Tumbleweed Real Estate and gives it an exclusive agency. After four months of attempting to locate a buyer, Tumbleweed learns that an interstate highway will proceed north from Denver and Cheyenne through McMillen's farmland, thus enhancing the purchase price. Tumbleweed contracts with McMillen to purchase the farmland for Dexter Brady, supposedly an out-of-state principal who has given Tumbleweed power of attorney to act on his behalf. Tumbleweed is actually purchasing the land for itself. Brady is a fictitious principal who does not exist. McMillen is happy with the purchase price until he learns about the interstate highway plan. He sues Tumbleweed Real Es-

tate and Dexter Brady, only to discover Brady is nonexistent. What recourse does McMillen have against Tumbleweed? Tumbleweed can be compelled to return the farmland to McMillen even though there were no other ready, willing, and able buyers. Tumbleweed attempted to defraud McMillen by purportedly acting for a principal who actually did not exist, while they were actually buying the land for themselves.

Assume that there was no interstate highway plan and that Dexter Brady actually existed and gave Tumbleweed authority to act for him. Suppose that Tumbleweed contracted with McMillen in its own name and that Brady later reneged on the purchase; would Tumbleweed be liable on the contract for the sale of McMillen's farmland? Yes! An independent contractor who signs in his or her own name is personally liable to a third party unless the employer admits he or she is liable by approving the agent's acts. Although Tumbleweed may be liable to McMillen, it may sue Brady for breach of his agency contract with the company. ◆

CASE

Sheffield, et al. v. State of New York, Education Department

N.Y. Sup.Ct. App.Div. (3rd Dept. 1991)

MIKOLL, Justice.

The facts underlying this proceeding are not in dispute but the litigants sharply contest the legal consequences based on the facts. Petitioners Genesee Hospital and Stanley S. Zack, the hospital's head pharmacist, were found guilty of misconduct in practicing pharmacy under two specifications: they permitted persons without pharmacy licenses (in this case nurses) to dispense and mix drugs and ingredients, and delegated to them the responsibility of measuring, weighing, compounding and mixing ingredients in preparation of hyper-alimentation, peripheral intravenous solutions and intravenous solutions, an activity reserved to a trained pharmacist. The hospital was censured and reprimanded and fined $250 under each specification. Petitioners Sandra Sheffield and Mary Kay Schroeder, nurses who worked for the hospital, were charged with two specifications of unprofessional conduct in the practice of nursing by practicing nursing beyond its scope in that they measured, weighed, compounded and mixed ingredients in preparation of intravenous solutions and prescriptions. They were censured and reprimanded and placed on probation for 18 months to insure their completion of a course of instruction in the legal aspects of nursing. Petitioners then commenced this proceeding challenging the determinations.

Petitioners contend that the determinations of professional misconduct were based on an arbitrary and capricious interpretation of vague regulatory provisions. They argue that statutory law fails to define "dispensing" of drugs and that the "Nurse Practice Act" fails to prohibit the conduct for which they were disciplined. They contend that the nursing practice in question has been going on at the hospital for more than 25 years and that since 1988 the Health Department regulations explicitly permit not only nurses but licensed practical nurses under the supervision of a nurse to prepare intravenous solutions, including those ultimately administered to patients by other nurses. They contend that the regulations codified accepted nursing practice.

The area of health-support services through intravenous use has apparently undergone substantial changes and has been in a state of flux for a considerable period. It is not disputed in this proceeding that Sheffield and Schroeder could prepare intravenous solutions, prescribed by a physician and pursuant to the physician's order, for patients to whom they personally administered the intravenous solutions without violating the law. However, respondents contend that nurses cannot prepare such solutions for administration by other nurses in that the latter practice constitutes "dispensing of drugs," an activity reserved to pharmacists. Respondents also argue that the law permits practical nurses, with special training, to perform certain intravenous therapy procedures and that this regulation only authorizes them to do what nurses may legally do, which does not include practical pharmacy. Respondents further argue that petitioners' interpretation would contradict Education Law section 6801 governing the practice of pharmacy.

Respondents' determination of guilt is required to be based upon a preponderance of evidence. Our review is limited to ensuring that the determinations here are supported by substantial evidence. When reviewing facts, "a court may not review administrative findings of fact as to the weight of the evidence or substitute its judgment for that of the administrative body".

Education Law section 6801 defined the practice of pharmacy as "the preparing, compounding, preserving, or the dispensing of drugs, medicines and therapeutic devices on the basis of prescriptions or other legal authority." Drugs are defined as, "[a]rticles intended for use in the diagnosis, cure, mitigation, treatment or prevention of disease in man or animals." Education Law section 6802 [7] (b) prohibits a person not licensed as a pharmacist from measuring, weighing, compounding or mixing ingredients. This language is broadly couched and permits only pharmacists to prepare or compound drugs or to compound or mix ingredients.

We conclude that the unrefused facts establish that the hospital and Zack improperly delegated the responsibility of preparing and compounding of drugs and compounding and mixing solutions and dispensing of drugs to unlicensed persons, namely the nurses at the hospital. It has also been established that Sheffield and Schroeder acted outside the scope of nursing since the activity of compounding of drugs is the practice of pharmacy and is not included in the practice of nursing.

Judgment for
State of New York
Education Dept.

LIABILITY OF EMPLOYERS

Contractual Liability

An employer is bound by his or her employee's or independent contractor's contract with a third party where the employee or independent contractor acted with actual authority, either express or implied, or with apparent authority. An employer is not liable for the unauthorized acts of the employee or independent contractor unless the employer ratifies the unauthorized acts.

Employment Perspective

Clifford Branch and James Alworth were both attending an auction at Porter's Auction House. Branch was representing the Ford Foundation as he had done on numerous occasions in the past. Alworth was representing a man named Vanderbilt, an undisclosed employer. During the auction, Branch was declared the highest bidder on paintings by Paul Cézanne and Henri Matisse for $850,000 and $700,000, respectively. Alworth was successful with his $1,450,000 bid for a Van Gogh. Both Branch and Alworth signed a contract agreeing to deliver the purchase price within two weeks, at which time the painting would be transferred. Branch signed "Ford Foundation by Clifford

Branch, Agent." Alworth signed his own name. If the Ford Foundation claimed that Branch exceeded his authority by paying a sum greater than the agreed-upon $500,000 for each painting, would this be a good defense to a suit by Porter? No! Branch had actual authority to pay up to $500,000 and apparent authority beyond that, since he had acted for the Ford Foundation on prior occasions. The Ford Foundation must pay for the painting. Its sole recourse lies against Branch for exceeding his actual authority. If Vanderbilt refuses to pay for the Van Gogh, will Alworth be liable? Yes! Porter's may sue Alworth because he signed the contract in his own name. The prudent move for Alworth would have been to disclose Vanderbilt's identity and produce the employment contract with Vanderbilt. Porter's may then proceed against either Alworth or Vanderbilt but most likely will choose the deepest pocket to be sure of collecting payment. If Alworth paid for the painting, would he have any recourse against Vanderbilt? Yes! Alworth would be entitled to sue Vanderbilt for indemnification of the loss Alworth suffered because of Vanderbilt's breach of duty. ◆

An employer is not liable for the unauthorized acts of an employee or independent contractor in cases where the third party has a duty to inquire about the agent's actual authority when that authority is not apparent. A third party who takes it for granted that the employee or independent contractor possesses the authority to contract and is not justified in so relying will have no recourse against the employer, but will be restricted to recovering from the employee or independent contractor alone.

CASE

Jessee v. Amoco Oil Co.

594 N.E.2d 1210 (Ill. App. 1 Dist. 1992)

DIVITO, Judge.

Amoco leased a service station to Tommy Baker. The lease provided that Amoco would be responsible for major repairs including the replacement of the furnace. Baker had full discretion over hiring. He hired Anna Jessee to work as cashier. Subsequently, the heating system did not function. Baker advised Amoco, which then hired Standard Heating to replace the system. After installation, Jessee became ill and was rushed to the hospital to be treated for carbon monoxide poisoning. She suffered brain damage. Because the fresh-air-return duct was not reconnected to the new furnace, the cashier's booth became filled with carbon monoxide. Standard Heating was hired to install the furnace but not to reconnect the ducts.

The issue is whether Amoco is liable for the work of Standard Heating, an independent contractor.

The court ruled, "Generally, an employer of an independent contractor is not liable for the acts or omissions of the independent contractor; however, an exception to the rule provides that an employer who retains control of any part of the work will be liable for injuries resulting from his failure to exercise his right of control with reasonable care."

Judgment for Jessee.

Tort Liability

An employer is liable for any *tort* committed by his or her employee if the tort is committed within the scope of employment—that is, if it is related to the business at hand. A tort is a private civil wrong as opposed to a crime which is a wrong committed against the public. Money damages are awarded to compensate a party who has been injured by a tort. Employers may contract for liability insurance to minimize their risk and to avoid paying for the damages out of the profits of the business. However, an employer is not liable for the torts of an independent contractor even if the torts are committed during the scope of employment because the employer has no control over the work of an independent contractor.

Employment Perspective

Luis Manulto is a construction worker who was hired by Valenti Construction Company. Currently, Luis is working on the forty-fourth floor of an office building in downtown Houston. Manulto has his toolbox at his feet, but when someone calls him abruptly, he accidentally knocks it off the beam. The toolbox falls onto a pedestrian walkway that was covered by a heavy plastic grating. Linda Anderson, who was walking through the passageway at the time, is severely injured. Is Manulto an employee or an independent contractor? Manulto is an employee because he works exclusively for Valenti and is under Valenti's direct control. Who is liable for Linda's injuries? Linda may sue both Luis Manulto (employee) and Valenti Construction Company (employer). Manulto acted negligently in knocking over the toolbox. Valenti Construction Company is liable for Manulto's negligence because it occurred during his scope of employment; the accident was related directly to the business at hand.

Suppose that at lunchtime, Manulto stops at a bar across the street to drown his sorrows and that a patron comments, "I saw the whole episode, and it was a real stupid thing you did." Manulto, angered by the patron's comments, punches him in the face, causing the patron to suffer a fractured nose and a concussion. Is the principal liable for Manulto's acts? No! Valenti Construction Company is not liable for Manulto's tort of assault and battery because it did not occur within the scope of employment—the tort was not related to the business at hand. Manulto will be solely liable. ◆

An employer is also liable for the fraud or misrepresentations committed by an employee where the principal has placed the employee in a position that leads people to believe that the agent has the apparent authority to make certain actual representations.

Employment Perspective

Keith Stewart, a representative of Super Duper Vacuum Company, calls on Thelma Williams at her house. Although at first Thelma is reluctant to make a purchase, Stewart convinces her when he makes the false representation that this household vacuum cleaner will also clean basements and garages, with the separate purchase of certain attachments. He does this intentionally to get the sale. Thelma purchases the vacuum cleaner as well as the attachments. When her husband comes home, she gives him a demonstration in the living room, where the vacuum cleaner works perfectly. Then using the attachments, Thelma's husband attempts to clean the garage floor. The machine breaks down. Thelma and her husband sue Super Duper Vacuum Company and Keith Stewart for fraud. Super Duper never instructed Stewart to make false statements of fact and never advertised its vacuum cleaner for anything more than household use. Who will be responsible for the fraud? If Keith is an employee working exclusively for Super Duper, then both Super Duper and Keith Stewart will be liable. Super Duper is liable for its employee's fraudulent representations because it placed Stewart in a position where people would reasonably believe that he had the authority to make such a statement. Super Duper may seek indemnification from Stewart because of his breach of duty of loyalty. Stewart breached the duty by exceeding his authority through the making of statements which were false and unauthorized. ◆

CASE

Hennessy v. Commonwealth Edison Co.

764 F.Supp. 495 (N.D. Ill. 1991)

ASPEN, District Judge.

The plaintiff, Michael J. Hennessy, has brought this three-count personal injury diversity action against the defendant, Commonwealth Edison Company ("ComEd"), for negligent infliction of emotional distress, strict liability and battery. Hennessy's claims arise as a result of receiving an internal contamination by radiation while he was working in ComEd's Dresden nuclear power station. ComEd has moved for summary judgment on all three counts of Hennessy's complaint. Hennessy in turn has moved for partial summary judgment on the question whether the doctrine of strict liability may be applied to the nuclear power industry. For the following reasons, we grant ComEd's motion for summary judgment on all three counts, and dismiss Hennessy's motion as moot.

Hennessy is a pipefitter and welder who worked for various contractors at two of ComEd's nuclear power plants from 1978–1985. Upon completing a job at ComEd's Dresden plant in 1981, Hennessy received what is known as an "exit whole body count" and several repeat counts, and was subsequently informed by a technician that he had an internal contamination of Cobalt-60. There appears to be a question, however, as to the precise date that Hennessy learned of this internal contamination. In his deposition Hennessy recalls Friday, April 3, 1981, as the date that a ComEd health physicist told him about the internal contamination. Yet Hennessy describes that day as the same day he received the exit whole body count and repeat counts on his last day of work at Dresden, which would have been in March. For the purposes of ruling on ComEd's motion for summary judgment, we will accept Hennessy's recollection of April 3, 1981, as the correct date.

According to his deposition testimony, Hennessy asked questions of Dresden workers and of Nuclear Regulatory Commission officials regarding the effects of the internal contamination. He specifically spoke with the NCR on-site inspector, Tom Tongue, who told him not to worry about the internal contamination and indicated that the level was not dangerous or potentially harmful. In a phone conversation, an NCR official in Washington told Hennessy the same thing. None of these individuals, or anyone else, ever told him that he would have any ill effects physically as a result of the contamination. ComEd's health physicists told him that the contamination would ultimately leave his body through bodily secretions.

Hennessy claims no physical injury as a result either of his internal or his external contamination and exposures. Hennessy has stated that no one has ever told him that he presently has, or in the future may have, any physical ill effects as a result of his internal exposures. No doctor has ever told Hennessy that he has an increased risk of cancer. According to the affidavit testimony of another ComEd witness, Dr. Eugene L. Saenger, Hennessy's internal 50-year committed dose of 24 millirem exposure was very small and there is no possibility of adverse biological effects from such an exposure. For the purposes of comparison, Dr. Saenger indicated that Hennessy's internal contamination presents no greater risk to his health than if he would receive one chest x-ray at any time during his life. A routine chest x-ray gives the patient a dose of approximately 20 millirem. Dr. Saenger concluded that Hennessy has suffered no acute health effects and has a zero percent chance of an increased risk of cancer or of any long term adverse health effects as a result of his internal Cobalt-60 contamination.

The only evidence that Hennessy has submitted that might pertain to the significance of his exposure is a page from a ComEd training manual which generally describes the possible effects of both acute and chronic doses of radiation exposures:

> The effect that radiation has on the body depends on how much exposure the body receives and how quickly it receives it. If we receive a large amount of radiation exposure within a short period of time (usually within a 24-hour period) it is called an **acute dose** and the effects upon the body will be actual physical symptoms.

Hennessy has indicated that he does not fear future injury or cancer from any of his external doses, totaling over 16,000 millirem (16 rems), but rather suffers emotional distress as a result solely of his concern about possible future effects from the 1981 incident resulting in 24 millirems of internal radiation dose exposure. Each of his three claims is predicated on that single incident. Hennessy has never sought professional help or advice from any psychiatrist, psychologist, or any other counsel for his alleged emotional distress.

Hennessy's emotional distress derives from a fear of cancer or other illness allegedly associated with the radiation exposure he received. Although often treated as distinct doctrinal category, fear of cancer claims effectively comprise a particular subset of emotional distress claims in general. On the issue of endangerment, the distinction between the typical emotional distress claim and a fear of cancer claim is simply a temporal one. As we have observed, the typical case is concerned with whether there was a significant possibility that plaintiff could have been injured by the negligent occurrence. Thus, the inquiry requires an after-the-fact consideration of what could have happened to a plaintiff who is presently no longer at risk of injury. By contrast, because fear of cancer claims usually arise from direct exposure to substances with latent disease-producing effects, such claims require a prospective inquiry as to whether the plaintiff is at risk of suffering and consequences in the future. Both inquiries are geared toward assessing whether a plaintiff's claimed distress is reasonable. "Whether a fear is reasonable is determined by the objective standard of whether a particular incident would produce fear in the person of ordinary sensibilities."

As evidence of the reasonableness of his fear, Hennessy claims to have read articles that informed him of the possible adverse consequences of exposure to radiation. Notwithstanding the overwhelming lack of specificity to this evidence, we acknowledge that there can be no doubt that it has been widely reported and is widely accepted that increased exposure to radiation yields an increased risk of contracting cancer. To establish the reasonableness of his distress, however, Hennessy must show something more than a general awareness of the risk of contracting cancer as a result of exposure tending to show that he actually experienced a particular event that placed him at risk, an event from which there appeared to be a real chance that he might come to harm.

Hennessy's claim is based solely on the internal radiation exposure he personally sustained. Hennessy has come forward with no competent evidence to provide a reasonable basis for his apprehension that the level of internal contamination he received would be expected to have any significant adverse effect upon him in his life-time. No one ever told Hennessy that he presently has, or in the future may have, some ill effects physically as a result of his internal contamination. No doctor has ever told him that he has an increased risk of cancer. In fact, Hennessy was specifically told that he was not at risk; his fear derives from his decision not to believe what he was told. His decision to disregard what he was told might be discounted if there was evidence to suggest that statement was untrue, but Hennessy has come forward with no such evidence.

In light of this, Hennessy ultimately relies on a claim of ignorance as the basis upon which his fear should be deemed reasonable. He maintains that he is not a physician, and therefore cannot be expected to understand the relative insignificance of his internal exposure. However, while such naivete concerning the actual ramifications of his internal exposure may make Hennessy's fears subjectively understandable, it does not provide a basis for finding his fears objectively reasonable. We are sympathetic to Hennessy's concerns about the potential dangers of working in his trade, as was Dr. Siebert. In addition, we can fully understand Hennessy's confusion as to the significance of the particular episode of internal exposure. Radiation poses a troubling threat and it is likely that radiation monitoring is a mysterious matter to the uninformed. Yet, absent a basis in fact that would support Hennessy's fear that he either was or will be at risk for cancer as a result of the episode of internal contamination, such a belief founders on pure speculation, and hence cannot be said to be reasonable. In sum, the record on summary judgment discloses that Hennessy had no tangible reason to believe he was actually endangered by the incident.

For the sake of completeness, we find the evidence sufficient to create an issue of fact as to whether Hennessy has manifested physical symptoms resulting from the distress. Dr. Siebert has loosely related Hennessy's duodenal ulcer to his alleged emotional distress. Although creating an issue of fact, we observe that this evidence is quite weak. Dr. Siebert did not directly relate the ulcer to Hennessy's concern about the single exposure giving rise to Hennessy's complaint, but rather, Dr. Siebert relates the ulcer to Hennessy's concern about the potential for radiation exposure at work in general. That testimony would tend to dilute any claim by Hennessy that the particular incident in question was the sole cause of his distress.

Within his claim for negligent infliction of emotional distress, Hennessy also seeks to recover for an increased risk of cancer. Such a claim is usually viewed as an element of damages arising from some other tort, and not a claim in and of itself. Thus, ComEd maintains that in order to recover damages for an increased risk of future injury, Hennessy must prove a present physical injury and that the claimed future injury is reasonably certain to occur. In responding to this, Hennessy confuses the difference between a claim for fear of cancer and a claim for increased risk of cancer. We need not address this matter in any detail, however, because as we have already found, Hennessy has failed to adduce any evidence to support the allegation that he is at any increased risk of harm as a result of this episode.

Accordingly, we grant summary judgment in favor of ComEd.

Employment Perspective

One day while strolling through Richmond Hill Mall, Bill Cominsky decides to browse around Peter's Jewelry Store. He spots what appears to be a gold necklace on sale for $49. He figures this would be perfect for his fiancee's upcoming birthday. Bill goes in and asks the clerk, Marjorie Travers, whether the necklace is made of gold. She excuses herself and goes into a back room where she questions Bernard Peters, the store owner. He replies that the necklace is 14K gold, knowing this to be false. Marjorie conveys the message to Bill, ignorant of its falsehood. Bill, relying on the statement, makes the purchase. On his fiancee's birthday, they discover that the necklace is not 14K gold. What recourse is available to Bill Cominsky? Bill may sue Marjorie Travers for misrepresentation and Bernard Peters for fraud. Marjorie Travers made a material misrepresentation of fact that Bill justifiably relied on to his detriment. She made this statement innocently, without an intent to defraud. Bernard Peters is guilty of fraud because his misrepresentation was intentional. ◆

Negligence

Negligence is the failure to perceive a risk which results in an injury that was foreseeable. Negligence is caused by conduct that falls below the standard established by law for the protection of others against risk of harm. The negligent party must have had a duty to perceive the risk of harm that he or she fails to meet. The key to negligence is that the defendant failed to act as a reasonable person would in light of the risk. The plaintiff has the burden of proving this. The elements that give rise to negligence are the following:

- Negligent act
- Duty owed
- Proximate cause
- Forseeable injury
- Resulting loss

CASE *Collum v. Argo*

599 So.2d 1210 (Ala. Civ. App. 1992)

Per Curiam.

Kenny Collum sold a mobile home to the Dawsons. He arranged with Stanley Wilson to have a septic tank installed. During installation, Wilson knocked over fifteen fruit trees on the adjacent property owned by the Argos. The Argos brought suit against Collum alleging that Wilson was in Collum's employ when Wilson committed the trespass.

The issues are whether Collum is Wilson's employer and whether an employer is liable for the torts of his or her employee.

The court ruled, "An employer's liability for general trespass is based on the doctrine of respondent superior; that is, an employer may be liable for consequential damages when his employee, acting within the course of the employer's business, wrongfully trespasses on the property of another. The employer need not have even been aware of the employee's actions, because liability arises from the employment relationship itself."

The court continued, "The test for determining whether one is an agent or employee, as opposed to an independent contractor, is whether the alleged employer has reserved the right of control over the means and method by which the work is done. We must conclude that there was no employer-employee relationship between Collum and Wilson. Instead, the record indicates that Collum merely acted as an agent of the Dawsons and engaged Wilson to install the septic tank at their behest. He did not have any right of control over the work to be performed and certainly did not direct Wilson to trespass onto the Argo property. Accordingly, Collum cannot be subjected to liability for the damage Wilson caused to the Argos, nor can he be held liable under a theory of trespass."

Judgment for Collum.

Negligence is an act performed in a careless manner, or an omission to act, that proximately causes injury to another. Liability for the negligence does not arise until it is established that the person who was careless owed a duty toward the person bringing the suit. A duty to exercise reasonable care arises whenever there is a danger of one person's causing injury to another. The injury to the plaintiff must have been proximately caused by the negligent act of the defendant.

Proximate cause means the negligent act must have been reasonably connected to the plaintiff's injury. The injury to the plaintiff must be foreseeable. A foreseeable injury is that which would be reasonably anticipated as a consequence of the defendant's negligence. In most states, the defendant is responsible for damages resulting from only foreseeable injuries. The plaintiff must sustain a definable loss or damage and prove that this loss or damage resulted from the injury caused by the defendant's negligence. The plaintiff's loss is recompensed with money damages.

The doctrine of foreseeability may also be applied to situations where one party's negligence has injured a person and caused others to attempt to rescue. Under the doctrine of "danger invites rescue," the negligent party is responsible for injury to the rescuers, where they act reasonably and where it is foreseeable that people might go to the rescue of the injured person.

Employment Perspective

The Laurens, a French-family owned corporation, is building a trestle bridge across Niagara Falls. The company employs Jack Hill as their chief carpenter and general contractor. One day Jack, who is rushing to finish work in order to leave for his home, omits three of the four nails securing one of the tracks. Two months later, the bridge opens and the first train rolls across. John Phillips and his cousin Fred Goodman are among the last to board the train. The two men are forced to stand between the cars because the train is overcrowded. Because the train's engineer, misjudges the correct speed needed to make a smooth transition around a curve, Phillips is sent flying out the door. The train stops 100 feet down the tracks. Fred Goodman bolts off the train to look for his cousin. When he steps onto the track that is not properly secured, it gives way, and he joins his cousin in Niagara Falls. Their estates sue the Laurens for wrongful death. The Laurens acknowledges its responsibility for Phillips only. What is the result? Fred Goodman's estate may also recover under the doctrine that danger invites rescue, because it was foreseeable that Fred Goodman might go to the rescue of his cousin. ◆

Ratification of an Employee's Unauthorized Acts

Ratification is the approval or sanction given by the employer to the unauthorized acts of an employee. The employer may ratify the unauthorized contracts made by the employee as well as the torts committed by the employee. The following requirements are necessary for ratification:

- Employee acts in excess of or without authority.
- Employer is made aware of all important facts.
- Employer ratifies entire act, not part of it.
- Ratification must be made in the same manner as the authority given to the employee.

CASE Hampton v. Rubicon Chemicals, Inc.

579 So.2d 485 (La. App. 1 Civ. 1991)

CATER, Judge.

This case arises out of the following set of the facts. Mack Hampton worked as a maintenance laborer for Barnard & Burk, Inc. (B & B), which had a contract with Rubicon's Chemicals, Inc. (Rubicon), to maintain Rubicon's production facilities at its Geismar plant. Hampton's job involved the cleanout and repair of equipment of a three-story plastics production rig, known as the MDI unit.

At that time, Dean Armstrong was the supervisor of the work which Hampton and his co-workers performed. He was the management employee who was the most involved with supervising B & B's operations at Rubicon's Geismar plant. Armstrong, as the immediate supervisor, was responsible for the day-to-day operations, worker training, and the conduction of safety programs. Over Armstrong was John Daniel, a senior executive officer for B & B, who was charged with the overall safety of B & B's operations. At the time of the accident, Fireman's Fund Insurance Company was the liability insurer of B & B and its executive officers.

At about 5:15 p.m. on January 29, 1974 Hampton and his co-workers were cleaning the area around the MDI unit, when a phosgene leak occurred, through the fault of Rubicon. Phosgene, commonly known as "mustard gas," is a highly toxic gas, which is used in the production of plastics. Phosgene has an almost sweet odor, it desensitizes one's sense of smell so that one may continue to breathe it without being aware of the extent of his exposure. Because it has a low solubility, the gas does not have an immediately irritating quality that other toxic gases have.

Hampton and several of his co-workers were exposed to phosgene for about ten minutes. Because of this exposure, Hampton and his co-workers were taken to the first aid station within the plant. No doctor was available, and they were given minimal, if any, medical treatment. They were then sent home with instruction to contact the plant doctor if they felt any effects from the gas.

After arriving home, Hampton became seriously ill, and his wife rushed him to the emergency room at Our Lady of the Lake Hospital in Baton Rouge. Despite all of the hospital's efforts, Hampton's condition rapidly worsened, and he died during the early morning hours of the following day, after suffering extreme pain for several hours. He was survived by his wife and minor daughter.

On January 3, 1975, Mrs. Georgia Parker Hampton, individually and as natural executrix of her minor child, Marge Lynette Hampton, commenced a survival and wrongful death action against Rubicon, Rubicon's insurer (Reliance Insurance Company), and Fireman's Fund Insurance Company, the liability insurer of B & B, whose policy, the petition asserted, covered as insurers the executive officers, management, safety officials, supervisors, and other employees of B & B.

Prior to trial a settlement was reached with Rubicon and its insurer, and they were subsequently dismissed from the suit reserving rights against all other persons.

After a number of years, the case went to trial by injury with Fireman's Fund as the sole party defendant. After a lengthy trial, a verdict was rendered in favor of Fireman's Fund, and judgment was signed in accordance with the jury's verdict.

Shortly thereafter, counsel for plaintiffs learned that counsel for Fireman's Fund had withheld pertinent information regarding insurance coverage. Upon this discovery, plaintiffs moved for a new trial based on newly discovered evidence. This motion was denied. On appeal, this court affirmed the judgment and the denial of a new trial.

On December 9, 1983, the Supreme Court granted writs. After hearing and rehearing, the Supreme Court determined that the original trial had been critically flawed, vacated its original opinion, reversed the decision of this court, and remanded the matter to the trial court for a new trial. The supreme court stressed that "the interests of justice require that a new trial be granted."

Prior to the new trial, plaintiffs amended their pleading naming certain B & B executive officers, including John Daniel and Dean Armstrong. . . .

Determination of Executive Officer Liability

Fireman's Fund contends that the trial judge was not entitled to re-determine Mr. Armstrong's liability. The trial judge's determination on the new trial was not a re-determination of Armstrong's liability, Armstrong was not a party defendant in the original trial, the only defendant in that trial was Fireman's Fund. For the most part, this argument was answered in our discussion of scope of the new trial, where we held that the trial judge correctly held a new, unlimited trial. There is no merit in Fireman's Fund's argument that "Armstrong was not liable." The question of Armstrong's liability has never been fairly litigated. The underlying basis for the supreme court's remand for a new trial was the essential unfairness of the original trial. It was incumbent upon the trial court to determine whether or not Mr. Armstrong, an executive officer of B & B, was at fault, on the new trial. The trial court correctly ruled on this question.

Fireman's Fund also argues that the trial judge's conclusion that Mr. Armstrong should have trained his men in escape procedures, rather than the Rubicon operatives who were in charge of the unit and the engineering control in place, is patently incorrect. The violation of OSHA regulations, if any, is not a decisive element in determining the fault of Mr. Armstrong.

The trial judge, in his oral reasons for judgment, remarked:

> The record is clear after hearing everything, quite frankly, that Mr. Hampton had not been trained for evacuation, had not been trained for the use of masks and in fact there was no evidence that there were masks available, that they had knowledge of the masks available.
>
> And whose fault was it that there was a lack of training? The record indicates that Mr. Daniel, executive officer, vice president of this large company with many jobs, many people, many diversified undertakings by the company [B & B], was given the job to be the safety person, so to speak. He looked to the people in the field, I gather from the overall testimony, the primary man at each location was the man really in charge of the safety, was a first line man on safety, and that was Mr. Armstrong in this particular case, and Mr. Armstrong's testimony is clear on that point. He knew that he had a responsibility for safety. In fact one of his comments that struck me, his job depends on safety. . . . He never testified, to my knowledge, about any drills, about evacuation, which common sense dictates ought to be a requirement of a safety procedure when something bad happens, how you should react. It's basic, you should train to some extent. . . . Had there been any, in my opinion, it seems that some of the workers at that plant would have been put on the stand to say yes, we had occasional drills; yes, we were instructed about the canisters, where they were, what we were supposed to do with them, etc. The record is completely void and it really stands out in my mind to the point that if there had been some training that some of the workers would have come in and explained and said yes, we had an occasional drill, we knew where they were, we had these . . . (respirators) to be used if we wanted to use them. . . .
>
> Mr. Hampton was lost because he got too much gas and was not watched closely enough. Mr. Armstrong knew about these latent effects (of phosgene gas), he testified to that effect. [He was told that there had been a massive escape of phosgene gas.]

[The trial court then determined that Mr. Armstrong was at fault.]

I find that Mr. Armstrong, as an executive officer, was at fault and that Mr. Hampton clearly died of the phosgene inhalation, and proper training and quicker medical attention could have certainly given him a better chance to have survived, no question, and I can say that fault was a substantial factor in his damage and demise.

The trial judge also points out that Armstrong was an executive officer of B & B and was covered under the Fireman's Fund policy.

It should be noted that Fireman's Fund's adjuster, Mr. David Williams, testified that Armstrong had the most to do with the supervision or control over B & B's Rubicon operation. He also said that Armstrong was responsible for the day-to-day safety training of B & B's employees. He also testified that Daniel was the next in line among the upper echelon of the organization.

It is well settled that an employer has an obligation to provide his employees with a working place and conditions which are reasonably safe considering the nature of the work. The obligation was not met by the performance of Mr. Armstrong in this case.

Two injured B & B employees testified they had no training in safety procedures to be used in case of a phosgene leak or other emergency. They were given no information concerning the toxicity of phosgene. They did not know that Scott air pack or other safety devices were available for their use if needed, and they were completely unaware of proper safety measures.

The landmark executive officers' suit prior to the 1976 amendment *Canter v. Koehring Company,* established the following criteria for imposing individual liability:

1. The principal or employer owes a duty of care to the third person (which in this sense includes a co-employee), breach of which has caused the damage for which recovery is sought.
2. This duty is delegated by the principal or employer to the defendant.
3. The defendant officer, agent, or employee has breached this duty through personal (as contrasted with technical or vicarious) fault. The breach occurs when the defendant has failed to discharge the obligation with the degree of care required by ordinary prudence under the same or similar circumstances whether such failure be due to malfeasance, misfeasance, or nonfeasance, including when the failure results from not acting upon actual knowledge of the risk to others as well as from a lack of ordinary care in discovering and avoiding such risk of harm which has resulted from the breach of duty.
4. With regard to the personal (as contrasted with technical or vicarious) fault, personal liability cannot be imposed upon the officer, agent, or employee simply because of his general administrative responsibility for performance of some function of the employment. He must have a personal duty towards the injured plaintiff, breach of which specifically has caused the plaintiff's damages. If the defendant's general responsibility has been delegated with due care to some responsible subordinate or subordinates, he is not himself personally at fault and liable for the negligent performance of this responsibility unless he personally knows or personally should know of its non-performance or mal-performance and has nevertheless failed to cure the risk of harm.

Accordingly, for one to be considered an "executive officer" within the scope of the cause of action asserted herein by the plaintiffs that person must have some personal contact with the responsibility toward the insured employee. The evidence in the record shows that Dean Armstrong, Hampton's immediate supervisor, personally had the responsibility for the safety of his workers, including Hampton, and that Armstrong failed to meet his responsibility for safety in that he failed to train the workers for evacuation in the event of a dangerous condition, failed to instruct his workers on the use of gas masks or even the availability of such masks, and failed to conduct evacuation drills or explain to his workers any safety procedures. There was a total lack of even minimum safety precautions taken by Armstrong in this case. Armstrong breached his duty through his own personal fault.

Thus, we affirm the trial judge's finding of fault on the part of Armstrong. However, we find that the trial judge erred in not finding that Mr. John Daniel was also an executive officer under the Canter criteria. Daniel, a senior executive officer of B & B, was the chief officer in charge of safety.

We disagree with the holding of the trial court that Daniel was not at fault. Under the "executive officer" jurisprudence, when a defendant executive officer breaches a duty of care owed to an employee through personal fault, the executive is liable for any resulting risk of harm. Therefore, we find that Daniel is also liable.

We reverse the judgment insofar as it finds no liability on the part of defendant Daniel and render judgment against him as a solitary obligor with Armstrong and Fireman's Fund.

Judgment for Hampton

CASE

Palsgraf v. Long Island Railroad Company

248 N.Y. 339, 162 N.E. 99 (1928)

CARDOZO, Judge.

Palsgraf sued the Long Island Railroad Company for injuries sustained as a result of the alleged negligence of its employees.

Mrs. Palsgraf was standing on a platform waiting for a train. A man carrying a package was running to catch a train that was already moving. As the man jumped aboard, two guards attempted to assist him for fear he might fall. One guard grabbed his arm, while the other pushed from behind. The package in the man's arms was dislodged in the process. It fell on the tracks and exploded because it contained fireworks. The explosion caused a set of scales several feet away on the platform to overturn and fall upon Mrs. Palsgraf.

The Long Island Railroad contended that it owed no duty of care to her because the injuries she received were not the result of any foreseeable harm.

The court agreed with the railroad's contention and established the doctrine of foreseeability, which states, "Negligence is not actionable unless it involves the invasion of a legally protected interest, the violation of a right." In this case, the railroad did not violate Mrs. Palsgraf's rights, because the risk of harm to her was not foreseeable. "One who jostles one's neighbor in a crowd does not invade the rights of others standing at the outer fringe when the unintended contact casts a bomb upon the ground. The wrongdoer as to them is the man who carries the bomb not the one who explored it without suspicion of danger. . . ."

Judgment for Long Island Railroad.

Ratification may be implied when an employer fails to condemn an employee's acts within a reasonable time after the employer acquires knowledge of all the important facts. Once the employer ratifies the employee's contractual acts and the third party is notified, a contract exists between the employer and the third party which the employer is now legally obligated to perform. When notice is conveyed to a third party that the employer assumes all responsibilities for an employee's torts, the employer will be liable for the injuries sustained by that third party.

Employment Perspective

Christopher Evans is a salesclerk in Montclair's Electronics Store. Evans is greeted one morning by an enthusiastic salesman offering to sell the store two hundred videotapes on consignment. Evans believes the sale of video movies will greatly enhance the store's business, especially the sale of its video players and recorders. Evans signs the contract on behalf of Montclair even though he has no authority to do so. When apprised of Evans's action, Montclair believes it to be a smart move and notifies the salesman of his approval. If Montclair changes his mind and claims Evans's acts were not authorized, who will be responsible, Evans or Montclair? Evans was originally liable for breaching his duty of loyalty by exceeding the authority given to him. How-

CASE

Roberts v. United States Fidelity and Guaranty Company

498 So. 2d 1037 (Fla. App. 1 Dist. 1986)

JOANOS, Judge.

Wilhem left his Blazer at Miller's service station for repair with the understanding that he would pick it up the next day. After making the repairs, Miller drove the Blazer to the beach. On his return, the Blazer struck another vehicle and injured Roberts, a passenger in that vehicle. Roberts brought suit against Wilhem and his insurer, USF&G, claiming under Florida's dangerous instrumentality doctrine, "The owner of a vehicle is liable to third persons for its negligent operation by anyone to whom it has been entrusted, even if the bailee grossly violates the owner's express instructions concerning its use."

The issue is whether Miller was acting as Wilhem's agent when the injuries to Roberts occurred.

Under the shop rule exception, the owner is relieved from liability caused by the mechanic's negligence with whom he has left his car as long as he did not exercise any control over the operation of the vehicle while it was being serviced. Roberts's recourse lies against Miller.

Judgment for United States Fidelity and Guaranty Company.

ever, once Montclair ratified Evans's actions, Evans is no longer liable. Montclair will be solely liable to the third party—the videotape distributor. Would it be the same if Evans advised Montclair of his unauthorized act and Montclair said nothing? Yes! Ratification may be implied by silence, if the employer fails to disaffirm responsibility for the employee's acts after learning all the facts. Would Montclair be liable to the videotape distributor if he immediately notified the distributor that he would not assume liability for Evans's unauthorized acts? It would depend on whether it was the usual practice in the trade for a salesclerk to order new merchandise. If so, Montclair would be liable because Evans acted with apparent authority. If it was not the usual practice, then the salesclerk should have known that a salesclerk does not possess the authority to contract with a new concern and the owner should have been consulted. ◆

LIABILITY OF THIRD PARTIES

A third party is liable only to the employer. A third party is not liable to an employee unless the employee signs the contract in his or her own name.

CASE

Kampen v. Department of Transportation

502 N.E.2d 31 (Ill. App. 2 Dist. 1986)

UNVERZAGT, Judge.

Delmar Kampen is the owner of two unincorporated businesses, Kampen Farms and Kampen Fertilizer. In 1981, he leased a cargo tanker for hauling anhydrous ammonia. Kenneth Pierson, an employee of Kampen, agreed to haul the chemical to Kampen's property. The tanker was equipped with several safety features. The outlet valve was to remain closed unless the chemical flow caused it to open. A sudden change in pressure would cause the outlet valve to close immediately, preventing the chemical from escaping.

Pierson, who had been trained on another type of tanker, believed that the outlet valve had to be opened manually to cause the liquid to flow before the pump could be started. Pierson opened the valve manually and used vise grips to keep it opened. Attachment of the vise grips rendered the safety devices immobile and placed the tanker in violation of the outlet valve regulations of the Illinois Hazardous Materials Transportation Regulations. As Pierson started the pump, one of the hoses ruptured, releasing a cloud of ammonia gas. This resulted in substantial property damage. The Department of Transportation assessed a civil penalty of $4,500 against Kampen for the alleged violations.

The issue is whether Kampen is liable in tort for Pierson's negligence. Kampen contends that he is not liable because he did not direct, coerce, or participate in his employee's conduct.

The court stated, "When he attached vise grips to the outlet valve, Pierson realized that he was locking it open and that the grips must be removed in order to close the valve. This knowledge was clearly sufficient for civil liability under the act."

The court declared, "... Pierson was his agent, acting within the scope of his employment. We conclude that the civil penalty was therefore properly imposed on plaintiff (Kampen) for Pierson's conduct."

Judgment for Department of Transportation.

Employment Perspective

In the prior example, on p. 38, concerning the Porter's art auction, if Porter's refused to sell the painting to Alworth after Alworth's bid had been accepted and a contract had been signed by Alworth and Porter's, then either Alworth or Vanderbilt, the undisclosed principal, could enforce the contract. Alworth has the right to enforce the contract against Porter's even though he is an independent contractor, because he signed the contract in his own name. The fact that he is personally liable on the contract also gives him the right to enforce it. ◆

REVIEW QUESTIONS

1. When is an employer contractually liable?
2. Explain the types of torts an employer may be liable for.
3. Which of these are intentional, and which are unintentional?

4. How does an employer ratify an employee's acts?
5. Is a third party ever liable to an employee?
6. In the Case on p. 49, why is the Long Island Railroad liable?
7. In the Case on p. 51, why should Kampen be held liable?
8. When is an employee personally liable?
9. The Hudgins entered into a contract with Bacon to build a house for them. Bacon hired an independent contractor, who poured the footings and laid the foundation. Within a few months after the Hudgins moved into the house, it began to fall apart. The Hudgins brought action against Bacon for negligence and for breach of contract for failure to build the house in a workmanlike manner. Bacon contends that he cannot be held liable for any negligence caused by the independent contractor. What was the result? *Hudgins v. Bacon,* 321 S.E.2d 359 (Ga. App. 1984)
10. Equitable Life Assurance instructed Dr. Arora to administer a stress test to Sidney Rosenberg, a fifty-one-year-old man with a history of heart problems. Rosenberg died a month after taking the stress test, and it was determined to be the proximate cause of his death. His estate sued Equitable for wrongful death. What was the result? *Rosenberg v. Equitable Life Assurance Society,* 584 N.Y.S.2d 765 (Ct. App. 1992).
11. Sparks sued the Northeast Alabama Regional Medical Center, her employer, claiming to be sexually harassed by Dr. Garland. Sparks alleged that Dr. Garland joked about her breast size and sex life and cursed at her for being late in front of her coworkers. The hospital claimed that this was outside the scope of Dr. Garland's employment. What was the result? *Sparks v. Regional Medical Center Bd.,* 792 F.Supp. 735 (N.D. Ala. 1992).
12. Power Equipment's president, Robert Ferguson, signed a promissory note without reading it. The note contained a provision that the bank could demand payment at any time. Power Equipment alleged that the bank breached its fiduciary duty to inform Ferguson of the demand provision before he signed the note. What was the result? *Power Equipment v. First Alabama Bank,* 585 So.2d 1291 (Ala. 1991)
13. Kimberly Bunce entered the Parkside Lodge for rehabilitation from a cocaine addiction. Bryan Brown, a senior counselor, comforted Bunce on a few occasions. This situation led to a sexual relationship. After several encounters, Bunce revealed her relationship with Brown to Parkside, then left the facility. Brown resigned. Bruce sued Parkside for sexual assault, malpractice, and intentional infliction of emotional distress. Parkside claimed that it was not responsible for the intentional torts of its employee. What was the result? *Bunce v. Parkside Lodge of Columbus,* 596 N.E.2d 1106 (Ohio App. 10 Dist. 1991)
14. Cory Grote, a 16-year-old, was a high school rodeo champion. After receiving permission from Bruce Bushnell, foreman, he was allowed to visit his brother Brad at Joy Ranch, a division of Meyers. During his visit, Cory helped Brad release twelve colts into a corral. One of the colts, known to the ranchers to be uncontrollable, kicked Cory, causing him to have a skull fracture. Cory sued the ranch, claiming that the ranch was negligent in not informing him of the colt's dangerous propensities. Is the ranch liable for its employees' failure to warn Cory? *Grote v. Meyers Land and Cattle Co.,* 485 N.W.2d 748 (Neb. 1992)
15. Baker entered into an agency contract with two separate real estate brokers, Wheeler and Fairchild, giving each of them authority to sell property he owned. He did not advise either one of them of the other's agency. Eventually Wheeler produced a ready, willing, and able buyer, who entered into a contract with Baker. At a later date, Fairchild

procured a prospective purchaser, unaware that the real estate had already been sold by Wheeler. In a suit for a commission, would Fairchild be successful because he did not have notice of any revocation of his agency? *Ahern v. Baker,* 34 Minn. 98, 24 N.W. 341 (1885)

16. Lenheim managed a store for his brother and acted as his brother's purchasing agent. A fire consumed the store in July. After this date, Lenheim's agency was terminated by his brother. Claflin contracted with Lenheim in November and December, unaware that the agency had been terminated. In a suit by Claflin for the unpaid price, would Lenheim's brother be responsible for the goods sold to Lenheim even though the agency was terminated? *Claflin v. Lenheim,* 66 N.Y. 301 (1876)

17. Shoenthal was hired as manager of a clothing store operated by Ruth Shops, Inc. The letter confirming this employment was signed by Aaron Bernstein, an agent of Ruth Shops. Subsequently, Shoenthal was fired without just cause. He then sued Bernstein personally. Although Bernstein signed his name without designating his agency, the letter was written on Ruth Shops stationery. The issue is whether Bernstein is personally liable or whether Shoenthal clearly understood that Bernstein was acting as an employee for Ruth Shops. What was the result? *Shoenthal v. Bernstein,* 276 App. Div. 200, 93 N.Y. S.2d 187 (1949)

18. In 1969, William Spence entered into a verbal contract with Manning, the Webster Parish School Board's assistant superintendent, to operate a bus route. This ongoing relationship was terminated in 1983 when the school board decided to operate the route itself. The school board claims that Manning's acts were unauthorized. Spence asserts that Manning's acts were ratified by the board in 1975 when it requested that Spence purchase another bus. What was the result? *Spence v. Webster Parish School Board,* 499 So.2d 217 (La. App. 2 Cir. 1986)

19. The Flynns, owners of a pecan grove, entered into a contract with Gold Kist, Inc., in which Gold Kist would plant, harvest, and market the Flynns' pecans. The farm manager, Brinkley, stole pecans from the groves. The Flynns brought suit, claiming Gold Kist was liable for the tort committed by its employee. Gold Kist contends that Brinkley's tort was intentionally committed outside the scope of his employment. What was the result? *Flynn v. Gold Kist, Inc.,* 353 S.E.2d 537 (Ga. App. 1987)

20. John Soderberg held controlling interest in Copco Corp., which in turn owned 100 percent of Constitutional Casualty Co. When he died, his shares passed to a trust for his wife, Georgina, and their daughters, Janet and Christine. When Constitutional began to have financial difficulties, Janet suggested the company hire her newfound boyfriend, Timothy Gem, an associate of the patent law firm of Winben and Gray. Gem suggested that Constitutional improve its financial position by acquiring other companies from which income would be derived. Gem created the acquired companies to perpetuate a fraud. When Copco was eventually sold, the purchaser required that the Copco shareholders buy back the assets of the newly acquired companies. The Soderbergs lost the entire share of the purchase price in return for the worthless securities. Is the patent law firm of Winben and Gray liable for Gem's conduct? *Soderberg v. Gem,* 652 F.Supp. 560 (N.D. Ill. 1987)

PART II

Employment Procedure

CHAPTER 4

Selection

DISCRIMINATION IN SELECTION

The purpose of recruitment and selection is to obtain the best possible workers for a business. Discrimination is permissible because employers can discriminate among candidates based on interpersonal relations, communication skills, training, and education. It is not permissible because of suspect classifications such as race, religion, gender, and national origin. Because employees are valuable assets to a business, employers must be able to choose those employees who will perform the best work for the business. Education, training, communication skills, and interpersonal relations are key qualities that employees must possess to help a business be more successful.

The easiest way to discriminate against individuals is to do so in the recruitment and selection process. Employers may use a myriad of methods to evaluate an individual and his or her particular traits. Testing, interviews, writing samples, demonstrations, and role playing are a few examples. If these methods are job-related, then the employer has every right to use them. What an employer may not do is discourage potential candidates who belong to a particular suspect classification as defined by Title VII of the Civil Rights Act, Age Discrimination in Employment Act, and the American Disabilities Act.

Employment Perspective

Speedy Delivery Service (SDS), delivers packages to residential and business customers. All the delivery personnel are men, and SDS would like to keep it that way. Sandra Musial applied for a position. SDS discouraged her by showing her extremely bulky and heavy parcels. Sandra was told she would have to carry these packages up two, sometimes three, flights of stairs. Sandra withdrew her application. Later, she learned that other female applicants were told the same story but males were not. Sandra filed a claim with the EEOC. Will she win? Yes! The selection process is tainted. Males are encouraged, females are not. They must be treated the same. Suppose SDS advertised the position only in a men's fitness magazine, would this be discriminatory? Yes! It would be designed to attract only male applicants. If the job entailed only minor lifting, but in its advertisements, SDS stated that heavy lifting was required in order to discourage female applicants, would this be discriminatory? Yes! SDS would be misrepresenting the requirements for the position. ◆

In the case that follows, the court speaks to the issue of whether a male-dominated selection committee assigned a woman applicant the appropriate number of points for her experience and education. She had not received the position and was claiming the selection procedure was biased against women.

CASE

Stukey v. U.S. Air Force

809 F.Supp. 536 (S.D. Ohio 1992)

SPIEGEL, District Judge.

The essential issue in this case is whether gender was a motivating factor in the Defendants' decision not to hire the Plaintiff. Furthermore, we must decide whether the Defendants retaliated against the Plaintiff for filing an EEO claim in pursuit of this lawsuit.

The Plaintiff, Linda S. Stukey, worked as a civilian employee in the Office of the Staff Judge Advocate at Wright-Patterson Air Force Base in Dayton, Ohio from 1981 until November 1985. The legal office, for which Ms. Stukey worked, gave advice to the Wing Commander who ran the day-to-day operations at Wright-Patterson.

Ms. Stukey received several promotions in her work in the legal office at Wright-Patterson. She began her employment as a GS-9, but moved up to GS-12 by September 1983. In 1984 and 1985, she received step increases, based upon satisfactory job performances.

However, Ms. Stukey experienced some difficulties in getting along with work colleagues. In her work in the environmental law area, the Base Staff Judge Advocate General's Office recommended that Ms. Stukey not attend meetings with personnel in the civil engineering department, because of Ms. Stukey's personality conflicts.

At one point, Ms. Stukey complained of her excessive workload, in comparison to her supervisor. An outside investigator, Mr. Pedersen, concluded that the workload was relatively equal between Ms. Stukey and her supervisor.

In 1982, Ms. Stukey was assigned to the Labor Law Division of the Base Staff Advocate Office. In this position, she became familiar with the mechanics and process of sex discrimination lawsuits.

During 1984, Ms. Stukey had several lunches with James Gill and James Mahoy. Mr. Gill, Mr. Mahoy, and Ms. Stukey were all friendly with one another. Mr. Gill and Mr. Mahoy were teachers at the School of Systems and Logistics at the Air Force Institute of Technology ("AFIT").

AFIT is a North Central accredited school of higher education at Wright-Patterson Air Force Base. The legal office, for which Ms. Stukey

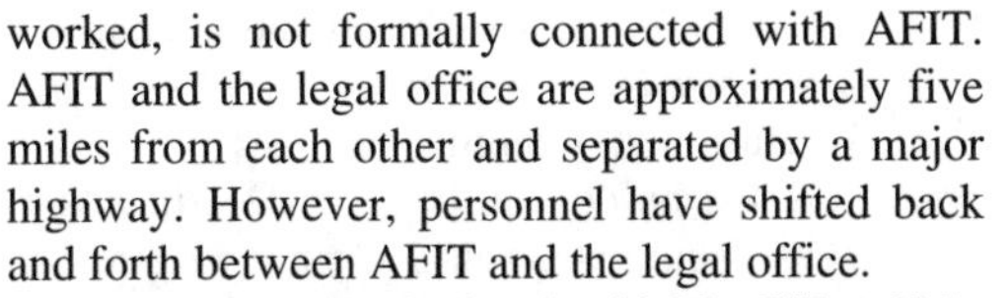

worked, is not formally connected with AFIT. AFIT and the legal office are approximately five miles from each other and separated by a major highway. However, personnel have shifted back and forth between AFIT and the legal office.

At one particular lunch with Mr. Gill and Mr. Mahoy, Ms. Stukey expressed dissatisfaction with her job in the legal office at Wright-Patterson. Mr. Gill and Mr. Mahoy informed Ms. Stukey that a teaching job might be opening at AFIT. Ms. Stukey had previously applied three times for a teaching job at AFIT, but never received an offer.

The teaching positions, or professorships, were appointments for not more than three years. At the end of the three years, tenure is generally granted, along with a substantial pay increase. In addition, AFIT professors are permitted to practice law part-time, outside of AFIT.

In December of 1984, two teaching positions at AFIT opened, and Ms. Stukey applied for the positions.

An affirmative action plan was established in part to guide AFIT in its hiring decision.

AFIT formed a five member subcommittee to conduct the selection process for the position. The members of the selection panel were William Dean, Ernest Spitzer, John Garrett, James Mahoy and Michael Schubert. All were male.

Mr. Mahoy had earlier told Major Mary Mudd, a teacher at AFIT but an applicant for the job, that it was embarrassing for a woman to correct a man. Mr. Mahoy specified that a female instructor, such as Ms. Mudd, should not correct a male student. Mr. Mahoy further felt that proof-reading was a proper task for women in law school.

Mr. Gill, a teacher at AFIT, frequently referred to Mr. Mahoy's secretary as "Miss Kitty." Ms. Mudd informed Mr. Gill that she considered this to be sexist, but he continued to call Mr. Mahoy's secretary "Miss Kitty."

Applicants first had to meet initial selection criteria. The selection committee then awarded points for different levels of professional attainment and teaching experience for those applicants who had met the initial selection criteria. Each member of the selection committee ranked the candidates separately and returned their scores to Mr. Dean. Mr. Dean compiled the scores and computed an average score for each applicant.

Selection committee members regularly disagreed with one another on how many points should be awarded to an applicant. For instance, no specific criteria existed for measuring teaching experience. Thus, the assignment of points for professional attainment and teaching experience involved some degree of subjectivity.

After the veterans' preference points were added in, Ms. Stukey ranked thirteenth out of sixteen qualified applicants.

Ms. Stukey had several experiences in teaching. Ms. Stukey directed educational seminars at Central State University and Antioch College from 1978 until 1981. In addition, Ms. Stukey had conducted seminars on a variety of legal topics, including labor law and housing law. Ms. Stukey had also been managing attorney for the Greene County Legal Aid Office from 1978 until 1981.

In contrast, one successful male candidate had only taught freshman chemistry at the University of Maryland in 1966–67. Nevertheless, the selection committee gave the male candidate substantially more teaching points than Ms. Stukey in the selection committee's evaluation.

After several applicants withdrew their applicants, the selection committee interviewed eight candidates, including Ms. Stukey, for the two positions at AFIT.

The interview process consisted of a mock teaching segment on the subject of termination for default in the government contracts area, followed by an informal interview consisting of questions about the candidate's background and experiences. The teaching segments were videotaped, as well as a portion of the informal interview.

Ms. Stukey received assistance in preparing for her presentation from James Gill, who was a member of the AFIT faculty. Mr. Gill recommended that Ms. Stukey contact Peg Arnold, the Wright-Patterson Terminations Contracting Officer, for additional assistance. As a result, Ms. Stukey consulted with Ms. Arnold to prepare for her interview.

Ms. Stukey arrived at the interview a few minutes early. Prior to the start of the March 25, 1985 interview, selection committee member Earnest Spitzer spoke with Ms. Stukey. In this conversation, Mr. Spitzer questioned Ms. Stukey about her divorce and her child care arrangements. Ms. Stukey claimed she was rattled by these questions, which as a labor lawyer, she knew were improper. Consequently, Ms. Stukey went to the water fountain to compose herself prior to her interview. Mr. Garrett then told Ms. Stukey that she looked nice.

Mr. Gill also sat in on Ms. Stukey's interview. Faculty members at AFIT were encouraged to attend the interviews of candidates. Mr. Gill, however, did not score Ms. Stukey's interview, because he was not a member of the selection committee.

Mr. Garrett and Mr. Dean, both selection committee members, testified that, prior to the interview, Ms. Stukey had a chance of being selected for one of the two positions.

Members of the selection committee testified that Ms. Stukey's teaching presentation was "disastrous." After carefully watching the videotape of Ms. Stukey's presentation and the videotape of one of the male selectees, we disagree. Despite being rattled by Mr. Spitzer's improper questions just prior to the start of the interview, Ms. Stukey gave a competent lecture on terminations for default. Although she was closely tied to her notes, Ms. Stukey was well-prepared and handled questions aptly.

Ms. Stukey has sued, alleging that the Defendants failed to select her for one of the AFIT teaching positions because of her gender in violation of Title VII, 42 U.S.C. 2000e (1991).

Congress enacted Title VII to ensure nondiscriminatory employment decisions. A plaintiff may prove sex discrimination by either direct or indirect evidence. Ms. Stukey has not presented any direct evidence that ". . . gender was a factor in the employment decision at the moment it was made. . . ." The selection committee awarded points to the candidates by consensus at a meeting following the interviews. No direct evidence came before the Court on how the selection committee actually arrived at the decision that Ms. Stukey should receive three points for her interview.

Therefore, we must now determine whether the Plaintiff can prove her case by indirect or circumstantial evidence. This determination must be made under the burden-shifting method of proof outlined in *McDonnell Douglas Corp. v. Green* (see Chapter 8). We must first determine whether Ms. Stukey has established a *prima facie* case. As a woman, Ms. Stukey is a member of a protected class. Ms. Stukey met the initial selection criteria in her application for a teaching position at AFIT, and as a result, she was one of the sixteen qualified applicants. Thus, Ms. Stukey has established a *prima facie* case.

Because the Plaintiff has met her *prima facie* case, the burden shifts to the Defendants to articulate a legitimate, non-discriminatory reason for not hiring Ms. Stukey. The Defendants articulated the reason that Ms. Stukey was not hired because she did poorly on her mock teaching exercise and because she did not have much teaching experience. Assuming these facts to be true, the Defendants have met their burden.

Thus, we must now consider whether the Plaintiff met her burden at trial to demonstrate by a preponderance of evidence at trial that the legitimate reason offered by the Defendants at trial were not the true reasons for their actions, but rather served as a pretext for discrimination.

The critical inquiry is whether gender was a factor in the employment decision at the moment the employment decision was made. It is impossible for this Court to crawl into the collective minds of the members of the selection committee to discover why they did not hire Ms. Stukey.

The Defendants also argue that even if Ms. Stukey had gotten the highest score on the interview, she still would not have received an offer for the position. This argument is supported by the facts. Mr. Garrett and Mr. Dean, both selection committee members, testified that prior to the interview, Ms. Stukey had a chance of being selected for one of the two positions. Furthermore, the assignment of points for professional attainment and teaching experience involved some degree of subjectivity. Selection committee members regularly disagreed with one another on how many points should be awarded to an applicant. In fact, Ms. Stukey received less credit for her teaching experience than one of the successful male candidates, despite the fact that Ms. Stukey had superior teaching experience.

Therefore, we conclude that gender was a factor in the Defendant's decision not to hire Ms. Stukey. The legitimate reason offered by the Defendants for her non-selection were not the true reasons for their actions, but rather as a pretext for discrimination.

We must now determine whether the Defendants retaliated against Ms. Stukey because she filed an EEO complaint in 1985 after not having been selected for a position at AFIT.

A *prima facie* case of retaliation or reprisal arises when a plaintiff establishes that: (1) she engaged in an activity protected under Title VII; (2) the employer subjected her to an adverse employment decision; and (3) a casual link exists between the protected activity and the employer's action.

However, in order to pursue a retaliation claim, a plaintiff must first exhaust her administration remedies. Ms. Stukey, an attorney with experience in labor law, never alleged retaliation in her informal administrative complaint or her formal administrative complaint. She filed her informal complaint on April 24, 1985 and her formal complaint on October 9, 1985. Many of the alleged acts of retaliation occurred prior to October 9, 1985. Therefore, Ms. Stukey is barred from asserting those instances of retaliation now, because she failed to exhaust her administrative remedies.

Additionally, Ms. Stukey fails to show that a causal link existed between the protected activity and her employer's action. In other words, Ms. Stukey has never demonstrated that filing of her complaint caused the unpleasant experiences she had at work in the summer and fall of 1985.

Ms. Stukey finally contends that her office was changed in retaliation. Indisputably, Ms. Stukey got moved to a less desirable office. Nevertheless, her new office was fit for an attorney, and the move was part of an office-wide reorganization which was announced at a staff meeting prior to the move. Two paralegals moved into Ms. Stukey's old office.

We must now determine what the appropriate relief is for the Plaintiff on her meritorious claim of sex discrimination. The Plaintiff asks for assorted injunctive relief. To reinstate Ms. Stukey would not be productive for either Ms. Stukey or the Air Force. Unfortunately, seven years of litigation have gone by since Ms. Stukey's non-selection. This litigation has helped to fester animosity on both sides. Therefore, we conclude that reinstatement is not proper.

We now examine the damages that Ms. Stukey had suffered. After leaving Wright-Patterson, Ms. Stukey started a private law practice. In her practice, Ms. Stukey earned \$243,775.00. If Ms. Stukey would have received the position at AFIT, she would have earned \$237,961.60 in wages. Plus, she would have earned benefits equal to some percentage of her wages. Ms. Stukey did not earn these same benefits in private practice. The Defendants asserted that 35.8 percent extra would have been earned, while the Plaintiff states that 40 percent should be used. As the Defendants have provided no reason for their 35.8 percent figure, we opt for the Plaintiff's recommended percentage, as the Plaintiff gave its reasons for the 40 percent figure at trial. Forty percent of \$237,961.60 is \$95,184.64. Therefore, Ms. Stukey would have earned \$333,146.24 in wages and benefits at AFIT, but only earned \$243,775.00 in private practice. Thus Ms. Stukey's damages are \$89,371.24.

We conclude that the Defendants impermissibly used gender in not selecting the Plaintiff for a position at AFIT. However, the Plantiff did not prove by a preponderance of the evidence that the Defendants retaliated against her for filing an EEO complaint.

Accordingly, judgment is granted to the Plaintiff in the amount of \$89,371.24.

Judgment for Stukey.

Employers may also not seek prospective applicants from pools that do not contain certain groups, such as recruiting from predominantly white male schools.

Employment Perspective

SDS is at it again. This time the company is recruiting candidates exclusively from Prestige College, a predominantly white male school. Is this practice discriminatory? Yes! ◆

Selection Process

The selection process must be free of discrimination. Great care must be taken to ensure that statements, overtures, and advertisements are not suspect. References to age must not be made because age is not a qualitative criterion to be used in the selection process. In an advertisement of a job description, the use of terms such as high school student, college student, recent college graduate, boy, girl, and only those under forty need apply are all examples of possible violations of the Age Discrimination in Employment Act.

Recruiting at colleges, graduate schools, and professional schools has long been a practice followed by many companies. This is a process in which a large pool of people seeking professional and office work are located and, for the most part, are unemployed. This practice may not in and of itself be discriminatory unless done exclusively. A company or professional firm that recruits only students at graduation is discriminating against people already in the labor force and possibly those without the mandated degree. Recruiting candidates solely from colleges for a position wherein a degree is not a justifiable necessity is discriminatory.

Employment Perspective

Rhodes, Lucas and Reed, is a prestigious accounting firm that recruits its entry level candidates solely from college. The firm advertises, "entry level positions available for this year's graduates only." Amanda Stewart graduated from college two years ago and has been working with a local accountant. She applies for the entry level position with Rhodes, Lucas and Reed because it would provide a sizeable salary increase and great experience. Amanda is rejected because of her experience. She claims discrimination. The firm argues that students right out of college can be trained and indoctrinated more easily. Amanda argues that her experience would not hamper that process in the least. Who wins? Amanda has a good chance of winning because of the exclusivity of the firm's policy with regard to hiring only college students. ◆

Employment Perspective

Safe T Alarm Systems advertises a position available for alarm-system planning and installation. Scott Feeney applies for the position but is rejected because he does not possess a college diploma. Scott argues an alarm system installer does not need a college education. Safe T recounts that college graduates have better interpersonal skills for dealing with people and possess sound reasoning skills for planning the layout of the alarm system. Who will be victorious? Scott! Safe T's argument will most likely fail because the college is not a justifiable business necessity for this type of position. Many individuals can and do perform this job adequately without possessing the college degree. While college graduates may be more qualified on average, it does not mean there are no qualified candidates among the remainder. To exclude this entire group because they do not possess a characteristic not crucial to the job is arbitrary and capricious. ◆

Employment Perspective

Simon, Matthews and Stevens, a Park Avenue law firm, consistently recruit new associates from three predominantly white male schools exclusively. Their firm is comprised of seventeen attorneys all of whom are protestant white males. They will not visit any other law schools. Simon, Matthews and Stevens conduct on-site interviews and, if interested, invite the select few for a visit to their office. Is the procedure discriminatory? Definitely! The firm is dismissing other qualified applicants without a justifiable reason. Simon, Matthews and Stevens may be looking to perpetuate the old-boy network by persisting in the maintenance of their policy of exclusivity. ◆

The following case addresses the question of whether an employment agency can address an advertisement toward recent college graduates. While the general rule is that such advertisements are discriminatory, this court carved out an exception for employment agencies when the ads are placed around the time of college graduation.

Hodgson v. Approved Personnel Serv.

529 F.2d 760 (1975)

CRAVEN, Circuit Judge.

The Department of Labor sued Approved Personnel Service, Inc., to enjoin alleged violations of the Age Discrimination in Employment Act of 1967, 29 U.S.C. ss 621, et seq. The complaint alleged that Approved Personnel Service, Inc. ("APS"), a Greensboro, North Carolina, employment agency, "has repeatedly violated, and . . . is violating . . . the Act by printing and publishing and causing to be printed and published notices and advertisements relating to classifications and referrals for employment by defendant indicating preferences, limitation, specifications, or discriminations based on age."

I.

In September 1968 a Department compliance officer visited APS to investigate certain company practices involving the wage-hour statutes. A discussion between the compliance officer and the president of APS touched incidentally upon the new Age Discrimination in Employment Act and its applicability to employment agencies. Although APS's president stated he knew the Act applied to his business, from November 1968 until October 1970, APS ran a number of advertisements soliciting job applicants using certain terms and phrases which the Department contends violate the Act. In October 1970 a compliance officer notified APS by telephone that help-wanted advertisements utilizing the term "recent college grad" were prohibited. The point was further impressed upon APS in December 1970 when another compliance officer visited the company's office and again warned that "recent grads" or similar terms could not be used. APS promised to discontinue the use of such terms.

The promise was not kept. On February 8th, 1972, the Area Director of the Department's Wage and Hour division notified APS by letter that help-wanted advertisements containing such terms as "young," "boy," and "recent college graduate" violated the Act. The letter included a copy of the Department's Interpretative Bulletin No. 860 and requested some assurance from APS that it would comply with the Act. APS's president responded by letter and advised the Area Director that changes in APS's advertising would be made.

Whatever changes were made did not satisfy the Department, for in July 1972 APS was again visited by a Department compliance officer. The officer advised APS's president that because of the company's repeated violations the Department was forced to turn the matter over for litigation.

At trial, the district judge found that some of the challenged advertisements violated the Act, while others did not. He further found that the Department had not "used proper methods of conciliation and persuasion as required by the Act." The district court denied an injunction, even against future use of advertisements clearly in violation of the Act, on two grounds: "first because of the confusion caused by the Secretary himself and, second, because the defendant has ceased using the terms in its advertisements."

II.

Congress passed the Age Discrimination Act "to promote employment of older persons based on their ability rather than age; to prohibit arbitrary age discrimination in employment; to help employers and workers find ways of meeting problems arising from the impact of age on employment."

The present appeal involves alleged violation under Section 4(e) of the Act, 29 U.S.C. ss 623 (e), dealing with employment agency practices. Section 4 (e) reads: (e) It shall be unlawful for an employer, labor organization, or employment agency to print or publish, or cause to be printed or published, any notice or advertisement related to employment by such an employer or membership in or any classification or referral for employment by such a labor organization, or relating to any classification or referral for employment by such an employment agency, indicating any preference, limitation, specification, or discrimination, based on age.

To assist employment agencies in their efforts to comply with the Act, the Department of Labor has issued Interpretative Bulletin No. 860. Section 860.92 of the Interpretative Bulletin provides in part:

> b) When help wanted notices or advertisements contain terms and phrases such as "age 25 to 35," "young," "boy," "girl," "college student," "recent college graduate," or others of a similar nature, such a term or phrase discriminates against the employment of older persons and will be considered in violation of the Act.

The relief sought here, an injunction against future violations of Section 4(e), is provided for in section 7(b) of the Act, 29 U.S.C. ss 626(b). In addition, Section 7(b) requires that:

> Before instituting any action under this section, the Secretary shall attempt to eliminate the discriminatory practice or practices alleged, and to effect voluntary compliance with the requirements of this chapter through informal methods of conciliation, conference, and persuasion. Only after such attempts have failed is the Secretary authorized to bring suit to compel obedience.

The district court felt that the Department had not made meaningful attempts to secure voluntary compliance from APS. We disagree. During the four-year period covered by this litigation, the Department contacted APS at least five times. Visits, telephone calls, and correspondence by Department personnel were part of a patient but unsuccessful effort to persuade APS to obey the law.

The earnest pledges given at trial by APS's management that it would not again violate the Act, if believed, are not dispositive of the Secretary's entitlement to injunctive relief. The fact is the company did not stop its use of prohibited advertisements until after the Department had filed suit. Understandably, the Secretary has had enough of APS's promises. If APS really intends to comply with the Act, its future business conduct will in no way be inhibited by an injunction. "It is to be noted that an injunction in this type of case is not a burdensome thing; it simply requires the employer to obey the law."

The most difficult problem presented by this appeal is the use by APS of the terms "recent college grads," "recent high school grads," and the like. The record reveals and the district court correctly discerned that APS used these phrases in different contexts and for different purposes, some of which violated the Act and others which did not. The Department urges that the Act absolutely forbids the use of these words in any context and for any purpose in employment advertisement. We are persuaded that the distinction drawn by the district court, while a subtle one, is correct. The district court held:

Defendant's use of terms such as "sharp recent grads," "recent college grads," "recent high school grads," "recent math grads," and other such broad, inclusive terms referring to recent graduates, when simply appealing generally to all such persons to avail themselves of defendant's services did not violate the Act. An extremely large number of graduates from various institutions enter the job market each year. They are usually inexperienced in job hunting. Defendant did not violate the Act by offering these people its services in finding employment. Therefore, it is not a violation of the Act for an employment agency to appeal to broad categories of individuals in such manner. It is not a violation of the Act for an employment agency to appeal to categories of people who have no prior experience in the job market when the sole purpose of the advertisement is to merely acquaint those individuals with defendant's services. This one time appeal to a category of people which would probably be composed mainly of the young does not discriminate against older individuals who, as a class, have had prior experience in the job finding process. All such appeals do is put the younger generation on a more even footing with their elders. To prevent the defendant from making such appeals would not benefit the older generation but would only penalize the younger. However, when such terminology is used in relation to a specific job, this likely would violate the Act. Most "recent graduates" are composed of young people. When the term is used with a specific job, it violates the Act since it is not merely informational to the job seeker but operates to discourage the older job hunter from seeking that particular job and denies them an actual job opportunity.

We hold that an employment agency advertisement directed to "recent graduates" as part of a broad, general invitation to a specific class of prospective customers coming into the job market at a particular time of year to use the services it offers does not violate the Act. But when these same words are used in reference to a specific employment opportunity, we think there is an implication that persons older than the normal "recent graduate" need not apply. Thus, such ads violate the Act. Acceptable advertisements of this type may emphasize the services and performance record of the agency itself, but must avoid representations of anticipated salaries as well as descriptions, general or specific, of job opportunities available to members of the class.

There may be other class advertisements that also escape the proscription of the Act. For example, when the Vietnam war ended it was not a violation of the Act to advertise services for "returning veterans." Perhaps presently an ad directed to "laid-off automobile workers" would not infringe, even though most of those laid off may be younger because of seniority rules. But generally an appeal to a younger class is suspect and in no event may be justified except as an infrequent effort to acquaint a class with the availability of employment service, as opposed to notice of availability of jobs restricted for that class only or preferentially.

The decision below is reversed.
Judgment for Hodgson.

Uniform Guidelines on Employee Selection Procedures

Uniform Guidelines on Employee Selection Procedures was enacted in 1978 to provide counsel in the proper methodology used in the selection process to avoid infringement of Title VII, Equal Employment Opportunity Act (Affirmative Action) and the Equal Pay Act. While not applying directly to the Age Discrimination in Employment Act and the American Disabilities Act, other guidelines are available for consultation in these areas.

Selection Procedure

The term *selection procedure* encompasses the use of aptitude testing, physical evaluations, educational credentials, employment experience, training programs, probationary terms, resumes, interviews, and application forms to evaluate prospective candidates. These guidelines apply to employers, employment agencies, testing organizations, and labor unions.

Employment Perspective

E. J. Roberts receives about fifty unsolicited resumes each month for positions with his marketing research firm. He dumps most of these in the garbage. Every once in a while he leafs through a few while he is having a cup of herbal tea. If something catches his eye, he notifies his secretary to contact the person for an interview. Is E. J.'s procedure in contradiction with the Uniform Guidelines on Employee Selection Procedures? Yes! There is no objective standard of judgment employed in E.J.'s procedure. It is arbitrary and capricious. ◆

The employer's right to investigate the employee's background including past criminal records is based on the employer's showing of a justifiable business necessity.

The following case addresses the question of whether an employer can question the applicant and do a follow-up check on prior convictions of theft where the job involves handling the personal belongings of customers.

CASE

Richardson v. Hotel Corporation of America

332 F.Supp. 519 (1971)

ALVIN B. RUBIN, District Judge.

The issue in this case is whether a hotel may lawfully discharge a bellman because, previous to his employment by the hotel, he has been convicted of theft and of receiving stolen goods. The argument that raises the issue is based on the thesis that it can be shown that more black persons than white have been convicted of serious crimes, and hence that the discharge of persons based solely on their criminal record is inherently discriminatory racially, hence violates Title VII.

The plaintiff filed an application for employment at the Royal Sonesta Hotel at a time when the newly constructed hotel was just beginning to operate. When asked on his application whether he had been convicted of a crime other than minor traffic violations, he responded in the affirmative. At this time, the hotel was hiring a large number of new employees and it could not secure police checks prior to its opening; as a result of this and a clerical error made in processing the plaintiff's application, he was hired as a bellman. As soon as his prior convictions of theft and receiving stolen goods were reported in a routine employment check, he was informed that he would not be eligible to continue as a bellman, but was offered other employment with the defendant. He refused the offer and was discharged. He was later replaced by a black bellman.

The plaintiff contends his discharge was discriminatory. *Griggs v. Duke Power Co.* (see Chapter 8) supplies the basic test: Congress has required "the removal of artificial, arbitrary, and unnecessary barriers to employment when the barriers operate invidiously to discriminate on the basis of racial or other impermissible classification." In *Griggs* the Court found that to require a high school diploma or the ability to pass a standardized general education test as a condition of employment in or transfer to certain jobs operated to disqualify Negroes at a substantially higher rate than whites. There had been no showing by the employer that there was any real relationship between this educational requirement and ability to do the job. "Congress has placed on the employer the burden of showing that any given requirement must have a manifest relationship to the employment in question."

The evidence here shows that the hotel rejects applicants for employment in positions it considers "security sensitive" if they have been convicted of a serious crime. Bellmen occupy one of the several positions that the hotel considers "security sensitive." They have access to guests' luggage and to guests' rooms. They are permitted to obtain room keys from the desk clerk, and even to go behind the desk for keys. They may go through hotel corridors unaccompanied without provoking inquiry. They may enter and leave the hotel by any exit during the day, carrying parcels, while most employees must use a special employees' entrance where they are subject to scrutiny by a guard, and packages are subject to inspection. Some effort is made by the Head Bellman to be aware of the whereabouts of bellmen during the day. Bellmen are expected to keep time records showing their activities. But these are not carefully scrutinized and they can of course be easily evaded: A bellman going to any specified room on a real errand might stop by another room en route without making any entry on his duty sheet. The crucial issue therefore is whether the hotel's policy has been shown to be required by its business needs. A past criminal record affords no basis to predict that a given person will commit a future crime. But the evidence indicates that a group of persons who have been convicted of serious crimes will have a higher incidence of future criminal conduct than those who have never been convicted. It is reasonable for management of a hotel to require that persons employed in positions where they have access to valuable property of others have a record reasonably free from convictions for serious property related crimes.

Furthermore, the evidence demonstrates that the policy followed with respect to the plaintiff has been followed with regard to white bellman. Moreover, the defendant has shown that it does not exact a similar requirement of employees who do not have access to guests' property, and that it has had an exemplary record with respect to affording equal opportunity in jobs at all levels to persons who are members of minority groups. While not decisive, these factors suggest that the requirement was not intentionally invidious. Because of this, it may be concluded that the discharge of the plaintiff was not the result of an artificial, arbitrary or unnecessary barrier, but resulted instead from a genuine business need.

No federal statute prohibits discrimination per se; rather, what is prohibited is discrimination that is racially motivated. Here, no racial discrimination is shown. For these reasons it is unnecessary to accept the invitation to explore issues of whether it would be acceptable to base an employment criterion on arrest records, or whether conduct that does not violate Title VII might violate Section 1981. Assuming jurisdiction under either or both statutes, the plaintiff has failed to show discrimination because of race, and the defendant has established that its criteria were reasonable and related to job necessities.

Judgment for Hotel Corporation of America.

Disparate Impact

Disparate impact may be defined as having an adverse or detrimental effect on a particular group. The main thrust of the Uniform Guidelines is to recognize and encourage the discontinuance of selection procedures that have a disparate impact on minorities and women. Men are also covered in situations where gender is a determining factor in the selection process. Minority groups include Blacks, Hispanics, Asians, and American Indians.

To eliminate a disparate impact, records must be kept of the number of each minority group and gender that apply and the number of each group selected. If the percentage of minorities selected is at least 80-percent of the percentage of whites selected, there is no adverse effect. If the 80-percent rule is not met, then a detriment in employment selection exists against the particular group of minority or women applicants.

Employment Perspective

ABC Mutual Fund places an advertisement for customer service representatives. One hundred positions are available. Three hundred applicants are received: 100 women and 200 men, including 150 whites, 50 Blacks, 50 Asians, and 50 Hispanics. The selections made were 20 women and 80 men, including 75 whites, 5 Blacks, 20 Asians, and 0 Hispanics. Does the selection procedure have an adverse effect on the minorities and women? Yes. A disparate impact exists against Blacks, Hispanics, and women. The percentage of whites chosen out of those whites who applied was 50 percent. That means all minority group selection rates must be within 80 percent of the 50 percent white rate. Minority groups selection rates must be at least 40 percent. The selection rate of Asians met the test, 50 applicants of which 20 were chosen—that is 40 percent. The Black selection rate was 10 percent, and the Hispanic selection rate was 0 percent. Both of these fall far short of the required rate and are evidence of discrimination, according to the Uniform Guidelines of Employee Selection Procedures. The selection rate of women was 20 percent: 20 out of 100. The selection rate of men was 40 percent: 80 out of 200. The women's percentage was only one-half, or 50 percent, of the men's percentage. This result does not meet the 80 percent rule and is evidence of discrimination. ◆

Disparate Treatment

Disparate treatment arises when an individual is not selected because of a suspect classification. Whereas disparate impact is directed against the group, disparate treatment is directed against the individual.

In the following case on p. 69, a white male believes he is not progressing within the company to the degree he should, based on his impressive qualifications and experience. He claims minority employees are being favored. The issue is whether his belief of disparate treatment can be supported by facts.

Investigation and Record-Keeping

To properly conduct an investigation, the EEOC has the right to evidence which has a bearing on the alleged unlawful employment practice. This would include the right of access to documentation, as well as to the coworkers, superiors, and subordinates of the employee alleging a Title VII violation for the purpose of questioning them.

CASE

Ulrich v. Exxon Co. U.S.A. A Div. of Exxon Corp.

824 F.Supp. 677 (S.D. Tex 1993)

CRONE, Judge.

Ulrich, a white male employee of Exxon, instituted this action on April 10, 1992, alleging that defendants have discriminated against him in employment on the basis of his race in violation of the Civil Rights Act of 1866, 42 U.S.C. 1981. He also contends that defendants, specifically Lawley, have intentionally inflicted emotional distress upon him and tortiously interfered with his beneficial relationship with Exxon. Lawley served as Ulrich's second level supervisor from 1983 through 1992, except for a one-year period from February 1987 to February 1988, when Ulrich was assigned to a special project.

Ulrich, who presently is classified either as a senior contract administrator or senior buyer, has been employed by Exxon since 1979. According to the complaint, Ulrich graduated *cum laude* in 1975 from Sam Houston State University with a B.S. degree in chemistry and mathematics, having received state and national recognition for his academic achievements in chemistry. In 1985, he earned his M.B.A. in finance and international business from the University of St. Thomas. In 1984, he was qualified as a Certified Purchasing Manager by the National Association of Purchasing Management, and was recertified in 1989. He also has completed numerous training courses in his professional area.

According to Ulrich, he has not progressed at Exxon to the level merited by his qualifications, abilities and performance. He complains that Exxon utilizes a highly subjective and arbitrary system for job performance evaluation, which includes a ranking system where employees who are determined to be within the same peer group are ranked from best to worst. Additionally, Exxon supervisors are required to prepare a "career potential assessment" of employees, which is critical to an employee's ability to advance within the company. Ulrich alleges that "in order to attempt to escape closer scrutiny by state and federal agencies enforcing statutory provisions for equal employment opportunity, Exxon has directed that individuals representing racial minorities be hired and promoted and placed in positions designed to provide maximum visibility to the incumbents." He contends that these efforts have been utilized to manipulate personnel decisions in disregard of individual ability and performance. He asserts, for example, that managers may artificially inflate the rating and ranking of selected minority employees to fill positions in preference to white employees of established merit and experience. As a result of these alleged practices, Ulrich asserts that he has been arbitrarily and capriciously ranked and assessed well below the level merited by his knowledge, training, experience and performance, leading to a loss of pay and promotional opportunities.

Defendants assert that Ulrich has not presented even a *prima facie* case of race discrimination.

Prior to the enactment of the Civil Rights Act of 1991 ("CRA") section 1981 provided, in pertinent part that "all persons within the jurisdiction of the United States shall have the same right in every State and Territory to make and enforce contracts . . . as is enjoyed by white citizens . . .". The pre-amendment 1981 protected only the right to enter into an employment contract and to enforce an employment contract through legal process. Section 1981 protection did not extend to discrimination in the conditions of employment once the initial employment relationship was entered. Thus, the conduct about which Ulrich complains prior to that date is actionable only if it involved discrimination in the formation of the employment contract or in the enforcement of the contract through legal process.

Failure to promote constitutes discrimination in the formation of a contract under pre-CRA 1981: "only where the promotion rises to the level of an opportunity to enter a new distinct relation between the employee and employer." A mere transfer to a different department performing essentially similar tasks is not a new and distinct relationship. This is true even when transfer to a particular division or group is a precondition to receiving a promotion or progressing within a company. Further, allegations of discrimination in evaluation and compensation were not cognizable under pre-CRA 1981.

Thus, Ulrich cannot now maintain his pre-CRA 1981 claims because they involve neither discrimination in the formation of an employment contract nor enforcement of the contract through legal process. Because all of Ulrich's promotion claims arose prior to November 21, 1991, and none encompasses the opportunity to enter into a new and distinct relationship with Exxon, they are not actionable under 1981. They are also barred by the two-year statute of limitations applicable in 1981 cases, as they occurred before April 10, 1990. Ulrich's evaluation and compensation claims that arose prior to November 21, 1991, likewise, are not actionable under 1981. The majority of them are also barred by the statute of limitations. Ulrich's reliance on the continuing violation theory is of no avail, because, prior to November 21, 1991, Ulrich's claims, even if proven, simply did not constitute a violation of 1981 that could be "continued." Accordingly, Ulrich's pre-CRA 1981 claims must be dismissed.

The United States Supreme Court has construed 1981 as affording a federal remedy against discrimination in private employment on the basis of race to white persons as well as to minorities. Thus, like Title VII, 1981 prohibits discriminatory preference for *any* racial group, *minority or majority*. Ultimately, to prevail on a 1981 claim, Ulrich must prove purposeful discrimination by defendants because he is white.

Section 1981, like Title VII, does not "give employers license to discriminate against some employees on the basis of race or sex merely because he favorably treats other members of the employees' group." Indeed, "a given employer may discriminate against an individual white worker even when no evidence demonstrates that the employer generally favors workers who belong to historically disadvantaged groups."

In this case however, the only evidence of employment discrimination that Ulrich offers is his own deposition testimony that lesser qualified racial minorities have advanced ahead of him in compensation and promotional opportunities. Ulrich contends that he has been "displaced" by every minority employee who ranked above him in his various peer grouping, meaning that although he did not aspire to their specific positions, because of the minority employees' relative rankings, "money flowed from [his] pocket into theirs." He also asserts that his educational credentials and professional certification make him a better-qualified employee than many of the whites who have ranked above him, and confirms that he has likewise been "displaced" by these higher-ranking whites.

The sole evidence of Ulrich's relative rankings, encompassing the years 1983 through 1992, was proffered by Exxon. Because Ulrich's pre-CRA 1981 claims are not actionable, the only evidence presently before the court that may be taken into consideration at this point is the relative rankings for 1991 and 1992. In 1991, Ulrich ranked 47th out of 60 employees (23%), ranking below 40 white and 6 minority employees. In 1992, Ulrich was ranked 42nd of 55 employees (25%) ranking below 38 white and 3 minority employees. Although in his deposition, Ulrich names a number of minorities whom he views as being less qualified and poorer employees than he, he fails to present any evidence concerning the specific identities, qualifications, experience, or performance of the 6 minority employees who ranked above him in 1991 or the 3 minority employees who ranked above him in 1992. Moreover, Ulrich presents no basis for his subjective beliefs concerning the performance of the minority employees he names; he has never supervised any of them. In addition, Ulrich admits that an employee holding an M.B.A. degree or Certified Purchasing Manager credentials would not always be a better performer in terms of what Exxon is seeking in a particular job.

To establish a claim of disparate treatment, Ulrich must show that Exxon gave preferential treatment to a minority. Without more specific information about the higher ranking minority em-

ployees, this court cannot say that their circumstances were "nearly identical" to that of Ulrich. The fact that a white employee is passed over in favor of a minority employee does not necessarily amount to discrimination or give rise to an inference of discrimination.

In an apparent effort to bolster his case, Ulrich states in his deposition that one of his supervisors told him that he had been "burned, snake bit, and screwed" in the ranking process. Yet, he does not claim that the supervisor attributed Ulrich's treatment to the fact that he is white, nor does he say that the supervisor thought he had been mistreated in relation to minority employees. Ulrich also asserts that he has not been placed in "high profile" positions, like some of the minorities, which might have highlighted his contributions. He admits, however, that white employees have also been placed in "high profile" positions and that minority employees should not be barred from such positions by virtue of their race.

Ulrich contends that the unfair advantages, which he perceives minority employees to enjoy, stem from Exxon's interpretation of its affirmative action plan. Once again, he fails to advance any specific facts in support of his contention. He does not even attach a copy of the affirmative action plan to his response or detail its relevant provisions, much less explain how the specific minority employees ranked above him benefitted from the plan. It is well established that the presence of an affirmative action plan is not evidence of discrimination against the majority. Yet, Ulrich makes no effort to tie any specific provisions of the plan, or their interpretation by Exxon officials, to his own situation and allegations of racial discrimination.

A subjective belief of discrimination, however genuine, cannot alone be the basis for judicial relief.

The court acknowledges that subjective evaluation procedures, like those involved in the instant case, which often appear to be arbitrary and are always susceptible to discriminatory application, should be carefully scrutinized.

Ulrich has made no showing, however, that the subjective evaluation procedures were applied to him in a discriminatory manner because of his race. Were the court to conclude that a different method of evaluation might operate more fairly, this would not assist Ulrich, as the discrimination laws are "not intended to be a vehicle for judicial second-guessing of business decisions, nor . . . to transform the courts into personnel managers."

In summary, Ulrich's proffered summary judgement evidence consists exclusively of conclusory and speculative allegations of race discrimination which are unsupported by specific facts. In the court's view, this evidence is insufficient to support a *prima facie* case of employment discrimination or to raise a genuine issue of material fact.

Judgment for Exxon Co. U.S.A.

Employers are obligated to keep records relating to their methods of selection, compensation, promotion, training, and termination of employees. Test scores and the chronological order of applications for hiring, training, and promotion, must be part of the record-keeping.

These records must be made available to the EEOC to enable them to determine whether unlawful employment practices have been committed. An employer may seek an exemption from the EEOC if it can prove the burden of record-keeping presents undue hardship. A notification of excerpts of Title VII is required to be posted by each employer in a conspicuous setting to apprise current employees as well as applicants of the existence of Title VII.

Record-keeping can be burdensome, especially for small firms that do not have a human resources department. In addition to keeping records denoting the number of persons who applied and the number of persons who were selected in each job category for each suspect classification, similar record-keeping must be kept for promotions and terminations as well.

Samples

Where the number of applicants and those selected are so numerous that maintaining records on every individual would be too burdensome, the Uniform Guidelines on Employee Selection Procedures permits the company to select samples and maintain records on them. The sample must be adequate in size and representative of the various groups. If it is not, then the sample may be challenged and an inference of discrimination may be drawn. If the sample is viable but results in a disparate impact, the company is bound by it. The company may not dispute the authenticity of its own sample.

The Bottom Line

The Uniform Guidelines on Employee Selection Procedures adopts the bottom line approach where a myriad of selection procedures are utilized. If one criterion is tainted, the selection process will not be found to be discriminatory where other criteria have offset it and the final results do not violate the 80 percent rule.

Employment Perspective

Thompson Meat Packing Plant employs three criteria in its employee selection process: a weight-lifting test, a dexterity test, and an application form. Hispanics, Asians, and women who apply have difficulty with the weight-lifting test because of their small stature. Their overall selection rate satisfies the 80 percent rule. Regardless, these groups claim that a greater number of them would have been selected but for this test and that weight-lifting is not a job necessity. Will they win? No! Since a significant number of women, Asians, and Hispanics are being selected, the bottom line is not discriminatory, the weight-lifting component does not have to be justified as a business necessity. ◆

Questioning

Questioning an applicant about his or her religion, national origin, race, and age is discriminatory. Inquiries regarding marital status, the number of children, or the prospects of having children are also suspect. An employer may not require an applicant to state whether he or she has a disability or to submit information concerning the disability. This would be an unfair employment practice. However, the employer may require the applicant to undergo a physical or mental examination to determine whether the person has the ability to perform the job. The examination must relate only to the essential job-related functions and must not be a fishing expedition. It must be required of all applicants, not just those with a perceived disability.

The American Disabilities Act (ADA), along with most state civil rights acts, prohibits discriminating against an individual in the selection process because of a disability. A disability is defined as a physical or mental condition that results in a substantial handicap. The employer may be required to reasonably accommodate disabled individuals to enable them to perform the jobs that but for their handicap they would be qualified to do.

Employment Perspective

Mary Thomas applied for a position as a computer programmer with Computer Wizard. She was given a computer language exam. Her references and educational background were checked, and she was required to undergo a physical examination. Mary's qualifications were superb except for the physical examination, which disclosed that she had had a breast removed four years ago because of cancer. Mary was not hired. She filed a claim with the EEOC, alleging disability discrimination. Computer Wizard claimed it did not want to hire someone with a history of cancer. Such a person might incur huge medical expenses in the future, and the company's medical insurance premiums might skyrocket. Is this a valid reason for not hiring her? No! Her breast removal is not related to an essential job-related function. Had she been missing fingers or an arm that related to her typing skills, that disability might be a consideration. However, even then a reasonable accommodation may be made or possibly the person may type as fast with one arm as someone with two arms. In that case, the disability would have no effect. ◆

DISCRIMINATION IN PROMOTIONS

The reason that certain groups are promoted less frequently is due in part to discrimination and in part to social factors. Promotions often entail more responsibility, longer hours, travel requirements, attendance at social affairs, decision-making requirements, and greater stress. Young people, a greater number of whom are single, may welcome the traveling and may not mind the longer hours. Older individuals with families, especially women who are mothers, may find the benefits of the promotion outweighed by their presumption that their quality of life will decline. The Equal Employment Opportunity Act presumes an equal percentage of all groups seek promotions. Overcoming this premise is a difficult task for the employer.

Promotion Criteria

When a possibility exists within a firm for a promotion or transfer, the employer must post the job along with its description in a conspicuous manner, and a formal evaluation procedure must be followed. The procedure must utilize criteria which are job-related, and the imposition of these criteria must be uniformly applied to every applicant. The managers who are in charge of recommending candidates for promotion must be judged on the basis of their recommendations to determine whether they are acting in conformity with equal employment opportunity guidelines. Finally, the racial, ethnic, and gender composition of the manager will be looked into where a breach of equal opportunity employment occurs.

In the next case, a female applicant questions the selection procedure used in the appointment over her of a male who is less experienced than she is. She claims that if not for her gender, she would have been selected.

824 F.Supp. 1345 (D. Neb. 1993)

PIESTER, Judge.

Plaintiff was first employed by the Box Butte County Weed District Board (weed board) in the spring of 1986, as a part-time sprayer during the summer months. She continued to work as a sprayer for the weed board over the next few years, during which time she also began taking on more responsibility and assisting the weed superintendent, Chris Burks, in nearly every facet of the weed board business.

In March of 1987, defendant Foley, a member of the weed board, headed an attempt to force Chris Burks to resign as weed superintendent, after he and others on the weed board became dissatisfied with her performance. At some point during the attempt to force the resignation of superintendent Burks, Gary Craig was first approached by defendant Foley about the prospect of applying for the superintendent position.

On November 7, 1989, at a regularly scheduled meeting of the county board, superintendent Burks resigned her position in order to accept employment with the Nebraska Department of Agriculture. At that meeting the county board appointed plaintiff as acting superintendent, effective immediately, pending the hiring of a permanent weed superintendent. Plaintiff's salary was set at $1,200.00 per month with no benefits. A public announcement was made regarding the permanent superintendent position, and an interview date was set.

At a meeting on November 21, 1989, the weed board and county board became aware that the only two applicants for the superintendent's position were plaintiff and Gary Craig. Kenneth Luce, a member of the weed board, testified that after discussing the applicants, three members of the weed board stood up and announced they wished to hire Gary Craig as the new superintendent. When Kenneth Luce reminded the three that interviews had not yet been held, they sat down and the meeting continued.

Interviews were held on December 19, 1989. Present during the interviews were all five members of the weed board and all three members of the county board. Gary Craig was interviewed first, because plaintiff was finishing weed board business in another office in the courthouse when the interviewers were ready to begin. Gary Craig testified that just prior to his interview he was provided with a written job description and a list of questions he may be asked during the interview. He was given an opportunity to review the job description and questions prior to the interview, and returned them to the interviewers after his interview.

Plaintiff was then interviewed. Unlike Gary Craig, she was not provided with a written job description and list of questions prior to or at any point during her interview. When asked about the number of categories on her EPA card, plaintiff informed the interviewers that she had recently been certified in two more categories, bringing her total EPA categories to five. This evidently angered certain weed board members, who refused to consider plaintiff's recently added categories and instead insisted on comparing the applicants on the basis of their EPA categories as they existed on the date the applications were submitted—when plaintiff had three categories and Gary Craig had four.

Following the interview, the weed board voted 3–2 to hire Gary Craig as weed superintendent. When it was pointed out that such a vote was improper—not having taken place at an official weed board meeting—it was agreed to postpone the taking of a vote until the next weed board meeting.

On January 4, 1990, the weed board met to vote on the hiring of a superintendent. The county board requested the vote and was present at the weed board meeting. At the meeting the weed board voted 3–2 to hire Gary Craig.

As a result of defendants' actions in rejecting her for the position of weed superintendent, plaintiff testified that she suffered both emotionally and physically. She became depressed, was unable to sleep, became emotional and cried when she saw people on the street, and felt as though her reputation in the community had been destroyed. She gained 40 pounds following the incident, and although she sought medical attention, she was able to afford only one visit.

Plaintiffs Title VII claim was brought against Box Butte County and the Box Butte County Weed Board.

The United States Supreme Court established a three-step framework for analyzing employment discrimination cases such as the one asserted by plaintiff. Recently, the Eighth Circuit Court of Appeals described the McDonnell Douglas–Burdine test as follows:

> Under the first stage of the McDonnell Douglas–Burdine framework, the plaintiff had the burden of production to establish a prima facie case of discrimination. A plaintiff must generally demonstrate four elements to establish a prima facie case: (1) that plaintiff is a member of a protected class, (2) that the plaintiff meets the minimum qualifications for the position, (3) that the plaintiff suffered some kind of adverse employment action, (4) that the employer continued to try to fill the position from among applicants with plaintiff's qualifications.

A plaintiff who establishes a prima facie case "in effect creates a presumption that the employer unlawfully discriminated against the employee," . . . and the analysis reaches the second stage of the McDonnell Douglas–Burdine framework. In the second stage, the burden of production "shifts to the defendant 'to articulate some legitimate nondiscriminatory reason for the employee's rejection.'"

A defendant who articulates a legitimate nondiscriminatory reason overcomes the presumption of discrimination raised by the prima facie case . . . and the case must then proceed to the third stage, the plaintiff must demonstrate that the defendant's proffered reason is mere pretext, "either directly, by persuading the court that a discriminatory reason more likely than not motivated the employer, or indirectly, by showing that the employer's proffered explanation is unworthy of credence."

In this instance I conclude plaintiff has established a prima facie case of sex discrimination by demonstrating that (1) she is a member of a protected class under Title VII; (2) she was qualified for the position of weed superintendent; (3) she was denied the position. Thus, plaintiff has, in effect, created a presumption that she was unlawfully discriminated against and the burden of production now "shifts to the defendant 'to articulate some legitimate nondiscriminatory reason for the employee's rejection.'"

Defendants articulate a number of reasons why they chose Gary Craig over plaintiff for the position of weed superintendent. Based upon the evidence adduced at trial, I find the proffered reasons to be pretextual.

First, defendants suggest Gary Craig was hired because he had the better resume. The evidence did not bear this out. A brief comparison of the resume and cover letters submitted by plaintiff and Gary Craig demonstrates the frailty of defendants' assertion.

Plaintiff's resume indicated she had been employed for the past four years with the weed control board, during which time she had an active part in the development and implementation of many programs. She conducted weed board business in the superintendent's absence, became familiar with the Weed Control Act and learned the mapping and record keeping procedures used by the weed board. Her resume further indicated that while working for the weed board she developed a working relationship with most of the Box Butte County landowners and had designed individual programs to meet their weed control needs. She supervised and trained new weed board employees, supervised the mixing and applying of herbicides, and educated the public regarding weed control practices. She had a working knowledge of weed inspection and enforcement procedures and had experience running the prairie dog control program in the off-season. She operated and maintained the vehicles and spray equipment used by the weed board, including installing and repairing small engines and electric pumps used in spraying.

In contrast, Gary Craig's resume indicated he had been employed by Box Butte County as a road grader for the past six years. Prior to that, he had been a self-employed farmer for seven years. He had no experience carrying out a weed eradication program, no experience administering a prairie dog program, no experience mapping weed infestations or documenting the spraying of weeds, and no experience maintaining the equipment used in the weed control program. His resume indicated he worked with chemical fertilizers a number of years prior to applying for weed superintendent, but he admitted in his cover letter that he was not familiar with newer chemicals. After comparing the two resumes in light of the specific duties of the superintendent, it is evident that defendants' assertion that Gary Craig was hired because he had the better resume is not worthy of credence.

Next, defendant asserts they hired Gary Craig over plaintiff because he had mechanical ability. Defendants acknowledge that mechanical ability was not identified specifically as a hiring criterion, but maintained it was nonetheless something they were looking for in a weed superintendent. There was no evidence that mechanical ability had ever before been a consideration.

Because the actions of the Box Butte County Commissioners can provide a basis for county liability, I conclude Box Butte County is liable to plaintiff for discriminating against her upon the basis of her gender in violation of the Equal Protection Clause.

Plaintiff requests declaratory, injunctive and monetary relief. Specifically, she requests: (1) she be employed as weed superintendent of Box Butte County with back pay and benefits; (2) she be awarded "liquidated" damages for defendant's willfull violation of Title VII; (3) she be awarded compensatory and punitive damages for violation of her constitutional rights; and (4) she be awarded costs and attorneys' fees.

Plaintiff has requested she be employed as weed superintendent of Box Butte County and be awarded back pay and benefits. Pursuant to 42 U.S.C. 2000e 5(g), I conclude plaintiff is entitled to such relief and I shall grant defendant Box Butte County a period of 60 days following the entry of judgement in which to employ plaintiff in the position of weed superintendent for the Box Butte County. I shall further order that plaintiff be awarded front pay in an amount equal to the salary provided the weed superintendent until such time as she is employed as weed superintendent.

Evidence showed that during 1990, 1991, and 1992 the weed superintendent was paid a total of $53,525.00. During this same period, the evidence showed plaintiff earned a total of $22,837.00. Therefore, under 2000e 5(g) interim earnings serve to reduce the back pay otherwise allowable), plaintiff is entitled to recover $30,688.00 as back pay from Box Butte County.

Evidence also showed that during 1990, 1991 and 1992 the weed superintendent was entitled to receive $802.00 in retirement benefits.

Judgment for Bruhn.

Nepotism and Promoting from Within

Nepotism is the hiring of family members. Some companies forbid this action; others allow it if the employed family member does not take part in the decision process. Still others encourage it wholeheartedly. This approach, as well as the concept of promoting from within, is incestuous because it may discourage diversity. If that is so, discrimination exists. Employers argue that promoting from within allows the company to reward an individual who is known and respected. While there is substance in that argument, if the result is the creation of a disparate impact against a suspect class, the tradition will be held to be discriminatory and will need to be abandoned.

The case that follows addresses the question of whether an employer who promotes from within can set promotion quotas for minorities and females. Nonminority males allege that they are being skipped over when promotions arise.

CASE *Dallas Fire Fighters v. City of Dallas*

885 F.Supp. 915 (N.D. Tex. 1995)

KENDALL, District Judge.

This lawsuit challenges the promotion practices of the Dallas Fire Department ("DFD") as discriminatory based upon race and gender-conscious promotions made under the City of Dallas' ("The City") Affirmative Action Plan ("AAP"). More specifically, the Plaintiffs challenge certain "skip promotions" which were made by the DFD in accordance with goals established by the City in its voluntary Affirmative Action Plan.

The Dallas Fire Fighters Association of Dallas file suit on behalf of individual white and Native American firefighters who sought, but did not receive, promotions between 1991 and 1993. In response to other challenges to its promotion program, the City has changed various features of the process, including eliminating the rank of Second Driver, reducing time-in-grade promotion eligibility requirements, and ending the practice of adjusting test scores upward for seniority. These actions were taken in addition to making the skip promotions at issue here.

The Dallas Fire Department's promotional process is not unlike many others across the nation. DFD does not make lateral hires from other fire departments, but fills positions above the entry level by promoting from within the department. Beginning with the entry level, current firefighter ranks are: fire and rescue officer, driver-engineer, lieutenant, captain, battalion chief, deputy chief, assistant chief and the fire chief. Among the various requirements for promotion for the ranks up to and including battalion chief is a promotional exam. Firefighters eligible for promotion are placed on a promotion list in descending order according to their scores on the exam. Unless a specific reason exists to pass over a particular candidate due to unsatisfactory job performance, disciplinary reasons, non-paramedic status or other reasons, members are promoted as vacancies occur by going down the eligibility list according to an individual's score on the exam.

Plaintiffs' complaints in these consolidated cases allege that all plaintiffs are now and were at the time the skip promotions were made, employed as firefighters by the Defendant City of Dallas. The Plaintiffs further allege that from 1991 to 1993, the City promoted various members of the Fire Department in the ranks of Driver, Lieutenant, Captain and Deputy Chief. Each of the Plaintiffs, all of whom are white males, with the exception of Plaintiff Wallace J. Graves who is a Native American, applied for promotions by taking and passing the promotional exam. The Plaintiffs were passed over for promotion in favor of lower ranked individuals. Plaintiffs' complaint asserts that they were passed over solely because of race or gender in an attempt by the City and DFD to promote minorities in accordance with the City's Affirmative Action Plan. Plaintiffs allege that these promotions violate the Equal Protection Clause of the United States Constitution. The Plaintiffs also assert claims under the Civil Rights Act of 1871. Plaintiffs further allege violation of the Equal Rights Clause of the Texas Constitution.

In Defendants' answer, the City denies that the skip promotions were made on the sole basis of sex or race. Further, the City denied that it acted in violation of either the United States Constitution, the Texas Constitution or any statutory prohibitions. The City asserts several affirmative defenses against the Plaintiffs. The City first asserts that the Plaintiffs have not been injured by a constitutionally defective policy or custom of the City. Second, the City asserts that some of Plaintiffs' claims are barred by the statute of limitations. Finally, the City asserts that a number of the Plaintiffs lack standing because they would not have been promoted even if the skip promotions had not been made.

This factor concerns the goals set by the AAP with relation to the labor pool of qualified applicants. As stated above, the Dallas Fire Department does not hire laterally from other fire departments. Therefore, each rank is composed of those individuals qualified for promotion from the rank below. The promotional goals should be statistically related to the number of qualified applicants in each rank below. The affirmative action goals of the City's 1992 adopted AAP state that annual promotion goals are based on a ratio of African-American and Hispanics in the population of Dallas, Texas at a level not to exceed 40%. The goals also show that representation goals for upper-ranks and executives are based on calculations of availability plus a five point acceleration factor when applicable. However, the promotion goals for all ranks within the fire department above Fire & Rescue Officer are the same. The City in the 1992 AAP, set promotion goals across the board in all ranks above Fire & Rescue Officer at 23.4% for African-Americans, 16.6% for Hispanics and 10% for Females. The percentage of qualified individuals in each rank below necessarily fluctuates, the Court does not find how a single broad percentage goal for each rank can be adequately related to the number of qualified applicants in the appropriate feeder pool.

The City argues that because no unqualified candidates were considered for promotion and the Plaintiffs were only denied an employment opportunity, not deprived of their existing jobs ("denial of a future employment opportunity is not as intrusive as loss of existing job") that the impact on the Plaintiffs is not significant. Certainly, "a DFFA member denied a promotion is not in as bad a position as the victim of a layoff." However, the City's interest in race-conscious promotion policies is not as strong as the rights and expectations surrounding seniority. DFD has validated its promotional exams, it no longer adjusts the scores for seniority and it has established policies and customs which are aimed at racial parity. The Plaintiffs have had their promotional opportunities affected and many are not eligible to take upcoming promotional exams. They would have been eligible for these exams had the City promoted according to its own promotional ranking. The policy of ranking scores on validated tests creates an expectation in *all* firefighters that promotion can be earned by studying for the test. The City should not undermine this expectation with skip promotions that are not narrowly tailored.

For the above reasons, the Court finds that the City's policy of skip promotions in the fire department is not narrowly tailored and the Plaintiff's motion for summary judgment, as to the Equal Protection violation, is granted.

The case before this Court is factually distinguishable from the *Johnson* case. While the legal standards set out in *Johnson* are applicable to this case, the promotional methodology at issue here is starkly different. The Dallas Fire Department utilizes two criteria in making its promotional decisions, a passing score on an exam and a ranked order of all passing scores. In the positions at the time, with the exception of a subjective interview, there is no evidence of a individual evaluation of the applicants to be promoted, there is no evidence of an evaluation of the applicants based upon their past job performance, experience or personal attributes. All of these factors are present in *Johnson.* In this case, there is evidence that race has become a trump card in the hands of a municipal government in its quest for a diverse workforce in the shortest amount of time. To paraphrase George Orwell, the City's argument seems to be that all factors are equal, but some factors are more equal.

The leading case in determining whether or not a race or gender-conscious remedy comports with Title VII is *Johnson v. Transportation Agency of Santa Clara.* In *Johnson,* the Santa Clara County Transit District Board promoted, in accordance with an affirmative action plan, a female employee with a lower qualifying score over a male employee who had scored two points higher on the interview scale. During the selection process, both applicants cleared the initial hurdle of being deemed qualified. Both applicants were included in a group of applicants interviewed by a two-person panel. Those applicants who scored above 70 on this interview were certified as eligible for selection by the appointing authority. The next step of the process was an interview by three Agency supervisors who made a final recommendation. Despite the panel's recommendation of the male applicant, the Affirmative Action Plan Coordinator recommended to the Director of the Agency that the female applicant be promoted. The Director of the Agency heeded that recommendation and promoted the female applicant. Subsequently, the male applicant filed a lawsuit.

The Supreme Court held that the Plan used by the Transit Board was permissible because the sex of the applicant was but one of numerous factors taken into account in arriving at the decision. "The Agency earmarks no positions for anyone; sex is but *one of several factors* that may be taken into account in evaluating qualified applicants for a position." The Supreme Court also stated that the decision to consider sex as one factor among many was made pursuant to an affirmative action plan that represented a moderate, flexible, case-by-case approach.

The Court acknowledges that "there is no precise formula for determining whether or not an affirmative action plan trammels the rights of [nonminorities]." When reviewing affirmative action plans involving race or gender-based entry-level hiring goals, the Supreme Court has noted that the impact on nonminorities is diffused, spread across all those in society who might deserve the entry-level position. Entry-level hiring goals, while burdening some innocent persons, do not impose the same type of injury on nonminorities as that imposed by the use of race or gender to determine layoffs. Because layoffs impose the entire burden on particular individuals, often causing serious disruption to their lives, the Supreme Court has determined that this burden is too intrusive. These two situations present the extremes of employment decisions based on race or gender. The instant situation, however, does not neatly fall at one end of the spectrum or the other.

This case involves neither hiring or layoffs, but instead concerns skip promotions made under the City's affirmative action plan. The Eleventh Circuit has held that a promotion situation lies between entry-level hiring and layoffs in terms of the burden permitted on nonminorities. This Court agrees with that holding. The burden of the City of Dallas' skip promotion policy is not diffused throughout society, nor even diffused throughout the entire fire department. Instead, this policy resembles the layoff situation because only specific individuals are burdened.

The Court does not find that in order to unnecessarily trammel on nonminorities rights, there must be a firing or a layoff decision based upon race or gender. As stated above in the discussion of the Equal Protection claim, this Court finds that the promotional goals adopted by the City in its AAP are not reasonably related to the applicable pools of qualified employees for each job classification in the Fire Department ranks. A single percentage for the promotional goal in each rank seem to be arbitrarily selected.

Judgment for Dallas Fire Fighters.

Negligent Hiring

Many job applications and résumés contain false representations made by prospective applicants specifically with regard to their employment history and educational background. Many candidates resort to this falsification to improve their prospects of being hired. Employers must be diligent in confirming the authenticity of the offered information. If the individual is hired and causes damage or injury to a third party, the employer will be liable.

Employment Perspective

Dennis Michaelson applied for a position as a resident gynecologist at Fairview Hospital in Brooklyn. According to Dennis's résumé, he graduated from one of the top medical schools and had an extensive private practice on the Kohala Coast on the big island of Hawaii. Dennis explained that after his wife's recent death, he wanted to return to his roots. Dennis's appearance, demeanor, and expertise convinced the hospital board to retain his services. The hospital was so impressed that it did not check with the medical school or on the references he had submitted. Dennis was at the hospital for fourteen months before he was questioned intensively about his diagnosing two cases of ovarian cancer as being benign growths. Dennis suddenly heard the call of the islands and disappeared. Fairview was sued by the two cancer victims as well as countless others who were treated by the fraud. When Fairview investigated, it learned that Dennis was not a licensed physician; he was just a con artist in disguise. Is the hospital liable? Yes! Fairview is liable for negligent hiring. ◆

The following case addresses the question of placement of liability for a negligent hiring that has resulted in the wrongful death of a twelve-year-old boy. Involved are a college who owned the property, the county, to whom it was leased, the firm hired by the county, and the firm's employee who committed the homicide.

CASE

Henley v. Prince George's County

503 A.2d 1333 (Md. 1986)

McAULIFFE, Judge.

On Saturday, June 17, 1978, Charles Wantland sexually assaulted and murdered Donald Alan Henley, age 12. Wrongful death and survival claims were filed by the personal representative of Donald's estate and by his parents in an action against Wantland, John H. Jones T/A Capitol building and remolding company (Jones), Prince George's County, Maryland (the "County"), and the Board of Trustees of Prince George's Community College. A default judgment was entered against Wantland, but all other claims were terminated in favor of the remaining defendants by summary judgment, and that action was affirmed by the court of special appeals.

In early 1978 the county embarked upon a skills training and improvement program in cooperation with the United States Department of Labor pursuant to the federal Comprehensive Employment and Training Act of 1973 (CETA). The purpose of the program was to provide specific construction skills training to 60 chronically unemployed persons, including but not limited to former convicts and convicts on work release status. The first phase of the program contemplated six months of classroom and practical training of all enrollees at a designated site, and the second phase contemplated supervised on the job training at various work sites. At the conclusion of this program the building contractor who had contracted with the County to provide the training was required to hire all enrollees (to a max of 50) who successfully completed the training cycle.

Because of irreconcilable differences, the County terminated its contract with the first building contractor selected, and on May 19th, 1978, it entered into a contract with Jones for the management of the program. At the same time the County contracted with the College for the use and occupancy of property known as the Clinton Center (and formerly known as the Berger mansion) for use as a training site.

Wantland originally came into the program as a trainee, at which time he was on work release status at Patuxent Institution in Jessup. Wantland was serving a sentence of 30 years for second degree murder, and had a record of various other crimes, including repeated instances of drunken and disorderly conduct. Shortly after Jones took over the program, Wantland was hired as a carpentry instructor. The record shows that Jones was involved with a number of construction projects in the metropolitan area, and that managerial responsibility for the running of the project was entrusted to Milton Gordon, Project Director, and to Albert Ruffin, Assistant Director. Wantland was hired by Gordon, who at that time as aware of Wantland's extensive crime background.

During the time he was enrolled as a trainee, and for a short time after he was employed as a carpentry instructor, Wantland continued to be an inmate of Patuxent Institution and was transported daily to and from the Clinton Center. Sometime prior to the murder Wantland was released from Patuxent, and arrangements were made for him to reside at the Clinton Center. At that time Ruffin was also residing at the Center, and was performing caretaker and security duties. Because of repeated acts of vandalism and theft that had occurred at the site after the inception of the program, an agreement was reached that Ruffin and Wantland would coordinate their activities so that one of them would be present on the property at all times.

William Rawles, a trainee in the program, offered the following evidence by affidavit:

> That on the Thursday or Friday prior to the murder of Donald Henley the following discussion took place between Charles M. Wantland and myself:
>
> *Wantland*—"I think I know who is doing the break-ins."
>
> *Me*—"Then why don't you call the police?"
>
> *Wantland*—"Fuck the damn police. I can take care of it myself. If I catch who's doing it I'm going to tie him to a tree and fuck him to death."

That I became concerned that Charles Wantland did intend to injure someone and that I therefore reported the conversation to the man in charge, Albert Ruffin, on that same Thursday or Friday. The following conversation took place:

> *Me*—"Is that fellow Charlie alright? If it's one of these dudes doing the break-ins they'd better be careful. He's talking about tying him to a tree and fucking him to death."
>
> *Ruffin*—"What the fuck are you worried about? Don't worry about it."

Wantland anally sodomized and stabbed Donald to death in a wooded area of the Clinton Center property at about 6:00 P.M. on the following Saturday, one or two days after the alleged statements had been made.

Liability of Jones

Appellants' claims against Jones is based upon a theory of negligent hiring or retention. Appellants concede that Jones was not negligent in hiring Wantland to perform the duties of a carpentry instructor. They contend, however, that Jones was negligent in later extending Wantland's duties to include caretaking and security functions, and that in any event Jones was negligent in retaining Wantland in any security or caretaking capacity after receiving notice of Wantland's statement to Rawles concerning his intended treatment of suspected vandals.

The record shows that Wantland was also furnished lodging at the site. Furthermore, there is evidence that the arrangement was similar to that made with Ruffin, in that the consideration was at least in part to provide additional security.

Additionally, the statement made by Wantland to Rawles concerning Wantland's alleged knowledge of the identity of a vandal and his intent if he was successful in catching him is sufficient to support the conclusion that Wantland believed he had been assigned security duties.

Considering the totality of this evidence, we conclude the trier of fact could find that Gordon and Ruffin were managerial employees of Jones with authority to assign additional duties to other employees of Jones, and that acting in that capacity, they assigned Wantland security duties to be carried out jointly with Ruffin, and compensated Wantland for these additional duties by arranging lodging for him on the site. Accordingly, summary judgment should not have been granted in favor of Jones on the basis of there being no evidence of a hiring or retention of Wantland for any duties other than as carpentry instructor.

Liability of the College

Appellants contend the College is liable as the owner and occupier of the land where these tragic events occurred. We conclude that summary judgment was properly entered in favor of the College because the uncontested facts demonstrate beyond dispute that the College had surrendered control of the premises to the County during the period of time involved in the action.

The Use Agreement entered into between the College and the county granted to the County the right to "use and occupy" the property for a specified term, and provided that "the County shall return said property to the College in a condition no worse than the condition of the property prior to the Use Agreement." The agreement conveyed the exclusive right of occupancy to the county, and therefore effectively transferred to the County the duties owed by an occupier of land.

Liability of the County

Appellants' claim against the County for negligence rests upon an alleged breach of duty arising from the County's occupancy of the land. The trial judge concluded that Wantland was a bare licensee residing on the premises as a result of the benevolence of the County, and that the County therefore owed no greater duty to Donald than it did to Wantland.

For the reasons set forth in this opinion we conclude the trier of fact could find that Wantland was furnished lodging in return for his agreement to perform security duties.

Judgment reversed as to Jones and the County. Judgment affirmed as to the College.

REVIEW QUESTIONS

1. Is discrimination possible in the selection process?
2. What is the Uniform Guidelines On Employee Selection Procedures?
3. Can an employer be guilty of negligent hiring?
4. Is nepotism permissible?
5. Are promotions from within the company discriminatory?
6. Are firms who recruit at colleges practicing discrimination?
7. What records is an employer required to keep with regard to its employees?
8. Can an employer specify "recent college graduates only" in an employment ad?
9. What is the procedure a company should follow when a job becomes available that would entail promoting someone within the company?
10. Does an employer have to be careful where it advertises for potential job applicants to avoid acting in a discriminatory manner?
11. May a municipality require that a candidate for a position be a resident prior to taking the examination for eligibility? *Matter of Hens v. Colucci* 235 N.Y.S. 2d 823
12. Sitgraves' request to be transferred was denied. Sitgraves filed suit claiming discrimination. Allied Signal argued that a new and distinct relationship would not have been

forthcoming had the request been granted. Therefore, Sitgraves has no grounds for bringing the suit. What was the result? *Sitgraves v. Allied Signal, Inc.* 953 F.2d 570 (9th Cir. 1992)

13. Carter applied for a transfer to a division through which eligibility for a promotion would occur. The transfer was denied. Carter brought suit claiming discrimination in the denial of a promotion. What was the result? *Carter v. South Central Bell,* 912 F.2d 832 (5th Cir. 1990)

14. Legrand satisfied the objective qualifications for the faculty position. The University of Arkansas did not select Legrand as a candidate. In a suit brought by Legrand, the University has asked for summary judgment because there was no case. Legrand contends that the initial burden of proof had been met because the qualifications for the job have been satisfied. What was the result? *Legrand v. Trustees of University of Arkansas, Pine Bluff,* 821 F.2d 478 (8th Cir. 1987)

15. Michelle LeGault applied to become a firefighter in Johnston, Rhode Island. Although she ranked among the highest on the written examinations, she was passed over because she did not complete the required run and hose pull within the allotted time period. She contended that these tests were never validated according to the National Fire Protection Association standards, which have no run or hose pull requirement. Mayor Arruso argued that he instituted a stringent test to find the best qualified people for this dangerous job. What was the result? *LeGault v. Arrusso,* 842 F.Supp. 1979 (D.N.M. 1994)

16. In the case on pp. 63, was the court correct in carving out an exception for college graduates?

17. In the case on pp. 80, does the fact that the boy committed a crime mitigate the responsibility of the parties?

18. Is the case on pp. 58, typical of male bias against women in the selection procedure?

19. In the case on pp. 66, should any or all of an individual's prior convictions be a decision factor in a new job?

20. In the case on pp. 69, the plaintiff claimed minority workers were favored. Is that true?

CHAPTER 5

Testing

The administration of tests must be job related, or else they will be discriminatory against an employee who is a member of a suspect classification.

APTITUDE TESTS

Employers must justify the use of employing an aptitude test by showing that the tests are job related and if so, are used for the sole purpose of identifying qualified applicants. If the tests are used as a pretext to disqualify members of a suspect classification, then the employer's action is discriminatory.

Opponents of general tests argue that they are biased against women and minorities. Proponents insist that scholarly individuals at impartial testing facilities established these tests. Their use is widespread and their reliability is reinforced by a long tradition.

The following case addresses the issue of whether the state may test the competency of its teachers through the administration of aptitude exams. The teachers felt that this was a violation of the Civil Rights Act and the Age Discrimination in Employment Act.

CASE *Frazier v. Garrison*

980 F.2d (5th Cir. 1993)

BROWN, Circuit Judge.

Texas Examination for Current Administrators and Teachers (TECAT). The teachers alleged that the TECAT, a state administered examination for teachers that tested basic reading and writing skills, violated Title VI and Title VII of the 1964 Civil Rights Act, the Age Discrimination in Employment Act (ADEA), the Equal Educational Opportunities Act of 1974, and the Due Process and Equal Protection Clauses of the Constitution. The Teachers also moved the trial court to certify them as a class for purposes of maintaining a class action. The trial court refused to certify the class, denied the Teachers' motion to consolidate, and granted summary judgment in favor of the School Districts on the Title VI claim, the Title VII claim, the ADEA claim, and the Due Process and Equal Protection claims. This is an appeal from the district court's final judgment. We affirm.

TECAT

On July 23, 1984, the Texas legislature passed into law House Bill 72 which contained numerous provisions for education reform including school funding, school finance reform, teacher raises, establishment of a teacher career ladder, provisions for school discipline management, restructuring of the State Board of Education and teacher competency testing. Section 13.047 of the act, which provides for teacher competency testing, is the section at issue on this appeal.

(a) The board shall require satisfactory performance on an examination prescribed by the board as a condition to continued certification for each teacher and administrator who has not taken a certification examination.

(b) The board shall prescribe an examination designed to test knowledge appropriate to teach primary grades and an examination designed to test knowledge appropriate to teach secondary grades. The secondary teacher examinations must test the knowledge of each examinee in the subject areas listed in Section 21.101 of this code in which the examinee is certified to teach and is teaching. If a teacher is not tested in an area of certification, the teacher must take the examination for that area within three years after beginning to teach that subject. The administrator examinations must test administrative skills, knowledge in subject areas, and other matters that the board considers appropriate. The examinations must also test the ability of the examinee to read and write with sufficient skill to perform satisfactorily as a professional teacher or administrator.

(c) In developing the examinations, the board shall solicit and consider the advice of classroom teachers and administrators.

(d) Each teacher must perform satisfactorily on the applicable examination on or before June 30, 1986, to teach the subject at a particular level unless a school district establishes to the satisfaction of the commissioner of education that there is an emergency need. A teacher may not teach under a determination of an emergency need for more than one school year.

(e) The board, in conjunction with school districts, shall provide teachers and administrators with an opportunity for board-developed preparation for the examination.

The teachers had not presented any direct evidence of intent to discriminate. Since the School Districts' knowledge of the allegedly adverse impact of the TECAT on minority teachers and the raising of the cutoff rate are the Teachers' only possible proof of intent to discriminate, we conclude that the district court's grant of summary judgment was appropriate on the disparate treatment claim. There is no evidence that the School Districts acted with discriminatory intent.

The teachers contend that the trial court erred in refusing to certify the Teacher's class for purposes of maintaining a suit under the Age Discrimination in Employment Act. This court held that the four elements that a plaintiff must initially prove under *McDonnell Douglas Corp. v. Green* to maintain a Title VII case are also required to support a claim under the ADEA. Specifically, the court held that a rejected job applicant must show the following in order to bring a discrimination suit: that he belongs to a racial minority, that he applied and was qualified for a job for which the employer was seeking applicants, that despite his qualifications, he was rejected, and that after his rejection, the position remained open and the employer continued to seek applicants from persons of complainant's qualifications. The district court concluded, that the Teachers had not applied for positions for which they were qualified (non-certified teaching positions) and therefore, could not bring suit under either Title VII or the ADEA.

Judgment for Garrison and the School Board.

RESIDENCY TESTS

Cities, towns, countries and municipalities may require that applicants for civil service positions be residents. In other localities, preference may be given to applicants. This mandate of preference must be clearly stated in a local ordinance.

The issue in the next case is whether a residency test was correctly applied against prospective employees.

CASE

Hanlon v. Harrolds

82 Misc. 2d 839 (Sup.Ct. Onondaga Cty. 1974)

TENNEY, Justice.

Petitioner requests a hearing for the purpose of determining the legality of certain acts of the Respondent. The Petitioner as the Chief of the Fire Department of the City of Syracuse was furnished by the Respondent, Commissioner of Personnel of Onondaga County, a list of persons eligible for appointment to the Syracuse Fire Department. On October 15, 1973, twenty-four firefighters were appointed from the list. The Chief gave preference to those on the list who were residents at the time of appointment. They were certified by the Commissioner and have completed their training as firefighters.

On January 2, 1974, the Commissioner advised the petitioner that he intended to decertify eleven of the twenty-four individuals. He stated that the appointments were improper because the eleven did not meet the residence requirements for a preference. He contends that they must have been residents for six months at the time of the examination to be eligible for a preference. It is conceded they were not residents at the time of examination.

There is no need for a hearing in this matter. The facts are clear and undisputed. The only issue which must be determined is whether or not the Commissioner has properly interpreted the residency requirements. This court finds that he has not. The appointments of the eleven individuals were proper and the decertification must be nullified.

There are conflicting statements regarding residence requirements. The notice prepared by the respondent Commissioner of Personnel advertised the position of firefighter for open competitive examination scheduled for January 27, 1973. It lists basic requirements stating the salary and the vacancy, specifically, in the City of Syracuse Fire Department, with a statement that "the resulting eligible list will be used to fill present and future vacancies and will be established for a two-year period." The contested portion is listed under Residence, which reads as follows:

> "Candidates must have been legal residents of Onondaga County for at least one (1) year immediately preceding date of examination. Preference and appointment may be given to City of Syracuse residents."

On an attached page there is a list of thirteen general instructions. There is no reference to the general instructions as to residence on the notice. However, Number 6 of the general instructions reads:

> "Unless otherwise stated, all candidates are required to be legal residents of the municipality in which they are seeking appointment for not less than six months, immediately preceding advertised date of examination. Candidates for City of Syracuse examinations must also meet City of Syracuse Charter requirements regarding residence at the time of appointment."

The use of the term "candidates" is the same. It appears that the residence requirement on the notice complies with the phrase "otherwise stated." This would nullify the need for candidates to be residents of the municipality (City of Syracuse) for six months. Reading both paragraphs it is clear that the only qualification to take the examination and for appointment is the individual be a resident of Onondaga County for one year prior to the examination.

The general rule in the construction of contracts would apply. An inconsistency between a specific provision and a general provision requires that the specific provision control. Although it is clearly stated on the notice, in the event of any potential ambiguity the specific provision on page one of the notice should prevail over any general provision which is designed to apply to all situations. To hold otherwise, would imply that the requirements established by the County Personnel Department were in violation of Section 3(4) of the Public Officers Law.

A municipality may require that a candidate for a position be a resident prior to examination. Neither Onondaga County nor the City of Syracuse have imposed such a condition in this case. Residence in the county is the only requirement for taking the examination. Furthermore, there is no indication that appointment would be limited to city residents only. Such a provision would violate Section 3(4) of the Public Officers Law.

It is agreed that any resident of the county on the list is eligible for appointment. The sole issue is the eligibility requirements for a preference which as stated "may be given to City of Syracuse residents."

The Commissioner's position is that residence for preference purposes is to be determined by the general provision "all candidates are required to be legal residents . . . for not less than six months preceding advertised date of examination." There is no indication on the notice that this condition is to be determinative of the issue of preference. There is no reference to preference nor is it anywhere stated in the Rules of the Civil Service Commission. The authority for granting preferential treatment is set forth in the Civil Service Law Section 23(4-a) which states that "an appointing authority of a department or agency of a city or civil division may require that eligible persons who are residents . . . shall be certified first. . . ."

There is no such requirement in the rules of the commission or in the City Charter. In the absence of a written requirement, the notice shall be determinative. It states that preference may be given. Reading Section 23(-a) and the notice whether a city resident is given preference is an option left to the appointing authority of the city, i.e., the Chief of Fire.

Since it is apparent that the six months residency requirement does not apply to candidates for this particular position, it cannot be arbitrarily construed as the criteria for granting a preference. Absent specific language, the only residence requirement for preferential treatment is that the certified person live in the City of Syracuse at the time of appointment. Such an interpretation is consistent with the Syracuse Charter and the Civil Service Law.

If the Commissioner seeks to impose other standards for preferential treatment, they should be clearly stated and accepted by the municipality. Otherwise, the conditions of residency for a preference shall be as determined by the appointing authority subject to any charter limitations.

Judgment for Petitioner Hanlon.

HONESTY TESTS

Honesty tests are those which measure physiological changes in the person tested. They are usually referred to as lie detector tests. Polygraphs, voice stress analyzers and psychological stress evaluators are the most prevalent types. Some employers also attempt to determine veracity through the use of psychological questionnaires of personal judgments based on demeanor or physical behavior.

Psychological Testing

Psychological tests may be administered only where the employer can show a compelling need. Employees are considered to be patients of the physicians conducting the examinations. In that respect, the patients are entitled to examine their medical reports.

Employment Perspective

Excelsior Bank, a specialist in investment banking, established along with a team of psychologists, a psychological profile of people who work best under pressure. Every new applicant is required to take the test. The result is a prime determinant as to whether the applicant is given the job. Susan Morgan, who was otherwise qualified, is refused employment as a result of her low score on the psychological profile. Excelsior Bank's employees are overwhelmingly white males. Susan claims the test is not job related and is used as a pretext to discriminate. Is she correct? Yes! Excelsior has not shown a compelling need for the administration of the psychological test. Its use by Excelsior is to eliminate women and minorities from the selection process. ◆

POLYGRAPH TEST

Polygraphs are a form of lie-detector test. Their use is prohibited in all but a select set of instances because the reliability is questionable and their use amounts to an invasion of privacy.

The issue in the next case is whether employees qualify within the definition of patients in their quest to obtain copies of their psychological test results.

CASE *Cleghorn v. Hess*

853 P.2d 1260 (Nev. 1993)

ROSE, Chief Justice.

Respondent Wackenhut Services, Inc. (Wackenhut) is under contract with the United States Department of Energy (DOE) to provide security services at the Nevada Test Site and related nuclear weapons facilities in Nevada. Appellant Michael Cleghorn (Cleghorn) is a security inspector for Wackenhut and has been a Wackenhut employee since May 24, 1982. Under a contract with Wackenhut, respondent Dr. Hess, a licensed psychologist, examines, tests, and evaluates Wackenhut employees and applicants for employment to determine their psychological suitability for employment. The psychological testing is conducted in accordance with the terms of a collective bargaining agreement between Wackenhut and appellant Independent Guard Association of Nevada, Local 1 (IGAN), and as part of a medical and psychological suitability testing program for the Doe Human Reliability Personnel Assurance Program (PAP). As a condition of employment for a security personnel, the DOE requires Wackenhut to employ only those persons who meet PAP medical standards.

Wackenhut referred Cleghorn to Dr. Hess for psychological testing on May 9, 1982 (pre-employment), and again on July 6, 1990. Cleghorn requested copies of his psychological records and test results. Dr. Hess and Wackenhut refused Cleghorn's repeated requests for copies of his psychological test results. Thereafter, Cleghorn brought an action for declaratory and injunctive relief, seeking to obtain the test results of his psychological testing.

The sole issue on review is whether the district erred in concluding that NRS 629.061 does not entitle Cleghorn and IGAN to obtain copies of their psychological test results. NRS 629.061 provides, in pertinent part: "1. Each provider of health care shall make the health care records of a patient available for physical inspection by: (a) the patient or a representative with written authorization from the patient. . . ." Cleghorn and IGAN argue that NRS 629.061 entitles them to receive copies of the test results of the psychological testing done by Hess for the following reasons: (1) Hess is a provider of health care as defined in NRS 629.031, (2) Cleghorn and the IGAN members are patients because they are persons seeking medical services for examination or treatment; and (3) the records requested are medical records as defined in NRS 629.021.

Dr. Hess and Wackenhut asserted that Hess is not a provider of health care under the statute. They further assert that Cleghorn and the IGAN members were not patients of Hess pursuant to NRS 629.061 because Hess did not provide health care to them, they did not expect any treatment from Hess, and the examinations were for the sole benefit of Wackenhut.

As a licensed psychologist, Dr. Hess is clearly a "provider of health care" under NRS 629.031. The information sought by Cleghorn and IGAN are written reports and records produced by Dr. Hess containing information relating to Dr. Hess' examination of Wackenhut employees, including Cleghorn, and thus are "health care records" as defined in NRS 629.021. Although there is no definition of patient provided in Chapter 629, a "patient" is defined in our evidence statute as "a person who consults or is examined or interviewed by a doctor for purposes of diagnosis or treatment." NRS 49.215(3). The word patient has similarly been defined as "a person seeking medical services for examination or treatment." The Wackenhut employees were undeniably interviewed and examined by Hess in order to determine their psychological suitability for employment.

Furthermore, to say in the instant case that the employees were not patients because they did not receive treatment is to split hairs. The employees were tested, examined, and evaluated by a psychologist. The definition of "patient" utilized by other jurisdictions when considering tort liability is not necessarily appropriate in the instant case, and a more liberal definition of "patient" would be in harmony with the legislative intent behind the enactment of NRS 629.061. The intent of the legislature is the controlling factor in statutory interpretation. When the language of a statute is clear on its face, its intention must be deduced from such language. The statute is clearly intended to provide, rather than prevent, access to medical records by specific persons, while at the same time protecting the patient's privacy rights: only the patient or patient's representative, the attorney general or grand jury or an authorized representative or investigator of the state licensing board may access the medical records. The Nevada Legislature set forth detailed requirements and procedures for the retention copying, and inspection of a patient's medical records to facilitate the obtaining of that information. A narrow interpretation of who is a patient would defeat the purpose of the statute. We therefore conclude that Cleghorn and the IGAN members are patients for the purpose of NRS 629.061.

Judgment for Cleghorn.

The issue in the next case is whether free speech and due process are violated by a state statute prohibiting an employer's use of polygraph testing.

CASE

State v. Century Camera, Inc.

309 N.W.2d 735 (Minn. 1981)

SHERAN, Chief Justice.

This case presents the question whether defendants' constitutional rights of free speech and due process of law, guaranteed by both federal and state constitutions, are infringed by Minn. State. 181.75-.76 (1980). Section 181.75 prohibits employers and their agents from "directly or indirectly soliciting or requiring" their employees or prospective employees to take a "polygraph, voice stress analysis, or any test purporting to test their honesty."

The district court found no violations of constitutional rights. That court considered the speech in issue under sections 181.75 and 181.76 to be commercial speech and therefore subject "to certain modes of regulation which might be impermissible in the realm of non-commercial expression." The trial court found the state's perception of the harm which employees may suffer "well founded," and the goal of preventing this harm "important and legitimate." The statutes survived overbreadth challenge because a "broad prophylactic" measure was necessary.

Commercial speech is "expression related solely to the economic interests of the speaker and its audience."

The state's interests here are several: encouraging the maintenance of a harmonious atmosphere in employment relationships which may be disturbed by the coercion to take a polygraph or similar examination; protecting an employee's expectation of privacy which he or she may have if the questions put during these examinations are personal, private, or confidential; discouraging practices which demean or appear to demean the dignity of an individual employee in a significant way; protecting employees from adverse inferences drawn if they refuse to take these tests; and avoiding the coercive impact present in the solicitation. No one can doubt the importance of regulating the employment relationship to discourage unfair or potentially unfair practices. In our courts we have questioned the validity of polygraph examinations and refused to allow the results of such tests to be admitted as competent evidence. We note that the State of Minnesota is not alone in prohibiting employers from compelling employees to take polygraph or similar tests.

It should be apparent that "indirect" means "not direct"; and neither of the adverbs "directly" or "indirectly" alters the meaning of the words "solicit" or "require" or lessens in any way the requirement that the employer be found to have solicited or required the employee or applicant to take a polygraph, voice stress analysis, or similar test. The phrase "directly or indirectly" in section 181.75 actually serves to warn employers that the prohibition extends to solicitation which may be subtle. "A statute will not be declared void for vagueness and uncertainty where the meaning thereof may be implied or where it employs words in common use, or words commonly understood or having an unmistakable significance in the connection in which they are employed." Section 181.75 will not be declared unconstitutionally vague merely because situations can be imagined in which it will be difficult to prove that what occurred was solicitation.

On the other hand, we feel that the phrase "any test purporting to test honesty" would render both sections 181.75 and 181.76 unconstitutionally vague in the absence of an authoritive construction. The two techniques enumerated in section 181.75, the polygraph and the voice stress analysis, both purport to measure physiological changes. Accordingly, we construe "any test purporting to test honesty" to be limited to those tests and procedures which similarly purport to measure physiological changes in the subject tested. Thus, we exclude from the current prohibitions of section 181.75 written psychological questionnaires, personal judgments made by an employer or his or her agent, even if based in part on observations of physical behavior or demeanor, and all other gauges of honesty which do not purport to measure physiological changes. With this construction, neither section 181.75 nor section 181.76 is unconstitutionally vague.

Judgment for the State of Minnesota.

Employee Polygraph Protection Act

Under the Employee Polygraph Protection Act, employers cannot directly or indirectly suggest or require an employee to take a lie-detector test, nor can an employer use an employee's results from a lie-detector test. The term "lie detector" encompasses a polygraph, voice stress analyzer, psychological stress evaluator, or any similar device used to determine the honesty of a person. A fine up to $10,000 is imposed on any employer found to be in breach of this act. If employee selection or termination is determined by the polygraph, the Secretary of Labor may order employment, promotion, reinstatement and reimbursement for lost wages and benefits. The employee may also seek these remedies in a private civil action. The Employee Polygraph Protection Act applies to all employers engaged in commerce. It does not apply to the federal government or to any state and local governments. There are other exemptions. Polygraphs may be used by an armored car company, a security alarm system firm, or a security personnel provider, with regard to their screening of employee applicants who are being hired to protect any facility impacting on the national health or safety of the United States, and any facility supplying electric, nuclear, or public water, shipments of radioactive or other toxic wastes, public transportation, currency, securities, precious commodities, or drug manufacture.

The following case expands the constitutional argument presented in the preceding case by alleging a violation of the equal protection clause.

Gawel v. Two Plus Two, Inc.

309 N.W. 2d 746 (Minn. 1981)

SHERAN, Chief Justice.

This case presents two of the same issues raised by the certified questions we considered at length in *State v. Century Camera:* Is Minn. Stat. 181.75 (1980) unconstitutionally overboard or vague, in violation of right of freedom of speech guaranteed by both the federal and state constitutions? On appeal, defendants have raised a new ground, claiming employers as a group are denied equal protection of the laws by section 181.75. This matter comes here as discretionary review pursuant to Minn.R.Civ. App.P. 105.01 of an order denying a motion for summary judgment. Our opinion in *State v. Century Camera* is in large a part controlling. We remand for further proceedings consistent with this opinion and *State v. Century Camera.*

Plaintiff Rose Gawel commenced an action against her former employer Two Plus Two, Inc., and Foresight Security, Inc., for injunction and damages under section 181.75, subd. 4. She claimed that Two Plus Two, a retail seller of jewelry and Foresight Security, Inc., a business administering polygraph examinations, directly or indirectly solicited or required her to take a polygraph examination in violation of section 181.75. Two Plus Two allegedly offered a polygraph examination to employees selected at random in order to reduce thefts by employees. The defendant's motion for summary judgment on free speech grounds was denied. We granted permission to appeal.

As to the first two issues, the alleged overbreath and vagueness of section 181.75, defendants' arguments are the same as the arguments of defendants in *State v. Century Camera.* Accordingly, we find section 181.75 is neither overbroad nor vague for the reasons given in that opinion.

Defendants' third argument, raised for the first time on appeal, is that section 181.75 violates the equal protection clause of U.S. Const. amend. XIV, 1, because employers and their agents are prohibited from soliciting or requiring polygraph, voice stress analysis, or similar tests while other persons are not. The standard of review applicable to an economic regulation under the equal protection clause is the "familiar 'rational basis' test." Since the speech affected by section 181.75 is commercial speech, *see State v. Century Camera,* the standard of review of an equal protection challenge to this statute is one requiring a showing of minimum rationality because of the lesser protection accorded commercial speech as compared to noncommercial expression. Applying this standard of review, it is apparent that any inequality of treatment of employers worked by section 181.75 is rationally related to the state's interest in regulating, in the employment context, the solicitation or requirement of polygraph, voice stress analysis, or similar tests.

Remanded for further proceedings consistent with this opinion.

Administration of the Polygraph Test

A polygraph test may be administrated to an employee against whom the employer has a reasonable suspicion for believing the employee is involved in a theft of property or information. The lie-detector test may be administrated as part of an investigation. The employer must submit a signed statement setting forth the specific property misappropriated or the damage which may be caused by the transfer of the secret in-

formation, the access the employee had to the property or information, and why the employer believes the employee was involved in a theft.

When a polygraph test is administered, the questions must relate to the job and to general matters for the purpose of determining the subject's veracity. Questions about private personal matters unrelated to the business are not permitted.

Employment Perspective

Linda Merrit applies for a job with Bull and Bear Securities Firm. The firm requires Linda to take a polygraph test. She consents. The questions include Linda's religious affiliation, political affiliation, beliefs on race relations, sex life and labor unions. Linda feels very uncomfortable about divulging her answers to these private matters. Has Bull and Bear conducted the polygraph examination in accord with the Employee Polygraph Protection Act? No! Questions relating to these matters are prohibited by the Act. ◆

In the case that follows, the employer suspected an employee to have stolen funds. The employer requested the employee take an polygraph test. He refused, citing state law. The company maintained that all employment disputes are subject to arbitration.

Saari v. Smith Barney

968 F.2d 877 (9th Cir. 1992)

T.G. NELSON, Circuit Judge.

In the employer's appeal of a district court order refusing to order arbitration of a discharged employee's claims, we hold that the Federal Employee Polygraph Protection Act does not prohibit arbitration of claims where required by contract. We further hold that the state law claims for violation of the California Labor Code and slander are likewise subject to arbitration.

Howard Saari was employed by Smith Barney, Harris Upham & Co., Inc. as an account executive beginning in July, 1988, and alleges that at all times his work was satisfactory. According to Saari's complaint, on or about December 14, 1988, a "sum of money, supposedly belonging to a client of Smith Barney, was supposedly stolen from the desk of a Smith Barney employee." Saari alleged he was questioned about the theft and was later asked to take a polygraph test concerning the incident, which he refused. Saari claims he was then terminated for his refusal to take the polygraph examination.

Saari filed an action in federal district court, alleging a violation of the employee Polygraph Protection Act (EPPA), USC. 2001-2009, a violation of California Labor Code 432.2, which makes it unlawful for an employer to demand or require that any employee submit to a polygraph test as a condition of continued employment, and a state law claim of slander, alleging that Smith Barney or its agent had slandered him by stating that he had engaged in a theft of money, or that Saari himself had been required to publish those statements in responding to questions from prospective employers concerning the cause of his termination from Smith Barney.

As a condition of his employment with Smith Barney, Saari signed a Uniform Application for Securities Industry Registration which provided in relevant part:

> I agree to arbitrate any dispute, claim or controversy that may arise between me and my firm, or a customer, or any other person, that is required to be arbitrated under the rules, constitutions, or by-laws of the organizations with which I register.

Saari became a registered representative of the New York Stock Exchange and thereby subject to its Rule 347 which provides that:

> Any controversy between a registered representative and any member or member organization arising out of the employment or termination of employment of such registered representative by and with such member or member organization shall be settled by arbitration.

Saari contends that the enforcement provisions of EPPA show no such flexibility.

Section 2002 of EPPA contains a broad general prohibition of employer use of lie detector tests. The prohibition is subject to exceptions listed in Sections 2006 and 2007 relating to governmental employers, national defense and security, F.B.I. contractors, certain private security firms, and a limited exemption for ongoing investigations. The enforcement provisions in Section 2005 permit an assessment of a civil penalty by the Secretary of Labor in an amount not to exceed $10,000 and injunctive actions by the Secretary of Labor to restrain violations of the Act. The redress the Secretary may seek includes orders of employment, reinstatement, promotion and payment of lost wages and benefits. The enforcement provisions also include a private civil action to be brought by the employee or prospective employee affected by such violation. The available relief is identical to that available to the Secretary by injunctive action in Section 2005. The enforcement provisions also include a bar on the waiver of rights which provides:

> The rights and procedures provided by this chapter may not be waived by contract or otherwise, unless such a waiver is part of a written settlement agreed to and signed by the parties to the pending action or complaint under this act.

Saari contends that EPPA relies on the judicial process for the resolution of claims. We think, however, that Saari's reliance on the flexibility comment follows certain "procedures." It is the type of procedure found in 2006(d) that an employer may attempt to have a prospective employee waive as a condition of employment, and that the anti-waiver provision would invalidate if extracted from the employee.

We conclude that Saari's claims under EPPA were subject to arbitration, and therefore the district court erred in denying Smith Barney's motion to compel arbitration and to stay the case pending arbitration.

Judgment for Smith Barney.

Polygraph Licensing

The polygraph examiner must be licensed by the state if so required and must post a $50,000 bond of professional liability coverage. The examiner's conclusion must be derived solely from the polygraph charts and cannot be based on a subjective evaluation. The examiner can give no opinion on whether the employer should hire the person examined. Disclosure of the results of a polygraph may be given only to the employee, employer who commissioned the test, and a court, should the matter arise in the course of litigation. The pertinent provisions of the Employee Polygraph Protection Act must be conspicuously posted in the workplace.

DRUG TESTING

Businesses lose many billions of dollars each year because of employee drug use. Employees using drugs are less productive; the quality of their work is suspect because of impairment to their reasoning capabilities. Drug users may be negligent in the assembly of a product; the driving of a motor vehicle, train, or airplane; the security of documents, currency, office, or other real or personal property, and the preparation of food and beverages. The list goes on and on. Employee drug users may also steal from their company to support their drug habit. Employers wish to safeguard against abuses by drug users that could jeopardize the safety of the company, its employees, and its customers. To do so, many companies beef up security, increase supervision, create drug-rehabilitation programs, propagate the antidrug message, advocate a drug-free work environment through a written policy conspicuously posted in the workplace, and test for drugs.

Fourth Amendment

The use of drug testing is a volatile issue because of concern about privacy. The argument put forth against drug testing because it infringes on a person's privacy is based on the Fourth Amendment. The Fourth Amendment affords individuals the right to be secure in their person, property, and effects; individuals do not have to submit to unreasonable searches and seizures. Opponents of drug testing claim that mandating a person to turn over a sample of his or her urine is an infringement on the right of that person to be secure in his or her person, because the urine is then seized for the purpose of subjecting it to a search for illegal drug contaminants. Proponents of drug testing argue that the search and seizure are not unreasonable in light of the pervasiveness of employee theft.

When applying the Fourth Amendment, there must be probable cause to believe that the person committed a crime before a warrant will be issued to conduct a search. The standard for employee drug testing is less. It may be justified under this theory when an employer can document its reasonable suspicion. There must be a reasonable suspicion that the employee is using drugs before a drug test can be required. A reasonable suspicion exists where a rational inference can be drawn from the facts and circumstances in the employment. The employer must document in writing the circumstances, which formed the basis for the reasonable suspicion that led to the requirement of the drug testing. The sources of information must be credible. The legitimate interests of the employer are balanced against the intrusion on an individual's physical solitude. In those cases where random drug testing has been found permissible, the need must overwhelmingly outweigh the unwanted invasion of privacy.

Employment Perspective

Victory College's administrators are arch conservatives who abhor the use of drugs and alcohol. The college institutes a policy that all faculty and staff submit to drug testing at the beginning of each semester. The faculty and staff claim the drug testing is an invasion of their privacy and that the invasion of privacy is not outweighed by the college's need to know. Who will win? Most likely the faculty and staff. While the use of drugs always impairs an employee's ability to function, the implementation of a drug testing program will be allowed where the safety of the public or the security of the workplace is at issue. The college has not shown this to be the case. ◆

The case that follows addresses the question of whether an employer had reasonable suspicion in ordering an employee to submit to a drug test.

Garrison v. Dept. of Justice

72 F.3d 1566 (Fed. Cir. 1995)

FRIEDMAN, Circuit Judge.

The petitioner, Daryel Garrison, challenges the decision of the Merit Systems Protection Board (Board) sustaining his removal by the Department of Justice due to his refusal to undergo a drug test. The principal issue is whether the Board correctly held that the agency official who ordered the testing had "reasonable suspicion" that the employee used drugs. We affirm.

The Department of Justice removed Daryel Garrison from his position at the Federal Bureau of Prisons (Bureau) in Kansas City in March 1994 after he refused to undergo a urinalysis drug test. The Department required the test after the Office of Personnel Management (OPM) informed it that, in a routine background reinvestigation, Mr. Garrison's brother Clarence had told the investigator that he had seen Daryel use marijuana "several times in the past few years," and as recently as 1993; that Clarence had stated where the marijuana use occurred; and that Clarence had seen Daryel purchase the drug from "Marvin." Based on this information Patrick R. Kane, the local Regional Director of the Bureau, determined in writing that although the investigation had "not yet been finalized," there was "reasonable suspicion" that Daryel Garrison was using drugs. He directed Mr. Garrison to undergo a urinalysis test.

When Daryel Garrison refused to provide a urine sample, Bureau staff warned him that he "should be well aware that refusal can lead to disciplinary action up to and including dismissal." He still refused to comply. After meeting with him and his attorney and considering "all the mitigating and aggravating factors in the case," Mr. Kane removed him.

Citing evidence presented at the hearing that Clarence Garrison was mentally ill and suffered from delusions, the Administrative Judge (AJ) found that he was not "a 'reliable and credible' source for the accusation as required by" the agency's drug-testing program. The AJ observed that although Kane was not aware of Clarence Garrison's mental problems at the time that he ordered the drug test, he "should have ensured that he had reliable and credible objective evidence, including dates and times of alleged off-duty drug use, and recognizable facts and circumstances which, to a trained supervisor, give rise to a 'reasonable suspicion' before ordering that a drug test be performed." According to the AJ, the failure to investigate further the allegations before ordering drug testing made the test "an unreasonable search under the Fourth Amendment," and therefore Mr. Garrison's removal for failure to submit to it was unconstitutional.

On the government's petition for review, the Board reversed the AJ and upheld the removal. Noting that "reasonable suspicion is a lesser standard than probable cause," which in itself "permits some degree of uncertainty," the Board concluded that "the administrative judge erred by evaluating the adequacy of the agency's reasonable suspicion determination based on facts that did not come to light until after the fact." Reviewing the information available to Mr. Kane at the time he made the testing decision, the Board concluded that "the agency had a reasonable suspicion sufficient to warrant directing the appellant to take a drug test, and that its instruction that he submit to a drug test was permissible under its drug-testing program."

The Bureau's Drug Free Workplace Program Statement allows mandatory drug testing of an employee if there is reasonable suspicion that the employee is under the influence of, or using drugs. Reasonable suspicion exists if the facts and circumstances known, warrant rational inferences that a person is using drugs. The official ordering the testing is required to "detail, for the record and in writing, the circumstances which formed the basis of the determination that reasonable suspicion exists to warrant the testing. A written report will be prepared to include, at a minimum . . . reliable/credible sources of information. . . ."

A. Daryel Garrison does not challenge the Bureau's use of the "reasonable suspicion" standard for determining when to require drug-testing. At least one other circuit has upheld, against challenge under the Fourth Amendment, the use of that standard for government employee drug-testing.

The determination of reasonable suspicion, like that of probable cause, necessarily turns upon the information the person making the determination had when that person acted. The facts then before that person either were or were not sufficient to create a reasonable suspicion that a particular individual used drugs. If that information was sufficient, it is immaterial that other information that weakened or undercut that conclusion subsequently was disclosed or could have been discovered by further inquiry. Stated another way, the AJ's theory that by making further inquiry Mr. Kane could and should have discovered other facts that weakened the reliability of the information upon which he acted, is but another way of stating that the information Mr. Kane had was not sufficient to create a reasonable suspicion.

B. The question, therefore, is whether Mr. Kane had reasonable suspicion that Daryel Garrison had used drugs when he ordered Garrison to undergo a urinalysis drug test.

Because "urine tests are searches," an employer's "drug-testing program must meet the reasonableness requirement of the Fourth Amendment." What is reasonable, however, depends upon all the facts and circumstances of the particular situation. "Reasonable suspicion is a less demanding standard than probable cause not only in the sense that reasonable suspicion can be established with information that is different in quantity or content than that required to establish probable cause, but also in the sense that reasonable suspicion can arise from information that is less reliable than that required to show probable cause."

We agree with the Board that this information was sufficient to create a reasonable suspicion in Kane's mind that Daryel had used marijuana. There was nothing about this information that should have led Kane, before acting upon it, to question its authenticity or reliability or to corroborate it.

Mr. Kane reasonably could have assumed that Mr. Garrison's brother was familiar with Daryel's behavior, and Kane had no reason even to suspect that Clarence might have fabricated the story as a result of his mental illness. "There is nothing about a sibling relationship," that would make suspect the information about his brother that Clarence had provided. To the contrary, the relationship enhanced the credibility of Clarence's statements.

Indeed, even in probable cause cases, where stronger evidence may be necessary, "the Court has never suggested that the police, with [eyewitness] information in hand, must conduct a further investigation." Several courts have held that the uncorroborated statements of eyewitnesses with no motive to falsify are enough to support a finding of probable cause. The drug-testing cases Daryel cites nowhere suggest that for its suspicion to be reasonable, an agency must make an affirmative investigation of its source's credibility.

CONCLUSION

The decision of the Merit Systems Protection Board sustaining Daryel Garrison's removal is

AFFIRMED.
Judgment for Dept. of Justice.

Drug-Free Workplace Act

A strong argument for random drug testing in cases involving public safety or national security can be made under the Drug-Free Workplace Act of 1988. This Act applies to contractors that provide more than $25,000 worth of property or services to the federal government and to those employers receiving federal grant monies. Under the Drug-Free Workplace Act, the employer must publish a conspicuous notice in the workplace that drug use is prohibited. This notice must also be sent to all employees. The employer must educate its employees about the dangers of drug use, the availability of counseling and drug treatment programs, and the consequences the employee will suffer if he or she does not seek assistance. Notification must be given to the appropriate federal agency by the employer within ten days of learning that an employee has been convicted for drug use. Employees must notify their employer if they have been convicted within five days of said conviction. The employer must in all respects make a good faith effort to ensure a drug-free workplace.

Job Relatedness

The Fourth Amendment applies to the federal government. Through the due process clause of the Fourteenth Amendment, the Fourth Amendment, along with the rest of the Bill of Rights, was applied to state and local governments. The application to others, including private employers, is essentially based on public policy decisions in court cases and the Privacy Act of 1974. The test applied, which is one of reasonableness, requires that the reason for the drug testing must be significantly job related. Adequate safeguards must be taken, and the intrusion on a person's physical solitude must be minimal. Job relatedness means that the purpose of the test must affect the public safety, the national security, or the safety and security of the workplace. Adequate safeguards must be instituted to assure that the testing is done by a qualified, independent laboratory.

Lab Testing

Laboratory drug testing has become a lucrative business. It is important that both the laboratory and the test it performs are reliable. Laboratories conducting drug testing for federal agencies are required to be certified. The initial tests, immunoassay, or thin-layer chromatography are usually expeditious and inexpensive to perform. If a positive result is found, a gas chromatography/mass spectrometry test may be used to confirm the finding. This test is more expensive and more reliable than the others.

The examination of hair follicles is an alternative method, which is said to provide more detailed information. The collection of the sample is less intrusive, but the results are more intrusive as they provide the quantity and duration of the drug use.

The case that follows addresses the question of when the importance of random drug testing overrides the invasion of privacy that it perpetrates. Although the case involves students, its practical effect is noteworthy for employers.

Vernonia School District 47J v. Wayne Acton

115 S. Ct. 2386 (1995)

Justice SCALIA delivered the opinion of the Court.

The Student Athlete Drug Policy adopted by School District 47J in the town of Vernonia, Oregon, authorizes random urinalysis drug testing of students who participate in the District's school athletics programs. We granted certiorari to decide whether this violates the Fourth and Fourteenth Amendments to the United States Constitution.

I

A

Petitioner Vernonia School District 47J (District) operates one high school and three grade schools in the logging community of Vernonia, Oregon. As elsewhere in small-town America, school sports play a prominent role in the town's life, and student athletes are admired in their schools and in the community.

Drugs had not been a major problem in Vernonia schools. In the mid-to-late 1980's, however, teachers and administrators observed a sharp increase in drug use. Students began to speak out about their attraction to the drug culture, and to boast that there was nothing the school could do about it. Along with more drugs came more disciplinary problems. Between 1988 and 1989 the number of disciplinary referrals in Vernonia schools rose to more than twice the number reported in the early 1980's, and several students were suspended. Students became increasingly rude during class; outbursts of profane language became common.

Not only were student athletes included among the drug users but, as the District Court found, athletes were the leaders of the drug culture. This caused the District's administrators particular concern, since drug use increases the risk of sports-related injury. Expert testimony at the trial confirmed the deleterious effects of drugs on motivation, memory, judgment, reaction, coordination, and performance. The high school football and wrestling coach witnessed a severe sternum injury suffered by a wrestler, and various omissions of safety procedures and misexecutions by football players, all attributable in his belief to the effects of drug use.

Initially, the District responded to the drug problem by offering special classes, speakers, and presentations designed to deter drug use. It even brought in a specially trained dog to detect drugs, but the drug problem persisted. According to the District Court:

> "[T]he administration was at its wit's end and . . . a large segment of the student body, particularly those involved in interscholastic athletics, was in a state of rebellion. Disciplinary problems had reached 'epidemic proportions.' The coincidence of an almost three-fold increase in classroom disruptions and disciplinary reports along with the staff's direct observations of students using drugs or glamorizing drug and alcohol use led the administration to the inescapable conclusion that the rebellion was being fueled by alcohol and drug abuse as well as the students' misperceptions about the drug culture."

At that point, District officials began considering a drug-testing program. They held a parent "input night" to discuss the proposed Student Athlete Drug Policy (Policy), and the parents in attendance gave their unanimous approval. The school board approved the Policy for implementation in the fall of 1989. Its expressed purpose is to prevent student athletes from using drugs, to protect their health and safety, and to provide drug users with assistance programs.

B

The Policy applies to all students participating in interscholastic athletics. Students wishing to play sports must sign a form consenting to the testing and must obtain the written consent of their parents.

Athletes are tested at the beginning of the season for their sport. In addition, once each week of the season the names of the athletes are placed in a "pool" from which a student, with the supervision of two adults, blindly draws the names of 10% of the athletes for random testing. Those selected are notified and tested that same day, if possible.

The student to be tested completes a specimen control form which bears an assigned number. Prescription medications that the student is taking must be identified by providing a copy of the prescription or a doctor's authorization. The student then enters an empty locker room accompanied by an adult monitor of the same sex. Each boy selected produces a sample at a urinal, remaining fully clothed with his back to the monitor, who stands approximately 12 to 15 feet behind the student. Monitors may (though do not always) watch the student while he produces the sample, and they listen for normal sounds of urination. Girls produce samples in an enclosed bathroom stall, so that they can be heard but not observed. After the sample is produced, it is given to the monitor, who checks it for temperature and tampering and then transfers it to a vial.

The samples are sent to an independent laboratory, which routinely tests them for amphetamines, cocaine, and marijuana. Other drugs, such as LSD, may be screened at the request of the District, but the identity of a particular student does not determine which drugs will be tested. The laboratory's procedures are 99.94% accurate. The District follows strict procedures regarding the chain of custody and access to test results. The laboratory does not know the identity of the students whose samples it tests. It is authorized to mail written test reports only to the superintendent and to provide test results to District personnel by telephone only after the requesting official recites a code confirming his authority. Only the superintendent, principals, vice-principals, and athletic directors have access to test results, and the results are not kept for more than one year.

If a sample tests positive, a second test is administered as soon as possible to confirm the result. If the second test is negative, no further action is taken. If the second test is positive, the athlete's parents are notified, and the school principal convenes a meeting with the student and his parents, at which the student is given the option of (1) participating for six weeks in an assistance program that includes weekly urinalysis, or (2) suffering suspension from athletics for the remainder of the current season and the next athletic season. The student is then retested prior to the start of the next athletic season for which he or she is eligible. The Policy states that a second offense results in automatic imposition of option (2); a third offense results in suspension for the remainder of the current season and the next two athletic seasons.

C

In the fall of 1991, respondent James Acton, then a seventh-grader, signed up to play football at one of the District's grade schools. He was denied participation, however, because he and his parents refused to sign the testing consent forms. The Actons filed suit, seeking declaratory and injunctive relief from enforcement of the Policy on the grounds that it violated the Fourth and Fourteenth Amendments to the United States Constitution and Article I, 9, of the Oregon Constitution. After a bench trial, the District Court entered an order denying the claims on the merits and dismissing the action. The United States Court of Appeals for the Ninth Circuit reversed, holding that the Policy violated both the Fourth and Fourteenth Amendments and Article I, 9, of the Oregon Constitution. We granted certiorari.

II

The Fourth Amendment to the United States Constitution provides that the Federal Government shall not violate "the right of the people to be secure in their persons, houses, papers, and effects, against unreasonable searches and seizures, . . ." We have held that the Fourteenth Amendment extends this constitutional guarantee to searches and seizures by state officers, including public school officials. In *Skinner v. Railway Labor Executives' Assn.,* we held that state-compelled collection and testing of urine, such as that required by the Student Athlete Drug Policy, constitutes a "search" subject to the demands of the Fourth Amendment.

As the text of the Fourth Amendment indicates, the ultimate measure of the constitutionality of a governmental search is "reasonableness." At least in a case such as this, where there was no clear practice, either approving or disapproving the type of search at issue, at the time the constitutional provision was enacted, whether a particular search meets the reasonableness standard "is judged by balancing its intrusion on the individual's Fourth Amendment interests against its promotion of legitimate governmental interests." Where a search is undertaken by law enforcement officials to discover evidence of criminal wrongdoing, this Court has said that reasonableness generally requires the obtaining of a judicial warrant. Warrants cannot be issued, of course, without the showing of probable cause required by the Warrant Clause. But a warrant is not required to establish the reasonableness of all government searches; and when a warrant is not required (and the Warrant Clause therefore not applicable), probable cause is not invariably required either. A search unsupported by probable cause can be constitutional, we have said, "when special needs, beyond the normal need for law enforcement, make the warrant and probable-cause requirement impracticable."

We have found such "special needs" to exist in the public-school context. There, the warrant requirement "would unduly interfere with the maintenance of the swift and informal disciplinary procedures that are needed," and "strict adherence to the requirement that searches be based upon probable cause" would undercut "the substantial need of teachers and administrators for freedom to maintain order in the schools."

III

The first factor to be considered is the nature of the privacy interest upon which the search here at issue intrudes. The Fourth Amendment does not protect all subjective expectations of privacy, but only those that society recognizes as "legitimate." What expectations are legitimate varies, of course, with context, depending, for example, upon whether the individual asserting the privacy interest is at home, at work, in a car, or in a public park. In addition, the legitimacy of certain privacy expectations vis-à-vis the State may depend upon the individual's legal relationship with the State. For example, we held that, although a "probationer's home, like anyone else's, is protected by the Fourth Amendment," the supervisory relationship between probationer and State justifies "a degree of impingement upon [a probationer's] privacy that would not be constitutional if applied to the public at large." Central, in our view, to the present case is the fact that the subjects of the Policy are (1) children, who (2) have been committed to the temporary custody of the State as schoolmaster.

Legitimate privacy expectations are even less with regard to student athletes. School sports are not for the bashful. They require "suiting up" before each practice or event, and showering and changing afterwards. Public school locker rooms, the usual sites for these activities, are not notable for the privacy they afford. The locker rooms in Vernonia are typical: no individual dressing rooms are provided; shower heads are lined up along a wall, unseparated by any sort of partition or curtain; not even all the toilet stalls have doors. As the United States Court of Appeals for the Seventh Circuit has noted, there is "an element of 'communal undress' inherent in athletic participation."

There is an additional respect in which school athletes have a reduced expectation of privacy. By choosing to "go out for the team," they voluntarily subject themselves to a degree of regulation even higher than that imposed on students generally. In Vernonia's public schools, they must submit to a preseason physical exam (James testified that his included the giving of a urine sample), they must acquire adequate insurance coverage or sign an insurance waiver, maintain a minimum grade point average, and comply with any "rules of conduct, dress, training hours and related matters as may be established for each sport by the head coach and athletic director with the principal's approval." Somewhat like adults who choose to participate in a "closely regulated industry," students who voluntarily participate in school athletics have reason to expect intrusions upon normal rights and privileges, including privacy.

IV

Having considered the scope of the legitimate expectation of privacy at issue here, we turn next to the character of the intrusion that is complained of. We recognized in *Skinner* that collecting the samples for urinalysis intrudes upon "an excretory function traditionally shielded by great privacy." We noted, however, that the degree of intrusion depends upon the manner in which production of the urine sample is monitored. Under the District's Policy, male students produce samples at a urinal along a wall. They remain fully clothed and are only observed from behind, if at all. Female students produce samples in an enclosed stall, with a female monitor standing outside listening only for sounds of tampering. These conditions are nearly identical to those typically encountered in public restrooms, which men, women, and especially school children use daily. Under such conditions, the privacy interests compromised by the process of obtaining the urine sample are in our view negligible.

The other privacy-invasive aspect of urinalysis is, of course, the information it discloses concerning the state of the subject's body, and the materials he has ingested. In this regard it is significant that the tests at issue here look only for drugs, and not for whether the student is, for example, epileptic, pregnant, or diabetic. Moreover, the drugs for which the samples are screened are standard, and do not vary according to the identity of the student. And finally, the results of the tests are disclosed only to a limited class of school personnel who have a need to know; and they are not turned over to law enforcement authorities or used for any internal disciplinary function.

The General Authorization Form that respondents refused to sign, which refusal was the basis for James's exclusion from the sports program, said only (in relevant part): "I . . . authorize the Vernonia School District to conduct a test on a urine specimen which I provide to test for drugs and/or alcohol use. I also authorize the release of information concerning the results of such a test to the Vernonia School District and to the parents and/or guardians of the student." While the practice of the District seems to have been to have a school official take medication information from the student at the time of the test, that practice is not set forth in, or required by, the Policy, which says simply: "Student athletes who . . . are or have been taking prescription medication must provide verification (either by a copy of the prescription or by doctor's authorization) prior to being tested." It may well be that, if and when James was selected for random testing at a time that he was taking medication, the School District would have permitted him to provide the requested information in a confidential manner—for example, in a sealed envelope delivered to the testing lab. Nothing in the Policy contradicts that, and when respondents choose, in effect, to challenge the Policy on its face, we will not assume the worst. Accordingly, we reach the same conclusion as in Skinner: that the invasion of privacy was not significant.

Taking into account all the factors we have considered above—the decreased expectation of privacy, the relative unobtrusiveness of the search, and the severity of the need met by the search—we conclude Vernonia's Policy is reasonable and hence constitutional.

We caution against the assumption that suspicionless drug testing will readily pass constitutional muster in other contexts. The most significant element in this case is the first we discussed: that the Policy was undertaken in furtherance of the government's responsibilities, under a public school system, as guardian and tutor of children entrusted to its care. Just as when the government conducts a search in its capacity as employer (a warrantless search of an absent employee's desk to obtain an urgently needed file, for example), the relevant question is whether that intrusion upon privacy is one that a reasonable employer might engage in; so also when the government acts as guardian and tutor the relevant question is whether the search is one that a reasonable guardian and tutor might undertake. Given the findings of need made by the District Court, we conclude that in the present case it is.

We may note that the primary guardians of Vernonia's schoolchildren appear to agree. The record shows no objection to this districtwide program by any parents other than the couple before us here—even though, as we have described, a public meeting was held to obtain parents' views. We find insufficient basis to contradict the judgment of Vernonia's parents, its school board, and the District Court, as to what was reasonably in the interest of these children under the circumstances.

* * *

The Ninth Circuit held that Vernonia's Policy not only violated the Fourth Amendment, but also, by reason of that violation, contravened Article I, -9 of the Oregon Constitution. Our conclusion that the former holding was in error means that the latter holding rested on a flawed premise. We therefore vacate the judgment, and remand the case to the Court of Appeals for further proceedings consistent with this opinion.

Judgment for Veronia School District.

Testing Procedure

It is important that the results be absolutely confirmed before aggressive action is taken. The procedure for gathering the urine specimen should be conducted by an independent source. The process from urination to labeling the vial to transportation to the laboratory to the performance of the actual test itself must be properly controlled. To allow the employer to do it would create a conflict of interest. Employees would find it intrusive and would allege tampering upon the determination of a positive finding. The collection of the urine sample must be observed to verify that the employee has not substituted another person's sample for his or her own. The observer may stand behind the man and outside the stall while listening for the sound of urination by the female. These methods are not unreasonably intrusive. The consequences of confirming drug use may be a warning, required counseling, admission to a drug-treatment program, or termination.

Employee Acceptance

The best approach is for employers to attempt to elicit an acceptance of the program by the employees. This can be accomplished by emphasizing safety, security, and a more productive work environment. The latter translates into greater profits, less theft, and possibly a sharing of this new-found wealth with the employees through better raises or bonuses. Advocating an employer/employee partnership in the fight against drugs will go a long way in easing the implementation of a drug-testing program into the workplace.

REVIEW QUESTIONS

1. What is a polygraph?
2. Are the use of polygraphs generally acceptable?
3. When can polygraphs be used?
4. What is the importance of the Fourth Amendment as it relates to testing?
5. Why are employers interested in testing their employees?
6. Are laboratory tests reliable?
7. What is the most informative method of testing for drug use?
8. When is random drug testing permissible?
9. What other types of testing devices can be utilized to determine an employee's honesty?
10. Explain the significance of the Drug-Free Workplace Act of 1988.
11. An employee was required as a condition of employment to submit to a medical examination. The employee asked to see the test results. The physician refused, arguing that the employee was not a patient and need only be notified if a dangerous condition was discovered. What was the result? *Green v. Walker* 910 F.2d 291 (5th Cir. 1990)
12. Skinner was compelled to subject himself to collection and testing of his urine. He claimed that this employment policy constituted a search subject to the Fourth Amendment. What was the result? *Skinner v. Railway Labor Executives Association,* 489 U.S. 602 (1989)

13. The constitutionality of the following statute was at issue: Minnesota statute Section 181.75 prohibits employers and their agents from "directly or indirectly soliciting or requiring their employees or prospective employees to take a polygraph, voice stress analysis, or any test purporting to test their honesty." What was the result? *C.M.C. v. A.P.F.*, 257 N.W.2d 282 (Minn. 1977)
14. Sibi Soroka applied for a position as a security officer with Target Stores. He was required to pass a psychological screening, the purpose of which is to judge the emotional stability of the applicants. Numerous questions related to the applicant's sex life, sexual orientation, and sexual thoughts. Soroka questioned the job-relatedness of this test. A security guard's primary function is to prevent shoplifting. What was the result? *Soroka v. Dayton Hudson Corporation,* 1 Cal. Rptr.2d 77 (1991)
15. Sidney Rosenberg applied to Equitable Life Assurance for a policy. He was 51 years of age and had had a heart attack seven years ago. Equitable required a stress test and arranged for him to see Dr. Arora. A month later he died of a heart attack. The stress test was found to be the proximate cause. Rosenberg's estate brought suit against Equitable for wrongful death. What was the result? *Rosenberg v. Equitable Life Assurance Society,* 584 N.Y.S. 2d 765 (Ct. App. 1992)
16. Referring to the case on pp. 85, should aptitude tests be given to all employees to insure that they are maintaining their job skills?
17. In the case on pp. 93, is the requiring of a polygraph test for an employee suspected of having stolen funds ethical?
18. Referring to the case on pp. 90, should free speech and due process be allowed to protect employees from polygraph tests?
19. Referring to the case on pp. 99, ethically, should schools be allowed to drug-test their students?
20. In the case on pp. 96, ethically, is having a reasonable suspicion enough for an employer to be allowed to drug-test an employee?

Employee Polygraph Protection Act, 29 U.S.C. 2001-2009

2001. DEFINITIONS

As used in this chapter:

(1) **Commerce.**—The term "commerce" has the meaning provided by section 203(b) of this title.

(2) **Employer.**—The term "employer" includes any person acting directly or indirectly in the interest of an employer in relation to an employee or prospective employee.

(3) **Lie detector.**—The term "lie detector" includes polygraph, deceptograph, voice stress analyzer, psychological stress evaluator, or any other similar device (whether mechanical or electrical) that is used, or the results of which are used, for the purpose of rendering a diagnostic opinion regarding the honesty or dishonesty of an individual.

(4) **Polygraph.**—The term "polygraph" means an instrument that—
(A) records continuously, visually, permanently, and simultaneously changes in cardiovascular, respiratory, and electrodermal patterns as minimum instrumentation standards; and
(B) is used, or the results of which are used, for the purpose of rendering a diagnostic opinion regarding the honesty or dishonesty of an individual.

(5) **Secretary.**—The term "Secretary" means the Secretary of Labor.

2002. PROHIBITIONS ON LIE DETECTOR USE

Except as provided in section 2006 of this title, it shall be unlawful for any employer engaged in or affecting commerce or in the production of goods for commerce—

(1) directly or indirectly, to require, request, suggest, or cause any employee or prospective employee to take or submit to any lie detector test;

(2) to use, accept, refer to, or inquire concerning the results of any lie detector test of any employee or prospective employee;

(3) to discharge, discipline, discriminate against in any manner, or deny employment or promotion to, or threaten to take any such action against—

(A) any employee or prospective employee who refuses, declines, or fails to take or submit to any lie detector test, or

(B) any employee or prospective employee on the basis of the results of any lie detector test;

(4) to discharge, discipline, discriminate against in any manner, or deny employment or promotion to, or threaten to take any such action against, any employee or prospective employee because—

(A) such employee or prospective employee has filed any complaint or instituted or caused to be instituted any proceeding under or related to this chapter,

(B) such employee or prospective employee has testified or is about to testify in any such proceeding, or

(C) of the exercise by such employee or prospective employee, on behalf of such employee or another person, of any right afforded by this chapter.

2006. EXEMPTIONS

(a) **No Application to the governmental employers**

This chapter shall not apply with respect to the United States Government, any State or local government, or any political subdivision of a State or local government.

(e) **Exception for security services**

(1) **In general**

Subject to paragraph (2) and sections 2007 and 2009 of this title, this chapter shall not prohibit the use of polygraph tests on prospective employees by any private employer whose primary business purpose consists of providing armored care personnel, personnel engaged in the design, installation, and maintenance of security alarm systems, or other uniformed or plainclothes security personnel and whose function includes protection of—

(A) facilities, materials or operations having a significant impact on the health or safety of any State or political subdivision thereof, or the national security of the United States, as determined under rules and regulations issued by the Secretary within 90 days after June 27, 1988, including—

(i) facilities engaged in the production, transmission, or distribution of electric or nuclear power,

(ii) public water supply facilities,

(iii) shipments or storage of radioactive or other toxic waste material, and

(iv) public transportation, or

(B) currency, negotiable securities, precious commodities or instruments or proprietary information.

(f) **Exemption for drug security, drug theft, or drug diversion investigations**

(1) In general

Subject to paragraph (2) and sections 2007 and 2009 of this title, this chapter shall not prohibit the use of a polygraph test by any employer authorized to manufacture, distribute, or dispense a controlled substance listed in schedule I, II, III, or IV of section 812 of Title 21.

2007. RIGHTS OF EXAMINEE

The exemptions provided under subsections (d), (e), and (f) of section 2006 of this title shall not apply unless the requirements described in the following paragraphs are met:

(1) **All phases**

Throughout all phases of the test—

(A) the examinee shall be permitted to terminate the test at any time;

(B) the examinee is not asked questions in a manner designed to degrade, or needlessly intrude on, such examinee;

(C) the examinee is not asked any question concerning—
(i) religious beliefs or affiliations,
(ii) beliefs or opinions regarding racial matters,
(iii) political beliefs or affiliations,
(iv) any matter relating to sexual behavior; and
(v) beliefs, affiliations, opinions, or lawful activities regarding unions or labor organizations; and

(D) the examiner does not conduct the test if there is sufficient written evidence by a physician that the examinee is suffering from medical or psychological condition or undergoing treatment that might cause abnormal responses during the actual testing phase.

(2) Pretest phase

During the pretest phase, the prospective examinee—

(A) is provided with reasonable written notice of the date, time, and location of the test, and of such examinee's right to obtain and consult with legal counsel or an employee representative before each phase of the test;

(B) is informed in writing of the nature and characteristics of the tests and of the instruments involved;

(C) is informed, in writing—
(i) whether the testing area contains a two-way mirror, a camera, or any device through which the test can be observed
(ii) whether any other device, including any device for recording or monitoring the test, will be used, or
(iii) that the employer or the examinee may (with mutual knowledge) make a recording of the test;

(D) is read and signs a written notice informing such examinee—
(i) that the examinee cannot be required to take the test as a condition of employment,
(ii) that any statement made during the test constitutes additional supporting evidence for the purposes of an adverse employment action subsection
(iii) of the limitations imposed under this section,
(iv) of the legal rights and remedies of the examinee if the polygraph test is not conducted in accordance with this chapter, and
(v) of the legal rights and remedies of the employer under this chapter; and

(E) is provided an opportunity to review all questions to be asked during the test and is informed of the right to terminate the test at any time.

(3) **Actual testing phase**

During the actual testing phase, the examiner does not ask such examinee any question relevant during the test that was not presented in writing for review to such examinee before the test.

CHAPTER

PRIVACY ACT OF 1974

The Privacy Act of 1974 was enacted to safeguard private information of Federal Employees from being disclosed by the Federal Government. Under the act, no information pertaining to an employee may be released before obtaining prior written consent of the employee. There are many exceptions to this procedure. Other employees of the agency may access the records of a particular worker on a need-to-know basis, if their position so requires. A court, civil or criminal law enforcement agency, Congress, the Census Bureau, or the National Archives may have access to an employee's records for a justifiable reason. Under the Freedom of Information Act of 1966, records relating to employment may be disclosed unless disclosure would constitute an invasion of privacy. A balance test is used between the need for disclosure and the intrusion. An individual may gain the employee's information upon the showing of a compelling reason relating to health or safety. A mailing to the employee's address is required for notification. A firm that is conducting a statistical analysis may have access to employee records for purely statistical reasons when the employee's identification has been deleted.

At all times, employees have the right to view their files. The employer must be able to justify why the files are kept and why the particular information contained in the files is needed. The employee must be afforded the opportunity to correct any information which is not accurate. Unless exempted under the Privacy Act, the infor-

mation should be kept in a secure facility that guards against easy access by unauthorized people. Civil and criminal penalties can be imposed for breaches of trust.

OMNIBUS CRIME CONTROL AND SAFE STREETS ACT

Title III of the Omnibus Crime Control and Safe Streets Act of 1968 prohibits employers from listening to the private telephone conversations of their employees or from publicly disclosing the contents of these conversations. Employers who eavesdrop intentionally when employees are justified in expecting their conversations to be private are in violation of the act. Employers may ban personal calls and then monitor conversations for violations, but they may not listen to the entire conversation for the purpose of discerning its content. Violators may incur fines up to $10,000.

Employment Perspectives

Sheena Whitmore placed a call to her physician concerning the results of a blood test she had taken to determine whether she had contracted a sexually transmitted disease. This call was intercepted by her employer, who then stayed on the line to hear the test results. Is this an invasion of privacy? Yes! The employer's actions are in violation of Title III of the Omnibus Crime Control and Safe Streets Act. Sheena was expecting privacy. Her employer invaded that privacy by listening to her test results. ◆

ELECTRONIC COMMUNICATIONS ACT

The Electronic Communications Act of 1986 extended employee's privacy protection to E-mail. Unauthorized access or interceptions are subject to stiff civil and criminal penalties. Federal law also prohibits tampering with mail directed to an employee. Fines up to $2,000 can be imposed along with incarceration.

FAIR CREDIT REPORTING ACT

The Fair Credit Reporting Act of 1970 allows consumer-reporting agencies to furnish credit reports for employment purposes. These reports contain basic information about the individual and his or her credit worthiness. The employers who seek this information need not notify the employee or prospective applicant of their intention to do so. If the employer wishes to have a more detailed background check done by the consumer-reporting agency with regard to interviews of the employee or of the applicant's friends, neighbors, and coworkers, then notice must be given to the individual. In all respects, the employer's reason for doing so must be job-related. If the report goes beyond what is considered to be a business necessity, an invasion of privacy suit may ensue. If the individual falls into a suspect classification (race, gender, religion, national origin, age, or disability), then grounds for a discrimination suit may exist.

DEFAMATION

Defamation is a false statement communicated to at least one other person orally or in a permanent form such as a writing, that causes harm to a third person's reputation. *Libel* is written defamation, while *slander* is oral defamation. Libel is actionable without proof of special damages because a writing remains in existence and could be distributed widely, whereas oral defamation is usually temporary and limited to the range of a person's voice, except when the oral statement is recorded and continuously broadcast on television, radio, or sound tracks.

Libel

The requirement for libel is a false statement that is published and read by someone other than the one about whom it is written. The true intention of the writer is that which is apparent from the natural and ordinary interpretation of the written words, and when applied to individuals, the interpretation placed upon those words by people acquainted with the plaintiff and the circumstances. General damages are automatically awarded for harm to reputation in the community or in business, and for personal embarrassment and mental anguish. Special damages may be awarded if the victim can prove he or she suffered an actual pecuniary loss from the harm to his or her reputation.

Employment Perspective

The *Star Gazette* published an article that accused Lawrence Binghamton, president of the town's savings bank, of pilfering depositors' money through the authorization of several large personal loans to himself. These statements are proven untrue. Nonetheless, Binghamton's bank loses numerous depositors. Has Binghamton any recourse? Yes! He may sue for libel by claiming that the statement was false and proving that it led to a decline in his business. ◆

Slander

Slander requires a defamatory statement that is heard by someone other than the person against whom it is directed. Special damages must be proved except in four situations where general damages are recoverable without proof. These situations include: derogating some characteristic important to a person in that person's trade or business, such as honesty or integrity; accusing a person of committing a crime of moral turpitude; denouncing someone by stating that he or she has contracted a loathsome disease; or imputing that a woman is unchaste.

Employment Perspective

Peter J. Roberts is a local attorney who has ambitions of running for city council. He is speaking at a town hall meeting when Matt Brady, his opponent's promoter, yells out that Peter J. Roberts is a swindler and a liar, and that he would cheat his constituents just as he has cheated his clients in several real estate deals. Even though Brady's statements are false, Roberts is not endorsed by his party, and his business suffers a severe decline as a result. Does Peter J. Roberts have any recourse? Yes! Roberts may recover general damages for the harm suffered to his business and political reputation. ◆

CASE

Piersall v. Sportsvision of Chicago

595 N.E.2d 103 (Ill. App. 1 Dist. 1992)

CAMPBELL, Judge.

Jimmy Piersall, a former major league all-star was hired by Jerry Reinsdorf, owner of the Chicago White Sox, to be a commentator for "Sports Vision," a cable TV program. Piersall was also a radio announcer for WMAQ. During the early 1980's Piersall made the following statements:

1. Wives of baseball players are "horny broads who say yes very easily."
2. "The writers for *The Sun Times* were a bunch of alcoholics."
3. There is no one in the White Sox organization smart enough to hold a gun to anyone's head," in response to a recent player trade.

After the first game of the 1983 season, Piersall was discharged. Reinsdorf made the following statements about Piersall and former White Sox announcer Harry Cary:

> "I don't mind criticism, but they both told a lot of lies. They wanted us to lose. They thought they were bigger than the club and did not want the attraction shifting to the field." (*Chicago Sun Times,* September 19, 1983);

and

> "The public could not know the truth about them; they are both liars. They both said things on the air they knew were not true." (*Chicago Tribune,* September 19, 1983).

Piersall sued Reinsdorf for libel. The issue is whether Reinsdorf's statements were made with actual malice.

The court held,

> "Nothing in the record, even with the benefit of reasonable inferences, supports a finding of knowing falsity on Reinsdorf's part. Therefore, Piersall has not established a genuine issue of material fact as to whether Reinsdorf acted with actual malice."

The court continued,

> "The general statement that someone is a liar, not being put in context of specific facts, is merely opinion."

Judgment for Sportsvision.

Truth and Malice

Truth is an absolute defense when the statement made is fully true. However, the truth must be proved. There is a special rule pertaining to defamatory statements made by the media concerning public figures. Even if the statement cannot be proved to be true, the media will not be liable unless malicious intent can be substantiated. *Malice* is the making of a false statement with the intent to injure another.

Employment Perspective

In the previous situation, assume that Matt Brady's allegations concerning Peter J. Roberts were the truest words ever spoken but that Brady has no way of proving them to be true. What would be the result? The result would be the same: Roberts will recover general damages. Although truth is an absolute defense, the burden of proof is on the person who made the statement. ◆

INVASION OF PRIVACY

Personal privacy is protected against invasions causing economic loss or mental suffering. There are four distinct invasions: intrusion on a person's physical solitude; publication of private matters violating ordinary decencies; putting a person in a false position in the public eye by connecting him or her with views he or she does not hold; appropriating some element of a person's personality for commercial use, such as photographs.

Employment Perspective

Statler Beer is introducing a new beer called Sparkling Lite. To market the product, Statler is featuring an unauthorized poster of the Reverend Luther Winthrop advocating the purchase of Sparkling Lite. The Reverend Winthrop is a well-known fundamentalist minister who openly decries the consumption of alcohol. Has Reverend Winthrop any recourse? Yes! He may sue Statler Beer, asserting that the poster was not consented to and that it puts him in a false position in the public eye by connecting him with a view that he does not hold and a product that he does not deem appropriate. ◆

CASE

Tyson v. L'Eggs Products, Inc.

351 S.E. 2d 834 (N.C. App. 1987)

BECTON, Judge.

L'Eggs Products, Inc. released an article to the press stating that tendonitis was not a work-related condition. Tyson and Bennett, employees, wrote a letter to the *Richmond County Daily Journal* accusing their employer of misstating the conclusion of the medical study. Later, they appeared on local television to further their cause. The management of L'Eggs responded in a company newsletter that the allegations of Tyson and Bennett were "a bunch of hog wash." A defamation suit against L'Eggs followed.

The issue is whether the statement was defamatory.

The court concluded that the opinion of the management of L'Eggs was written with hostility. But Tyson and Bennett expressed their own feelings with strong accusations and cannot therefore have a thin skin. The statements of both parties were within the realm of proper debate and were not of a defamatory nature.

Judgment for L'Eggs.

Publication of private matters that are newsworthy is privileged as long as it does not violate ordinary decencies. A false report by the media of a matter of public interest is protected by the First Amendment right of free press, in the absence of proof that it was published with malice.

INTERFERENCE WITH BUSINESS RELATIONS

A person who intentionally interferes in a business relationship through the use of fraudulent inducement or other unethical means that result either in an unfavorable contract or in the loss or breach of a favorable contract is liable for damages. The victim must prove damages, such as the specific loss of a customer, except where the nature of the falsehood is likely to bring about a general decline in business.

This lawsuit involves a libel action brought by a police commissioner against the New York Times because of an advertisement which had purportedly defamed him.

CASE

New York Times v. Sullivan

376 U.S. 254 (1964)

BRENNAN, Justice

The *New York Times* published an advertisement, signed and paid for by several individuals, that complained about the conduct of the police in dealing with a racial disturbance in Montgomery, Alabama. The police commissioner claimed that statements in the advertisement defamed him personally because he was in charge of the police during the racial disturbance. Under Alabama law, the published opinion of the press is accorded only the privilege of "fair comment." The argument presented here was that the *New York Times* overstepped their privilege. Based on this reasoning, the *jury* awarded Sullivan $500,000. This award was affirmed in the Alabama Supreme Court.

The issue is whether the First Amendment confers a privilege concerning false statements made by the press.

The United States Supreme Court held the First Amendment does grant a qualified privilege to the press concerning false statements provided they are not made with malice. The press must not be limited merely to fair comment or opinion. The reasoning behind the First Amendment is that the freedom to discuss issues of public concern will aid individuals in drawing more truthful conclusions.

Judgment for the *New York Times*.

Employment Perspective

Phil Murray owns a service station in Mobile, Alabama. The On-The-Spot Car Service Company approaches Phil about maintaining their twelve-car fleet. This opportunity would greatly enhance Phil's business. While they are still negotiating, Michael Dean, owner of a rival service station, circulates a false rumor that Phil Murray is incompetent and unreliable when it comes to servicing cars. As a result, Phil loses the contract with On-The-Spot Car Service. Thereafter, he discovers that Michael Dean originated the false rumor and sues him for damages. Will Phil be successful? Yes! Michael Dean's intentional interference with the contractual negotiations between Phil Murray and On-The-Spot Car Service caused Phil to lose the contract. Phil is entitled to the profits that he lost because of Michael Dean's interference. ◆

CASE

Morgan v. Hustler Magazine, Inc.

653 F. Supp. 711 (N.D. Ohio 1987)

KRENZLER, Judge.

In January 1973, Donda Morgan posed for a professional fashion model photographer in connection with her career as a fashion model. Hustler Magazine, Inc. published one of these pictures on the front cover of its December 1975 magazine. Donda brought this action based on libel and invasion of privacy. Donda alleges that this was done without her consent and that her prominent display on the front cover implies that she supports the views of Hustler Magazine, which she does not. Donda argues further that this event placed her in a false light in the public eye and that her personal esteem, her character, and her peace of mind have been destroyed.

Hustler argues that Donda executed a release covering the photograph in question which was given to the photographer. The words "or distorted in character or form" were deleted by Donda from the provisions of the release.

Since this action was brought approximately ten years after the publication, Hustler argues that the lawsuit is governed by the one-year statute of limitation for libel. Donda argues that she did not become aware of the publication until 1984 and that the one-year time limitation should run from this date.

The issue is whether the libel action is timely and whether the release prohibits the invasion of privacy claim.

The court held, "It has been held that a cause of action for libel when there is a publication in a national magazine accrues on the date of publication. This is known as the single publication rule."

As to the invasion of privacy claim, "It is the view of this Court that the release signed by the plaintiff Donda R. Morgan was clear and unambiguous. . . . In addition, the plaintiff Donda R. Morgan excised certain language from the printed form of the release to distortions. If she had wanted to or had intended to exclude the use of her pictures from a magazine such as Hustler, she could have included this language in the release."

Judgment for Hustler.

EMPLOYEE THEFT

Theft by employees accounts for billions of dollars in losses for businesses each year. Employee theft can be narrowly or broadly defined. The narrow definition is the appropriating of personal property belonging to the business for an employee's own personal use. This appropriation can be temporary, but most often it is permanent.

Employment Perspective

Harry Tubbs and Pete Jackson work as a team for Moving On Van Lines. They often make long-distance moves. After being assigned a job, they often complete it in less time by working late hours. Then they use the company van for making short moves from which they derive a profit. Harry and Pete believe that as long as they perform their assigned work within the allotted time, they are doing their job, and the company should not be concerned. Are they guilty of employee theft? Yes! Their theft is temporary, but the consequences are still severe. A van's useful life and maintenance costs will directly correspond to its mileage. Harry's and Pete's ventures are lowering the van's useful life to the company and increasing its maintenance costs. There is no difference between doing this and keeping the equivalent amount of money from a customer's cash payment. Both acts are theft. In addition, if they are in an accident while performing their personal work, the accident could subject Moving On to liability for damages and injuries. If Harry and Pete are injured, most likely Moving On will incur medical expenses, and workers' compensation benefits will be paid out. Harry and Pete are not entitled to any of this because this occurrence happened outside the scope of their employment, but Moving On may have to pay for it if the theft is not known. Some companies will want their employees prosecuted, but most will not because of the bad publicity it would bring. Dismissal with or without restitution is the most likely consequence. ◆

Employment Perspective

When Marge Adams resigned from Pentangel Publishing, everything in her office was intact. That evening, Phil Thomas took the computer, printer, lamp, office supplies, and fax machine from Marge's office and brought them home. Phil believed his actions were justified because most likely Marge was not going to be replaced. Is Phil's reasoning sound? No! Phil has stolen company property for his own personal aggrandizement. ◆

Conversion

Conversion is the unlawful taking of personal property from the possession of another. It is the converting of another's property for one's own use. Conversion may be made by mistake, but if it is done intentionally it amounts to criminal theft, which is considered under the headings of larceny, embezzlement, and robbery.

Employment Perspective

Mary Rodgers works as a cashier in Macy's Department store. She takes a break one afternoon to go to the powder room. She mistakenly leaves her pocketbook at the register. When she returns, her pocketbook is there but her wallet has been removed. The store detective apprehends Debbie Wilson, a stock clerk, with Mary's wallet in her hand. Has Mary Rodgers any civil recourse for Debbie Wilson's theft? Yes! Mary may sue Debbie in tort for conversion. Debbie may also be criminally prosecuted for the crime of larceny or theft. ◆

Employee theft occurs when a worker, usually a cashier or someone in billing, charges a customer, who is generally a friend, less than the amount owed. Although the employee may not be benefiting directly, the employee is instrumental in making the theft happen. There would be no difference between the preceding example and that of an employee stealing the merchandise and giving it to a friend. Both acts are thefts.

Employment Perspective

Missy Atkins is a waitress at the Busy Body Diner. Missy, who is shy and unassuming, wants to become more popular with the in-crowd at school. Whenever they come in for burgers, fries, and sundaes, Missy charges them only for the sundaes. Missy's popularity is increasing fast, but is she gaining it at Busy Body's expense? Yes! Missy is guilty of employee theft. ◆

Padded Payroll

A padded payroll is one to which a dishonest employee has added names that are unauthorized and frequently fictitious. Checks are issued to these fictitious payees and endorsed by the dishonest employee. The person or bank receiving the endorsed instrument is not liable if they acted in good faith and exercised ordinary care.

Employment Perspective

Jonathan Rhodes worked as the treasurer for the Whitney and Myers Department Store. There were ninety-two employees of the store. Rhodes issued ninety-five checks each week. The three additional checks were issued to Kelly, Paige, and Evan—fictitious employees of the department store who supposedly worked with mannequins. Rhodes endorsed the names of the payees and negotiated the checks to the Williamsburg Savings Bank in return for cash. When the department store discovered Rhodes's scheme, he had left for a permanent vacation in the Bahamas. Has the department store any recourse against the bank? No! The endorsement of Rhodes, the impostor, are effective against the company as long as the bank acted in good faith. ◆

Theft of Time

The broad definition of employee theft would also include theft of time. This would encompass longer lunch breaks, arriving late, leaving early, conducting personal business on company time, and just goofing off. The old expression "time is money" is true. An employee who commits this theft of time is not giving the employer adequate work in return for the wage bargained for. The employee is wrongfully inflating his or her wage at the employer's expense, which is a form of theft. Theft of time will not result in prosecution but may result in dismissal or demotion.

Employment Perspective

Pamela Hall is a research assistant at Bull and Bear Stockbrokerage. She often spends time in the firm's library researching information on companies that her father, an avid market player, is interested in investing in. Is this act employee theft? Yes! Pamela is guilty of theft of time. What if Pamela had no work assigned? Then she should ask her supervisor for an assignment or educate herself on some aspect of the company's business. ◆

Employment Perspective

Justin Sheldon is a data entry clerk for Miracle Drug Pharmaceutical Company. Justin often spends an hour or two a day making personal calls and running errands. He then works overtime at time-and-a-half to accomplish what he could not do in the eight-hour day. Obviously, Justin is not closely supervised. In any event, is he guilty of employee theft? Yes! Justin is not only stealing time but also charging the company at the overtime rate for the time he spent on personal business. ◆

Fourth Amendment

Employee theft is a very serious problem. It undermines business profitability as well as giving the unethical employees an unfair advantage over their honest counterparts. Some solutions are closer supervision through time sheets, electronic surveillance, desk and office searches, security guards, and tape-recorded-phone lines. Many employees feel that such steps are an invasion of privacy, but what degree of privacy should an employee have at the workplace? The Fourth Amendment to the United States Constitution guarantees the right of the People to be secure in their person, property, and effects from unreasonable searches and seizures. In the workplace, absent an overcoat or a briefcase, what personal effects or property belong to the employee? Aren't the office and the desk company property? That would seem to be the case.

SURVEILLANCE

Many companies use time sheets and electronic surveillance. Time sheets require an employee to justify his or her time spent during the workday, but they can be doctored. However, supervisors should be able to distinguish fabrications by comparisons with other similarly engaged employees and from experience with the work habits of the employee in question. Electronic surveillance is often installed by retail companies under the guise of identifying shoplifters, but equally important to the company is the electronic supervision of the work habits of its employees and the recognition of those who steal. Tape-recorded conversations are often used in the securities industry to record conversations between broker and customer for the purpose of verification should a miscommunication occur. Tape-recorded conversations can also discourage an employee from receiving personal calls. Desk and office searches are often used

primarily to locate drug use but also to identify the conducting of work unrelated to the company by the employee while on the job. Many employees find this to be particularly intrusive and an invasion of privacy. Most courts come down on the side of the employer if it has a justifiable business reason. The use of polygraphs, otherwise known as lie-dectector tests, is severely restricted to cases in which the employer has a reasonable suspicion that an employee has committed a theft.

SECURITY

The mere presence of security guards is a deterrence to many employees who would otherwise want to steal. Security guards, though, cannot be everywhere and see everything. They are also expensive when compared with the other alternatives. An additional method would be the use of inventory control. This requires limiting access to inventory to certain employees and instituting accounting controls and physical checks for verification. Inconsistencies can be investigated, and thefts are more easily traceable. When companies are lax in determining the existence of theft, it encourages employees so inclined to steal because there is little chance of detection. When controls are instituted, employees are more wary.

The following case addresses the question of whether the contents of a physician's office can be searched by the hospital that employs him. The resolution revolves around the issue of whether the fourth amendment protects the physician's privacy.

480 U.S. 709 (1986)

O'CONNOR, Justice

This suit under 42 U.S.C. 1983 presents two issues concerning the Fourth Amendment rights of public employees. First, we must determine whether the respondent, a public employee, had a reasonable expectation of privacy in his office, desk, and file cabinets at his place of work. Second, we must address the appropriate Fourth Amendment standard for a search conducted by a public employer in areas in which a public employee is found to have a reasonable expectation of privacy.

Dr. Magno Ortega, a physician and psychiatrist, held the position of Chief of Professional Education at Napa State Hospital for 17 years, until his dismissal from that position in 1981. As Chief of Professional Education, Dr. Ortega had primary responsibility for training young physicians in psychiatric residency programs.

In July 1981, Hospital officials, including Dr. Dennis O'Connor, the Executive Director of the Hospital, became concerned about possible improprieties in Dr. Ortega's management of the residency program. In particular, the Hospital officials were concerned with Dr. Ortega's acquisition of an Apple II computer for use in the residency program. The officials thought that Dr. Ortega may have misled Dr. O'Connor into believing that the computer had been donated, when in fact the computer had been financed by the pos-

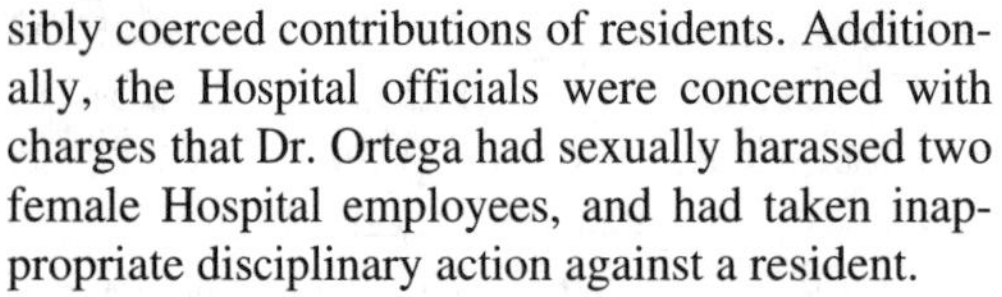

sibly coerced contributions of residents. Additionally, the Hospital officials were concerned with charges that Dr. Ortega had sexually harassed two female Hospital employees, and had taken inappropriate disciplinary action against a resident.

Dr. O'Connor selected several Hospital personnel to conduct the investigation, including an accountant, a physician, and a Hospital security officer. Richard Friday, the Hospital Administrator, led this "investigative team." At some point during the investigation, Mr. Friday made the decision to enter Dr. Ortega's office. The petitioners claim that the search was conducted to secure state property. Initially, petitioners contended that such a search was pursuant to a Hospital policy of conducting a routine inventory of state property in the office of a terminated employee. At the time of the search, however, the Hospital had not yet terminated Dr. Ortega's employment; Dr. Ortega was still on administrative leave. Apparently, there was no policy of inventorying the offices of those on administrative leave. Before the search had been initiated, however, petitioners had become aware that Dr. Ortega had taken the computer to his home. Dr. Ortega contends that the purpose of the search was to secure evidence for use against him in administrative disciplinary proceedings.

The resulting search of Dr. Ortega's office was quite thorough. The investigators entered the office a number of times and seized several items from Dr. Ortega's desk and file cabinets, including a Valentine's Day card, a photograph, and a book of poetry, all sent to Dr. Ortega by a former resident physician. These items were later used in a proceeding before a hearing officer of the California State Personnel Board to impeach the credibility of the former resident, who testified on Dr. Ortega's behalf. The investigators also seized billing documentation of one of Dr. Ortega's private patients under the California Medicaid program. The investigators did not otherwise separate Dr. Ortega's property from state property because, as one investigator testified, "trying to sort State from non-State, it was too much to do, so I gave it up and boxed it up." Thus, no formal inventory of the property in the office was ever made. Instead, all the papers in Dr. Ortega's office were merely placed in boxes, and put in storage for Dr. Ortega to retrieve.

Dr. Ortega commenced this action against petitioners in Federal District Court under 42 U.S.C.1983, alleging that the search of his office violated the Fourth Amendment.

The Fourth Amendment protects the "right of the people to be secure in their persons, houses, papers, and effects, against unreasonable searches and seizures. . . ." Our cases establish that Dr. Ortega's Fourth Amendment rights are implicated only if the conduct of the Hospital officials at issue in this case infringed "an expectation of privacy that society is prepared to consider reasonable."

Because the reasonableness of an expectation of privacy, as well as the appropriate standard for a search, is understood to differ according to context, it is essential first to delineate the boundaries of the workplace context. The workplace includes those areas and items that are related to work and are generally within the employer's control. At a hospital, for example, the hallways, cafeteria, offices, desks, and file cabinets, among other areas, are all part of the workplace. These areas remain part of the workplace context even if the employee has placed personal items in them, such as a photograph placed in a desk or a letter posted on an employee bulletin board.

Not everything that passes through the confines of the business address can be considered part of the workplace context, however. An employee may bring closed luggage to the office prior to leaving on a trip, or a handbag or briefcase each workday. While whatever expectation of privacy the employee has in the existence and the outward appearance of the luggage is affected by its presence in the workplace, the employee's expectation of privacy in the contents of the luggage is not affected in the same way. The appropriate standard for a workplace search does not necessarily apply to a piece of closed personal luggage, a handbag, or a briefcase that happens to be within the employer's business address.

Within the workplace context, this Court has recognized that employees may have a reasonable expectation of privacy against intrusions by police. As with the expectation of privacy in one's home, such as expectations that have deep roots in the history of the Amendment.

Given the societal expectations of privacy in one's place of work, we reject the contention made by the Solicitor General and petitioners that public employees can never have a reasonable expectation of privacy in their place of work. Individuals do not lose Fourth Amendment rights merely because they work for the government instead of a private employer. The operational realities of the workplace, however, may make some employees' expectations of privacy unreasonable when an intrusion is by a supervisor rather than a law enforcement official. Public employees' expectations of privacy in their offices, desks, and file cabinets, like similar expectations of employees in the private sector, may be reduced by virtue of actual office practices and procedures, or by legitimate regulation.

The Court of Appeals concluded that Dr. Ortega had a reasonable expectation of privacy in his office, and five Members of this Court agree with that determination. Because the record does not reveal the extent to which Hospital officials may have had work-related reasons to enter Dr. Ortega's office, we think the Court of Appeals should have remanded the matter to the District Court for its further determination. But regardless of any legitimate right of access the Hospital staff may have had to the office as such, we recognize that the undisputed evidence suggests that Dr. Ortega had a reasonable expectation of privacy in his desk and file cabinets. The undisputed evidence discloses that Dr. Ortega did not share his desk or file cabinets with any other employees. Dr. Ortega had occupied the office for 17 years and he kept materials in his office, which included personal correspondence, medical files, correspondence from private patients unconnected to the Hospital, personal financial records, teaching aids and notes, and personal gifts and mementos.

On the basis of this undisputed evidence, we accept the conclusion of the Court of Appeals that Dr. Ortega had a reasonable expectation of privacy at least in his desk and file cabinets.

Judgment for Ortega.

COMPANY POLICY

Establishing a policy against employee theft is an important consideration for a company. The policy should include a definition encompassing all the property that the company feels if taken or allowed to be taken would constitute theft. The policy should spell out what the consequences for thefts will be and whether the company intends to have the employee prosecuted. A statement should be included stipulating that the policy applies to all employees from executives on down. The company must disseminate this policy to all its employees along with conspicuous posting. Finally the company should follow through rigorously, identifying and then enforcing breaches of this policy in a consistent manner.

WHISTLE-BLOWING

Whistle-blowing is the notification by an employee to management about a coworker's unlawful activities or to the appropriate federal and state agencies about the company's illegal activities. It takes a lot of courage on the part of the employee to make the report. While ethically the employee's action is commendable, it may result in the employee's being ostracized by others in the company or it may result in discharge. While the authorities encourage whistle-blowing, more could be done to protect people who do risk their jobs for the truth to be known.

In the following case, a teacher claimed to have been dismissed for whistle-blowing. She brought an action for wrongful discharge based on public policy reasons. The school superintendent claimed that the discharge was not retaliatory but rather based on substantial grounds reflected in the evaluation of the teacher.

CASE *Wytrwal v. Mowles*

886 F.Supp. 128 (D.Me. 1995)

CARTER, Judge.

Plaintiff Barbara Wytrwal started teaching behaviorally impaired students at Saco Middle School in the fall of 1990. Wytrwal, like all other new teachers, was in probationary status for the first two years. At the end of the second probationary year, teachers are considered for continuing contract status, which is similar to being awarded tenure. After two years, Wytrwal's contract at Saco school was not renewed. Wytrwal claims that she was not continued because, at a school board meeting, she criticized the special education department and alleged that Saco Middle School was violating special education laws. Wytrwal's complaint seeks recovery for violation of the Civil Rights Act. The court finds for Defendants on all counts.

The decision whether to renew Wytrwal's contract rested with Dr. Cynthia Mowles, who served as Superintendent of Schools for Saco School District during both the 1990–91 and 1991–92 school years. David Stickney was Director of Special Education for Saco School District and served as Wytrwal's direct supervisor for the 1990–91 school year, but during Wytrwal's second year at Saco, although he was ultimately responsible for special education, he was not Wytrwal's direct supervisor. During the 1990–91 school year, Gregory T. Goodness was the interim principal at Saco Middle School. The following year, the 1991–92 school year, Joseph Voci held the position of principal at Saco Middle School and served as Wytrwal's direct supervisor during that year. During the 1991–92 school year, Goodness was assistant principal of Saco Middle School.

When Wytrwal started teaching at Saco, the special education department was moving toward "mainstreaming," and the students were being housed, for the first time, inside the Saco Middle School building. Mainstreaming means incorporating special education students into the regular classroom as much as possible, with the goal being for the student to make the transformation back to full time in the regular classroom. Because of the emphasis on mainstreaming, the expectation was for the special education teachers to work very closely with classroom teachers to facilitate the transition of students back and forth between special education and regular classrooms.

During the 1990–91 school year, the majority of students were placed in Wytrwal's classroom as an option to avoid more expensive placements out of the district. Wytrwal received a note in her mailbox requesting she go to Voci and Goodness' office on her lunch break. When she arrived, Voci handed her an evaluation that he had completed, and then he informed her that he had recommended to Mowles that her contract not be renewed. Wytrwal testified that Voci and Goodness asked her if she wanted to discuss anything regarding the nonrenewal of her contract, and then Wytrwal testified that Voci leaned back in his chair with his feet up on the desk, put his hands behind his head, and said, "We hate to see a seventeen year career down the tubes, but I guess yours is." Wytrwal testified that she was shocked when she learned that she was not going to be renewed. A few days later, Mowles wrote a letter to Wytrwal informing her that she would not be continued as a teacher in special education at the Saco Middle School.

Wytrwal based her suit on section 1983. The law controlling the violation of section 1983 is quite clear. First, plaintiff must show that her conduct was constitutionally protected and that this conduct was a "substantial" or "motivating" factor in the Board's decision not to re-hire her.

The court does not find, as Defendant suggests, that Wytrwal's presentation to the school board was benign. The court is satisfied that Wytrwal told the school board at the February 11 meeting that Saco Middle School was violating special education laws by failing to appropriately place students. Here the Court draws the inference, despite testimony to the contrary, that Wytrwal's presentation to the board was a motivating factor in the decision not to renew her contract.

At this point, Defendants argue that the same decision would have been made absent the constitutionally protected activity. Defendant's claim that there were a number of other problems with Wytrwal that supported the decision not to renew her contract. Most significantly, Defendants produced evidence that Wytrwal's functionally nonexistent working relationship with Stickney, the special education director, lead the administrators not to nominate Wytrwal for renewal.

Under the Maine Whistle Blowers Protection Act, an employer may not discriminate against an employee because:

The employee, acting in good faith . . . reports orally or in writing to the employer or a public body what the employee has reasonable cause to believe is a violation of a law or rule adopted under the laws of this State, a political subdivision of this State, or the United States.

To prevail on a claim under this statute, Wytrwal must first establish a prima facie case of reprisal, which requires that she show that (1) she engaged in activity protected by the statute; (2) she was the subject of adverse employment action; and (3) there was casual link between the protected activity and the adverse employment action. Because the elements of this tripartite test are essentially the same as those required to establish a prima facie case under section 1983, the Court finds, for the reasons discussed above, that Wytrwal has met this standard. With Plaintiff's prima facie case established, however, this court has been unable to find any Maine case law on what burden Defendants bear.

Under McDonnell Douglas, its progeny and Maine law, the employee has the initial burden of establishing a prima facie case. Wytrwal having already made this showing, the burden shifts to the employer to rebut the presumption of discrimination by producing evidence that the employer made the questionable employment decision for a legitimate reason. The employer's explanation of its actions must be "clear and reasonably specific." If the employer meets its burden of production, the legal presumption that would justify a judgment as a matter of law based on the plaintiff's prima facie case "simply drops out of the picture," and the plaintiff bears the burden of persuading the factfinder that the proffered reasons are pretextual and that the employment decision was the result of discriminatory intent. Pretext may be demonstrated either by the presentation of additional evidence showing that "the employer's proffered explanation is unworthy of credence," or by reliance on the evidence comprising the prima facie case coupled with disbelief of the reasons put forward by defendant. Defendants have presented persuasive evidence that Wytrwal was discharged for reasons other than her board presentation. Although Defendants have failed to show written documentation establishing any problems with Wytrwal prior to the school board meeting, the Court is satisfied that this is because, under state law, they are not required to create documentation as a basis for a decision not to renew a probationary teacher. These problems occurred prior to, and independent of, any concern about her presentation at the school board meeting. Accordingly, Defendants have satisfied their burden.

Without question, Wytrwal's evaluations reflected that the administrators were more than satisfied with her performance. There were two classroom observation evaluations done on Wytrwal during the 1990–91 school year. On both evaluation forms, Wytrwal received highest marks, that is, she "exceeded expectations" in all but one category. In the final category, she received a mark of "meets expectations" for effective performance.

During the second year, Goodness engaged in ongoing discussions with Wytrwal regarding her students and her classroom. In addition, Voci discussed with Wytrwal her problems in getting along with other teachers and specialists as well as her difficulty getting and keeping the special education students mainstreamed. When the administrators spoke with Wytrwal about these discrete issues it was never indicated that her continuing employment contract was in jeopardy. The Court is satisfied that despite the dearth of criticism in Wytrwal's evaluations, the administrators attempted, albeit halfheartedly, to point out some of the areas where Wytrwal was having trouble. Therefore, Wytrwal has failed to establish that the reasons given for not renewing her contract are pretextual.

Although the Maine Law Court has not recognized the tort of wrongful discharge, it has not foreclosed the possibility of such recognition if the employer's motives violate some strong public policy. Because the Court finds that Wytrwal's discharge was not done in retaliation for the remarks she made at the school board meeting, her discharge does not contravene any strong public policy. Therefore, even if this Court were to recognize the existence of a common law claim under Maine law for wrongful discharge, Wytrwal would not prevail.

Judgment for Mowles.

In the following case, a border patrol agent gave an unfavorable evaluation of a trainee. The trainee, in turn, complained about the unlawful actions of the agent while on patrol. The supervisor recommended that the trainee not be retained. The trainee claimed retaliation for whistle-blowing.

CASE

Frederick v. Department of Justice

73 F.3d 349 (1996)

LOURIE, Circuit Judge.

Thomas B. Frederick petitions for review of the December 7, 1994 final decision of the Merit Systems Protection Board, holding that he violated the Whistleblower Protection Act (WPA), and sustaining the agency's 21-day suspension. Because the board's decision was not supported by substantial evidence and was not in accordance with law, we reverse.

Background

The Department of Justice, Immigration and Naturalization Service (the agency), employed Frederick as a Patrol Agent In Charge at the Sonoita, Arizona Border Patrol Station from December 1988 to January 1994. Frederick supervised Border Patrol Agents, including Esker Mayberry. He also supervised Kenneth Womack, a trainee who entered on duty at Sonoita after completing academy training at the federal law enforcement training center in Glynco, Georgia.

After completing academy training, trainees at the Station received field training from Border Patrol Agents who were required to complete Conduct and Efficiency (C&E) evaluations for each trainee. The C&E evaluations were recorded on a standard two-page form containing various categories that the evaluator used to rate the trainee. The evaluator also had to make a recommendation either for or against retention of the trainee. Each trainee typically received several C&E evaluations over the course of the field training. After a trainee had passed a required Spanish exam, a Probationary Review Board made a recommendation for retention or non-retention based on the trainee's C&E evaluations and grades on a law exam and Spanish exam. The Probationary Review Board's recommendation was forwarded to the Sector office and then to the Region office, which made the final decision of retention or non-retention.

Following a field training session, Mayberry completed an unfavorable C&E evaluation of Womack on October 27, 1989. Immediately thereafter, Womack reported to Frederick incidents that occurred during his field training session with Mayberry. Those incidents consisted of: (1) throwing stones at a railroad car that contained illegal aliens, which Womack alleged was a human rights violation; (2) performing a license plate check, which he alleged was unethical; and (3) crossing over the border between the United States and Mexico while on duty, which he alleged was a violation of international law.

Frederick discussed these incidents individually with Womack and Mayberry. He determined that the incidents were not violations of law and that Womack had made the allegations in order to divert attention from Mayberry's unfavorable C&E evaluation. As the Patrol Agent In Charge, Frederick was required to complete his own C&E evaluation of Womack by October 31, 1989, which was the date on which Womack was scheduled to take the required Spanish exam. When discussing the incidents with Womack, Frederick urged him to take the Spanish exam regardless of any concerns Womack had regarding the C&E evaluation that Frederick had not yet completed. Frederick also sought guidance from his superiors on how to handle Womack's disclosure, but received none. Frederick completed his C&E evaluation on the evening of October 30, 1989, and recommended against retention of Womack. Womack voluntarily resigned on October 31, 1989.

Eventually, Womack complained to the Office of Special Counsel (OSC). The OSC determined that Frederick retaliated against Womack because of protected disclosures and recommended that the agency take disciplinary action against Frederick. The agency suspended him for twenty-one days.

Frederick appealed to the Merit Systems Protection Board. In an initial decision, the administrative judge (AJ) found that Womack could not have reasonably believed that the license plate check was unlawful. The AJ based his finding on Mayberry's testimony, in which he stated that he explained to Womack that the license plate check was necessary because the occupants of the house where the vehicle was parked were suspected of drug dealing, and the agents had not previously observed the vehicle at that house. The AJ similarly found that Womack could not have reasonably believed that the rock-throwing incident was unlawful because the rocks were thrown at the side of the railroad car to gain the attention of the aliens observed to have been inside. The AJ further found the the railroad car had no openings on the side at which the rocks were thrown, and the aliens were in no danger of being hit by the rocks.

The AJ found, however, that Womack's allegation of a border crossing was a protected disclosure. The AJ also found that the protected disclosure was the "sole reason" for Frederick's recommendation that Womack not be retained, and the AJ thus held that Frederick violated the WPA. Because Frederick did not know that he was violating the law and did not act with malicious motivation, the AJ held that there was only a technical violation and that a letter of warning was the maximum reasonable penalty for the violation.

The agency petitioned for review by the full board and Frederick cross-petitioned. The board affirmed the AJ's holding that Frederick violated the WPA; however, the board vacated the mitigation of the penalty and reinstated the agency's twenty-one day suspension. Frederick petitions for review by this court.

The WPA provides that:

(b) Any employee who has authority to take, direct others to take, recommend, or approve any personnel action, shall not, with respect to such authority . . .

(8) take or fail to take, or threaten to take or fail to take, a personnel action with respect to any employee or applicant for employment because of

 (A) any disclosure of information by an employee or applicant which the employee or applicant reasonably believes evidences

 (i) a violation of any law, rule, or regulation. . . . We have interpreted the

WPA to require proof of four elements to establish a violation: "(1) the acting official has the authority to take, recommend, or approve any personnel action; (2) the aggrieved employee made a protected disclosure; (3) the acting official used his authority to take, or refuse to take, a personnel action against the aggrieved employee; (4) the acting official took, or failed to take, the personnel action against the aggrieved employee because of the protected disclosure."

We agree with Frederick that there was no substantial evidence to support a reasonable belief by Womack that a violation occurred. The alleged border crossing occurred when Womack and Mayberry were "cutting sign," which involved inspecting for tracks, such as tire tracks or footprints, indicative of illegal entry into the United States. During this activity, Mayberry and Womack crossed over a fence between the United States and Mexico in order to evaluate "sign." Mayberry testified that he did not know if in the process of jumping the fence they crossed into Mexico because the fence was not exactly on the border and in most situations is on the United States' side; the exact location of the border is determined by monuments. Mayberry also testified that he did not believe that he went far enough beyond the fence to enter Mexico. At the time, Mayberry had almost four years of service and had never been the subject of an adverse action.

The WPA was enacted to protect employees who report genuine infractions of law, not to encourage employees to report arguably minor and inadvertent miscues occurring in the conscientious carrying out of one's assigned duties. As noted in the legislative history of the WPA: What is needed is a means to protect the Pentagon employee who discloses billions of dollars in cost overruns, the GSA employee who discloses widespread fraud, and the nuclear engineer who questions the safety of certain nuclear plants. . . . Nor would the bill protect employees who claim to be whistle blowers in order to avoid adverse action based on inadequate performance.

The WPA was thus not intended to encompass such a minor transgression as took place even if Mayberry and Womack stepped into Mexico while doing their work. If supervisors have to fear that every trivial lapse in their own behavior will be the subject of a whistleblowing complaint when they critically appraise their employees, as they are obligated to do, they will be deterred from carrying out honest appraisals. Poor performers will be protected by any minor lapse in a supervisor's conduct. This was not the purpose of the WPA, which was intended to root out real wrongdoing. Thus, the alleged action by Mayberry was of such a trivial nature that Womack could not have had a reasonable belief that Mayberry was violating a law, rule, or regulation within the meaning of the WPA.

Considering all the evidence presented, including that which detracts from a "reasonable belief," the record does not contain substantial evidence to support a reasonable belief by Womack that the border crossing was a violation of law. Thus, no reasonable fact-finder could conclude that Womack's disclosure of the alleged border crossing was a protected disclosure.

In addition, Frederick's act of completing the C&E evaluation was not a "personnel action." The WPA defines "personnel action" as: (i) an appointment; (ii) a promotion; (iii) an action under chapter 75 of this title or other disciplinary or corrective action; (iv) a detail, transfer, or reassignment; (v) a reinstatement; (vi) a restoration; (vii) a reemployment; (viii) a performance evaluation under chapter 43 of this title; (ix) a decision concerning pay, benefits, or awards, concerning education or training if the education or training may reasonably be expected to lead to an appointment, promotion, performance evaluation, or other action described in this subparagraph; (x) a decision to order psychiatric testing or examination; and (xi) any other significant change in duties, responsibilities, or working conditions. The agency conceded that the C&E evaluation was not a "performance evaluation." Instead, the agency first argues that the C&E evaluation was an appointment. However, Womack had already received an appointment, and Frederick did not have authority to appoint or transfer border patrol agents. Without such authority, Frederick's C&E evaluation could not have been an appointment. Moreover,

the C&E evaluation only recommended against retention; it did not effectuate any such action and had no binding effect on the agency.

The WPA specifically distinguishes between those who recommend personnel actions and those who take or fail to take personnel actions. In terms of being within the scope of the WPA, the act applies to those who have authority to recommend a personnel action. However, the WPA only attaches liability to those who take or fail to take a personnel action. Supervisors such as Frederick are fully encouraged to make honest recommendations concerning employees, but they must be more careful of actions they take (or fail to take) concerning employees.

Frederick did not take or fail to take a personnel action against Womack. On the contrary, his C&E evaluation was merely a recommendation to the agency. It is only when one takes or fails to take a personnel action against an employee because of a protected disclosure that liability attaches under the relevant section of the WPA, and no such action occurred here. The board's holding that Frederick took a personnel action and that the third element of the test was met, was thus not in accordance with law because it resulted from an erroneous interpretation of the WPA.

Conclusion

The decision of the Merit Systems Protection Board is reversed because it was not supported by substantial evidence and was not in accordance with law; it misconstrued the meaning and scope of the WPA. Frederick is entitled to back pay to compensate for the twenty-one day suspension, and we remand to the board for a determination of such back pay.

Judgment for Frederick.

Employment Perspective

Stellar Industries, a manufacturer of brake pads for commercial aircraft, is located in Oklahoma City. Times have been tough for Stellar.

The last recession had caused Stellar to trim its workforce by 40 percent. Recently Stellar was awarded a contract by Heavenly Airlines for designing a lightweight brake pad. This contract will triple Stellar's revenues over a five-year period. Also, the contract enabled Stellar to rehire half the people it had laid off as well as some new people.

One of the people rehired was Megan Thomas. Her assignment is to run the testing of the brake pads. She will work directly under Russ Heflin, who is the chief engineer and the person directly responsible for the design of the lightweight brake pads. The purpose of the testing is to assure Heavenly that the plane will stop fifty times before the pads have to be replaced. After the first round of tests, the pads disintegrate after the thirty-sixth landing. Megan Thomas informs Russ of the result. He instructs her to test again. This time the pads last through the thirty-fourth landing. Both Megan and Russ realize that a mistake has been made. Megan asks Russ if he will inform Heavenly that Stellar can guarantee only thirty landings and that the pads will have to be replaced more frequently. Russ explains that the failure to guarantee fifty landings is a breach of contract. Heavenly will go elsewhere to have the brakes manufactured and will sue for the difference between the contract price and the market price, the price paid elsewhere. Stellar not only will have to pay damages but also will lose the revenue guaranteed over the next five years. Stellar's reputation for quality will also be harmed, and its financial stability will be undermined.

Russ orders Megan to do whatever is necessary to see to it that the pads work fifty times, such as allowing the plane to coast after landing rather than applying full pressure to the brake pads. Russ's behavior is clearly unethical. What should Megan do?

A likely response is to speak to Russ's boss. Fred Worthingham, vice president for manufacturing, is Russ's superior. Fred is also the one who negotiated the contract with Heavenly and who signed his name thereto. He is the person ultimately responsible for the deal. Upon learning this, should Megan still seek out Fred?

Megan decides to talk the situation over with Fred. Fred informs Megan that her duty is to follow the orders given by her direct superior. He says that the responsibility for those decisions lies with the company. Megan tells Fred that she cannot live with this decision and would rather resign.

Fred tells Megan that he will assign her to a different job. Does that relieve Megan from ethical responsibility, or must she whistle-blow by informing Heavenly Airlines, the FAA, and/or the Attorney General's office? Whistle-blowing would be the most ethical decision, but the consequences can often be severe: loss of job; black-balled from the industry, threats of physical harm, or even murder, as was intimated by the movie about Karen Silkwood.

The possibility of loss of life from the brake pads is a major consideration for whistle-blowing as compared with defective tray tables or food carts on an airplane. Although ethical responses should be unconditional, is it realistic to expect a person to whistle-blow or lose a job over defective tray tables or food carts? Ethically, no one should produce defective equipment regardless of the consequences of the defect, because to do so would be to breach the duty to act in good faith.

When the rehirings took place, Russ Heflin specifically asked for Megan because she is a diligent worker. Megan was thrilled because her husband, Phil, was recently placed on disability from his job because of a back injury. She is now the primary supporter of her husband and four children. Knowing her gratefulness for being rehired and her personal financial dilemma, Russ emphasizes that his favor to her must be repaid; otherwise, the consequences of losing her job would leave Megan and her family in dire financial straits. Now Megan must balance her desire to do the right thing against her family's livelihood. Megan decides to discuss the matter with her husband. Phil tells her that as long as the vice president accepts full responsibility and relieves her from any responsibility, then she should do as they say. Now lacking support from her husband, Megan gives in. She is practical, but is she unethical? Must she sacrifice everything to do the right thing? What if a plane crashes because she followed orders by doctoring the tests or failed to prevent that from happening by remaining silent and accepting the transfer? What if she whistle-blows, loses her job, ruins her family life, and no one believes her accusations, and furthermore, no plane ever crashes? ◆

REVIEW QUESTIONS

1. Explain the significance of the Privacy Act of 1974.
2. What implications does the Omnibus Crime Control and Safe Streets Act of 1968 have on privacy?
3. How has the right to privacy been affected by the Electronic Communications Act of 1986?

4. In what respect has the Fair Credit Reporting Act of 1970 improved the right to privacy?
5. What types of property are encompassed under the heading of employee theft?
6. What types of action have been taken by employers to combat employee theft?
7. Do any of these security actions infringe on an employee's right to privacy?
8. How can both interests be effectively balanced?
9. Is an employer entitled to conduct office searches?
10. Tuttle owned a barbershop in a small town in Minnesota. Buck, a town banker, financed the operation of a competing barbershop for the sole purpose of putting Tuttle out of business. Buck spread false and malicious lies about Tuttle, threatened his customers, and continued to finance the competing barbershop even though it was losing money. Tuttle sued Buck for loss of profits resulting from the loss of many of his customers. Buck asserted that he was lawfully diverting customers to make his barbershop profitable. What result? *Tuttle v. Buck,* 107 Minn. 145, 199 N.W. 946 (1909)
11. Thomas worked as a security manager for E.J. Korvette in its store located in King of Prussia, Pennsylvania. Thomas was about to purchase a game for his child's birthday when he was diverted by a suspected shoplifter, whom he followed out of the store with the game still in hand. He put the game in the trunk of his car and paid for it later. The assistant manager had observed what Thomas did and asked him to produce the sales receipt. Thomas could not produce the receipt because he had misplaced it, and he resigned because of the accusation. Later Thomas was arrested on the grounds of larceny. Subsequently, he found the sales receipt, but it did not match the price of the game. Thomas said the cashier had erred. The store then circulated a notice to all employees that Thomas had been arrested. When Thomas attempted to get employment in the same field, a prospective employer who was checking references was told by Korvette not to hire Thomas unless the employer wanted a thief working for it. After the criminal charge was dismissed, Thomas sued Korvette for false arrest, malicious prosecution, and defamation of character. What result? *Thomas v. Korvette Inc.,* 329 F. Supp. 1163 (E.D. Pa. 1971)
12. Is it possible for some government offices to be open to the public so that no reasonable expectation of privacy can exist? *Katz v. United States,* 389 U.S. 347 (1967)
13. Deforte, a union employee, shared an office with other union employees. A warrantless search was made of the office. Deforte argued notwithstanding the sharing of the office, that an expectation of privacy exists. What was the result? *Mancusi v. DeForte,* 392 U.S. 364 (1968)
14. Johnson, an employee of Boeing Airplane Co., appeared in a photograph with one of the company's planes. He made no complaint at the time the picture was taken or when it appeared posted around the company. Later Johnson sued for invasion of privacy when the company used it in a national magazine advertisement. What was the result? *Johnson v. Boeing Airplane Co.,* 262 P.2d 808 (1953)
15. Lenzer was employed as a physician assistant by Arc under the supervision of Drs. Baucom and Harman. She was in the process of satisfying the requirement for state certification. However, Drs. Baucom and Harman withdrew supervision from Lenzer, causing her to lose the certification she needed to maintain her position with Arc. The physicians' reason was that Lenzer counseled patients about child abuse. This action was outside the scope of a physician assistant's duties. There was no dispute over Lenzer's competence, and actually her counseling had been tolerated for a long time. Lenzer claims that her counseling is protected by the First Amendment's Free Speech. Lenzer is

suing for Drs. Baucom's and Harman's interference with her contract with Arc. What was the result? *Lenzer v. Flaherty,* 418 S.E. 2d 276 (N.C.App. 1992)

16. Richard Bloom worked as an associate dentist in Allan Dampf's office. While the plaintiff took a vacation, Dr. Bloom made a photostatic copy of the plaintiff's computer-generated recall list, which contained all his patients' names, addresses, telephone numbers, dates of last appointments, and dates due for next checkup. This list was kept in Dr. Dampf's home for security reasons. After he was fired, Dr. Bloom opened his own office and began soliciting the plaintiff's patients. What was the result? *Allan Dampf, P.C. v. Bloom,* 512 N.Y.S. 2d 116 (A.D. 2 Dept. 1987)

17. In the case on pp. 117, is it ethical for an employer to conduct an office search?

18. In that same case, is the fact that the office is the property of the owner significant?

19. Ethically, should employers be allowed to tape-record the conversations of their employees?

20. In the case on pp. 113, should Morgan have to suffer because of a poor decision she made when she was young?

Selective Amendments to the Constitution of the United States of America

AMENDMENT I (1791)

Congress shall make no law respecting an establishment of religion, or prohibiting the free exercise thereof; or abridging the freedom of speech, or the press, or the right of the people peaceably to assemble, and to petition the Government for a redress of grievances.

AMENDMENT IV (1791)

The right of the people to be secure in their persons, houses, papers, and effects, against unreasonable searches and seizures, shall not be violated, and no warrants shall issue, but upon probable cause, supported by oath or affirmation, and particularly describing the place to be searched, and the persons or things to be seized.

AMENDMENT XIV (1868)

Section 1. All persons born or naturalized in the United States, and subject to the jurisdiction thereof, are citizens of the United States and of the State wherein they reside. No State shall make or enforce any law which shall abridge the privileges or immunities of citizens of the United States; nor shall any State deprive any person of life, liberty, or property, without due process of law; nor deny to any person within its jurisdiction the equal protection of the law. [Sections 2–5 omitted.]

AMENDMENT XV (1870)

Section 1. The rights of citizens of the United States to vote shall not be denied or abridged by the United States or by any State on account of race, color, or previous condition of servitude. [Section 2 omitted.]

Whistleblower Protection Act

1214. INVESTIGATION OF PROHIBITED PERSONNEL PRACTICES; CORRECTIVE ACTION

(a) (1) (A) The Special Counsel shall receive any allegation of a prohibited personnel practice and shall investigate the allegation to the extent necessary to determine whether there are reasonable grounds to believe that a personnel practice has occurred, exists, or is to be taken.

(b) Within 15 days after the date of receiving an allegation of a prohibited personnel practice under paragraph (1), the Special Counsel shall provide written notice to the person who made the allegation that—

(i) the allegation has been received by the Special Counsel; and

(ii) Shall include the name of a person at the Office of Special Counsel who shall serve as a contact with the person making the allegation.

(c) Unless an investigation is terminated under paragraph (2), the Special Counsel shall—

(i) within 90 days after notice is provided under subparagraph (B), notify the person who made the allegation of the status of the investigation and any action taken by the Office of the Special Counsel since the filing of the allegation.

1215. DISCIPLINARY ACTION

(a) (1) If the Special Counsel determines that disciplinary action should be taken against any employer for having—

(A) committed a prohibited personnel practice,

(B) violated the provisions of any law, rule, or regulation, or engaged in any other conduct within the jurisdiction of the Special Counsel as described in section 1216, or

(C) knowingly and willfully refused or failed to comply with an order of the Merit Systems Protection Board, the Special Counsel shall prepare a written complaint against the employer containing the Special Counsel's determination, together with a statement of supporting facts, and present the complaint and statement to the employee and the Board, in accordance with this subsection.

Privacy Act of 1974

Sec 2.

(a) The Congress finds that—

(1) the privacy of an individual is directly affected by the collection, maintenance, use, and dissemination of personal information by Federal agencies;

(2) the increasing use of computers and sophisticated information technology, while essential to the efficient operations of the Government, has greatly magnified the harm to individual privacy that can occur from any collection, maintenance, use, or dissemination of personal information;

(3) the opportunities for an individual to secure employment, insurance and credit, and his right to due process, and other legal projections are endangered by the misuse of certain information systems;

(4) the right to privacy is a personal and fundamental right protected by the Constitution of the United States; and

(5) in order to protect the privacy of individuals identified in information systems maintained by Federal agencies, it is necessary and proper for the Congress to regulate the collection, maintenance, use and dissemination of information by such agencies.

(b) The purpose of the Act is to provide certain safeguards for an individual against invasion of personal privacy by requiring Federal agencies, except as otherwise provided by law, to—

(1) permit an individual to determine what records pertaining to him are collected, maintained, used, or disseminated by such agencies;

(2) permit an individual to prevent records pertaining to him obtained by such agencies for a particular purpose from being used or made available for another purpose without his consent;

(3) permit an individual to gain access to information pertaining to him in Federal agency records, to have a copy made of all or any portion thereof, and to correct or amend such records;

(4) collect, maintain, use, or disseminate any record of identifiable personal information in a manner that assures that such action is for a necessary and lawful purpose, that the information is current and accurate for its intended use, and that adequate safeguards are provided to prevent misuse of such information;

(5) permit exemptions from the requirements with respect to records provided in this Act only in those cases where there is an important public policy need for such exemption as has been determined by specific statutory authority; and

(6) be subject to civil suit for any damages which occur as a result of willful or intentional action which violates any individual's rights under this Act.

Sec. 3

(b) CONDITIONS OF DISCLOSURE.—No agency shall disclose any record which is contained in a system of records by any means of communication to any person, or to another agency, except pursuant to a written request by, or with the prior consent of, the individual to whom the record pertains, unless disclosure of the record would be—

(1) to those officers and employees of the agency which maintains the record who have a need for the record in the performance of their duties;

(4) to the Bureau of the Census for purposes of planning or carrying out a census of survey or related activity pursuant to the provisions of title 13;

(5) to a recipient who has provided the agency with advance written assurance that the record will be used solely as a statistical research or reporting record, and the record is to be transferred in a form that is not individually identifiable;

(8) to a person pursuant to a showing of compelling circumstances affecting the health or safety of an individual if upon such disclosure notification is transmitted to the last known address of such an individual;

(d) ACCESS TO RECORDS.—Each agency that maintains a system of records shall—

(1) upon request by any individual to gain access to his record or to any information pertaining to him which is contained in the system, permit him and upon his request, a person of his own choosing to accompany him, to review the record and have a copy made of all or any portion thereof in a form comprehensible to him, except that the agency may require the individual to furnish a written statement authorizing discussion of that individual's record in the accompanying person's presence;

(2) permit the individual to request amendment of a record pertaining to him and—

(A) not later than 10 days (excluding Saturdays, Sundays, and legal public holidays) after the date of receipt of such request, acknowledge in writing such receipt; and

(B) promptly either—

(i) make any correction of any portion thereof which the individual believes is not accurate, relevant, timely, or complete, or

(ii) inform the individual of its refusal to amend the record in accordance with his request, the reason for the refusal, the procedures established by the agency for the individual to request a review of that refusal by the head of the agency or an officer designated by the head of the agency, and the name and business address of that official;

(e) AGENCY REQUIREMENTS.—Each agency that maintains a system of records shall—

(1) maintain in its records only such information about an individual as is relevant and necessary to accomplish a purpose of the agency required to be accomplished by statute or by executive order of the President;

(2) collect information to the greatest extent practicable directly from the subject individual when the information may result in adverse determinations about an individual's rights, benefits, and privileges under Federal programs;

(i) CRIMINAL PENALTIES.—Any officer or employee of an agency, who by virtue of his employment or official position, has possession of, or access to, agency records which contain individually identifiable information the disclosure of which is prohibited by this section or by rules or regulations established thereunder, and who knowing that disclosure of the specific material is so prohibited, willfully discloses the material in any manner to any person or agency not entitled to receive it, shall be guilty of a misdemeanor and fined not more than $5,000.

CHAPTER 7 Termination

TERMINATION OF EMPLOYMENT

Termination is the discharge of an employee by an employer with or without cause. An employment relationship may terminate in the following ways:

- Revocation of authority
- Agreement
- Fulfillment of purpose
- Unfulfilled condition
- Operation of law

Revocation of Authority

An employee's or an independent contractor's authority may be revoked if the duration of the contract is indefinite or if no time limit has been specified. The employer may also revoke an employee's or an independent contractor's authority for cause where the employee or independent contractor has breached one of the duties owed. The employee or independent contractor must be notified that his or her authority is revoked. If the employment contract was in writing, then the revocation must also be in writing. Under other circumstances, it may be oral. This notice is effective when the employee or independent contractor receives it.

Notice of termination by revocation or mutual agreement must also be communicated to third persons who have dealt with the employer through the employee or independent contractor. Otherwise, the employer will be liable to third persons who

contract with the employee or independent contractor. The employer's liability is based on apparent authority to act based on prior dealings that the third party is justified in believing. Third parties who have dealt with the employee or independent contractor on prior occasions must be sent actual notice of termination. This becomes effective when the third party receives it. For all other third parties, the employer's duty to notify may be satisfied by publishing a statement regarding termination of authority in a newspaper.

Employment Perspective

Bob Kaufman was the managing agent for the Barons, a singing group that performed at clubs and weddings. When it came time to renew his contract, Kaufman demanded that his commission be increased from 10 percent to 15 percent of the band's gross earnings. Although Barons informed him that they would consider his request, they subsequently informed him that they would not accede to his request and terminated his employment. Infuriated by their reply, Kaufman, who was in the process of negotiating with several clubs for bookings, informed each of the clubs that the Barons would perform on the dates requested for $250 less than their usual price. Kaufman said, "They're glad to get the work." The Barons were familiar with these particular clubs but never informed them of the termination of Kaufman's employment. Are they bound to perform at the club for the lower fee? Yes! The Barons, as employer, have a duty to inform the clubs of Kaufman's termination. Otherwise, as in the case here, the clubs are justified in relying on Kaufman's apparent authority because they have dealt with the Barons through him on past occasions. ◆

Agreement

An employment contract can be terminated, like any other contract, by the mutual agreement of the parties. This termination is valid even if the contract had called for a longer term of employment.

Fulfillment of Purpose

The authority of an employee or an independent contractor hired for a specific term of employment, as in an employee-employer relationship, will terminate upon the expiration of that term. An agency relationship created for the fulfillment of a specific purpose will terminate when that purpose is completed.

Employment Perspective

Jonathan Murrow, a lawyer, was engaged by Marvelous Mini-Bikes, Inc., to represent it in several product liability suits. Murrow hired Timothy Hines, a paralegal, to assist him by researching the numerous cases in point and writing a legal memorandum of the principles of law applicable to the issues presented. Hines was hired for two years, by which time Murrow figured the suits would be settled. What is the status of the employment relationships created, and when will they terminate? Jonathan Murrow is an independent contractor hired by Marvelous Mini-Bikes and is free to use his own methods to handle the case. This employment will terminate when all of the product liability suits against Marvelous Mini-Bikes have been settled. Timothy

Hines is an employee of Jonathan Murrow. Hines must follow Murrow's instructions with regard to the work he undertakes. This employment relationship will expire at the end of the two-year term of employment. ◆

Unfulfilled Condition

The creation of an employment relationship may be conditioned on the happening of an event. If the condition precedent fails, the employment will not be created. Employment may also be created with its continued existence dependent on the fulfillment of a condition subsequent. If this condition should fail, the employment will be terminated.

Employment Perspective

George Larsen applied to Chevrolet for a franchise in order to open a dealership. Confident that his request would be approved, Larsen called Kenneth Washburn and asked him to be a sales agent for the new dealership if the franchise was approved. If the franchise is approved, the condition precedent has been met, and an employment relationship has been created between Larsen and Washburn. If not, there will be no employment relationship. Suppose that the franchise is approved and Larsen hires Washburn on the condition that Washburn sells seventy cars each year. During the first two years of his employment, Washburn meets his quota, but in the third year he sells only fifty-seven cars and is dismissed. Has he any recourse? No! Washburn's employment is terminated because he failed to continue to meet the required condition. ◆

Prohibited by Operation of Law

Employment may terminate by operation of law in the following ways:

- Bankruptcy of the employer or the employee terminating the employee's authority in financial transactions.
- Insanity or death of the employee or employer if he or she is a sole proprietor.
- Destruction or loss of the subject matter, if the employment was created for a purpose related to that subject matter.

If the termination is not legally justifiable, then it is considered wrongful. This discussion does not apply to instances in which an employee voluntarily resigns or in which an employment contract for a designated period has reached its end. An employer may dismiss an employee for cause when the employee is in breach of contract or has committed a tort or a crime or has not otherwise compiled with the rules and regulations set forth by the employer. These regulations would include those laws imposed upon the employer such as the Occupational Safety and Health Act, Title VII of the Civil Rights Act, or the Americans with Disabilities Act. Termination with cause protects employees from being arbitrarily dismissed.

The issue in the following case is whether the employment contract was amended to require termination by cause.

CASE

Brennan v. National Telephone Directory Corp.

881 F.Supp. 986 (E.D.Pa. 1995)

JOYNER, District Judge.

The defendants in this case are National Telephone Directory Corporation ("NTD"), a New Jersey corporation with its principal offices in Somerset, New Jersey; Penn-Del Directory Corporation ("Penn-Del"), a related corporation with offices in Bensalem and Harrisburg, Pennsylvania; and Bell Atlantic Enterprises International, Inc. ("Bell Atlantic"), which became a general partner in both NTD and Penn-Del after purchasing the two companies from Bell of Canada Enterprises ("BCE") in January of 1993. The plaintiff, Amy Brennan, is a New Jersey resident who was hired in April 7, 1986, and began working as a sales training coach in Penn-Del's office in Bensalem, a Philadelphia suburb.

By January 1, 1987 Brennan had been promoted to the position of district sales manager and transferred to Penn-Del's office in Harrisburg. In November of 1988, Ms. Brennan returned to Bensalem and assumed the position of account executive. As an account executive, Ms. Brennan was responsible for the selling and servicing of advertising in the Yellow Pages of the telephone directory. One of the more important aspects of her position was to ensure the accuracy of the paperwork for a given account. A minor lapse in the accuracy of the paperwork could result in a crucial error, such as an incorrect address or phone number, appearing in an advertisement.

To combat sales errors, the defendants employed a written policy regarding "chargeable errors." Pursuant to that policy, the division manager and customer service manager would, once an error was discovered, investigate the circumstances and make a determination as to whether to charge the error to the sales representative. After the investigation, the account executive was given the opportunity to discuss the matter and offer his or her version of the events. The division manager and customer service manager would then decide whether to charge the account representative with the sales error. A sales representative would be assessed a chargeable error if he or she was either fully or partially responsible for the error. The account executive would then sign an acknowledgment form, which alerted the account executive as to the following company policy: (1) an account executive was to be counseled after each chargeable error; (2) the account executive would be given an in depth interview with the vice president of sales after four chargeable errors; and (3) the company could take "drastic measures," including termination, if the account executive were assessed with four chargeable errors in a given calendar year.

The record reflected Brennan was one of the defendants' more valuable employees. Indeed, she was twice recognized as sales representative of the month and also won trips to Cancun, Mexico and Aruba as rewards for her performance. The record also reflects, however, that Ms. Brennan had some difficulty with the paperwork involved in processing the accounts, and that she was criticized, on more than one occasion, for a lack of attention to detail. During 1990 and 1991, Ms. Brennan was assessed five chargeable errors, but she was not terminated because she collected less than four errors in each year.

In January of 1992 Brennan went on disability leave due to the complicated nature of her pregnancy. She was scheduled to return to work in July of 1992. In the spring of 1992, however, six sales errors surfaced involving accounts assigned to Ms. Brennan. Ms. Brennan's division manager, James Schmitt, contacted her in June of 1992 and informed her of the six potential chargeable errors that were pending against her. The evidence presented suggests that Mr. Schmitt had already decided to charge her with three of the errors at the time they informed her of the pending charges. Documentation regarding the errors was forwarded to Ms. Brennan on June 18, 1992. On June 28, 1992, Ms. Brennan was again contacted by Mr. Schmitt to discuss the errors. Ms. Brennan admitted that she was at fault with respect to one account, but denied making any mistakes regarding the remaining five chargeable errors. Nonetheless, Mr. Schmitt decided to terminate Ms. Brennan. After consulting with the vice president of sales, who concurred with the decision to terminate, Mr. Schmitt informed Ms. Brennan that she would be fired effective July 9, 1992. Ms. Brennan never received counseling after each chargeable error, never signed an acknowledgment form regarding the errors, and was never interviewed by the vice president of sales.

The defendants argue that they are entitled to summary judgment to the extent that Count II of the amended complaint requests relief under the theory that the defendants discriminated against Ms. Brennan on the basis of her "pregnancy disability." The defendants correctly note that while Title VII prohibits discrimination based upon a person's "race, color, religion, sex, or national origin," it does not prohibit disability discrimination. Thus, such claims are not cognizable under Title VII.

Under New Jersey law, the traditional rule is that an at-will employee may be discharged at any time, for any reason or for no reason at all. Generally, an employment contract running for an indefinite term is presumed to be terminable at-will. In some circumstances, however, language in an employment manual can create an implied promise to terminate only for just cause that may be enforceable against the employer, even when the relationship would otherwise be terminable at-will. Thus, Ms. Brennan argues that Penn-Del's Employee Resolution Process ("ERP") operated to change her employment status from that of an at-will employee to one who would be discharged only for cause. The ERP provides, in pertinent part, as follows:

The ERP is established to assure that all employees are accorded fair and honest treatment in all aspects of their employment.

It provides employees with a method by which they may obtain full review decisions concerning problems or complaints arising from the application of company policy or rules, in order to avoid any arbitrary actions.

The issue thus presented is whether the ERP conferred upon Ms. Brennan the right to be discharged only in accordance with the ERP's terms. The Supreme Court of New Jersey has recently set forth the considerations to be applied in resolving such questions, noting that "the key consideration in determining whether an employment manual gives rise to contractual obligations is the reasonable expectations of the employees." Since, under New Jersey law, the question of whether Ms. Brennan could reasonably have expected that the ERP created an implied modification to the employment contract is one for the jury to decide, our present task is to determine whether an issue of fact has been raised regarding the existence of the modification.

Applying these principles to the matter at hand, it is clear that Ms. Brennan has created an issue of fact as to whether the ERP modified the employment contract to provide for termination for cause. First, while the parties have provided no information regarding the extent to which the ERP was distributed, we note that it was addressed to "All Employees," raising the inference that Penn-Del intended for it to be read and considered by all of the employees. We further note that Penn-Del intended for the ERP to supplement the company's employee manual. Finally, we note that the policy sets forth a three-step procedure under which an employee can discuss incidents which could lead to adverse employment actions, including termination. The stated goal of the ERP is "to avoid any arbitrary actions," which can be construed as indicative of management's intent to terminate its employees only for cause. Thus, under these circumstances, we cannot say that there is no dispute as to whether the ERP operated to alter Ms. Brennan's employment status. Accordingly, we must deny Penn-Del's summary judgment motion.

Judgment for Brennan.

Employment Perspective

Molly Player, Caitlin Dempsey, and Jason Simington are employees of the Texas Gentlemen, a fine men's-apparel store. One of Molly's responsibilities was to fold sweaters after customers had unfolded them to get a better idea as to whether they liked the sweaters. Molly continuously neglected her duty despite her recognition of the Texas Gentlemen's image of being meticulous in appearance.

Caitlin's function was to replenish the retail inventory from storage in the back of the store. On occasion, she would remove an article of clothing from the premises as a present for her boyfriend. Finally, she was apprehended by the security guard.

Jason was in charge of safety maintenance. One day a fire broke out in the storage area. The sprinklers malfunctioned, and the fire extinguishers, which were placed in the rear of the store, could not be reached, so that substantial damage resulted. Molly, Caitlin, and Jason were all terminated for cause. They claim that Texas Gentlemen's actions amount to wrongful discharges. Are they correct? No! Molly was insubordinate and therefore was in breach of contract. Caitlin was guilty of the tort of conversion and the crime of larceny. Jason violated OSHA laws by failing to adhere to federal safety standards. ◆

An employer may dismiss an employee without cause where the employment relationship is considered to be at will. *At will* means either the employer or the employee can terminate the relationship upon giving proper notice. Proper notice is considered to be the duration of the pay period, i.e., one week, two weeks, or one month. (That is where the phrase "two-week notice" is derived from.) Employers feel that if employees are free to leave at will, then employers should be free to discharge employees at will, too. However, some employers provide in their employee handbooks that employees will not be dismissed except for cause or in case of layoffs. In this context, the employer has given up its ability to terminate at will.

In the next case, an employee claims to have been wrongfully discharged because of age. The employer claims it is justified in doing so because the employment was at-will.

CASE

Finch v. Hercules, Inc.

809 F.Supp. 309 (D.Del 1992)

SCHWARTZ, District Judge.

Hercules, motivated by bad faith and malice, wrongfully discharged the Plaintiff in violation of the public policy against employment discrimination based on age, as codified in the ADEA and the Delaware Fair Employment Practices Act (FEPA).

First, it could be a claim for discharge of an at-will employee in violation of public policy. Second, it could be read as alleging a common law tort claim of malicious discharge.

The Delaware Supreme Court has never recognized a public policy exception to an employer's ability to dismiss an at-will employee. However, in *Merrill v. Crothall American, Inc.*, the Delaware Supreme Court recognized that an implied covenant of good faith and fair dealing may be breached in some circumstances by termination of an at-will employee.

In at least two instances, however, the Delaware Superior Court has recognized exceptions, albeit not public policy exceptions.

In *Heller v. Dover Warehouse Mkt., Inc.*, the Delaware Superior Court found a "statutory exception to the at-will employee doctrine." In *Heller,* the employee had been forced to undergo a polygraph test, despite a statutory prohibition of such a practice. The analysis in the case, however, did not focus on gleaning public policy from Delaware statutes. Instead, the court found an implied right of action under the statute upon which plaintiff could sue. Because this implied right allowed an at-will employee to sue for wrongful discharge, the implied right by necessity formed an exception to the at-will employee doctrine.

In a second case, the employer had allegedly directed the plaintiff to "set prices on the government contracts in excess of that provided for in the federal regulations." Referring to the growing number of states which recognize a public policy exception to the at-will doctrine, the court found a valid cause of action. In so doing the Superior Court effectively identified a second exception to the at-will employee doctrine.

Turning to the instant case, the State of Delaware has in place a statutory scheme governing matters related to employment discrimination.

The FEPA parallels Title VII and the ADEA in many respects. It contains no exclusive remedy provision. Even if it did, however, Plaintiff did not seek to invoke it.

The FEPA allows claims to be filed at the Delaware Department of Labor (the "Department"). After a charge is filed, the Department will send the employer the Charge of Discrimination, a No Fault Settlement Invitation, a Fact Finding Conference Form, and a questionnaire. If the parties cannot negotiate a settlement, the Department will proceed with its investigation. The Department usually holds a fact finding conference as part of its investigation, and the parties are required to attend. After completing its investigation, if no "reasonable cause" is found to believe that the charging party's allegations of discrimination were correct, the charge will be dismissed. If "reasonable cause" is found, the Department will attempt to reach a conciliation agreement with the employer.

In the event that no agreement can be reached, the Department will prepare a Complaint for a hearing before the Equal Employment Review Board. The parties are permitted to submit briefs up to five days before the hearing. The Board will conduct a hearing on the record in which each side may present its case. If the Board finds discrimination it will also prescribe a remedy.

Either party may appeal the decision of the Board to the Superior Court. The court's only function is to determine whether there is "substantial evidence" in the record to support the Board's findings of fact and determination of law. In addition, the Attorney General may file suit in the Court of Chancery when he or she has reasonable cause to believe an employer or group of employers is engaged in a pattern or practice of violation of the Act.

Given that only careful incursions have thus far been made upon the employment at-will doctrine, the Court is convinced the Delaware Supreme Court would not create a common law public policy exception to the employment at-will doctrine where there is in place an elaborate statutory scheme addressing the same public policy concerns.

Therefore, insofar as the plaintiff's complaint may be read to allege a claim for discharge of an at-will employee in violation of public policy of the State of Delaware, this Court determines such claim must fail as a matter of law.

Judgment for Hercules, Inc.

The issue in the next case is whether the employer breached a contract implied in fact that permitted termination only for cause. The employer's argument is that the employment contract is at-will.

Jones v. UNISYS Corp.

54 F.3d 624 (10th Cir. 1995)

LOGAN, Circuit Judge.

Unisys was formed by a merger of the Burroughs and Sperry Corporations in 1986. It is a computer and computer products company which maintained commercial and defense divisions in Salt Lake City, Utah. Because of serious financial losses in the late 1980s and early 1990s it implemented drastic cost cutting measures including layoffs at its various facilities. Unisys closed the Salt Lake distribution center (a part of its commercial division) in late 1991 and shifted its remaining work to San Jose, California.

Plaintiffs asserted that in laying them off Unisys breached an implied-in-fact employment contract term that provided for termination only for cause. They also allege that employees with more seniority had the right to bump less senior employees to survive layoff or avoid a transfer. The district court found that plaintiffs failed to establish any issues of material facts on the employment contract claim and that plaintiffs had not rebutted the presumption under Utah law of employment at will.

In Utah "any employment contract which has no specified term of duration is an at-will relationship." At-will employment may be terminated at any time by the employer or the employee. This presumption of at-will employment may be rebutted by an employee showing "that the parties expressly or impliedly intended a specified term or agreed to terminate the relationship for cause alone." The employee must establish the existence of an implied-in-fact contract provision. The court looks for objective manifestations of the parties' intent when evaluating the factual issue whether they agreed to modify what would otherwise be an at-will relationship.

Plaintiffs produced evidence that Unisys and its predecessors, Sperry and Burroughs, considered seniority in reduction in force decisions from the 1950s until sometime in the late 1980s. The seniority system allowed employees with more service to bump employees with less service. Plaintiffs produced evidence that when they were originally hired employee handbooks and other documents stated that seniority would be followed in layoff decisions. They pointed to numerous statements in employee handbooks that seniority was the determining factor in such circumstances and noted that during earlier force reductions Unisys followed a seniority policy.

Apparently sometime in 1988 Unisys decided to replace seniority-based layoffs with a skills-based system, in which retention decisions accommodated the following in descending priority: (1) demonstrated performance, (2) skills mix, (3) length of experience, and (4) length of service as a tiebreaker. The skills based system also eliminated bumping. Plaintiffs contend that this changed their employment contract without notice. The district court found . . . that their employment was terminable at will. We agree.

Judgment for UNISYS Corp.

The following case addresses the question of whether the court should create a public policy exception to the at-will doctrine.

CASE *Howard v. Wolff Broadcasting Corp.*

611 SO.2d 307 (Ala. 1992)

MADDOX, Justice.

The plaintiff was fired by Wolff Broadcasting Corporation ("Wolff"). The principal question presented here is whether this Court should carve out an exception to the employee-will doctrine and hold that plaintiff stated a cause of action for breach of an implied contract of employment. The basic facts are not significant. In October 1987, the plaintiff, Patricia Williams Howard, inquired about employment with Wolff, which operated a radio station. She was unemployed at the time. Shortly thereafter, Keith Holcombe, the manager of the station, called her and set up an interview. Wolff hired her as a disc jockey and advertising salesperson. Howard had had no prior experience of any kind in the radio business. Howard presented evidence that, during the process of her hiring she noted in the lobby of the station a sign stating that Wolff would not discriminate against "females, blacks, or any others." There was no written contract of employment.

On January 26, 1988, while Howard was on the air, Keith Holcombe drove to the station and informed her that she was fired. When he fired her, Holcombe told her that she was being fired because Karen Wolff, whose husband owned Wolff, did not want any females on the air. On that same night, Howard typed a letter stating that she was fired because Karen Wolff did not want any females on the air. Howard says this letter was signed by Keith Holcombe.

On October 2, 1989, Howard filed a complaint against Wolff, alleging fraud and breach of contract, and against Karen Wolff, alleging intentional interference with business relations.

The determinative question on that issue is whether Howard's employment contract was terminable at will.

"Employees at-will can terminate their employment, or can be terminated by their employer, at any time, with or without cause or justification."

It is undisputed that Howard was not offered lifetime employment or employment of any definite duration. However, Howard argues that her employment was not terminable at will because, she says, she comes within the exception recognized in *Hoffman–La Roche, Inc. v. Campbell.* Under *Hoffman–La Roche,* an employment contract is not terminable at will if three conditions are met:

"(1) that there was a clear and unequivocal offer of lifetime employment or employment of a definite duration;

(2) that the hiring agent had authority to bind the principal to a permanent employment contract; and

(3) that the employee provided substantial consideration for the contract separate from the services to be rendered."

Howard contends that when she entered into her contract with Wolff, there was an implied covenant that Wolff would not discriminate against her on the basis of race, gender, religion, or national origin. Howard argues that this covenant is implied in every contract of employment that is governed by the regulation of the Federal Communication Commission ("FCC"), the relevant provisions of which state:

"Equal employment opportunity (EEO) policy. Equal opportunity in employment shall be afforded by all licensees or permittees of commercially or noncommercially operated AM, FM, TV or international broadcast stations (as defined in this part) to all qualified persons, and no person shall be discriminated against in employment by such stations because of race, color, religion, national origin or sex.

"(b) EEO program. Each broadcast station shall establish, maintain, and carry out a positive continuing program of specific practices designed to ensure opportunity in every aspect of station employment policy and practice. Under the terms of its programs, a station shall:

"(1) Define the responsibility of each level of management to ensure a positive application and vigorous enforcement of its equal opportunity, and establish a procedure to review and control managerial and supervisory performance;

"(2) Inform its employees and recognized employee organization of the positive equal employment opportunity policy and program and enlist their cooperation;

"(3) Communicate its equal employment opportunity policy and program and its employment needs to sources of qualified, color, religion, national origin or sex, and solicit their recruitment assistance on a continuing basis;

"(4) Conduct a continuing program to exclude all unlawful forms of prejudice or discrimination based on race, color, religion, national origin or sex from its personnel policies and practices and working conditions; and

"(c)(1) disseminate its equal opportunity program to job applicants and employees. For example, this requirement may be met by:

"(i) Posting notices in the station's office and other places of employment, informing employees and applicants for employment of their equal opportunity rights."

This court has held that employment policies, especially those in writing can become a binding promise once it is accepted by the employee through his continuing to work when he is not required to do so. Certain employment policies were contained in an employee handbook. The Court held that the provisions contained in the employee handbook when combined with the employee's continuation of employment following the employee's receipt of the handbook, created a unilateral contract modifying the at-will employment relationship. The court stated:

"Language contained in a handbook can be sufficient to constitute an offer to create a binding unilateral contract. The existence of such a contract is determined by applying the following analysis to the facts of each case: First, the language contained in the handbook must be examined to see if it is specific enough to constitute an offer. Second, the offer must have been communicated to the employee by the issuance of the handbook, or otherwise. Third, the employee must have accepted the offer by retaining employment after he has become generally aware of the offer. His actual performance supplies the necessary consideration."

It has long been the law in Alabama that employment is terminable at will by either party for any reason unless there is an express and specific contract for lifetime employment or employment for a specific duration. "Absent an agreement on a definite term, any employment is considered to be 'at will,' and may be terminated by either party, with or without cause or justification."

Instead, Howard argues that the sign in the station lobby stating the general policy that the station was an "equal opportunity employer" constituted a false representation under the law of this State and thus embodied a present intent to deceive. However, Howard never asked anyone at Wolff about the sign or about any related policy of the station. The summary judgment was properly entered in favor of Wolff on Howard's claim of promissory fraud.

Finally, Howard argues that, even assuming that a unilateral contract did not exist and that the "at-will" doctrine applies, there should be a public policy exception to that doctrine in this case.

The employment "at-will" doctrine was first recognized in Alabama in 1891. It stated, "that an employment contract terminable at the will of either the employer or the employee may be terminated by either party at any time with or without cause." Howard argues that because the doctrine is a judicially created one, the judiciary can and should abolish or modify it. However, this court has so far declined to judicially create a public policy exception to the employment "at-will" doctrine.

The Court has consistently refused to create a cause of action for wrongful the charge on "public policy" ground, for three reasons: (1) to do so would abrogate the inherent right of contract between employer and employee; (2) to do so would be to overrule well-established employment law; and (3) "contrary to public policy" is too vague or nebulous a standard to justify creation of a new tort.

Howard urges the Court to adopt a narrow public policy exception to the employment "at-will" doctrine based on principles of non-discrimination. Indeed, many states have carved out exception to the employment "at-will" doctrine. Howard, in her brief, recognizes that this court "has so far refused to allow a public policy exception to the employment 'at-will' doctrine," but she says that "it is clear that the national trend exists for the adoption of a public policy exception to the employment "at-will" doctrine in the State of Alabama.

On the public policy issues, the Congress of the United States has elected to exempt Wolff from the provisions of law relating to discrimination in employment. While we recognize that Wolff is prohibited from discriminating on the basis of sex, we do not think, especially in view of the principle stated in Hinrichs, that we should judicially create a wrongful discharge action based on "public policy" grounds in this case involving a licensee of the FCC. In refusing to adopt a "public policy" exception, we should not be understood as condoning a person's discharge because of gender. We merely hold that it is the province of the legislature to create such an exception, if it should determine that employees such as Howard, who cannot come within the provisions of the Equal Employment Act, should be given the right to sue for damages.

The legislature, when it meets, may desire to create an action in circumstances such as those presented here. In short, the legislature has shown its willingness and ability to respond to perceived injustices that can result by a strict application of the long-standing doctrine of employment "at-will." Thus, we again decline to modify the employee-at-will doctrine by creating a public policy exception and defer to the judgment of the legislature.

For the foregoing reasons, the judgment of the trial court is affirmed.

Judgment for Wolff Broadcasting Corp.

CONTESTING THE TERMINATION

Claims for wrongful termination are filed with the department of labor in the state of employment. The department of labor will forward a claim of discrimination to the employer. The employer will be afforded the opportunity to settle the claim pursuant to a no-fault agreement. If a settlement can not be reached, the department will proceed with its fact finding investigation. A fact finding conference may be held with mandatory attendance required of the employer and the employee. A decision regarding the employer's fault will then be made. If the employer is at fault, the Department will attempt to reach a conciliation agreement with the employer regarding damages and/or reinstatement of the employee. If an agreement can not be reached, a complaint will be filed by the Department of Labor with the Equal Employment Review Board. The parties may submit written briefs prior to the hearing. After the hearing, the Board will make its decision and pronounce a remedy. The Board's decision can be appealed to the State's General Trial Court. The court's function is to determine whether the Board's decision was substantiated by sufficient evidence.

Because downsizing has become a widespread phenonomen among companies, hundreds of thousands of employees have been laid off as a result. When a company downsizes for economic reasons, the employee has no recourse. Economic reasons may encompass a broad spectrum from saving a company from filing for bankruptcy to improving the price of the stock by increasing earnings.

MODEL EMPLOYMENT TERMINATION ACT

The Model Employment Termination Act was designed to permit employers to discharge employees only for cause. In turn, employees would have to relinquish their right to sue in favor of arbitration. The advantage to the employer is to forgo the time and expense of litigation. The advantage to the employee is that he or she could no longer be terminated at will.

An employer may terminate for good cause when the employee has been: derelict in his or her duties of loyalty, duty to act in good faith and duty to account; acting in excess of or without authority; performing work outside the scope of employment; harassing coworkers or subordinates; and engaging in employee theft. The employer may also discharge for good cause when the employer downsizes its workforce because of a consolidation, reorganization, or divestiture.

Under the Act, termination refers to dismissal for cause, layoff pursuant to downsizing and resigning by an employee due to the employer's intolerable actions.

Within 180 days of termination, the employee may file a complaint. The matter will then be arbitrated. After the arbitration hearing, a decision will be rendered within thirty days. If the arbitrator finds for the employee, an award may be made for reinstatement, back pay, reimbursement for benefits lost, or a lump sum if reinstatement is not permissible.

Wrongful Discharge

An employer is guilty of wrongful discharge where its motivation for termination is discriminatory. This situation gives the employee the right to sue under Title VII of the Civil Rights Act, the Americans with Disabilities Act, the Age Discrimination in Employment Act, or The Equal Pay Act to name a few. Furthermore, employees may not be discharged for exercising their constitutional rights such as freedom of speech or freedom of religion.

The case that follows addresses the question of whether an employer can dismiss an employee for his or her political affiliation.

Pierce v. Montgomery County Opportunity Bd., Inc.

884 F.Supp. 965 (E.D.Pa. 1995)

JOYNER, District Judge.

This litigation arises out of the termination of Plaintiff Frances Pierce from her position as Executive Director of the Montgomery County Opportunity Board, Inc. (MCOB). Pierce is and has been a Republican Committeewoman at all material times and votes for Republican political candidates. In August, 1990, Pierce was made the Acting Executive Director of MCOB. At some point after August 1990, State Defendants, presumably Democrats, resolved to have Pierce removed from the head of MCOB, allegedly for political reasons. In June 1991, Pierce was appointed MCOB's Executive Director for a 5-year term at a certain salary and with certain benefits.

In November 1991, State Defendants arranged to terminate MCOB's federal funding, allegedly because Pierce's active Republicanism created a prohibited conflict of interest under Federal regulations. In May 1992, MCOB Defendant Harvey Portner was appointed to the MCOB Board and at some point became its President. He apparently asked Pierce to resign as Executive Director, and when she refused, embarked upon a campaign to impugn Pierce's reputation. In August 1992, the MCOB's Defendants (including at least one Republican) joined in a conspiracy with Portner and the State Defendants to remove Pierce from MCOB on account of her Republicanism.

In December 1992, Portner resigned as President of the Board so as to "create an aura of non-involvement," but nonetheless, "maintained effective control over the Opportunity Board." He was replaced by MCOB Defendant Aaron Schell, a Republican.

On December 16, 1992, Schell informed Pierce that the MCOB Board was to meet with the Department of Community Affairs, told Pierce that he did not know the purpose of the meeting, and then did not attend the meeting himself. At this meeting, State Defendants informed the board that they were there to close down MCOB. According to the Amended Complaint, the "purpose of the attendance of defendants Darling and Weisberg was to give a basis for the actions which were planned sub rosa to remove Frances Pierce as Executive Director." One month later the MCOB Board voted to remove Pierce as Executive Director.

In Pennsylvania, an at-will employee can be discharged for any reason or for no reason at all. The exception to this rule is the public policy exception. This provides that when there is no plausible and legitimate reason for a termination, and a clear mandate of public policy is violated by the termination, even an at-will employee has a claim for wrongful discharge. Pennsylvania does not, however, permit a wrongful discharge claim if statutory relief is available to the plaintiff.

Here, Pierce alleges that "The Opportunity Board of Montgomery County, Inc. could not discharge an employee for utilizing the right to freedom of speech in the employee's off hours, such discharge as here complained of, being in violation of the public policy of the Commonwealth of Pennsylvania." Elsewhere in the Amended Complaint, Pierce alleges that she was terminated solely on account of her participation in Republican party politics. As the Third Circuit has held, "an important public policy is in fact implicated wherever the power to hire and fire is utilized to dictate the term of employee political activities." Pierce alleges that she was terminated for engaging in protected First Amendment activities. We find that this states a claim for wrongful discharge, for which, if the allegations are proved, relief can be granted.

Judgment for Pierce.

In the next case, an employee claimed that he was discharged because of his involvement in politics. He is an American citizen employed by a foreign corporation. The issue is whether the employer had the requisite number of employees mandated by statute.

CASE

Mochelle v. J. Walter, Inc.

823 F.Supp. 1302 (M.D.L.A. 1993)

POLOZOLA, District Judge.

J. Walter Company Ltd. ("Walter Ltd.") is a Canadian corporation with its principal place of business in Quebec, Canada. Walter Ltd. is involved in the engineering, importation, distribution, and sale of industrial products. Manfred Thiede was employed by Walter Ltd. In April of 1989, Thiede hired Patrick Mochelle as the district representative for Walter Ltd. in the United States. After hiring Mochelle, Thiede explained to him the relevant terms of employment, such as base salary, commission rates, and reimbursement policies of Walter Ltd. Mochelle continued to work for Walter Ltd. until November 1990.

In November 1990, Walter Ltd. formed J. Walter Inc. ("Walter Inc.") as an independent corporation responsible for the sale of Walter products in the United States. Walter Inc. is a Delaware corporation with its principal place of business in Hartford, Connecticut. On November 1, 1990, Thiede was hired as the president of Walter Inc. and Mochelle was hired as a salesman for Walter Inc. and continued to sell Walter products in the United States.

On January 14, 1992, Thiede fired Mochelle from Walter Inc. for failing to perform his job duties and for failing to communicate with his supervisor, Thiede, despite repeated warnings. Mochelle filed a charge of age discrimination against Walter Inc. with the Equal Employment Opportunity Commission ("EEOC") in July of 1992. In August 1992, Mochelle sued Walter Inc., alleging that he was fired because he ran for political office. Mochelle also alleged fraud and breach of contract in his initial suit against Walter Inc. In September 1992, plaintiff amended his complaint to name Walter Ltd. as a defendant. Although Walter Ltd. was named as a defendant in the federal suit, it was not named in the charge filed with the EEOC. Both Walter Inc. and Walter Ltd. have filed motions to dismiss.

Plaintiff claims that he was fired from his employment at "Walter" because of his political aspirations and his desire to run for political office. Plaintiff relies on La.R.S. 23:961, which provides, in part:

> Except as otherwise provided in R.S. 23:962, no employer having regularly in his employ twenty or more employees shall make, adopt or enforce any rule, regulation, or policy forbidding or preventing any of his employees from engaging or participating in politics, or from becoming a candidate for political office.

Mochelle informed his employer in August 1991 of his intention to run for Clerk of Court. The election was held on October 19 of the same year. Mochelle was fired in January 1992.

Walter Ltd. contends that it cannot be liable under La.R.S. 23:961 because it was not the employer of Mochelle during the period of the alleged political interference. Walter Inc. admits that it was the employer of Mochelle at the time of the alleged political interference, but contends that it cannot be liable under 23:961 because it does not have the requisite twenty employees mandated by the statute.

In response to defendants' arguments, plaintiff contends that both Walter Ltd. and Walter Inc. may be liable under 23:961 because the two entities are deemed to be the single or joint employer of Mochelle.

The Fifth Circuit addressed the "single employer" doctrine in *Trevino v. Celanese Corp.* In that case, the court set forth the following factors to be used in determining whether superficially distinct entities actually represent a single integrated enterprise: (1) interrelation of operations, (2) centralized control of labor relations, (3) common management, and (4) common ownership or financial control. Courts which have applied this four-part standard have focused on the second factor—centralized control of labor relations. Specifically, the courts have stated that "the critical question to be answered is: What entity made the final decisions regarding employment matters related to the persons claiming discrimination?" While the second factor is critical to the Court's analysis, the Court will discuss each of the Trevino factors.

The first factor of the Trevino test is interrelation of operations. The Court finds that there exists little or no interrelation of operations between Walter Inc. and Walter Ltd. Each corporation has its own employees, pays its own taxes, and maintains separate accounting records, bank accounts and lines of credit. Furthermore, the corporations have separate offices and telephone numbers, use different forms and letterheads, and distribute different sales catalogs. Employees of Walter Ltd. and Walter Inc. do communicate frequently with each other by telephone. Plaintiff contends that these frequent communications demonstrate the interrelated operations of the two companies. However, plaintiff ignores the fact that Walter Inc. is in the business of selling Walter Ltd. products in the United States. Therefore, it would not be unquestionable or unexpected that Walter Inc. kept in close contact with Walter Ltd. in order to keep its product lines up to date and to process orders rapidly.

The second, and most important, factor of the Trevino test is centralized control of labor relations. As stated, this Court must determine which entity made the final decision regarding Mochelle's termination. The Court finds that Thiede, the president of Walter Inc., fired Mochelle. In fact, Mochelle has introduced no evidence to show that anyone at Walter Ltd. played a part in his termination. It is also clear that Walter Ltd. was neither consulted nor had any control over the hiring and firing of Walter Inc. employees. Furthermore, Walter Ltd. has no involvement in the promulgation of rules or conditions of employment at Walter Inc. For example, the record reveals that the conditions of work such as holidays benefits, insurance coverage, work hours, and personnel policies vary significantly from Walter Inc. to Walter Ltd.

The third Trevino factor is common management. Two members of the Walter Ltd. board of directors, Walter J. Somers and Pierre Somers, are on the board of Walter Inc. In addition, Walter J. Somers and Pierre Somers are the secretary and vice president, respectively, of Walter Inc. However, the Somers, who are also on the board of the Canadian holding company, have no recognizable management duties whatsoever. Neither Walter J. Somers nor Pierre Somers has ever taken any role in the operation of Walter Inc. other than to attend annual board meetings in 1991 and 1992. Each meeting lasted approximately one hour. Walter Somers has never visited Walter Inc.'s offices. Pierre Somers' visits to Walter Inc. are limited to discussions of products and marketing, and do not pertain to the operations of Walter Inc. Thiede has never attended a meeting of Walter Ltd. and is in no way affiliated with the management of Walter Ltd.

The final Trevino factor is common ownership or financial control. The holding company, 159585 Canada, Inc., owns both Walter Inc. and Walter Ltd. However, Walter Ltd. owns no part of Walter Inc. and exerts no financial control over Walter Inc.

After careful review of the Trevino factors, the Court finds that Walter Ltd. and Walter Inc. are not the single employer of Mochelle.

Plaintiff also contends that Pierre Somers and Walter J. Somers, as vice president and secretary of Walter Inc. should be considered as employees of Walter Inc. The addition of these two men as employees would place Walter Inc. at the twenty employee level and, therefore, within the purview of La.R.S. 23:961.

The Court finds the facts fail to support plaintiff's contention. Neither Walter J. Somers nor Pierre Somers are on the Walter Inc. payroll. Furthermore, Walter J. Somers has never visited the Walter Inc. offices, and Pierre Somers' visits are limited to discussions of products and marketing. Thus, the court finds as a matter of fact and law that the total number of persons employed by Walter Inc. is less than 20.

Plaintiff filed an EEOC charge on July 8, 1992, alleging Walter Ltd. discriminated against him because of his age when it fired him on January 31, 1992. The period of the discrimination as set forth by the charge filed with the EEOC is from January 14 to January 31, 1992. The EEOC charge only names Walter Inc. Walter Ltd. is not included in the EEOC charge. After the plaintiff amended his complaint to add the ADEA claim, the EEOC found that it had no jurisdiction to hear the plaintiff's ADEA complaint because Walter Inc. did not have the requisite 20 employees required by the 29 U.S.C. 630 (b).

Defendants' arguments in defense of the ADEA claim are similar to those asserted in the response to plaintiff's political interference claim. Walter Ltd. claims that it was not the employer of Mochelle during the period of the alleged discrimination. Walter Inc. claims that it does not have the requisite 20 employees for ADEA liability.

In summary, the Court finds that the defendants' motions for summary judgment as to the ADEA claim should be granted for the following reasons: (1) Walter Ltd. was not the employer of Mochelle during the period of the alleged discrimination; (2) Walter Inc. does not employ 20 employees and is, therefore, precluded from ADEA liability. No single employer, joint employer or agency theories are applicable to the facts of this case. Walter Ltd. as a foreign company not controlled by an American employer is specifically excluded from ADEA liability under 623(h)(2).

Judgment for Walter, Inc.

RETALIATORY DISCHARGE

It is wrongful when a worker is discharged for appearing as a witness in a discrimination action, filing a worker's compensation claim, or blowing the whistle on a company's illegal activity. The employee may bring an action for retaliatory discharge against the employer.

Employment Perspective

Carly Fisher worked the night shift at Top Cat Chemical Corporation. One evening while on a break, she observed several workers emptying barrels into the Pristine River adjacent to the plant. Carly notified the Environmental Protection Agency. Because their investigation revealed that toxic waste had been dumped, the company was fined heavily. One month later, Carly was discharged after a poor performance rating. For six years, Carly had received satisfactory ratings. Is this a case of retaliatory discharge? Yes! Top Cat's actions in dismissing Carly were motivated by its desire for revenge against her for whistle-blowing. ◆

The next case presents the question of whether an applicant was not chosen for a government job because he would not support the political party in power.

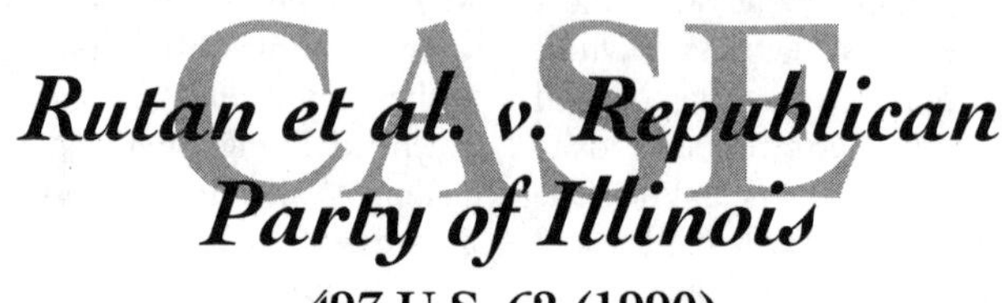

Rutan et al. v. Republican Party of Illinois

497 U.S. 62 (1990)

BRENNAN, Justice.

To the victor belong only those spoils that may be constitutionally obtained. The First Amendment forbids government officials to discharge or threaten to discharge public employees solely for not being supporters of the political party in power, unless party affiliation is an appropriate requirement for the position involved. Today we are asked to decide the constitutionality of several related political patronage practices—whether promotion, transfer, recall, and hiring decisions involving low-level public employees may be constitutionally based on party affiliation and support. We hold that they may not.

The petition and cross-petition before us arise from a lawsuit protesting certain employment policies and practices instituted by Governor James Thompson of Illinois. On November 12, 1980, the Governor issued an executive order proclaiming a hiring freeze for every agency, bureau, board, or commission subject to his control. The order prohibits state officials from hiring any employee, filling any vacancy, creating any new position, or taking any similar action. It affects approximately 60,000 state positions. More than 5,000 of these become available each year as a result of resignations, retirements, deaths, expansion, and reorganizations. The order proclaims that "no exceptions" are permitted without the Governor's "express permission after submission of appropriate requests to his office." Requests for the Governor's "express permission" have allegedly become routine. Permission has been granted or withheld through an agency expressly created for this purpose, the Governor's Office of Personnel (Governor's Office). Agencies have been screening applicants under Illinois' civil service system, making their personnel choices, and submitting them as requests to be approved or disapproved by the Governor's Office. Among the employment decisions for which approvals have been required are new hires, promotions, transfers, and recalls after layoffs. By means of the freeze, according to petitioners, the Governor has been using the Governor's Office to operate a political patronage system to limit state employment and beneficial employment-related decisions to those who are supported by the Republican Party. In reviewing an agency's request that a particular applicant be approved for a particular position, the Governor's Office has looked at whether the applicant voted in Republican primaries in past election years, whether the applicant has provided financial or other support to the Republican Party and its candidates, whether the applicant has promised to join and work for the Republican Party in the future, and whether the applicant has the support of Republican Party officials at state or local levels.

Five people (including the three petitioners) brought suit against various Illinois and Republican Party officials in the United States District Court for the Central District of Illinois. They alleged that they had suffered discrimination with respect to state employment because they had not been supporters of the State's Republican Party and that this discrimination violates the First Amendment. Cynthia B. Rutan has been working for the State since 1974 as a rehabilitation counselor. She claims that since 1981 she has been repeatedly denied promotions to supervisory positions for which she was qualified because she had not worked for or supported the Republican Party.

Franklin Taylor, who operates road equipment for the Illinois Department of Transportation, claims that he was denied a promotion in 1983 because he did not have the support of the local Republican Party. Taylor also maintains that he was denied a transfer to an office nearer to his home because of opposition from the Republican Party chairmen in the counties in which he worked and to which he requested a transfer. James W. Moore claims that he has been repeatedly denied state employment as a prison guard because he did not have the support of Republican Party officials. We explained the viability of his First Amendment claim as follows:

> "For at least a quarter-century, this Court has made clear that even though a person has no 'right' to a valuable governmental benefit and even though the government may deny him the benefit for any number of reasons, there are some reasons upon which the government may not rely. It may not deny a benefit to a person on a basis that infringes his constitutionally protected interests—especially, his interest in freedom of speech. For if the government could deny a benefit to a person because of his constitutionally protected speech or associations, his exercise of those freedoms would in effect be penalized and inhibited. This would allow the government to 'produce a result which it could not command directly.' Such interference with constitutional rights is impermissible."

We therefore determine that promotions, transfers, and recalls after layoffs based on political affiliation or support are an impermissible infringement on the First Amendment rights of public employees. What we decide today is that such denials are irreconcilable with the Constitution and that the allegations of the four employees state claims under 42 U.S. C. MDRV 1983 for violations of the First and Fourteenth Amendments. Therefore, although we affirm the Seventh Circuit's judgment to reverse the District Court's dismissal of these claims and remand them for further proceedings, we do not adopt the Seventh Circuit's reasoning.

Petitioner James W. Moore presents the closely related question whether patronage hiring violates the First Amendment. Patronage hiring places burdens on free speech and association similar to those imposed by the patronage practices discussed above. A state job is valuable. Like most employment, it provides regular paychecks, health insurance, and other benefits. In addition, there may be openings with the State when business in the private sector is slow. There are also occupations for which the government is a major (or the only) source of employment, such as social workers, elementary school teachers, and prison guards. Thus, denial of a state job is a serious privation. The question . . . is . . . whether the government, without sufficient justification, is pressuring employees to discontinue the free exercise of their First Amendment rights. If Moore's employment application was set aside because he chose not to support the Republican Party, as he asserts, then Moore's First Amendment rights have been violated. Therefore, we find that Moore's complaint was improperly dismissed.

Judgment for Rutan, et al.

Constructive Discharge

As opposed to outright termination, an employer may make the work environment so intolerable that the employee may be forced to resign. This process amounts to constructive discharge. These actions may be motivated by discrimination, general dislike, or retaliation. The employer may act directly or through the targeted employee's coworkers. The coworkers themselves may act on their own initiative.

The next case deals with an employee's claim that the workplace environment became so intolerable that a reasonable person would be forced to resign.

CASE *Clowes v. Allegheny Valley Hosp.*

911 F.2d 1159 (3rd Cir. 1993)

ALITO, Circuit Judge.

The ADEA prohibits, among other things, the "discharge" of a covered individual "because of such individual's age." In this case, Clowes's ADEA claim and the judgment she won were predicated on the assertion that she has been constructively discharged. "We employ an objective test in determining whether an employee was constructively discharged from employment: whether 'the conduct complained of would have the foreseeable result that working conditions would be so unpleasant or difficult that a reasonable person in the employee's shoes would resign.'"

Even if subject to review only for clear error, the district court's holding that Clowes was constructively discharged cannot be sustained.

We first note that Clowes cannot rely on many of the factors commonly cited by employees who claim to have been constructively discharged. Clowes was never threatened with discharge; nor did her employer ever urge or suggest that she resign or retire. Similarly, Clowes's employer did not demote her or reduce her pay or benefits. Clowes was not involuntarily transferred to a less desirable position, and her job responsibilities were not altered in any way. She was not even given unsatisfactory job evaluations but merely received ratings of "fair."

It is also highly significant that Clowes, prior to leaving her position with the hospital, never requested to be transferred to another position, never advised the hospital that she would feel compelled to leave if changes regarding the manner in which she was being supervised were not made, and did not even attempt to file a grievance until long after she had stopped working at the hospital. As other courts of appeals have noted, a reasonable employee will usually explore such alternative avenues thoroughly before coming to the conclusion that resignation is the only option.

Moreover, it is significant, in our view, that Clowes's complaint focused exclusively on Malloy's allegedly overzealous supervision of her work. Clowes has not brought to our attention a single case in which a constructive discharge has been found based solely upon such supervision. While we do not hold that an employer's imposition of unreasonably exacting standards of job performance may never amount to a constructive discharge, we are convinced that a constructive discharge claim based solely on evidence of close supervision of job performance must be critically examined so that the ADEA is not improperly used as a means of thwarting an employer's nondiscriminatory efforts to insist on high standards.

In support of her claim of constructive discharge, Clowes relies heavily on evidence regarding the impact that the events in question had on her. But as we have noted, "'the law does not permit an employee's subjective perceptions to govern a claim of constructive discharge.'"

We recognize that the jury, which heard testimony by both Clowes and Malloy, presumably concluded that Malloy treated Clowes unfairly and that her criticisms of Clowes were not entirely warranted. We accept these apparent conclusions for purposes of this appeal, but it is clear that unfair and unwarranted treatment is by no means the same as constructive discharge.

In sum, we hold that the evidence in this case was insufficient to show that Clowes was constructively discharged. The judgment of the district court is therefore reversed.

Judgment for Allegheny Valley Hospital.

Employment Perspective

Sean Stockton works for Premier Motors Manufacturing in their quality control division. He uncovers a scheme to shortcut the process by continuing assembly before the adhesives dry. Sean notifies his superiors, but he is told to ignore the problem. Sean approaches senior management, who appreciate his forthrightness. Sean's superiors and coworkers are severely disciplined. Later, though, he begins to receive threatening notes, his car windshield has been smashed, his tires have been flattened, and he has been demoted. Sean complains to senior management, but they tell him to deal with the problems in his own way. After being assaulted, Sean leaves the company, claiming constructive discharge. Is he correct? Yes! His coworkers and superiors have made the work environment so intolerable that it is no longer conducive to Sean's mental and physical well-being to continue on the job. If the individuals responsible had been discharged because of Sean's whistle-blowing, then Premier's duty to protect Sean and safeguard his property extends only while Sean is on the premises. Once he departs, he is on his own. This is a major risk that a whistle-blower must bear on his or her own. It may not be foreseeable to the whistle-blower that retaliatory acts will be directed against him or her. However, it would be wise for the employee to consider all of the possible ramifications for whistle-blowing and the recourses available for protection. ◆

The following case presents the question of whether the state is in breach of contract for failing to pay certain workers while compensating others who do the same kind of work. The employees brought this action because their not getting paid would constitute constructive discharge from their jobs.

883 F.Supp. 816 (N.D.N.Y. 1995)

McAVOY, Chief Judge.

Plaintiffs are legislative employees of the State of New York ("State"). They have been employed to provide services either for the duration of each legislative session or on an annual basis. Each of these legislative employees is generally paid a bi-weekly salary pursuant to New York State Finance Law 200. Plaintiffs have not been paid for work performed for the State since March 31, 1995 notwithstanding the fact that payment for work performed through April 5, 1995 was due on April 19, 1995.

Each plaintiff has supplied reasons why he or she has been specifically harmed by not being paid on a timely bi-weekly basis. Plaintiff Haley is a single mother of three teenage children who earns $10,000 annually. Plaintiff Verbal is a single mother earning $24,000 annually and is the sole support of two sons with asthma. Plaintiff Scott is the primary family wage earner at $19,000 per year. Plaintiff Watson is the father of two sons and earns $23,000. Plaintiff King provides full support for herself and her two children, one of whom requires special medical and day care. Plaintiff Jones earns $17,000 per year and supports herself. Plaintiff Matthews earns $28,000 annually and is scheduled to purchase a new house in the unspecified future. Plaintiff Allen earns $21,000 and is the sole support of a totally disabled husband and minor child. Plaintiff Ehrlich is the sole source of support of a totally disabled ex-wife. All plaintiffs claim that they will not be able to feed, clothe and house themselves, and in many cases their families, if not paid on a bi-weekly basis. Plaintiffs note that the work they have performed is identical to work performed by other state employees who continue to be paid. The nature of their employment, except the fact that they have been classified as "legislative employees," has nothing to do with the State's failure to pay their wages.

As background, Governor Pataki took office on January 1, 1995 and has since repeatedly stated that he would take a series of actions if the legislature did not pass a timely budget by April 1, 1995. If the budget was not passed on time he stated that he would, along with other actions, refuse to take any steps necessary to pay members of the legislature and its employees. To date, the budget has not been passed and the Governor has carried out the plan to refuse payment to legislative employees while ensuring continuing salary payments to most employees of the executive and judiciary branches through supplemental appropriation bills.

Under 40 of New York State Finance Law, appropriations cease to be effective on March 31 except for payment obligations incurred prior to the end of the fiscal year. As a result, historically, when budgets have not been enacted prior to the start of the fiscal year, the governor has submitted special appropriation bills which have provided money for salary payments to all state employees until passage of the new budget. On April 13, 1995, the Governor submitted a special appropriation bill to pay the salaries of certain employees in the executive, legislative and judicial branches for the period of March 23, 1995 to April 5, 1995. This bill covered the salaries of almost all state employees except a few in the executive chamber and certain officers and employees of the judiciary. In the legislative branch, however, the bill only covered the salaries of the legislative library employees, nurses and messengers.

Under Article VII, 5 of the New York State Constitution, in the absence of action on all the appropriation bills submitted by the Governor, the legislature may not consider any other appropriation bill "except on message from the governor certifying to the necessity of the immediate passage of such a bill." Therefore, without the Governor's consent by way of a message of necessity, the legislature has no power to appropriate money for the salaries of the legislative employees. Governor Pataki has repeatedly stated that he would not request an appropriation for the payment of such salaries and would not sign a bill providing for such salaries.

The Contract Clause at Article I, 10 of the United States Constitution provides that "[n]o state shall . . . pass any . . . law impairing the obligation of contracts." U.S. Const. art. I, 10. Each plaintiff is employed by the year or by the legislative session at a certain rate of pay. Despite defendants' argument to the contrary, plaintiffs clearly work under contracts regardless of the lack of a written agreement. "A contract implied in fact is just as binding as an express contract arising from declared intention, since the law makes no distinction between agreements made by words and those made by conduct."

Furthermore, "as a general rule, an employee who has performed services in accordance with a contract of employment has a right to recover either the amount expressly agreed upon for such services or, in the absence of such an agreement, the reasonable value of the services." The Contract Clause is applicable to both implied and express contracts.

Additionally, the court is unlikely to find that such a substantial impairment of contracts is "reasonable and necessary to serve an important public purpose." While the quick passage of the state budget can be viewed as an important public purpose, assuming for sake of this argument that it is the purpose, it is certainly far from clear that nonpayment of the legislative staff is a reasonable and necessary step to achieving this goal. The withholding of wages can only be seen either as a token showing of solidarity with the taxpayers who bear the ultimate financial brunt of an untimely state budget, as the defendants attest, or as a backhanded method of getting disgruntled employees to coax the legislators into adopting Governor Pataki's budget proposals more quickly, as the plaintiffs assert. In either scenario the withholding of plaintiffs' wages is not a reasonable and necessary step toward passage of the budget. It is far from necessary to make such a showing to the public. Furthermore, under New York law, state employees are banned from lobbying activities, and so, legally cannot attempt to coerce their employers into passing the budget. Thus, the court believes plaintiffs have shown a likelihood of success on the merits of their Contract Clause claim, for the Contract Clause "is especially vigilant when a state takes liberties with its own obligations."

This finding does not leave the court powerless to act, however. Based upon the court's finding of irreparable harm and likelihood of success on the merits of the Contract Clause claim, plaintiffs have established their right to a preliminary injunction consistent with principles of federalism. In keeping with the spirit of the relief requested by the plaintiffs, and mindful of the limitations on mandatory injunctive relief as outlined herein, the court finds that although it may be unable to require the Governor to seek the appropriation of state funds, it can lawfully require the Governor to include the legislative employees in any further appropriations for the payment of state employees that he does seek.

Judgment for Haley.

In the following case, a female filed a complaint alleging sexual harassment and sex discrimination. She claimed that her supervisor retaliated against her by making the work environment so hostile that she was forced to leave. A claim for constructive discharge resulted.

CASE

Gary v. Washington Metropolitan Area Transit Authority

886 F.Supp. 78 (D.D.C. 1995)

SPORKIN, District Judge.

This matter comes before the Court on Defendant Washington Metropolitan Area Transit Authority's ("WMATA") motion for summary judgment. Plaintiff Coramae Ella Gary has brought suit under Title VII of the Civil Rights Act, 42 U.S.C. 2000e, alleging that WMATA retaliated against and constructively discharged Plaintiff because of her complaints of sexual discrimination and harassment.

Plaintiff was hired by WMATA in 1983 as a custodian in WMATA's Department of Rail Service. In May of 1987, she became a stock clerk at WMATA's Brentwood facility. Her immediate supervisor at Brentwood was Mr. Charles Brown. Mr. Edward Long was Mr. Brown's supervisor and Plaintiff's second-level supervisor.

In this action, Plaintiff alleges that WMATA retaliated against her because she took the following actions: 1) filed a written complaint with WMATA on February 28, 1990 against

Mr. Long, alleging sexual harassment; 2) filed an EEOC charge on Mary 16, 1990, alleging sexual harassment; and 3) filed an action in District Court in December 1990 against WMATA and Long relating to the sexual harassment.

Plaintiff alleges that due to the stress from work she was forced to take a week sick leave in July of 1990. Upon her return, her supervisor Anthony Johnson reprimanded Plaintiff for excessive sick leave absences. Moreover, Plaintiff alleges that Supervisor Woodward told her that he did not want her working at WMATA because of the sexual harassment charges that she filed and that he would find a way to get rid of her.

Upon her transfer to the Southeast facility, Plaintiff alleges that several supervisors retaliated against her. Supervisor Brown told her that he had heard about the sexual harassment charges and that he did not want her working at Southeast. Supervisor Michael Johnson and Supervisor Gerald Hobbs each stated that he was going to find a way to get rid of her because of the charges.

Over Labor Day weekend in 1991, Plaintiff agreed to work overtime shifts at the Metro Supply Facility. When Plaintiff arrived, Mr. Long, her alleged harasser, was present and Plaintiff was sent home. According to Plaintiff, Supervisor Jorgensen told Plaintiff that he never wanted Plaintiff working at his facility regardless of whether Long was present. Plaintiff filed a grievance over this incident and she received 54 hours of overtime pay in settlement.

Plaintiff did not work from September 12 through September 19, 1991. According to Plaintiff, she was suffering from acute stress disorder related to the hostile environment at work.

Upon her final rotation to Bladensburg, Plaintiff's first paycheck was sent to her prior work location. Plaintiff was permitted to pick up her paycheck at the old location during work hours. Plaintiff further alleges that Supervisor Tompkins said that she did not want Plaintiff working at the facility because of the several harassment charges and that Tompkins watched Plaintiff more closely than other employees.

On June 9, 1992 Plaintiff returned to work for two hours. After that day, she did not return to work due to stress and severe depression which Plaintiff attributes to the retaliation at work. On January 28, 1993, Plaintiff resigned.

Based on the above precedent, this Court finds that Title VII claims can be subject to compulsory arbitration. The question before the Court is whether under the circumstances of this case the Plaintiff's Title VII claims should be subject to compulsory arbitration under Section 66(c) of the WMATA Compact. This case does not involve a compulsory arbitration clause in a collective bargaining agreement. Nor does it involve a compulsory arbitration clause in an agreement signed by an employee. The Compact contains an arbitration clause mandated by Congress. The legislative history indicates that "all unsettled labor disputes between parties will be referred to final and binding arbitration."

Judgment for WMATA.

REVIEW QUESTIONS

1. What constitutes a wrongful discharge?
2. Is downsizing a form of discriminatory conduct?
3. What does at-will employment mean?
4. Explain retaliatory discharge.
5. Is retaliatory discharge ever justifiable?
6. How can an employee be constructively discharged?
7. What does it mean to be dismissed for cause?

8. Define termination.

9. Can an employee be dismissed without cause?

10. Explain the significance of the Model Employment Termination Act.

11. How can a termination be contested?

12. R.C. Foster was in the employ of Hickman Datsun as their used car manager until April 1983 when he was discharged. Foster claimed that Hickman Datsun breached its employment contract with him. Datsun reported that the contract was for an indefinite period and therefore can be terminated by either party at will. What was the result? *Hickman Datsun, Inc. v. Foster,* 351 S.E. 2d 678 (Ga. App. 1986)

13. Meeks was injured while on the job and filed a worker's compensation claim. The company terminated Meeks in retaliation, claiming employment at-will. What was the result? *Meeks v. Opp. Cotton Mills, Inc.,* 459 So.2d 814 (Ala. 1984)

14. Stevens was called for jury duty. He decided to go in spite of his employer's objections and was terminated as a result. The employer claimed the employment was terminated at-will. Stevens implored the court to create a public policy exception. What was the result? *Bender Ship Repair, Inc. v. Stevens,* 379 So.2d 594 (Ala. 1980)

15. When is a contract not terminable at will? *Hoffman La Roche, Inc. v. Campbell,* 512 So.2d 725 (Ala. 1987)

16. In 1969, William Spence entered into a verbal contract with Manning, the Webster Parish School Board's assistant superintendent, to operate a bus route. This ongoing relationship was terminated in 1983 when the school board decided to operate the route itself. The school board claimed that Manning's acts were unauthorized. Spence asserts that Manning's acts were ratified by the board in 1975 when it requested that Spence purchase another bus. What was the result? *Spence v. Webster Parish School Board,* 499 So.2d 217 (La. App. 2 Cir. 1986)

17. Should all states have public policy exceptions to employment at-will?

18. Referring to the case on pp. 135, is termination for cause a more ethical method for deciding when an employee is to be discharged?

19. In the case on pp. 144, should politics be allowed to play a part in the termination process?

20. Referring to the case on pp. 137, is employment at-will ethical?

Model Employment Termination Act of 1991

DEFINITION

Section 1. In this Act:

(4) "Good cause" means (i) a reasonable basis related to an individual employee for termination of the employee's employment in view of relevant factors and circumstances, which may include the employee's duties, responsibilities, conduct on the job or otherwise, job performance, and employment record, or (ii) the exercise of business judgment in good faith by the employer, including setting its economic or institutional goals and determining methods to achieve those goals, organizing or reorganizing operations, discontinuing, consolidating, or divesting operations or positions, or parts of operations or positions, determining the size of its workforce and the nature of the positions filled by its workforce, and determining and changing standards of performance for positions.

(8) "Termination" means:
(i) a dismissal, including that resulting from the elimination of a position, of an employee by an employer;
(ii) a layoff or suspension of an employee by an employer for more than two consecutive months; or
(iii) a quitting of employment or a retirement by an employee induced by an act or omission of the employer, after notice to the employer of the act or omission without appropriate relief by the employer, so intolerable that under the circumstances a reasonable individual would quit or retire.

SCOPE

Section 2. (a) This Act applies only to a termination that occurs after the effective date of this Act.

(b) This Act does not apply to a termination at the expiration of an express oral or written agreement of employment for a specified duration, which was valid, subsisting, and in effect on the effective date of this Act.

PROHIBITED TERMINATIONS

Section 3. (a) Unless otherwise provided in an agreement for severance pay under Section 4(c) or for a specified duration under Section 4(d), an employer may not terminate the employment of an employee without good cause.

AGREEMENTS BETWEEN EMPLOYER AND EMPLOYEE

Section 4. (a) A right of an employee under this Act may not be waived by agreement except as provided in this section.

(b) By express written agreement, an employer and an employee may provide that the employee's failure to meet specified business-related standards of performance or the employee's commission or omission of specified business-related acts will constitute good cause for termination in proceedings under this Act. Those standards or prohibitions are effective only if they have been consistently enforced and they have not been applied to a particular employee in a disparate manner without justification. If the agreement authorizes changes by the employer in the standards or prohibitions, the changes must be clearly communicated to the employee.

(c) By express written agreement, an employer and employee may mutually waive the requirement of good cause for termination, if the employer agrees that upon the termination of the employee for any reason other than willful misconduct of the employee, the employer will provide severance pay in an amount equal to at least one month's pay for a maximum total pay-

ment equal to 30 months' pay at the employee's rate of pay in effect immediately before the termination.

PROCEDURE AND LIMITATIONS

Section 5. (a) An employee whose employment is terminated may file a complaint and demand for arbitration under this Act with the Commission; Department; Service not later than 180 days after the effective date of the termination, the date of the breach of an agreement for severance pay under Section 4(c), or the date the employee learns or should have learned of the facts forming the basis of the claim, whichever is latest. The time for filing is suspended while the employee is pursuing the employer's internal remedies and has not been notified in writing by the employer that the internal procedures have been concluded.

AWARDS

Section 7. (a) Within 30 days after the close of an arbitration hearing or at a later time agreeable to the parties, the arbitrator shall mail or deliver to the parties a written award sustaining or dismissing the complaint, in whole or in part, and specifying appropriate remedies, if any.

(b) An arbitrator may make one or more of the following awards for a termination in violation of this Act:

(1) reinstatement to the position of employment the employee held when employment was terminated or, if that is impractical, to a comparable position;

(2) full or partial backpay and reimbursement for lost fringe benefits, with interest, reduced by interim earnings from employment elsewhere, benefits received, and amount that could have been received with reasonable diligence;

(3) if reinstatement is not awarded, a lump-sum severance payment at the employee's rate of pay in effect before the termination, for a period not exceeding 36 months after the date of the award, together with the value of fringe benefits lost during that period, reduced by likely earnings and benefits from employment elsewhere, and taking into account such equitable considerations as the employee's length of service with the employer and the reasons for the termination; and

(4) reasonable attorney's fees and costs.

PART III

Employment Discrimination

CHAPTER 8
Civil Rights Act

INTRODUCTION

A basis was laid for equal rights in employment with the adoption of the 14th Amendment's Equal Protection Clause. In *Plessy v. Ferguson* the Supreme Court interpreted this to mean separate, but equal facilities would satisfy the 14th Amendment requirement. This segregation of minority and whites continued until the *Brown v. Board of Education* decision in 1954.

CASE
Brown v. Board of Education of Topeka

347 U.S. 483 (1954)

Chief Justice WARREN

The decision in this lawsuit was rendered in response to a number of cases having the same constitutional question concerning the segregation of white and colored children in public schools.

In each case, colored children have made applications to schools attended by white children and in most cases they have been denied admission based on the separate but equal doctrine formulated in 1896. That doctrine provided that equal treatment of races is satisfied when the races are provided separate, but equal facilities. The parties bringing these lawsuits contended that segregated public schools are not "equal."

The issue is whether segregation in public schools is unconstitutional in violation of the Equal Protection clause of the Fourteenth Amendment.

In 1954, the United States Supreme Court held that segregation in public schools was unconstitutional. They cited as their reasoning a finding made by the court in the Kansas case which, although holding segregation to be constitutional, declared "Segregation of white and colored children in public schools has a detrimental effect upon the colored children. The impact is greater when it has the sanction of the law; for the policy of separating the races is usually interpreted as denoting the inferiority of the Negro group. A sense of inferiority affects the motivation of a child to learn." The Supreme Court added "In these days, it is doubtful that any child may reasonably be expected to succeed in life if he or she is denied the opportunity of an education. Such an opportunity, where the state has undertaken to provide it, is a right which must be made available to all on equal terms."

Judgment for Brown.

Ten years later, the Civil Rights Act was introduced to codify existing statutes and case law. Enforcement of the Civil Rights Act continued to wane until the *Griggs v. Duke Power* case set forth the criteria for bringing a discrimination suit based on the disparate impact of an employer's selection and promotion procedure.

Three years later, the Supreme Court laid out the process for an individual to bring a discrimination action based on disparate treatment.

Title VII of the Civil Rights Act of 1964 is the main authority governing employment discrimination. Because it is a federal law, it is binding on all employers throughout the United States. An employer is a person or business employing at least fifteen individuals for twenty weeks of the year. The employer's business must have some connection with interstate commerce for Title VII to be applicable. Basically, a business is engaged in interstate commerce if it ships goods to a state other than the one in which it is located, performs services in another state or performs services intrastate for individuals traveling interstate. Interstate commerce has been construed so broadly that it would be difficult for a business to seek exemption from Title VII under the auspices of not participating in interstate commerce.

The main thrust of Title VII is that it is an unlawful practice to discriminate in failing or refusing to hire, train, discharge, promote, compensate, or in any other aspect of the employment relationship because of an individual's religion, race, color, sex or, national origin. Employers may not segregate employees or classify them in such a way as to deprive any of them of employment opportunities or adversely to affect their status as employees.

Employment Perspective

Redeye truck stop is located on interstate 80 in Pennsylvania. It refuses to serve women and minority truckers. Redeye argues that it is not subject to the Civil Rights Act because all of its business is transacted in Pennsylvania. Is this argument valid? No! Although Redeye's business is conducted intrastate, it services truckers who are traveling interstate. Therefore, its business affects interstate commerce. ◆

In the next case, the question presented is whether the female employee can bring a discrimination action against her employer. The issue revolves around whether the employer has the requisite number of employees to be covered under the Civil Rights Act.

CASE

Lattanzio v. Security Nat. Bank

825 F.Supp. 86 (E.D.Pa. 1993)

JOYNER, District Judge.

Betty Lattanzio initiated this employment discrimination action against Security National Bank (the Bank) pursuant to Title VII of the Civil Rights Act of 1964 (Title VII), and the Pennsylvania Human Relations Act (PHRA), Lattanzio alleges that the Bank discriminated against her on the basis of her age and sex in discharging her from employment on December 19, 1990. The Bank contends that because it employed fewer than fifteen individuals during 1989 and 1990, the Plaintiff's complaint fails to state a cause of action and this Court lacks subject matter jurisdiction under Title VII.

On or about June 1, 1988, the Bank hired Lattanzio as Vice-President and she served in that capacity until August, 1990 when the then President of the Bank resigned. The Bank subsequently promoted Lattanzio to Executive Vice President in charge of the Bank's day-to-day operations. Although Lattanzio applied for the position of bank president and had more than twenty years of experience in the banking industry, the bank hired a thirty-four-year-old male candidate with only ten years experience in the field. After two months in this position, the new President terminated Lattanzio's employment without prior notice or explanation. Lattanzio, 56 years old at the time of her firing and who received numerous honors, accolades and pay raises throughout her tenure with the Bank, then filed complaints raising sex and age discrimination claims with both the Pennsylvania Human Relations and the Equal Employment Opportunity Commission. After receiving the right to sue letter from the EEOC, Lattanzio commenced this lawsuit.

Title VII prohibits employees from engaging in unlawful employment practices against any individual. However, to fall within Title VII's purview, an employer must be "a person engaged in an industry affecting commerce who has fifteen or more employees for each working day in each of twenty or more calendar weeks in the current or preceding calendar year."

Resolution of the Defendant's motion to dismiss for want of subject matter jurisdiction hinges upon first determining who is considered an "employee" under Title VII, and second, whether or not the Bank had fifteen or more employees during either 1989 or 1990. Specifically, Lattanzio alleges that five individuals, Carolyn Gibbs, James J. Lennon, Howard E. Kalis, III, Robert Hartenstine and Joseph M. Wheeler should be considered "employees" under Title VII. Any two of these five, if found to be "employees," bring the Bank within Title VII's purview.

However, for the reasons outlined below, we find that none of the five individuals can be considered employees as contemplated by Title VII. As a result, we must conclude that the Bank is not an "employer" under Title VII and the Bank's motion to dismiss the complaint shall be granted.

The common law agency test examines the totality of the circumstances in determining who is an employee. It contains "no shorthand formula or magic phrase that can be applied to find the answers, . . . all of the incidents of a relationship must be assessed and weighed with no one factor being decisive."

The test, however, places its greatest emphasis on the hiring party's right to control the manner and means by which the work is accomplished. Other factors include means of the employment; the skills required; the source of the instrumentalities and tools; the location of the work; the duration of the relationship between the parties; the hiring party's right to assign additional duties; the hiring party's discretion over hours; method of payment; the hiring party's role in hiring and paying assistants; whether the work is part of the regular business of the hiring party; whether

the hiring party is in the business; the provisions of employee benefits; and the hiring party's tax treatment.

A. Carolyn Gibbs

The Third Circuit previously had adopted the "hybrid test," a combination of the common-law agency and economic realities tests, in determining whether an individual is an "employee" under Title VII. Recently, however, the Supreme Court in *Nationwide Mutual Insurance Co. v. Darden,* held that in statutes where Congress does not helpfully define "employee," the court should employ the common-law agency test to determine who is an employee.

Under this test, Ms. Gibbs cannot be counted as an employee against the Bank for Title VII purposes. First Moonlight Office Cleaners hired, trained, and supervised Ms. Gibbs. They controlled how she did her work in the Bank. Moonlight paid her on a weekly basis and withheld the appropriate taxes. Moonlight also provided and resupplied the materials Ms. Gibbs needed to do her job.

Second, the Bank had no control over her performance. Ms. Gibbs controlled her own hours as long as it was after banking hours. Outside of minor tasks, additional duties or tasks were coordinated through Moonlight who then decided by whom, when and how the task was to be accomplished. If the Bank was unsatisfied with Ms. Gibbs's performance for any reason, Moonlight reserved the right to make the decision to replace her.

Lastly, the Bank had no control over her employment opportunities. Of her own choice, Ms. Gibbs turned down other employment opportunities under Moonlight and opted to quit Moonlight because of physical ailments. The Bank, therefore, was not an economic necessity for her.

B. James J. Lennon

The Plaintiff asserts that although Lennon was an independent contractor, he received compensation for his services and should therefore be considered an "employee" under Title VII. However, the fact that he received compensation alone is not dispositive. Given the totality of the circumstances, Lennon is not an employee under Title VII.

Similarly, the Bank had no control over the "means and manner" over which Lennon performed his duties as an accounting and business consultant to the Bank. First, Lennon's primary business was as a managing partner for the accounting firm of Maillie, Falcomiero and Co. As such, his duties included consulting for a number of businesses of which the Bank was but one. Outside of attending those Bank committee meetings that he was a member of, Lennon managed his own time and assets.

Second, Lennon performed his duties purely in his capacity as a partner of his firm. He exercised his own judgment apart from Bank supervision; he frequently used his parents' firm's facilities; and all consulting fees were received by and deposited in the firm's bank account and recorded as income. Additionally, the Bank did not deduct any taxes from the compensation paid to Lennon as a consultant to the Board of Directors.

C. Robert Hartenstine and Joseph M. Wheeler

The Plaintiff contends that although Hartenstine and Wheeler are directors, they performed duties traditionally within the realm of an employee and, therefore, should be considered employees pursuant to Title VII. However, although Hartenstine and Wheeler were very involved in the Bank's success, their actions were in keeping with the traditional employer's role. Consequently, neither Hartenstine nor Wheeler are employees under Title VII.

Although a director has traditionally been considered an employer, "a director may accept duties that make him also an employee."

Central to the inquiry is whether an employer-employee relationship exists. Courts have capsuled the common-law agency test into three factors: 1) whether the director has undertaken traditional employee duties; 2) whether the director was regularly employed by a separate entity; and 3) whether the director reported to someone higher.

Here, however, both Hartenstine and Wheeler performed duties traditionally expected of directors. The Comptroller's Handbook for National Examiners details the board director's duties to include: effectively supervising the bank's affairs; adopting and following sound policies and objectives; and being informed of the bank's conditions and management policies. The Plaintiff has not asserted that Hartenstine and Wheeler participated in any activities that were inconsistent with a director's duties and responsibilities.

Second, both were regularly employed by separate organizations. Hartenstine worked full-time as vice-president and treasurer of both Sunnybrook Enterprises, Inc. and Sunnybrook Foods, Ltd. Wheeler served as First Vice-President of a non-profit organization and had a controlling interest in an electronics business.

Third, the evidence does not demonstrate that either Hartenstine or Wheeler answered to anyone other than themselves.

Lastly, their compensation was in keeping with their position as bank directors. Additionally, the Bank did not deduct taxes from their compensation.

D. Howard E. Kalis, III

The Plaintiff contends that Kalis should be considered an "employee" because of his services as the Acting Chief Executive Officer. However, the determination of who is an "employee" should not turn on a label but rather on the individual's particular duties. Giving all reasonable inferences to the non-moving party, the Plaintiff failed to provide evidence that Kalis actually performed day-to-day duties as CEO. Additionally, he was regularly employed as a partner in a law firm, and, similar to Hartenstine and Wheeler, he received compensation commensurate to a director, he answered to no one but the Board itself, and the Bank did not withhold taxes.

Even if Kalis had performed CEO duties, he served as CEO for only eight weeks, well short of the "twenty or more calendar weeks" required by Title VII.

AND NOW, this 17th day of June, 1993, following a careful review of all evidence in a light most favorable to the non-moving party and finding that the Security National Bank at no time had fifteen or more employees during the years 1989 and 1990 and, therefore, is not subject to Title VII, 42 U.S.C. 2000e *et seq.*, it is hereby ORDERED that the Defendant's motion to dismiss the Plaintiff's complaint is GRANTED without prejudice to Plaintiff's right to raise her state law claim in the appropriate forum.

Judgment for Security Nat. Bank.

The term *employer* includes individuals, partnerships, corporations, associations, unincorporated organizations, and governments. Employment agencies and labor unions are also subject to Title VII. For purposes here, *employer* will also refer to employment agencies and labor unions where appropriate. It does not include the United States, an American Indian tribe, or a tax exempt, bona fide private membership club. Religious societies and religious educational institutions are also exempt insofar as they have the right to employ only individuals of their religion.

Employment Perspective

George Feinstein, who is Jewish, has just received a college degree in education. Neither the public schools nor the Jewish schools have openings for teachers. George applied to the Catholic Diocese, where positions are readily available. He was turned down because he is not a practicing Catholic. Is this discrimination? No! Catholic schools, as well as any other religious-affiliated institutions, may restrict employment to members of their own particular faith. ◆

DISPARATE TREATMENT

Disparate treatment exists where an employer treats an individual differently because that individual is a member of a particular race, religion, gender, or ethnic group. The complaining party must show that he or she is a member of a particular Title VII class; that the employer in question was seeking applicants for a position; that he or she was rejected; and that the employer continued to seek applicants with similar qualifications. Disparate treatment is done with intent, whereas intent is not required in a disparate impact case.

Employment Perspective

Thomas Johnson, who is black, responded to an advertisement offering a position with the law firm of Mayer, Morgan and Marconi. The law firm was seeking a person who graduated in the top half of his or her class from an Ivy League law school. Johnson met those qualifications. However, he was told that the position had already been filled. The same advertisement continued to run in the newspaper, though. Johnson claimed disparate treatment. Is he correct? Yes! The law firm lied to Johnson about the position's being filled, because it did not want to hire a black person. ◆

The following case, which set the standard for qualifying for disparate treatment, is a landmark case. To qualify for Title VII protection, a person must show that (1) he or she is a member of a protected class; (2) he or she applied for a position for which he or she was qualified and for which the employer had openings; (3) he or she was rejected; (4) the position remained open. At this point, the burden of proof has been met by the employee or the applicant and then shifts to the employer to establish a justifiable reason for its action. Finally, the employee must prove that the employer's reason was just a pretext for its refusal to hire.

CASE

McDonnell Douglas Corp. v. Green

411 U.S. 792 (1972)

MR. JUSTICE POWELL delivered the opinion of the Court.

The case before us raises significant questions as to the proper order and nature of proof in actions under Title VII of the Civil Rights Act of 1964, 42 U.S.C. 2000e.

Petitioner McDonnell Douglas Corp., is an aerospace and aircraft manufacturer headquartered in St. Louis, Missouri, where it employs over 30,000 people. Respondent, a black citizen of St. Louis, worked for petitioner as a mechanic and laboratory technician from 1956 until August 28, 1964 when he was laid off in the course of a general reduction in petitioner's work force. Respondent, a long-time activist in the civil rights movement, protested vigorously that his discharge and the general hiring practices of petitioner were racially motivated. As part of this protest, respondent and other members of the Congress on Racial Equality illegally stalled their cars on the main roads leading to petitioner's plant for the purpose of blocking access to it at the time of the morning shift change. The District Judge described the plan for, and respondent's participation in, the "stall-in."

Some three weeks following the "lock-in" on July 25, 1965, petitioner publicly advertised for qualified mechanics, respondent's trade, and respondent promptly applied for re-employment. Petitioner turned down respondent, basing its rejection on respondent's participation in the "stall-in" and "lock-in." Shortly thereafter, respondent filled a formal complaint with the Equal Employment Opportunity Commission, claiming that petitioner has refused to rehire him because of his race and persistent involvement in the civil rights movement, in violation of 703 (a)(1) and 704 (a) of the Civil Rights Act of 1964. The former section generally prohibits racial discrimination in any employment decision while the latter forbids discrimination against applicants or employees for attempting to protest or correct allegedly discriminatory conditions of employment.

The language of Title VII makes plain the purpose of Congress to assure equality of employment opportunities and to eliminate those discriminatory practices and devices which have fostered racially stratified job environments to the disadvantage of minority citizens.

The complainant in a Title VII trial must carry the initial burden under the statute of establishing a prima facie case of racial discrimination. This may be done by showing (1) that he belongs to a racial minority; (ii) that he applied and was qualified for a job for which the employer was seeking applicants; (iii) that, despite his qualifications, he was rejected; and (iv) that, after his rejection, the position remained open and the employer continued to seek applicants from persons of complainant's qualifications. In the instant case, we agree with the Court of Appeals that respondent proved a prima facie case. Petitioner sought mechanics, respondent's trade, and continued to do so after respondent's rejection. Petitioner, moreover, does not dispute respondent's qualifications and acknowledges that his past work performance in petitioner's employ was "satisfactory."

The burden then must shift to the employer to articulate some legitimate, nondiscriminatory reason for the employer's rejection. We need not attempt in the instant case to detail every matter which fairly could be recognized as a reasonable basis for a refusal to hire. Here petitioner has assigned respondent's participation in unlawful conduct against it as the cause for his rejection. We think that this suffices to discharge petitioner's burden of proof at this stage and to meet respondent's prima facie case of discrimination.

Respondent admittedly had taken part in a carefully planned "stall-in," designed to tie up access to and egress from petitioner's plant at a peak traffic hour. Nothing in Title VII compels an employer to absolve and rehire one who has engaged in such deliberate, unlawful activity against it.

> "We are unable to conclude that Congress intended to compel employers to retain persons in their employ regardless of their unlawful conduct, to invest those who go on strike with an immunity from discharge for acts of trespass or violence against the employer's property."

Petitioner's reason for rejection thus suffices to meet the prima facie case, but the inquiry must not end here. While Title VII does not, without more, compel rehiring of respondent, neither does it permit petitioner to use respondent's conduct as a pretext for the sort of discrimination prohibited by 703(a)(1). On remand, respondent must, as the Court of Appeals recognized, be afforded a fair opportunity to show that petitioner's stated reason for respondent's rejection was in fact pretext. Especially relevant to such a showing would be evidence that white employees involved in acts against petitioner of comparable seriousness to the "stall-in" were nevertheless retained or rehired. Petitioner may justifiably refuse to rehire one who was engaged in unlawful, disruptive acts against it, but only if this criterion is applied alike to members of all races.

In sum, respondent should have been allowed to pursue his claim under 703(a)(1). If the evidence on retrial is substantially in accord with that before us in this case, we think that respondent carried his burden of establishing a prima facie case of racial discrimination and that petitioner successfully rebutted that case. But this does not end the matter. On retrial, respondent must be afforded a fair opportunity to demonstrate that petitioner's assigned reason for refusing to reemploy was a pretext or discriminatory in its application. If the District Judge so finds, he must order a prompt and appropriate remedy. In the absence of such a finding, petitioner's refusal to rehire must stand.

The judgment is vacated and the cause is hereby remanded to the District Court for further proceedings consistent with this opinion.
Judgment for Green.

DISPARATE IMPACT

Employers may not institute an employment practice that causes a *disparate impact* on a particular class of people unless they can show that the practice is job related and necessary. If there is intent to discriminate, then proof of business necessity will not save the employer from being in violation of Title VII.

The following case, which established the standard for disparate impact, is a landmark case. When an employer establishes a test or other barrier with the intention of using it to discriminate against a protected class, this act creates a disparate impact against the class. The burden, having been met, shifts to the employer to justify its actions as being job related or a business necessity.

CASE

Griggs v. Duke Power Co.

401 U.S. 424 (1971)

CHIEF JUSTICE BURGER delivered the opinion of the Court.

We granted the writ in this case to resolve the question whether an employer is prohibited by the Civil Rights Act of 1964, Title VII, from requiring a high school education or passing of a standardized general intelligence test as a condition of employment in or transfer to jobs when (a) neither standard is shown to be significantly related to successful job performance, (b) both requirements operate to disqualify Negroes at a substantially higher rate than white applicants, and (c) the jobs in question formerly had been filled only by white employees as part of a longstanding practice of giving preference to whites.

The District Court found that prior to July 2, 1965, the effective date of the Civil Rights Act of 1964, the Company openly discriminated on the basis of race in the hiring and assigning of employees at its Dan River plant. The plant was organized into five operating departments: (1) Labor, (2) Coal Handling, (3) Operations, (4) Maintenance, and (5) Laboratory and Test. Negroes were employed only in the Labor Department where the highest paying jobs paid less than the lowest paying jobs in the other four "operating" departments in which only whites were employed. Promotions were normally made within each department on the basis of job seniority. Transfers into a department usually began in the lowest position.

In 1955 the Company instituted a policy of requiring a high school education for initial assignment to any department except Labor, and for transfer from the Coal Handling to any "inside" department (Operations, Maintenance, or Laboratory). When the Company abandoned its policy of restricting Negroes to the Labor Department in 1965, completion of high school also was made a prerequisite to transfer from Labor to any other department. From the time the high school requirement was instituted to the time of trial, however, white employees hired before the time of the high school education requirement continued to perform satisfactorily and achieve promotions in the "operating" departments. Findings on this score are not challenged.

The Company added a further requirement for new employees on July 2, 1965, the date on which Title VII became effective. To qualify for placement in any but the Labor Department it became necessary to register satisfactory scores on two professionally prepared aptitude tests, as well as to have a high school education. Completion of high school alone continued to render employees eligible for transfer to the four desirable departments from which Negroes had been excluded if the incumbent had been employed prior to the time of the new requirement. In September 1965 the Company began to permit incumbent employees who lacked a high school education to qualify for transfer from Labor or Coal Handling to an "inside" job by passing two tests—the Wonderlic Personnel Test, which purports to measure general intelligence, and the Bennett Mechanical Comprehension Test. Neither was directed or intended to measure the ability to learn to perform a particular job or category of jobs. The requisite scores used for both initial hiring and transfer approximated the national median for high school graduates.

After careful analysis a majority of that court concluded that a subjective test of the employer's intent should govern, particularly in a close case, and that in this case there was no showing of a discriminatory purpose in the adoption of the diploma and test requirements. On this basis, the Court of Appeals concluded there was no violation of the Act.

Congress did not intend by Title VII, however, to guarantee a job to every person regardless of qualifications. In short, the Act does not command that any person be hired simply because he was formerly the subject of discrimination, or because he is a member of a minority group. Discriminatory preference for any group, minority or majority, is precisely and only what Congress has prescribed. What is required by Congress is the removal of artificial, arbitrary, and unnecessary barriers to employment when the barriers operate invidiously to discriminate on the basis of racial or other impermissible classification.

The Act proscribes not only overt discrimination but also practices that are fair in form, but discriminatory in operation. The touchstone is business necessity. If an employment practice which operates to exclude Negroes cannot be shown to be related to job performance, the practice is prohibited. On the record before us, neither the high school completion requirement nor the general intelligence test is shown to bear a demonstrable relationship to successful performance of the jobs for which it was used. Both were adopted, as the Court of Appeals noted, without meaningful study of their relationship to job-performance ability. Rather, a vice president of the Company testified, the requirements were instituted on the Company's judgment that they generally would improve the overall quality of the work force.

The evidence, however, shows that employees who have not completed high school or taken the tests have continued to perform satisfactorily and make progress in departments for which the high school and test criteria are now used. The promotion record of present employees who would not be able to meet the new criteria thus suggests the possibility that the requirements may not be needed even for the elicited purpose of preserving the avowed policy of advancement within the Company. In the context of this case, it is unnecessary to reach the question whether testing requirements that take into account capability for the next succeeding position or related future promotion might be utilized upon a showing that such long-range requirements fulfill a genuine business need. In the present case the Company has made no such showing.

The Court of Appeals held that the Company had adopted the diploma and test requirements without any "intention to discriminate against Negro employees." We do not suggest that either the District or the Court of Appeals erred in examining the employer's intent; but good intent or absence of discriminatory intent does not redeem employment procedures or testing mechanisms that operate as "built-in headwinds" for minority groups and are unrelated to measuring job capability.

The facts of this case demonstrates the inadequacy of broad and general testing devices as well as the infirmity of using diplomas or degrees as fixed measures of capability. History is filled with examples of men and women who rendered highly effective performance without the conventional badges of accomplishment in terms of certificates, diplomas, or degrees. Diplomas and tests are useful servants, but Congress has mandated the common-sense proposition that they are not to become masters of reality.

The Company contends that its general intelligence tests are specifically permitted by 703 (h) of the Act. That section authorizes the use of "any professionally developed ability test" that is not "designed, intended or *used* to discriminate because of race. . . ."

The Equal Employment Opportunity Commission, having enforcement responsibility, has issued guidelines interpreting 703(h) to permit only the use of job related tests.

Nothing in the Act precludes the use of testing or measuring procedures; obviously they are useful. What Congress has forbidden is giving these devices and mechanisms controlling force unless they are demonstrably a reasonable measure of job performance. Congress has not commanded that the less qualified be preferred over the better qualified simply because of minority origins. Far from disparaging job qualifications as such, Congress has made such qualifications the controlling factor, so that race, religion, nationality, and sex become irrelevant. What Congress has commanded is that any tests used must measure the person for the job and not the person in the abstract.

The judgment of the Court of Appeals is, as to that portion of the judgment appealed from, reversed.
Judgment for Griggs.

Employment Perspective

Skyscraper Construction Company was awarded a contract by the Detroit Downtown Redevelopment Agency with the provision that all of the workers used in the project must live within the city of Detroit. In response to the company's advertisement, two-thirds of the applicants were minorities. Skyscraper, afraid that is would have to hire mostly minorities, instituted a standardized achievement test as a prerequisite to the job, knowing that on average, whites score higher than do minorities. As a result of selecting workers by the test scores, 75 percent of those hired were white. Is this disparate impact? Yes! The use of the standardized test could not be proven to constitute a business necessity, because it was not related to performance on the job. Although the test may be indiscriminate, the purpose for which it was used was to discriminate intentionally against minorities, a protected class. ◆

The "80-Percent Rule"

The EEOC issued the *80-percent rule* as a statistical measure to ascertain when an employment practice has had a disparate impact on a minority group. The selection rate of minorities must be within the eighty percent of the selection rate of nonminorities; otherwise, the selection procedure utilized is discriminatory.

Employment Perspective

In 1993, 1,000 people applied for a position with Zip, Inc, and 230 people were selected.

Group	*Applied*	*Selected*	*Selection Rate*
Minorities	200	30	15%
Nonminorities	800	200	25%

Minorities Selection Rate 15% divided by Nonminorities Selection Rate 25% = 60%

Is this selection procedure discriminatory? Yes! This shows only a 60 percent selection rate, which falls short of the 80-percent rule. Therefore, Zip's selection procedure has an adverse impact on minorities. Zip, Inc. must enact a plan to remedy this. ◆

RETALIATION

If an employee has made a claim of discrimination or is to appear as a witness in a discrimination investigation, the employer may not take retaliatory action against the employee.

Employment Perspective

Cindy Thomas has filed a gender-based discrimination claim against Star Enterprises for not receiving a promotion. Nicole Robinson will be appearing as a witness on Cindy's behalf. In the interim, Cindy has been discharged, and Nicole has been demoted. Do they have a recourse? Yes! Cindy may amend her claim to include the charge of retaliation. Nicole may commence an action for violation of Title VII against Star Enterprises based on its retaliatory behavior. ◆

EQUAL EMPLOYMENT OPPORTUNITY COMMISSION

The Equal Employment Opportunity Commission was established in 1972 when the Equal Employment Opportunity Act amended Title VII of the Civil Rights Act of 1964. It is composed of five members, no more than three of which may be Republican or Democrat. The President of the United States shall appoint these members with the advice and consent of the U.S. Senate for a period of five years. Although the Civil Rights Act of 1964 is the cornerstone of the movement against employment discrimination, it is important to understand that legislative policy on employment discrimination has developed over time through the enactment of several different laws.

The Commission's responsibility is to enforce the provisions of Title VII against unlawful employment practices. A person claiming a violation of Title VII has 180 days to file the complaint with the EEOC. There is no cost to file.

Violations of Title VII are brought before the Equal Employment Opportunity Commission (EEOC). Within ten days of receipt of a complaint, the EEOC notifies the employer and conducts an investigation that entails questioning employees and/or obtaining physical evidence. A determination must be made by the EEOC. If there is a reasonable cause to believe the charges are true, the EEOC will attempt to persuade the offender to change its practices. None of these proceedings are made public. The offender has thirty days to comply. If the violation is charged against a government or one of its agencies, the EEOC shall refer the matter to the Attorney General of the United States, who may then proceed in Federal District Court. There are ninety-eight Federal District Courts located throughout the United States. These are the general trial courts in the Federal Court System. Appeals from them go to one of the eleven Circuit Courts of Appeals and then to the United States Supreme Court.

If a state or local law exists prohibiting the unlawful employment practice, the complainant must first proceed within the state or locality before filing with the EEOC. After sixty days of instituting the suit with the state, the time limit for filing with the EEOC shall be extended to the earlier of three hundred days or thirty days after the state or local action has been resolved.

If at the time of filing, the EEOC or Attorney General's office believes that irreparable harm will result if the employer's unlawful employment practices are not immediately halted, they can apply for a temporary restraining order or a preliminary injunction against the employer.

After the initial investigation, the EEOC will determine whether there is a reasonable basis to believe that the allegation is true. If the EEOC believes that there is no basis, the complaining party is informed and is free to proceed with a civil suit in a Federal District Court within ninety days of notification.

The District Court may enter a permanent injunction against the employer to refrain from engaging in the unlawful employment practice cited in the complaint. Furthermore, the Court may authorize the employer to hire the individual or individuals issuing the charge, reinstate them if they have been discharged, reimburse them with back pay, promote them, or give them any other type of equitable relief that the Court deems necessary. The Court may also allow the prevailing party reasonable fees for attorney representation, as well as for expert testimony. The charge for discrimination under Title VII is limited to race, religion, national origin, or sex. Discrimination for age and disability are covered under separate acts discussed later.

Investigation and Record-Keeping

To conduct an investigation properly, the EEOC has the right to evidence that has a bearing on the alleged unlawful employment practice. This evidence would include the right of access to documentation, as well as to the coworkers, superiors, and subordinates of the employee alleging a Title VII violation for the purpose of questioning these people.

Employees are obligated to keep records relating to their methods of selection, compensation, promotion, training, and termination of employees. Test scores and the chronological order of applications for hiring, training, and promotion must be part of the record-keeping. These records must be made available to the EEOC to enable it to determine whether unlawful employment practices have been committed. An employer may seek an exemption from the EEOC if it can prove the burden of record-keeping presents undue hardship. A notification of excerpts of Title VII is required to be posted by each employer in a conspicuous setting to apprise current employees as well as applicants of the existence of Title VII.

Equal Opportunity Plan

In addition to the application of the preceding stated requirements of Title VII, the EEOC shall be responsible for approving an equal employment opportunity plan for each department and agency, and also reviewing progress reports at least twice a year from each department and agency, and evaluating on an annual basis the operation of the equal opportunity plan for each department and agency.

CIVIL RIGHTS ACT OF 1991

The Civil Rights Act of 1991 amended in part the Civil Rights Act of 1964. Jury trials are permitted. Juries are primarily comprised of workers who may be more sympathetic to the plight of employees with whom they can identify. Compensatory and punitive damages are now recoverable. Individuals who are covered by the Americans with Disabilities Act of 1990 and the Rehabilitation Act of 1973 are now covered by the Civil Rights Act of 1964 for the purpose of recovering compensatory and punitive damages. Punitive damages are recoverable when the employer has acted with malice or in reckless disregard of an individual's civil rights.

Compensatory and Punitive Damages

Compensatory damages include emotional pain and suffering, mental anguish, loss of enjoyment of life, inconvenience, as well as other nonpecuniary losses. Compensatory and punitive damages are in addition to back pay, which is still recoverable under the Civil Rights Act of 1964. The total of compensatory and punitive damages may not exceed $50,000 for employers with 15 to 100 employees; $100,000 for employers with 101 to 200 employees; $200,000 for employers with 201 to 500 employees; and $300,000 for employers with more than 500 employees. The employee claiming the violation may request a jury trial. The term *complaining party* now encompasses a disabled person as well as a member of a minority race, religion, sex, and national origin.

Business Necessity

The Civil Rights Act of 1991 adopted the concepts of "business necessity" and "job related" as enunciated by the Supreme Court in *Griggs vs. Duke Power Company* (1971). The test for business necessity is not met where the employment practice that excludes a particular class is not job related. In such a case, the practice is prohibited.

It shall be an unlawful practice to adjust scores, establish different cutoff scores, or alter scores on employment-related tests for a particular race, religion, gender, or national origin.

Glass Ceiling Commission

Congress has found that there still exists barriers to the advancement of women and minorities in the workplace. They remain underrepresented in management decision-making positions. Under the Civil Rights Act of 1991, Congress established the Glass Ceiling Commission to rectify this problem. The Commission must consider how prepared women and minorities are for advancement, what opportunities are avail-

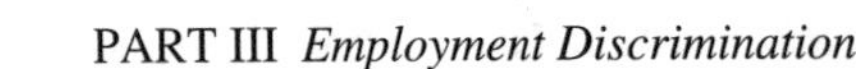

able, and what policies businesses follow in making such promotions, as well as making comparisons with businesses that have actively promoted women and minorities and their reasons for success.

EXEMPTIONS

There are a number of classifications which are exempt from the Civil Rights Act. In these situations, discrimination would be permissible.

Bona Fide Occupational Qualification

Employers may discriminate because of religion, gender, and national origin if they can establish that there is a bona fide occupational qualification. This condition does *not* apply to race and color.

Employment Perspective

Mary Jacobs applied for a position as a rest-room attendant at the Nautilus Health and Fitness Club. A total of seven women, but no men, applied for the position. After another woman was selected for the position of attendant to the female locker-room, Mary asserted that she should be considered for attendant to the male locker-room. Nautilus refused on the ground that Mary is a woman. Is this discrimination? No! Gender is bona fide occupational qualification in the selection of a locker-room attendant. ◆

Communists

Title VII does not apply to individuals who are members of the Communist party of the United States.

Employment Perspective

Igor Musnovec, a Communist party member, applied for a job as a checkout clerk at a local Foodway supermarket. His application was not considered because he is a Communist. Is this discrimination? No! It is lawful to discriminate against a Communist. ◆

Drug Addicts

It is lawful for an employer to refuse to hire individuals who are using illegal drugs as long as this practice was not adopted intentionally to discriminate against a particular class.

Employment Perspective

Julio Gonzalez, who is currently participating in drug rehabilitation, has applied for a job as a clerk in Save Mart Department Store. Save Mart refuses to hire Julio because of his drug addiction. Does Julio have any recourse? No! Julio's only recourse would be if he could prove that Save Mart had instituted the stipulation with the intention of enforcing it only against Hispanics. ◆

Merit Pay

Employers may compensate individuals differently on the basis of merit, seniority, quality, or quantity of work performed, or location of employment. It is understood that employers cannot discriminate under the guise of the protected categories of the Civil Rights Act. If it turns out that discrimination is the employer's intention, then the employer will be in violation of Title VII. Professionally developed ability tests may be designed and administered to determine hiring and promoting as long as the test is job related not intended to discriminate.

ADVERTISING

Employers are barred from indicating in any advertisement for employment that they prefer an applicant of a particular race, religion, gender, or national origin. An exception to this condition exists if it can be shown that a bona fide occupational qualification requires a person of a particular religion, gender, or national origin. There is no exception for race and color.

Employment Perspective

Lilly's Lingerie Shop places an advertisement in a local paper for a position admitting women to its dressing room area. The ad stated that only females need apply. Is this advertisement in violation of Title VII? Most likely not! Lilly's must establish that it is a business necessity that only a woman should work in this position where the attendant is in such close proximity to an area where female customers are undressing. ◆

CONCLUSION

In hindsight, the Civil Rights Act of 1964, along with subsequent amendments, has had the most profound impact on employment since the proliferation of unions. The Civil Rights Act opened the door to employment opportunities and promotions for minorities and women. These two groups comprise more than half the work force. Neglecting them for so long was an egregious mistake. Forgetting them in the future would be economically disastrous.

Securing a well-paying job is the main step for an individual to increase his or her standard of living and to secure better housing. Without employment opportunities, women and minorities are relegated to welfare, unemployment, or ministerial positions with low pay. In turn, minorities and women providing sole support for a family have the lowest economic status. Making ends meet is a day-to-day goal. The Civil Rights Act, while not being a panacea, provided an area of opportunity for those on the lowest levels of society. Women and minorities are now significantly represented in professional and graduate school programs. They are also present in middle-level management positions. Attaining upper-level positions is much harder to realize because it is easier for decision-makers to integrate those departments that are beneath them than it is to integrate their own. Also, while it takes time for qualified candidates to work their way up through the ranks, that moment is at hand because enough time has passed for these candidates to emerge. It is now that access to the executive level and the boardroom should begin to increase. It will likely remain a slow process, though, for these positions involve sizeable amounts of pay and more importantly, power.

Societies should not be judged on the basis of their most wealthy citizens. If they were, Mexico and certain Arabian countries would score very high. The average standard of living is not the most satisfactory basis either, because great wealth can give the average an upward bias. Instead, societies should be judged on how well their poor are doing. The greater the number of people in this classification, the more likely the society has failed to serve the needs of all its people. When a society can boast that even the least of its members has a job that provides the means for a satisfactory subsistence, then a society has achieved its greatest goal.

The Civil Rights Act has provided an impetus for achieving this goal. Raising the bottom up is its underlying purpose. However, improvements in education, life at home, and the community have not kept pace with the advancement made in employment opportunities. Employment opportunities are the goal for a young person who has honed his or her intellect and been brought up in a stable community, with a family oriented toward principles and values. When education and environment leave a lot to be desired, employment opportunities are difficult to take advantage of. In order for the Civil Rights Act to fulfill its main purpose of lifting the lower echelon of society to a more suitable level, similar strides must take place in education and the community and family environment.

REVIEW QUESTIONS

1. Explain the significance of the Civil Rights Act of 1964.
2. Who is covered under the Civil Rights Act?
3. What changes were made by the 1991 Civil Rights Act?
4. What is a Bona Fide Occupational Qualification?
5. Are Communists covered by the Civil Rights Act?
6. Is the use of merit pay permissable?
7. Elucidate the difference between disparate treatment and disparate impact.
8. Give an example of the 80 percent rule.
9. Does the employee have recourse if the employer retaliates?
10. May drug addicts be discriminated against?
11. What is the function of the EEOC?
12. What is the purpose of the Glass Ceiling Commission?
13. When are punitive damages awarded?
14. What is the test for business necessity?
15. Does the EEOC have the right to access employment records regarding the makeup of a company's employees?

16. If a plaintiff has established a prima facie case and further shows that the employer's articulated reasons are pretextual, is the plaintiff entitled to recovery for illegal discrimination? *Blare v. Husky Injection Molding Systems Boston, Inc.,* 646 N.E.2d 111 (1995)

17. J. Walter, Inc. and J. Walter, Ltd. are two separate companies. In November 1990, Mochelle was hired by J. Walter, Inc., as a salesman. In August 1991, Mochelle informed his supervisor of his intention to run for political office. In October 1991, he lost the election. In January 1992, Mochelle was fired for failing to perform his duties. Mochelle claimed he was fired because he ran for political office and brought suit against J. Walter, Ltd., contending that the two companies were interrelated. The reason for this was that Walter, Inc., does not have enough employees to qualify for a Title VII action. Walter, Ltd., contended that it has separate offices, employees, records, phone numbers, and tax returns. What was the result? *Mochelle v. J. Walter, Inc.,* 823 F.Supp. 1302 (M.D. LA. 1993)

18. When does a joint employer relationship exist? *Texas World Service Co., Inc. v. NLRB,* 928 F.2d 1426 (5th Cir. 1991)

19. Zimmerman filed a suit against North American Signal Co., charging it with age discrimination. Signal contended that it did not have the required number of employees to be held accountable. Zimmerman charged that the requirement was met when unpaid, inactive officers were included. What was the result? *Zimmerman v. North American Signal Co.,* 704 F.2d 347 (7th Cir. 1983)

20. Plaintiff brought a civil rights action against the company. The company claimed it did not have the requisite number of employees to be held responsible. Plaintiff argued that the company did have by including the Board of Directors, the reason being that they were paid for attending the directors' meetings. What was the result? *Chavero v. Local 241, Division of the Amalgamated Transit Union,* 787 F.2d 1154 (7th Cir. 1986)

21. Is the 80 percent rule ethical?

22. Are the standards set forth in the case on pp. 166 the best requirements for determining the viability of a lawsuit under Title VII?

23. Was the case on pp. 166 decided in an ethical manner?

24. If the case on pp. 168 was decided again today, would the result be the same?

25. Are the requirements of "job relatedness" and "business necessity" fair in the manner in which they are applied?

Civil Rights Act of 1964

2000e. DEFINITIONS

For the purposes of this subchapter

(a) The term "person" includes one or more individuals, governments, governmental agencies, political subdivisions, labor unions, partnerships, associations, corporations, legal representatives, mutual companies, joint-stock companies, trusts, unincorporated organizations, trustees, or receivers.

(b) The term "employer" means a person engaged in an industry affecting commerce who has fifteen or more employees for each working day in each of twenty or more calendar weeks in the current or preceding calendar year, and any agent of such a person, but such term does not include (1) the United States, a corporation wholly owned by the Government of the United States, an Indian tribe, or any department or agency of the District of Columbia subject by statute to procedures of the competitive service, or (2) a bona fide private membership club (other than a labor organization) which is exempt from taxation except that during the first year after March 24, 1972, persons having fewer than twenty-five employees (and their agents) shall not be considered employers.

(c) The term "employment agency" means any person regularly undertaking with or without compensation to procure employees for an employer or to procure for employees opportunities to work for an employer and includes an agent of such a person.

(d) The term "labor organization" means a labor organization engaged in an industry affecting commerce, and any agent of such an organization, and includes any organization of any kind, any agency, or employee representation committee, group, association, or plan so engaged in which employees participate and which exists for the purpose, in whole or in part, of dealing with employers concerning grievances, labor disputes, wages, rates of pay, hours, or other terms or conditions of employment, and any conference, general committee, joint or system board, or joint council so engaged which is subordinate to a national or international labor organization.

(e) A labor organization shall be deemed to be engaged in an industry affecting commerce if (1) it maintains or operates a hiring hall or hiring office which procures employees for an employer or procures for employees opportunities to work for an employer, or (2) the number of its members (or, where it is a labor organization composed of other labor organizations or their representatives, if the aggregate number of the members of such other labor organization) is (A) twenty-five or more during the first year after March 24, 1972, or (B) fifteen or more thereafter, and such labor organization—

(1) is the certified representative of employees under the provisions of the National Labor Relations Act, or the Railway Labor Act,

(2) although not certified, is a national or international labor organization or a local labor organization recognized or acting as the representative of employees of an employer or employers engaged in an industry affecting commerce; or

(3) has chartered a local labor organization or subsidiary body which is representing or actively seeking to represent employees of employers within the meaning of paragraph (1) or (2); or

(4) has been chartered by a labor organization representing or actively seeking to represent employees within the meaning of paragraph (1) or (2) as the local or subordinate body through which such employees may enjoy membership or become affiliated with such labor organization; or

(5) is a conference, general committee, joint or system board, or joint council sub-

ordinate to a national or international labor organization, which includes a labor organization engaged in an industry affecting commerce within the meaning of any of the preceding paragraphs of this subsection.

(f) The term "employee" means an individual employed by an employer, except that the term "employee" shall not include any person elected to public office in any State or political subdivision of any State by the qualified voters thereof, or any person chosen by such officer to be on such officer's personal staff, or an appointee on the policy making level or an immediate adviser with respect to the exercise of the constitutional or legal powers of the office. The exemption set forth in the preceding sentence shall not include employees subject to the civil service laws of a State government, governmental agency or political subdivision. With respect to employment in a foreign country, such term includes an individual who is a citizen of the United States.

(g) The term "commerce" means trade, traffic, commerce, transportation, transmission, or communication among the several States; or between a State and any place outside thereof; or within the District of Columbia, or a possession of the United States; or between points in the same State but through a point outside thereof.

(h) The term "industry affecting commerce" means any activity, business, or industry in commerce or in which a labor dispute would hinder or obstruct commerce or the free flow of commerce and includes any activity or industry "affecting commerce" within the meaning of the Labor-Management Reporting and Disclosure Act of 1959 and further includes any governmental industry, business, or activity.

(i) The term "State" includes a State of the United States, the District of Columbia, Puerto Rico, the Virgin Islands, American Samoa, Guam, Wake Island, the Canal Zone, and Outer Continental Shelf lands defined in the Outer Continental Shelf Lands Act.

(j) The term "religion" includes all aspects of religious observance and practice, as well as belief, unless an employer demonstrates that he is unable to reasonably accommodate to an employee's or prospective employee's religious observance or practice without undue hardship on the conduct of the employer's business.

(k) The terms "because of sex" or "on the basis of sex" include, but are not limited to, because of or on the basis of pregnancy, childbirth, or related medical conditions; and women affected by pregnancy, childbirth, or related medical conditions shall be treated the same for all employment-related purposes, including receipt of benefits under fringe benefit programs, as other persons not so affected but similar in their ability or inability to work, and nothing in this title shall be interpreted to permit otherwise. This subsection shall not require an employer to pay for health insurance benefits for abortion, except where the life of the mother would be endangered if the fetus were carried to term, or except where medical complications have arisen from an abortion: Provided, That nothing herein shall preclude an employer from providing abortion benefits or otherwise affect bargaining agreements in regard to abortion.

(l) The term "complaining party" means the Commission, the Attorney General, or a person who may bring an action or proceeding under this subchapter.

(m) The term "demonstrates" means meets the burdens of production and persuasion.

(n) The term "respondent" means an employer, employment agency, labor organization, joint labor-management committee controlling apprenticeship or other training or retraining program, including an on-the-job training program, or Federal entity.

2000e-1. APPLICABILITY TO FOREIGN AND RELIGIOUS EMPLOYMENT

(a) Inapplicability of subchapter to certain aliens and employees of religious entities

This subchapter shall not apply to an employer with respect to the employment of aliens outside any State, or to a religious corporation, association, educational institution, or society with respect to the employment of individuals of a particular religion to perform work connected with the carrying on by such corporation, association, educational institution, or society of its activities.

(b) Compliance with statute as violative of foreign law

It shall not be unlawful for an employer (or a corporation controlled by an employer), labor organization, employment agency, or joint labor-management committee controlling apprenticeship or other training or retraining (including on-the-job training programs) to take any action otherwise prohibited by such section, with respect to an employee in a workplace in a foreign country if compliance with such section would cause such employer (or such corporation), such organization, such agency, or such committee to violate the law of the foreign country in which such workplace is located.

(c) Control of corporation incorporated in foreign country

(1) If an employer controls a corporation whose place of incorporation is a foreign country, any practice prohibited by this title engaged in by such corporation shall be presumed to be engaged in by such employer.

(2) This title shall not apply with respect to the foreign operations of an employer that is a foreign person not controlled by an American employer.

(3) For purposes of this subsection, the determination of whether an employer controls a corporation shall be based on—

(A) the interrelation of operations;

(B) the common management;

(C) the centralized control of labor relations; and

(D) the common ownership or financial control, of the employer and the corporation.

2000e-2. UNLAWFUL EMPLOYMENT PRACTICES

(a) Employer practices

It shall be an unlawful employment practice for an employer—

(1) to fail or refuse to hire or to discharge any individual, or otherwise to discriminate against any individual with respect to his compensation, terms, conditions, or privileges of employment, because of such individual's race, color, religion, sex, or national origin; or

(2) to limit, segregate, or classify his employees or applicants for employment in any way which would deprive or tend to deprive any individual of employment opportunities or otherwise adversely affect his status as an employee, because of such individual's race, color, religion, sex, or national origin.

(b) Employment agency practices

It shall be an unlawful employment practice for an employment agency to fail or refuse to refer for employment, or otherwise to discriminate against, any individual because of his race, color, religion, sex, or national origin, or to classify or refer for employment any individual on the basis of his race, color, religion, sex, or national origin.

(c) Labor organization practices

It shall be an unlawful employment practice for a labor organization—

(1) to exclude or to expel from its membership, or otherwise to discriminate against, any individual because of his race, color, religion, sex, or national origin;

(2) to limit, segregate, or classify its membership or applicants for membership, or to classify or fail or refuse to refer for employment any individual, in any way which would deprive or tend to deprive any individual of employment opportunities, or would limit such employment opportunities or otherwise adversely affect his status as an employee or as an applicant for employment, because of such individual's race, color, religion, sex, or national origin; or

(3) to cause or attempt to cause an employer to discriminate against an individual in violation of this section.

(d) Training programs

It shall be an unlawful employment practice for any employer, labor organiza-

tion, or joint labor-management committee controlling apprenticeship or other training or retraining, including on-the-job training programs to discriminate against any individual because of his race, color, religion, sex, or national origin in admission to, or employment in, any program established to provide apprenticeship or other training.

(e) Businesses or enterprises with personnel qualified on basis of religion, sex, or national origin; educational institutions with personnel of particular religion

Notwithstanding any other provision of this subchapter, (1) it shall not be an unlawful employment practice for an employer to hire and employ employees, for an employment agency to classify, or refer for employment any individual, for a labor organization to classify its membership or to classify or refer for employment any individual, or for an employer, labor organization, or joint labor-management committee controlling apprenticeship or other training or retraining programs to admit or employ any individual in any such program, on the basis of his religion, sex, or national origin in those certain instances where religion, sex, or national origin is a bona fide occupational qualification reasonably necessary to the normal operation of that particular business or enterprise, and (2) it shall not be an unlawful employment practice for a school, college, university, or other educational institution or institution of learning to hire and employ employees of a particular religion if such school, college, university, or other educational institution or institution of learning is, in whole or in substantial part, owned, supported, controlled, or managed by a particular religion or by a particular religious corporation, association, or society, or if the curriculum of such school, college, university, or other educational institution or institution of learning is directed toward the propagation of a particular religion.

(f) Members of Communist Party or Communist-action or Communist-front organizations

As used in this subchapter, the phrase "unlawful employment practice" shall not be deemed to include any action or measure taken by an employer, labor organization, joint labor-management committee, or employment agency with respect to an individual who is a member of the Communist Party of the United States or of any other organization required to register as a Communist-action or Communist-front organization by final order of the Subversive Activities Control Board pursuant to the Subversive Activities Control Act of 1950.

(g) National security

Notwithstanding any other provision of this subchapter, it shall not be an unlawful employment practice for an employer to fail or refuse to hire and employ any individual for any position, for an employer to discharge any individual from any position, or for an employment agency to fail or refuse to refer any individual for employment in any position, or for a labor organization to fail or refuse to refer any individual for employment in any position, if—

(1) the occupancy of such position, or access to the premises in or upon which any part of the duties of such position is performed or is to be performed, is subject to any requirement imposed in the interest of the national security of the United States under any security program in effect pursuant to or administered under any statute of the United States or any Executive order of the President; and

(2) such individual has not fulfilled or has ceased to fulfill that requirement.

(h) Seniority or merit system; quantity or quality of production; ability tests; compensation based on sex and authorized by minimum wage provisions

Notwithstanding any other provision of this subchapter, it shall not be an unlawful employment practice for an employer to apply different standards of compensation, or different terms, conditions, or privileges of employment pursuant to a bona fide seniority or merit system, or a system which measures earnings by quantity or quality of production or to employees who work in different locations, provided that such differences are not the result of an intention to discriminate because of race, color, religion, sex, or national origin, nor shall it be an unlawful employment practice for an employer to give and to act upon the results of any professionally developed ability test provided that such test, its administration or action upon the results is not designed, intended or used to discriminate because of race, color, religion, sex or national origin. It shall not be an unlawful employment practice under this subchapter for any employer to differentiate upon the basis of sex in determining the amount of the wages or compensation paid or to be paid to employees of such employer if such differentiation is authorized by the provisions of this title.

(i) Businesses or enterprises extending preferential treatment to Indians

Nothing contained in this subchapter shall apply to any business or enterprise on or near an Indian reservation with respect to any publicly announced employment practice of such business or enterprise under which a preferential treatment is given to any individual because he is an Indian living on or near a reservation.

(j) Preferential treatment not to be granted on account of existing number or percentage imbalance

Nothing contained in this subchapter shall be interpreted to require any employer, employment agency, labor organization, or joint labor-management committee subject to this subchapter to grant preferential treatment to any individual or to any group because of the race, color, religion, sex, or national origin of such individual or group on account of an imbalance which may exist with respect to the total number or percentage of persons of any race, color, religion, sex, or national origin employed by any employer, referred or classified for employment by any employment agency or labor organization, admitted to membership or classified by any labor organization, or admitted to, or employed in, any apprenticeship or other training program, in comparison with the total number or percentage of persons of such race, color, religion, sex, or national origin in any community, State, section, or other area, or in the available work force in any community, State, section, or other area.

(k) Burden of proof in disparate impact cases

(1)(A) An unlawful employment practice based on disparate impact is established under this subchapter only if—

(i) a complaining party demonstrates that a respondent uses a particular employment practice that causes a disparate impact on the basis of race, color, religion, sex, or national origin and the respondent fails to demonstrate that the challenged practice is job related for the position in question and consistent with business necessity; or

(ii) the complaining party makes the demonstration described in subparagraph (C) with respect to an alternative employment practice and the respondent refuses to adopt such alternative employment practice.

(B)(i) With respect to demonstrating that a particular employment practice causes a disparate impact as described in subparagraph (A)(i), the complaining party shall demonstrate that each particular challenged employment practice causes a disparate impact, except that if the complaining party can demonstrate to the court that the elements of a respondent's decisionmaking process are not capable of separation for analysis, the decisionmaking process may be analyzed as one employment practice.

(ii) If the respondent demonstrates that a specific employment practice does not cause the disparate impact, the respondent shall not be required to demonstrate that such practice is required by business necessity.

(C) The demonstration referred to by subparagraph (A)(ii) shall be in accordance with the law as it existed on June 4, 1989, with respect to the concept of "alternative employment practice."

(2) A demonstration that an employment practice is required by business necessity may not be used as a defense against a claim of intentional discrimination under this subchapter.

(3) Notwithstanding any other provision of this subchapter, a rule barring the

employment of an individual who currently and knowingly uses or possesses a controlled substance, as defined in schedules I and II of section 102(6) of the Controlled Substances Act other than the use or possession of a drug taken under the supervision of a licensed health care professional, or any other use or possession authorized by the Controlled Substances Act or any other provision of Federal law, shall be considered an unlawful employment practice under this subchapter only if such rule is adopted or applied with an intent to discriminate because of race, color, religion, sex, or national origin.

(l) Prohibition of discriminatory use of test scores

It shall be an unlawful employment practice for a respondent, in connection with the selection or referral of applicants or candidates for employment or promotion, to adjust the scores of, use different cutoff scores for, or otherwise alter the results of, employment related tests on the basis of race, color, religion, sex, or national origin.

(m) Impermissible consideration of race, color, religion, sex, or national origin in employment practices

Except as otherwise provided in this subchapter, an unlawful employment practice is established when the complaining party demonstrates that race, color, religion, sex, or national origin was a motivating factor for any employment practice, even though other factors also motivated the practice.

(n) Resolution of challenges to employment practices implementing litigated or consent judgments or orders

(1)(A) Notwithstanding any other provision of law, and except as provided in paragraph (2), an employment practice that implements and is within the scope of a litigated or consent judgment or order that resolves a claim of employment discrimination under the Constitution or Federal civil rights laws may not be challenged under the circumstances described in subparagraph (B).

(B) A practice described in subparagraph (A) may not be challenged in a claim under the Constitution or Federal civil rights laws—

(i) by a person who, prior to the entry of the judgment or order described in subparagraph (A), had—

(I) actual notice of the proposed judgment or order sufficient to apprise such person that such judgment or order might adversely affect the interests and legal rights of such person and that an opportunity was available to present objections to such judgment or order by a future date certain; and

(II) a reasonable opportunity to present objections to such judgment or order; or

(ii) by a person whose interests were adequately represented by another person who had previously challenged the judgment or order on the same legal grounds and with a similar factual situation, unless there has been an intervening change in law or fact.

(2) Nothing in this subsection shall be construed to—

(A) alter the standards for intervention under rule 24 of the Federal Rules of Civil Procedure or apply to the rights of parties who have successfully intervened pursuant to such rule in the proceeding in which the parties intervened;

(B) apply to the rights of parties to the action in which a litigated or consent judgment or order was entered, or of members of a class represented or sought to be represented in such action, or of members of a group on whose behalf relief was sought in such action by the Federal Government;

(C) prevent challenges to a litigated or consent judgment or order on the ground that such judgment or order was obtained through collusion or fraud, or is transparently invalid or was entered by a court lacking subject matter jurisdiction; or

(D) authorize or permit the denial to any person of the due process of law required by the Constitution.

(3) Any action not precluded under this subsection that challenges an employment consent judgment or order described in paragraph (1) shall be brought in the court,

and if possible before the judge, that entered such judgment or order.

2000e-3. OTHER UNLAWFUL EMPLOYMENT PRACTICES

(a) Discrimination for making charges, testifying, assisting, or participating in enforcement proceedings

It shall be an unlawful employment practice for an employer to discriminate against any of his employees or applicants for employment, for an employment agency, or joint labor-management committee controlling apprenticeship or other training or retraining, including on-the-job training programs, to discriminate against any individual, or for a labor organization to discriminate against any member thereof or applicant for membership, because he has opposed any practice made an unlawful employment practice by this subchapter, or because he has made a charge, testified, assisted, or participated in any manner in an investigation, proceeding, or hearing under this subchapter.

(b) Printing or publication of notices or advertisements indicating prohibited preference, limitation, specification, or discrimination; occupational qualification exception

It shall be an unlawful employment practice for an employer, labor organization, employment agency, or joint labor-management committee controlling apprenticeship or other training or retraining, including on-the-job training programs, to print or publish or cause to be printed or published any notice or advertisement relating to employment by such an employer or membership in or any classification or referral for employment by such a labor organization, or relating to any classification or referral for employment by such an employment agency, or relating to admission to, or employment in, any program established to provide apprenticeship or other training by such a joint labor-management committee, indicating any preference, limitation, specification, or discrimination, based on race, color, religion, sex, or national origin, except that such a notice or advertisement may indicate a preference, limitation, specification, or discrimination based on religion, sex, or national origin when religion, sex, or national origin is a bona fide occupational qualification for employment.

2000e-4. EQUAL EMPLOYMENT OPPORTUNITY COMMISSION

(a) Creation; composition; political representation; appointment; term; vacancies; Chairman and Vice Chairman; duties of Chairman; appointment of personnel; compensation of personnel

There is hereby created a Commission to be known as the Equal Employment Opportunity Commission, which shall be composed of five members, not more than three of whom shall be members of the same political party. Members of the Commission shall be appointed by the President by and with the advice and consent of the Senate for a term of five years. Any individual chosen to fill a vacancy shall be appointed only for the unexpired term of the member whom he shall succeed, and all members of the Commission shall continue to serve until their successors are appointed and qualified, except that no such member of the Commission shall continue to serve (1) for more than sixty days when the Congress is in session unless a nomination to fill such vacancy shall have been submitted to the Senate, or (2) after the adjournment of the session of the Senate in which such nomination was submitted. The President shall designate one member to serve as Chairman of the Commission, and one member to serve as Vice Chairman. The Chairman shall be responsible on behalf of the Commission for the administrative operations of the Commission, and, except as provided in subsection (b) of this section, shall appoint, in accordance with the provisions of title 5 governing appointments in the competitive service, such officers, agents, attorneys, administrative law judges, and employees as he deems necessary to assist it in the performance of its functions and to fix their compensation in accordance with the provisions relating to classification and General Schedule pay rates: Provided, That assignment, removal, and compensation of administrative law judges shall be in accordance with title 5.

(b) General Counsel; appointment; term; duties; representation by attorneys and Attorney General

(1) There shall be a General Counsel of the Commission appointed by the President, by and with the advice and consent of the Senate, for a term of four years. The General Counsel shall have responsibility for the conduct of litigation as provided in this title. The General Counsel shall have such other duties as the Commission may prescribe or as may be provided by law and shall concur with the Chairman of the Commission on the appointment and supervision of regional attorneys. The General Counsel of the Commission on the effective date of this Act shall continue in such position and perform the functions specified in this subsection until a successor is appointed and qualified.

(2) Attorneys appointed under this section may, at the direction of the Commission, appear for and represent the Commission in any case in court, provided that the Attorney General shall conduct all litigation to which the Commission is a party in the Supreme Court pursuant to this subchapter.

(c) Exercise of powers during vacancy; quorum

A vacancy in the Commission shall not impair the right of the remaining members to exercise all the powers of the Commission and three members thereof shall constitute a quorum.

(d) Seal; judicial notice

The Commission shall have an official seal which shall be judicially noticed.

(e) Reports to Congress and the President

The Commission shall at the close of each fiscal year report to the Congress and to the President concerning the action it has taken and the moneys it has disbursed. It shall make such further reports on the cause of and means of eliminating discrimination and such recommendations for further legislation as may appear desirable.

(f) Principal and other offices

The principal office of the Commission shall be in or near the District of Columbia, but it may meet or exercise any or all its powers at any other place. The Commission may establish such regional or State offices as it deems necessary to accomplish the purpose of this subchapter.

(g) Powers of Commission

The Commission shall have power–

(1) to cooperate with and, with their consent, utilize regional, State, local, and other agencies, both public and private, and individuals;

(2) to pay to witnesses whose depositions are taken or who are summoned before the Commission or any of its agents the same witness and mileage fees as are paid to witnesses in the courts of the United States;

(3) to furnish to persons subject to this subchapter such technical assistance as they may request to further their compliance with this subchapter or an order issued thereunder;

(4) upon the request of (i) any employer, whose employees or some of them, or (ii) any labor organization, whose members or some of them, refuse or threaten to refuse to cooperate in effectuating the provisions of this subchapter, to assist in such effectuation by conciliation or such other remedial action as is provided by this subchapter;

(5) to make such technical studies as are appropriate to effectuate the purposes and policies of this subchapter and to make the results of such studies available to the public;

(6) to intervene in a civil action brought under this title by an aggrieved party against a respondent other than a government, governmental agency or political subdivision.

(h) Cooperation with other departments and agencies in performance of educational or promotional activities; outreach activities

(1) The Commission shall, in any of its educational or promotional activities, cooperate with other departments and agencies

in the performance of such educational and promotional activities.

(2) In exercising its powers under this subchapter, the Commission shall carry out educational and outreach activities (including dissemination of information in languages other than English) targeted to–

(A) individuals who historically have been victims of employment discrimination and have not been equitably served by the Commission; and

(B) individuals on whose behalf the Commission has authority to enforce any other law prohibiting employment discrimination, concerning rights and obligations under this subchapter or such law, as the case may be.

(i) Personnel subject to political activity restrictions

All officers, agents, attorneys, and employees of the Commission shall be subject to the provisions of title 5, notwithstanding any exemption contained in such section.

(j) Technical Assistance Training Institute

(1) The Commission shall establish a Technical Assistance Training Institute, through which the Commission shall provide technical assistance and training regarding the laws and regulations enforced by the Commission.

(2) An employer or other entity covered under this subchapter shall not be excused from compliance with the requirements of this subchapter because of any failure to receive technical assistance under this subsection.

(3) There are authorized to be appropriated to carry out this subsection such sums as may be necessary for fiscal year 1992.

(k) EEOC Education, Technical Assistance, and Training Revolving Fund

(1) There is hereby established in the Treasury of the United States a revolving fund to be known as the "EEOC Education, Technical Assistance, and Training Revolving Fund" (hereinafter in this subsection referred to as the "Fund") and to pay the cost (including administrative and personnel expenses) of providing education, technical assistance, and training relating to laws administered by the Commission. Monies in the Fund shall be available without fiscal year limitation to the Commission for such purposes.

(A) The Commission shall charge fees in accordance with the provisions of this paragraph to offset the costs of education, technical assistance, and training provided with monies in the Fund. Such fees for any education, technical assistance, or training—

(i) shall be imposed on a uniform basis on persons and entities receiving such education, assistance, or training,

(ii) shall not exceed the cost of providing such education, assistance, and training, and

(iii) with respect to each person or entity receiving such education, assistance, or training, shall bear a reasonable relationship to the cost of providing such education, assistance, or training to such person or entity.

(B) Fees received under subparagraph (A) shall be deposited by the Fund by the Commission.

(C) The Commission shall include in each report made under subsection (e) of this section information with respect to the operation of the Fund, including–

(i) the identity of each person or entity to which the Commission provided education, technical assistance, or training with monies in the Fund, in the fiscal year for which such report is prepared,

(ii) the cost to the Commission to provide such education, technical assistance, or training to such person or entity, and

(iii) the amount of any fee received by the Commission from such person or entity for such education, technical assistance, or training.

(3) The Secretary of the Treasury shall invest the portion of the Fund not required to satisfy current expenditures from the Fund, as determined by the Commission, in obligations of the United States or obligations guaranteed as to principal by the United States. Investment proceeds shall be deposited in the Fund.

(4) There is hereby transferred to the Fund $1,000,000 from the Salaries and Expenses appropriation of the Commission.

2000e-5. ENFORCEMENT PROVISIONS

(a) Power of Commission to prevent unlawful employment practices

The Commission is empowered, as hereinafter provided, to prevent any person from engaging in any unlawful employment practice as set forth in this title.

(b) Charges by persons aggrieved or member of Commission of unlawful employment practices by employers, etc.; filing; allegations; notice to respondent; contents of notice; investigation by Commission; contents of charges; prohibition on disclosure of charges; determination of reasonable cause; conference, conciliation, and persuasion for elimination of unlawful practices; prohibition on disclosure of informal endeavors to end unlawful practices; use of evidence in subsequent proceedings; penalties for disclosure of information; time for determination of reasonable cause

Whenever a charge is filed by or on behalf of a person claiming to be aggrieved, or by a member of the Commission, alleging that an employer, employment agency, labor organization, or joint labor-management committee controlling apprenticeship or other training or retraining, including on-the-job training programs, has engaged in an unlawful employment practice, the Commission shall serve a notice of the charge (including the date, place and circumstances of the alleged unlawful employment practice) on such employer, employment agency, labor organization, or joint labor-management committee (hereinafter referred to as the "respondent") within ten days, and shall make an investigation thereof. Charges shall be in writing under oath or affirmation and shall contain such information and be in such form as the Commission requires. Charges shall not be made public by the Commission. If the Commission determines after such investigation that there is not reasonable cause to believe that the charge is true, it shall dismiss the charge and promptly notify the person claiming to be aggrieved and the respondent of its action. In determining whether reasonable cause exists, the Commission shall accord substantial weight to final findings and orders made by State or local authorities in proceedings commenced under State or local law pursuant to the requirements of subsections (c) and (d) of this section. If the Commission determines after such investigation that there is reasonable cause to believe that the charge is true, the Commission shall endeavor to eliminate any such alleged unlawful employment practice by informal methods of conference, conciliation, and persuasion. Nothing said or done during and as a part of such informal endeavors may be made public by the Commission, its officers or employees, or used as evidence in a subsequent proceeding without the written consent of the persons concerned. Any person who makes public information in violation of this subsection shall be fined not more than $1,000 or imprisoned for not more than one year, or both. The Commission shall make its determination on reasonable cause as promptly as possible and, so far as practicable, not later than one hundred and twenty days from the filing of the charge or, where applicable under subsection (c) or (d) of this section, from the date upon which the Commission is authorized to take action with respect to the charge.

(c) State or local enforcement proceedings; notification of State or local authority; time for filing charges with Commission; commencement of proceedings

In the case of an alleged unlawful employment practice occurring in a State, or political subdivision of a State, which has a State or local law prohibiting the unlawful employment practice alleged and establishing or authorizing a State or local authority to grant or seek relief from such practice or to institute criminal proceedings with respect thereto upon receiving notice thereof, no charge may be filed under subsection (a) of this section by the person aggrieved before the expiration of sixty days after proceedings have been commenced under the State or local law, unless such proceedings have been earlier terminated, provided that such sixty-day period shall be extended to one hundred and twenty days during the first year after the effective date of such State or local law. If any requirement for the commencement of such proceedings is imposed by a State or local authority other than a requirement of the filing of a written and signed statement of the facts upon which the proceeding is based, the proceeding shall be deemed to have been commenced for the purposes of this subsection at the time such statement is sent by registered mail to the appropriate State or local authority.

(d) State or local enforcement proceedings; notification of State or local authority; time for action on charges by Commission

In the case of any charge filed by a member of the Commission alleging an unlawful employment practice occurring in a State or political subdivision of a State which has a State or local law prohibiting the practice alleged and establishing or authorizing a State or local authority to grant or seek relief from such practice or to institute criminal proceedings with respect thereto upon receiving notice thereof, the Commission shall, before taking any action with respect to such charge, notify the appropriate State or local officials and, upon request, afford them a reasonable time, but not less than sixty days (provided that such sixty-day period shall be extended to one hundred and twenty days during the first year after the effective day of such State or local law), unless a shorter period is requested, to act under such State or local law to remedy the practice alleged.

(e) Time for filing charges; time for service of notice of charge on respondent; filing of charge by Commission with State or local agency; seniority system

(1) A charge under this section shall be filed within one hundred and eighty days after the alleged unlawful employment practice occurred and notice of the charge (including the date, place and circumstances of the alleged unlawful employment practice) shall be served upon the person against whom such charge is made within ten days thereafter, except that in a case of an unlawful employment practice with respect to which the person aggrieved has initially instituted proceedings with a State or local agency with authority to grant or seek relief from such practice or to institute criminal proceedings with respect thereto upon receiving notice thereof, such charge shall be filed by or on behalf of the person aggrieved within three hundred days after the alleged unlawful employment practice occurred, or within thirty days after receiving notice that the State or local agency has terminated the proceedings under the State or local law, whichever is earlier, and a copy of such charge shall be filed by the Commission with the State or local agency.

(2) For purposes of this section, an unlawful employment practice occurs, with respect to a seniority system that has been adopted for an intentionally discriminatory purpose in violation if this subchapter (whether or not that discriminatory purpose is apparent on the face of the seniority provision), when the seniority system is adopted, when an individual becomes subject to the seniority system, or when a person aggrieved is injured by the application of the seniority system or provision of the system.

(f) Civil action by Commission, Attorney General, or person aggrieved; preconditions; procedure; appointment of attorney; payment of fees, costs, or security; intervention; stay of Federal proceedings; action for appropriate temporary or preliminary relief pending final disposition of charge; jurisdiction and venue of United States courts; designation of judge to hear and determine case; assignment of case for hearing; expedition of case; appointment of master

(1) If within thirty days after a charge is filed with the Commission or within thirty days after expiration of any period of reference under subsection (c) or (d) or this section, the Commission has been unable to secure from the respondent a conciliation agreement acceptable to the Commission, the Commission may bring a civil action against any respondent not a government, governmental agency, or political subdivi-

sion named in the charge. In the case of a respondent which is a government, governmental agency, or political subdivision, if the Commission has been unable to secure from the respondent a conciliation agreement acceptable to the Commission, the Commission shall take no further action and shall refer the case to the Attorney General who may bring a civil action against such respondent in the appropriate United States district court. The person or persons aggrieved shall have the right to intervene in a civil action brought by the Commission or the Attorney General in a case involving a government, governmental agency, or political subdivision. If a charge filed with the Commission pursuant to subsection (b) of this section, is dismissed by the Commission, or if within one hundred and eighty days from the filing of such charge or the expiration of any period of reference under subsection (c) or (d) of this section, whichever is later, the Commission has not filed a civil action under this section or the Attorney General has not filed a civil action in a case involving a government, governmental agency, or political subdivision, or the Commission has not entered into a conciliation agreement to which the person aggrieved is a party, the Commission, or the Attorney General in a case involving a government, governmental agency, or political subdivision, shall so notify the person aggrieved and within ninety days after the giving of such notice a civil action may be brought against the respondent named in the charge (A) by the person claiming to be aggrieved or (B) if such charge was filed by a member of the Commission, by any person whom the charge alleges was aggrieved by the alleged unlawful employment practice. Upon application by the complainant and in such circumstances as the court may deem just, the court may appoint an attorney for such complainant and may authorize the commencement of the action without the payment of fees, costs, or security. Upon timely application, the court may, in its discretion, permit the Commission, or the Attorney General in a case involving a government, governmental agency, or political subdivision, to intervene in such civil action upon certification that the case is of general public importance. Upon request, the court may, in its discretion, stay further proceedings for not more than sixty days pending the termination of State or local proceedings described in subsection (c) or (d) of this section or further efforts of the Commission to obtain voluntary compliance.

(2) Whenever a charge is filed with the Commission and the Commission concludes on the basis of a preliminary investigation that prompt judicial action is necessary to carry out the purposes of this Act, the Commission, or the Attorney General in a case involving a government, governmental agency, or political subdivision, may bring an action for appropriate temporary or preliminary relief pending final disposition of such charge. Any temporary restraining order or other order granting preliminary or temporary relief shall be issued in accordance with rule 65 of the Federal Rules of Civil Procedure. It shall be the duty of a court having jurisdiction over proceedings under this section to assign cases for hearing at the earliest practicable date and to cause such cases to be in every way expedited.

(3) Each United States district court and each United States court of a place subject to the jurisdiction of the United States shall have jurisdiction of actions brought under this subchapter. Such an action may be brought in any judicial district in the State in which the unlawful employment practice is alleged to have been committed, in the judicial district in which the employment records relevant to such practice are maintained and administered, or in the judicial district in which the aggrieved person would have worked but for the alleged unlawful employment practice, but if the respondent is not found within any such district, such an action may be brought within the judicial district in which the respondent has his principal office. For purposes of title 28, the judicial district in which the respondent has his principal office shall in all

cases be considered a district in which the action might have been brought.

(4) It shall be the duty of the chief judge of the district (or in his absence, the acting chief judge) in which the case is pending immediately to designate a judge in such district to hear and determine the case. In the event that no judge in the district is available to hear and determine the case, the chief judge of the district, or the acting chief judge, as the case may be, shall certify this fact to the chief judge of the circuit (or in his absence, the acting chief judge) who shall then designate a district or circuit judge of the circuit to hear and determine the case.

(5) It shall be the duty of the judge designated pursuant to this subsection to assign the case for hearing at the earliest practicable date and to cause the case to be in every way expedited. If such judge has not scheduled the case for trial within one hundred and twenty days after issue has been joined, that judge may appoint a master pursuant to rule 53 of the Federal Rules of Civil Procedure.

(g) Injunctions; appropriate affirmative action; equitable relief; accrual of back pay; reduction of back pay; limitations on judicial orders

(1) If the court finds that the respondent has intentionally engaged in or is intentionally engaging in an unlawful employment practice charged in the complaint, the court may enjoin the respondent from engaging in such unlawful employment practice, and order such affirmative action as may be appropriate, which may include, but is not limited to, reinstatement or hiring of employees, with or without back pay (payable by the employer, employment agency, or labor organization, as the case may be, responsible for the unlawful employment practice), or any other equitable relief as the court deems appropriate. Back pay liability shall not accrue from a date more than two years prior to the filing of a charge with the Commission. Interim earnings or amounts earnable with reasonable diligence by the person or persons discriminated against shall operate to reduce the back pay otherwise allowable.

(2)(A) No order of the court shall require the admission or reinstatement of an individual as a member of a union, or the hiring, reinstatement, or promotion of an individual as an employee, or the payment to him of any back pay, if such individual was refused admission, suspended, or expelled, or was refused employment or advancement or was suspended or discharged for any reason other than discrimination on account of race, color, religion, sex, or national origin or in violation of this title.

(B) On a claim in which an individual proves a violation under this title and a respondent demonstrates that the respondent would have taken the same action in the absence of the impermissible motivating factor, the court—

(i) may grant declaratory relief, injunctive relief (except as provided in clause (ii)), and attorney's fees and costs demonstrated to be directly attributable only to the pursuit of a claim under this title; and

(ii) shall not award damages or issue an order requiring any admission, reinstatement, hiring, promotion, or payment, described in subparagraph (A).

(h) Provisions of title 29 not applicable to civil actions for prevention of unlawful practices

The provisions of title 29 shall not apply with respect to civil actions brought under this section.

(i) Proceedings by Commission to compel compliance with judicial orders

In any case in which an employer, employment agency, or labor organization fails to comply with an order of a court issued in a civil action brought under this section, the Commission may commence proceedings to compel compliance with such order.

(j) Appeals

Any civil action brought under this section and any proceedings brought under subsection (i) of this section shall be subject to appeal as provided in sections 1291 and 1292, title 28.

(k) Attorney's fee; liability of Commission and United States for costs

In any action or proceeding under this subchapter the court, in its discretion, may allow the prevailing party, other than the Commission or the United States, a reasonable attorney's fee (including expert fees) as part of the costs, and the Commission and the United States shall be liable for costs the same as a private person.

2000e-6. CIVIL ACTIONS BY THE ATTORNEY GENERAL

(a) Complaint

Whenever the Attorney General has reasonable cause to believe that any person or group of persons is engaged in a pattern or practice of resistance to the full enjoyment of any of the rights secured by this subchapter, and that the pattern or practice is of such a nature and is intended to deny the full exercise of the rights herein described, the Attorney General may bring a civil action in the appropriate district court of the United States by filing with it a complaint (1) signed by him (or in his absence the Acting Attorney General), (2) setting forth facts pertaining to such pattern or practice, and (3) requesting such relief, including an application for a permanent or temporary injunction, restraining order or other order against the person or persons responsible for such pattern or practice, as he deems necessary to insure the full enjoyment of the rights herein described.

(b) Jurisdiction; three-judge district court for cases of general public importance: hearing, determination, expedition of action, review by Supreme Court; single judge district court: hearing, determination, expedition of action

The district courts of the United States shall have and shall exercise jurisdiction of proceedings instituted pursuant to this section, and in any such proceeding the Attorney General may file with the clerk of such court a request that a court of three judges be convened to hear and determine the case. Such request by the Attorney General shall be accompanied by a certificate that, in his opinion, the case is of general public importance. A copy of the certificate and request for a three-judge court shall be immediately furnished by such clerk to the chief judge of the circuit (or in his absence, the presiding circuit judge of the circuit) in which the case is pending. Upon receipt of such request it shall be the duty of the chief judge of the circuit or the presiding circuit judge, as the case may be, to designate immediately three judges in such circuit, of whom at least one shall be a circuit judge and another of whom shall be a district judge of the court in which the proceeding was instituted, to hear and determine such case, and it shall be the duty of the judges so designated to assign the case for hearing at the earliest practicable date, to participate in the hearing and determination thereof, and to cause the case to be in every way expedited. An appeal from the final judgment of such court will lie to the Supreme Court.

In the event the Attorney General fails to file such a request in any such proceeding, it shall be the duty of the chief judge of the district (or in his absence, the acting chief judge) in which the case is pending immediately to designate a judge in such district to hear and determine the case. In the event that no judge in the district is available to hear and determine the case, the chief judge of the district, or the acting chief judge, as the case may be, shall certify this fact to the chief judge of the circuit (or in his absence, the acting chief judge) who shall then designate a district or circuit judge of the circuit to hear and determine the case.

It shall be the duty of the judge designated pursuant to this section to assign the case for hearing at the earliest practicable date and to cause the case to be in every way expedited.

(c) Transfer of functions, etc., to Commission; effective date; prerequisite to transfer; execution of functions by Commission

Effective two years after March 24, 1972, the functions of the Attorney General under this section shall be transferred to the Commission, together with such personnel, property, records, and unexpended balances of appropriations, allocations, and other funds employed, used, held, available, or to be made available in connection with such functions unless the President submits, and neither House of Congress vetoes, a reorganization plan pursuant to title 5, inconsistent with the provisions of this subsection. The Commission shall carry out such functions in accordance with subsections (d) and (e) of this section.

(d) Transfer of functions, etc., not to affect suits commenced pursuant to this section prior to date of transfer

Upon the transfer of functions provided for in subsection (c) of this section, in all suits commenced pursuant to this section prior to the date of such transfer, proceedings shall continue without abatement, all court orders and decrees shall remain in effect, and the Commission shall be substituted as a party for the United States of America, the Attorney General, or the Acting Attorney General, as appropriate.

(e) Investigation and action by Commission pursuant to filing of charge of discrimination; procedure

Subsequent to March 24, 1972, the Commission shall have authority to investigate and act on a charge of a pattern or practice of discrimination, whether filed by or on behalf of a person claiming to be aggrieved or by a member of the Commission. All such actions shall be conducted in accordance with the procedures set forth in this title.

2000e-7. EFFECT ON STATE LAWS

Nothing is this subchapter shall be deemed to exempt or relieve any person from any liability, duty, penalty, or punishment provided by any present or future law of any State or political subdivision of a State, other than any such law which purports to require or permit the doing of any act which would be an unlawful employment practice under this subchapter.

2000e-8. INVESTIGATIONS

(a) Examination and copying of evidence related to unlawful employment practices

In connection with any investigation of a charge filed under this title, the Commission or its designated representative shall at all reasonable times have access to, for the purposes of examination, and the right to copy any evidence of any person being investigated or proceeded against that relates to unlawful employment practices covered by this subchapter and is relevant to the charge under investigation.

(b) Cooperation with State and local agencies administering State fair employment practices laws; participation in and contribution to research and other projects; utilization of services; payment in advance or reimbursement; agreements and rescission of agreements

The Commission may cooperate with State and local agencies charged with the administration of State fair employment practices laws and, with the consent of such agencies, may, for the purpose of carrying out its functions and duties under this subchapter and within the limitation of funds appropriated specifically for such purpose, engage in and contribute to the cost of research and other projects of mutual interest undertaken by such agencies, and utilize the services of such agencies and their employees, and, notwithstanding any other provision of law, pay by advance or reimbursement such agencies and their employees for services rendered to assist the Commission in carrying out this subchapter. In furtherance of such cooperative efforts, the Commission may enter into written agreements with such State or local agencies and such agreements may include provisions under which the Commission shall refrain from processing a charge in any cases or class of cases specified in such agreements or under which the Commission shall relieve any person or class of persons in such State or locality from requirements imposed under this section. The Commission shall rescind any such agreement whenever it determines that the agreement no longer serves the interest of effective enforcement of this subchapter.

(c) Execution, retention, and preservation of records; reports to Commission; training program records; appropriate relief from regulation or order for undue hardship; procedure for exemption; judicial action to compel compliance

Every employer, employment agency, and labor organization subject to this subchapter shall (1) make and keep such records relevant to the determinations of whether unlawful employment practices have been or are being committed, (2) preserve such records for such periods, and (3) make such reports therefrom as the Commission shall prescribe by regulation or order, after public hearing, as reasonable, necessary, or appropriate for the enforcement of this subchapter or the regulations or orders thereunder. The Commission shall, by regulation, require each employer, labor organization, and joint labor-management committee subject to this subchapter which controls an apprenticeship or other training program to maintain such records as are reasonably necessary to carry out the purposes of this subchapter, including, but not limited to, a list of applicants who wish to participate in such program, including the chronological order in which applications were received, and to furnish to the Commission upon request, a detailed description of the manner in which persons are selected to participate in the apprenticeship or other training program. Any employer, employment agency, labor organization, or joint labor-management committee which believes that the application to it of any regulation or order issued under this section would result in undue hardship may apply to the Commission for an exemption from the application of such regulation or order, and, if such application for an exemption is denied, bring a civil action in the United States district court for the district where such records are kept. If the Commission or the court, as the case may be, finds that the application of the regulation or order to the employer, employment agency, or labor organization in question would impose an undue hardship, the Commission or the court, as the case may be, may grant appropriate relief. If any person required to comply with the provisions of this subsection fails or refuses to do so, the United States district court for the district in which such person is found, resides, or transacts business, shall, upon application of the Commission, or the Attorney General in a case involving a government, governmental agency or political subdivision, have jurisdiction to issue to such person an order requiring him to comply.

(d) Consultation and coordination between Commission and interested State and Federal agencies in prescribing recordkeeping and reporting requirements; availability of information furnished pursuant to recordkeeping and reporting requirements; conditions on availability

In prescribing requirements pursuant to subsection (c) of this section, the Commission shall consult with other interested State and Federal agencies and shall endeavor to coordinate its requirements with those adopted by such agencies. The Commission shall furnish upon request and without cost to any State or local agency charged with the administration of a fair employment practice law information obtained pursuant to subsection (c) of this section from any employer, employment agency, labor organization, or joint labor-management committee subject to the jurisdiction of such agency. Such information shall be furnished on condition that it not be made public by the recipient agency prior to the institution of a proceeding under State or local law involving such information. If this condition is violated by a recipient agency, the Commission may decline to honor subsequent requests pursuant to this subsection.

(e) Prohibited disclosures; penalties

It shall be unlawful for any officer or employee of the Commission to make public in any manner whatever any information obtained by the Commission pursuant to its authority under this section prior to the institution of any proceeding under this subchapter involving such information. Any officer or employee of the Commission who shall make public in any manner whatever any information in violation of this subsection shall be guilty, of a misdemeanor and upon conviction thereof, shall be fined not more than $1,000, or imprisoned not more than one year.

2000e-9. CONDUCT OF HEARINGS AND INVESTIGATIONS PURSUANT TO SECTION 161 OF TITLE 29.

For the purpose of all hearings and investigations conducted by the Commission or its duly authorized agents or agencies, title 29 shall apply.

2000e-10. POSTING OF NOTICES; PENALTIES

(a) Every employer, employment agency, and labor organization, as the case may be, shall post and keep posted in conspicuous places upon its premises where notices to employees, applicants for employment, and members are customarily posted a notice to be prepared or approved by the Commission setting forth excerpts, from, or summaries of, the pertinent provisions of this subchapter and information pertinent to the filing of a complaint.

(b) A willful violation of this section shall be punishable by a fine of not more than $100 for each separate offense. . . .

2000e-14. EQUAL EMPLOYMENT OPPORTUNITY COORDINATING COUNCIL; ESTABLISHMENT; COMPOSITION; DUTIES; REPORT TO PRESIDENT AND CONGRESS

The Equal Employment Opportunity Commission shall have the responsibility for developing and implementing agreements, policies and practices designed to maximize effort, promote efficiency, and eliminate conflict, competition, duplication and inconsistency among the operations, functions and jurisdictions of the various departments, agencies and branches of the Federal Government responsible for the implementation and enforcement of equal employment opportunity legislation, orders, and policies. On or before October 1 of each year, the Equal Employment Opportunity Commission shall transmit to the President and to the Congress a report of its activities, together with such recommendations for legislative or administrative changes as it concludes are desirable to further promote the purposes of this section. . . .

2000e-16. EMPLOYMENT BY FEDERAL GOVERNMENT

(a) Discriminatory practices prohibited; employees or applicants for employment subject to coverage

All personnel actions affecting employees or applicants for employment (except with regard to aliens employed outside the limits of the United States) in military departments as defined in title 5, in executive agencies as defined in title 5 (including employees and applicants for employment who are paid from nonappropriated funds), in the United States Postal Service and the Postal Rate Commission, in those units of the Government of the District of Columbia having positions in the competitive service, and in those units of the legislative and judicial branches of Federal Government having positions in the competitive service, and in the Library of Congress shall be made free from any discrimination based on race, color, religion, sex, or national origin.

(b) Equal Employment Opportunity Commission; enforcement powers; issuance of rules, regulations, etc.; annual review and approval of national and regional equal employment opportunity plans; review and evaluation of equal employment opportunity programs and publication of progress reports; consultations with interested parties; compliance with rules, regulations, etc.; contents of national and regional equal employment opportunity plans; authority of Librarian of Congress

Except as otherwise provided in this subsection, the Equal Employment Opportunity Commission shall have authority to enforce the provisions of subsection (a) of this section through appropriate remedies, including reinstatement or hiring of employees with or without back pay, as will effectuate the policies of this section, and shall issue such rules, regulations, orders and instructions as it deems necessary and appropriate to carry out its responsibilities under this section. The Equal Employment Opportunity Commission shall—

(1) be responsible for the annual review and approval of a national and regional equal employment opportunity plan which each department and agency and each appropriate unit referred to in subsection (a) of this section shall submit in order to maintain an affirmative program of equal employment opportunity for all such employees and applicants for employment;

(2) be responsible for the review and evaluation of the operation of all agency equal employment opportunity programs, periodically obtaining and publishing (on at least a semiannual basis) progress reports from each such department, agency, or unit; and

(3) consult with and solicit the recommendations of interested individuals, groups, and organizations relating to equal employment opportunity. The head of each such department, agency, or unit shall comply with such rules, regulations, orders, and instructions which shall include a provision that an employee or applicant for employment shall be notified of any final action taken on any complaint of discrimination filed by him thereunder.

The plan submitted by each department, agency, and unit shall include, but not be limited to—

(1) provision for the establishment of training and education programs designed to provide a maximum opportunity for employees to advance so as to perform at their highest potential; and

(2) a description of the qualifications in terms of training and experience relating to equal employment opportunity for the principal and operating officials of each such department, agency, or unit responsible for carrying out the equal employment opportunity program and of the allocation of personnel and resources proposed by such department, agency, or unit to carry out its equal employment opportunity program. With respect to employment in the Library of Congress, authorities granted in this subsection to the Equal Employment Opportunity Commission shall be exercised by the Librarian of Congress.

(c) Civil action by employee or applicant for employment for redress of grievances; time for bringing of action; head of department, agency, or unit as defendant

Within 90 days of receipt of notice of final action taken by a department, agency, or unit referred to in subsection (a) of this section, or by the Equal Employment Opportunity Commission upon an appeal from a decision or order of such department, agency, or unit on a complaint of discrimination based on race, color, religion, sex or national origin, brought pursuant to subsection (a) of this section, Executive Order 11478 or any succeeding Executive orders, or after one hundred and eighty days from the filing of the initial charge with the department, agency, or unit or with the Equal Employment Opportunity Commission on appeal from a decision or order of such department, agency, or unit until such time as final action may be taken by a department, agency, or unit, an employee or applicant for employment, if aggrieved by the final disposition of his complaint, or by the failure to take final action on his complaint, may file a civil action as provided in this title, in which civil action the head of the department, agency, or unit, as appropriate, shall be the defendant.

(d) The provisions of this title, as applicable, shall govern civil actions brought hereunder, and the same interest to compensate for delay in payment shall be available as in cases involving nonpublic parties.

(e) Government agency or official not relieved of responsibility to assure nondiscrimination in employment or equal employment opportunity

Nothing contained in this Act shall relieve any Government agency or official of its or his primary responsibility to assure nondiscrimination in employment as required by the Constitution and statutes or of its or his responsibilities under Executive Order 11478 related to equal employment opportunity in the Federal Government.

2000e-17. PROCEDURE FOR DENIAL, WITHHOLDING, TERMINATION, OR SUSPENSION OF GOVERNMENT CONTRACT SUBSEQUENT TO ACCEPTANCE BY GOVERNMENT OF AFFIRMATIVE ACTION PLAN OF EMPLOYER; TIME OF ACCEPTANCE OF PLAN

No Government contract, or portion thereof, with any employer, shall be denied, withheld, terminated, or suspended, by any agency or officer of the United States under any equal employment opportunity law or order, where such employer has an affirmative action plan which has previously been accepted by the Government for the same facility within the past twelve months without first according such employer full hearing and adjudication under the provisions of title 5, and the following pertinent sections: Provided, That if such employer has deviated substantially from such previously agreed to affirmative action plan, this section shall not apply: Provided further, That for the purposes of this section an affirmative action plan shall be deemed to have been accepted by the Government at the time the appropriate compliance agency has accepted such plan unless within forty-five days thereafter the Office of Federal Contract Compliance has disapproved such plan.

Civil Rights Act of 1991

DAMAGES IN CASES OF INTENTIONAL DISCRIMINATION IN EMPLOYMENT

Sec 1977A

(a) Right of Recovery.—

(1) Civil Rights.—In an action brought by a complaining party under section 706 or 717 of the Civil Rights Act of 1964 against a respondent who engaged in unlawful intentional discrimination (not an employment practice that is unlawful because of its disparate impact) prohibited under section 703, 704, or 717 of the Act, and provided that the complaining party cannot recover under section 1977 of the Revised Statutes (42 U.S.C. 1981), the complaining party may recover compensatory and punitive damages as allowed in subsection (b), in addition to any relief authorized by section 706(g) of the Civil Rights Act of 1964, from the respondent.

(2) Disability.—In an action brought by a complaining party under the powers, remedies, and procedures set forth in section 706 or 717 of the Civil Rights Act of 1964 (as provided in section 107(a) of the Americans with Disabilities Act of 1990, and section 505(a)(1) of the Rehabilitation Act of 1973, respectively) against a respondent who engaged in unlawful intentional discrimina-

tion (not an employment practice that is unlawful because of its disparate impact) under section 501 of the Rehabilitation Act of 1973 and the regulations implementing section 501, or who violated the requirements of section 501 of the Act or the regulations implementing section 501 concerning the provision of a reasonable accommodation, or section 102 of the Americans with Disabilities Act of 1990, or committed a violation of section 102(b)(5) of the Act, against an individual, the complaining party may recover compensatory and punitive damages as allowed in subsection (b), in addition of any relief authorized by section 706(g) of the Civil Rights Act of 1964, from the respondent.

(3) Reasonable accommodation and good faith effort.—In cases where a discriminatory practice involves the provision of a reasonable accommodation pursuant to section 102(b)(5) of the Americans with Disabilities Act of 1990 or regulations implementing section 501 of the Rehabilitation Act of 1973, damages may not be awarded under this section where the covered entity demonstrates good faith efforts, in consultation with the person with the disability who has informed the covered entity that accommodation is needed, to identify and make a reasonable accommodation that would not cause an undue hardship on the operation of the business.

(b) Compensatory and Punitive Damages.—

(1) Determination of Punitive Damages.—A complaining party may recover punitive damages under this section against a respondent (other than a government, government agency or political subdivision) if the complaining party demonstrates that the respondent engaged in a discriminatory practice or discriminatory practices with malice or with reckless indifference to the federally protected rights of an aggrieved individual.

(2) Exclusions from Compensatory Damages.—Compensatory damages awarded under this section shall not include backpay, interest on backpay, or any other type of relief authorized under section 706(g) of the Civil Rights Act of 1964.

(3) Limitations.—The sum of the amount of compensatory damages awarded under this section for future pecuniary losses, emotional pain, suffering, inconvenience, mental anguish, loss of enjoyment of life, and other nonpecuniary losses, and the amount of punitive damages awarded under this section, shall not exceed, for each complaining party—

(A) in the case of a respondent who has more than 14 and fewer than 101 employees in each of 20 or more calendar weeks in the current or preceding calendar year, $50,000;

(B) in the case of a respondent who has more than 100 and fewer than 201 employees in each of 20 or more calendar weeks in the current or preceding calendar year, $100,000; and

(C) in the case of a respondent who has more than 200 and fewer than 501 employees in each of 20 or more calendar weeks in the current or preceding calendar year, $200,000; and

(D) in the case of a respondent who has more than 500 employees in each of 20 or more calendar weeks in the current or preceding calendar year, $300,000.

Section 1981, Equal Rights Under the Law

(a) All persons within the jurisdiction of the United States shall have the same right in every State and Territory to make and enforce contracts, to sue, be parties, give evidence, and to the full and equal benefit of all laws and proceedings for the security of persons and property as is enjoyed by white citizens, and shall be subject to like punishment, pains, penalties, taxes, licenses, and exactions of every kind, and to no order.

(b) For purposes of this section, the term "make and enforce contracts" includes the making, performance, modification, and termination of contracts, and the enjoyment of all benefits, privileges, terms, and conditions of the contractual relationship.

(c) The rights protected by this section are protected against impairment by nongovernmental discrimination and impairment under color of State law.

Glass Ceiling Act of 1991

FINDING AND PURPOSE

Section 202. (a) findings.—Congress finds that—

(1) despite a dramatically growing presence in the workplace, women and minorities remain underrepresented in management and decisionmaking positions in business;

(2) artificial barriers exist to the advancement of women and minorities in the workplace;

(3) United States corporations are increasingly relying on women and minorities to meet employment requirements and are increasingly aware of the advantages derived from a diverse work force;

(4) the "Glass Ceiling Initiative" undertaken by the Department of Labor, including the release of the report entitled "Report on the Glass Ceiling Initiative," has been instrumental in raising public awareness of—

(A) the underrepresentation of women and minorities at the management and decisionmaking levels in the United States work force;

(B) the underrepresentation of women and minorities in line functions in the United States work force;

(C) the lack of access for qualified women and minorities to credential-building developmental opportunities; and

(D) the desirability of eliminating artificial barriers to the advancement of women and minorities to such levels;

(5) the establishment of a commission to examine issues raised by the "Glass Ceiling Initiative" would help—

(A) focus greater attention on the importance of eliminating artificial barriers to the advancement of women and minorities to management and decisionmaking positions in business; and

(B) promote work force diversity;

(6) a comprehensive study that includes analysis of the manner in which management and decisionmaking positions are filed, the developmental and skill-enhancing practices used to foster the necessary qualifications for advancement, and the compensation programs and reward structures utilized in the corporate sector would assist in the establishment of practices and policies promoting opportunities for, and eliminating artificial barriers to, the advancement of women and minorities to management and decisionmaking positions; and

(7) a national award recognizing employers whose practices and policies promote opportunities for, and eliminate artificial barriers to, the advancement of women and minorities will foster the advancement of women and minorities into higher level positions by—

(A) helping to encourage United States companies to modify practices and polices to promote opportunities for, and eliminate artificial barriers to, the upward mobility of women and minorities; and

(B) providing specific guidance for other United States employers that wish to learn how to revise practices and policies to improve the access and employment opportunities of women and minorities.

(b) Purpose.—The purpose of this title is to establish—

(1) a Glass Ceiling Commission to study—

(A) the manner in which business fills management and decisionmaking positions;

(B) the developmental and skill-enhancing practices used to foster the necessary qualifications for advancement into such positions; and

(C) the compensation programs and reward structures currently utilized in the workplace; and

(2) an annual award for excellence in promoting a more diverse skilled work

force at the management and decisionmaking levels in business.

ESTABLISHMENT OF GLASS CEILING COMMISSION

Section 203. (a) In general.—There is established a Glass Ceiling Commission (referred to in this title as the "Commission"), to conduct a study and prepare recommendations concerning—

(1) eliminating artificial barriers to the advancement of women and minorities; and

(2) increasing the opportunities and developmental experiences of women and minorities to foster advancement of women and minorities to management and decisionmaking positions in business.

RESEARCH ON ADVANCEMENT OF WOMEN AND MINORITIES TO MANAGEMENT AND DECISION POSITIONS IN BUSINESS

Section 204. (a) Advancement Study.—The Commission shall conduct a study of opportunities for, and artificial barriers to, the advancement of women and minorities to management and decisionmaking positions in business. In conducting the study, the Commission shall—

(1) examine the preparedness of women and minorities to advance to management and decisionmaking positions in business;

(2) examine the opportunities for women and minorities to advance to management and decisionmaking positions in business;

(3) conduct basic research into the practices, policies, and manner in which management and decisionmaking positions in business are filed;

(4) conduct comparative research of business and industries in which women and minorities are promoted to management and decisionmaking positions, and business and industries in which women and minorities are not promoted to management and decisionmaking positions;

(5) compile a synthesis of available research on programs and practices that have successfully led to the advancement of women and minorities to management and decisionmaking positions in business, including training programs, reward programs, employee benefit structures, and family leave policies; and

(6) examine any other issues and information relating to the advancement of women and minorities to management and decisionmaking positions in business.

(b) Report.—Not later than 15 months after the date of enactment of this Act, the Commission shall prepare and submit to the President and the appropriate committees of Congress a written report containing—

(1) the findings and conclusions of the Commission resulting from the study conducted under subsection (a); and

(2) recommendations based on the findings and conclusions described in paragraph (1) relating to the promotion of opportunities for, and elimination of artificial barriers to, the advancement of women and minorities to management and decisionmaking positions in business, including recommendations for—

(A) policies and practices to fill vacancies at the management and decisionmaking levels;

(B) developmental practices and procedures to ensure that women and minorities have access to opportunities to gain the exposure, skills, and expertise necessary to assume management and decisionmaking positions;

(C) compensation programs to reward structures utilized to reward and retain key employees; and

(D) the use of enforcement (including such enforcement techniques as litigation, complaint investigations, compliance reviews, conciliation, administrative regulations, policy guidance, technical assistance, training, and public education) of federal agencies as a means of eliminating artificial barriers to the advancement of women and minorities in employment.

(c) Additional Study.—The Commission may conduct such additional study of the advancement of women and minorities to management and decisionmaking positions in business as a majority of the members of the Commission determines to be necessary.

CHAPTER 9

Affirmative Action

INTRODUCTION

Affirmative action attempts to achieve equal employment opportunity by actively selecting minorities and women where they have been underrepresented in the workforce. Although affirmative action programs are considered temporary, many remain in force for a long time until equilibrium is achieved. To determine whether an affirmative action program is needed, a number of factors must be considered: the minority population of the area and their percentage of the total population in the area; the number of minorities employed and unemployed, together with their respective percentages; the skills of the minority; the labor pool; the amount of training the employer can reasonably undertake; and the availability of other minorities or women in the organization who can be promoted or transferred. The same criteria are considered in determining the need for an affirmative action program for women. After procedures are in place, the goals must be achieved following reasonable timetables. The rate of success must be measured.

In the case that follows, a white employee received a promotion over a black employee. The black male alleged that he had been the victim of racial discrimination because the promotion was not made in accordance with the employer's affirmative action plan.

CASE

Lawson v. Dept. of Health and Hospitals

618 So.2d 1002 (La.App. 1 Cir. 1993)

WATKINS, Judge.

Earl Lawson, Jr., appellant, was employed by the Louisiana Department of Health and Hospitals (DHH) at Central Louisiana State Hospital and was serving with permanent status as a DHH Police Lieutenant when a position for Police Chief at the hospital became open in October of 1990. Although he was considered by the hospital's committee that interviewed candidates for the position, Mr. Lawson did not receive the promotion to Police Chief. Thereafter he appealed to the State Civil Service Commission (Commission), and he was granted a hearing before a civil service referee. On his appeal to the Commission, and again to this court, Mr. Lawson complained that he was denied the promotion and not selected to fill the vacancy as DHH Police Chief at the hospital solely because of his race.

On appeal to the Civil Service Commission Mr. Lawson argued that the denial was a violation by DHH of La. Cont. Art. I, Sec. 3 and 12, La. Const. Art. 10, 8, and Civil Service Rule 14.1(a). As relief, Mr. Lawson sought to have the position of DHH Police Chief vacated, to have the application process reopened, and to have the position filled in accordance with the Affirmative Action Plan for the hospital and the civil service rules. The Commission concluded that appellant failed to bear his burden of proving that the denial of promotion to Police Chief was based on prohibited discrimination or violations of civil service rules.

Mr. Lawson served as coordinator for the security department of the Central Louisiana State Hospital (CLSH) for six months during the illness of the previous Police Chief. When applications for the vacancy were accepted, Mr. Lawson ranked first on the promotional certificate of eligibles issued by the Department of State Civil Service and third on the probational certificate.

Insisting that he was discriminated against, appellant points to the fact that two of the top three eligibles on the probational certificate were black, but that the caucasian, Samuel J. Mayeux, Jr., was selected. Mr. Mayeux was second on the probational certificate, and he had a score of 86, one point higher than Mr. Lawson's score. The civil service referee found for a fact that no evidence was presented that Mr. Mayeux was not qualified for the position.

Mr. Lawson also notes that he was interviewed by a five-member, all white committee appointed by the hospital's associate administrator and that the committee was not refereed according to the hospital's Affirmative Action Plan. It is undisputed that in the hospital's Affirmative Action Plan, the position of DHH Police Chief falls within Group 4-A, specialty staff consisting of one black male, one white female, and nine white males; the group bears the label: "underutilization of minority employees."

Acknowledging that the Affirmative Action Plan was not considered, the Commission, through its referee, concluded that appellant presented no evidence that racial bias or prejudice affected the results of the selection process for Police Chief. The referee pointed out that appellant neither alleged nor proved that the questions asked during the interview were designed to disadvantage a minority applicant such as himself, nor that any member of the selection committee exhibited a predisposition against him either before, during, or after the interview.

Promotions do not take place automatically or as a matter of right. The appointing authority has much discretion in choosing employees properly certified as eligible, and the appointing authority may pass over a name on the eligible list.

The mere fact that there are few or no females or minority persons in supervisory positions does not constitute proof of sexual or racial discrimination. This court previously has pointed out that statistical evidence, such as the number of minorities in certain positions, is proper evidence for cases brought pursuant to Title VII of the United States Code, but such evidence is not sufficient to meet an employee's burden of proof of discrimination under Louisiana law. Title VII actions provide a remedy entirely distinct from that afforded by state civil service appeals. A plaintiff who wishes to rely on Title VII must first file a charge with the Equal Employment Opportunities Commission and give that body a chance to attempt to obtain voluntary compliance with the statue.

Thus, in the instant case, Mr. Lawson's use of the statistical data of the hospital's Affirmative Action Plan as the major support for his charge of discrimination might be appropriate for a Title VII claim; however, raw data does not prove discrimination under the Louisiana Constitution and the civil service rules.

Accordingly, we conclude the appointing authority made the appointment of Police Chief on the basis of race-neutral criteria, and we decline to disturb the decision.

Likewise, we find no merit in the appellant's argument that the appointing authority failed to consider his length of service when making its selection from the list of candidates. Appellant overlooks the fact that the Constitution provides that length of service is one of the elements to be used by the appropriate civil service department in compiling the certificates of eligibility. There is nothing in the record to indicate that appellant's length of service was not used in calculating his "score" for purposes of the eligibility certificates. The appointing authority's discretion in making the appointment is not limited by the constitutional provision because length of service has received proper consideration.

Accordingly, we affirm the decision of the Commission.
Judgment for Dept. of Health and Hospitals.

The concept of affirmative action first arose out of an Executive Order promulgated by President Lyndon Johnson in 1964. It provided that contractors who were supplying goods or services to the federal government were required to take an affirmative action, that employees are to be hired without regard to race, color, religion, sex, or national origin, and that once selected, promotion, compensation, training and termination are made without discrimination. Subcontractors hired by federal contractors were held to the same standards.

Those federal contractors whose employees were underrepresented with regard to women and minorities were forced to correct that injustice by developing an affirmative action plan designed to hire and/or promote more women and minorities.

Employment Perspective

Blackwell Enterprises is a federal contractor located in the city of Atlanta, which employs one hundred workers, ten of whom are minorities. The minority population of the city of Atlanta is approximately 50 percent. Will Blackwell jeopardize its federal contracts because of the underrepresentation of minorities in its workforce? Yes, unless it establishes an affirmative action plan designed to increase the number of minorities hired! How should this plan be designed? Blackwell may create a plan that for every three new positions that become open, two must be filled by qualified minorities. Thus, when the first position becomes available, if there is a qualified minority applicant, he or she will receive the job. With the second position, if there are no qualified minority applicants, a white person may be hired; but then preference will be given to the minority applicant for the third position. ◆

What if an employer is having difficulty finding qualified minority candidates? The employer must make every effort to locate potential candidates through advertisement in newspapers that are likely to be read by minorities. The employer must also contact employment agencies who service minority job-seekers. The burden is on the employer to put the word out in the minority community.

Employment Perspective

The CPA firm of Glick, Worthington and Sutherland has 50 accountants and 150 staff members. The latter includes administrative assistants, typists, and file clerks. During tax season, the firm's accountants put in 80 plus hour workweeks. For this reason, the firm refuses to hire women during their child bearing years. Women accountants claim this provision creates a disparate impact on young women. Is this correct? Yes! The Court will impose an order on the CPA firm to establish an affirmative action plan to hire female accountants during their child bearing years. If females make up 40% of accountants, then a plan to hire two out of three will suffice. Does the firm have to discharge men and replace them with women? No! The entire injustice does not have to be remedied immediately, as long as the process begins in a timely manner. As long as an affirmative action plan is implemented as the accounting firm expands or as existing accountants leave, justice is served. ◆

TITLE VII VIOLATORS

Those employers who have intentionally discriminated or who have been guilty of creating an employee environment where a disparate impact exists against a class of people of race, color, religion, sex, or national origin, may receive a court order to establish an affirmative action plan to remedy the discrimination.

Employment Perspective

Fredericks Meat Packing in Kansas City has 150 managers and 500 workers. Minority employees consist of 400 workers and no managers, although the population of Kansas City is approximately one-third minority. A claim is registered with the EEOC against Fredericks for discrimination. The EEOC files suit in Federal District Court and secures a judgment. How will the court remedy this injustice? The District Court will issue a court order mandating Fredericks to establish an affirmative action plan to increase the number of minority managers to reflect more adequately the percentage of minorities in the Kansas City population. This plan may be achieved either through recruitment or promotion. ◆

Voluntary Action

Rather than wait for potential lawsuits to force the correction of Title VII violations, many employers instituted their own voluntary plans. In many instances quotas were instituted to increase the number of women and minorities; the quotas require a set number of women and minorities to be hired. In effect, if qualified applicants cannot be found, unqualified ones must be hired. Quotas are not mandated by law and are thought to be necessary only where the racial imbalance is severe and has been intentionally disregarded. Although the word *quota* sparks controversy, it seems that every plan designed must have a goal of some fraction or percentage allocating two out of three or 60 percent of new hirings or promotions. This would appear to be equivalent to a quota, but strictly speaking it is not.

Affirmative action plans require that only qualified women and minorities have to be hired, unlike quotas where the hiring is done without regard to qualification. If there are no qualified women or minorities, white males may be hired in their place. But as mentioned earlier, the employer must make every effort to attempt to locate qualified women and minority applicants.

Affirmative action plans are designed to address manifest imbalances in the racial makeup of the work force. Once the imbalance is eradicated, the affirmative action plan will be discontinued. Affirmative action plans are not designed to remain indefinitely to maintain equilibrium. If a discrepancy occurs in the future, then the affirmative action plan can be put into effect again.

Affirmative action plans do not place existing employees in jeopardy regarding termination or disciplinary action; which must be applied equally to all employees. However, it is lawful for an employer to hire qualified women and minorities over white men who are more qualified. The key is that the women and minorities must be qualified.

Employment Perspective

Express Airlines requires that applicants who wish to be considered for the job of pilot must have completed 750 hours of air flight-training. Currently, Express employs 100 pilots, none of whom are women or minorities. Express then implements an affirmative action program. The next 5 openings are filled by 2 women, 2 minorities, and 1 white male. There were 15 qualified applicants. The women and minorities chosen were among them. Although the women and minorities selected were not among the top 5 persons most qualified, they were chosen to fulfill the affirmative action plan. Is this lawful? Yes, because they were qualified! If they had not been qualified, Express would have been justified in hiring all white male employees, as long as its requirement met the strict standard of being a business necessity. ◆

The following case addresses the question of whether a private employer and a union can in a collective bargaining agreement provide for an affirmative action plan. The plan reserved 50 percent of the openings for black applicants until the racial makeup of the workplace was indicative of the local community.

United Steelworkers of America v. Weber

443 U.S. 193 (1978)

Mr. JUSTICE BRENNAN delivered the opinion of the Court.

Challenged here is the legality of an affirmative action plan—collectively bargained by an employer and a union—that reserves for black employees 50 percent of the openings in an in-plant craft-training until the percentage of black craftworkers in the plant is commensurate with the percentage of blacks in the local labor force. The question for decision is whether Congress in Title VII of the Civil Rights Act of 1964, left employers and unions in the private sector free to take such race-conscious steps to eliminate manifest racial imbalances in traditionally segregated job categories. We hold that Title VII does not prohibit such race-conscious affirmative action plans.

In 1974, petitioner United Steelworkers of America (USWA) and petitioner Kaiser Aluminum & Chemical Corp. (Kaiser) entered into a master collective-bargaining agreement covering terms and conditions of employment at 15 Kaiser plants. The agreement contained an affirmative action plan designed to eliminate conspicuous racial imbalances in Kaiser's then almost exclusively white craftwork forces. Black crafthiring goals were set for each Kaiser plant equal to the percentage of blacks in the respective local labor forces. To enable plants to meet these goals, on-the-job training programs were established to teach unskilled production workers—black and white—the skills necessary to become craftworkers. The plan reserved for black employees 50 percent of the openings in these newly created in-plant training programs.

This case arose from the operation of the plan at Kaiser's plant in Gramercy, La. Until 1974, Kaiser hired as craft-workers for that plant only persons who had had prior craft experience. Because blacks had long been excluded from craft unions, few were able to present such credentials. As a consequence, prior to 1974 only 1.83 percent (5 out of 273) of the skilled craftworkers at the Gramercy plant were black, even though the work force in the Gramercy area was approximately 39 percent black.

Pursuant to the national agreement Kaiser altered its craft-hiring practice in the Gramercy plant. Rather than hiring already trained outsiders, Kaiser established a training program to train its production workers to fill craft openings. Selection of craft trainees was made on the basis of seniority, with the proviso that at least 50 percent of the new trainers were to be black until the percentage of black skilled craftworkers in the Gramercy plant approximated the percentage of blacks in the local labor force.

During 1974, the first year of the operation of the Kaiser-USWA affirmative action plan, 13 craft trainees were selected from Gramercy's production work force. Of these, seven were black and six white. The most senior black selected into the program had less seniority than several white production workers whose bids for admission were rejected. Thereafter one of those white production workers, respondent Brian Weber (hereafter respondent), instituted this class action in the United States District Court for the Eastern District of Louisiana.

The complaint alleged that the filling of craft trainee positions at the Gramercy plant pursuant to the affirmative action program had resulted in junior black employees' receiving training in preference to senior white employees, thus discriminating against respondent and other similarly situated white employees in violation of Section 703 (a) and (d) of Title VII. The District Court entered a judgment in favor of the plaintiff class, and granted a permanent injunction prohibiting Kaiser and the USWA "from denying plaintiffs, Brian F. Weber and all other members of the class, access to on-the-job training programs on the basis of race." A divided panel of the Court of Appeals for the Fifth Circuit affirmed, holding that all employment preferences based upon race, including those preferences incidental to bona fide affirmative action plans, violated Title VII's prohibition against racial discrimination in employment. We granted certiorari. We reverse.

We emphasize at the outset the narrowness of our inquiry. Since the Kaiser-USWA plan does not involve state action, this case does not present an alleged violation of the Equal Protection Clause of the Fourteenth Amendment. Further, since the Kaiser-USWA plan was adopted voluntarily, we are not concerned with what Title VII requires or with what a court might order to remedy a past proved violation of the Act. The only question before us is the narrow statutory issue of whether Title VII forbids private employers and unions from voluntarily agreeing upon bona fide affirmative action plans that accord racial preferences in the manner and for the purpose provided in the Kaiser-USWA plan.

Congress' primary concern in enacting the prohibition against racial discrimination in Title VII of the Civil Rights Act of 1964 was with "the plight of the Negro in our economy." Before 1964, blacks were largely relegated to "unskilled and semi-skilled jobs." Because of automation the number of such jobs was rapidly decreasing. As a consequence, "the relative position of the Negro worker was steadily worsening. In 1947 the nonwhite unemployment rate was 64 percent higher than the white rate; in 1962 it was 124 percent higher." As Senator Humphrey explained to the Senate:

> "What good does it do a Negro to be able to eat in a fine restaurant if he cannot afford to pay the bill? What good does it do him to be accepted in a hotel that is too expensive for his modest income? How can a Negro child be motivated to take full advantage of intergrated educational facilities if he has no hope of getting a job where he can use that education?
>
> "Without a job, one cannot afford public convenience and accommodations. Income from employment may be necessary to further a man's education, or that of his children. If his children have no hope of getting a good job, what will motivate them to take advantage of educational opportunities?"

These remarks echoed President Kennedy's original message to Congress upon the introduction of the Civil Rights Act in 1963:

> "There is little value in a Negro's obtaining the right to be admitted to hotels and restaurants if he has no cash in his pocket and no job."

Accordingly, it was clear to Congress that the crux of the problem was to open employment opportunities for Negroes in occupations which have been traditionally closed to them and it was to this problem that Title VII's prohibition against racial discrimination in employment was primarily addressed.

Clearly, a prohibition against all voluntary, race conscious, affirmative action efforts would disserve these ends. We therefore hold that Title VII's prohibition in section 703(a) and (d) against racial discrimination does not condemn all private, voluntary, race-conscious affirmative action plans.

We need not today define in detail the line of demarcation between permissible and impermissible affirmative action plans. It suffices to hold that the challenged Kaiser-USWA affirmative action plan falls on the permissible side of the line. The purposes of the plan mirror those of the statute. Both were designed to break down old patterns of racial segregation and hierarchy. Both were structured to "open employment opportunities for Negroes in occupations which have been traditionally closed to them."

At the same time, the plan does not unnecessarily trammel the interest of the white employees. The plan does not require the discharge of white workers and their replacement. Nor does the plan create an absolute bar to the advancement of white employees; half of those trained in the program will be white. Moreover, the plan is a temporary measure; it is not intended to maintain racial balance, but simply to eliminate a manifest racial imbalance.

Judgment for United Steelworkers
of America.

HISTORY OF AFFIRMATIVE ACTION

Equal employment opportunity had its roots in a series of executives orders and acts. In 1940, President Roosevelt issued Executive Order 8587, which prohibited the denial of public employment based on race. Several orders and acts followed that were designed to prohibit other forms of discrimination in public employment, such as on the basis of religion and color. The emphasis was on what the administrative agencies could *not* do. There was no mandate as to what they *should* do.

1955 marked the beginning of a transformation from passive to active programs. In Executive Order 10050, President Eisenhower stipulated, " . . . it is the policy of the United States Government that equal opportunity be afforded all qualified persons, consistent with law, for employment in the Federal Government." Equal employment opportunity was formally recognized and confirmed by President Kennedy in 1961; Executive Order 10925 called for ". . . . positive measures for the elimination of any discrimination, direct or indirect, which now exist."

In 1965, President Johnson, through Executive Order 11246, placed the responsibility for equal employment opportunity with the Civil Service Commission. Johnson followed that in 1967 with Executive Order 11375 that added sex discrimination. However, it was not until 1969 that affirmative action was used to address the problem of those seeking employment as well as those stuck in low-level positions.

President Nixon's Executive Order 11478 issued in 1969 provided that equal employment opportunity " . . . applies to and must be made an integral part of every aspect of personnel policy and practice in the employment, development, advancement and treatment of civilian employees of the Federal Government." It also set forth the procedure for affirmative action, as well as the requirement for training programs to enable low-level employees to gain the experience necessary to be eligible for upper-level positions.

The Executive Order resulted in the Equal Employment Opportunity Act of 1972.

EQUAL EMPLOYMENT OPPORTUNITY ACT

This was the first major amendment to Title VII of the 1964 Civil Right Act. The Act provided the Civil Service Commission with the power to address all federal employment issues and to remedy injustices with reinstatement and back pay. Each agency director was required to apply the law. The Equal Employment Opportunity Act of 1972 states that all employment decisions " . . . shall be made free from any discrimination based on race, creed, color, religion, sex, or national origin."

To insure compliance, evaluation will be made and record-keeping will be required on the employment of women and minorities. " . . . nothing contained in the act shall relieve any Government agency or official of its or his primary responsibility to assure non-discrimination in employment as required by the Constitution and statutes or its or his responsibility under Executive Order 11478 relating to equal employment opportunity in the Federal Government."

Each administrative agency, as well as each department within the agency, was required to set forth an affirmative action plan. This was even required to be done on regional basis to help the Civil Service Commission identify areas in need of particular attention. Agencies were required to develop education and training programs geared to aiding its employees achieve their greatest potential. To implement these programs, agencies were required to secure qualified personnel to administer these programs. Program content and personnel size and competency were both subject to scrutiny by the Civil Service Commission. On-site inspections were conducted routinely. After annual review, the Civil Service Commission would publish reports on each agency's progress. Employees were encouraged to file complaints if they have not been afforded an equal employment opportunity. The Commission would reach a resolution after investigation. If dissatisfied with the resolution, access to the courts was now available to an aggrieved employee. Court decisions over time have developed a body of case law, which now provide legal precedent in certain areas of employment discrimination (i.e., the U.S. Supreme Court decisions of *Griggs v. Duke Power Co.* and *McDonnell Douglas Corp. v. Green*).

Agencies were required to administer Skill Utilization Surveys to identify the skill that each employee had and to determine whether those skills were being utilized. Nonutilization of a skill may be grounds for an adaptation of the current job or a transfer or a promotion of that employee to a job in which the skill will be more fully utilized. An illustrative questionnaire was given to all employees for purposes of eliciting meaningful responses regarding their skills. Then the supervisors were asked to evaluate each response to determine whether the skills were being utilized in the current job and whether they could be utilized there or at another position within the agency.

Many deficiencies were noted by the Civil Service Commission in reviewing the affirmative action plans of the administrative agencies. These included lack of specificity in the development of employment opportunities, failure to file timely reports, refusal to set timetables for achievement of plan goals, many generalized statements, inadequate and inexperienced personnel devoted to the plan, and relegating employment and supervision to human resource departments rather than integrating them throughout the agency.

The Civil Service Commission redefined its mandate to correct these deficiencies. In developing the plan, the commission called for agencies to file an assessment report to single out departments where access had been denied or rarely given to women and minorities. Consultation with women and minority groups was strongly suggested for the valuable input they could give. Next, specific remedies were required to address the problems identified in the assessment report. Each department was to tailor the plan to meet its respective needs. Timetables were then required to be attached to each plan of action to monitor progress and ultimately resolution. Although the plans permitted flexibility, movement toward the goal was necessary. These plans would then be reviewed by the Commission annually, and agency directors would be called to explain noncompliance.

A breakdown of the composition of women and minorities for each department and each grade level in the administrative agency should be an integral part of the assessment. The percentage of women and minorities in maintenance, clerical, managerial, technical, and professional areas should also be included. Once jobs become available, each agency should endeavor to discover those women and minorities in their workforce who have the capability for advancement. In addition, agencies should seek out potential recruiting venues for women and minority employment candidates.

Discriminatory complaints must be grouped according to job category and grade level. Solutions should be proposed for reoccurring complaints, while unique dilemmas must be handled on an ad hoc basis. The goal of an affirmative action plan is not an instantaneous resolution, but one of constant movement toward the accomplishment of equal opportunity in employment for all.

With the assessment report in hand, specific actions can be taken. Expeditious resolution of discriminatory complaints is the key toward ensuring that women and minorities continue to have faith in the system. Advertising job opportunities in promotional mediums, which are earmarked specifically toward recruiting women and minorities, is imperative to secure greater applicants from that cohort. Instituting programs in the community to enhance the potential pool of prospective employees is a proactive step. These might include helping an employee find adequate housing, aiding the community in establishing day-care centers or providing on-site day-care centers instead, and fostering relations with women and minority groups. The designing of proficient training programs will enable women and minority employees to become the most qualified they can be. Self-evaluation of the affirmative action program's proficiency is an important tool when future reassessment is made.

AFFIRMATIVE ACTION PLAN GUIDELINES FOR THE PRIVATE SECTOR

The key to establishing an affirmative action plan is to garner the commitment of management. Once committed, management can emphasize its importance and lead by example. An assessment must be made of the number of women and minorities and their current status within the organization. This data will prove invaluable as a benchmark against which the program's progress can be measured. Once the problem areas are identified, then recruitment and promotion issues must be addressed. A critical look at the current methods utilized must be taken, and a plan must be instituted to remedy its deficiencies. To bolster recruitment, notification should be sent to the placement offices of schools with significant or exclusive women or minority populations. Women and minority organizations can also be advised of the need for prospective candidates. Advertisements in newspapers, magazines, radio, and television designed for women and minorities will enable a company to tap into that particular circle. Company tours for students and community groups are also beneficial. Relying solely on referrals and traditional recruitment techniques will only reinforce discrimination.

Career counseling to direct women and minorities toward career paths and training programs to help them realize these accomplishments must be created or embellished. The fact that counseling and training programs exist is not sufficient. They must be made available or specifically developed with women and minorities in mind.

Job descriptions must also be perused for possible barriers against women and minorities. If found, the descriptive narration must be rethought. All requirements must be job-related. Any which are not should be eliminated, especially unnecessary education or experience; otherwise, discrimination will continue. Testing should also be restricted to when it is absolutely necessary and its reality and job-relatedness can be proved. The assignment of grade levels to jobs must also be reviewed for bias in favor of men. If discovered, such bias must be readjusted. Interviewers must be indoctrinated to no longer believe that women and minorities can perform only certain jobs—those involving routine ministerial tasks. They must avoid asking women and minorities personal questions about marital status, other sources of income, number of children, criminal record, and other issues that are not job-related and are not routinely asked of white men.

Job categories, job description, promotional material, and in-house rules and regulations must be redrafted to be gender-neutral, both in written communications and pictorials.

Employment Perspective

In an advertisement brochure, Sunshine Chemicals states that the men in its employ are the most qualified in the industry. Several pages of pictorials of white men follow. Is this material discriminatory toward the women and minorities who are employed there? Yes! The language is not gender-neutral, and the pictorials are neither gender- nor racially-neutral. ◆

The affirmative action plan should be in written form and distributed throughout the company. A director should be appointed to administer the plan. A letter from the director as well as the CEO should confirm that it is the company's intention to refrain from discrimination both maliciously as well as accidentally and that the company expects all of its employees to act accordingly or face disciplinary measures. Lip service will not be tolerated.

The director should be developing companywide goals for recruitment, training, promotion, and termination; companywide applies to top management equally. There can be no exceptions, or else a good example will not be set, and the plan will fail because of selective application. Each of the goals should be tailored appropriately to work within individual departments. Discussions should be held at all levels to explain the reasoning behind the plan. Getting as much support as possible from top to bottom will thwart divisiveness, prejudice and subversion. Unions should be encouraged to embrace and promote the plan. Whenever a positive attribute of the plan is realized, it should be publicized throughout the company as well as externally. It is wise to clear up any misunderstanding or resentment about the purpose of the plan by counseling those feeling so inclined. Educating employees goes a long way to resolving prejudice and conflict. The director should have an open-door policy for all employees and should communicate periodically with the CEO.

REVERSE DISCRIMINATION

Reverse discrimination exists when the affirmative action plan is unfair to white males in that it selects unqualified women and minorities over them, establishes mandatory quotas, or bars the selection of white males completely. Often reverse discrimination is claimed when qualified women and minorities are given preference over higher-qualified white males. Although there have been conflicting cases, it is generally agreed that this is an acceptable practice when a racial imbalance exists.

Employment Perspective

Oakland is going to employ twenty new police officers. Oakland has very few women and minority police officers. A score of 70 on the police exam is required to be qualified. Oakland plans to hire ten minorities and five women, if they are qualified. The ten minorities selected scores 74 to 90. The five women selected scored 78 to 87. Jim Newman, a white male, scored 94 but was not selected because five other white males scored higher. He sues Oakland, claiming reverse discrimination. Will he win? Most likely not. The issue is not who is more qualified, but whether the individuals selected are qualified. As long as they are qualified, as is the case here, the affirmative action plan will be upheld. If they were not qualified, then Jim's claim of reverse discrimination would be granted, and he would be given a position. ◆

Without affirmative action plans, it is unlikely that women and minorities would have the opportunity of obtaining certain jobs, especially those involving managerial positions.

The following case addresses the issue of whether a school can set aside a definitive number of seats for minority applicants. A white applicant argued that race should not be the determining factor in making an admissions decision.

CASE

University of California Regents v. Bakke

438 U.S. 265 (1977)

Mr. JUSTICE POWELL announced the judgment of the Court.

This case presents a challenge to the special admissions program of the petitioner, the Medical School of the University of California at Davis, which is designed to assure the admission of a specified number of students from certain minority groups. The Superior Court of California sustained respondent's challenge, holding that petitioner's program violated the California Constitution, Title VII of the Civil Rights Act of 1964, and the Equal Protection Clause of the Fourteenth Amendment. The court enjoined petitioner from considering respondent's race or the race of any other applicant in making admissions decisions.

Following the interviews, each candidate was rated on a scale of 1 to 100 by his interviewers and four other members of the admissions committee. The rating embraced the interviewers' summaries, the candidate's overall grade point average, grade point average in science courses, scores on the Medical College Admissions Test (MCAT), letters of recommendation, extracurricular activities, and other biographical data. The ratings were added together to arrive at each candidate's "benchmark" score. Since five committee members rated each candidate in 1973, a perfect score was 500; in 1974, six members rated each candidate, so that perfect score was 600. The full committee then reviewed the file and scores of each applicant and made offers of admission on a "rolling" basis. The chairman was responsible for placing names on the waiting list. They were not placed in strict numerical order; instead, the chairman had discretion to include persons with "special skills."

The special admissions program operated with a separate committee, a majority of whom were members of minority groups. On the 1973 application form, candidates were asked to indicate whether they wished to be considered as "economically and/or educationally disadvantaged" applicants; on the 1974 form the question was whether they wished to be considered as members of a "minority group," which the Medical School apparently viewed as "Blacks," "Chicanos," "Asians," and "American Indians." If these questions were answered affirmatively, the application was forwarded to the special admissions committee. No formal definition of "disadvantaged" was ever produced, but the chairman of the special committee screened each application to see whether it reflected economic or educational deprivation. Having passed this initial hurdle, the applications then were rated by the special committee in a fashion similar to that used by the general admissions committee, except that special candidates did not have to meet the 2.5 grade point average cutoff applied to regular applicants. About one-fifth of the total number of special applicants were invited for interviews in 1973 and 1974. Following each interview, the special committee assigned each special applicant a benchmark score. The special committee then presented its top choices to the general admissions committee. The latter did not rate or compare the special candidates against the general applicants, but could reject recommended special candidates for failure to meet course requirements or other specific deficiencies. The special committee continued to recommend special applicants until a number prescribed by faculty vote were admitted. While the overall class size was still 50, the prescribed number was 8; in 1973 and 1974, when the class size had doubled to 100, the prescribed number of special admissions also doubled, to 16.

Allan Bakke is a white male who applied to the Davis Medical School in both 1973 and 1974. In both years Bakke's application was considered under the general admissions program, and he received an interview. His 1973 interview was with Dr. Theodore C. West, who considered Bakke "a very desirable applicant to the medical school." Despite a strong benchmark score of 468 out of 500, Bakke was rejected. His application had come late in the year, and no applicants in the general admissions process with scores below 470 were accepted after Bakke's application was completed. There were four special admissions slots unfilled at that time, however, for which Bakke was not considered. After his 1973 rejection, Bakke wrote to Dr. George H. Lowrey, Associate Dean and Chairman of the Admissions Committee, protesting that the special admissions program operated as a racial and ethnic quota.

Bakke's 1974 application was completed early in the year. His student interviewer gave him an overall rating of 94, finding him "friendly, well tempered, conscientious and delightful to speak with." His faculty interviewer was, by coincidence, the same Dr. Lowrey to whom he had written in protest of the special admissions program. Dr. Lowrey found Bakke "rather limited in his approach" to the problems of the medical profession and found disturbing Bakke's "very definite opinions which were based more on his personal viewpoints than upon a study of the total problem." Dr. Lowrey gave Bakke the lowest of his six ratings, at 86; his total was 549 out of 600. Again, Bakke's, application was rejected. In neither year did the chairman of the admissions committee, Dr. Lowrey, exercise his discretion to place Bakke on the waiting list. In both years, applicants were ad-

Class Entering in 1974

			MCAT **[Percentiles]**			
	SGPA	*OGPA*	*Verbal*	*Quantitative*	*Science*	*Gen. Info.*
Bakke	3.44	3.46	96	94	97	72
Average of regular admittees	3.36	3.29	69	67	82	72
Average of special admittees	2.42	2.62	34	30	37	18

mitted under the special program with grade point averages, MCAT scores, and benchmark scores significantly lower than Bakke's.

After the second rejection, Bakke filed the instant suit in the Superior Court of California. He sought mandatory, injunctive, and declaratory relief compelling his admission to the Medical School. He alleged that the Medical School's special admissions program operated to exclude him from the school on the basis of his race, in violation of his rights under the Equal Protection Clause of the Fourteenth Amendment. The University cross-complained for a declaration that its special admissions program was lawful.

Applicants admitted under the special program also had benchmark scores significantly lower than many students, including Bakke. Bakke was rejected under the general admissions program, even though the special rating system apparently gave credit for overcoming "disadvantage."

The special admissions program is undeniably a classification based on race and ethnic background. To the extent that there existed a pool of at least minimally qualified minority applicants to fill the 16 special admissions seats, white applicants could compete only for 84 seats in the entering class, rather than the 100 open to minority applicants. Whether this limitation is described as a quota or a goal, it is a line drawn on the basis of race and ethnic status.

The guarantees of the Fourteenth Amendment extend to all persons. Its language is explicit: "No State shall . . . deny to any person within its jurisdiction the equal protection of the laws." The guarantee of equal protection cannot mean one thing when applied to one individual and something else when applied to a person of another color. If both are not accorded the same protection, then it is not equal.

If petitioner's purpose is to assure within its student body some specified percentage of a particular group merely because of its race or ethnic origin, such a preferential pupose must be rejected not as insubstantial but as facially invalid. Preferring members of any one group for no reason other than race or ethnic origin is discrimination for its own sake. This the Constitution forbids.

In such an admissions program, race or ethnic background may be deemed a "plus" in a particular applicant's file, yet it does not insulate the individual from comparison with all other candidates for the available seats. The file of the particular black applicant may be examined or his potential contribution to diversity without the factor of race being decisive when compared, for example, with that of an applicant identified as an Italian-American if the latter is thought to exhibit qualities more likely to promote beneficial educational pluralism. Such qualities could include exceptional personal talents, unique work or service experience, leadership potential, maturity, demonstrated compassion, a history of overcoming disadvantage, ability to communicate with the poor, or other qualifications deemed important. In short, an admissions program operated in this way is flexible enough to consider all pertinent elements of diversity in light of the particular qualifications of each applicant, and to place them on the same footing for consideration, although not necessarily according them the same weight. Indeed, the weight attributed to a particular quality may vary from year to year depending upon the "mix" both of the student body and the applicants for the incoming class.

This kind of program treats each applicant as an individual in the admissions process. The applicant who loses out on the last available seat to another candidate receiving a "plus" on the basis of ethnic background will not have been foreclosed from all consideration for that seat simply because he was not the right color or had the wrong surname. It would mean only that his combined qualifications, which may have included similar nonobjective factors, did not outweigh those of the other applicant. His qualifications would have been weighed fairly and competitively, and he would have no basis to complain of unequal treatment under the Fourteenth Amendment.

It had been suggested that an admissions program which considers race only as one factor is simply a subtle and more sophisticated—but no less effective—means of according racial preference than the Davis program. A facial intent to discriminate, however, is evident in petitioner's preference program and not denied in this case. No such facial infirmity exists in an admissions program where race or ethnic background is simply one element—to be weighed fairly against other elements—in the selection process.

In summary, it is evident that the Davis special admissions program involves the use of an explicit racial classification never before countenanced by this Court. It tells applicants who are not Negro, Asian, or Chicano that they are totally excluded from a specific percentage of the seats in an entering class. No matter how strong their qualifications, quantitative and extracurricular, including their own potential for contribution to educational diversity, they are never afforded the chance to compete with applicants from the preferred groups for the special admissions seats. At the same time, the preferred applicants have the opportunity to compete for every seat in the class.

The fatal flaw in petitioner's preferential program is its disregard of individual rights as guaranteed by the Fourteenth Amendment. Such rights are not absolute. But when a State's distribution of benefits or imposition of burdens hinges on ancestry or the color of a person's skin, that individual is entitled to a demonstration that the challenged classification is necessary to promote a substantial state interest. Petitioner has failed to carry this burden. For this reason, that portion of the California court's judgment holding petitioner's special admissions program invalid under the Fourteenth Amendment must be affirmed.

In enjoining petitioner from ever considering the race of any applicant, however, the courts below failed to recognize that the State has a substantial interest that legitimately may be served by a properly devised admissions program involving the competitive consideration of race and ethnic origin. For this reason, so much of the California court's judgment as enjoins petitioner from any consideration of the race of any applicant must be reversed.

With respect to respondent's entitlement to an injunction directing his admission to the Medical School, petitioner has conceded that it could not carry its burden of proving that, but for the existence of its unlawful special admissions program, respondent still would not have been admitted. Hence, respondent is entitled to the injunction, and that portion of the judgment must be affirmed.

Judgment for Bakke.

The following case brought by a white male concerns the validity of an affirmative action plan. The question presented is whether sufficient statistical facts have been introduced to show the plan has a reverse discrimination effect on white males.

CASE *Hannon v. Chater*

887 F.Supp. 1303 (N.D. Cal. 1995)

INFANTE, Judge.

In the instant case, the OHA's (Office of Housing Administration) Affirmative Action Plan is designed to increase over a five-year period, and by varying specific percentages, the numbers of women and minorities who are ALJs (Administrative Law Judges) through "reaching out to inform potential applicants about ALJ employment opportunities at OHA."

The Government's "latest statistics" indicate that five of every six ALJs nationwide are white males. Hannon has not shown, nor even suggested, that the entire United States is an inappropriate labor market for the purpose of evaluating an affirmative action plan for hiring ALJs for Los Angeles. Nor has he supplied evidence whatsoever suggesting that the Government's statistics are mistaken or that such statistics are disproportionate to the qualified labor force. Finally, Hannon has not established that women and minorities are not "underutilized" as ALJ's—i.e., that there does not exist a "manifest imbalance" between the percentage of women and minorities who are ALJs and the percentage of women and minorities qualified to be ALJs. Without the comparative statistics, Hannon cannot carry his burden of showing, on the basis of the undisputed facts, that OHA's Affirmative Action Plan is invalid.

Hannon has also failed to make any showing establishing that the OHA's Affirmative Action Plan unnecessarily trammels the rights of white male ALJ applicants or creates a bar to their advancement. The OHA's plan is, by its terms, "limited to reaching out to inform potential applicants about ALJ employment opportunities at OHA." Insofar as affirmative action policies are necessary evils, the OHA's plan could hardly be more benign. It does not establish quotas nor set aside positions for women or minorities. Moreover, Hannon did not have an "absolute entitlement" to or "legitimate firmly rooted expectation" of obtaining a position as an ALJ.

Finally, Hannon has not offered an iota of proof that the OHA's Affirmative Action Plan is a permanent feature of the OHA's landscape which seeks to establish in perpetuity a work force whose sexual composition mirrors that of the relevant labor force. Indeed, to the contrary, Hannon argues that the Affirmative Action Plan lapsed, and was no longer in force, prior to 1993.

In sum, Hannon has not made a showing sufficient to establish the existence of any elements essential to his disparate impact claim, on which he would bear the burden of proof at trial, and as such the Government is entitled to summary adjudication of Hannon's disparate impact claim.

Judgment for Chater.

In the next case, a white male claims that an injustice has been perpetrated against him by the employer's affirmative action plan and that this amounts to reverse discrimination.

CASE

Stock v. Universal Foods Corp.

817 F.Supp. 1300 (D.Md. 1993)

LEGG, Judge.

Plaintiff David Stock ("Stock") is a white male who unsuccessfully sought a position as a maintenance mechanic at Universal's Red Star Yeast plant in Baltimore. Stock, whose experience as a tool and dye maker qualifies him for the job, contends that he was rejected solely because of his race.

Defendant Kenneth Randall ("Randall") is Universal's Plant Manager. Defendant Dennis Cassidy ("Cassidy") is Universal's General Superintendent, and is responsible for the implementation of Universal's AAP (Affirmative Action Plan). Defendant Ronald C. Miller ("Miller") is Universal's Maintenance Superintendent; he supervises the maintenance mechanics.

Universal bought the Red Star Yeast plant in 1981 from Diamond Shamrock. At that time, it was the practice at the plant to recruit new employees by word of mouth. As a result, new employees were typically friends or relatives of old employees. One consequence of this practice was an almost complete absence of minorities and women in the workforce. When Universal bought the plant, there were only two minority employees.

Although Universal's management made some effort to recruit minority employees, the company did not adopt a formal affirmative action program until 1991, after an Equal Employment Opportunity Commission ("EEOC") audit revealed violations of Executive Order 11246 and various federal fair employment statutes and regulations. In an effort to remedy these violations and to avoid potential legal liability, Universal, on June 28, 1991, entered into a conciliation agreement with the EEOC. Under that agreement, Universal developed and adopted an AAP, which described Universal's past deficiencies, its new hiring policies, and its hiring goals for fiscal year 1991.

The May 1991 workforce analysis, prepared for the EEOC audit, reflected an underutilization of minorities in the "craft" category. Of the twenty-one craft positions at the Baltimore plant, only two were filled by blacks. Four of the last six craft hires were white, two black. At Universal, maintenance mechanics were included in the craft category. All of the fourteen maintenance mechanics were white; the two previous hires for the position were white.

Universal's AAP provides that the primary considerations in hiring decisions are knowledge, skill, job competence, willingness to work, and the ability to work with others. In an effort to meet Universal's hiring goals and its need for a competitive workforce, the AAP provides that each employee shall be competent and shall have experience which demonstrates qualifications for the job, including loyalty and productivity. The AAP specifically states that its goals are not rigid quotas, but are rather targets "reasonably attainable by means of applying every good faith effort to make all aspects of the entire affirmative action plan work."

In late August or early September 1991, a position in the plant's maintenance department became available. This position was for a general mechanic on the night shift whose primary responsibility is servicing the packaging equipment. This night mechanic works alone, in contrast to the day shift mechanics who work in pairs. About half of the Universal plant's maintenance mechanics are "papered" machinists, the other half are not. The two previous hires into the maintenance department were not papered.

The night shift position became available when a day shift machinist quit and the old night shift machinist switched to the day shift. Neither of these two men were papered. A night shift machinist, therefore, could effectively perform the job without being a papered machinist.

Despite the AAP requirement that all job openings be listed with the state job service and be advertised, Stock learned about the Universal job opening from Preston Sealover ("Sealover"), a Universal maintenance mechanic, who told Stock that Universal was looking for a journeyman machinist. Sealover approached Stock after Miller asked his maintenance mechanics whether they knew anyone who would be interested in filling the department's vacancy.

Miller, who was unfamiliar with the new AAP, interviewed Stock for the open position on September 9, 1991. Miller told Stock he was impressed with Stock's qualifications and arranged for Stock to be interviewed the next day by the plant manager, Allan Brethauer ("Brethauer"). After this second interview, Miller again told plaintiff that everything "looked good," and Miller began arranging for a physical examination for Stock.

It then came to the attention of Dennis Cassidy, the Assistant Plant Manager, that Miller had interviewed an applicant before the position had been publicly advertised. Cassidy contacted Miller and informed him of the AAP's requirements. Miller in turn told Stock that the company needed to advertise and interview more applicants to comply with its affirmative action plan, but that Miller was still very impressed by plaintiff's qualifications.

Universal listed the opening with the Maryland State Job Service, and placed a print advertisement in the Baltimore *Sun* on September 14 and 15, 1991. The ad read:

> MACHINIST-MECHANIC
>
> Familiarity with high speed packaging equipment preferred. Experience in plant maintenance is essential. Hours will be primarily third shift.

The Maryland State Job Services ad was similar, though not as detailed regarding specific qualifications.

Some thirty-two men applied. After reviewing the applications, Miller chose the five men who were most qualified on paper and interviewed them. Of these applicants, three were journeymen machinists and two were tool and dye makers. Miller thereafter told both Stock and the maintenance workers at Universal that Stock was still the most qualified applicant.

None of the initial interviewees were minority group members. This fact, Cassidy suspected, was not because there were no qualified minority applicants, but rather because Miller was prejudiced and had weeded out applicants who appeared on paper to be minorities. Consequently, Cassidy urged Miller to find qualified minority applicants and call them in for interviews. At no time, however, did Cassidy tell Miller that he must hire a minority.

Miller went back through the applications and located two he suspected had been submitted by blacks. On October 10, 1991, Miller asked Sealover to apologize to Stock for the delay in a hiring decision, and to inform him that Universal intended to interview a black applicant in order to comply with its AAP.

Tyrone Anderson ("Anderson") was interviewed and subsequently hired by Universal for the maintenance vacancy. Anderson, who is black, had vocational training from a respected school and had production line equipment experience. His former employer gave him an unqualified recommendation and expressed disappointment that he was leaving. Despite his admitted prejudice against minorities, Miller was impressed by Anderson's qualifications and decided Universal should hire him. Anderson began work on November 4, 1991.

Although the other maintenance mechanics were upset that a black man had been chosen, Anderson soon impressed them with his quality work and amiable personality. There have been no complaints about Anderson's work since the initial grumbling.

The essence of Count I of Stock's complaint is that Tyrone Anderson was not qualified for the maintenance mechanic position. The undisputed material facts of this case, however demonstrate beyond legitimate dispute that (i) Anderson was qualified, (ii) Universal's AAP was bona fide, and (iii) Anderson was hired pursuant to the plan. Accordingly, all defendants are entitled to summary judgment.

Stock alleges that Universal Foods, in violation of 1981, refused to hire him for a job vacancy solely on the basis of his race. Plaintiff contends that he was not hired into the position for which he interviewed solely because he is white, and that Tyrone Anderson was hired for that position solely because he is black. Despite its language "as is enjoyed by white citizens," 1981 prohibits intentional racial discrimination against whites in hiring decisions.

A 1981 plaintiff must prove that he is a victim of intentional race discrimination.

The most commonly used and best understood proof scheme in a discrimination case is the one announced by the Supreme Court in *McDonnell Douglas Corp. v. Green.* Because direct proof of discrimination is usually difficult to produce, the *McDonnell Douglas* burden shifting scheme, which allows a plaintiff to proceed with circumstantial evidence, was an important development in discrimination law.

Under the *McDonnell Douglas* scheme, a plaintiff must carry the initial burden of creating an inference that the challenged employment decision was based on a discrimination criterion. A minority plaintiff bringing a failure to hire suit under 1981 raises an inference of discrimination by establishing (i) that he is a minority (ii) who applied for and was qualified for a job, (iii) that he was rejected for the job, and (iv) that the job was filled by a non-minority candidate.

The burden of proof then shifts to the employer to come forward with a legitimate non-discriminatory reason for its decision. If the defendant does this, then the plaintiff must prove by a preponderance of the evidence that the reason offered by the employer is a pretext, masking a discriminatory motive, and is unworthy of credence.

In the context of a reverse discrimination suit brought pursuant to 1981, the Court must decide whether the *McDonnell Douglas* test applies. The Eleventh Circuit has held that a white plaintiff is entitled to the same inference of discrimination as a minority plaintiff when he proves a prima facie case.

Other courts, including the Courts of Appeals for the District of Columbia Circuit and the Sixth Circuit have held, however, that a white male plaintiff who otherwise makes out a prima facie case is not entitled to an inference of discrimination. Those courts reason that the *McDonnell Douglas* proof scheme is premised upon this country's history of racial discrimination against minority groups, particularly blacks. Thus, they apply *McDonnell Douglas* to the minority but not the majority.

The Sixth Circuit and the District of Columbia Circuit have held that a reverse discrimination plaintiff raises an inference of impermissible racial discrimination when he satisfies the *McDonnell Douglas* prima facie case and also shows that "background circumstances support the suspicion that the defendant is that unusual employer who discriminates against the majority."

Whether a white plaintiff is entitled to an inference of impermissible racial discrimination when he satisfies the *McDonnell Douglas* prima facie case is a question of first impression in the Fourth Circuit. This Court will apply the standard *McDonnell Douglas* test. In this Court's view, the extra factor required by the Sixth, Eighth, and District of Columbia Circuits is vague and difficult to apply. The *McDonnell Douglas* test is well-established, generally understood, and also focuses attention upon the bona fides of the defendant's AAP, which, in a reverse discrimination case, is the usual "legitimate reason" cited by the employer for its hiring decision.

In the reverse discrimination context, therefore, the plaintiff raises an inference of racial discrimination when he proves:

(1) that he belongs to a class;
(2) that he applied for and was qualified for a job;
(3) that he was rejected for the job; and
(4) that the job was filled by a minority group member.

Once this inference is raised, the employer must come forward with a legitimate, nondiscriminatory reason for the hiring decision. In the instant case, Universal has done this by adverting to its AAP. Thus, the burden of persuasion rests on the plaintiff to prove that (i) the AAP is not bona fide, or (ii) the AAP was not followed in the instant case.

An AAP is bona fide if it is substantially related to its remedial purpose. An AAP is substantially related to a remedial purpose if:

> (1) its implementation results or is designed to result in the hiring of a sufficient number of minority applicants so that the racial balance of the employer's work force approximates roughly, but does not exceed, the balance that would have been achieved absent the past discrimination; (2) the plan endures only so long as is reasonably necessary to achieve its legitimate goals; (3) the plan does not result in hiring unqualified applicants; and (4) the plan does not completely bar whites from all vacancies or otherwise unnecessarily or invidiously trammel their interests.

A defendant satisfies his burden of production by coming forward with facts that would tend to establish each of the elements set forth above. This would include evidence that the AAP was a response to a conspicuous racial imbalance in the workforce, and that the plan is reasonably tailored to cure this imbalance.

The disposition of defendant's motion for summary judgment turns upon two issues: (i) whether Universal's AAP is bona fide, and (ii) whether the Universal employees were acting pursuant to the AAP when they hired Anderson.

Stock contends (i) that Anderson was not qualified for the maintenance mechanic position, (ii) that Universal's employees acted for a discriminatory, and not a remedial, purpose when they implemented Universal's affirmative action plan (i.e., that they did not act pursuant to the AAP), and (iii) that implementation of Universal's program unnecessarily trammeled the rights of white applicants (i.e., the AAP is not bona fide).

Plaintiff offers no direct evidence of intentional racial discrimination, so he must proceed according to the *McDonnell Douglas* proof scheme. Here, plaintiff Stock satisfies the four part *McDonnell Douglas* scheme. He (i) applied for the open position, (ii) was undeniably qualified for the job, (iii) was rejected, and (iv) the job was filled by a black applicant.

Because Stock has met his initial burden of raising an inference of impermissible racial discrimination, Universal must enunciate a legitimate, non-discriminatory reason for its decision not to hire Stock. Universal satisfies this burden by presenting evidence that the challenged employment decision was made pursuant to its bona fide AAP.

Judgment for Universal Foods.

In the following case, the question is whether a white male claiming reverse discrimination must meet the same criteria set forth in the McDonnell Douglas case as required of minorities.

CASE

Kelsay v. Milwaukee Area Technical College

825 F.Supp. 215 (E.D.Wis. 1993)

GORDON, Judge.

Mr. Kelsay's statement of claim is repeated below in its entirety:

> As a Limited Term Employee at MATC (Milwaukee Area Technical College), I was entitled to retain the teaching position to which I had been appointed until such time as a permanent hiring took place. Instead, at the beginning of the second semester of the 1990-91 school year MATC transferred a black male NON-APPLICANT into this position in violation of the Collective Bargaining Agreement then in effect between the teachers, union AFT (of which I am a member) and the administration of MATC. I filed a grievance and was reinstated but lost wages as a result of this incident.

When he declined the position, he was fired. Mr. Kelsay requests the following relief,

> I would like to be compensated for my lost wages, for the sullying of my reputation as a teacher, and I would like my job back on a permanent basis with full tenure and other rights retroactive to the date of hire of my replacement, as well as additional sums for emotional distress caused by their discriminatory practices.

Mr. Kelsay's complaint does not declare his race. However, a decision of the State of Wisconsin Department of Industry, Labor and Human Relations attached to his complaint, as an addendum, reveals that Mr. Kelsay is a white male. That addendum also states that Carol Brady, a black female, was hired by MATC on August 26, 1991, to fill the permanent paralegal instructor position that Mr. Kelsay had applied for on August 1, 1990, and was qualified for, and had filled for MATC as a limited term employee from August 1990 through May 1991.

Mr. Kelsay's complaint along with its addendum treated as part of his complaint, suggests that he is seeking relief for alleged reverse discrimination by the defendant, MATC, pursuant to Title VII of the Civil Rights Act of 1964. Specifically, he appears to be contending that MATC discriminated against him because of his race and sex in failing to hire him for the permanent paralegal instructor job offered to Carol Brady.

"It shall be an unlawful employment practice for an employer . . . to fail or refuse to hire . . . any individual with respect to his compensation, terms, conditions, or privileges of employment, because of such individual's race, color, religion, sex, or national origin." This section "applies on the same terms to discrimination against males or whites as it does to discrimination against women or racial ethnic minorities."

As a general rule, in a disparate treatment case under Title VII:

First, the plaintiff has the burden of proving by the ponderance of the evidence a prima facie case of discrimination.

> In the first semester of the 90–91 school year, I applied for the position which I was serving as the Limited Term Employee. A round of interviews were held. Recommendations were made as to whom to hire by the interview panel. These recommendations were rejected by MATC, allegedly due to their racial and/or sexual makeup. The panelists resigned enmasse in protest of this action and a second panel was convened. This panel selected a lesser-qualified black female in part to retaliate against the undersigned for grieving the actions complained of. . . .
>
> The qualifications for this position were lowered with each subsequent posting of this position to enable a larger "Pool" of targeted (i.e. non-white, non-male) applicants to be considered for this position. The position for which I was serving as a Limited Term Employee was offered to a black male. . . .

In reverse discrimination cases, the first of the McDonnell Douglas factors has been interpreted to allow a majority plaintiff to establish a prima facie case of intentionally disparate treatment when "background circumstances support the suspicion that the defendant is that unusual employer who discriminates against the majority."

Mr. Kelsay has alleged enough facts to state a prima facie claim for reverse discrimination. . . .

Judgment for Kelsay.

CONCLUSION

Whenever one group constitutes the majority of the population or has political, military, or economic control, there is going to be unequal discrimination; that is, one group which is in control is capable of affecting the employment of the other groups, and with it, their lifestyle. If all groups were equally represented in numbers as well as political, military, and economic strength, there would still be discrimination, but it would be equal. Group A would associate, work, and live predominantly with Group A people. Group B would do the same, and so on. It would be predominantly, not exclusively, because some people enjoy intermingling or may, in fact, prefer another group entirely. Group A employers would predominantly hire Group A people, assuming that the general abilities of the group were similar. Why? Because people usually feel more comfortable with people with whom they can identify—those similar to themselves. The main categories that create similarities are race, national origin, gender, religion, age, economic status or standard of living, domicile, education, and associations or clubs.

In the hypothetical situation of equal representation, the discrimination, while having societal drawbacks, would not have affected the employment and, as a result, the income, education, housing, and standard of living of any one of the groups. In the United States, where the white race has been the majority in population and the white male the dominant force in politics, the military, and business, the result has been an unequal discrimination against women and minorities. How does the United States measure up against other countries?

It may be true that other countries are doing the same, if not, worse. They may be acting discriminatorily to their minority white populations. But the old adage "two wrongs don't make a right" rings clear. As proponents of human rights, Americans should be solving our own problems and teaching other nations through the good examples of promoting equality among peoples. To accomplish this, the majority does not have to give handouts to women and minorities. All that is required is to remove the obstacles in their path to job hiring and subsequent promotions. Let them be judged on their content rather than on their cover. Equal opportunity is the answer. The pendulum was stuck on one side. Swinging it to the other side is not the answer. Stopping it in the middle is. Giving women and minorities preference will only incite prejudices more and undermine their ability to perform. With multinationals downsizing work forces and relocating them to foreign countries, American jobs can only be saved by ability. Successful businesses will not survive by employing minimally qualified people, they must employ the most qualified people. The players in the National Football league are qualified, but the most successful teams are the ones who have employed the most qualified players. This is the philosophy which will rule in the world of global business. Helping women and minorities to be the most qualified they can be should be the philosophy adopted. The American business who will not hire women or minorities may end up losing business to a competitor who will hire women and what we call minorities overseas, i.e., Pakistan women and Sri Lanka men. Discrimination will be phased out in favor of ability. The most qualified will rule.

REVIEW QUESTIONS

1. What is affirmative action?
2. When did this concept first arise?
3. How is a quota different from an affirmative action plan?
4. Why would a company voluntarily institute an affirmative action plan?
5. What is meant by equal employment opportunity?
6. Explain the affirmative action plan guidelines for the private sector.
7. Explain the concept of reverse discrimination.
8. How can the EEOC enforce its ruling against an employer who refuses to comply?
9. Are affirmative action plans ethical?
10. Once an affirmative action plan is implemented, can it remain indefinitely?
11. Gonzalez brought an action against the United States Army, claiming he had been the victim of racial discrimination. Specifically, Gonzalez argued he was denied a promotion because of his race. The Army retorted that the judiciary should defer the decision making to the Army because of its expertise in military affairs. What was the result? *Gonzalez v. Department of Army,* 718 F.2d 926 (9th Cir. 1983)
12. When is an Affirmative Action Program bona fide? *Valentine v. Smith,* 654 F.2d 503 (8th Cir. 1981)
13. Are employees entitled to promotions automatically or as a matter of right? *Blake v. Giarrusso,* 263 So.2d 392 (LA. App. 4th Cir.)
14. Fullilove and several contractors brought suit, claiming that they lost substantial sums as a result of the Congressional requirement that 10 percent of federal funds used for local projects must be used to purchase supplies or service from minority groups. The contractors claimed that this affirmative action plan is discriminatory against nonminorities.

What was the result? *Fullilove v. Klutznick, Secretary of Commerce of the U.S.*, 448 U.S. 448 (1980)

15. To ease racial tension, the Jackson Board of Education adopted a layoff plan in 1972 that provided the percentage of minorities currently employed must be maintained when employees are discharged. In 1974, when layoffs occurred, this plan was not followed. After several lawsuits, nonminority teachers were laid off, while minority teachers with less seniority were kept. Wygant, a nonminority teacher brought suit, claiming that the affirmative action plan was unfair in that it was put in place in response to possible fluctuations in the student body. What was the result? *Wygant v. Jackson Board of Education, etc. et al.* 106 S.Ct. 1842 (1986)

16. Referring to the case on pp. 215, is reverse discrimination a real threat, and what is an equitable solution?

17. With regard to the case on pp. 202, is affirmative action ethical?

18. When white people claim reverse discrimination, should the same tests apply to them as to minorities? Refer to the case on pp. 220.

19. Was the decision in the caseon pp. 206 ethical?

20. How can the judgment in the case on pp. 212 be reconciled with the judgment in case on pp. 206?

Uniform Guidelines on Employee Selection Procedures (1978)

ADVERSE IMPACT

The fundamental principle underlying the guidelines is that employer policies or practices which have an adverse impact on employment opportunities of any race, sex, or ethnic group are illegal under title VII and the Executive order unless justified by business necessity.

If adverse impact exists, it must be justified on grounds of business necessity. Normally, this means by validation which demonstrates the relation between the selection procedure and performance on the job.

The guidelines adopt a "rule of thumb" as a practical means of determining adverse impact for use in enforcement proceedings. This rule is known as the "4/5ths" or "80 percent" rule.

WHERE ADVERSE IMPACT EXISTS: THE BASIC OPTIONS

Once an employer has established that there is adverse impact, what steps are required by the guidelines? As previously noted, the employer can modify or eliminate the procedure which produces the adverse impact, thus taking the selection procedure from the coverage of these guidelines. If the employer does not do that, then it must justify the use of the procedure on grounds of "business necessity." This normally means that it must show a clear relation between performance on the selection procedure and performance on the job.

General Principles

1. Relationship between validation and elimination of adverse impact, and affirmative

action. Federal equal employment opportunity law generally does not require evidence of validity for a selection procedure if there is not adverse impact; e.g., *Griggs v. Duke Power Co.* Therefore, a user has the choice of complying either by providing evidence of validity (or otherwise justifying use in accord with Federal law), or by eliminating the adverse impact. These options have always been present under Federal law and the Federal Executive Agency Guidelines. The December 30 draft guidelines, however, clarified the nature of the two options open to users.

2. The *"bottom line"* (section 4C). The guidelines provide that when the overall selection process does not have an adverse impact the Government will usually not examine the individual components of that process for adverse impact or evidence of validity. The concept is based upon the view that the Federal Government should not generally concern itself with individual components of a selection process, if the overall effect of that process is nonexclusionary. Many commenters criticized the ambiguity caused by the word "generally" in the December 30 draft of section 4C which provided, "the Federal enforcement agencies generally will not take enforcement action based upon adverse impact of any component" of a process that does not have an overall adverse impact. Employer groups stated the position that the "bottom line" should be a rule prohibiting enforcement action by Federal agencies with respect to all or part of a selection process where the bottom line does not show adverse impact. Civil rights and some labor union representatives expressed the opposing concerns that the concept may be too restrictive, that it may be interpreted as a matter of law, and that it might allow certain discriminatory conditions to go unremedied.

Sec. 5. *General Standards for validity studies.*

A. Acceptable types of validity studies. For the purposes of satisfying these guidelines, users may rely upon criterion-related validity studies, content validity studies or construct validity studies, in accordance with the standards set forth in the technical standards of the guidelines. New strategies procedures will be evaluated as they become accepted by the psychological profession.

B. *Criterion-related content, and construct validity.* Evidence of the validity of a test or other selection procedure by a criterion-related validity study should consist of empirical data demonstrating that the selection procedure is predictive of or significantly correlated with important elements of job performance. Evidence of the validity of a test or other selection procedure by a content validity study should consist of data showing that the content of the selection procedure is representative of important aspects of performance on the job for which the candidates are to be evaluated. Evidence of the validity of a test or other selection procedure through a construct validity study should consist of data showing that the procedure measures the degree to which candidates have identifiable characteristics which have been determined to be important in successful performance in the job for which the candidates are to be evaluated.

C. *Guidelines are consistent with professional standards.* The provisions of these guidelines relating to validation of selection procedures are intended to be consistent with generally accepted professional standards for evaluating standardized tests and other selection procedures, such as those described in the Standards for Educational and Psychological Tests prepared by a joint committee of the American Psychological Association, the American Educational Research Association, and the National Council on Measurement in Education (American Psychological Association, Washington, D.C., 1974) (hereinafter "A.P.A. Standards") and standard textbooks and journals in the field of personnel selection.

D. *Need for documentation of validity.* For any selection procedure which is part of a selection process which has an adverse impact and which selection procedure has an adverse impact, each user should maintain and have available such documentation as is described in section 15 below.

E. *Accuracy and standardization.* Validity studies should be carried out under conditions which assure insofar as possible the adequacy and accuracy of the research and the report. Selection procedure should be administered and scored under standardized conditions.

F. *Caution against selection on basis of knowledges, skills, or ability learned in brief orientation period.* In general, users should avoid making employment decisions on the basis of measures of knowledges, skills, or abilities which are normally learned in a brief orientation period, and which have an adverse impact.

G. *Method of use of selection procedures.* The evidence of both the validity and utility of a selection procedure should support the method the user chooses for operational use of the procedure, if that method of use has a greater adverse impact than another method of use. Evidence which may be sufficient to support the use of a selection procedure on a pass/fail (screening) basis may be insufficient to support the use of the same procedure on a ranking basis under these guidelines. Thus if user decides to use a selection procedure on a ranking basis, and that method of use has a greater adverse impact than use on an appropriate pass/fail basis (see section 5H below), the user should have sufficient evidence of validity and utility to support the use on a ranking basis.

H. *Cutoff scores.* Where cutoff scores are used, they should normally be set so as to be reasonable and consistent with normal expectations of acceptable proficiency within the work force. Where applicants are ranked on the basis of properly validated selection procedures and those applicants scoring below a higher cutoff score than appropriate in light or no chance of being selected for employment, the higher cutoff score may be appropriate, but the degree of adverse impact should be considered.

Documentation of Impact and Validity Evidence

Sec. 15. *Documentation of impact and validity evidence.*

A. *Required information.* Users of selection procedures other than those users complying with section 15 A(1) below should maintain and have available for each job information on adverse impact of the selection process for that job and, where it is determined a selection process has an adverse impact, evidence of validity as set forth below.

(1) *Simplified recordkeeping for users with less than 100 employees.* In order to minimize recordkeeping burdens on employers who employ one hundred (100) or fewer employees and other users not required to file EEO-1, et seq., reports, such users may satisfy the requirements of this section 15 if they maintain and have available records showing, for each year:

(a) The number of persons hired, promoted, and terminated for each job, by sex, and where appropriate by race and national origins;

(b) The number of applicants for hire and promotion by sex and where appropriate by race and national origin; and

(c) The selection procedures utilized (either standardized or not standardized).

These records should be maintained for each race or national group constituting more than two percent (2%) of the labor force in the relevant labor area. However, it is necessary to maintain records by race and/or national origin if one race or national origin group in the relevant labor area constitutes more than ninety-eight percent (98%) of the labor force in the area. If the user has reason to believe that a selection procedure has an adverse impact, the user should maintain any available evidence of validity for that procedure.

Definitions

Sec. 16. *Definitions.* The following definitions shall apply throughout these guidelines:

A. *Ability.* A present competence to perform an observable behavior or a behavior while results in an observable product.

B. *Adverse impact.* A substantially different rate of selection in hiring, promotion, or other employment decisions which work to the disadvantage of members of a race, sex, or ethnic group.

C. *Compliance with these guidelines.* Use of a selection procedure is in compliance with these guidelines if such use has been validated in accord with these guidelines, or if such use does not result in adverse impact on any race, sex, or ethnic group, or, in unusual circumstances, if use of the procedure is otherwise justified in accord with Federal law.

D. *Content Validity.* Demonstrated by data showing that the content of a selection procedure is representative of important aspects of performance on the job.

E. *Construct Validity.* Demonstrated by data showing that the selection procedure measures the degree to which candidates have identifiable characteristics which have been determined to be important for successful job performance.

F. *Criterion-related Validity.* Demonstrated by empirical data showing that the selection procedure is predictive of or significantly correlated with important elements of work behavior.

G. *Employer.* Any employer subject to the provisions of the Civil Rights Act of 1964, as amended, including State or local governments and any Federal agency subject to the provisions of section 717 of the Civil Rights Act of 1964, as amended, and any Federal contractor or subcontractor or federally assisted construction contractor or subcontractor by Executive Order 11246, as amended.

H. *Employment Agency.* Any employment agency subject to the provisions of the Civil Rights Acts of 1964, as amended.

I. *Enforcement action.* A proceeding by a Federal enforcement agency such as a lawsuit or an administrative proceeding leading to debarment from withholding, suspension, or termination of Federal Government contracts or the suspension or withholding of Federal Government funds; but not a finding of reasonable cause or a conciliation process or the issuance of right to sue letters under title VII or under Executive Order 11246 where such finding, conciliation, or issuance of notice of right to sue is based upon an individual complaint.

J. *Enforcement agency.* Any agency of the executive branch of the Federal Government which adopts these guidelines for purposes of the enforcement of the equal employment opportunity laws or which has responsibility for securing compliance with them.

K. *Job analysis.* A detailed statement of work behaviors and other information relevant to the job.

L. *Job descriptions.* A general statement of job duties and responsibilities.

M. *Knowledge.* A body of information applied directly to the performance of a function. Evidence for intermittent leave, or leave on a reduced leave schedule, for planned medical treatment, the dates on which such treatment is expected to be given and the duration of such treatment.

Section 102. Employee Leave

In the case of certification for intermittent leave, or leave on a reduced leave schedule, a statement of the medical necessity for the intermittent leave or leave on a reduced leave schedule, and the expected duration of the intermittent leave or reduced leave schedule; and in the case of certification for intermittent leave, or leave on a reduced leave schedule, a statement of the employee's intermittent leave or leave on a reduced leave schedule is necessary for the care of the son, daughter, parent, or spouse who has a serious health condition, or will assist in their recovery, and the expected duration and schedule of the intermittent leave or reduced leave schedule.

Second Opinion.—

(1) IN GENERAL.—In any case in which the employer has reason to doubt the validity of the certification, the employer may require, at the expense of the employer, that the eligible employee obtain the opinion of a second health care provider designated or approved by the employer concerning any information certified under subsection (b) for such leave.

Resolution of Conflicting Opinions.—

(1) IN GENERAL.—In any case in which the second opinion differs from the opinion in the original certification, the employer may require, at the expense of the employer, that the employee obtain the opinion of a third health care provider designated or approved jointly by the employer and the employee.

(2) FINALITY.—The opinion of the third health care provider shall be considered to be final and shall be binding on the employer and the employee.

Sec. 104. Employment and Benefits Protection.

(a) Restoration to Position.—

(1) IN GENERAL.—Any eligible employee who takes leave under section 102 for the intended purpose of the leave shall be entitled, on return from such leave—

(A) to be restored by the employer to the position of employment held by the employee when the leave commenced; or

(B) to be restored to an equivalent position with equivalent employment benefits, pay, and other terms and conditions of employment.

(2) Loss of Benefits.—The taking of leave under section 102 shall not result in the loss of any employment benefits accrued prior to the date on which the leave commenced.

(3) Limitations.—Nothing in this section shall be construed to entitle any restored employee to—

(A) the accrual of any seniority or employment benefits during any period of leave; or

(B) any right, benefit, or position of employment other than any right, benefit, or position to which the employee would have been entitled had the employee not taken the leave.

(b) Exemption Concerning Certain Highly Compensated Employees.—

(1) Denial of Restoration.—An employer may deny restoration under subsection (a) to any eligible employee described in paragraph (2) if—

(A) such denial is necessary to prevent substantial and grievous economic injury to the operations of the employer;

(c) Maintenance of Health Benefits.

(1) Coverage.—Except as provided in paragraph (2), during any period that an eligible employee takes leave under section 102, the employer shall maintain coverage under any "group health plan" (as defined in section 5000(b)(1) of the Internal Revenue Code of 1986) for the duration of such leave at the level and under the conditions coverage would have been provided if the employee had continued in employment continuously for the duration of such leave.

(2) Failure to Return from Leave.—The employer may recover the premium that the employer paid for maintaining coverage for the employee under such group health plan during any period of unpaid leave under section 102.

CHAPTER 10

Racial Discrimination

INTRODUCTION

Racial discrimination exists where employees of one race are favored by the employer over another. Usually it is the white race favored over the black race, but there are also many instances of Hispanics, Orientals, Asians, and American Indians being subjected to racial discrimination. There are even isolated instances of white people being victimized as well.

Employment Perspective

Mary Jones, who is black, and Martha Thomas, who is white, were both salespersons for the Fashion Boutique, a women's apparel store. In concert, they stole over $4,000 worth of merchandise. Upon discovery, Martha was terminated, but Mary was not. Fashion Boutique felt that if Mary was terminated, she might file a complaint with the EEOC, claiming discrimination since she was the only black employee. Martha filed a claim for racial discrimination. Is she correct? Yes! Although both could be terminated for the theft, by choosing one race over the other, the employer racially discriminated against Martha. The argument that Title VII does not cover white people is without merit. It applies to *all* races. ◆

In the following case, a black professor was denied tenure at a college. He brought a racial discrimination suit. The college claimed it was justified in denying tenure because of a failure to produce scholarly work. The professor claimed the college's argument was just a pretext in order to racially discriminate.

CASE

Jiminez v. Mary Washington College

57 F.3d 369 (4th Cir. 1995)

HAMILTON, Circuit Judge.

Anthony Jiminez, a black professor from Trinidad, West Indies, instituted suit pursuant to Title VII of the Civil Rights Act of 1964, against Mary Washington College (MWC) and Philip Hall, Vice President of Mary Washington College, for alleged employment discrimination based on race and national origin. According to Jiminez, he was impermissibly given a terminal contract instead of remaining in a tenure-track teaching position. Following a bench trial, the district court rendered judgment in favor of Jiminez, ruling that he had established a prima facie case of race and national origin discrimination, and he had demonstrated MWC's proffered reason for the adverse action was pretextual and unworthy of credence. MWC appeals, contending that the district court erred in ruling in favor of Jiminez, and Jiminez cross-appeals, asserting that the damages are inadequate. Concluding that the factual findings of the district court are clearly erroneous, we reverse.

Jiminez applied for an assistant professorship in the Department of Economics at MWC on March 4, 1989. In connection with his application, Jiminez represented that he would receive his doctorate degree in economics in June of 1989 from the University of New Mexico. A divided Economics Department extended Jiminez an offer, even though he was not the most qualified applicant; he only met MWC's minimal standards. The department was split in its decision to offer Jiminez a position since he garnered inauspicious evaluations at the University of New Mexico. Despite this knowledge, MWC offered Jiminez the position because the college was seeking to increase the number of blacks on its faculty. To a degree, therefore, Jiminez was hired because he was black. By letter dated August 3, 1989, William Anderson, President of MWC, notified Jiminez of MWC's offer, expressly explaining that Jiminez' appointment was "contingent upon his being granted his Ph.D. by August 16, 1989." This contingency reflected MWC's policy applicable to Jiminez that professors seeking tenure have terminal degrees, as reflected in the faculty handbook, which provided that for consideration for promotion to assistant professor "possession of the appropriate earned terminal degree, in most cases, the Doctorate in one's discipline in unusual circumstances, equivalent professional achievement" was necessary. Thus, on extension of the offer, Jiminez was aware that obtaining his Ph.D. was necessary for promotion. In this respect, Jiminez' offer differed from that of his colleague in the Economics Department, Professor Steve Greenlaw, because according to the 1982 faculty handbook in effect when Greenlaw was hired, attaining a terminal degree was not a prerequisite for advancement. Thus, Greenlaw was given tenure even though he did not obtain a terminal degree until 1986.

As a nontenured professor seeking tenure, Jiminez was subject to a six-year probationary period after which he could be awarded tenure. Consistent with MWC's procedures, Jiminez initially was awarded a one-year contract as a newly-hired, tenure-track faculty member. Subsequent to his initial year, a tenure-track faculty member can be awarded a two-year contract, followed by a three-year contract, provided, of course, his performance satisfied MWC's standards. Following successful completion of the three-year contract, a faculty member could be considered for tenure. If a tenure-track professor is not considered for further advancement because of unsatisfactory performance, however, MWC grants him a one-year terminal contract, which expires at the termination of the academic year.

Tenure is based largely on teacher evaluations. The faculty at MWC is evaluated annually according to three criteria: (1) teaching effectiveness; (2) service to MWC; and (3) scholarship or professional activity. Of these criteria, teaching effectiveness is paramount and is based largely on evaluations from students, the department chairman, and other faculty within the department. Scholarship or professional activity includes publication or presentation of scholarly works.

After his first semester of teaching, MWC evaluated Jiminez' performance on February 22, 1990. This evaluation was a compendium of faculty observations, student course ratings, and the annual Faculty Activities Report. The gist of this initial evaluation was that Jiminez' skills as a professor were lacking, but his personal fortitude was commendable. Specifically with respect to the tenure criteria, this evaluation concluded: 1. Concerning teaching effectiveness, students were critical of the clarity and loudness of his voice, his speaking to the chalk board instead of the class, poorly worded tests, and covering material too fast." These negative conclusions were countered by the generic observation that they were "shortcomings any new teacher is bound to have and are things easily corrected by experience. Additionally, Jiminez was "praised . . . for caring about his students, holding review sessions, encouraging questions, and taking the time to make sure students understand the material." 2. Regarding service to MWC, Jiminez was rated highly for his participation in college organizations. 3. Respecting scholarship, the evaluation admonished that Jiminez' major focus for the immediate future must be completion of this dissertation." Significantly, Jiminez neither protested nor contradicted the initial evaluation's conclusions.

On April 2, 1991, MWC again evaluated Jiminez' performance, this evaluation again being an amalgam of the faculty observations, student course ratings, and the annual Faculty Activities Report. Focusing on the three primary criteria for tenure, this second MWC evaluation concluded: 1. With respect to teaching effectiveness, the evaluation reported that while Jiminez was dedicated, his "student evaluation scores were below average for both the Economics Department and College-wide faculty," but expressing the hope that time would cure this failure. 2. With respect to service Jiminez again rated highly; and 3. With respect to scholarship, the evaluation observed that Jiminez had attended various meetings. As with the initial MWC evaluation, Jiminez conspicuously took no exception to the conclusions, nor did he request consideration for a merit award.

> An example, a letter from former student Laura Kasley recited:
>
> It is my understanding that several students have either given Mr. Jiminez poor evaluations, or have written negative letters of complaint concerning his teaching. . . . Last semester (Fall 1991), I . . . witnessed, on evaluation day, a collaborative effort on the part of the majority of students to give Mr. Jiminez poor evaluations. They have also written negative letters of complaint concerning his teaching. It is my opinion that the students in this class, who gave Mr. Jiminez poor evaluations, did not take the time required by the course to fully understand the material. Since the first day of classes, Mr. Jiminez forewarned us to ask him to repeat himself if we couldn't understand his accent. . . . I have acclimated to his accent and find no trouble understanding him. Ultimately, Kasley opined that despite the fact that Jiminez was not the best qualified candidate, on hiring him MWC assumed particular or additional burdens "to protect Jiminez from racial and national origin animus." MWC's duty was only to refrain from taking adverse employment action against him because of invidious racial discrimination, and MWC's obligation did not extend to protecting Jiminez against any alleged racial and national origin animus by others in the employment community, nor to excusing derelictions in the job performance because the animus of others may have contributed to it.

Jiminez produced no scholarly work. While he was somewhat excused from this requirement while working on his Ph.D. he did not complete his Ph.D. in the prescribed time, nor by the time he was given a terminal contract: hence, he cannot take refuge in this safe harbor. Jiminez himself testified that during his entire stint at the college, he never published a single work in a peer-review publication. We note that Jiminez' failure to produce scholarly publications presents a legitimate rationale for issuing a terminal contract. (See *King v. Board of Regents of Univ. of Wis. Sys.* explaining that a Title VII plaintiff "was not qualified for tenure renewal," because she failed to produce "scholarly publications" and noting that scholarship is an integral factor in assessing tenure-type decisions). As with the other evidence, the district court disregarded the fact that Jiminez had defaulted on this obligation and in so doing, clearly erred.

We hold that Jiminez failed to satisfy the obligations imposed on him in that he failed to prove that he was a victim of invidious discrimination.

The judgment of the district court, therefore, is reversed.
Judgment for Mary Washington College.

The following case addresses the question of whether a supervisor's criticism, marginal evaluation, and decision to transfer a Hispanic employee constituted racial discrimination. The supervisor claimed that his actions were justified because of the employee's poor performance.

CASE

De La Cruz v. New York City Human Resources Dept.

184 F.Supp. 112 (S.D.N.Y.)

MOTLEY, District Judge.

Plaintiff Sergio de la Cruz, a caseworker for the Human Resources Administration of the City of New York (HRA), commenced this Title VII and Section 1983 action alleging that a supervisor's criticism, marginal rating of his communication skills, and a transfer to another unit without any loss of pay or benefits, constitute anti-Hispanic discrimination. Defendants have moved for summary judgment pursuant to Rule 56(e). Plaintiff was first employed as a caseworker by New York City Human Resources Administration ("Human Resources") in August 1988. He was assigned to the Division of Adoption and Foster Care Services (DAFCS), Centralized Services, of the HRA. DAFCS is responsible for evaluating prospective parents and foster parents, which requires, among other matters, personal visits by caseworkers to perform home studies and to personally interview applicants and their references. In DAFCS several units perform various services. These units are Inquiry/Recruitment, which handles the initial inquiries from prospective applicants; Adoption/Interstate Compact (unit 703), which is responsible for adoption home studies, interstate adoption and foster care home studies and special adoption and foster care home studies; Placement/Coordination, which oversees the placement of children under the auspices of DAFCS; and Foster Care/Home Finding (units 704 and 705), which assess prospective foster parents. DAFCS was under the supervision of Site Director Constance Weinberg. Because the home studies reports were ultimately submitted to Family Court in connection with adoption or foster care proceedings, these reports needed to be done in a comprehensible, professional manner.

During the first two years of his employment, Plaintiff received very good performance evaluations. In September 1990, plaintiff was transferred to unit 703 (adoption unit) and given the title of "acting" supervisor I position. At the same time twelve other caseworkers were placed in "acting" positions and performed "out-of-title" duties. Acting supervisors received no additional pay or benefits. Unit 703 required special investigatory and creative problem solving skills. In January 1991, Myra Berman, who is Caucasian, became the unit supervisor for the adoption unit and plaintiff's direct supervisor. Berman's supervisor who was Doris Ayala, who is Hispanic. The employees of unit 703 at the time of plaintiff's assignment included plaintiff; Donald Williams, an African-American; Brahaspatie Ramsaroop, an East-Indian-Guyanese; and Ira Sohmer, a Caucasian. All of these employees had the title of "supervisor I." In this unit, all employees with the title of "supervisor I" performed caseworker duties, rather than supervision of a unit which is the traditional duty of a supervisor. However, they carried a higher caseload than caseworkers in other units.

Although plaintiff was generally a good employee, he frequently made errors in his written work, particularly concerning articles, word usage, and use of prepositions. He also demonstrated comprehension problems in gathering and recording information presented to him by English-speaking clients. Plaintiff concedes that he makes grammatical errors in the course of his work.

When Berman gave plaintiff a performance evaluation for the period of October 31, 1991, to January 30, 1992, she gave plaintiff an overall rating of good but she also gave him a marginal rating in his verbal and writing skills. The subsequent performance evaluation given for the period of January 31, 1992, to April 10, 1992, had him upgraded from marginal to good in his verbal and written communication skills. At about this same period of time, Berman also evaluated Donald Willliams, an African-American and gave similar criticism of Mr. Williams' deficits in communication skills.

On March 30, 1992, Child Welfare Administration Executive Deputy Director Robert Little ended the agency policy of permitting employees to perform "out-of-title" work. As a result, all thirteen workers in "acting" titles, including plaintiff and Berman, were restored to their original civil service titles effective April 10, 1992. In total, 5 Hispanics, 2 whites, and 6 African-Americans were reassigned to their former titles. Along with the reassignment, some of these employees were transferred to other units. Plaintiff himself was transferred to unit 704, based on the Little directive and Weinberg's belief that plaintiff could perform better in a unit where the written work would not be as demanding on limited writing skills. Plaintiffs direct supervisor, Berman, did not participate in the decision. Plaintiff claims that Berman's remarks that plaintiff's problems were "cultural" and that she wanted to replace him with a black female and Weinberg's comment that plaintiff and his new Hispanic supervisor "will understand each other better" are direct evidence of discrimination. These remarks are supported by plaintiff's affidavit and not supported elsewhere in the record. These remarks standing along appear to be the only "evidence" that plaintiff presents in his attempt to make out his claim for discrimination. However, defendants correctly indicate these ambiguous statements cannot be "evidence which, if believed, prove the fact without interference or presumption." In a discrimination case, explicit and unambiguous statements of racial or ethnic hostility would be direct evidence (statement by company official that if it were his company he would not hire black people); (supervisor's repeated use of term "nigger"). For further guidance on the issue of direct evidence, Justice O'Connor's concurrence stated that "stray remarks in the workplace," "statements by non-decision-makers," and "statements by decision-makers unrelated to the decisional process itself do not "justify requiring the employer to prove that its hiring or promotion decisions were based on legitimate criteria." Berman was not involved in the decision to transfer plaintiff to unit 704 so her remarks cannot qualify as direct evidence. Moreover, Weinberg's comment that plaintiff and his new Hispanic supervisor would understand each other better is lacking in racial animus and cannot be considered in and of itself to be direct evidence of discrimination.

Even if this court did consider this statement to be direct evidence and the burden to defendants to show that plaintiff would have been transferred for a legitimate business purpose as required by Price Waterhouse, there is clear evidence that plaintiff made numerous and critical errors in his written reports. It should be noted for the record that defendants have clearly articulated a legitimate business reason for its business decision which is supported by documentary evidence.

Judgment for N.Y.C.
Human Resources Department.

Employment Perspective

Fishers Oil Drilling Equipment prides itself on being an equal opportunity employer because it has numerous employees of all races. However, the minority employees are all factory workers. Each time a minority worker applies for a managerial position, he or she is rejected. Fisher feels that it is better that the minorities work among their own kind. Is this racial discrimination? Yes! Fisher Oil is prejudicing the ability and competence of its minority workers on the basis of the color of their skin or of their origin. Fisher Oil may know that its white managers may feel uncomfortable with minorities working with them rather than underneath them, but this privilege of racial dominance can no longer be sustained. Everyone must be given an equal opportunity. ◆

In the next case, a black female alleged that she was hired for a position subordinate to the one she applied for because of her race. When she informed her employer of her intent to file a racial discrimination claim, she claims she was discharged in retaliation.

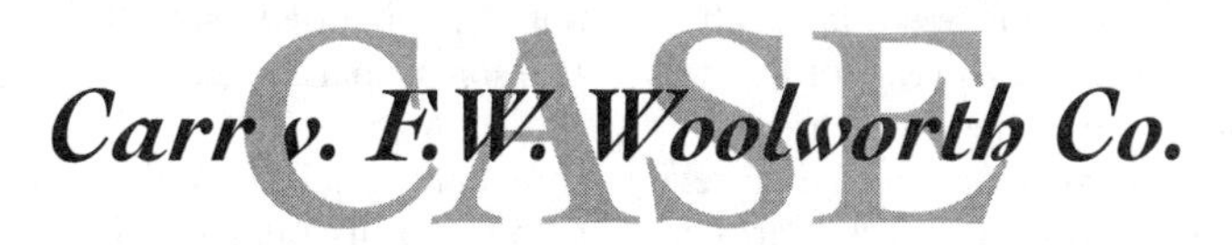

Carr v. F.W. Woolworth Co.

883 F.Supp. 10 (E.D.N.C. 1992)

BOYLE, Judge.

Plaintiff Brentley Jean Carr has charged defendant Woolworth Company and its employee, Carol McCullen, with violating both Title VII of the Civil Rights Act of 1964 and Section 1981. Specifically, Carr contends that defendants hired her as assistant manager at a retail outlet, rather than for the manager's position, based on unlawful considerations of race, and subsequently discharged her in retaliation for her announced intent to file a complaint concerning the hiring decision. Defendants have denied these charges, and now seek dismissal of all claims against them.

On June 13, 1990, defendant Woolworth, solicited applications for manager and assistant manager of AfterThoughts, a newly opened retail subsidiary of Woolworth's specializing in moderately-priced ladies' fashion accessories. Plaintiff Carr, 33-year-old black female, applied for both positions on the following day. The printed application form Carr filled out warned applicants that any misrepresentation would be grounds for denial of employment or dismissal.

Carr's application showed that she had held six jobs over the previous six years, all in either banks and credit unions or in the cashier's of retail sales outlets such as Montgomery Ward's. She listed her most recent position as "interviewer" in the loan department of Seymour Johnson Federal Credit Union. Carr described her duties there as primarily involving processing loan applications, but including assisting as a teller or in collections when needed. Plaintiff's educational background consisted of a high school degree, one year as a nursing major at a community college, and further community college course work to become a notary. In an aptitude test administered by Woolworth at the time of her application, Carr scored a 98 out of 100.

Plaintiff was interviewed by defendant Carol McCullen, a white female then serving as AfterThoughts Area manager. Shortly thereafter, Plaintiff was offered the assistant manager's post, which she accepted. As part of her administrative in-processing, Carr filled out two personal reference forms, which were mailed to Carr's previous employers with the understanding that her position as assistant manager was contingent on Woolworth's receiving satisfactory responses.

Soon after assuming her duties at AfterThoughts, Carr became skeptical of the professional and interpersonal skills of Emily Jackson, the white woman chosen as manager. Examining Jackson's personnel file, Carr learned that Jackson had scored eight points lower on her aptitude test than she, was 11 years younger, and had, in Carr's opinion, inferior work experience. Jackson had previously worked short stints as insurance sales agent, sign company office manager, hospital payroll supervisor, a clerk, and day-care teacher. In addition, Jackson and her husband had briefly owned and operated an aluminum siding and window company. Her resume also listed periods of employment at Reed's Jewelers and D.A. Kelly's under the heading "Odd Jobs-Retail." Jackson was a high school graduate who had completed two years of business courses at local community colleges.

Based solely on her evaluation of their relative qualifications and respective races, Carr concluded that Jackson had been chosen for the manager's position over her because of racial prejudice. On July 28, 1990, she questioned Area Manager McCullen on her hiring decision. Although allegedly admitting having made a mistake, McCullen defended her initial choice, saying she had been impressed by Jackson's more recent sales experience, more extensive college education, management background, and more enthusiastic and outgoing attitude, which McCullen thought would benefit sales. According to plaintiff, McCullen then offered her the manager's position at another AfterThoughts outlet, and asked her to keep notes on Jackson's poor performance to support her eventual discharge. Carr did not mention her suspicions concerning racial discrimination during this conversation.

Over the next four weeks, Carr continued to complain to McCullen about Jackson's poor performance. During this period, McCullen allegedly learned that Jackson had been fired from her previous job, and had written a bad check to another AfterThoughts outlet—both grounds for dismissal—yet took no action. On August 19, 1990, McCullen told Carr that she was considering firing Jackson. However, Carr would not be moved up to the manager's spot; McCullen allegedly stated that she had chosen a woman from Ohio as replacement manager. This seemed further evidence of discrimination to plaintiff, although she did not ascertain the race of the prospective replacement manager. On August 22, 1990, Carr informed McCullen that she had spoken with the Equal Opportunity Employment Commission (EEOC) concerning this situation, and was considering filing a discrimination complaint. Plaintiff claims that McCullen became angry when she learned of her contact with the EEOC, and ordered her to work immediately for a meeting on the subject.

Carr, McCullen and McCullen's superior, AfterThoughts Regional Manager Mike Marshal, met the same afternoon to discuss Carr's grievances. While Marshal promised to investigate the charges against Jackson and take appropriate action, he supported McCullen's initial selection of Jackson as manager. Carr told her supervisors that she now intended to go forward with her complaint against Woolworth's. Marshal did nothing to discourage plaintiff from this, merely asking that all relevant papers be forwarded to his office.

On August 28, 1990, McCullen informed Carr that she had spoken with Mildred Hodgin, Carr's former supervisor at Seymour Johnson Federal Credit Union. Contrary to statements contained in her AfterThoughts application, Hodgin told McCullen that Carr had not been employed as a loan interviewer who occasionally filled in as a teller, but rather the reverse; Carr had worked primarily as a teller, but did loan interviews and collections work when needed. Hodgin also returned a reference form in which she rated Carr's performance as "fair," and indicated that she would not re-hire Carr based on her spotty attendance and professed need for a better-paying job. After a brief argument concerning these revelations, McCullen dismissed Carr for falsifying her application and for poor references.

Carr proceeded to file Title VII charges against Woolworth's, accusing the corporation of racial discrimination in hiring and retaliatory discharge. The complaint did not name McCullen as an individual defendant. After its own investigation uncovered no evidence to support Carr's claims, the EEOC dismissed both charges against Woolworth's, and gave Plaintiff notice of her right to sue. Plaintiff subsequently filed this action.

Plaintiff has satisfied the minimal requirements of a prima facie case. She is a black female who applied and was qualified for the manager's position at AfterThoughts, and was rejected for that position in favor of Jackson, a white female. Moreover, Carr has provided evidence sufficient to create "fair doubt" as to who was better qualified to be manager, thus raising the possibility that the proffered rationale behind the hiring decision is pretextual. By her own admission, however, plaintiff does not expect to produce any evidence to sustain her ultimate burden of proving that defendants' stated reasons for hiring Jackson were not only pretextual, but also were a pretext for race-based discrimination.

Faced with this formidable evidentiary task, Carr states with admirable perhaps, unintentional candor that her only proof of defendants discriminatory intent is that she is black, Jackson is white, and plaintiff believes herself to be better qualified than Jackson. In some instances Carr lacks even this minimal basis; she notes McCullen's decision to replace Jackson with a woman from Ohio, rather than plaintiff, as further evidence of racial discrimination, without even knowing the proposed replacement's race. Plaintiff must have some proffer of evidence which reaches beyond speculation and conjecture and which could support an inference that her employer's decision was other than a business decision and impermissibly based on race. Plaintiff has failed to produce such evidence and the absence of this evidence of pretext is fatal.

Judgment for F.W. Woolworth Co.

Employment Perspective

Marshall Jackson, who is black, has been a sales representative for Tucker Machinery Corp. for twenty years. His district has a predominantly black population. He has applied for promotion to sales manager. Although his credentials are superior to those of the other candidates, Jackson is overlooked because management feels that he will not command the respect of the sales force, which is overwhelmingly white. Is this employment discrimination? Yes! Tucker Machinery has violated Title VII because the sole reason that Jackson was not selected was because he was black. Jackson would be entitled to the promotion, together with the pay differential from the date when he should have been selected. ◆

In the case that follows, a black male claimed he was discharged from his position as a disc jockey because of his race. He satisfied his initial burden under the McDonnell Douglas test. The employer, in turn, met its burden of justifiable action. The question presented is whether the employer's reason for discharge was a pretext.

CASE *Thompson v. Price Broadcasting Co.*

817 F.Supp. 1538 (D. Utah 1993)

ANDERSON, District Judge.

Wayne Thompson (hereafter "Thompson") brought this race discrimination action against his former employer, Price Broadcasting Company KCPX (hereafter referred to as "Price" or "KCPX"), for allegedly discharging him in violation of Title VII of the 1964 Civil Rights Act.

Thompson is a 36-year-old African male who has worked since 1980 in the broadcasting industry. During that time Thompson has worked in radio production, and has acted as a radio personality ("Jockey"). As a Disk Jockey, Thompson is aware that listeners develop listening habits and loyalty to radio stations because of the particular personalities involved. Thus, radio stations require their Disk Jockeys to make every effort possible to be at work in sufficient time to go "on the air" for assigned time slots.

On October 14, 1988, Thompson was hired by Price to work part time as a KCPX Jockey for the Sunday afternoon time slot 2:00 p.m. to 9:00 p.m. Prior to working for Price, Thompson worked as a Disk Jockey for Radio Station KDAB in Ogden, Utah, where Thompson resided. KCPX is located in Salt Lake City, Utah, and Thompson agreed to provide his own transportation to and from work on Sundays.

Shortly after going to work for Price, Thompson brought a Title VII lawsuit against his former employer KDAB for allegedly firing him because of his race. This lawsuit was publicized in the local newspapers, and a copy of an article relating to the suit was cut out by an unknown employee of Price, and placed on the desk of supervisor David Leppink, whose radio name is Morgan Evans (hereafter "Evans"). Evans acknowledged seeing the article, but testified that it played no part in his decision making with regard to Thompson.

A few days after the local newspapers publicized Thompson's suit against KDAB, a snow storm hit the northern parts of Utah. By 4:00 p.m., Mountain Standard Time, on Saturday, November 26, 1988, driving conditions in the Ogden area became hazardous as a result of snowy and icy roads. Thompson, being concerned about the driving conditions, telephoned Evans' home at 4:43 p.m. to inform Evans that he would not be coming into KCPX the next day for his radio slot. Evans was not home, and Thompson left a message on Evans' answering machine.

When Evans returned home at approximately 4:50 p.m. he listened to the telephone message from Thompson and telephoned Thompson's house. Mrs. Thompson answered the telephone, and informed Evans that her husband was not at home, and was at Lionel Playworld in Ogden where he had a second job. Evans informed Mrs. Thompson that roads in Salt Lake City were not too bad, and that he expected Thompson to be at work at 2:00 p.m. the next day. Evans further informed Mrs. Thompson that she should contact her husband to tell him that he was expected to report to work, and that if there was a problem Thompson should call Evans to talk about it.

Mrs. Thompson did as she was instructed and telephoned Evans' home thirty minutes later with her husband's reply. Evans had gone out, however, and Mrs. Thompson had to leave another message on Evans' answering machine. She stated that her husband still felt the same way, and that he would not be coming into work the next day. Five hours later, when Evans returned home and listened to his messages, Evans telephoned Mrs. Thompson to get Thompson's telephone number at Lionel Playworld.

When Evans spoke with Thompson at Lionel Playworld, he asked Thompson what the problem was. Thompson responded that KCPX did not pay him enough to risk his life driving down to Salt Lake City to do a shift. Evans responded that he needed someone he could count on every Sunday, regardless of the weather. When Thompson stated he would not be coming down to

Salt Lake City the next day for the 2:00 p.m. shift, Evans fired him.

Following his firing by KCPX, Thompson brought race discrimination claims against Price before the Anti-Discrimination Division of the Industrial Commission of Utah ("ICU") and the Equal Opportunity Commission of the United States ("EEOC"). The ICU and EEOC found no basis for Thompson's discrimination charges.

There are two theories of employment discrimination under Title VII: disparate treatment and disparate impact. The disparate treatment theory focuses on the employer's intent to discriminate. Disparate impact, on the other hand, requires no proof of discriminatory intent. Rather, a plaintiff need only show that the employer's practices are "discriminatory in operation."

At trial, Thompson only sought relief for disparate treatment under Title VII, specifically, discriminatory discharge and retaliatory discharge. Consequently, Thompson needed to show discriminatory intent on the part of Price. Thompson failed to do so.

Title VII of the 1964 Civil Rights Act makes it unlawful for an employer to discharge any individual, or to otherwise discriminate against any individual . . . because of such individual's race.

To establish a prima facie case for discrimination under Title VII, the plaintiff must show that: (1) he belongs to a protected group; (2) he was qualified for his job; (3) he was terminated despite his qualifications; and (4) after his termination, the employer hired someone or sought applicants for the plaintiff's vacated position, whose qualifications were no better than the Plaintiff's.

The court is persuaded that Thompson met the burden of establishing a prima facie case of discriminatory discharge. In that regard, Thompson, an African-American, is a member of a protected class. Further, Price did not dispute that Thompson was qualified for the Disk Jockey job. Price conceded that Thompson has been involved in the radio broadcast industry for a number of years, and had performed his job at KCPX for six weeks without complaint from management as to his performance. Despite being qualified for the job, Thompson was discharged. Finally, while there was a dispute between the parties as to who took over Thompson's radio time slot, there is no question that someone handled the air time.

The Court is also persuaded that Thompson met his burden to establish a prima facie cause of action for retaliatory discharge under Title VII of the 1964 Civil Rights Act. The Act provides:

> It shall be unlawful . . . for an employer to discriminate against any of his employees . . . because the employee has made a charge, testified, assisted, or participated in any manner in an investigation, proceeding, or hearing under this subchapter.

The Tenth Circuit Court of Appeals has held that in order for a plaintiff to establish a prima facie cause of action for retaliation, the plaintiff must show by a preponderance of the evidence that: (1) Plaintiff engaged in protected opposition to discrimination or participation in a proceeding arising out of discrimination; (2) adverse action by the employer subsequent to the protected activity; and (3) a causal connection between the employee's activity and the adverse action.

Thompson established that he was engaged in a protected activity at the time of his discharge from KCPX. In that regard, although there exists no business relationship between KDAB, the station against whom Thompson brought his discrimination suit and KCPX, the law does not require such a relationship. If a relationship between employers was required, claimants would be discouraged from filing discrimination claims against former employers because of the fear that their present employers, upon learning of the claims, would fire them. The purposes of Title VII would, therefore, be frustrated.

Thompson also established the second requirement of a retaliation claim, by showing that subsequent to his filing of a suit against KDAB, he was fired by Price. Termination of employment clearly constitutes an "adverse action by the employer subsequent to the protected activity."

Finally, Thompson established, as a result of the timing of his discharge by KCPX and the filing of the claim against KDAB, that a causal connection existed between the protected activity and the adverse action, at least for purposes of proving a prima facie case.

A "causal connection may be demonstrated by the proximity of the adverse action to the protected activity, provided, the employer . . . had knowledge of the plaintiff's protected activity."

Having found a prima facie case for Thompson's discriminatory discharge claim and retaliatory discharge claim, the burden of production shifts to Price to show "a legitimate nondiscriminatory reason for terminating the employee."

In meeting its burden, Price need not prove that it was actually motivated by its non-discriminatory reason.

As noted by the United States Supreme Court:

> "The burden that shifts to the defendant, therefore, is to rebut the presumption of discrimination by producing evidence that the plaintiff was rejected . . . for a legitimate, nondiscriminatory reason. The defendant need not persuade the court that it was actually motivated by the proffered reasons. . . . It is sufficient if the defendant's evidence raises a genuine issue of fact as to whether it discriminated against the plaintiff. To accomplish this, the defendant must clearly set forth, through the introduction of admissible evidence the reasons for the plaintiff's rejection. The explanation must be legally sufficient to justify a judgment for the defendant.

The question of Price's actual motivation is only addressed after Price shows a legitimate nondiscriminatory reason for termination, and the burden of proof shifts back to Thompson under McDonnell Douglas.

At trial, Price presented credible evidence that on the day before Thompson was to report to work, Thompson telephoned his superior at KCPX, Morgan Evans, to inform Evans that he was not going to come to work because of adverse weather conditions. Evans informed Thompson that the weather was not that bad, and that he expected him to report to work. When Thompson continued to refuse to come to work, he was fired.

A refusal to work is a legitimate nondiscriminatory reason for terminating an employee. In *E.E.O.C. v. Wendy's of Colorado Springs, Inc.*, the reason for terminating the employee that Defendant articulated was that he "refused to work necessary time periods necessary to meet store needs." Refusal to work the time periods necessary to meet the demands of business demonstrates a lack of qualification for the job. Lack of qualifications is a legitimate, nondiscriminatory reason for terminating an employee.

In the radio broadcast industry, management is constantly concerned with the concept of "listener expectation." That concept is that listeners have expectations that when they tune to a certain radio station at a certain time, a particular music or news format will be in the process of being presented, and that a certain disk jockey will be on the air. By consistently fulfilling the listener's expectations, the radio station keeps the listener's loyalty, and can ask advertisers to pay for the privilege of broadcasting their messages to the listener. For this reason, broadcast employers legitimately expect their Disk Jockeys to make every effort possible to be on the air when scheduled. Thompson was unable to satisfy Price that he would make that effort. The Court determines, therefore, that Price had a legitimate reason to terminate Thompson.

Price did not discuss the KDAB suit with Thompson and did not look for an excuse to fire Thompson after finding out about the lawsuit. On the contrary, the evidence shows that when Evans was first informed by Thompson that Thompson was not coming in to work the next day, Evans did not fire Thompson but, rather, gave Thompson an opportunity to say that he would be coming into work. The Court is convinced that if Thompson had simply informed Evans on November 26, 1988, that he would be at the radio station for his assigned time slot on Sunday, Thompson would not have been fired. Even if Evans "had in mind" the KDAB lawsuit at the time that he fired Thompson, and there is no direct evidence that he did, Thompson's Title VII claim would still fail.

As noted by the Tenth Circuit Court of Appeals:

> Once a plaintiff in a Title VII case shows that an illegitimate reason played a motivating part in an employment decision, the defendant may avoid a finding of liability only by proving that it would have made the same decision even if it had not allowed the improper motive to play such a role.

The Court finds that Price would have discharged Thompson on November 21, 1988, even if no lawsuit had been filed by Thompson against his former employer, KDAB. Price needed Disk Jockeys that it could count on to make every rea-

sonable effort possible to make their assigned shifts regardless of the weather. Thompson was not willing to make that effort.

While Thompson established a prima facie case under Title VII on both his retaliatory discharge and discriminatory discharge claims, he was unable to show by a preponderance of the evidence that Price's legitimate nondiscriminatory reason for discharge was a pretext. No violation of Title VII was shown and judgment will be entered for the defendant.

Judgment for Price Broadcasting.

The question presented in the next case is at what point does the statute of limitations begin to run. The black male bringing the action claimed it should begin at the time he learned of the preselection criteria on which his action is based. The employer claimed it should commence when the selection took place.

CASE

Zervas v. District of Columbia

817 F.Supp. 148 (D.D.C. 1993)

HARRIS, District Judge.

Plaintiff's claim . . . is based on the promotion of Danny Mott, an African American, to the position of Deputy Director of Emergency Ambulance Bureau (EAB) of the DCFD in March of 1988. Plaintiff alleges that the selection was made on the basis of race. Plaintiff also alleges that defendants Barry, Coleman, and Thornton preselected Mott for the position in October 1987. Mott was "acting" Deputy Director at the time and remained in the "acting" position until the official announcement of his selection after a purported competitive selection process in March of 1988.

Defendants argue that the plaintiff's claim is time-barred because he alleges that the actual selection occurred in October 1987. Plaintiff's claim as to the March 1988 selection process was filed within the three year statute of limitations. Plaintiff's claim was also timely to the extent that he relies on the alleged preselection in October 1987. Plaintiff was not aware of the facts constituting that cause of action until April 1989, when his counsel obtained a document referring to the alleged preselection through discovery. Until that time, plaintiff could not reasonably have known the facts surrounding the alleged preselection. It appeared that no permanent selection had been made for the position because Mott was "acting" Deputy Director and the DCFD solicited applications for the post. The statute of limitations did not begin to run until April of 1989. Thus, plaintiff's claim is not time-barred.

Judgment for Zervas.

RACIAL HARASSMENT

Racial harassment in the workplace exists when conduct by coworkers, superiors, or the company itself has created a hostile work environment in which the victimized employee's ability to do his or her job has been impaired. Evidence of the severity of the incidents is equally as important as the frequency.

When an employee claims that he or she is being racially harassed by a coworker, the employee must notify the employer. The employer must not condone this activity and must investigate the complaint in a timely fashion. If the employer finds a reasonable basis for believing that the harassment exists, it must take corrective action immediately, or otherwise it will be held liable. When the harassment originates with the employer itself, then no notification is needed. The employer will be held liable.

Employment Perspective

Todd Washington was hired as a management trainee in Bulls and Bears Brokerage House. He was the first black person in a managerial position in the Jackson, Mississippi office. Towards the end of the first week, he found his desk covered by a white sheet with a burnt cross lying across it. Washington complained to his superiors, who told him that the boys just have a warped sense of humor. Similar incidents followed. Does this constitute racial harassment? Yes! Todd Washington was harassed by his coworkers. He made a timely complaint to his employer, which made no attempt to investigate and took no corrective action. For its failure to act, Bulls and Bears is liable. ◆

In the following case, a black female claimed she was constructively discharged because she was black. The issue is whether the working conditions were so deplorable that no reasonable person could continue working there.

CASE *Harriston v. Chicago Tribune Co.*

992 F.2d 697 (7th Cir. 1993)

MANION, Circuit Judge.

The Tribune hired Harriston as a voluntary advertisement taker. During the next fifteen years of Harriston's career with the Tribune, she was promoted to various positions within the Advertising Department.

When Harriston became the EEO/Employment Manager, the position was not eligible for participation in the Tribune's Management Incentive Fund. . . .

In April 1987, John Sloan replaced Veon as the Vice President of Employee Relations. Sloan found Harriston's work performance as EEO/Employment Manager unsatisfactory, mainly because she lacked the skills a human resource manager needed. Sloan thought Harriston better suited for the work done in the Advertising Department, and he contacted Robert Holzkamp, the Vice President of Advertising, to determine the availability of any positions suitable for Harriston. Sloan later learned that an opening would be occurring for a Senior Sales Representative for the Michigan Avenue territory.

Sloan informed Harriston about the opening. Harriston accepted the position, effective June 1987. Her new salary was $51,500.00 per year, which was $2,000.00 more than she had made as the EEO/Employment Manager. Ronald Williams, a black man, replaced Harriston as the EEO/Employment Manager. Unlike Harriston, Williams had considerable experience in the area of human resources, something that was needed in light of the change in the Employee Relations Department. Sloan thereafter restructured the EEO/Employment Manager position, making it eligible for participation in the Incentive Fund.

In June 1988, after working as a Senior Sales Representative for one year Harriston received her first performance appraisal. Riordan gave her a "satisfactory" rating, but criticized her sales level. Owing to her "satisfactory" evaluation, Harriston received a $2,060.00 salary increase, which brought her annual salary to $53,560.00. Still, throughout the remainder of 1988 Riordan continued to observe problems with Harriston's work. She failed to serve properly some of her advertising accounts, and the annual revenue in her territory had declined approximately $257,000.00 from the previous year.

To help Harriston increase her sales performance, Riordan removed her from the RECAS project in January 1989. Her sales did not improve. Revenue in her territory for the first four months of 1981 was down nearly $75,000.00. In May 1989, Riordan sent Harriston a memorandum expressing his displeasure with her sales performance and requested her to inform him how she planned to improve. Riordan did not threaten to fire Harriston. Harriston, however, failed to respond to the memorandum. Instead, she submitted a letter of resignation in June 1989. In the letter, she alleged age and race discrimination as well as retaliation against her both because she had filed complaints with the Equal Employment Opportunity Commission in the past concerning employment discrimination against her and because she had an employment discrimination lawsuit against the Defendants pending in federal district court.

Harriston has not, however, presented us with evidence to show that participation in the Incentive Fund would have provided her with greater benefits and, therefore, has not supported her position that she was demoted when she took the job as Senior Sales Representative. Second, Harriston has not shown that she was excluded from participation in the Incentive Fund because she was black. Harriston has not shown that she was constructively discharged. To establish a constructive discharge claim, Harriston needed to show that the Tribune made her working conditions so intolerable that she was forced to resign involuntarily. Harriston alleged that she was subjected to such forms of discrimination as being excluded from office activities, being reprimanded without reason, and being given one of the least lucrative sales territories, as well as not being assigned new accounts, not being allowed to supervise two white employees, and not being assisted by Riordan. We agree with the district court that the alleged conduct was not intolerable. Harriston's allegations do not show that her working conditions were so onerous or demeaning that she was compelled to leave her employment with the Tribune.

Accordingly, we affirm the district court for granting summary judgment in favor of the Defendants.

Judgment for Chicago Tribune Co.

COLOR DISCRIMINATION

Title VII prohibits discrimination against color in addition to race. Color could apply to people of mixed races, as well as to the different color of pigmentation of people of the same race. In Europe, white people from southern Europe have darker pigmentation than white people from northern Europe. Black, Asian, and Hispanic people have different shades of pigmentation.

Employment Perspective

Rachel Blake, who is a dark-skinned black woman, is employed as a teller in the Bank of Los Angeles. Dena Perry, a light-skinned black woman, is the bank manager. For eight years Rachel has been passed over for promotions by whites and light-skinned blacks. Rachel claims that she has been discriminated against by her superior. Dena disagrees, claiming that discrimination cannot exist where both parties are of the same race. Who is correct? Rachel! Dena has discriminated against Rachel because of the color of her skin and not because of her race. ◆

RECONSTRUCTION ACT

Following the abolition of slavery with the passage of the Thirteenth Amendment to the Constitution, Congress passed the Reconstruction Era Act in 1866. The Act provided blacks with the right "to make and enforce contracts . . . as enjoyed by white citizens." The right to make and enforce contracts includes employment contracts. The Civil Rights Act of 1991 has amended and incorporated this Act within it. There are several distinctions between bringing a claim under the Reconstruction Act and under Title VII.

Title VII applies to employers with fifteen or more employees. The Reconstruction Act applies to all employees. Title VII has a statute of limitations for filing. The Reconstruction Act does not. Title VII places monetary limitations on the recovery of compensatory and punitive damages. The Reconstruction Act has no such limitations.

The availability of the Reconstruction Act is limited to race, color, and national origin. It does not apply to sex, religion, disability, or age. The reason that not all claims for racial discrimination are filed under the Reconstruction Act is that there is a more stringent requirement for proving intentional discrimination. Under Title VII, proving intentional discrimination is not required, only that a disparate impact exists.

Employment Perspective

The Beanery, a cafeteria-style restaurant, required that all employees be clean-shaven and free of facial hair. Because Edward Jordan refused to shave his beard, he was discharged. Jordan sued under the Reconstruction Act. His claim was based on the fact that many black men have a facial skin condition that becomes very irritated when they shave. To require them to do so is discriminatory. Will he win? No! Jordan will be unable to prove that the Beanery's requirement was intended to discriminate purposely against black men. He would be better off instituting a claim for disparate impact under Title VII, where no intent on the part of the employer is required. If Jordan sued under Title VII, he would most likely win. However, if more than 180 days from the date of his discharge has elapsed, he will be barred from proceeding under Title VII because of its statute of limitations. ◆

U.S. CONSTITUTION

The Fifth Amendment to the U.S. Constitution provides that no person shall be deprived of "life, liberty or property, without due process of the law." This Amendment, which originally applied only to the federal government, was later applied to the states through the Fourteenth Amendment. The Fourteenth Amendment also guarantees to all persons "the equal protection of the laws." Bringing an action under the Constitution does not relieve a party from the statute of limitations under Title VII. The amendments only embellish the validity of the argument against discrimination.

The following case addresses the question of whether the equal protection clause is applicable to black applicants who were equally qualified with the white applicants selected for the position in question.

CASE

Sims v. Montgomery County Com'n

887 F.Supp. 1479 (M.D.Ala. 1995)

THOMPSON, Chief Judge.

This litigation consists of two consolidated class-action lawsuits . . . a class of black employees sought relief from the Montgomery County Sheriff's Department's racially discriminatory employment practices.

On December 15 and 16, 1993, the Sheriff's Department made its selections for promotion to sergeant and lieutenant from among the candidates in band A, the highest band, certified for each rank. Ten white males, one African-American male, and one African-American female scored in the sergeant's band A certification, and two white males, one white female, and one African-American female scored in the lieutenant's band A certification. Because there were no court-approved guidelines to govern the choice of candidates considered equally qualified within a band, the department's selections "were made with consideration of any adverse impact as to race or gender and thereafter, based upon seniority first as to 'time in grade' and second as to time served as a deputy sheriff." The department selected two white males, Robert L. Ingram and Mark C. Thompson, for promotion to sergeant and lieutenant in the enforcement division.

On December 21, 1993, the Sims plaintiffs and the Scott intervenors objected to the selection of two white males, and moved to enjoin the selections. They alleged, among other things, that the Sheriff's Department's selections from within the bands was "unaided by any judicially approved guidelines and was based on seniority, as the determining factor . . . , thereby perpetuating the Department's proven policy and practice of discriminating against African-Americans, who were not even employed in the enforcement division until 1988 and remain woefully under-represented in the 'rank' positions of Sergeant and Lieutenant.' "

On October 20, 1994, the Sims plaintiffs, the Scott intervenors, and the defendants moved for approval of an agreement settling the Sims plaintiffs' and the Scott intervenors' objection to the 1993 selections for promotion to sergeant and lieutenant. Under the agreement, in addition to the two whites selected for promotion to sergeant and lieutenant, the department must select two African-Americans from the top scoring band of most qualified candidates.

Under the equal protection clause, this court must apply strict scrutiny to race conscious relief voluntarily implemented by a public employer . . . . The Sims plaintiffs, the Scott intervenors, and the defendants contend that strict scrutiny analysis is not required because all those in the sergeant and lieutenant bands from which the African-Americans are to be selected are equally qualified, that is, African-Americans were not selected over more qualified whites. The court agrees with the Sims plaintiffs, the Scott intervenors, and the defendants that African-Americans were not selected over more qualified whites. The record is clear that all those in band A for both the sergeant and lieutenant positions were equally qualified.

Judgment for Sims.

CONCLUSION

When baseball finally opened its doors to blacks and Hispanics, they proliferated. The same situation may be true in the future for Asian baseball players. Blacks have also flourished in basketball and football. The integration of minorities into sports has not caused a decline; instead, sports are growing at unprecedented rates because people want to see the best players compete. The same is true in the business arena. If businesses give minorities the opportunity to work but with their jobs contingent upon performance, then minorities will have the impetus to perform to the highest potential they are capable of. Only opportunities can be guaranteed, not lifetime jobs. In sports, minorities must perform up to their potential or otherwise be released. It is rare to hear of a player suing for racial discrimination. In turn, businesses must act like sports teams and hire the most qualified. They must also be color blind.

As the population of the United States is made up of approximately one-quarter minorities, it is too formidable a size to be ignored. This country must embrace the fact that it is racially diverse. There are strengths in this situation that must be recognized. People who come from different backgrounds and cultures have different viewpoints, work habits, traits, traditions, and decision-making methods that they bring to the workplace. These must be exploited, not suppressed. In addition, workers often rise to the level of an employer's expectations. If the expectation is low, the result will be, too. Employers need to present a common color-blind–gender-blind level for their workers.

Leading by example is very important. Businesses can do this, and so can successful business people in the minority community. Minorities that become successful must not abdicate their community in favor of white ones and then allege white people discriminate. They must do their part being role models. Communicating the message that education enables people to become the best that they can be is essential. Education, like a career, is something to be embraced for life.

In a global world, every country is a team, and every person on the team must be a player. There can be no benchwarmers. If there are, the team will be operating at a disadvantage in the global league. This will be the fault of the team for not giving these nonparticipatory members the opportunity and encouragement to become team players with the goal of enabling these individuals to make a significant contribution to the team's success. Teams that meet the challenge will have a successful quest in the global bowl.

REVIEW QUESTIONS

1. Define racial discrimination.
2. What groups could be the subject of racial discrimination?
3. Explain the difference between color discrimination and racial discrimination.
4. Define racial harassment.
5. What impact has the Reconstruction Act had on racial discrimination?
6. Can a bona fide occupational qualification ever exist with regard to race?
7. What effect does the United States Constitution have with respect to race?

8. Why is it preferable to sue under Title VII rather than the Reconstruction Act?
9. In what situation must a victim of racial discrimination sue under the Reconstruction Act because Title VII is unavailable?
10. Are the tensions involving racial discrimination decreasing?
11. Plaintiff's employment discrimination claim is based on the denial of his applications for promotion to either Dean of the School of Engineering at TSU or Head of the Mechanical Engineering Department at TSU. Rather than include all of the bio-data from Plaintiff's personnel file, Defendant Rogers gave to the selection committee only Plaintiff's faculty profile on file with the university for accreditation purposes. After learning of the university's recommendation to offer the position to Dr. Okeke, Plaintiff filed an objection with the Tennessee Board of Regents, claiming that he was more qualified for the position and that his application was not given appropriate consideration. As a result of this objection, the recommendation was withdrawn. The following year, Defendant Rogers began a new search for the Head of the Mechanical Engineering Department. Defendant Rogers also altered the published requirements for the position. Initially, the job announcement required only a Ph.D. in Mechanical Engineering. The second job announcement included the requirement of a B.S. degree in Mechanical Engineering as well. Plaintiff does not have a B.S. degree in Mechanical Engineering but in another related field. Unfortunately, virtually all of the records regarding the selection of the Dean of the School of Engineering in 1988 cannot be found. Plaintiff contends that the very fact that these documents have been "lost" renders Defendants' promotion decision suspect. What was the result? *Chaudmuri v. State of Tennessee,* 886 F.Supp. 1374 (M.D. Tenn. 1995)
12. Is a white plaintiff entitled to the same inference of discrimination as a minority plaintiff? *Wilson v. Bailey,* 934 F.2d 301 (11th Cir. 1991)
13. McAlester was able to point to specific examples in the workplace in which white employees who violated similar rules were merely suspended, while minority employees were terminated. He claimed that this conduct on the part of United Airlines amounted to racial discrimination. United retorted that no such treatment had been directed against McAlester, and, therefore, he had no basis for bringing the lawsuit. What was the result? *McAlester v. United Air Lines, Inc.,* 851 F.2d 1249 (10th Cir. 1988)
14. Chaney was terminated from his employ with Southern Railway when a drug test disclosed that he was using marijuana. He claimed that white employees possessing or using marijuana were not discharged and that, therefore, Southern Railway's motivation was a pretext for racial discrimination. What was the result? *Chaney v. Southern Ry. Co.,* F.2d 718, (11th Cir. 1988)
15. McDonald was one of four employees who were caught stealing. Three of those employees were white, including McDonald; they were discharged. The fourth, who was black, was not. McDonald claimed that Santa Fe racially discriminated against him. What was the result? *McDonald v. Santa Fe Trail Transportation Co.,* 427 U.S. 273 (1976)
16. Referring to the case on pp. 229, are pretexts often used to cover up discriminatory behavior?
17. Referring to the case on pp. 231, when poor performance and racist behavior are both involved, what takes precedence?
18. With regard to the case on pp. 233, are minorities as racist as whites? In other words, if minorities had equal power as whites have, would they be equally racist?

19. In the case on pp. 236, was the plaintiff using race as an excuse, or was the employer unreasonable?

20. Referring to the case on pp. 243, should white people be afforded the same protection under the Equal Protection Clause as minorities?

Reconstruction Era Act of 1866

CIVIL ACTION FOR DEPRIVATION OF RIGHTS

Every person who, under color of any statute, ordinance, regulation, custom, or usage, of any State or Territory or the District of Columbia, subjects, or causes to be subjected, any citizen of the United States or other person within the jurisdiction thereof to the deprivation of any rights, privileges, or immunities secured by the Constitution and laws, shall be liable to the party injured in an action at law, suit in equity, or other proper proceeding for redress. For the purposes of this section, any Act of Congress applicable exclusively to the District of Columbia shall be considered to be a statute of the District of Columbia.

AMENDMENT XIV (1868)

Section 1. All persons born or naturalized in the United States, and subject to the jurisdiction thereof, are citizens of the United States and of the State wherein they reside. No State shall make or enforce any law which shall abridge the privileges or immunities of citizens of the United States; nor shall any State deprive any person of life, liberty, or property, without due process of law; nor deny to any person within its jurisdiction the equal protection of the law. (Sections 2–5 omitted.)

AMENDMENT XV (1870)

Section 1. The rights of citizens of the United States to vote shall not be denied or abridged by the United States or by any State on account of race, color, or previous condition of servitude. (Section 2 omitted.)

CHAPTER 11

Sex Discrimination

INTRODUCTION

In the past, sex was considered a bona fide occupational qualification. Stereotypes ruled. Men were physicians, lawyers, construction workers, and policemen. Women were nurses, flight attendants, secretaries, and teachers. This arrangement had the effect of discriminating against men and women in certain job classifications. The effect on women, particularly with regard to higher-paying positions, was noticeable. Prescribing limits for lifting or carrying weight or for working before or after childbirth is prohibited. Any provisions or benefits must be provided to both sexes.

Employment Perspective

Eric Freeman is a vice-president at Bulls and Bears, Inc., an investment banking firm. There is an opening for an assistant vice-president to work directly underneath Freeman. There are two in-house candidates: Tom Folino, a competent securities trader with two years of experience, and Mary Michaels, a senior bond trader with seven years of experience. Mary's experience and competence is clearly superior, but Freeman selects Tom because they have common interests. They go to the hockey games after work and have a few beers together. Eric and Tom are both single, whereas Mary is married with children. Eric and Mary have nothing in common outside of work. Does this qualify as sexual discrimination? Yes! Eric's decision is not based on job performance, but rather on personal interests he shares with one candidate. ◆

In the case that follows, an error was made by two employees in dispatching a fire call. One employee, who was a female, claims that she was terminated, while the other, a male employee, was not disciplined.

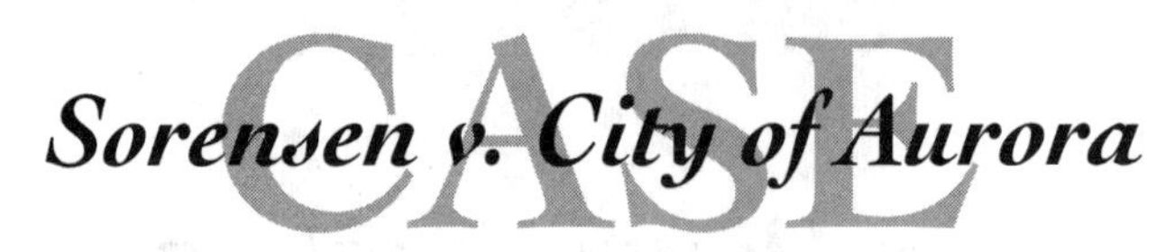

Sorensen v. City of Aurora

984 F.2d 349 (10th Cir. 1993)

LUNGSTRUM, District Judge.

On February 23, 1990, plaintiff-appellant, Mary J. Sorensen (plaintiff) filed a complaint with the U.S. District Court for the District of Colorado against defendant appellee City of Aurora ("City") and others alleging that defendants had violated Title VII in terminating her employment as a fire dispatcher. The City filed a motion for summary judgment . . . which was granted by the District Court.

When alleging disparate treatment on the basis of sex, the plaintiff must prove by a preponderancee of the evidence that the defendant had a discriminatory motive or intent. This may be done either by direct proof of discriminatory intent, or, more commonly, through the series of shifting evidentiary burdens that are intended progressively to sharpen the inquiry into the elusive factual question of intentional discrimination.

Thus, pursuant to the shifting burden of proof scheme of *McDonnell Douglas* and subsequent cases, plaintiff must first establish a prima facie case of discrimination. Once plaintiff establishes a prima facie case of discrimination the burden of production shifts to the defendant to rebut the presumption of discrimination.

If the defendant succeeds in rebutting the presumption of discrimination raised by the plaintiff's prima facie case, then the inquiry returns, as in any civil case, to whether or not the plaintiff has met its burden of persuasion. In that event, the plaintiff must prove by a preponderance of all the evidence in the case that the legitimate reasons offered by the defendant were a pretext for discrimination.

The Supreme Court has cautioned that this shifting burden of proof scheme is only intended to assist in marshalling and presenting relevant evidence. "The ultimate burden of persuading the trier of fact that the defendant intentionally discriminated against the plaintiff remains at all times with the plaintiff." Further, the ultimate question in a Title VII disparate treatment case is whether the defendant intentionally discriminated against the plaintiff.

Thus when such a case is fully tried, as here, we need only consider that ultimate question of whether plaintiff proved that the defendant intentionally discriminated against her. The crux of plaintiff's sex discrimination claim is a comparison of the treatment of her and the treatment of Mr. Mann for the handling of the Hanlon Call. Plaintiff was eventually terminated for her actions while Mann did not receive discipline. Plaintiff also contends that Mann shared the responsibility and some degree of culpability for the alleged errors in the handling of the Hanlon call. Plaintiff also contends that the district court failed to properly analyze her sex discrimination claim, improperly categorizing it as a sexual harassment claim.

We cannot conclude that the district court's ultimate finding that plaintiff failed to prove that the City had a discriminatory motive or intent in discharging the plaintiff was clearly erroneous. Similarly, we find no clear error in the district court's failure to find plaintiff and Mann to be similarly situated employees. The burden is on the plaintiff to demonstrate that the plaintiff and Mann were similarly situated employees. Plaintiff admitted in her brief, and in her oral arguments before this court, that she had primary responsibility for the Hanlon call. An internal affairs investigation directed by John C. Driscoll determined that plaintiff's confusion as to Hanlon's location at the mall had caused her to commit several serious errors, including failure to ask any questions from the EMD protocol cards; failure to determine that the Hanlon call was an injury type call; an inappropriate delay of dispatch; and an inappropriate dispatch. Plaintiff argues that the fact that the dispatchers used a team concept and that Mann was involved with the Hanlon call created a shared responsibility and some degree of culpability on Mann's part for the errors in the handling of the Hanlon call. However, the City presented evidence indicating Mann's role in the call to be less than that claimed by plaintiff. Based upon the record before us, we do not find the district court's determination that plaintiff was not a victim of intentional discrimination to be clearly erroneous.

A plaintiff must first establish a prima facie case of retaliation. If a prima facie case is established, then the burden of production shifts to the defendant to produce a legitimate, nondiscriminatory reason for the adverse action. If evidence of a legitimate reason is produced, the plaintiff may still prevail if she demonstrates the articulated reason was a mere pretext for discrimination. The overall burden of persuasion remains on the plaintiff.

The district court concluded that plaintiff did establish a prima facie case of retaliation. The court further found that the City articulated legitimate, nondiscriminatory reasons for discharging plaintiff and that plaintiff did not demonstrate by credible evidence that the articulated reasons were pretextual. The district court concluded that the City "discharged plaintiff for valid, nondiscriminatory reasons, i.e., undue delay in answering calls, erratic performance, leaving her position on the console unattended, excessive tardiness, and failure to deal effectively with emergency dispatch—a function critical to the lives and safety of citizens in the community."

Plaintiff claims that various alleged procedural irregularities involving the internal investigation, which resulted in the plaintiff's dismissal, show a clear, organized attempt to "get rid of" plaintiff and that in light of these alleged procedural irregularities the City's proffered reasons for terminating plaintiff cannot be considered worthy of belief. Among the procedural irregularities specified by plaintiff are the fact that the original internal affairs file, along with one of the working files, turned up missing, the fact that the original master tape of the Hanlon call was taped over, the fact that the audit trail regarding the call was shredded, and the fact that Chief Speed refused to meet with plaintiff's attorney during the investigation. Plaintiff also claims that for the period following her discrimination complaint in 1981 through her termination she was subjected to discrimination and unfair treatment. Plaintiff claims this discriminatory treatment included reprimands for reasons that ranged from "trivial to absurd," being unfairly subjected to weekly evaluations, and being put on probationary status.

We see no clear error in the district court's finding that plaintiff failed to show that the City's articulated nondiscriminatory reasons for discharging her were pretextual. The record demonstrates that the plaintiff had an erratic history of performance on the job. The District Court heard all of the evidence before it with respect to the plaintiff's allegations of procedural irregularities and prior discriminatory conduct on the part of the City and determined that the plaintiff had not proven that the stated reasons for her discharge were pretextual. It is true that plaintiff and the City have offered conflicting testimony on many of these issues. However, where there are two permissible views of the evidence, the factfinder's choice between them cannot be clearly erroneous. Our independent review of the record indicates ample evidence supporting the trial court's determination that the plaintiff was discharged for valid, nondiscriminatory reasons, and that plaintiff failed to prove those stated reasons were pretextual. Because our review of the record does not leave us with a "definite and firm conviction that a mistake has been committed," we affirm the finding of the district court on plaintiff's retaliation claim.

Judgment for the City
of Aurora Affirmed.

The case that follows addresses the question of whether an employee who has not received severance pay has been subject to sex discrimination. Plaintiff has requested a one-year leave of absence but never returned. She was terminated as a result.

CASE *Zelewski v. American Federal Sav. Bank*

811 F.Supp. 456 (D.Minn. 1993)

DOTY, Judge.

In January 1990, Plaintiff asked the bank if she could work only in the afternoons and use accumulated sick leave to pay for the mornings that she would not be working. The bank granted her request, and plaintiff continued to receive the same salary even though she worked only afternoons.

On May 4, 1990, plaintiff requested a one-year leave of absence for health reasons. In addition to her lung condition, plaintiff had been suffering from depression since 1987, had been on anti-depressants since 1988 and had been suffering from rheumatoid arthritis since 1989. The bank again granted plaintiff's request, combining the maximum disability leave, vacation time, sick leave and personal leave available to permit the requested leave of absence. Plaintiff began her leave on May 21, 1990.

In July 1990, plaintiff asked the bank to send her copies of all staff memoranda or newsletters, including those that she had missed after beginning her leave. Although the bank informed plaintiff that it would not be practical to send all bank memoranda and other internal correspondence to employees who were not actually in the work place, the bank nonetheless sent its most recent newsletter and employee handbook revisions to plaintiff. The bank subsequently sent plaintiff copies of job postings and newsletters.

Plaintiff's leave ended in May 1991. Plaintiff, however, failed to inform the bank when or if she would be able to return to work. Although the bank wanted plaintiff to return, it believed that she was terminating her employment.

Plaintiff further contends that the bank created a hostile working environment for older employees, and that she suffered mental anguish and depression as a result. She claims that her depression caused and aggravated her physical ailments.

Plaintiff . . . alleges claims of sex discrimination under the Minnesota Human Rights Act ("MHRA") and Title VII of the Civil Rights Act.

Plaintiff also asserts claims of sex discrimination under Title VII and the MHRA as a result of the bank's failure to pay her severance pay. Plaintiff's complaint alleges that the bank agreed to pay three male bank officers whose employment had been terminated severance pay of at least $250,000. In her deposition, however, plaintiff identified only two such officers, Gowan and Devig, and further conceded that Devig received no severance pay but was retained as a consultant for one year after his employment terminated. Thus, plaintiff's claim of sex discrimination is based solely on the fact that one male employee, Gowan, received severance payments while she did not.

To support a claim of sex discrimination, a plaintiff must show that she suffered an adverse employment action because of her sex. The court is to analyze such claims under the framework set forth in *McDonnell-Douglas.* Plaintiff's failure to receive severance payments does not constitute an adverse employment action unless such payments were a benefit normally offered to bank employees. In the present case, however, it is undisputed that the bank had no written or unwritten policy of providing severance pay to any employee, and the bank's decision to provide severance pay to one employee is insufficient to create such a policy. It is also undisputed that at least two other male bank officers terminated their employment with the bank but failed to receive any severance or settlement payments. Plaintiff further concedes that the bank's decision was not related to her sex. The court thus concludes that plaintiff fails to establish a prima facie case because she is unable to show that she was subject to any adverse employment action or that the bank treated her differently than nonmembers of the protected class.

Moreover, even if the court were to determine that the severance payments to Gowan constitute a bank practice, the court concludes that plaintiff would not be entitled to such payments because her situation is clearly distinguishable from the circumstances surrounding Gowan's termination. The bank sought Gowan's termination while he was still an active employee. Thus, the bank paid him in exchange for his agreement to end his employment, execute a general release and perform certain other things. In contrast, although plaintiff was unable to work at the end of her leave, the bank was nontheless willing to have her return to work if she had been willing or able to do so. The bank thus had no reason to pay her in exchange for an agreement to leave. The court therefore concludes that even if the bank's payments to Gowan were to constitute a bank policy, plaintiff would not be entitled to such payment because her situation was distinguishable.

Based on the foregoing, the court concludes that plaintiff's sex discrimination claims under MHRA and Title VII are fatally flawed because she fails to demonstrate an adverse employment action or that she was treated differently than nonmembers of the protected class. The court thus granted defendants' motion for summary on plaintiff's sex discrimination claims.

Judgment for American Savings Bank.

The case that follows resolves the conflict between protecting employees from sexual discrimination and upholding a firm's freedom of choice in granting associates partnership status.

CASE

Ezold v. Wolf, Block, Schorr and Solis-Cohen

983 F.2d 509 (3rd Cir. 1992)

HUTCHINSON, Judge.

Ezold was hired by Wolf as an associate on a partnership track in July 1983. She had graduated in the top third of her class from the Villanova University School of Law in 1980 and then worked at two small law firms in Philadelphia. Before entering law school, Ezold had accumulated thirteen years of administrative and legislative experience, first as an assistant to Senator Edmund Muskie, then as contract administrator for the Model Cities Program in Philadelphia, and finally as Administrator of the Office of the Special Prosecutor of the Pennsylvania Department of Justice.

Ezold was hired at Wolf by Seymour Kurland, then chairman of the litigation department. The district court found that Kurland told Ezold during an interview that it would not be easy for her at Wolf because "she was a woman, had not attended an Ivy League law school, and had not been on law review." Subsequent to this meeting, but prior to accepting Wolf's offer of employment, Ezold had lunch with Roberta Liebenberg and Barry Schwartz, both members of the litigation department. She did not ask them anything about the firm's treatment of women.

Ezold was assigned to the firm's litigation department. From 1983–87, Kurland was responsible for the assignment of work to associates in the department. He often delegated this responsibility to partner Steven Arbittier. As Ezold acknowledged, many partners bypassed the formal assignment procedure and directly assigned matters to associates. The District Curt found that Arbittier assigned Ezold to actions that were "small" by Wolf standards.

Ezold's performance was reviewed regularly throughout her tenure pursuant to Wolf's evaluation process, which operated as follows: The Associates Committee, consisting of ten partners repre-

senting each of the firm's departments, first reviews the performance of all the firm's associates and makes recommendations to the firm's five-member Executive Committee as to which associates should be admitted to the partnership. The Executive Committee then reviews the partnership recommendations of the Associates Committee and makes its own recommendations to the full partnership. The firm's voting partners consider only those persons whom the Executive Committee recommends for admission to the partnership.

Senior associates within partnership consideration are evaluated annually; non-senior associates semi-annually. The firm's partners are asked to submit written evaluations. . . . Kurland was at one time a decision maker and eventually supported Ezold's admission to the partnership; he took no vote in the final votes or evaluation concerning Ezold because he had by that time left the firm.

Though Kurland's initial comments, if made, were crude and unprofessional, we do not believe they are sufficient in and of themselves to sustain the district court's judgment in favor of Ezold. They may reflect unfavorably on Kurland's personality or his views, but they are not sufficient to show that there was such a pervasive hostility toward women at Wolf sufficient to show that Ezold's partnership decision was more likely the result of discriminatory bias than Wolf's perception of Ezold's legal ability. Ezold has made no claim that Kurland's comments created a hostile working environment. If we were to hold that several stray remarks by a nondecisionmaker over a period of five years, while inappropriate, were sufficient to prove that Wolf's associate evaluation and partnership admission process were so infected with discriminatory bias that such bias more likely motivates Wolf's promotion decision than an articulated legitimate reason we would spill across the limits of Title VII. (Title VII strikes a balance between protecting employees from unlawful discrimination and preserving for employers their remaining freedom of choice.)

We have reviewed the evidence carefully and hold that it is insufficient to show pretext. Despite Ezold's disagreement with the firm's evaluations of her abilities, and her perception that she was treated unfairly, there is no evidence of sex discrimination here.

Judgment for Wolf.

Men are also protected against gender discrimination under Title VII. Although it does not happen very often, there are occasions when men have been treated unfavorably because of their gender.

The following case addresses the question of whether a female superior could be found to have sexually discriminated against a male subordinate.

824 F.Supp. 969 (D.Colo. 1993)

FINESILVER, Chief Judge.

Plaintiff, Harry Hastings, began work with Defendant Small Business Administration ("SBA") on or about August 1976 in the Denver Regional Office. From August 1980 until his retirement from the federal government in December 1986, Hastings was employed by the SBA as a Surety Bond Officer in the Surety Bond Division of the Regional Office. Hastings' responsibilities in the surety bond program included reviewing surety bond applications and making recommendations either to accept or reject the applications. The applications and Hastings' recommendations were then reviewed by Hastings' superiors, who would then make their own recommendations for accepting or rejecting the applications.

The performance of SBA employees was evaluated on the Performance Management Appraisal System ("PMAS").

Until February 1983, Hastings' immediate, first line supervisor was Senior Surety Bond Officer Helen Edwards. Edwards was transferred to the Denver District Office after filing numerous complaints for sex and age discrimination against the SBA and several individuals, including Hastings.

In February 1985, Edwards prevailed on portions of her sex discrimination case, and in May of that year she was transferred back to the Denver Regional Offices Surety Bond Division. Edwards once again became Hastings' first line supervisor and Berry was moved to Hastings' second line supervisor and Edwards' immediate supervisor. Hastings claims after Edwards' return to the bond surety program, she began subjecting him to various forms of hostile treatment, including delays in reviewing his work that caused his performance evaluations to suffer and public abuse of Hastings in the presence of his coworkers.

In order to prevail in an individual disparate treatment case, a plaintiff must generally satisfy a three-pronged test. First, the plaintiff must prove by a preponderance of the evidence a prima facie case of discrimination. Second, once the plaintiff establishes his prima facie case, the burden of production shifts to the defendant to articulate some legitimate, nondiscriminatory reason for its action. Finally, if the defendant is able to advance such a reason, the plaintiff has the burden of proving the defendant's reason as merely a pretext for discrimination. The plaintiff has the ultimate burden of proving a defendant treated him less favorably than others because of his age or sex.

To prevail upon a claim of disparate treatment based on age or sex, a plaintiff must establish a prima facie case of discrimination by showing (1) the plaintiff was a member of the protected class; (2) the plaintiff was adversely affected by a personnel action; (3) the plaintiff's performance was satisfactory; and (4) persons outside the protected class were not adversely affected by the personnel action. The plaintiff must produce either direct or circumstantial evidence from which a factfinder could reasonably conclude that the employer intended to discriminate in reaching the employment decision. Although the prima facie standard originated in the context of Title VII, it has also been adopted for cases brought under the Age Discrimination in Employment Act ("ADEA"). In alleging age discrimination, a plaintiff must also show that his age was a determining factor in his employer's decision.

Beginning with the third criterion, we note that Hastings' performance appears to have been more than satisfactory. Defendant points out that he generally received performance evaluations ranging from above average to the highest possible score.

In order to show constructive discharge in a discrimination context, a plaintiff must show the employer "by its illegal discriminatory acts had made working conditions so difficult that a reasonable person in the employee's position would feel compelled to resign." The key phrase here is "by its discriminatory acts." We do not believe Hastings has met his burden of showing that any actions by Defendants were discriminatory.

Federal antidiscrimination laws do not require that employers treat all employees equally. The laws exist, rather, to prevent employers from discriminating on the basis of race and gender, as well as age. To establish a prima facie case of illicit discrimination, a plaintiff must produce evidence of a discriminatory intent or motive on the part of the defendant. While a plaintiff need not show that a defendant was personally prejudiced against the plaintiff, some evidence of individualized disparate treatment or statistical disparity is necessary.

Hastings realized that statements he made in his deposition and affidavits in concluding that "the emotional outbursts of his supervisor, the failure of the agency to address issues of concern to Hastings, the failure of the agency to provide appropriate evaluations of his performance and other forms of disparate treatment to which plaintiff Hastings was subjected did in fact make his working conditions intolerable." Hastings does indeed describe in detail what appeared to be highly undesirable working conditions. Nowhere, however, does Hastings suggest any facts tying those working conditions to his age or sex. Hastings does not dispute Defendant's assertion that his supervisor, Edwards, has personality conflicts with most or all of the people with whom she works. It also appears that she had running battles with Hastings; Berry stated in his deposition that both Edwards and Hastings continually went to him to complain about each other, prompting Berry to investigate and mediate their disputes.

Hastings does not adduce any reason for a finder of fact to infer that Defendants possessed not merely intent to make his work miserable, but discriminatory intent or motive. The former is an unfortunate occurrence in the workplace; only the latter provides a cause of action under Title VII and the ADEA. Hastings asserts "Defendants have given no legitimate nondiscriminatory reason for the intolerable state of Plaintiff Hastings' work life," but Hastings fails to suggest, as he must, a prima facie discriminatory reason in the first place.

For example, in McAlester, the plaintiff was able to point to specific examples in the workplace where white employees who violated similar rules were merely suspended while minority employees were terminated. In *Chaney v. Southern Ry. Co.,* a black plaintiff was discharged as a result of his positive drug test met his prima facie burden by showing the defendant had discovered white employees possessing or using marijuana without also discharging them. Hastings' constructive discharge claim must therefore be dismissed.

Hastings also claims that he was subject to reprisal for filing his various discrimination complaints. To establish a prima facie case of unlawful reprisal, he must show:

> (1) protected opposition to discrimination or participation in a proceeding arising out of discrimination; (2) adverse action by the employer contemporaneously or subsequent to the employee's protected activity; and (3) a causal connection between such activity and the employer's action.

However, he has alleged no adverse action taken, after May 1986, as a result of his complaints. His claim of reprisal must therefore be dismissed.

Judgment for Saiki.

SEX PLUS DISCRIMINATION

Discrimination may occur against an individual not solely because of his or her gender, but that fact coupled with another may be its cause. Women with small children, women in child-bearing years, and women taking care of elderly parents are all examples.

As part of their interview process, some companies endeavor to discover if a female applicant has small children. It has been their experience that mothers are preoccupied with worrying about their children. In addition, if the child becomes ill or gets hurt, the mother will leave work immediately. This behavior can be disruptive to the workplace. For that reason, the company may nonchalantly ask the female applicant where her children go to school. The response will indicate whether the woman has children and, if so, what their ages are. The company can then generally refuse her or deny her for another reason. This is discriminatory behavior.

In the next case, a female worker told her employer she was going to marry and relocate to Atlanta. She asked the company whether they would relocate her. The company agreed to do so, but they later reneged. She claimed retaliation and constructive discharge based upon sex plus age discrimination.

CASE

West v. Marion Merrell Dow, Inc.

34 F.3d 493 (8th Cir. 1995)

LOKEN, Circuit Judge.

Myrna West commenced this employment discrimination suit against her former employer, Marion Laboratories, Inc., now Marion Merrell Dow, Inc. ("Marion"), alleging sex, age, and retaliation discrimination. After a six-day trial, the jury awarded West $350,000 in compensatory damages on her claim that Marion had retaliated after West filed a charge accusing Marion of sex and age discrimination. The district court awarded additional front-pay damages and attorney's fees, and Marion appealed.

West's retaliation claim is that Marion reneged on a promise that it would find her a position in Atlanta if she married and moved there. After West committed to the move, Marion advised that it had no openings in Atlanta, and West took the position she was constructively discharged. However, before West resigned, Marion reconsidered and offered her a choice of Atlanta-based positions. West nonetheless immediately resigned her employ with Marion. Because West unreasonably refused Marion's attempt to accommodate her desire to transfer, we conclude that there was insufficient evidence that Marion reneged on a promise, or that West was constructively discharged. Accordingly, we reverse.

The jury rejected West's claims of sex and age discrimination, so we limit our discussion to the facts relevant to her retaliation claim. We view the evidence in the light most favorable to West and give her the benefit of all reasonable inferences that may be drawn from that evidence.

Marion hired West in February 1978. In late 1986, she was promoted to district manager of the Wound Care Division, marketing products used in treating major wounds and burns. As District Manager, West was based in Dallas, Texas, and managed eight field sales representatives who covered the western half of the country.

In November 1988, West told her supervisor, James Laufenberg, that she was planning to marry an Atlanta resident in June 1989. West advised that she wanted to remain with Marion but, following the marriage, would need to relocate to Atlanta, or to Marion in Kansas City where her new husband could relocate. West hoped that she would be promoted to Regional Manager for the Wound Care Division in Kansas City, but Laufenberg was "not particularly positive" that she would attain that position.

On May 5, 1989, West again expressed concern about her upcoming wedding and need to relocate. Laufenberg assured her that she could remain with the Wound Care Division and transfer to Atlanta. At a minimum, Laufenberg explained, he would split an existing sales territory and give West an entry level field sales position until the division grew enough to justify creating a new district manager position in Atlanta.

On August 29, West met with both Laufenberg and Gianini. Laufenberg advised that there was no opening in the Wound Care Division in Atlanta. Gianini advised that he had looked but was unable to find her an Atlanta position elsewhere in the company. West then wrote a lengthy letter to Laufenberg on September 2, and she filed a charge of retaliation discrimination on September 5. In both documents, she asserted that Laufenberg had withdrawn his offer to find her a Wound Care Division position in Atlanta, that Gianini had made a perfunctory effort to find her an alternative opportunity in Atlanta and therefore that she was forced to leave Marion because the company refused to offer her "the same transfer opportunities that countless others had received."

On September 11, Laufenberg wrote West and asked that she provide the specific date of her move to Atlanta to "help me to start the process of interviewing for a district manager in Dallas. Treating this as a request to resign, West again wrote to Laufenberg on September 20th, asserting that she had endured eleven years of sexual discrimination and harassment and concluding, "I am now forced to tender my resignation effective September 30, 1989. It is my belief that because I have protested the treatment I have received that the position you promised to make for me in Atlanta was withdrawn."

On September 21, apparently before he received West's September 20 resignation letter, Laufenberg responded to her September 2 letter. Expressing his surprise at this letter, Laufenberg commented, "You know very well that I sincerely want you to remain with Marion, in the Wound Care Division if possible." Laufenberg stated that the Wound Care Division's expansion plans were on hold, so he could not add a new Atlanta district manager. He suggested the following alternatives to permit West to remain with Marion:

"Remain in your District Manager position in Dallas pending resolution of these workforce scale-up issues." Apply for any of five executive positions then available at Marion's Kansas City headquarters. (None was a regional manager's position, the subject of West's discrimination charge.)

Although Marion has no open field sales positions in the Atlanta area, "You may take any of several territories open in the southeastern United States."

Alternatively, Marion's Prescription Products Division "will provide you with a rover position in Field Sales. . . . This will permit you to move to Atlanta and remain with Marion at no loss in base pay while we wait for a regular opening to develop" in Atlanta.

After receiving Laufenberg's September 21 letter, West declined all of the positions offered and resigned on September 30. She testified that, by late September 1989, she had committed to reside in Atlanta after her marriage. She rejected Laufenberg's offer of sales positions in Atlanta because they were "too little, too late," they were not bona fide offers but only invitations to "interview for a position" and she was not willing to accept an insulting demotion to a field sales position.

At trial, the parties differed as to why Laufenberg in May had assured West of at least a sales position with the Wound Care Division in Atlanta, but then in August told her that nothing was available. West argued this was retaliation for her May 16 discrimination charge. She presented evidence that Marion had specially accommodated many other employees who asked to relocate. On the other hand, Laufenberg testified that the Wound Care Division's business conditions changed dramatically between May 5 and August 8, 1989, eliminating his ability to offer West a Wound Care Division position in Atlanta. First, the Division encountered production problems with two significant products. Then, in mid-July, Marion agreed to merge with Merrell Dow Pharmaceuticals, Inc. The merger froze Laufenberg's expansion plans for the Wound Care Division. Laufenberg explained in October 1989 after West resigned that Marion decided to divest the entire Wound Care Division because its product line did not fit the post-merger company's global marketing strategy.

An employer may not retaliate against an employee for bringing charges of age or sex discrimination. To prove unlawful retaliation discrimination, a plaintiff must show "(1) statutorily protected participation in Title VII or ADEA process adverse employment action; and (2) a connection between the two." An employee is constructively discharged when an employer deliberately renders the employee's working condition intolerable and thus forces her to quit her job." The standard is an objective one. "An employee may not be unreasonably sensitive to her working environment. A constructive discharge arises only when a reasonable person would find her working conditions intolerable.

Turning to the issue of constructive discharge, we note that West rejected Laufenberg's September 21 offers without any investigation and immediately resigned. She testified that Laufenberg's September 21 letter was not "a bona fide offer" because the Atlanta positions offered were simply, invitations to interview." But this is contrary to the plain meaning of Laufenberg's letter, which said that "You may take" any open Southeastern sales territory, and that the Prescription Products Division "will provide" a rover sales Position. West admitted that Laufenberg's prior plan to expand the Wound Care Division had been derailed by the recent merger. She could not continue to serve as District Manager for the Western

United States while living in Atlanta. In these circumstances, her decision to quit one week after receiving the offers contained in Laufenberg's September 21 letter was unreadably precipitous.

"Part of an employee's obligation to be reasonable is an obligation not to assume the worst and not to jump to conclusions too fast." An employee who quits without giving the employer a reasonable chance to work out a problem is not constructively discharged. Indeed, even if Marion had made the decision to transfer West to a position she opposed, she would not necessarily have been constructively discharged.

Unless the transfer is, in effect, a discharge, the employee has no right simply to walk out. . . . The employee cannot recover damages for losses that he could have avoided without risk of substantial loss or injury.

Here, the problem was caused by West's desire to relocate for personal reasons, so she had an even greater obligation to be flexible and reasonable. West also testified that she rejected Laufenberg's September 21 offers because she considered them a "visible insult" and "another effort on Marion's part to humiliate me." Given West's belief that she had been the victim of longstanding sex and age discrimination, these subjective reactions were no doubt genuine. However, frustration and embarrassment at not being promoted do not make work conditions sufficiently intolerable to constitute constructive discharge.

Judgment for Marion Merrell Dow.

In the next case, a professor was denied tenure. She claimed that she received lower pay raises, shared an office, carried a heavier teaching load, and had little access to secretarial assistance. The University argued that she lacked scholarly publications, and her denial was supported by female colleagues. The issue is whether sex plus discrimination exists because her complaint is based upon sex plus religious discrimination.

CASE

Merrill v. Southern Methodist University

806 F.2d 600 (5th Cir. 1986)

GARWOOD, Circuit Judge.

December 28, 1979, Southern Methodist University (SMU) notified Dr. Janet I. Merrill (Merrill) that it would not extend tenure to her. Consequently, she sued SMU, charging it with violating Title VII of the 1964 Civil Rights Act by discriminating against her on the basis of sex and religion. After a three-day bench trial, the district court held that many of the allegedly discriminatory acts were time-barred. As to the remaining claims, the court found that Merrill failed to establish intentional discrimination and held in SMU's favor. Merrill appeals. We affirm.

Facts and Proceedings Below

Appellant Merrill holds a master's degree from the University of Notre Dame and a doctorate in education from Columbia University. Her doctoral emphasis was in guidance, particularly in elementary education. In 1968, after receiving her degree from Columbia, she moved with her husband to Lenox, Massachusetts, where they taught at Berkshire Christian College, which had an enrollment of about 150 students and offered no graduate work. Merrill also taught part-time at the College of Our Lady of the Elms, a nearby Catholic women's institution with an enrollment of about 600. Merrill was a tenured full professor at Berkshire Christian College and had the title of "Lecturer at Our Lady of the Elms."

In 1975, Merrill's husband accepted an invitation to teach at the Dallas Theological Seminary. Merrill inquired about job openings at several colleges and universities in the Dallas area. Apparently, SMU was the only institution with an opening in her field. Merrill was one of 107 persons who applied for that position—Assistant Professor of Education—and though SMU ultimately hired a male, Dr. Ronald E. Pound, Merrill, along with two other women, was one of the six finalists. Merrill now asserts that SMU's 1975 selection of Dr. Pound over her was an act of intentional sex discrimination.

Some time later, a similar position became available at SMU. Dr. Pound perused the applications that had been received for the job he now held and chose Dr. Merrill to teach part-time during the spring of 1976. At the end of the semester, SMU offered Merrill a full-time, three-year contract, beginning August 30, 1976, as an untenured assistant professor in the Department of Education at the first-year salary of $13,250. Although she had been a tenured full professor at Berkshire Christian College, Merrill acceded to SMU's terms in writing. SMU gave Merrill three years' credit toward tenure eligibility and pledged to consider her for promotion no later than the last year of her contract. Merrill now contends that the terms of this contract—her rank, salary, and untenured status—were the result of intentional sex discrimination.

During the span of this contract, Merrill shared an office with another female teacher, and had difficulty procuring secretarial help to type her manuscripts. She alleged that this was the result of sex discrimination because most male teachers had private offices and secretarial services. She allegedly carried heavier teaching loads and received lower pay raises than her male colleagues. The primary evidence supporting these two aspects of discriminatory treatment consisted of various charts and tables, which the district court admitted but did not greatly credit because the underlying data was largely hearsay and the faculty sample underlying the statistical comparisons was very small.

Until she was denied tenure, Merrill was satisfied with conditions at SMU. None of these circumstances seemed discriminatory to her and she apparently never vigorously protested any of them. In September 1978, the tenured faculty of the Department of Education, eight men and two women, reviewed Merrill's performance and voted to deny tenure to her. She then requested, and was given, the opportunity to make a personal appeal to the faculty. However, the faculty reaffirmed its previous unfavorable decision. Her colleagues evaluated Merrill in four areas: teaching ability, published research, service to SMU and her profession, and needs of the department. Only her teaching received a favorable vote. Not one of the ten tenured faculty members voted her publications sufficient to merit advancement. Her articles were unfocused, short, and not published in referred journals. At trial, Merrill admitted that she had not published widely or impressively. She fared somewhat better in the area of service to SMU and her profession, though even here a heavy majority of the department faculty rated her deficient. Her most significant contribution was sponsoring a student group that assembled a project designed to teach the virtues of the free enterprise system to elementary and high school students. This project, entered in a national competition sponsored by General Motors, placed second. The final area of evaluation focused more on Merrill than it did on the needs of the Department of Education. Not one faculty member voted that a need existed for Merrill in the department. Indeed, enrollment was dwindling.

The tenured faculty voted as follows:

	Yes	*No*	*Abstain*
Teaching	7	2	1
Research	0	9	1
Service	3	6	1
Needs	0	9	1

After the faculty's second rejection, in November 1978, Merrill appealed to James Early, Dean of the College of Humanities and Science, of which the Department of Education was a part. Early convened the College Executive Committee.

This committee included two women. The committee unanimously affirmed the Education Department faculty decision. Early informed Merrill of this result on December 13, 1978. Merrill next appealed to the SMU Provost, James Brooks, who assembled an ad hoc committee to review Merrill's case. She was permitted to nominate two persons, one of whom the provost appointed to a position on the three-person committee. Merrill's representative on this ad hoc committee, a woman, joined the other two members in voting against her. Brooks informed Merrill of this decision on December 28, 1979.

Dr. Merrill asserts that this tenure decision was the result of intentional sex discrimination. She asserts that she had written as prolifically as her male colleagues who had tenure. She contends that she was a victim of discrimination on the basis of religion because many of her articles were published in religious-type magazines or were based on religious assumptions, and that her colleagues must have therefore discredited the articles. She stresses that her service to SMU and her profession was exemplary, citing the General Motors project, workshops conducted for various groups, and professional meetings attended.

Merrill argues that the faculty had no right to consider the department's needs in voting against her because this was criterion she had not been forewarned to address in her presentation. She alleged that it was applied for the first time in her case.

After denying her tenure, SMU gave Merrill a "terminal" contract for 1979–80, at the end of which Merrill's employment at SMU ended. She subsequently secured a teaching position at Dallas Baptist University, where her starting salary was about $6,000 more per year than her final salary at SMU. Merrill testified that she would not return to SMU except as a tenured full professor.

The district court held that several of Merrill's claims were time-barred. She filed her first complaint with the EEOC on November 16, 1979, and followed this with a second complaint on May 23, 1980. The court barred recovery on any alleged discriminatory act occurring more than 180 days before November 19, 1979. This eliminated many of her claims, such as those based on the initial terms of employment. Thus the court was left to try only claims based on the denial of tenure and allegedly unequal pay. In findings of fact and conclusions of law recited from the bench, the court held that Merrill had failed to show that she was a victim of intentional discrimination.

On appeal, Merrill raises five issues: (1) the district court's holding that certain claims were barred by the statute of limitations, (2) (3) the district court's decision that the tenure denial and pay differentials were not motivated by intentional discrimination, (4) the District Court's refusal to certify a class of SMU employees and its failure to hold an evidentiary hearing on certification, and (5) the District Court's refusal to admit evidence of a settlement between SMU and the Department of Labor both regarding alleged sex discrimination at SMU.

The District Court upheld that any Title VII claim arising prior to May 20, 1970, i.e., more than 180 days prior to November 16, 1979, the date Merrill lodged her first charge of discrimination with the EEOC, was barred. We agree. This ruling excluded I&II claims except those based on wage discrimination and the tenure denial, including claims based on Merrill's original terms of employment, the lack of secretarial assistance, the lack of research leave, and the fact that Merrill shared an office with another professor.

Section 706(e) of Title VII, 42 U.S.C. 2000e-5(e), requires a discrimination victim to file a complaint with the EEOC within 180 days of the act's occurrence. Any act occurring more than 180 days prior to filing "may constitute relevant background evidence in a proceeding in which the status of a current practice is at issue, but separately considered, it is merely an unfortunate event in history which has no present legal consequences." Merrill does not dispute this rule, nor has she ever sought redress for discrimination under the "continuing violations" theory.

Merrill chose to frame her claim as a case of disparate treatment. The Pretrial Order makes this clear. In a disparate treatment case, as the district court understood, "the plaintiff bears the burden of proving intentional discrimination."

The record discloses ample evidence that SMU had legitimate justifications for denying Merrill tenure. Merrill's publications were sufficiently weak to prevent us from saying that the district court clearly erred in finding that SMU's reliance on this justification was not a pretext for intentional discrimination. Merrill asserted that she published as frequently as her male colleagues. However, academic scholarship is not measured by volume alone, but by the comprehensiveness and direction of the research. Moreover, much of Merrill's work was printed in journals with little or no recognition in the academic community. Merrill's colleagues, including females, overwhelmingly rated her deficient in this area.

Merrill's complaints that SMU should not have weighed its needs in deciding whether to grant her tenure are also not well-founded. There was testimony at trial that enrollment in the education graduate programs was "dangerously shrinking" at the time Merrill was denied tenure, and the subsequent dissolution of the Education Department lends credence to SMU's position that it did not need Merrill as a tenured faculty member. Title VII does not require employers to ignore harsh economic realities; the district court did not clearly err in rejecting Merrill's arguments based on this factor.

Merrill presented a number of charts and tables comparing her teaching load, salary, and other characteristics with those of her male colleagues. This evidence tended to show unequal treatment of Merrill, but the district court gave these charts and tables little weight because many of them were based on hearsay evidence and they all drew from a very small sample. We have cautioned against over-reliance on raw numbers in Title VII litigation because numbers can be misleading if not properly compiled. After carefully examining the entire record in this case, we hold that the district court's finding that SMU did not intentionally discriminate in its tenure decision is not clearly erroneous.

Judgment for SMU.

BONA FIDE OCCUPATIONAL QUALIFICATION (BFOQ)

The bona fide occupational qualification (BFOQ) operates as a defense to a suit for discrimination with regard to religion, national origin, gender, and age. The first three defenses are found in Title VII, while the age BFOQ is found in the Age Discrimination in Employment Act. The courts have narrowly construed this defense, limiting it to job requirements that are essential to the job or are at the core purpose of the business. Mere job relatedness is not sufficient.

Employment Perspective

Nancy Hartwick attended Podunk University where she was a star basketball player. She later became a women's basketball coach at Premier College where she won the national championship four times. When a vacancy arose for the men's basketball coach at her alma mater, she applied. Although Podunk's administration had fond affection for Hartwick, they refused her application after consulting the school's students, players, and alumni. The students and alumni said that they would boycott the games. The players said they would have no confidence in her ability. Nancy claimed sex discrimination. Podunk argued that requiring a man to fill the position of men's basketball coach is a BFOQ. Are they correct? No! The preference of the constituents of Podunk does not qualify as a BFOQ. Nancy Hartwick's qualification must be judged in its face alone. Gender preference may not play a part. ◆

Employment Perspective

Gail Dudack is a sports reporter for the Minnesota Moon, an evening daily newspaper. Gail had been covering women's sporting events, but now with the retirement of Charlie Scofield, she has been elevated to the major team sports. Her first assignment is a pro basketball game. During the game, Shorty Williams scores his 25,000th point. After the contest, all the reporters are rushing into the locker room to interview Shorty. Gail is refused entry because the men are changing and showering and she is a woman. Gail files a claim with the EEOC, alleging pro basketball is discriminating against women reporters. The team argues that the closed-door policy toward women is a BFOQ. Is her claim viable? Yes! The locker-room policy makes it impossible for a woman to be a first-rate reporter. Either the team must allow unrestricted entry or forbid all reporters from the locker room and conduct all interviews in the press room where equal access can be given. ◆

Employment Perspective

Roger Bishop is a registered nurse at Sumner County Hospital. Roger is on duty one evening when Mildred Dirkson calls for assistance. When Roger attempts to assist Mildred, she admonishes him that she called for a nurse. Roger explains that he is a nurse, but she wants no part of him. Roger queries Mildred about the fact that if he were a physician, she would have no problem having him touch her. The next day Mildred's family complains to the hospital administration, and Roger is assigned to an all-male ward. The hospital justifies its action by asserting it is a BFOQ. Roger claims that this behavior is discriminatory because female nurses are not confined to servicing exclusively female patients. Who is correct? Roger! The hospital's action was not justified. BFOQ's do not apply to one sex but not the other. Hospitals cannot discriminate in deference to their patients' preferences. The patients must accept the hospital staff as long as they are qualified. What if Mildred's request concerned applying medication to or washing the genital area? Every accommodation should be made in this regard if there are female nurses available. Respecting privacy is important. But patients who are hospitalized must have physicians on duty, who are predominantly male, view their private parts if the need arises and their private physician is not available. So, too, with nurses. ◆

EQUAL PAY

The Equal Pay Act of 1963 is an amendment to the Fair Labor Standards Act, which regulates child labor, minimum wage, and overtime pay. The Equal Pay Act prohibits the payment of different wages to men and women who are performing the same job. This Act covers all types of job categories from clerical to executive. The jobs must be equal with regard to skill, knowledge, or experience, and the conditions under which the work is performed must be similar. For example, a person working overseas is entitled to a pay differential for the same job performed domestically.

In the following case, a female veterinarian claimed that her employer paid her less than similarly experienced male colleagues. The issue is whether the employer discriminated against her in violation of the Equal Pay Act.

CASE

McMillan v. Massachusetts Soc. of Cruelty to Animals

880 F.Supp. 900 (D. Mass. 1995)

STEARNS, District Judge.

Dr. Marjorie McMillan began her career as Director of Radiology at Angell in 1981. She worked continuously until December of 1983, when she took a leave of absence lasting through 1985. Angell maintains some twenty veterinarians on staff who provide direct care as well as instructional guidance to interns and post-graduate residents. McMillan's salary complaint dates from her return as Director of Radiology in 1985.

Until 1989, Thornton served as Angell's Chief of Staff. In that position, he was responsible for setting salary levels for new employees and determining annual increases. In 1989, Thornton became President of the MSPCA and Gambardella designed and implemented a salary system which assigned a grade to every veterinarian and awarded annual increases in pay based on performance evaluations and ranges within each grade. In the year following the implementation of this new pay system, McMillan's salary jumped from $58,295 to $72,000. Notwithstanding this increase, it is undisputed that from 1985 until the termination of her employment on November 26, 1991, McMillan was paid less than any other Director/Department Head, while her job description was for all practical purposes indistinguishable from that of her male colleagues.

McMillan first discovered the pay disparity in August of 1989. She filed a gender discrimination claim with the MCAD in October of 1989. In January of 1990, McMillan entered into negotiations with Angell over the purchase of Windhover, a private aviary practice established by McMillan in Walpole, Mass. McMillan sought to rent space at Angell to carry on the new practice.

To establish a prima facie case under the Equal Pay Act, a plaintiff must show: 1. that her employer is subject to the Act; 2. that discrimination regarding wages occurred within the same working establishment; 3. that she performed work in a position requiring equal skill, effort and responsibility under similar working conditions; and 4. that she was paid less than a comparable employee of the opposite sex. The plaintiff is not required to show that the compared jobs are identical, only that they are "substantially equal." Once a prima facie case is made out under the Equal Pay Act, the employer must resort to the Act's statutory defenses, that is, that pay differentials can be explained by seniority, merit, quantity or quality of production or by "any other factor other than sex."

The affirmative defenses of the Equal Pay Act were incorporated by Congress into Title VII by way of the so-called Bennett Amendment. The Amendment is intended to prevent plaintiffs from using Title VII to circumvent the Equal Pay Act when the pay difference at issue can be justified by one or more of the Equal Pay Acts' affirmative defenses. However, as construed by the Supreme Court, the Amendment does not confine Title VII sex-based wage discrimination claims to the four corners of the Equal Pay Act. The Court's concern was with the "equal work" requirement of the Act. If strictly applied in the Title VII context, "this requirement would mean that a woman who is discriminatorily underpaid could obtain no relief—no matter how egregious the discrimination might be—unless her employer also employed a man in an equal job in the same establishment, at a higher rate of pay." Equal Pay Act litigation, therefore, has been structured to permit employers to defend against charges of discrimination where their pay differentials are based on a bona fide use of facts other than sex.

Equal Pay

The MSPCA argues that because McMillan as Director/Department Head of Radiology did not have the same supervisory, budgetary, or administrative responsibilities as did other Directors/Department Heads (that is, her job was not "substantially equivalent"), she cannot establish a prima facie case under the Equal Pay Act. Thornton and Gambardella also deny that gender formed the basis of any of their salary decisions. They justify the significant salary differential between McMillan and the others by asserting that her job was less time consuming, produced less revenue for the MSPCA, and involved fewer functions. Specifically, they point to the fact that Radiology had the smallest staff and no actual responsibility for interns or residents.

Because a material dispute of fact exists concerning the comparability of McMillan's position with that of other department heads, the defendant's motion for summary judgment must be denied with respect to a claim of a violation of the Equal Pay Act.

Judgment for McMillan.

Employment Perspective

Keith Peterson and Jennifer Rivers were both hired after graduation for entry level positions by an accounting firm. Their scholastic achievements were comparable. Keith was offered $32,000, but Jennifer was offered $30,000. Does this constitute sex discrimination? Yes! This is in violation of the Equal Pay Act because the jobs are exactly the same. ◆

In the case that follows, a female professor argued that she was paid a salary inferior to that of her male colleagues. Her premise was based on the fact that males dominated the reviewal process.

CASE

Chance v. Rice University

989 F.2d 179 (5th Cir. 1993)

DUHE, Circuit Judge.

Dr. Jane Chance is a full professor of English literature at Rice University. Her colleague, Dr. Allen Grob, is chairperson of the English Department. Dr. Chance began her career at Rice in 1973, and in 1980 achieved her present status as a full professor.

In 1985, if not earlier, Dr. Chance began airing her grievances regarding compensation and promotions within the English Department. Specifically, Dr. Chance complained to Rice officials that her salary was not commensurate with that of her male colleagues, and that she was not given adequate consideration for two "endowed chairs," prestigious positions within the department that carry a title and increased compensation. She complained that these inequities resulted from the subjected determination of compensation and promotion within her department, a process controlled by males.

In response to Dr. Chance's allegations, Rice officials reviewed her past internal evaluations and asked other scholars, both within and outside Rice, to critique her published works. Based upon this investigation, the officials concluded that Dr. Chance's salary was commensurate with her abilities, and that she was not a victim of sexual discrimination within the English Department.

Dr. Chance's dissatisfaction continued, and in 1988 she filed suit alleging that Rice violated Title IX of the Education Amendments of 1972 as well as the Equal Pay Act.

To establish a prima facie case under the Equal Pay Act, Dr. Chance must show:

1. her employer is subject to the Act;
2. she performed work in a position requiring equal skill, effort, and responsibility under similar working conditions; and
3. she was paid less than the employee of the opposite sex providing the basis of comparison.

The district court's detailed and meticulous Findings of Fact included a finding that "Rice University does not pay appropriate male comparators higher compensation than Plaintiff for equal work on jobs, the performance of which require equal skill, effort, and responsibility under similar working conditions." Our review of the record reveals that this finding is fully supported by the evidence and is not clearly erroneous. Dr. Chance has therefore failed to establish a prima facie case under the Equal Pay Act.

To prevail on a claim for intentional infliction of emotional distress, Texas law requires Dr. Chance to show that:

(a) Dr. Grob acted intentionally or recklessly,
(b) his conduct was extreme and outrageous,
(c) his actions caused Dr. Chance emotional distress, and
(d) the emotional distress was severe.

Dr. Chance argues that she introduced sufficient evidence of depression, sleeplessness, and derogatory comments made by Dr. Grob, to create an issue of material fact. We disagree. Having reviewed the record, we find no evidence that Dr. Grob acted intentionally or recklessly, and find extensive evidence that other problems in Dr. Chance's life, other than the alleged behavior of Dr. Grob, may have caused Dr. Chance's emotional distress. Finding the evidence overwhelmingly in favor of Dr. Grob, we affirm the district court's grant of a directed verdict in his favor.

For the foregoing reasons, the district court's judgment in favor of Rice University and the directed verdict in favor of Dr. Grob are AFFIRMED.

Judgment for Rice University.

COMPARABLE WORTH

Comparable worth is an attempt to assign values to male-dominated and female-dominated jobs based on worth. Where the values are equated, equal pay would be required. The theory behind this doctrine was that most female-dominated jobs pay less than male-dominated jobs. This argument has not found favor with the courts because assigning values is arbitrary and interferes with payments based on supply and demand.

Employment Perspective

Gary Josephson is a construction worker. Jessica Tremont is a stenographer. He earns $36,000. She earns $22,000. Jessica argues that both jobs have comparable worth and that she should earn the same as Gary. Is she correct? No! Although her argument is based on comparable worth, the courts have decided not to enforce this doctrine. ◆

GROOMING

When employers attempt to regulate grooming, i.e., length of hair, beards, and mustaches, courts have usually found in favor of the employer. Their reasoning is that grooming codes are more closely related to the manner in which an employer decides to operate its business then to equal opportunity. Good grooming standards have always been required in the business world. Imagine walking into a bank and seeing a long-haired branch manager who has not shaved or showered, wearing jeans and a wrinkled shirt. This kind of appearance is not allowed because it would not be a good business policy. Customers may lose confidence in the bank and move their accounts elsewhere.

Arguments against grooming codes have come in the form of the First Amendment's rights of speech through personal expression, the Fourteenth Amendment Equal Protection Clause, and Title VII's provision regarding terms and conditions of employment.

Employment Perspective

Richard Masters is twenty-nine, and he is becoming bald. He is very self-conscious, so he has started wearing a hat all the time. Richard works as a bond trader for Bulls and Bears, Inc. While his manager empathizes with Richard's dilemma, Richard is told to remove the hat while in the office. Richard objects, claiming that baldness is a disability, and files a claim with the EEOC. Will he win? Probably not! Richard is not being subjected to discrimination because of his disability. If Richard is harassed by coworkers, he may sue for harassment. That is not the problem here, though. It revolves around Richard's vanity and his own perception of himself. This reasoning cannot outweigh Bulls and Bears' maintenance of dress codes as the way it conducts its business. ◆

Employment Perspective

Mary Jo Worthington, a longtime customer at Grasmere Bank is informed by Felix Farnsworth that he will be leaving the branch for a new position. On Monday, his replacement will begin. When Mary Jo enters the bank on Monday, she is horrified to see a long-haired man who has neither showered or shaved, wearing jeans, cowboy boots, and a T-shirt, sitting behind Felix's old desk. The scruffy man smiles, then introduces himself as Jesse Mickelson, new branch manager. Mary Jo dashed out of the bank and calls its customer service department reporting what she saw. Mickelson is informed of the bank's grooming policy and told never to be seen like that again. The next day, Mickelson looks the same and therefore is immediately terminated. He files a Title VII claim with the EEOC asserting that his actions are protected by freedom of speech through personal expression. Jesse also claims the grooming policy as a term and condition of employment is discrimination. Is he correct? Most likely not! Although there have been conflicting cases, the bank will be able to enforce its grooming policy because it is requiring of Mickelson only what is considered to be the norm in American business. He is not being deprived of an equal opportunity. He is only being asked to conform to the generally accepted standards of our society. ◆

Employment Perspective

Sonja Hendricks was a trader at First Financial in Buffalo. Their company dress code requires women to wear skirts, dresses, or suits with skirts. In the winter, the temperature is often below freezing. Sonja wore pants to keep her legs warm. First Financial dismissed her for being uncooperative. She claimed that the dress code manifested sex discrimination because it subjected women to show their legs and to be subjected to the cold weather. Is she correct? Probably! This restriction places an undue burden on women in that it does not give them the choice to protect themselves from the cold during the winter months. First Financial's business reasons are not paramount to a woman's health. ◆

In the next case, a female contests an employer's dress code as being discriminatory in that the women's attire is demeaning as compared with the men's attire. The women were suspended when they wore the same business attire as the men.

CASE

O'Donnell v. Burlington Coat Factory Warehouse

706 F.Supp. 263 (S.D.Ohio 1987)

SPIEGEL, District Judge.

In this sex discrimination action, plaintiffs, female sales clerks at defendants' retail store, challenge defendants' dress code as being violative of Title VII of the Civil Rights Act of 1964. The dress code in question requires female sales clerks to wear a "smock," while male sales clerks only are required to wear business attire consisting of slacks, shirt and a necktie. The smocks are supplied to the female sales clerks at no cost. After complaining that the smock requirement for women is discriminatory, plaintiffs refused to wear the smocks and instead wore regular business attire. Plaintiffs filed sex discrimination charges with the EEOC on August 18, 1983. Thereafter, plaintiffs reported for work wearing a blouse and tie and each day they were suspended. On August 30, 1983, plaintiffs were discharged when they refused to wear smocks. Plaintiffs filed charges with the EEOC claiming their discharge was sex discrimination and retaliation. Subsequently, the EEOC determined that there was reasonable cause to believe that the charge was true. After attempts at conciliation proved futile, plaintiffs commenced the present action in this Court. Both parties agree that the issue before this Court on summary judgment is whether defendants' dress code requiring female sales clerks to wear a smock while allowing male sales clerks to wear a shirt and tie is discriminatory under Title VII. The defendants' contend that distinctions between the sexes that do not adversely effect the terms and conditions of employment or employment opportunities do not violate Title VII. In Barker, the Court upheld an employer's grooming code which mandated shorter hair lengths for men than for women. Importantly, this grooming code set standards for both sexes: it regulated the length of men's hair and the styles for women's hair. According to defendants, the question we must decide is whether the differences in treatment created disadvantages for women in their compensation, terms, conditions or privileges of employment or employment opportunities. Because plaintiffs stipulated that wearing the smocks had no effect on their salary, benefits, hours of employment, raises, employment evaluations or any other term or condition of employment, defendants argue that the distinction in question is not discriminatory. Analogizing the dress requirement here to the grooming code in Barker, defendants claim both sexes had equal burdens with respect to their dress requirements: female employees had to wear a smock and male employees had to wear a shirt and tie. Plaintiffs acknowledge that Title VII does not prohibit all differences in treatment between the sexes but claim that a rule requiring only women to wear a smock does violate Title VII. In support of the position, plaintiffs claim that the instant case should not be governed by the "hair length/grooming" line of decisions cited by defendants. Rather, plaintiffs direct our attention to cases directly addressing "uniform" requirements that mandate different dress standards for male and female employees. In the lead case of *Carroll v. Talman Fed. Sav. & Loan,* a bank required its female tellers, officers and managerial employees to wear a uniform while male employees working in the same positions were required only to wear customary business attire. Unlike the case at bar, the female employees in Talman incurred the initial cost of their uniforms as well as subsequent cleaning and maintenance expenses. The employer expressly maintained that the purpose of the uniform requirement was to reduce fashion competition among women. Since men do not engage in such competition, they do not need a uniform requirement.

The Seventh Circuit held that personal appearance regulations with differing requirements for men and women do not violate Title VII as long as there is "some justification in commonly accepted social norms and are reasonably related to the employer's business needs." However, an employer who imposes separate dress requirements for men and women performing the same jobs will violate Title VII when one sex can wear regular business attire and the other must wear a uniform. Finding the uniform requirement demeaning to women, the Talman Court stated; "while there is nothing offensive about uniforms per se, when some employees are uniformed and others are not there is a natural tendency to assume that the uniformed women have lesser professional status than their colleagues. Even though defendants have expressed no discriminatory motive for the "smock" rule, we find that the blatant effect of such a rule is to perpetuate sexual stereotypes. We believe the cornerstone of the Talman decision is that it is demeaning for one sex to wear a uniform when members of the other sex holding the same positions are allowed to wear professional business attire. In contrast to the "hair length" standards for male employees, the smock requirement finds no justification in accepted social norms. Moreover, as plaintiffs point out, defendants have several non-discriminatory alternatives for achieving the goal of sales clerk identification: both sexes could wear the smock, a distinguishing blazer or identifying badges on their professional attire. Thus, we find that the smock rule creates disadvantages to the conditions of employment of females sales clerks and hence, is a violation of Title VII.

Judgment for O'Donnell.

CUSTOMER PREFERENCES

Although we are in an age in which customer service and satisfaction rules, acceding to customer preferences for service exclusively by one gender to the exclusion of the other is contradictory to Title VII's prohibition against gender discrimination.

Employment Perspective

Tooters, a sports bar and restaurant chain, known for its voluptuous female servers, has recently received applications from Ken, Frank, and Nick, who seek employment as servers. Tooters polls its clientele, who resoundingly state that they will no longer frequent the premises if male servers appear. Tooters denies the position to Ken, Frank, and Nick because of their gender. Ken, Frank, and Nick sue for sex discrimination arguing as long as they were otherwise qualified, they cannot be refused employment on the basis of their gender. Is the customer always right and will they be toiling at Tooters? This issue has been left in doubt in light of the EEOC's recent decision not to pursue its case involving a similar situation against Hooters Restaurant. ◆

Job selection cannot be based on customer preference for a particular gender; otherwise, it is discriminatory.

Employment Perspective

Thomas Stockwell applies for a position with "Workouts For Women Only," a health club exclusively for women. He is denied employment because he is a man. The proprietors are concerned with respecting the privacy rights of women. They argue that requiring only women employees is a bona fide occupational qualification. Thomas argues that assisting women with fitness instruction, teaching aerobics, and performing desk duties do not qualify as a BFOQ. Besides, he adds there are female employees available for locker-room maintenance. Is he correct? Yes! The preference of women customers to refrain from working out in front of men does not qualify as a BFOQ sufficient enough to override perpetuating discrimination against men by requiring their exclusion. ◆

The following case addresses the question of whether requiring only women to work in women's correctional institutions is a bona fide occupational qualification.

CASE *Carl v. Angelone*

883 F.Supp. 1433 (D.Nev. 1995)

REED, JR., District Judge.

Plaintiff alleges that Mr. Angelone is the director of Nevada Department of Prisons (NDOP). Plaintiffs are Correctional Officers (C/Os within NDOP). They allege that Mr. Angelone intentionally discriminated against them on the basis of their gender.

Plaintiffs allege that Mr. Angelone transferred Plaintiff male C/Os out of two women's correctional facilities and transferred plaintiff female C/Os from other correctional facilities to fill the vacancies. Mr. Angelone concedes that he did this and that he did so based on the plaintiff's gender: i.e., Mr. Angelone admits he made the transfers because he wanted female correctional officers at the women's correctional facilities and therefore transferred the male officers out because they were men and transferred the female officers in because they were women.

Qualified immunity protects government officials from civil liability for actions taken in the performance of discretionary functions when their actions do not violate clearly established statutory or constitutional rights of which a reasonable person should have known. However, no official can in good faith impose discriminatory burdens on a person or group by reason of a racial or ethnic animus against them. The constitutional right to be free from such invidious discrimination is so well established and so essential to the preservation of our constitutional order that all public officials must be charged with knowledge of it.

In cases involving intentional discrimination there can be no qualified immunity defense, and the dispositive issue of the defendant's intent merge. If the plaintiff fails to establish that the discrimination was intentional, the claim fails. If the plaintiff does establish such intent, there can be no qualified immunity. Thus, it seems simpler to say that qualified immunity is not a defense in such cases rather than that the defense prevails where proof of intentional discrimination is not established.

There is substantial evidence that the motivating factor for Mr. Angelone's actions was the gender of each of the individual plaintiffs. Mr. Angelone not only admits that he took the challenged actions solely on the basis of gender. Mr. Angelone contends that because he thought his actions were legal and appropriate responses, . . . his actions were non-discriminatory.

Mr. Angelone's belief that his actions were legal and appropriate . . . does not remove discriminatory intent from his actions. This raises the affirmative defense of bona fide occupational qualification (bfoq) in which a defendant admits the discriminatory intent motivating the actions, but claims that such actions were otherwise necessary.

The bfoq is an affirmative defense in itself. To allow defendants to elevate it into a qualified immunity appears improper for several reasons. First, the bfoq is an affirmative defense to liability. No good reason is presented why qualified immunity should flow from the assertion of an affirmative defense on which defendant has the burden of proof. This would in essence reverse the burden of proof, requiring plaintiff to demonstrate that defendant could not have reasonably believed the bfoq defense applied, even though the defendant would bear the burden of proving the bfoq defense.

Where discrimination on the basis of gender exists, the employer bears the burden of proving:

> 1) that the job qualification or function justifying the discrimination is reasonably necessary to the essence of the defendant's particular business; and 2) that gender is a legitimate proxy for the qualification or function because (a) there is a substantial basis for believing that all or nearly all employees of the affected gender lack the qualification or ability to perform that function, or (b) it is impossible or highly impractical for the defendant to insure by individual testing that its employees will have qualifications for the job.

A defendant Prison must demonstrate why it cannot reasonably rearrange job responsibilities within the prison to minimize the clash between the privacy interests of the inmates and the safety of the Prison employees on the one hand and the non-discriminatory requirement of Title VII on the other, before the prison will be entitled to the bfoq exception.

First, Mr. Angelone argues a per se rule making it illegal for male correctional officers to conduct routine or random body searches of female prisoners. If that were so, such a rule would be binding upon Mr. Angelone. . . .

. . . there is no per se rule upon which Mr. Angelone may rely which would permit him to take the challenged actions. There is no per se rule providing a substantial basis for believing that male C/Os lack the legal ability to perform random or routine body searches of female inmates.

Judgment for Carl.

CONCLUSION

In the past, American society excluded women from many positions in the labor market because they could afford to. The American society was the most affluent in the world while its economy was flourishing almost exclusively at the hands of men. In today's global environment no brain can be left untapped. Women should be encouraged by men to realize their potential in the workplace. Some men fear that employing women in business will reduce the number of positions for them. Their fear is misdirected. "Us against them" should not mean men against women. It should mean keeping the jobs in the United States as opposed to losing them to foreign labor. If the power of each American male and female is not used to its fullest to become innovators and entrepreneurs to develop newer, faster, cheaper, and better products, services and technologies, then the positions that men are trying to safeguard from women will be lost to overseas competitors. The key is that the number and quality of jobs are elastic and can expand or contract, depending upon how well we perform.

REVIEW QUESTIONS

1. Define sex discrimination.
2. What is sex plus discrimination?
3. Explain the significance of the Equal Pay Act.
4. Define comparable worth.
5. Is comparable worth in effect today?
6. Are grooming standards permissible?
7. Can a man be discriminated against because of his gender?
8. Why is a BFOQ a defense to a gender discrimination suit?
9. Ethically, should women tennis players be paid the same as the men in the U.S. Open, even though the women play 2 out of 3 sets in comparison to the 3 out of 5 sets played by the men?
10. Are employers justified in practicing sex discrimination in hiring because of customer preferences?
11. Marilyn A. Doerter was hired as Assistant Dean at Bluffton College by Dean William Hawk. Less than a year later, she was terminated because of her lack of skills and her inability to communicate effectively with Dean Hawk. She was replaced by a woman. Doerter claimed sex discrimination, arguing Dean Hawk was unfriendly toward her and preferred the company of other men. Doerter acknowledged that a personality conflict existed that contributed to the communications problem. What was the result? (*Doerter v. Bluffton College,* 647 N.E.2d 876 (Ohio App. 3 Dist. 1994)
12. An employee questioned the employer's grooming code, which required a different maximum hair length for men than for women. He claimed that the code was sexually discriminatory. What was the result? *Barker v. Taft Broadcasting Co.*, 549 F.2d 400 (6th Cir. 1977)
13. A bank required its female tellers to wear a uniform, while male employees working in the same position were required only to wear customary business attire. The female em-

ployees incurred the initial cost of their uniforms as well as subsequent cleaning and maintenance expenses. The employer expressly maintained that the purpose of the uniform requirement was to reduce fashion competition among women. Since men do not engage in such competition, they do not need a uniform requirement. What was the result? *Caroll v. Talman Fed. Sav. & Loan,* 604 F.2d 1030 (7th Cir.)

14. King, a professor at the University of Wisconsin, applied for tenure. Her tenure review was not granted because she did not provide any scholarly publications. King claimed sex discrimination. What was the result? *King v. Board of Regents of Wisconsin System,* 898 F.2d 533 (7th Cir. 1990)

15. What must a plaintiff prove to establish a prima facie case under the Equal Pay Act?

16. Once a prima facie case is made out under the Equal Pay Act, what factors must employers show that will operate as justifiable defenses? *Corning Glass Works v. Brennan,* 417 U.S. 188 (1974)

17. The MSPCA argues that because McMillan as Director/Department Head of Radiology did not have the same supervisory, budgetary, or administrative responsibilities as did other Director/Department Heads (that is, her job was not "substantially equivalent"), she cannot establish a prima facie case under the Equal Pay Act. Thornton and Gambardella also deny that gender formed the basis of any salary differential between McMillan and the others by asserting that their job was less time consuming, produces less revenue for the MSPCA, and involves fewer functions. Specifically, they point to the fact that Radiology had the smallest staff and no actual responsibility for interns or residents. What was result? *McMillan v. Massachusetts Soc. of Cruelty to Animals,* 880 F.Supp 900 (D. Mass 1995)

18. In the case on pp. 266, should grooming codes be the same for men as for women?

19. Referring to the case on pp. 262, is the Equal Pay Act helping women to achieve equality in pay?

20. Is there any reason why women should not be paid at the same rate as a man?

CHAPTER 12
Sexual Harassment

INTRODUCTION

Sexual harassment encompasses the request for sexual favors as well as touching, joking, commenting, or distributing material of a sexual nature that an employee has not consented to and finds offensive. The aggrieved individual may initiate a lawsuit against the individual personally or may proceed against the company. If there was unpermitted touching, this gives rise to the torts of civil assault and battery. If there were sexual comments made with a particular individual in mind, that would constitute slander. If sexual comments were written or sexual pictorials were drawn, it would be libel. If generic comments were made that degraded the gender, an individual could claim the tort of infliction of emotional distress.

Requirements

There are six requirements that must be satisfied for sexual harassment to exist:

1. The victimizing employee alleging sexual harassment must be a member of a protected class, that is a man or a woman.
2. The complaint must be gender related, for example, a female must assert there would have been no harassment if she were not a woman.
3. The employee must not have consented to the sexual advances or participated in the hostile work environment.
4. The harassment must be based on sex.
5. The conduct complained of must have had a deleterious effect on the employee's job.

6. Respondent superior exists, that is, the harassment must have occurred during the scope of employment, thus making the employer liable for the sexual harassing conduct of its employees.

The following case addresses the issue of whether off-color jokes, glaring, or rubbing up against a subordinate is severe and pervasive enough to amount to sexual harassment.

Canada v. Boyd Group, Inc.

809 F.Supp. 771 (D.Nev. 1992)

PRO, District Judge.

Plaintiff Canada's first contact with Defendants was on January 16, 1990, when she applied for employment as a poker dealer at Defendants California Hotel & Casino, d/b/a Sam's Town. This was the first time Plaintiff met Steve Strauss, the poker-room manager for Defendants. As poker-room manager, Mr. Strauss had authority to hire, fire, make personnel decisions, and act as supervisor of all poker-room employees at Sam's Town. According to Plaintiff, on one occasion prior to her employment with Defendants, but after she submitted her application for employment, Mr. Strauss asked Plaintiff to dinner. The Plaintiff refused. This is the only time during Plaintiff's contact with Defendants that Plaintiff was ever asked out by Mr. Strauss.

In March of 1990, Plaintiff learned the position for which she had originally applied had been filled. Plaintiff returned to Defendants' establishment in April 1990, and spoke to Mr. Strauss who stated that if a position became available he would contact her. That same evening, around 9:30 p.m., Mr. Strauss called Plaintiff at home and offered Plaintiff a job. Plaintiff accepted. Because Mr. Strauss was the poker-room manager he would act as Plaintiff's supervisor upon hiring her.

On approximately April 24, 1990, Plaintiff reported for work at Defendants' establishment where she received her Employee Handbook. The Handbook included a section on sexual harassment. According to Plaintiff, over the next two to three weeks, Mr. Strauss's conduct included the following: Two incidents of telling "off-colored" jokes (from which Plaintiff walked away); comments on how good Plaintiff looked in her uniform; smiling and looking at Plaintiff a great deal; one incident in which Mr. Strauss leaned or rubbed the front of his body on the back of Plaintiff's body and placed his hand on Plaintiff's shoulder (from which Plaintiff moved away); one other incident in which Mr. Strauss placed his hand on Plaintiff's shoulder; and, one phone call to Plaintiff at home.

Soon after these incidents, Plaintiff asked Mr. Strauss if she could work the "swing" shift, a shift Mr. Strauss did not work. Mr. Strauss told Plaintiff she would have to work whatever shifts she could get, but in fact she was assigned mostly swing shifts from that point on until her discharge.

Subsequent to this request, over approximately a five week period, Plaintiff's and Mr. Strauss's relationship was strained. On several occasions Plaintiff asked Mr. Strauss if another dealer could work her shift. According to Plaintiff, Mr. Strauss rudely refused each request. On another occasion Plaintiff was sick and asked Mr. Strauss if she could leave early. Mr. Strauss refused this request. Later that same day Mr. Strauss allowed other dealers to leave early.

On June 14, 1990, plaintiff spoke with Robert Neuman, manager of Sam's Town and Mr. Strauss's boss. Plaintiff told Mr. Neuman about the incidents with Mr. Strauss and stated that she thought Mr. Strauss was going to fire her because she had been unresponsive to his overtures. Mr. Neuman referred Plaintiff to Stan Roth, manager of Sam's Town casino, and also Mr. Strauss's boss. On June 15, 1990, Plaintiff related the same incidents about Mr. Strauss to Mr. Roth who told her that her allegations were serious and that he would initiate an investigation. Mr. Roth reminded Plaintiff that she was an at-will employee and as such could be fired for no reason at all. Additionally, Plaintiff admits she signed an employment application that included a statement that she was an at-will employee.

On June 16, 1990, Plaintiff reported for her shift in her uniform with a doctor's note indicating she was too ill to work. Plaintiff gave the note to Mr. Strauss who sent her home without commenting on the fact that she had failed to comply with General Rule No. 7 of Defendants' Employee Handbook. The Handbook clearly indicates that an employee is to give four hours notice when she in unable to report for a shift. Approximately five days later, Plaintiff's first day back to work, she received a disciplinary notice. Plaintiff refused to sign the notice, and after asking for but receiving no explanation as to why she was not put on notice immediately, Plaintiff stated she would speak to a higher authority. That same night Plaintiff was handed a suspension notice and told to leave.

A prima facie case of hostile environment sexual harassment exists when a female employee alleges conduct that "a reasonable woman would consider sufficiently severe or pervasive to alter the conditions of employment and create an abusive working environment." Thus, after drawing all favorable inferences to Plaintiff, this Court will grant summary judgment to Defendants only if no reasonable woman would find Defendant's conduct sufficiently severe or pervasive to have caused a hostile working environment.

The required showing of severity of conduct varies inversely with the required showing of frequency of conduct when a court is to determine whether a reasonable woman would find her employment environment hostile. Thus, Defendants repeatedly urge this Court to note that no incidents of sexual harassment are alleged to have occurred after the first two to three weeks of Plaintiff's employment. But while frequency and severity of conduct are important factors to consider when assessing whether a hostile environment was created, ultimately it is the effect or consequences of conduct on the working environment that must be evaluated. Thus, while none of Defendants may have considered Mr. Strauss's conduct to be severe or frequent enough to be offensive, the question is whether a reasonable woman, who had worked with Mr. Strauss, would consider his conduct severe and/or frequent enough to create an abusive working environment. The answer to that question is not sufficiently clear to warrant a grant of summary judgment in favor of Defendants.

Within a two to three week period approximately six separate incidents occurred in which Mr. Strauss's conduct could be considered abusive. The most severe of these incidents included Mr. Strauss leaning or rubbing himself against Plaintiff. In fact, according to Plaintiff, she may have been encountering Mr. Strauss's alleged abusive conduct as frequently as every other day during her first few weeks of employment. This Court cannot conclude that these facts present no material issue as to whether Mr. Strauss's conduct was severe and frequent enough to have created a hostile working environment for Plaintiff.

Under Title VII of the Civil Rights Act, a claim for quid pro quo sexual harassment is one in which an employer conditions "employment benefits on sexual favors." This is clearly distinguished from a hostile environment case in which an abusive environment is alleged. Although the Court clearly views these as distinct causes of action, it is certainly feasible that the factual basis for a quid pro quo allegation and a hostile environment allegation may overlap. Plaintiff's factual allegations do not, however, rise to the level of quid pro quo.

In *Miller v. Bank of America,* the court defined the essence of a quid pro quo allegation as a case in which a supervisor relies upon his authority to "extort sexual consideration from an employee." In the case at bar, Plaintiff has presented no evidence to support a claim that any supervisor used his authority to extort sexual favors from her. Plaintiff offers no evidence of statements or actions by any Defendants, including those dismissed from this action, that indicate that Plaintiff's continued employment, or other employment benefits, were contingent on her granting sexual favors. The fact that Plaintiff believed Mr. Strauss treated her badly because she was unresponsive to him is not sufficient to support an allegation that

Mr. Strauss was using sex as a criterion for employment benefits. There is no evidence to suggest employment benefits were withheld from Plaintiff. Rather, Plaintiff claims that she was subjected to sexually inappropriate conduct by Mr. Strauss and that she was not allowed to leave early or have others work her shifts. To some extent the denial of these favors may be considered employment benefits; however, they much more directly reflect the environment in which Plaintiff had to work. Moreover, the allegation that Mr. Strauss may have treated other employees of Sam's Town in a manner arguably sufficient to constitute a claim for quid pro quo harassment is not relevant to show that Plaintiff's employment benefits were contingent on a quid pro quo.

Furthermore, this Court rejects Plaintiff's suggestion that the "reasonable woman" standard should be used to determine when quid pro quo occurs. Unlike hostile environment, for which the "reasonable woman" test was developed, quid pro quo sexual harassment does not need a gender-conscious reasonable person test to determine whether a violation of Title VII has occurred. If an employer conditions employment benefits on the granting of sexual favors, a civil rights violation occurs and the employer is strictly liable. No further evidence need be presented.

Plaintiff fails to state a claim for quid pro quo sexual harassment. Therefore, Defendants' Motion for Summary Judgment as to quid pro quo sexual harassment must be granted.

Judgment for Boyd Group, Inc.

Employment Perspective

George Miles works as an insurance underwriter. In the office, he has openly stated his view that women are good only for sex and do not belong in the workplace because they are always crying about PMS. Susan cringes when she hears these remarks and tries to hide from George's view lest she become a target. George continues to fondle Amanda's backside when she has repeatedly admonished him. He photostated a caricature of Debbie, a coworker, as a naked woman with large breasts. George speaks about the pornographic films that he has viewed and describes them in detail. He also has commented that he is due for a promotion after having sex with Margaret, the vice president for operations. What recourse do these women have against George? Amanda may sue George for the tort of battery because it was unpermitted touching that she has found offensive and embarrassing. Margaret may sue for slander because George's remarks are untrue and damaging to her reputation. Debbie may sue for libel because the sexually offensive drawing has been distributed. Susan may sue for infliction of emotional distress because his comments, although not directed at her personally, are degrading to her because she is a woman. ◆

The predominant number of instances of sexual harassment have been men harassing women, but there are occasions when men have been harassed by women or other men and when women have been harassed by other women. These instances are equally unacceptable.

The following case addresses the question of whether a female employee's allegations of sexual harassment are mitigated by the fact that she appeared nude in a magazine. In addition, the case also raises the point concerning what prompted her to leave the job. Was it the alleged sexual harassment, or was it because of other circumstances?

CASE

Burns v. McGregor Electronic Industries, Inc.

807 F.Supp. 506 (N.D.Iowa 1992)

STUART, Judge.

This is a sex discrimination case brought under Title VII of the Civil Rights Act of 1964. Plaintiff claims that she was subjected to sexual harassment in the workplace creating such a hostile working environment that the quitting of her job constituted a constructive discharge.

In *Meritor Savings Bank, FSB v. Vinson,* the Supreme Court held "that a plaintiff may establish a violation of Title VII by proving that discrimination based on sex has created a hostile or abusive work environment." Not all workplace conduct that may be described as harassment affects a "term, condition, or privilege" of employment within the meaning of Title VII.

The plaintiff, Lisa Burns, quit school in the middle of the 9th grade because she didn't get along with other students. She felt that they picked on her because she was poor. She testified that she felt sexually harassed. At age 18-1/2, plaintiff got her first regular job at McGregor Electronic Industries, Inc. (McGregor Electronics). She worked there from October 14, 1980 to August 10, 1981. Plaintiff testified that during this period of time she got along well with most of the employees, but that Marla Ludvik, a co-worker, made derogatory comments about her, tried to get her to date male employees, and accused her of seeing Paul Oslac, the owner of McGregor Electronics. Ludvik denied any such conduct. Plaintiff testified that she complained to supervisors but that nothing changed.

Plaintiff also testified that after she began working on the main floor of the factory Oslac talked to her about sex, showed her pictures from Penthouse magazine, tried to get her to go out with him, and invited her to his apartment on the top floor of the factory to watch pornographic movies. She said that she did not say "no" outright because she was afraid of losing her job. Rather, she would decline his advances with one reason or another and try to change the subject. She testified further that Oslac directed lewd gestures at her once while she was working. During the first period of employment Oslac was at the factory approximately two days each week. Plaintiff testified that she eventually became emotionally upset and quit because it was affecting her work. There were, however, no complaints about the quality of her work, and Oslac denied any such conduct. Plaintiff claims she did not file for unemployment compensation because she did not know she could apply.

Plaintiff was rehired by Virginia Kelley about five weeks later and worked from September 15, 1981 to June 20, 1983 as a tester at better pay. Virginia Kelley managed the plant from August 19, 1981 to February 28, 1982. Plaintiff's mother, Marlene Bouska, had been working at McGregor Electronics since October 14, 1980. Plaintiff and her mother testified that Kelley asked Marlene to ask plaintiff to come back to work. Kelley, on the other hand, testified that Marlene asked her to rehire plaintiff.

As a tester, plaintiff tested speakers manufactured at the plant as they passed through her testing booth on the assembly line. The testing booth was open on the top, on the front below the assembly line, and on the sides at the points of entry and exit of the assembly line. A door at the back of the booth ordinarily was open. Plaintiff testified that while she was working, Oslac would come into the booth alone and proposition her. She testified that Oslac spent "almost all" of the time that he was at the plant in her testing booth and that on at least two occasions he improperly touched her. Oslac testified to the contrary. During this second period of employment Oslac was at the plant from about Monday noon to Tuesday mid-morning each week.

In the spring of 1982, plaintiff appeared nude in *Easy Riders* "In the Wind" magazine. In April 1983, she appeared nude in *Easy Riders* magazine. The magazine circulated throughout the plant, and employees saw them. In these photographs she had ornaments or earrings attached to her nipples. One picture revealed a tattoo in the pelvic region. Her father had pierced her nipples and had taken the photographs in her brother's presence.

Plaintiff testified that she once agreed to have dinner with Oslac because she feared losing her job. She accepted on the condition that her mother could come too. Her mother refused to go with her, but her father went with her instead. Plaintiff testified that as they were leaving after the meal, her father told Oslac to "leave the girls alone," and that Oslac nodded in agreement. Oslac testified that he invited the plaintiff and her father to dinner in order to persuade her not to quit working at the factory. The Court finds that Oslac was surprised when the father appeared instead of the mother.

Plaintiff testified that some of her co-workers missed her. In particular, she testified that Marla Ludvik circulated a petition to get her fired because of the nude pictures. Only one witness testified that she saw the petition. The rest had heard that a petition was being circulated but did not see it. No one signed the petition. Two other male co-workers subjected her to offensive name-calling. Plaintiff testified that she quit because of the harassment. She said that her work slowed. However, no one complained about the quality of her work.

Plaintiff was rehired and worked from September 26, 1983 to July 19, 1984. By this time Virginia Kelley was managing the plant again. Plaintiff testified that Virginia Kelley persuaded her to return to work by promising that Oslac would leave her alone. Kelley denied this. During the third period of employment, plaintiff started as a tester and was then transferred to the laboratory. Plaintiff testified that she again was subjected to advances from Oslac and harassment from co-workers.

On July 19, 1984, plaintiff walked off the job following a work dispute with Eugene Ottaway. Ottaway had moved a stack of speakers to the plaintiff's work area. Plaintiff asked Ottaway to move them into her workroom and then asked him to lower the stack and not to stack them so high in the future. Plaintiff testified that Ottaway began throwing down the stack of speakers. Ottaway admitted cursing and subjecting her to offensive name-calling. He testified the plaintiff also called him names. He testified that the speakers simply fell down after he moved the stack into plaintiff's workroom. Plaintiff testified she got upset, left, and that weekend decided to quit her job.

Plaintiff did not see Oslac in the plant during the last four to six weeks of her employment with McGregor Electronics. During plaintiff's last period of employment, Oslac arrived at the plant Monday about noon and left before noon on Tuesday each week. Oslac occasionally would pass through the work area briefly on his way to or from the plant's office.

Plaintiff filed an unemployment compensation claim. McGregor Electronics did not contest the claim before the hearing officer. Plaintiff received unemployment compensation benefits after leaving McGregor Electronics. Plaintiff obtained employment in 1987 with another employer. The Court has had some difficulty in determining what actually went on at McGregor Electronics. Rumor and gossip ran rampant. As one witness testified:

> It's probably a last resort of anybody that needs a job. If they need a job bad enough that they need money. They're always hiring, because they can't keep their help. Like I say, I worked there five times, and if I got to the point where I absolutely had to have a job, I'd probably go back. If I could find another job, I would be gone again.

The general working conditions; gossip about plaintiff's working attire and the nude pictures in a crude and lewd publication and her resulting treatment by co-employees; unwanted sexual advances by Oslac—the 65 year old owner of the plant; and the running dispute with other employees about whose duty it was to move and stack speakers for the laboratory workers—all contributed to plaintiff's decision to quit her job. But the primary reason she left work and did not return was the incident on the last day during which she and Eugene Ottaway got into a violent name calling argument and speakers were knocked about.

Judgment for McGregor Electronics Industries.

In the following case, the issue is whether sexual harassment may be perpetrated against a member of the same sex.

Vandeventer v. Wabash Nat. Corp.

CASE

887 F.Supp. 1178 (N.D.)

SHARP, Judge.

Same-Sex Sexual Harassment Under Title VII

Mr. Feltner's only allegation of sexual harassment involved a male co-worker who aimed obscene language at him. In ruling against the plaintiff, this court stated that "Same-sex harassment is not actionable under Title VII." That statement may have been overbroad.

The holding against plaintiff Feltner in his same-sex harassment claim was correct, and based on solid law.

It may be that same-sex harassment is never cognizable under Title VII, but that is still a murky area of the law and was not the basis of the decision in this case. Discrimination because of homosexuality is not covered by Title VII.

("Congress manifested an intention to exclude homosexuals from Title VII coverage. . . . The phrase in Title VII prohibiting discrimination based on sex, in its plain meaning, implies that it is unlawful to discriminate against women because they are women and against men because they are men. . . . Congress never considered nor intended that this 1964 legislation apply to anything other than the traditional concept of sex.")

People who are harassed because they are homosexual (or are perceived as homosexual) are not protected by Title VII any more than are people who are harassed for having brown eyes. However, it is imperative to note that being homosexual does not deprive someone of protection from sexual harassment under Title VII, it is merely irrelevant to it. The issue is and remains whether one is discriminated against because of one's gender. If a male homosexual is discriminated against because he is male, such violates Title VII regardless of his particular sexual orientation. Not surprisingly, cases of male prejudice against males or female prejudice against females is rare.

There seems to be significant confusion regarding the distinctions between sexual harassment and gender discrimination. There is no law specifically outlawing sexual harassment. Sexual harassment is illegal because and only because it is a form of gender discrimination under Title VII. Sexual harassment is a subset of gender discrimination under Title VII. The concept of sexual harassment is an acknowledgement that when a male employer requires a woman to submit to him sexually for a promotion, or creates a sexually hostile environment, he is discriminating against her on the basis of her gender. Gender discrimination is the root; absent a base in gender discrimination, there can be no actionable sexual harassment. One can most certainly be the victim of gender discrimination without being a victim of sexual harassment; however, the reverse is not true. One cannot be the victim of actionable sexual harassment if one is not a victim of gender discrimination.

No evidence was produced by Mr. Feltner that he was harassed because he was a male. The EEOC's Compliance Manual Section 615.2(b)(3) states that "the crucial inquiry is whether the harasser treats a member or members of one sex differently from members of the other sex," whether or not the victim is of the opposite sex from the harasser. That means that a man can state a claim under Title VII for sexual harassment by another man only if he is being harassed because he is a man; the relative genders are irrelevant. There may or may not be homosexual aspects to such harassment. There may or may not be a prejudice against one's own gender involved.

The words "sex" and "sexual" create definitional problems because they can mean either "relating to gender" or "relating to sexual/reproductive behavior." The two are not the same, but are certainly related and easily confused. Title VII only recognizes harassment based on the first meaning, although that frequently involves the second meaning. However, harassment which involves sexual behavior or has sexual behavior overtones (i.e. remarks, touching, display of pornographic pictures) but is not based on gender bias does not state a claim under Title VII.

Conclusion

It is being the victim of anti-male or anti-female bias that forms the basis of a Title VII sexual harassment claim, not simply being exposed to "sexual" type comments or behavior. Title VII is meant to rectify gender bias in the workplace, not per se to outlaw foul mouths or obscenities. Sometimes sexually-explicit comments are evidence of or constitute gender bias, and sometimes not. Absent extenuating circumstances, it would seem difficult to prove that sexually explicit words or conduct between men would demonstrate an anti-male atmosphere. Evidence of such was not presented here.

Judgment for Wabash Nat. Corp.

Employment Perspective

Phil Thomas is a construction worker who lives with his mother. After work every day he rushes home to tend to her needs. When he won't join them for a few beers, his coworkers taunt him continuously, claiming that he's a Momma's boy, a wimp tied to his mother's apron strings. This taunting happens continuously throughout the day. The coworkers leave notes, photostat caricatures, and openly make remarks. Is this sexual harassment? Probably not! Phil's coworkers are inflicting emotional distress upon him. But this isolated instance of teasing alone is not sufficient to constitute sexual harassment. ◆

The following case addresses the question of whether a male employee who has had an affair with a female supervisor can later claim sexual harassment. When the affair ended, she tried to have him discharged. Her superiors refused to comply.

Carter v. Caring for the Homeless of Peekskill

821 F.Supp. 225 (S.D.N.Y. 1993)

BRIEANT, District Judge.

In this Title VII action, based on sexual harassment of a male employee by a woman who at relevant times was Chairman of the Board of Directors of the corporate employer, this Court now considers a motion by defendants for judgment in their favor not withstanding the jury verdict. The verdict was for loss of wages (back pay) in the amount $6,100.00, the maximum recoverable under the applicable facts. Liability depends upon a jury finding of constructive discharge. A claim for plaintiff's legal fees in the requested amount of $84,000 has been presented for consideration by the Court.

The conduct complained of occurred prior to November 21, 1991, the date of enactment of Pub.L. 102–166 (The Civil Rights Act of 1991). Although plaintiff is an African American and Dr. Janet Foy is white, the Amended Complaint docketed September 14, 1992 does not invoke 42 U.S.C. 1981.

The Parties

At the time of the incidents complained of, plaintiff was receiving a pension from the Veterans

Administration based on 100% disability. He is a reformed alcoholic and former substance abuser, divorced with at least one adult child. Defendant, Dr. Janet Foy, is a psychologist practicing in the City of Peekskill, who specializes in marital counseling. She also is divorced with at least one adult child. While the ages of these parties do not appear in the record, both are mature adults.

Defendant, Caring for the Homeless of Peekskill, is a Not-for-Profit New York corporation also referred to by its acronym, CHOP, Inc. It was founded by PAPA, another acronym, which stands for "Peekskill Area Pastors Association." Dr. Janet Foy was the non-salaried Chairman of the Board of Directors of CHOP, Inc. a group of approximately twenty community volunteers of various faiths, races and backgrounds brought together by PAPA and the Mayor of Peekskill, all of whom served without pay. Assisted by local service clubs, the officials of the City of Peekskill, and the public, these people were successful in establishing and opening a facility known as the Jan Peek House as a shelter for the homeless of that community.

In January 1988, Mr. Larry Carter was employed at Jan Peek House as a part-time Client Care worker, and became a full-time Case Manager on May 9, 1988. This promotion was offered by Terri Powers, the salaried Director of Jan Peek House, and was based on the understanding that he would initiate training towards becoming qualified as a "C.A.C." or "Certified Alcohol Counselor," which is a trained counselor in the field of alcohol and substance abuse.

A consensual sexual relationship developed between Mr. Carter and Dr. Foy in about September 1989.

Throughout the course of his employment at Jan Peek House, Mr. Carter received satisfactory or better performance evaluations. The corporate defendant maintained throughout this litigation that Mr. Carter was an outstanding employee, and was so regarded by his peers and by the Board, and there is no evidence to the contrary. Dr. Foy wrote a glowing recommendation and personal reference to permit him to enter the C.A.C. training program, as did Terri Powers, the Director of the Jan Peek House until mid or late 1989. Mr. Carter developed additional skills working at the Jan Peek House. With tuition paid by the Veterans Administration, he successfully completed his C.A.C. accreditation shortly before his resignation dated October 15, 1990, which he claims and the jury found to be the result of a constructive discharge.

Following the resignation of Terri Powers and after a brief period during which Carter was Acting Director, the Executive Director of the shelter became Jeanette Quinn (Lardiere). The written job description of Ms. Quinn, approved by the Board of Directors, included the power to hire and fire personnel employed at the shelter. Dr. Foy, as Chairman of the Board, had neither statutory nor apparent authority to hire and fire, not did she purport to exercise such powers, which remained with the entire Board as a matter of New York law, unless expressly delegated.

The path of true love seldom runs smoothly. Mr. Carter testified that he first attempted to "break-off" the relationship with Dr. Foy in November of 1989, and again in December of 1989, because he felt that Dr. Foy was "very controlling and critical" of his participation in support groups and AA. The couple had joint consultations, paid for by plaintiff, with Dr. James W. Walkup in November 1989, to "identify the issues in their relationship." By plaintiff's own admission, however, Dr. Foy and he continued their tumultuous personal relationship until April or May of 1990. At this time, Mr. Carter advised Dr. Foy that he wanted to end the relationship, and that he no longer wanted her to attend his son's graduation from medical school or his own graduation from his C.A.C. certification program, to both of which he had previously invited her. Nevertheless, Mr. Carter testified that, in March of 1990, the two opened a joint savings account to save, in part, "for us to get married" and that sometime after their "final" breakup the two met on one or two occasions at her apartment for sex.

According to Mr. Carter, on June 4, 1990, he appeared at Dr. Foy's own professional office in Peekskill to recover a passbook for the joint savings account containing funds belonging only to him, and that the two engaged in a shouting match before Dr. Foy surrendered the passbook. This incident was off the work premises, not related to his employment at Jan Peek House and, by Mr. Carter's own admission, was instigated by him in the first place.

After this incident in Dr. Foy's professional office, Mr. Carter testified that Dr. Foy harassed him sexually when she attended his graduation from the C.A.C. certification program on June 4, 1990. The alleged harassment by Dr. Foy during the graduation ceremony included her unwelcome attendance at the graduation (after having been invited, with the invitation subsequently withdrawn), her taking pictures and her kissing Mr. Carter when she presented him with a gift and flowers. Mr. Carter characterized this episode as "embarrassing." While this may have been embarrassing for Mr. Carter and may demonstrate that Foy lacked judgment in attending a ceremony to which her prior invitation had been withdrawn, this does not constitute sexual harassment in any sense in connection with the employment relationship. Mr. Carter did not even suggest that this incident had any consequence in the work place.

The next alleged incident of sexual harassment also occurred in June of 1990. Mr. Carter testified, and defendant Foy concedes, that on June 5, 1990 at 10:00 a.m., Dr. Foy called Mr. Carter at work, and asked him to meet over dinner that evening to reconsider their relationship. After Mr. Carter declined the invitation, Dr. Foy then suggested that he resign from his position at Jan Peek House "as a personal consideration" to her and asked him to take a one week vacation to consider his options. Dr. Foy memorialized this conversation in a memorandum of the same date.

Mr. Carter acknowledged during his direct and cross examination that he was assured immediately and directly by Ms. Quinn, the Director of Jan Peek House, and also by the Board of Directors of the corporate defendant, that his job was not in jeopardy. He was further advised that Jeannie Quinn would act as an intermediary between him and Dr. Foy and that he would no longer have to report directly to Dr. Foy, if that had ever been a requirement of his job.

Mr. Carter could cite no other examples of alleged harassment that occurred during the four month period between June 5, 1990 and October 15, 1990, the date he resigned.

Jeannie Quinn gave two week's notice of her resignation as Director of Jan Peek House, on October 1, 1990, and on the following day the Board caused her to be removed from the premises.

Mr. Carter testified that after Jeannie Quinn resigned he was required to report directly to Dr. Foy, yet he could cite no specific examples of when his job required him to do so. The uncontroverted evidence is that Mr. Carter was out sick between October 8, 1990 and the date of his resignation. Accordingly, the only period of time in which any events relied on to constitute a constructive discharge could have occurred between the second and the eighth of October, and there was no evidence of any incidents occurring between Dr. Foy and Mr. Carter during this period of time, except that on one occasion Dr. Foy yelled because she could not find the secretary and sent plaintiff to look for her.

While there clearly was a history of sexual tension between Mr. Carter and Dr. Foy, it cannot be said that this was the result of sexual harassment in the work place. Instead, the tension was the result of a failed relationship. And in the realm of private affairs people do have the right to react to rejection, jealousy and other emotions attendant to a failed relationship.

The standard for a constructive discharge is the objective one of the reasonable person, and is not altered in this case by the fact that Mr. Carter had a problem with his blood pressure. Plaintiff now argues that the change in his working environment was "the discharge of Jeannie Quinn, leading to Dr. Foy becoming his direct supervisor, and the rise in his blood pressure to a level which his cardiologist testified was unacceptable." This amounts to mere suspicion that Dr. Foy, as Acting Director, might change his working conditions before a new Director could be chosen and is an insufficient basis in law for a finding of constructive discharge.

For the reasons set forth above, if the issues of sexual harassment and constructive discharge are for trial to the Court in a pre-amendment Title VII case, then judgment in this case clearly must be for the defendants. I find that there is no evidence of any changes, deliberate or otherwise, in the job conditions of plaintiff which would force a reasonable employee into an involuntary resignation. Nor was there an "abusive work environment." At most, the case presents the trivial fallout of a faded affair; a "personal request" for a resignation Dr. Foy knew she could not compel, which was promptly disowned by the Director, Mrs. Quinn, who had the power to hire and fire, by the Personnel Committee of the Board of Directors, and the Board itself. The case must be dismissed for a failure of proof of the sexual harassment claim.

Judgment for Caring for the Homeless.

Employment Perspective

Steve Hart is a happily married man with three children. His superior, Linda Evert, finds him very attractive. She invites him to dinner, a show, and her apartment. Steve politely declines each time. Linda stresses to Steve that if he wants to get promoted, he must have a close, intimate relationship with her. Is this sexual harassment? Yes! It is an unwelcome sexual advance. ◆

In the next case, a superior involved a male subordinate in a ménage à trois relationship. The employee claimed he was forced to accede to his boss's request.

CASE

Showalter v. Allison Reed Group, Inc.

767 F.Supp. 1205 (D.R.I. 1991)

LAGUEUX, District Judge.

These consolidated cases were instituted by plaintiffs Gary Showalter and Nenh Phetosomphone alleging that they were sexually harassed while employed at Techni-Craft Plating Company, a jewelry plating firm located in Cranston, Rhode Island. Essentially, they both claim that defendant Noel Smith, the General Manager of Techni-Craft, forced them to engage in various sexual activities with his secretary, defendant Carol Marsella, by threatening them with the loss of their jobs if they did not acquiesce in his demands.

The evidence establishes that an environment of sexual innuendo was prevalent at Techni-Craft during the time in question. Evidence of two particular incidents serves to prove the existence of such an environment. For example, Marsella wore two tee-shirts with sexually suggestive slogans. One shirt was introduced into evidence and marked as Plaintiff's Exhibit 7. It says "All I want is a little peace and quiet. Give me a little piece and I'll be quiet." A photograph of the second shirt was introduced into evidence and marked as Defendant's Exhibit K3. It says "Big cats are dangerous but a little pussy won't hurt anyone." Another photograph, marked as Defendant's Exhibit H4, shows Marsella holding a present she received of black panties.

Second, the testimony of Daniel Salzillo, a retired letter carrier for the United States Postal Service, helps establish the existence of an environment charged with sexual innuendo at Techni-Craft. Salzillo testified that he was the regular carrier for Techni-Craft for seventeen years. He also testified that Marsella "flashed" him by showing him "everything she had" one day in the Spring of 1989. Showalter testified that Marsella flashed the mailman on a fifty dollar bet from Smith. Although Smith and Marsella denied the incident occurred, the Court believes that both Salzillo's and Showalter's testimony are more credible.

Showalter certainly did not refrain from interacting with his peers at Techni-Craft. One co-worker, Maurice Szarko, testified that he and Showalter, as a "joke," used to jockey for position in order to look down Marsella's blouse or up her skirt. Szarko testified that this happened numerous times, and he was able to describe in detail the design pattern of Marsella's panties. The evidence also shows that Showalter participated in giving "gag" gifts of a sexual nature at the 1988 Christmas party. For example, Nicholas Ruzzano, another Techni-Craft employee, testified that Showalter gave him a package of condoms at the party. Defendant's Exhibit H2 is a photograph that shows Ruzzano holding up the condoms. In addition, several co-workers testified that Showalter bragged about his supposed sexual exploits with various women, and about his possession of x-rated videos. There is also credible evidence that Showalter made lewd proposals to a female co-worker on several occasions. In short, the evidence establishes that Showalter willingly contributed to the environment of sexual innuendo at Techni-Craft.

In the Spring of 1988, Smith began talking incessantly, and obsessively, about Marsella to Showalter. These talks were invariably of a sexual nature, and usually described Smith's sexual relationship with Marsella. Smith also shared with Showalter his various artistic expressions of his relationship with Marsella: nude photographs, pornographic drawings, and x-rated letters. Also, beginning in the Spring of 1988, Smith attempted to change Showalter's physical appearance in order to make him more pleasing to Marsella. Most notably, Smith told Showalter to begin wearing a long sleeve button down shirt to work instead of his customary tee-shirt. Smith explained the request as follows: "Carol Marsella wants to see you in a shirt." Showalter's initial refusal to change the type of shirt he wore to work caused Smith to repeat the demand.

By the end of the summer of 1988, Smith began directly prodding Showalter to join his sexual liaison with Marsella. Smith began telling Showalter that Marsella was interested in Showalter, and that he should join their sexual activity. Showalter declined on the grounds that he was married. Smith immediately stated that both he and Marsella were also married and that what their spouses didn't know wouldn't hurt them. Angrily, Smith told Showalter that Marsella controlled the hiring and firing decisions at Techni-Craft, and that if he valued his job he would follow Smith's demands. It is clear from the evidence that at this time Smith was attempting to install at the workplace a modified ménage à trois.

Unfortunately for Smith, Showalter indeed proved to be more a man of words than of action. Thus, Smith was forced to make repeated threats to Showalter. For example, Smith reminded Showalter of his extensive connections in the jewelry business in Rhode Island implying that Showalter would be blackballed from the industry if he did not comply. Smith also told Showalter that he had to please Marsella in order for everything between Smith and Marsella "to be okay." At one point, Smith also threatened Showalter with the loss of his medical benefits if he failed to participate in the sexual activity. Smith knew that the medical benefits were especially important to Showalter because Showalter's eldest son had a heart defect and had undergone three open heart surgeries. Showalter had had discussions in the past with Smith apprising him of his son's condition.

Showalter first acceded to Smith's demands in September of 1988, when Smith orchestrated an after hours strip-tease performance by Marsella on company premises. Before the actual event, Smith gave explicit instructions to Showalter outlining the various sexual activities Smith expected Showalter to engage in with Marsella and him. Although Marsella failed to show up a couple of times as scheduled by Smith, she eventually did perform a strip-tease in front of Smith and Showalter. She also performed a second strip-tease about a month later.

Each time, Marsella stripped off all her clothes while dancing to music emanating from a portable tape recorder. When she finished undressing, Showalter followed Smith's earlier instructions and joined him in performing sexual acts with Marsella. Each time Showalter was unable to fully follow Smith's instructions because he could not attain an erection. The first time Marsella told Showalter that he was "out of luck," and left the area. The second time Smith asked Showalter what was wrong with him and even suggested that he take vitamins to remedy that situation.

Showalter was also forced to observe and engage in other sexual activity at Techni-Craft from September 1988 until June 1989. On a regular basis, when Showalter worked overtime and other employees had left, Smith required him to engage in sexual activity with Marsella. The sexual harassment was also present during the regular workday hours. Once Showalter witnessed Marsella and Smith engaging in oral sex in Marsella's office as he walked by. Twice Showalter changed the outside storm windows at Marsella's office, once in the fall of 1988 and once in the spring of 1989. Both times, Smith and Marsella fondled each other and engaged in oral sex in full view of the window. Another time, Marsella grabbed him by his genitals.

Showalter also was required to participate in a strip poker game on company premises following the 1988 Techni-Craft Christmas party. The game broke up when a driver from United Parcel Service unexpectedly opened up an unlocked door.

During the spring of 1989 Smith attempted to coerce Showalter to get Showalter's wife involved in Smith's broadening sexual net. Showalter resisted all of Smith's efforts, having to suddenly uninvite his wife to a jewelry convention to spare her from exposure to Smith's sexual circus.

Title VII of the Civil Rights Act of 1964 prohibits discrimination because of sex in employment situations. A claim of sexual harassment is a form of sex discrimination actionable under Title VII. Two broad types of sexual harassment violate Title VII; quid pro quo sexual harassment and hostile work environment sexual harassment. Because only "employers" can be held liable under either theory of sexual harassment, or for any Title VII violation, it is appropriate to analyze the status of the three defendants before discussing the law concerning the two types of sexual harassment.

1. "Employers" Under Title VII

Title VII defines an employer as "a person engaged in an industry affecting commerce who has fifteen or more employees for each working day in each of twenty or more calendar weeks in the current or preceding calendar year, and any agent of such a person."

Defendant Allison Reed Group clearly is an "employer" for purposes of this case. So too is defendant Smith, who was Allison Reed's agent in charge at Techni-Craft. Smith performed the functions of a general manager at Techni-Craft and had the sole authority to hire and fire Techni-Craft workers. Defendant Marsella, however, is not an "employer" within the meaning of Title VII. Marsella was simply Smith's secretary, and merely a co-worker of the plaintiffs. She had no authority to make any personnel decisions. The plaintiffs' erroneous belief that Marsella could make such decisions can not overcome the reality that she, in fact, had no such power. A co-worker who is not the employer's agent with the power to supervise can not be held liable under Title VII.

2. Quid Pro Quo Sexual Harassment

Quid pro quo sexual harassment occurs when "a supervisor conditions the granting of an economic or other job benefit upon the receipt of sexual favors from a subordinate, or punishes that subordinate for refusing to comply." A claim of quid pro quo sexual harassment must meet the five-part test set out by the First Circuit in *Chamberlin v. 101 Realty, Inc.* Chamberlin requires a plaintiff to show that "(1) the plaintiff-employee is a member of a protected group; (2) the sexual advances were unwelcome; (3) the harassment was sexually motivated; (4) the employee's reaction to the supervisor's advances affected a tangible aspect of his employment; and (5) respondent superior liability has been established." An analysis of these factors shows that both plaintiffs have proved that they were subjected to quid pro quo sexual harassment.

First, both plaintiffs are members of a "protected group." Title VII protects both males and females from sexual harassment.

Second, both plaintiffs were subjected to unwelcome sexual advances. The essence of an inquiry into unwelcomeness is whether the sexual advances were "uninvited and offensive or unwanted from the standpoint of the employee." Although both plaintiffs contributed to the general tone of sexual innuendo at Techni-Craft, there is no evidence that either plaintiff invited or desired intimate physical sexual contact with Marsella. Indeed, neither plaintiff welcomed sexual relations with Marsella. Both eventually participated only because they feared that noncompliance would cost them their jobs. Showalter expressly and verbally rejected Smith's invitation to join his sexual affair with Marsella.

An important factor in determining whether the plaintiffs welcomed the sexual advances is the availability and practical viability of an employer's grievance procedure. Allison Reed Group had no formal procedure in place for processing employee grievances. Its "Employee Handbook" introduced into evidence as Defendant's Exhibit A, states that employees should consult their supervisor or the Personnel Department if clarification of any Allison Reed Group employment policy is desired. The Handbook, however, does not set out any policy for processing of employment complaints. The failure of the plaintiffs to register a complaint about the sexual advances does not at all indicate that the advances were welcome. Rather, the plaintiffs' failure to complain to someone at Allison Reed Group, which operates out of a separate facility in Warwick, is a reflection of Allison Reed Group's failure to have a policy or readily accessible personnel available to handle sexual harassment complaints.

Third, there is no question that the harassment of the plaintiffs was sexually motivated. Fourth, the sexual harassment affected a "tangible" aspect of the plaintiffs' jobs.

Here, the plaintiffs have shown that the harassment affected a tangible aspect of the conditions of their employment. Indeed, this is the quintessential quid pro quo case—the plaintiffs understood that they would lose their jobs if they did not submit to the sexual demands of Smith. In short, the harassment imposed a new condition on the plaintiff's employment: if they wanted to keep their jobs, they needed to comply with the condition of sexual harassment.

Fifth, not only is Smith directly liable under Title VII for his acts, but Allison Reed Group is also liable under the doctrine of respondent superior. Employers are held strictly liable in cases of quid pro quo sexual harassment.

In sum, each plaintiff has satisfied Chamberlin's five requirements for making out a case of quid pro quo sexual harassment. The clear weight of the credible evidence indicates that the plaintiffs were forced to engage in intimate sexual contact as a condition of retaining their employment at Techni-Craft. Smith's boldfaced denials of the sexual incidents is unconvincing, and Allison Reed Group's legal argument that such conduct is outside the scope of his employment is meaningless in the face of strict liability.

3. Hostile Work Environment Sexual Harassment

The sexual harassment inflicted upon the plaintiffs also can be characterized as hostile environment sexual harassment. Unlike quid pro quo harassment which occurs when a supervisor promises an economic job benefit in exchange for sexual favors, hostile environment harassment occurs when "verbal or physical conduct of a sexual nature . . . has the purpose or effect of . . . creating an intimidating, hostile, or offensive work environment."

Although all quid pro quo cases do not per se qualify as hostile environment cases, here the harassment drastically altered the conditions of plaintiffs' employment and created a hostile and abusive work environment. Sexual advances to the plaintiffs were made for months, and the harassment completely infested their work environment. Smith is obviously liable for creating the hostile work environment.

In this case, Showalter was not forced out of his job by the harassment. Rather, a back injury has put him on worker's compensation, Clearly, Showalter is not entitled to back pay. There is, however, the likelihood that Showalter will recover from his back injury and find himself working again at Techni-Craft. Although Smith is no longer employed by Allison Reed Group, the company still suffers from the lack of a grievance procedure for harassed employees. Therefore, it is appropriate for the Court to enjoin Allison Reed Group from allowing the future sexual harassment of Showalter. Allison Reed Group is directed to the E.E.O.C.'s Guidelines on Sexual Harassment:

> Prevention is the best tool for the elimination of sexual harassment. An employer should take all steps necessary to prevent sexual harassment from occurring, such as affirmatively raising the subject, expressing strong disapproval, developing appropriate sanctions, informing employees of their right to raise and how to raise the issue of harassment under Title VII, and developing methods to sensitize all concerned.

It is also the judgment of the Court that Allison Reed Group be required to designate an officer at its headquarters to receive and process sexual harassment complaints, and that this be set forth in the Employee Handbook. In this manner, employees at Techni-Craft will have a repository outside that firm for consideration of sexual harassment claims to the end that this sorry episode at Allison Reed Group's corporate subsidiary will never again be repeated.

Because Smith is no longer employed by Allison Reed Group, there is no need for the injuction to run against him. As against Smith, Showalter is only entitled to nominal damages in the amount of one dollar.

Because defendant Marsella is not an "employer" under Title VII, she is entitled to judgment on plaintiffs' Title VII claims. The Court finds that both plaintiffs were subjected to sexual harassment. The harassment can be characterized as both quid pro quo sexual harassment and hostile work environment sexual harassment. As against defendant Allison Reed Group, Showalter is entitled to an injunction barring the company from allowing any sexual harassment of him when, and if, he returns to work there. In addition, Allison Reed Group is mandatorily enjoined to designate an officer at its headquarters to receive and process sexual harassment complaints and to state this information in its employee handbook.

Judgment for Showalter.

The majority of the victims who are harassed seek recovery from the company, the rule of thumb being to sue the deepest pocket.

The following case addresses the question of whether an employee can sue her supervisor individually for sexual harassment.

CASE

Parsons v. Nationwide Mutual Ins. Co.

899 F.Supp. 465 (M.D. Fla. 1995)

KOVACHEVICH, Judge.

Plaintiffs (Parsons, Selph and MacDonald) were employed on the office staff at Nationwide Mutual Insurance. Defendant Walker was also employed by Nationwide, and during the scope of this employment Defendant Walker alleged orally published "rude and offensive remarks" about Plaintiffs sexual practices, gave detailed accounts of his own sexual exploits, made unwelcome sexually suggestive comments to Plaintiffs and generally created a sexually graphic and offensive work environment. After the occurrence of the alleged events, each of the Plaintiffs were discharged from employment at Nationwide. As a result of these supposed actions, Plaintiffs brought suit against Defendants Walker and Nationwide.

Plaintiffs allege that Defendants (hereinafter "Walker" and "Nationwide") are joint employers of Plaintiffs because of Nationwide's "exercise of substantial control of the business of Defendant Walker including ownership of accounts, equipment and contracts, the interrelationship of operations, and the centralized control of labor relations and common management." However, Plaintiffs fail to specifically allege in the complaint what Walker's role is within Nationwide. Further, there is no mention of Walker's official capacity or job title at Nationwide; it may only be inferred that Walker held some form of supervisory control over Plaintiffs.

Walker moves to dismiss the sexual harassment and retaliation claims against him because he alleges that he is being sued in his individual capacity as a result of his employment at Nationwide.

The court professed that, "The relief granted under Title VII is against the employer, not individual employees whose actions constitute a violation of the Act," and "the proper method for a plaintiff to recover under Title VII is by suing the employer, either by naming the supervisory employees, as agents of the employer or by naming the employer directly." The crux . . . is that, even though Congress defined "employer" to include any "agent" this provision does not impose individual liability but only holds the employer accountable for the acts of its individual agents. Even though such a definition might be construed so as to impose liability on individual employees as "agents" the Eleventh Circuit Court has held that agents of employers who violate

Title VII provisions only trigger an action against the employer, and not an action against the individual agent/employee. Moreover, the law in the Eleventh Circuit has been settled that there is no individual liability under Title VII. "If Congress had envisioned individual liability under Title VII for compensatory or punitive damages, it would have included individuals in this litany of limitations and would have discontinued the exemption for small employers."

Judgment for Nationwide.

QUID PRO QUO

There are two distinct situations for which the company may be liable; quid pro quo and hostile work environment. *Quid pro quo* means "this for that." It involves situations in which a superior is eliciting sexual favors from a subordinate in return for some form of sexual activity.

Employment Perspective

Clarence Conklin, a hospital administrator, approaches one of the nurse's aides and informs her that he can arrange a schedule change from nights, weekends, and holidays to day work if she is willing to sleep with him. Is this quid pro quo? Yes! The hospital is liable for the sexual harassment of its employee because a benefit was denied to the nurse's aide unless she agreed to have sex. ◆

In the case that follows, a female employee quit her job because of sexual advances by two of her supervisors. When she filed for unemployment benefits, she was refused because she did not file a complaint within the company. The question is whether reporting sexual misconduct is a condition precedent to unemployment benefits.

CASE

Allen v. Dept. of Employment Training

618 A.2d 1317 (Vt.1992)

MORSE, Justice.

The Employment Security Board denied Plaintiff unemployment benefits because before quitting her job, she did not give notice to her employer's business manager or someone in similar authority that she was being sexually harassed by her supervisor. Plaintiff appealed. We reverse and remand.

Plaintiff worked at Vermont Academy as a secretary for the housekeeping and maintenance departments. From 1989 to April 1990, plaintiff alleged and the Board expressly found, that one of plaintiff's two supervisors, the head of maintenance, made sexual advances toward her on at least three occasions. The first incident occurred in Dec. 1989 when the supervisor grabbed the Plaintiff and kissed her. Plaintiff informed no one of the incident. Several days later, the supervisor apologized and stated that it would not happen again. In January 1990, the supervisor asked Plaintiff for a New Year's kiss and Plaintiff objected. He later apologized and made another promise to stop the conduct. In April 1990, however, the supervisor for a third time insisted that she kiss him. Plaintiff refused, pushed the supervisor away, and left. Finally, in August, 1990, the supervisor requested that the Plaintiff accompany him to the gym basement and take inventory. Although Plaintiff agreed to perform the task, she refused to do so in the isolated basement. No incident occurred during the inventory; however, Plaintiff, claiming she feared further unwanted sexual advances, shortly thereafter quit her job.

Several days later Plaintiff wrote a letter to the supervisor in which she demanded that the harassment stop and stated that she wanted to return to work. He allowed her to return, but within a short period of time the supervisor became "very friendly" again, although no unwanted sexual contact or comments occurred. Plaintiff believing that the harassment would recommence, quit for good in October 1990. Except for one occasion, Plaintiff never personally complained, by formal grievance or otherwise, to anyone other than the offending supervisor. The Board found that Plaintiff, after returning to work in September 1990, informed the head of housekeeping that the head of maintenance attempted to kiss her, to which she objected. Vermont Academy's business manager, the offending supervisor's supervisor, had not been told by anyone of the offending behavior toward the Plaintiff.

The Academy did not submit in evidence, a personnel policy or grievance procedure at the hearing. Instead, it presented the testimony of the head of housekeeping at the Academy. She stated that she had been aware of a posted personnel policy but she was unsure whether it outlined grievance procedure in general or one specifically addressing complaints of sexual harassment. Because the business manager and therefore Vermont Academy as the employing unit, was without notice, the Board denied the Plaintiff benefits. We conclude that actual notice to a person's superior or to the offending supervisor was not required. Generally, notice to the employer is required when an employee leaves a job for unsatisfactory working conditions so that the employer has an opportunity to rectify the situation before becoming responsible for unemployment compensation payments. In the context of sexual harassment, however, notice to the employer is problematic. Women, understandably may not complain about sexual harassment in the workplace out of fear of not being believed, embarrassment about making it known, and fear of reprisals. Nevertheless, the sexual harassment victim is "precisely the type of claimant unemployment compensation benefits are designed to assist."

Judgment for Allen.

There are also instances in which a person uses sex to gain advancement, sometimes called "sleeping the way to the top."

Employment Perspective

Christine Wiley was an administrative assistant at Bay Ridge Publishing when she met Joe Flanagan, the president, at a company picnic. Joe immediately became infatuated with Christine, and they began an affair. During the next two years, she was promoted seven times, eventually to vice president of corporate affairs. Her skills were not particularly impressive. Every other vice president had been in a managerial position at least fourteen years before attaining the position of vice president. Is this sexual harassment? Yes! In the opposite, though. The employees who were passed over for promotion have been sexually harassed because of the favoritism exhibited to Christine. ◆

In some cases, sexual harassment can be used as a threat against management, in that an employee may demand a promotion or else will file a claim against the management.

Employment Perspective

It was obvious to everyone at Parker Management Co. that Charlie Harris was very fond of Marie Copley, a marketing research assistant. He would compliment her every day and often bring her flowers. One day Marie learned of an opening for a sales representative within the company. Marie was tired of doing research—she wanted to earn commissions and work with people. This would be tantamount to a transfer and promotion. Marie approached Charlie, who was vice president of marketing and asked him to grant her request. Charlie informed Marie that although he was fond of her, he could not grant the request because she was not qualified. Marie told Charlie that unless he granted her wish, she would file a complaint against him, alleging that he demanded sex for the promotion. What should Charlie do? This action is blackmail. Charlie is in a delicate situation because his conduct, although not constituting sexual harassment, has laid the foundation for a false claim to be leveled against him. Charlie should seek the advice of upper management and legal counsel. Ethically, Marie's request should not be granted because it is false. Practically, it may be granted by Charlie or the company to avoid future public embarrassment and litigation. If Charlie adopts an ethical viewpoint and refuses Marie's request and the company is sued, Charlie must be prepared to be severely reprimanded at best or to lose his job at worst as a consequence of the damage done to the company. ◆

In the next case, a female employee and her male superior conducted an open affair for many years. The employer did not discourage this until she became pregnant for the second time. At this point, both were discharged. The company claimed that the termination was necessary to prevent potential sexual harassment suits by the female employee involved for quid pro quo and the coworkers for hostile work environment.

CASE

Cumpiano v. Banco Santander Puerto Rico

902 F.2d 148 (1st Cir. 1990)

SELYA, Circuit Judge.

The Bank hired Cumpiano in 1978. In due time, she came in contact with, and worked under the supervision of, Humberto Rodriguez Calderon (Rodriguez), the Bank's assistant comptroller. In 1980, Cumpiano and Rodriguez became enmeshed in an amorous relationship. Although Rodriguez was married, the record reflects that the affair was conducted in a public and notorious fashion. In 1982, a child was born to the couple out of wedlock. The Bank clearly knew of the affair and of its consequences; indeed, Rodriguez presented a copy of the infant's birth certificate to appellant's human resources director, Arturo Thurin, and secured coverage for his offspring under an employer-paid health insurance policy. The lovers stayed on the payroll after the baby was born. Plaintiff was not reprimanded, admonished, or cautioned in any way. And the affair continued "openly."

Although appellant denies that it was aware of the romance's prolongation, the evidence amply sustains the opposite inference. To cite one example, there was proof, credited by the court below, that at an office softball tournament in 1983, Rodriguez's adult son (who also worked for the Bank) argued publicly with his father about Cumpiano's presence. Several officials of the

Bank, including its assistant personnel officer, witnessed this episode and overheard the discussion. Thurin was told about it shortly thereafter. So was the Bank's senior vice president.

Cumpiano had various assignments over the years. After 1982, she and Rodriguez worked in different departments. They still spent time together out of the office. In December 1986, following a brief vacation, Cumpiano returned to work dressed in maternity clothes and visibly pregnant. She was handed a letter promoting her, on an interim basis, to operations officer (a position in which she directly supervised 7 to 9 employees at the Bank's San Juan branch). Weeks later, the axe fell. Thurin fired both Rodriguez and Cumpiano on January 29, 1987. Cumpiano received no notice, but Thurin offered her $5,000 in exchange for a letter of resignation and a general release. When Cumpiano asked for an explanation of her dismissal, Thurin refused to give her any reason, saying only that he did not wish to discuss things she already knew.

At trial, appellant claimed that Cumpiano was dismissed because her conduct violated the Bank's internal regulations. Specifically, appellant protested that plaintiff's affair with a married man made her guilty of the crime of adultery under Puerto Rico law and was therefore violative of Norm 14 of the Bank's Manual of General Norms of Work and Conduct (Manual). Plaintiff asserted that the stated reason was pretextual. After evaluating the evidence the district court found in Cumpiano's favor, reinstating her and awarding backpay, compensatory damages, counsel fees, and costs.

A "disparate treatment" claim arises when an employer treats an employee less favorably than others because of her race, color, religion, sex, or national origin. On the other hand, "disparate impact" claims stem from employment practices, often facially neutral, which (1) cannot be justified by business necessity and (2) in fact impose harsher burdens on employees who share a protected characteristic. In the latter type of case, statistical evidence may be highly relevant to a determination of the employer's motive. In a disparate treatment case, however, the issue is less whether a pattern of discrimination existed and more how a particular individual was treated, and why. In that regard, statistical comparisons, although often relevant, are obviously less crucial. Were the rule otherwise, the employer's first bite at the apple would be for free: if the firm had never before discriminated on the basis of gender, it could with impunity discharge one woman.

Appellant argues that it must have had the right to discharge Cumpiano because the trysters' relationship, if ignored by the Bank, could have become the basis of a sexual harassment suit under both federal law (citing Title VII) and local law. In essence, the Bank contends that, since Cumpiano was on a lower rung of the management ladder than Rodriguez, she could have successfully prosecuted a claim of *quid pro quo* harassment. Alternatively, the Bank contends that other employees could have made such a claim because the affair's "pervasive" sexuality created a hostile workplace environment. So, the thesis runs, the Bank was forced to take disciplinary action against Cumpiano and Rodriguez in order to avoid liability arising out of their affair. We regard the argument as fallacious and believe that the trial judge acted well within his discretion in rejecting it.

In the first place, the court was entitled to deem the alleged fear of sexual harassment suits to be bogus. After all, the Bank was apparently content to let the relationship continue, publicly and openly, for several years, although Title VII was firmly in place.

The sockdolager is this: any supposed concern about potential sexual harassment claims, whether on behalf of Cumpiano herself or some hypothetical third party, vanished once the Bank terminated Rodriguez, since only Rodriguez, as Cumpiano's superior, was in a position to harass.

The key finding, of course, was that defendant intentionally discriminated against Cumpiano because of her pregnancy. Having carefully canvassed the record, we believe the finding was sustainable.

The record permits a finding that Cumpiano and Rodriguez had been engaged in a longstanding affair of which management had full awareness. Norm 14 was on the books throughout this period, but appellant chose not to explore its use. Far from expressing disapproval regarding Cumpiano's behavior, the Bank instead rewarded her by placing her in positions of increased responsibility. It was not until early 1987, when Cumpiano was obviously pregnant, that the Bank ousted her.

There is one final point which demands our attention. In addition to reinstatement, backpay, and other relief, the district court awarded plaintiff compensatory damages in the amount of $10,000. That award must be reversed. It is clearly established in this circuit that "compensatory and punitive damages are not available to Title VII plaintiffs."

Judgment for Cumpiano.

HOSTILE WORK ENVIRONMENT

Hostile Work Environment is intimidating and offensive conduct perpetrated by a superior or co-worker against an employee. The hostile action must be severe and pervasive so as to interfere with the performance of the employee's work. Touching, joking, commenting and distributing material of a sexual nature all fall within the confines of a hostile work environment.

The case that follows presents the question of whether the presentation of a sexual gift to a female employee for her birthday constitutes sexual harassment. Furthermore, the case addresses the issue of whether the complainant's acceptance of the gift and participation in the event preclude her from winning the lawsuit.

CASE

Hansen v. Dean Witter Reynolds, Inc.

887 F.Supp. 669 (S.D. N.Y. 1995)

BAER, District Judge.

Plaintiff's Hostile Work Environment Claim

Plaintiff focused primarily on three incidents in her effort to show that defendant maintained a hostile work environment. Two of them involved sexually explicit birthday cakes, while the other concerned what a female employee, Lynn Jerome, described as an "act of terrorism" perpetrated against her by a male Dean Witter manager. As explained below, I find that the birthday cake incidents are not attributable to defendant Dean Witter; the incident that Jerome called an act of "terrorism," meanwhile, is at best an exaggeration and at worst calls into question Jerome's judgment generally.

One of the birthday cakes in question was presented to plaintiff in 1986 by several co-workers. The cake was in the shape and color of a black man's penis, was filled with Devil Dog cream, and bore the dubious greeting, "Happy Birthday, Bitch." Hansen did not file a complaint or otherwise report this incident to management. In fact, there was testimony by a former co-worker that Hansen was so proud to receive the cake that she stored the remaining portion in her freezer and brought it to her parents' home for their July 4th barbecue.

While food for thought, it is unnecessary to decide whether Hansen considered the cake an insult or a joke. There was evidence that she partook enthusiastically in the event, and there was testimony that she was proud of being referred to as the "bitch" and that the name was in fact a self-professed title as she considered herself "a tough cookie." The fact is that she failed to inform any supervisory personnel, and thus there is nothing on which to base a determination that Dean Witter tolerated, prohibited, or encouraged such activity. There was, however, a similar situation that was reported to management; Dean Witter's reaction left no doubt as to its stance towards such cakes. In 1982, Ms. Jerome received a cake from co-workers "in the shape of a man's anatomy." Upon being made aware of the nature of the cake, Dean Witter's Chairman issued a memorandum stating that such behavior would not be tolerated and that any persons involved in such activity would be terminated. In light of this response, there is hardly support that the birthday cake incident is indicative of a sanctioned hostile work environment for women at Dean Witter.

The same is true of the event that Jerome referred to at trial as an act of terrorism. Jerome stated during her initial testimony that she had complained about "sexual matters" in 1989 based on her being "called in and terrorized" at Dean Witter. When asked to provide greater detail, Jerome offered, "It's very strong male intimidation to the point of, without touching a person, there is a physical reaction by the strength of the words."

When asked to what she was referring regarding the 1989 complaint, Jerome testified to only one event, an incident where she and a male colleague were called into a conference room by Ray Anderson, a Dean Witter manager. Jerome and her colleague had been reading newspapers on the trading floor. According to Jerome, Anderson "rose himself up in an intimidating male stature." Jerome conceded that Anderson never got within three and one-half feet of her, nor did he make any sexist or off-color remarks. Finally, as Jerome acknowledged, no adverse personnel action resulted, notwithstanding Anderson's statement that if Jerome and her colleague "had nothing better to do than read the paper, he wanted their resignations." Jerome then pointed out that Anderson had made the statement "in an extremely loud tone of voice." It is beyond peradventure that one would be hard pressed to consider this an act of terrorism.

Judgment for Dean Witter.

The composition of sexual harassment will vary among different types of employment. Conduct and language which is accepted in certain manual labor jobs may be regarded as offensive in an office environment. Each employment environment will have a different set of standards. These will be determined by company policy and female employees themselves. If employees participate, encourage or accept what would otherwise constitute sexual harassment, they will be precluded from claiming such behavior was intimidating and offensive to them.

In the next case, a female construction worker claimed her supervisor created a hostile work environment when he used profane language in her presence and directed some of it at her. The question presented is whether the profanity must contain language relating to the female gender to be actionable.

CASE

Gross v. Burggraf Construction Co.

53 F.3d 1531 (10th Cir. 1995)

ANDERSON, Circuit Judge.

Gender discrimination can be based on sexual harassment or a hostile work environment. Gross has not asserted that she was subjected to sexual harassment, in the form of "unwelcome sexual advances, requests for sexual favors, and other verbal or physical conduct of a sexual nature." Therefore, there is only one issue on appeal: did the district court err in granting summary judgment because there is a genuine issue of material fact in dispute regarding whether Anderson's conduct and statements created a hostile work environment for Gross?

Burggraf is a road construction company. Most of Burggraf's employees are hired on a seasonal basis. The construction season generally runs from May to October of each year. Gross drove a water truck for Burggraf in 1989. Her employment was terminated on October 20, 1989.

Gross was hired again by Burggraf as a truck driver for the 1990 construction season. In mid-May, Gross was assigned to drive a water truck for the Jenny Lake Project in the Grand Teton National Park. Anderson was the supervisor of the Jenny Lake Project. He was responsible for supervising more than 100 individuals.

Gross was an hourly employee. She was subject to being released from work at any time that her services were no longer needed. Gross was initially paid $12.50 per hour for her work on the Jenny Lake Project. Toward the end of the summer, her salary was increased to $13.50 per hour. Gross worked more hours on the Jenny Lake Project than any other truck driver employed by Burggraf.

It is undisputed that Gross was laid off on October 2, 1990, because Burggraf no longer needed the services of a water truck driver on the Jenny Lake Project. Paving operations on the Jenny Lake Project were commenced on September 10, 1990; the final paving was completed on October 3, 1990. As the paving operations began to wind down, the need for the water truck diminished. On September 30, 1990, Gross was sent home early because there was nothing for her to do. On October 2, 1990, Gross was informed that she was being laid off because the water truck was no longer needed for the Jenny Lake Project. The water truck was not used on the Jenny Lake Project after October 2, 1990.

On September 28, 1993, Gross filed this action against Burggraf and Anderson. In count one, Gross alleged that she was subjected to gender discrimination in violation of Title VII and retaliation because she contemplated filing a claim with the EEOC.

In *Meritor Sav. Bank, FSB v. Vinson,* the Supreme Court stated that "for sexual harassment to be actionable it must be sufficiently severe or pervasive to alter the conditions of the victim's employment and create an abusive working environment." The existence of sexual harassment must be determined "in light of the record as a whole 'and courts must examine the totality of the circumstances, such as the nature of the sexual advances and the context in which the alleged incidents occurred.'" The mere utterance of a statement which "engenders offensive feelings in an employee would not affect the conditions of employment to a sufficiently significant degree to violate Title VII."

Any harassment of an employee that would not occur but for the sex of the employee . . . may, if sufficiently patterned or pervasive comprise an illegal condition of employment under Title VII. "If the nature of an employee's environment, however unpleasant, is not due to her gender, she has not been the victim of sex discrimination as a result of that environment."

In determining whether Gross has established a viable Title VII claim, we must first examine her work environment. In the real world of construction work, profanity and vulgarity are not perceived as hostile or abusive. Indelicate forms of expression are accepted or endured as normal human behavior. As is clear from Gross' deposition testimony, she contributed to the use of crude language on the job site:

Q. As a construction worker, you had occasion to use profane or obscene language, didn't you?

A. [Gross] Yes.

Q. Can you describe for me or give me examples of the type of language that you would use?

A. Only to say that it was no different than the language that anyone else around here was using.

Q. So you basically could profane equally with the men who were on the job.

A. That's a difficult comparison. I wasn't in competition with anybody.

Q. And I understand that and I'm not calling it competition. I'm just indicating, you say that you used the same language that other people on the job—I guess I'm saying that when you say other people on the job, you're talking about the male construction workers in addition to the female construction workers, right?

A. Yes.

Q. You didn't have any reluctance on the construction job to use profanity, did you?

A. No.

Q. You were not offended by the use of profanity on the construction site, were you?

A. No.

Q. Did you in fact tell off-color jokes at the construction site?

A. I can't recall specifics, but I told jokes similar to the same jokes that I was hearing.

Q. And I understand you can't remember the same jokes. I can't remember the jokes I told last week, Patty. So I don't expect you to remember the specific jokes, but you don't know that you would have told off-color jokes like they were telling on the construction site.

A. Yes.

Q. And probably if you heard one at the end of the construction site, when you got to the other end, you would tell it down there because that's—I mean, that's just part of the society on a construction job, isn't it?

A. Yes.

Clint Guthrie, another Burggraf employee who worked with Gross during the 1990 season on the Jenny Lake Project, testified that Gross used profanity in the workplace:

Q. Did Patty Gross use profanity on the job site?

A. Yes.

Q. Did she use profanity as much as George Anderson did or more or less?

A. Everybody was pretty equal on that aspect.

Accordingly, we must evaluate Gross' claim of gender discrimination in the context of a blue collar environment where crude language is commonly used by male and female employees. Speech that might be offensive or unacceptable in a prep school faculty meeting, or on the floor of Congress, is tolerated in other work environments. We agree with the following comment by the district court in *Rabidue v. Osceola Refining Co.*:

The standard for determining sexual harassment would be different depending upon the work environment. Indeed, it cannot seriously be disputed that in some work environments, humor and language are rough hewn and vulgar. Sexual jokes, sexual conversations and girlie magazines may abound. Title VII was not meant to or can change this. It must never be forgotten that Title VII is the federal court mainstay in the struggle for equal employment opportunity for the female workers of America. But it is quite different to claim that Title VII was designed to bring about a magical transformation in the social mores of American workers.

Gross maintains that Anderson made several vulgar and "harassing" statements in her presence that demonstrate that she was subject to a hostile work environment. We discuss each allegation under separate headings.

1. Anderson's reference to a portion of Gross' body

   One afternoon, at 4:00 p.m., Anderson yelled at Gross: "What the hell are you doing? Get your ass back in the truck and don't you get out of it until I tell you." It is undisputed that Gross was aware that compaction and density tests were being performed that afternoon. Further, Gross testified that she knew that some members of the roadcrew, of both genders, were needed to perform such tests and that Anderson insisted that the employees stay on the site until all of the tests were completed. The term "ass" is a vulgar expression that refers to a portion of the anatomy of persons of both sexes. Thus, the term is gender-neutral. Its usage on a construction site does not demonstrate gender discrimination.

2. Anderson's use of demeaning terms

   Gross maintains that Anderson referred to her as "dumb." Gross did not present any evidence that he characterized her as "dumb" when she was present. The only evidence that Gross presented that Anderson referred to her in this manner, is the portion of Guthrie's deposition quoted in the section entitled "Alleged inflammatory sexual epithets." Guthrie's deposition testimony establishes that when Anderson was upset, he called Gross "dumb."

Guthrie's deposition, however, also establishes that Anderson used crude or harsh language in reprimanding each of his employees. The term "dumb" is gender-neutral. Guthrie's testimony does not demonstrate that Anderson subjected Gross to gender discrimination.

Gross argues that "she was not alone in finding Mr. Anderson's conduct intolerable." She maintains that we can infer that Anderson's treatment of women created a hostile work environment from the fact that only two women, out of the forty who worked under Anderson's supervision, completed the 1990 construction season. The only evidence in the record concerning the reason that women left the Jenny Lake Project before the construction season ended is that most of them departed to return to college. No evidence was presented that any of them left early because of a hostile work environment. The mere fact that only two women employees remained on the job at the end of the season does not support an inference that Anderson created a hostile work environment for Gross and the other female employees at the Jenny Lake Project.

Gross maintains that "Anderson acknowledged that he hired Ms. Gross not because he wanted to, but in order to meet federal opportunity requirements on the Jenny Lake Project. According to Gross, the fact that Anderson hired her to comply with federal law is evidence that she was subjected to a hostile work environment. Gross submitted the following portion of Anderson's deposition testimony to support this theory:

> Q. Would you explain to me what your relationship to Patricia Gross was during the 1990 construction season?
>
> A. I was her supervisor.
>
> Q. Had she ever worked for you before?
>
> A. No.
>
> Q. Had she ever worked for Burggraf before?
>
> A. Yes, she had. She had worked for Burggraf, I think, the preceding summer under Richard Neff as supervisor.
>
> Q. Was that the basis under which you hired her, that she had previous experience with the company?
>
> A. No.
>
> Q. Tell me why you hired her.
>
> A. I hired her—I asked Richard Neff for some women truck drivers, so we could meet our women minor for the participation on the Jenny Lake Project. I asked Richard for some women that could drive trucks. Tracey, I forget her last name, and Patty.
>
> Q. Did you hire Patty?
>
> A. I contacted Tracey first because that was Richard's recommendation, that Tracey would be his first choice. Patty was second choice. I could not get ahold of Tracey, she had obtained employment elsewhere, so I got ahold of Patty.

This evidence establishes that Anderson hired Gross because he was required to do so under federal law. Thus, it demonstrates his compliance with a law that compels the hiring of women. It does not support an inference of gender discrimination. The record shows that Anderson approached Gross after work one day, and stated that he had heard that Rick had "chewed her out." Gross replied "yeah, I fucked up." Anderson stated that he would buy Gross a case of beer if she told Rick to "go fuck himself the next time he chewed her out." Although Anderson's comment is clearly offensive in certain settings, and to many persons, he merely repeated the same vulgar verb that had been previously used by Gross. Anderson's use of this term does not support Gross' contention that she was subject to discrimination because of her gender.

Gross alleges that Anderson embarrassed and humiliated her in the presence of employees when he told her that if she ruined the transmission on the truck she was driving, she would be fired because her truck would be inoperable. It is undisputed that the clutch in Gross' truck required extensive repairs.

In *Steiner,* a female blackjack dealer testified that her supervisor referred to her in her presence as a "dumb fucking broad," a "cunt," and a "fucking cunt." Additionally, the record showed that he yelled profanities at her in front of customers and other casino employees while moving toward her in a threatening manner. In reversing an order granting summary judgment, the Ninth Circuit held that while the evidence established that the Supervisor was "abusive to men and women alike; . . . his abusive treatment and remarks to women were of a sexual or gender-specific nature." In this action, Gross has failed to submit any admissible evidence that Anderson used a gender based vulgarity in reference to her or that he engaged in any physically threatening conduct. Instead, the admissible evidence in the record demonstrates that Anderson criticized her in the presence of others because of his belief that she had abused company equipment. She has not presented any evidence that his criticism of her driving was sexual or gender specific.

In *Huddleston,* the evidence showed that a supervisor yelled at Huddleston every day in front of her co-workers. On one occasion, her supervisor "grabbed her by the arm and forcibly moved her a few feet." She was called a "bitch" and a "whore" to her face and in front of her customers. Her appearance was frequently ridiculed, and she was told "'we're going to take your pants off and put a skirt on you,' and 'we're going to take your clothes off to see if you are real.'"

The Eleventh Circuit concluded that this evidence was sufficient to demonstrate gender discrimination.

After reviewing the admissible evidence in the record, we conclude that Gross has failed to demonstrate that there is a genuine issue of material fact in dispute that she was subjected to a hostile work environment because of her gender. None of the alleged instances cited by Gross to support her Title VII claim is sufficient on its own to establish that she was discriminated against because of her gender. We have examined the evidence as a whole to determine whether the totality of the circumstances supports a viable Title VII claim.

Therefore, after considering the totality of the circumstances we hold that Gross has failed to establish that there is a genuine issue of material fact to establish gender based harassment that was pervasive and severe enough to alter the terms, conditions or privileges of employment.

Judgment for Burggraf Construction Co.

Severe and Pervasive

The sexual harassment complained of must be severe enough to create an abusive work environment and to disrupt the victim's employment. Casual comments or insignificant events that are isolated or happen only intermittently are not sufficient. In order to come to a determination, the accused's conduct must be viewed in light of all of the circumstances, including the victim's behavior. If the victim consented to, participated in, or initiated the hostile work environment, then that will severely mitigate the victim's claim. If the work environment becomes intolerable because the employer refuses to remedy the situation, thus forcing the victim to resign, the victim can claim constructive discharge. The victim must resign in response to the sexual harassment. If the resignation is for another reason, constructive discharge will not apply.

Reasonable Person Standard

The standard by which sexual harassment will be judged is a reasonable person standard. A reasonable person must believe that the conduct complained of must have substantially interfered with the victim's ability to work or created an environment that was intimidating and offensive.

In the following case, because a female employee was forcibly restrained by her employer in an attempt to kiss and touch her, she resigned from her job. The question is whether this conduct substantially interferes with her employment by creating a hostile work environment.

CASE *Radtke v. Everett*

501 N.W. 2d 155 (Mich. 1993)

RILEY, Judge.

Plaintiff Tamama Radtke was employed as an unregistered veterinary technician for defendant Clarke-Everett Dog and Cat Hospital P.C., beginning in January 1984. The hospital is owned in equal shares by defendant Dr. Stuart Everett and Dr. James Clarke. As of May 1988, her duties included supervising staff, assisting the doctors during surgery, scheduling, and performing minor janitorial tasks. She assisted each doctor nearly equally, and possessed a "good working relationship" with each. There were no incidents of sexual harassment before the date in issue.

As commonly occurred, on Sunday, May 29, 1990, plaintiff was working alone with defendant Everett to provide weekend emergency veterinarian services. In her deposition plaintiff stated that after a lengthy day of work, she suggested that they take a break. Everett agreed. Plaintiff proceeded to the hospital's lounge and poured them each a cup of coffee. She then relaxed on the couch, with her back leaning onto its corners and her legs on the sofa.

After finishing a few phone calls, Everett joined her and proceeded to sit next to her. Plaintiff, believing that Everett's behavior was inappropriate, attempted to leave the couch "the minute he sat down." Everett, however physically restrained her by firmly placing his arm around her neck and holding her down. Plaintiff, both frightened and surprised by Everett's behavior, described what followed during her deposition:

> "I tried to pull my head up three times and, on the third time, I realized he was not going to let me go. And then finally, when his arm relaxed, I sprung forward, and I told him, 'You don't want to do this.'"

Although plaintiff forcefully escaped his grip, Everett began to flatter her. Plaintiff rebuffed his newest advances by stating. "You don't want to do this. I don't want to do this. You're married. I'm married." Everett responded by caressing plaintiff's neck. Again she protested, but he simply ignored her pleas. Indeed, he then attempted to kiss her by grabbing her neck and pushing his face towards hers. Plaintiff successfully pushed his face away, left the couch, and walked across the room. Plaintiff then stated that she wished to smoke outside, and encouraged Everett to accompany her in public, which he did. The working day was finished without incident.

Plaintiff further stated when deposed that she did not know or could not know whether the defendant was trying to hurt her, but she stated that he "would have or could have." She acknowledged that he might have mistakenly believed she wished to kiss him and that he did not condition the terms or conditions of her employment upon the acceptance of his advances.

That evening plaintiff discussed the incident with her husband, and she tendered her resignation, along with a list of requests, to Everett's office the next morning. The following day, Dr. Clarke and plaintiff cursorily discussed the incident. Plaintiff also began psychological counseling that day. Although plaintiff suffered no physical injuries, she alleges severe emotional pain stemming from the incident.

In December 1988, plaintiff filed a four-count civil suit against Everett and the hospital in the Grand Traverse Circuit Court. Plaintiff alleged that she was (1) sexually harassed in violation of the Civil Rights Act, (2) constructively discharged on the basis of sex, (3) the victim of assault and battery, and (4) denied access to her personnel files in violation of the Employee Right to Know Act. The crux of plaintiff's case is that Everett's actions constituted sexual harassment because they create a hostile work environment thereby forcing her resignation.

The court then found that under the reasonable woman standard, a "single incident could be sufficiently severe under some circumstances to support a finding" of a hostile work environment.

The Civil Rights Act "is aimed at 'the prejudices and biases' borne against persons because of their membership in a certain class, and seeks to eliminate the effects of offensive or demeaning stereotype, prejudices, and biases." Accordingly, the act declares that "an employer shall not . . . discriminate against an individual with respect to employment, compensation, or a term, condition, or privilege of employment, because of . . . sex. . . ."

In pursuit of equality in the workplace, the act broadly defines discrimination to include sexual harassment:

> Discrimination because of sex includes sexual harassment which means unwelcome sexual advances, requests for sexual favors, and other verbal or physical conduct or communication of sexual nature when:
>
> "(i) Submission to such conduct or communication is made a term or condition either explicitly or implicitly to obtain employment. . . .
>
> "(ii) Submission to or rejection of such conduct or communication by an individual is used as a factor in decisions affecting such individual's employment. . . .
>
> "(iii) Such conduct or communication has the purpose or effect of substantially interfering with an individual's employment . . . or creating an intimidating, hostile, or offensive . . . environment."

Sexual harassment was targeted by the Civil Rights Act because it is both "pervasive" and "destructive, entailing unacceptable personal, organizational, and societal costs."

Perhaps more important, sexual harassment is prohibited in the workplace because it violates civil liberty: "Sexual harassment should be explicitly defined and prohibited because it is a demeaning, degrading, and coercive activity directed at persons on the basis of their sex, the continuation of which is often contingent on the harasser's economic control over the person being harassed. It should be outlawed because it violates basic human rights of privacy, freedom, sexual integrity, and personal security."

An examination of the Michigan Civil Rights Act reveals that there are five necessary elements to establish a prima facie case of a hostile work environment:

> (1) the employee belonged to a protected group;
>
> (2) the employee was subjected to communication or conduct on the basis of sex;
>
> (3) the employee was subjected to unwelcome sexual conduct or communication;
>
> (4) the unwelcome sexual conduct or communication was intended to or in fact did substantially interfere with the employee's employment or create an intimidating, hostile, or offensive work environment; and
>
> (5) respondent superior.

A prima facie case of sexual harassment under the Michigan Civil Rights Act begins by showing that the plaintiff "was a member of a class entitled to protection under the statute and that, for the same or similar conduct, she was treated differently than a man." Plaintiff meets the first element of the action because she is a member of a protected class—she is an employee who has been the object of unwelcomed sexual advances.

Plaintiff also meets the second element of the action because she alleges that she was subjected to harassment on the basis of sex. Defendants argue that the conduct at issue was not sexual in nature, but was rather an innocent romantic overture, yet plaintiff need only show that "but for the fact of her sex, she would not have been the object of harassment."

In the instant case, plaintiff alleges that Everett forcefully held her down, caressed, and attempted to kiss her. Furthermore, implicitly underlying plaintiff's deposition testimony is an allegation that Everett was seeking unwelcome intimate sexual conduct with plaintiff. The overtures at issue were certainly inferentially sexually motivated: but for her womanhood, Everett would not have held plaintiff down and attempted to solicit romance, if not sex, from her. Plaintiff's allegations are not sufficient to meet the minimum prima facie showing necessary to establish that the conduct in question was based on sex.

Plaintiff also meets the third element of the action because she alleges that she was subjected to unwelcome sexual conduct or communication. Not unlike Title VII, the gravamen of a Michigan Civil Rights Acts sexual harassment claim is that the alleged sexual advances were unwelcome. "The threshold for determining that conduct is unwelcome is 'that the employee did not solicit or incite it, and the employee regarded the conduct as undesirable or offensive.'"

In the instant case, plaintiff alleges that Everett physically restrained her against her will, as well as attempted to force her to kiss him. Viewing the testimony in the light most favorable to plaintiff, she has provided sufficient evidence to meet the unwelcomeness element.

The crux of the instant case is whether the unwelcome sexual conduct or communication was intended to or in fact did substantially interfere with plaintiff's employment or created an intimidating, hostile, or offensive work environment. The essence of a hostile work environment action is that "one or more supervisors or co-workers create an atmosphere so infused with hostility toward members of one sex that they alter the conditions of employment for them." Hence, "a loss of a tangible job benefit is not necessary since the harassment itself affects the terms or conditions of employment." This is so because "the employer can thus implicitly and effectively make the employee's endurance of sexual intimidation a 'condition' of her employment."

Plaintiff, however, also maintains that the reasonableness standard should be gender-conscious. Hence, plaintiff urges the application of a "reasonable woman" standard when the plaintiff is female or a "reasonable man" standard when the plaintiff is a male. The Court of Appeals agreed:

"We believe that in a sexual harassment case involving a woman, the proper perspective to view the offensive conduct from is that of the 'reasonable woman,' not that of the 'reasonable person.' Thus, the severity or pervasiveness of the conduct should be viewed from the perspective of the victim, not that of a hypothetical employee irrespective of gender. We believe that a standard which views harassing conduct from the 'reasonable person' perspective has the tendency to be male-biased and runs the risk of reinforcing the prevailing level of discrimination which the state Civil Rights Act and Title VII were designed to eliminate. In such a case, harassers could continue to discriminate merely because such harassment was the norm at the workplace."

However, this Court disagrees. Hence, we reaffirm the application of the reasonable person standard. We hold that whether a hostile work environment existed shall be determined by whether a reasonable person, in the totality of circumstances, would have perceived the conduct at issue as substantially interfering with the plaintiff's employment or having the purpose or effect of creating an intimidating, hostile, or offensive employment environment.

However, with all respect, we conclude that a gender-conscious standard must be rejected.

Hence, we hold that plaintiff has alleged a prima facie case of a hostile work environment and affirm the ruling of the Court of Appeals, albeit on different grounds.

Judgment for Radtke.

The incidents of sexual harassment must be at the workplace or otherwise work related. If the sexual harassment has no connection with work, then action against the employer is without merit. A criminal harassment complaint against the accused may be more appropriate.

Economic dependence has long placed women in vulnerable positions with their fathers, husbands, and employers. A feeling of inferiority has long caused women to have inadequate self-esteem. On the job, verbal and physical sexual abuse are rampant. Almost every woman will be subject to an incident of this during her working career. Most women accept this conduct begrudgingly because they have felt powerless in an employment environment where men are powerful.

They fear reporting sexual harassment because of subtle reprisals. Instances of sexual harassment at work often make women feel anxious, embarrassed, and insecure. Their emotional distress and mental anguish interfere with their ability to perform well at work.

In an age in which women are exercising greater freedom in the control of their bodies, they should not submit to unwarranted sexual comments and advances. Women should stand firm in their refusal to accept this treatment and be proactive in seeking a resolution from the company. However, this will happen only when women feel more secure in protecting themselves. Men must be admonished that they have no right to mistreat women, expect sexual gratification at work, and use their positions to extort sex from women in return for promotions, raises, easier work schedules, or just allowing them to keep their jobs. Companies should be educated that permitting the harassment of women results in their decreased performance on the job and the possibility of a long, protracted, and expensive law suit.

Respect for women means more than just paying lip service to them. It means speaking to them as a man would speak to his mother, sister, wife, or daughter. Building women's self-esteem on the job will enable women to become more productive in the work environment.

In the next case, a female worker claimed that derogatory comments and a demotion constituted sexual discrimination. The employer claimed that her work performance was unsatisfactory, in part because of her third-grade reading level.

CASE

Lord v. Kerr-McGee Coal Corp.

809 F.Supp 87 (D.Wyo. 1992)

BRIMMER, District Judge.

This matter comes before the Court on defendant's motion for summary judgment. The Court, having considered the materials in support of and in opposition to the motion, having weighed the arguments of counsel, and being fully advised in the premises, FINDS and ORDERS as follows:

Background

Jeraldine Lord ("Lord") is an employee at Kerr-McGee's surface coal mine near Wright, Wyoming, where she has been employed since 1979. Lord has been demoted and promoted several times in both the production and maintenance departments. In July of 1990, Lord was demoted from the job of Component Repairer to her previous job, Maintenance Laborer. The litigation stems from this demotion, and an earlier demotion in 1987.

In January of 1987, Lord applied for and was promoted to the job of Component Repairer for the Jacobs Ranch Mine. The job entailed organizing and maintaining the tool room and repairing small tools. From 1987 through 1990, Lord performed her job at an allegedly less than satisfactory level.

Apparently, training for Component Repairer was of the "on the job" sort. Kerr McGee had only one Component Repairer prior to Lord and he was a mechanic with over thirty years experience. Kerr-McGee evaluated each employee's performance annually. At the end of Lord's first year as Compo-

nent Repairer, she received the lowest possible job performance rating. Kerr-McGee decided Lord was in need of "more formal" training which was administered over the next two years.

In November of 1989, Kerr-McGee sought to find out why Lord was doing poorly at her new job. Kerr-McGee suggested to Lord that she be tested regarding specific functions of her job. The test appeared to be job-related and involved mechanical jargon and other simple mechanical concepts. Lord failed the first test. After an unrelated leave of absence, Lord took the test a second time and again failed it. After Lord was demoted in 1990, another woman, a former payroll clerk, passed the test and is now employed as Component Repairer.

During the course of her three years as Component Repairer, Kerr-McGee offered to pay 90% of the tuition and fees for which might improve Lord's skills. However, Lord did not take advantage of this offer.

During this period of time generally, one of Lord's supervisors was Paul Keithan. Lord and Keithan never related well to each other. Keithan talked about Lord behind her back, was generally rude and insensitive to her, and told outside vendors she was "dumb."

In the Spring of 1990, Kerr-McGee brought in an outside professional to analyze the situation. The professional determined that Lord had a third grade reading and comprehension level which caused, in part, her inability to properly perform her new job.

On July 12, 1990, Lord was demoted to her previous job of Maintenance Laborer with no loss of seniority. Lord did not avail herself of the internal complaint procedure as specified in the employee handbook of Kerr-McGee. Neither the State of Wyoming nor the EEOC found Lord's case to have merit. Lord sued pursuant to her option to do so provided in the EEOC response letter. She alleged both sexual harassment and intentional infliction of distress.

Kerr-McGee contends that Lord's complaints do not constitute an "intimidating, hostile, or offensive working environment as a matter of law. Kerr-McGee urges that Lord has failed to articulate sufficient evidence to refute the reason that she was demoted, i.e., poor job performance.

In contrast, Lord alleges she was unlawfully harassed based on her gender. To wit, supervisors never said nice things to her, supervisor Keithan called her "dumb" and talked about her behind her back; male employees were treated better than she was at the warehouse area; foremen were not nice to her, and supervisor Elliot treated her as "mentally retarded" by virtue of the test Elliot administered to her regarding her job skill level. Lord argues that the real reason she was demoted from her job in the toolroom was due to gender discrimination against her. She seeks back-wages and desires to be returned to her toolroom job.

A careful review of Lord's deposition and the accompanying exhibits reveals that the evidence does not support a legitimate claim of hostile work environment sexual harassment. The evidence presented by Lord in her deposition can be usefully reduced to three related areas: (1) Plaintiff's supervisors regularly referred to her as "dumb" or "retarded" when speaking with other employees and vendors; (2) plaintiff's supervisors regularly ignored her or spoke badly about her; (3) men, generally, were treated with more respect and more fairly than women at Kerr-McGee.

Furthermore, Lord's own deposition contains substantial evidence that she was demoted because she performed her job inadequately. The record established that Lord had little, if any, of the mechanical skills needed to succeed in the toolroom. Plaintiff's deposition contains substantial evidence that she was demoted because she performed her job inadequately. Prior to the promotion to the toolroom, Lord had no experience with tools. Lord consistently received poor evaluations on her work performance evaluations. More than one supervisor observed that her skills were lacking and her performance was poor.

Sexual Discrimination: Lord's claims also may be analyzed under the legal theory of gender discrimination in particular, "mixed motive" gender discrimination. *Price Waterhouse* established that plaintiff must bear the burden of proving by direct evidence that an impermissible criterion was a "substantial factor" in the adverse employment decision at issue.

As a result, this Court holds that the facts alleged by Lord do not establish a prima facie case of either hostile environment sexual harassment or actionable gender discrimination.

Judgment for Kerr-McGee.

Companies should draft a sexual harassment policy and have it well publicized throughout the firm. The policy should clearly define the types of sexual harassment as well as set forth examples of verbal and physical abuse that will not be tolerated. Investigations will be thorough and the consequences severe.

A MODEL SEXUAL HARASSMENT POLICY

Sexual harassment is defined as (1) a sexual advance or request for sexual favor made by one employee to another which is unwelcome and not consented to; and (2) touching, joking, commenting or distributing material of a sexual nature that an employee has not consented to and finds offensive.

Sexual advance may be defined as embracing, touching, cornering or otherwise restricting an individual's freedom to move with the intent of pursuing sexual intimacy.

Request for sexual favors may be defined as asking an individual to engage in some type of sexual behavior such as but not limited to sexual intercourse, oral sex, intimate touching and kissing.

Touching may be defined as placing hands on or rubbing against some part of another individual's body that is unwelcome and not consented to. The part of the person's body includes not only the breast, genitals, and buttocks, but also leg, knee, thigh, arm, shoulder, neck, face, and hair.

Joking may be defined as encouraging, participating or telling sexual jokes which are offensive and demeaning.

Commenting may be defined as passing remarks of a sexual nature about an individual's anatomy, sex life, or personality or about that individual's gender, which is offensive and demeaning.

Distributing material of a sexual nature encompasses pornography, photostatic sheets which depict sexual cartoons or sexual jokes or libelous statements of an individual's sex life.

Although the court appointed test for determining what constitutes sexual harassment is a reasonable person standard and what is reasonable may vary depending on the work environment, it is the purpose of this policy on sexual harassment to avoid litigation, not to win lawsuits. Therefore, employees are forewarned that the use of the terms "babe, broad, bitch and chick" when spoken either alone or coupled with hot, foxy, dumb, stupid, and like words may give rise to a woman filing a sexual harassment complaint and are therefore prohibited.

If a complaint is filed with the company's human resources department on any of the above allegations, it will be investigated immediately. The investigation shall consist of questioning the complainant, alleged perpetrator, co-workers, superiors and subordinates. If a determination is made that a valid complaint had been issued against an employee, that employee will be entitled to a hearing to which he or she may be assisted by outside council. If a conclusion is reached that the conduct complained of meets one of the above criteria, then the employee shall be dismissed forthwith.

Furthermore, the victim will be afforded counseling services if needed. Every effort will be made by the company to aid the victimized employee in overcoming the emotional trauma of the unfortunate ordeal.

Finally, the company will sponsor in house workshops explaining this policy on sexual harassment, cautioning employees against engaging in it and encouraging those affected by sexual harassment to come forward with the details of their encounter with it in order for the company to investigate and resolve the dilemma and service the needs of the victimized employee.

Employment Perspective

Dawn West, an employee of Bull and Bear Stockbrokers, appeared one Monday morning with a new hairstyle and wearing a royal blue dress. Jack Olsen, a coworker, couldn't take his eyes off Dawn. Finally, he said, "Boy don't you look fantastic." Dawn, embarrassed in front of her coworkers, filed a claim for sexual harassment. Will she be successful? No! This incident was not severe nor did it reoccur. It was an isolated occurrence. What if Jack's behavior is repeated on a daily basis? The answer would depend upon whether Dawn communicated to Jack her distaste for his conduct or whether it was blatantly obvious from Dawn's reaction each day that she did not welcome Jack's behavior. ◆

Employment Perspective

Susan Jennings is speaking to Jessica Randolph in the latter's cubicle about the terrible cramps she is experiencing this month. John Woods, a coworker happens to overhear their conversation and interjects, "Why don't you let Dr. John have a look down there and see what the problem is? You know I have magic fingers not to mention. . . ." "No thanks, John, now take a walk," was their response. Later, they filed a sexual harassment claim against John. Will they win? Again, this is an isolated occurrence during which the women made clear to John that they did not appreciate his comments. By filing the complaint, they are putting the company on notice that they will not tolerate further harassment from John. The company should investigate their complaint and upon satisfying itself about its accuracy, notify John that future behavior will result in suspension or dismissal. ◆

Employment Perspective

Kay Stevens was 5 feet tall and weighed 250 pounds at the age of thirty-two. She worked in a meat-packing plant, where she was subjected to constant criticisms by her coworkers: "You're eating the company's profits, no man would sleep with you because he could not fit in the bed, and your mother thought she was having twins, then you appeared." For many years Kay endured the belittling behavior because she was ashamed to repeat what had been said. She has been very depressed. Should Kay file a complaint? Yes! If she does not, the harassment will never stop. By filing a complaint, Kay is putting the onus on the company to stop what she cannot end herself. ◆

Damages

The 1991 Amendment to the Civil Rights Act has now made compensatory and punitive damages available to Title VII plaintiffs including those victimized by sexual harassment.

If victims of sexual harassment suddenly were in a superior position, they would make the aggressor end the abuse. Having inferior status, they must rely on the company to act as their guardian. The company must act accordingly or subject itself to liability.

The following case presented the question of whether a male coworker's sexual antics were severe and pervasive enough to constitute a hostile work environment.

CASE *Dombeck v. Milwaukee Valve Co.*

823 F.Supp. 1473 (W.D. 1993)

SHABAZ, District Judge.

Evidence was presented that defendant Carpenter forcefully placed his foot in plaintiff's crotch and wiggled it, pulled the waistband on her pants and disclosed her undergarments on at least two occasions, slapped her on the buttocks, and pushed her in a threatening manner. Plaintiff complained to John Schmidt, her supervisor, that Carpenter had been mean to her and frequently used sexual language in her presence. The jury had every reason to accept this overwhelming evidence when determining that plaintiff was subjected to a hostile working environment. Defendant's argument in support of its motion for judgment as a matter of law after plaintiff's presentation of evidence in the liability phase suggested counsel for plaintiff lacked sufficient familiarity with factory conditions. The jury had every reason to determine that regardless of those factory conditions which may exist, defendant could not close its eyes to that intolerable sexual harassment accorded plaintiff by Carpenter which did, indeed, meet the pervasive level of a hostile working environment. There was considerable testimony that in 1990, plaintiff complained to her supervisor, John Schmidt, about Carpenter's offensive sexual language.

Jayne Carlson, the defendant's occupational health nurse, was advised by Dr. Haakon P. Carlson of complaints of sexual harassment made to him by plaintiff in May 1991. The jury had evidence before it from which members could have reasonably determined that the defendant knew or certainly should have known of the hostile working environment and failed to take appropriate remedial action. In 1990 a female employee, Joanne Neuheusel, complained to Schmidt that Carpenter was harassing her and threatened to disrupt her marriage, for which Carpenter was given a written warning that if his conduct continued he would be terminated.

The jury was instructed it was to determine the amount of money that would reasonably compensate plaintiff for anguish and emotional pain she suffered and which she is reasonably certain to suffer in the future as the direct result of defendant's conduct. Plaintiff testified to bad anxiety, her headaches, her frequent crying, her shaking and her nervous condition which she and her psychologist, Elizabeth E. Seebach, attributed to the sexual harassment to which plaintiff was subjected in the workplace. Seebach further testified that plaintiff suffered a generated anxiety disorder caused by sexual harassment at the workplace which is the same determination previously made and referred to Nurse Carlson by Dr. Haakon P. Carlson. Although the amount of $25,000 may arguably be somewhat high, this Court is unable to determine that it is excessive to the point where a new trial or remitter should be granted.

Under these circumstances the award is not excessive and the $25,000 for compensatory damages shall stand, the Court believing that, regardless of the anxiety which the plaintiff experienced in her home life, the jury could have well determined that the conduct she endured in the workplace was so egregious as to justify the amount awarded as compensatory damages. Certainly, it was not as suggested by defendant "monstrously excessive" and there was sufficient testimony to provide a "rational connection between the evidence on damages and the verdict. Defendant further argues that there is evidence to support an award of punitive damages. Without objection the jury instructed that if it should find that: The act or emission of the defendant which proximately caused actual injury or damages to the plaintiff was maliciously or wantonly done, then the Jury may, if in the exercise of discretion they unanimously choose so to do, award such amount as the jury shall unanimously agree to be proper as punitive and exemplary damages. An act or failure to act is maliciously done if promoted or accompanied by ill will, or spite, or grudge, either toward the injured person individually, or toward all persons in one or more groups or categories of which the injured person is a member.

An act or failure to act is "wantonly" done if done in reckless or callous disregard of, or indifference to, the rights of one or more persons, including the injured person.

Judgment for Milwaukee Valve Co.

CONCLUSION

In the competitive global environment in which businesses operate, employees should be instructed that their work hours should be spent productively, not taking time for idle chatter, much less for abusing coworkers and subordinates. The team concept should be promoted, and personal favoritism should be discarded for the success of the team. Encouragement and a willingness to help one another should displace personal aggrandizement at the expense of demeaning one's coworker. Employees who embrace these concepts will make positive contributions to the firm in a future in which employees will be judged not only on their positive contributions but also on what their negative actions are likely to cost the company.

REVIEW QUESTIONS

1. Define sexual harassment.
2. Explain hostile work environment.
3. Define the concept of quid pro quo.
4. What should be included in a company policy on sexual harassment?
5. Can sexual harassment be directed against management?
6. Is it possible for a man to be a victim of sexual harassment?
7. Can sexual harassment occur outside the work environment?
8. Does using the term "babe" constitute sexual harassment?
9. Can sexual harassment involve an aggressor and a victim from the same sex?
10. In situations involving sexually harassing comments, is truth an absolute defense?

11. A female employee sued her employer for sexual harassment, claiming that a supervisor referred to her as a "worthless broad." The employer argued that the supervisor's alleged abuse was not gender-oriented in that he treated men the same way. What was the result? *Steiner v. Showboat Operating Co.,* 25 F.3d 1459 (9th Cir. 1994)
12. The workplace was permeated with discriminatory intimidation, ridicule, and insult that is sufficiently severe or pervasive to alter the conditions of the victim's employment and create an abusive working environment. The employer argued that this was not sufficient unless the employee had suffered psychological distress. What was the result? *Harris v. Forklift Systems, Inc.,* 114 S.Ct. 367 (1994)
13. This case involved the display and posting of pornographic photographs, and the use of derogatory language directed at women. Does this qualify as a hostile work environment? What was the result? *Jenson v. Eveleth Taconite Co.,* 824 F.Supp. 847 (D.Minn. 1993)
14. Sparks sued the Northeast Alabama Regional Medical Center, her employer, claiming to be sexually harassed by Dr. Garland. Sparks alleged that Dr. Garland joked about her breast size and sex life and cursed at her for being late in front of her coworkers. The hospital claimed that this was outside the scope of Dr. Garland's employment. What was the result? *Sparks v. Regional Medical Center Bd.,* 792 F.Supp. 735 (N.D. Ala. 1992)
15. Byron Brown, a senior counselor at a drug rehabilitation facility engaged in sexual intercourse with Kimberly Bunce, a patient. This happened several times with her consent. Thereafter, she sued Brown in civil court for sexual assault, battery, and malpractice. Brown argued that consent is a defense. What was the result? *Bunce v. Parkside Lodge of Columbus,* 596 N.E. 2d 1106 (Ohio App. 10 Dist. 1991)
16. In the case on pp. 282, should the plaintiff's acquiescence in the relationship preclude him from recovery?
17. In the case on pp. 273, if off-color jokes are acceptable to everyone, should an employer still prohibit this type of behavior?
18. In the case on pp. 292, if an employee has participated in the offensive behavior, can he or she later claim hostile work environment?
19. In the case on pp. 279, would the employer have been ethical if it fired them both?
20. In the case on pp. 289, is the company ethical for being indifferent to the employee's affair until such time as the female employee became pregnant, at which time both she and her lover were discharged?

CHAPTER 13

Family Leave and Pregnancy Discrimination

FAMILY LEAVE

The Family and Medical Leave Act of 1991 permits an employee in any twelve-month period to take up to twelve weeks of unpaid leave for the birth or adoption of a child; for the care of a spouse, child, or parent who has a serious health condition; or because of a serious health problem that makes the employee unable to work.

To be eligible, the employee must have worked for the employer for at least one year and must have earned 1,250 hours of service during the previous twelve months. The Family and Medical Leave Act applies only to employers who have *fifty* or more employees who have worked for each day during twenty weeks of the current or preceding calendar year.

Serious Health Condition

Serious health condition means that the person is in a hospital, hospice, or nursing home or requires continuous medical treatment. Biological, adopted, foster, and stepchildren are covered by the Act.

The case on the next page, deals with the issue of whether an employee has the right to a leave of absence due to her pregnancy. She was discharged because of her request.

E.E.O.C. v. Lutheran Family Services

884 F.Supp. 1022 (E.D.N.C. 1994)

FOX, Chief Judge.

On March 16, 1992, Denise Savage filed a charge of discrimination with the Equal Employment Opportunity Commission (hereinafter "Plaintiff") alleging that her employer, defendant herein, discriminated against her on the basis of her pregnancy. Plaintiff conducted an investigation and, on March 23, 1993, issued a finding that defendant had impermissibly discriminated against Savage on the basis of her pregnancy by denying her a leave of absence that was requested for reasons related to her pregnancy and, subsequently, terminating her employment. Consequently, plaintiff filed a complaint against defendant in this action on September 30, 1993, alleging violations of Title VII of the Civil Rights Act of 1964.

Defendant is a church-affiliated social services agency that provides a variety of social services and group homes for orphans, neglected and abused children, problem teenagers, and developmentally disabled children and adults. Among the various group homes defendant operates is Woodhouse, a group home located on a former dairy farm in a rural area of Halifax County, near Rapids, North Carolina. Woodhouse is designed to provide a stable home environment and counseling center for teenagers below the age of sixteen who have exhibited aggressive or assaultive behavior and delinquency or truancy in school. At all times relevant to this lawsuit, five such male teens resided at Woodhouse. State licensing requirement for group homes of this type required that the home have on duty at all times a minimum of two properly trained and qualified adult staff members for every five residents.

On April 21, 1988, defendant hired Savage as a residential counselor for Woodhouse on a part-time, hourly wage basis. In October 1988, Savage became a part-time salaried employee, working as an Overnight Awake Residential Counselor I at Woodhouse. In this capacity, Savage worked night shifts seven days per week, every other week. Her position required her to assist the residents in getting to bed in the evening; to remain awake at night to address emergencies or other problems that might arise with the residents; and to assist the residents in getting up, fed, and off to school in the morning. During the time of her employment with defendant, Savage was also employed on a full-time basis as an elementary school teacher in Weldon, North Carolina.

On or about September 24, 1991, Savage learned that she was pregnant. Due to sickness associated with the early period of her pregnancy, Savage took sixty hours of accrued sick leave between September 24 and 29, 1991. Shortly thereafter, on October 25, 1991, Savage approached Bob Scott, Program Director for Woodhouse, with a note from her doctor advising that she take two months leave of absence due to complications with her pregnancy. On that same date, Savage submitted a written request to Scott for a leave of two months pursuant to her doctor's order. Savage indicated to Scott in her request that she would like to apply her accrued sick and vacation time—then totalling twenty-one days—to her leave of absence. Following her notification to Scott, Savage began her leave on October 28, 1991.

At the time Savage made her leave request, defendant had in place two policies regarding medical leaves. The first, designated as a "Sick Leave" policy with a revision, effective date of "8/3/91", provided that employees may take sick leave with pay up to their accrued amounts. Such leave could have been requested of the employee's immediate supervisor without the need for the President's approval. In the case of injury or illness requiring an extended absence beyond the leave then accrued in favor of the employee, the employee would be required to exhaust his or her accrued sick leave and vacation leave and then begin "leave without pay" status with the approval of the president. For extended absences, the President also would determine for what period of time the employee's position would be held open pending the employee's return.

In fact, the Pregnancy Discrimination Act, as discussed below, mandates only that pregnant employees receive equal treatment to employees suffering from other medical disabilities; it does not specify any required or special considerations that must be given them. Accordingly, the only relevant inquiry is whether defendant gave Savage's leave request consideration and treatment under its "Sick Leave" policy equal to that which defendant would give any other medically related leave request.

Although she had not received the needed authorization for an extended leave without pay from either Larry Paul, defendant's Area Director, or William Brittain, defendant's President, Savage began her leave on October 28, 1991.

In this letter, Paul also informed Savage that her request for accrued vacation and sick leave pay would not be honored because Savage gave defendant only two days' notice of her intent to take leave, instead of the four week notice required by defendant's policies. In conclusion, Paul informed Savage that, because she would not tender her resignation as requested, he would proceed with her termination.

Title VII of the Civil Rights Act of 1964, as amended by the Equal Employment Opportunity Act of 1972, prohibits discrimination in the work place on the basis of race, color, religion, sex or national origin.

In 1978, the enactment of the Pregnancy Discrimination Act (hereinafter "PDA") amended Title VII to include discrimination based on pregnancy within the coverage of its general prohibition on sex based discrimination. Specifically, this amendment provides, in relevant part, "the terms 'because of sex' or 'on the basis of sex' include, but are not limited to, because of or on the basis of pregnancy, childbirth, or related medical conditions and women affected by pregnancy, childbirth, or related medical conditions shall be treated the same for all employment-related purposes, including receipt of benefits under fringe benefit programs, as other persons not so affected but similar in their ability or inability to work." The legislative history of the PDA, as noted by both plaintiff and defendant, emphasizes that the Act provides not for preferential treatment of pregnant employees, but rather for treatment equal to that given other employees laboring under a similar disability.

The PDA does not require employers to treat pregnant employees in any particular manner with respect to hiring, permitting them to continue working, providing sick leave, furnishing of medical and hospital benefits. . . . The bill would simply require that pregnant women be treated the same as other employees on the basis of their ability or inability to work. . . .

As discussed above, Plaintiff has made a prima facie showing of discrimination through a combination of both direct evidence tending to show that defendant impermissibly considered Savage's pregnancy as a factor in making its decisions with regard to her leave request and subsequent discharge. There is indirect evidence sufficient to raise a judicial inference of discrimination under the McDonnell Douglas model. Plaintiff has shown that Savage was a pregnant employee of defendant who was qualified for the position she held and who had otherwise performed her duties in a satisfactory manner but who was denied a pregnancy-related medical leave and was subsequently terminated and replaced by a male. In making such a showing, plaintiff has also adduced evidence to support its claim that such treatment was less favorable than that given to various other employees of defendant who were similarly disabled by medical conditions other than pregnancy.

Judgment for EEOC.

In cases of birth or adoption, the employee is required to provide the employer with at least thirty days notice of his or her intent to request family leave. When a serious health condition is forseeable, the employee must provide thirty days notice and take into consideration the employer when scheduling treatment, if this is practicable.

Employment Perspective

Joseph Woodward is an accountant with Bean, Brower and Boseman, CPA firm. In early December, his father had been advised to undergo a cataract operation within the next six months. The recovery period is up to three months. Joseph, dreading the upcoming tax season, schedules his father's operation for mid-January, and gives the required thirty days' notice of his intent to take twelve weeks leave. Is Joseph acting in good faith? No! He has violated the provision of making a reasonable effort to schedule the leave with his employer in mind. Moreover, the operation could have been scheduled in April, thus being in accord with the physician's directive and lessening the burden on his employer. ◆

In the following case, a female employee was discharged upon returning from a leave of absence taken for pregnancy. The company argued a suitable position was not available when she returned.

CASE

California Federal S. & L. Assn. v. Guerra

479 U.S. 272 (1987)

JUSTICE MARSHALL delivered the opinion of the Court.

The question presented is whether Title VII of the Civil Rights Act of 1964, as amended by the Pregnancy Discrimination Act of 1978, pre-empts a state statute.

California's Fair Employment and Housing Act (FEHA) is a comprehensive statute that prohibits discrimination in employment and housing. In September 1978, California amended the FEHA to proscribe certain forms of employment discrimination on the basis of pregnancy. Section 12945 Subdivision (b) (2)—the provision at issue here—is the only portion of the statute that applies to employers subject to Title VII. It requires these employers to provide female employees an unpaid pregnancy disability leave of up to four months. Respondent Fair Employment and Housing Commission, the state agency authorized to interpret the FEHA, has construed Section 12945 (b) (2) to require California employers to reinstate an employee returning from such pregnancy leave to the job she previously held, unless it is no longer available due to business necessity. In the latter case, the employer must make a reasonable, good-faith effort to place the employee in a substantially similar job. The statute does not compel employers to provide paid leave to pregnant employees. Accordingly, the only benefit pregnant workers actually derive from Section 12945 (b) (2) is a qualified right to reinstatement.

Title VII of the Civil Rights Act of 1964, also prohibits various forms of employment discrimination, including discrimination on the basis of sex. However, in *General Electric Co. v. Gilbert* (1976), this Court ruled that discrimination on the basis of pregnancy was not sex discrimination under Title VIII.

In response to the Gilbert decision, Congress passed the Pregnancy Discrimination Act of 1978 (PDA). The PDA specifies that sex discrimination includes discrimination on the basis of pregnancy.

Petitioner California Federal Savings & Loan Association (Cal Fed) is a federally chartered savings and loan association based in Los Angeles; it is an employer covered by both Title VII and Section 12945 (b) (2). Cal Fed has a facially neutral leave policy that permits employees who have completed three months of service to take unpaid leaves of absence for a variety of reasons, including disability and pregnancy. Although it is Cal Fed's policy to try to provide an employee taking unpaid leave with a similar position upon returning, Cal Fed expressly reserves the right to terminate an employee who has taken a leave of absence if a similar position is not available.

Lillian Garland was employed by Cal Fed as a receptionist for several years. In January 1982, she took a pregnancy disability leave. When she was able to return to work in April of that year, Garland notified Cal Fed, but was informed that her job had been filled and that there were no receptionist or similar positions available. Garland filed a complaint with respondent Department of Fair Employment and Housing, which issued an administrative accusation against Cal Fed on her behalf. Respondent charged Cal Fed with violating Section 12945 (b) (2) of the FEHA. Prior to the scheduled hearing before respondent Fair Employment and Housing Commission, Cal Fed, joined by petitioners Merchants and Manufacturers Association and the California Chamber of Commerce, brought this action in the United District Court for the Central District of California.

They sought a declaration that Section 12945 (b) (2) is inconsistent with and pre-empted by Title VII and an injunction against enforcement of the section. The District Court granted petitioners' motion for summary judgment. The court stated that "California employers who comply with state law are subject to reverse discrimination suits under Title VII brought by temporarily disabled males who do not receive the same treatment as female employees disabled by pregnancy. . . . " On this basis, the District Court held that "California state law and the policies of interpretation and enforcement . . . which require preferential treatment of female employees disabled by pregnancy, childbirth, or related medical conditions are preempted by Title VII and are null, void, invalid and inoperative under the Supremacy Clause of the United States Constitution."

Title VII, as amended by the PDA, and California's pregnancy disability leave statute share a common goal. The purpose of Title VII is "to achieve equality of employment opportunities and remove barriers that have operated in the past to favor an identifiable group of . . . employees over other employees." By taking pregnancy into account, California's pregnancy disability-leave statute allows women, as well as men, to have families without losing their jobs.

As Senator Williams, a sponsor of the Act, stated: "The entire thrust . . . behind this legislation is to guarantee women the basic right to participate fully and equally in the workforce, without denying them the fundamental right to full participation in family life."

Section 12945 (b) (2) also promotes equal employment opportunity. By requiring employers to reinstate women after a reasonable pregnancy disability leave, Section 12945 (b) (2) ensures that they will not lose their jobs on account of pregnancy disability.

Thus, petitioners' facial challenge to Section 12945 (b) (2) fails. The statute is not preempted by Title VII, as amended by the PDA, because it is not consistent with the purposes of the federal statute, nor does it require the doing of an act which is unlawful under Title VII.

The judgment of the Court
of Appeals is Affirmed.
Judgment for California S&L Association.

If the employee has unused paid leave in the form of vacation, personal days, or sick time, he or she may elect, or the employer may require that time be used toward the twelve-week family and medical leave. Use of sick time would apply only to medical leave for the employee himself or herself or for a family member.

Employment Perspective

Henry Marceni's five-year-old daughter has been diagnosed with leukemia and has to be hospitalized immediately. Henry informs his employer, Apple Valley Bank, that he must take twelve weeks leave. Henry currently has ten vacation days, four personal days, and five sick days remaining. He asks Apple Valley to apply those nineteen days of paid leave to the twelve weeks. Apple Valley agrees except for the sick time, asserting that this may only be used when he is sick. Is Apple Valley's reasoning correct? No! The use of sick time may be applied when leave is taken for a serious health condition of a family member. ◆

The following case addresses the issue of whether accumulated sick leave can be taken in combination with maternity leave when a teacher becomes pregnant.

CASE *U.S. v. Bd. of Educ. of Consol. High Sch. D. 230*

761 F.Supp. 524 (N.D.Ill. 1990)

LEINENWEBER, District Judge.

This case originated from a timely charge brought by a District 230 teacher, Sharon Carlson, before the Equal Employment Opportunity Commission ("EEOC") on June 25, 1984, complaining that District 230's leave policies discriminated on the basis of sex. The EEOC subsequently issued a reasonable cause determination, and because the challenged practices and policies affected other female teachers referred the matter to the Department of Justice, which brought this pattern or practice case.

The gist of the United States' complaint is the CBA provisions and the practices of District 230 prohibiting pregnant teachers from taking sick leave for pregnancy-related disability and then taking maternity leave at the expiration of the sick leave, and the Collective Bargaining Agreement (CBA) provision excluding maternity benefits from the sick leave bank ("SLB"), violate Title VII.

The relevant CBAs cover the years 1982 through June 1, 1987. The complained-of provisions were eliminated on the latter date.

During the relevant time period maternity leave policy as established by the CBA provided, the following:

> "A teacher shall not be required to resign or take a leave of absence because of pregnancy. Said teacher, however, may in writing, request a leave of absence without pay. *A maternity leave of absence may begin when the pregnant teacher desires, but not later than when she is unable to perform her duties satisfactorily.* A maternity leave of absence for a period longer than one semester shall end on the day prior to the beginning of any school year up to and including five school semesters after the maternity leave of absence begins."

Under this subsection, maternity leave may begin whenever a pregnant teacher chooses, but must begin no later than the date when the teacher actually becomes disabled due to her pregnancy or because of childbirth. Her maternity leave need not end when her medical disability ceases, and may extend for a period of up to five semesters.

The relevant provisions of the CBA for use of sick leave by a pregnant teacher were as follows:

> "A teacher *not requesting maternity leave* may utilize accumulative sick leave under the following conditions:

(1) A pregnant teacher shall notify her principal in writing when her pregnancy is confirmed in order to be eligible to utilize her accumulated sick leave.

(2) Such accumulated sick leave shall be allowed during the time period that the teacher's physician determines, in writing, that she is unable to perform her teaching duties as a result of the pregnancy or delivery of the child. The teacher shall submit periodic statements from her physician attesting to the condition of her health. If a teacher shall have exhausted her accumulated sick leave prior to her ability to return to work, she will be granted an unpaid leave of absence for such period.

(3) Failure of the teacher to return after her physician determines she is medically able to perform her teaching duties shall be considered as having waived all rights to continued employment in the District."

A pregnant teacher therefore who requested to use sick leave for her pregnancy disability could not take maternity leave and vice versa. A pregnant teacher who took sick leave in lieu of maternity leave was required, as was the case with any teacher who took sick leave for any other illness or condition, to return to her teaching position as soon as her medical (pregnancy) disability ceased.

A pregnant teacher who elected to take maternity leave instead of sick leave could however use accumulated paid sick leave for any non-maternity related disability.

At all times relevant, the CBA contained a provision for parental leave. It was worded as follows:

"A teacher may request a parental leave of absence without pay to rear his children. A teacher who adopts a child may request a parental leave of absence without pay to rear his/her adopted child. A teacher on maternity or parental leave shall not accept employment outside his/her home during the hours he/she otherwise would be teaching, except to be employed as a substitute for District 230, or except where the teacher is denied her initial request that her maternity leave of absence should end on the day prior to the beginning of a school semester.

A teacher who requests a parental leave of absence shall follow the procedures, where applicable, in this Section 6.04."

District 230 and the union agreed that the use of the masculine pronoun "his" in the first sentence of Section 6.045 was a misprint and this paragraph should be read to make parental leave available to natural mothers. While there is evidence that some of the faculty read the provision literally to deny parental leave to natural mothers, District 230 did grant Mary Parkhurst, a natural mother, a parental leave. There was no evidence that District 230 ever denied a natural mother parental leave. Therefore, the court finds that at all relevant times parental leave was, in fact, available to natural mothers as well as natural fathers and adoptive parents.

District 230's current leave policy embodied in Section 6.04 of the 1987–1990 CBA allows a pregnant teacher to use accumulated sick leave prior to taking maternity leave.

A SLB was first established in the 1980–1982 CBA. Subsection 6.015 of the 1982–1984, 1984–1986, and 1987–1990 CBAs provided that:

"Withdrawals from the sick leave bank shall be available only for a teacher's *prolonged and extended catastrophic illness and shall not be available for maternity benefits, elective surgery,* illness of family or household members, and/or death of family or household members."

Pregnancy is the only non-elective medical condition resulting in disability that is specifically excluded from the SLB use.

Conclusions of Law

1. Title VII of the Civil Rights Act of 1964, as amended, provides that it shall be an unlawful employment practice for an employer to:

"(1) fail or refuse to hire or to discharge any individual, or otherwise to discriminate against any individual with respect to his compensation, terms, conditions, or privileges of employment because of such individual's race, color, religion, sex or national origin."

2. The (Pregnancy Discrimination Act) PDA, enacted by Congress in 1978 as an amendment to Title VII, defines all discrimination on the basis of "pregnancy, childbirth or related medical conditions" as discrimination on the basis of sex. Specifically, Congress added Section 701 (k) to Title VII, which provides, in relevant part, that:

"The terms 'because of sex' or 'on the basis of sex' include, but are not limited to, because of or on the basis of pregnancy, childbirth or related medical conditions; and women affected by pregnancy, childbirth or related medical conditions should be treated the same for all employment-related purposes, including the receipt of benefits under fringe benefit programs, as other persons not so affected but similar in their ability or inability to work, and nothing in this section 703 (h) of this shall be interpreted to permit otherwise."

Here, the District 230 CBA permits a pregnant teacher to take sick leave for disability up to and including birth disability and then take parental leave for the period after birth. Thus a pregnant teacher under the District 230 CBA has precisely the same rights to take sick leave and parental leave as a non-pregnant teacher, but one additional right: a pregnant teacher has the option open to her to take maternity leave in lieu of sick leave and paternal leave, an option not available to non-pregnant teachers. She may take maternity leave as a matter of right at any time after she becomes pregnant and remain on leave for up to five semesters.

Accordingly, the court finds that the sick leave and maternity leave provisions of the CBA do not violate Title VII and therefore the government has failed to prove a pattern or practice of discrimination on the part of District 230 with respect to its leave policies.

On the other hand, the court does find that District 230 has engaged in a pattern or practice of sex discrimination in violation of Title VII in the implementation and maintenance of its SLB policies established in the CBA against pregnant women who opt for use of accumulated sick leave for their pregnancy. The court has found that District 230 almost never refused to grant use of the SLB for any disabling condition that required hospitalization. District 230 has adopted no definition of "catastrophic" and has allowed SLB use for such minor disabling conditions as back strain, requiring hospitalization for traction, and gall bladder surgery. The only medically disabling conditions expressly excluded from the SLB are maternity and those conditions involving elective surgery. All other ailments and medical conditions causing disability are at least eligible for District 230 consideration. Maternity in no sense can be considered to be "elective" in the same sense as "elective" surgery. Accordingly, the CBA SLB provisions, by automatically excluding maternity benefits, discriminate against pregnant teachers who elected to utilize accumulated sick leave for their pregnancy-related disability. The court holds therefore that District 230 has engaged in a pattern or practice of sex discrimination against pregnant women in the implementation and maintenance of its SLB policies in violation of Title VII.

It is so ordered.
Judgment for U.S.

Maintenance of Health Benefits

When an employee takes family and medical leave, he or she is entitled to the maintenance of health benefits while on leave. If an employee does not return, he or she may be charged by the employer for the health care premiums while on leave, unless it is due to a continuation of the serious health problem. With regard to pension, life insurance, and other employment benefits, these may be suspended during the period of the leave but must be restored immediately upon the return of the employee.

Employment Perspective

Two months before giving birth, Jessica McCormick applied for family leave for the twelve-week period after the birth of her child. At the expiration of the twelve-week period, Jessica has decided to resign her position and stay home with her child. Can she be charged for the health care premiums paid on her behalf? Yes! In not returning

to work, it was as though she resigned when she gave birth. There is no indication in the Act for how long a period of time she must return. ◆

The next case deals with an employee whose position was eliminated while she was on maternity leave. She claimed discrimination because of her pregnancy. The company argued that it was in the process of downsizing and that the employee was aware of the situation before she took maternity leave.

Rudolph v. Hechinger Co.

884 F.Supp. 184 (D.Md. 1995)

MESSITTE, District Judge.

This is another case, of a type seen with increasing frequency in federal courts, in which an employee seeks to transform arguably harsh treatment by an employer into a claim of statutory discrimination. Beyond pure speculation, however, the evidence in no way suggests that the employer's actions were unlawfully discriminatory, a burden of proof which the employee ultimately bears. Plaintiff Carol Rudolph has brought this suit against her former employer Hechinger Company, alleging discrimination on the basis of sex and pregnancy, in violation of Title VII of the Civil Rights Act of 1964.

Hechinger's is a publicly held company which operates retail do-it-yourself home centers in Washington, D.C., Maryland, Virginia, North Carolina, Pennsylvania, New York, Ohio, Delaware, New Jersey and Connecticut. Rudolph began her employment with Hechinger's as a part-time cashier in its Rockville, Maryland, store in 1975. She was transferred to Hechinger's Alexandria, Virginia facility, where she trained as a bookkeeper in a full-time position. By 1991, located in Richmond, she had progressed to the position of loss prevention supervisor for Hechinger's stores in the Richmond/Tidewater, Virginia geographical region. In this position she was responsible for preventing store losses, whether in the form of inventory or cash, at the stores assigned to her.

In March of 1992, Rudolph, unmarried at the time, was pregnant. She worked until March 27 before taking leave for the birth of her child, who was born on April 3. She did not return to her job until June 15, 1992. On that date, Tom Riley, a loss prevention regional manager for Hechinger's, and Carol Stevens, the company's Vice-President of Human Resources, met with Rudolph and informed her that her loss prevention supervisor position had been eliminated, that her employment was over. Rudolph's request to be demoted to loss prevention coordinator was denied.

At the time Rudolph went on maternity leave, Hechinger's was in the process of closing a number of its stores in the Tidewater region. By January of 1992, closures had taken place in all its stores in North Carolina as well as in Harrisonburg and Newport News, Virginia. All other stores in the Richmond/Tidewater area were being considered for closure. Prior to her leave, Stevens was aware that such closures were in process.

Riley, aware that stores in the Richmond/Tidewater area were going to close, also needed to make arrangements to cover Rudolph's store during her absence. Accordingly, Stores No. 71 and 72 were permanently reassigned to Alfred Baird, a second loss prevention supervisor responsible for the Richmond/Tidewater market, primarily North Carolina. Riley knew that Baird, having closed nine stores in the past, was experienced in that regard. The two Tidewater stores were in fact closed in July 1992. Rudolph's Richmond stores, Nos. 73, 74 and 78, as to which a final decision on closure had not been made when Rudolph went on leave, were temporarily assigned to Baird. These stores ultimately closed in January 1993.

Prior to departing on leave, Rudolph discussed with Riley the possibility that, due to store closings, her position might be eliminated. As it happened, Hechinger's acted on that possibility while Rudolph was away, deciding to terminate both her and Baird. Loss prevention coverage for the Richmond/Tidewater market was arranged through the Washington, D.C. region, with Felton Gilliam, a loss prevention supervisor from the D.C. market, assigned to supervise the remaining Richmond/Tidewater stores until they were closed.

Rudolph claims that, before going on leave, Stevens informed her that, if lay-offs were necessary, individuals would be selected on the basis of their past three performance reviews, with the poorest performers being selected for termination. On the basis of Hechinger's guidelines for selecting employees for lay off, Rudolph contends that her performance was superior to that of Gilliam, her replacement, since she had been ranked "very good," while he had only received a "satisfactory" ranking.

On this foundation, Rudolph constructs her claim that Hechinger's decided to terminate her based upon her sex, specifically because she was an "unwed mother" and because of "her inability to relocate."

McDonnell Douglas posits two ways in which to establish a prima facie case of discrimination. First, the employee may attempt to establish the case by direct evidence supporting an inference of discrimination. Alternatively, the employee may meet the four-part test originally articulated in *McDonnell Douglas* in the illegal hiring context, later adapted to the illegal discharge context. Rudolph offers no direct evidence of discrimination, seeking instead to meet the four-part test.

Although the parties spar over whether Rudolph's termination was a "reduction in force" (RIF) as opposed to a "market closing," for present purposes the Court will accept Rudolph's view that a RIF was involved. The four-part *McDonnell Douglas* calculus, then, adapted to the RIF situation, requires the following showing:

1) That the employee was protected under the employment discrimination statute;
2) That she was selected from the group or territory for termination;
3) That she was performing at a level substantially equivalent to the lowest level of those retained in the group or territory; and
4) That the process of selection produced a residual work force of persons in the group or territory containing some unprotected persons who were performing at a level lower than that at which the plaintiff was performing.

The Court will assume for present purposes that Rudolph has made out a prima facie case by this approach. Under the *McDonnell Douglas* scheme, the burden then shifts to Hechinger's to rebut an inference of discrimination by articulating a legitimate non-discriminatory reason for Rudolph's treatment. This burden Hechinger's unquestionably meets. A number of store closings were taking place throughout Rudolph's region, actually and prospectively, at the time of her termination. Whether her termination is viewed as a result of a RIF or a market closure, the point is that Hechinger's had a reason for her dismissal that was legitimate and non-discriminatory—a reduction in work force brought about by apparently lagging sales or other operational inefficiencies. Upon that proof, any presumption of discrimination created by Rudolph's prima facie showing "drops from the case," and she bears the ultimate burden of persuasion to prove that Hechinger's intentionally discriminated against her. Rudolph must do more than simply disprove Hechinger's articulated reason. She must instead establish that the articulated reasons were a pretext. "A reason cannot be proved to be 'a pretext for *discrimination*' unless it is shown *both* that the reason was false, *and* that discrimination was the real reason."

She presents, quite simply, no evidence that consideration of sex and pregnancy played any part in the termination process. Her own opinion, without more, cannot suffice to establish either a prima facie case or pretext. In other words, the record is devoid of any evidence raising a genuine issue of fact that Hechinger's action in this case was in any way based on illegal discrimination. From all that appears, her claim could be equally premised on her race, age, national origin, or religion. That gender or pregnancy had anything to do with her termination is no more evident than that any of these other statutorily prohibited factors played a role.

Judgment for Hechinger Co.

Employment Perspective

Christie Wesley, a financial analyst with Magnificent Mutual Funds, was a senior member of her department. While Christie was on family leave, Kurt Walker was promoted to department manager on the basis of being the senior member at the time that the promotion was made. Christie claimed that she did not forfeit her position of seniority while on family leave. Is she correct? Yes! Although she did not accrue time toward seniority while on leave, she must be accorded her status as senior member even though she is not there. ◆

Certification of a serious health problem may be required by an employer. The health care provider shall provide the date when the condition began, its likely duration, and a medical explanation of the condition. If the request for leave is to care for a spouse, child, or parent, then a statement by the health care provider is required, stating that the employee's services are needed and indicating the amount of time likely to be expended. If the employer doubts the validity of the certification, it can, at its own expense, require the employee to get a second opinion. If that opinion is in conflict, the employer may again, at its own expense, request a third opinion, which shall be the final arbitrator.

If the employee requests intermittent leave, then a certification of the medical necessity must be presented. The employer may temporarily transfer the employee to another position of equal pay and benefits that is less disruptive to the employer's work environment.

Employment Perspective

Pamela Whalen's daughter Julia has cancer. She is required to go for treatments three days a week during the afternoon. Pamela requests medical leave on an intermittent basis for three afternoons a week. In this manner, her twelve-week unpaid leave can be taken over a much longer period. Is this situation acceptable? Yes! ◆

PREGNANCY DISCRIMINATION

In 1978, discrimination on the basis of pregnancy became illegal in the United States, with passage of the Pregnancy Disability Act, an amendment to Title VII of the 1964 Civil Rights Act.

Pregnant women must be treated the same as other applicants or employees. They must be judged by their ability to perform rather than on their physical condition.

Pregnant Women in the Workplace

One half of all women who give birth each year are returning to their jobs before the child is one year old. On the other hand, an increasing number of women are choosing to remain at their jobs until they give birth. These women are working well into their ninth month.

In the next case, an unmarried teacher in a religiously affiliated school became pregnant. The church discharged her because that behavior was not in accord with its theology. She claimed that the church discriminated against her because of her pregnancy.

CASE

Boyd v. Harding Academy of Memphis, Inc.

887 F.Supp. 157 (W.D.Tenn. 1995)

McCALLA, District Judge.

Plaintiff, who is unmarried, was employed by defendant Harding Academy of Memphis, Inc., ("Harding Academy"), in January of 1992 as a teacher in a preschool facility known as Little Harding. Harding Academy is a religious school affiliated with the Church of Christ, and as such, expects that its teachers will adhere to the religious tenets it supports. All faculty members are required to be Christians with a preference given to Church of Christ members. Harding Academy uses as its religious tenets the teachings of the New Testament, and one of the religious principles embodied therein is that sex outside of marriage is proscribed. Plaintiff knew that Harding Academy was a church-related school and indicated on her employment application that she had a Christian background and believed in God.

In early February, 1993, Brenda Rubio, the director of the Little Harding program, was told by her assistant Sharon Cooper that plaintiff may be pregnant. That information, if true, would inequivocally establish that plaintiff had engaged in sex outside of marriage. Upon receiving this information, Brenda Rubio reported the information through her superior to Dr. Harold Bowie, the President and Chief Executive Officer of Harding Academy. Dr. Bowie required that the information be confirmed by direct conversation with plaintiff, and further directed that plaintiff be terminated if the information was true. At trial, Dr. Bowie testified that he determined to terminate plaintiff if it were verified that plaintiff was pregnant and unmarried, not because of the pregnancy per se, but because the facts would indicate that plaintiff engaged in sex outside of marriage.

At Dr. Bowie's instruction, a meeting was scheduled between plaintiff, Brenda Rubio, and Sharon Cooper. At that meeting, plaintiff admitted that she was pregnant. Plaintiff was then informed that she would be terminated but that she would be eligible for re-employment if she were to marry the father of the child. During this meeting, Brenda Rubio used words to the effect that plaintiff was being terminated because she was "pregnant and unwed." Plaintiff relies on the statements made by Brenda Rubio at this meeting in support of her allegations that her discharge from Harding Academy under the circumstances of her out of wedlock pregnancy constitutes impermissible gender discrimination. However, Brenda Rubio's testimony at trial also indicates that in explaining the reason for plaintiff's termination, Brenda Rubio used the phrase "pregnant and unwed" to mean plaintiff engaged in sex outside of marriage in violation of the religious principles subscribed to by Harding Academy. It is not disputed that Brenda Rubio did not have the power or authority to terminate plaintiff or any other employee of Harding Academy.

It is also undisputed that Dr. Bowie is the only person with the authority to terminate the employment of teachers at Harding Academy. Throughout Dr. Bowie's tenure as the chief administrative officer of Harding Academy, Dr. Bowie has discharged teachers, both male and female, for engaging in acts of sex outside of marriage, whether or not pregnancy resulted from the proscribed sexual conduct. No deviation from this doctrine-based policy was shown to the Court under circumstances where knowledge of an employee's sexual activity outside of marriage was made known to Dr. Bowie. Furthermore, it was not shown that women employees at Harding Academy are terminated solely on the basis of pregnancy. In fact, the testimony at trial demonstrated that many married women have become pregnant while working at Harding Academy and have remained employed during and after their pregnancies.

Conclusions of Law

Title VII of the Civil Rights Act of 1964 prohibits employment discrimination based on sex. Section 2000e-2 (a) states that:

> [i]t shall be an unlawful employment practice for any employer—
>
> (1) to fail or refuse to hire or to discharge any individual, or otherwise to discriminate against any individual with respect to his compensation, terms, conditions, or privileges of employment, because of such individual's race, color, religion, sex or national origin.

Title VII further defines sex discrimination as follows:

> The terms "because of sex" or "on the basis of sex" include, but are not limited to, because of or on the basis of pregnancy, childbirth, or related medical conditions; and women affected by pregnancy, childbirth, or related medical conditions shall be treated the same for all employment-related purposes. . . .
>
> Section 2000e (k), referred to as the Pregnancy Discrimination Act, makes clear that sex discrimination includes any adverse employment decision based upon pregnancy.
>
> (a) Inapplicability of subchapter to certain aliens and employees of religious entities
>
> This subchapter shall not apply to . . . a religious corporation, association, educational institution, or society with respect to the employment of individuals of a particular religion to perform work connected with the carrying on by such corporation, association, educational institution, or society of its activities.

Although this provision permits religious organizations to discriminate based on religion, religious employers are not immune from liability for discrimination based on race, sex, or national origin. In order for the religious entities exemption in Title VII to apply, a religious employer must make its employment decision upon a religious basis or criteria. In the present case, defendant Harding Academy asserts that plaintiff's termination was based on her violation of the religious tenet proscribing sex outside of marriage, which was evidenced by the fact of her out of wedlock pregnancy. Plaintiff, however, contends that the religious reason cited by defendant for her termination is simply a pretext for sex discrimination.

If the defendant can show a legitimate nondiscriminatory reason for its employment decision, the plaintiff must then show that the defendant's proffered reason is just a pretext for discrimination. In the present case, plaintiff asserts that she was terminated because she was pregnant, not because she violated Harding Academy's proscription against sex outside of marriage and that defendant's proffered reason for her termination is merely pretext for unlawful gender discrimination.

In support of this contention, plaintiff relies upon statements made to her by her supervisor, Brenda Rubio, on February 10, 1993, when plaintiff was terminated. During this meeting, Brenda Rubio used words to the effect that plaintiff was being terminated because she was "pregnant and unwed." Plaintiff asserts that such statements by Brenda Rubio demonstrate that her discharge from Harding Academy was based solely on her pregnancy and therefore constitutes impermissible gender discrimination.

At trial, Dr. Bowie's testimony clearly established that he did not receive information regarding plaintiff's prior miscarriage and that if he had received such information and it was confirmed then plaintiff would have been terminated according to Harding Academy's doctrine-based policy. Dr. Bowie also testified that plaintiff was terminated not because of her pregnancy per se, but because her pregnancy indicated that plaintiff engaged in sex outside of marriage as proscribed by Harding Academy. Dr. Bowie was a very credible witness and was not materially impeached in any respect. Based on Dr. Bowie's testimony, the fact that Dr. Bowie was the only person with the authority to terminate plaintiff, and the fact that Harding Academy has consistently discharged both male and female employees who engaged in sex outside of marriage, whether or not pregnancy resulted from the conduct, the Court finds that plaintiff has failed to show that defendant's proffered nondiscriminatory reason for plaintiff's termination was mere pretext for gender discrimination. Plaintiff having failed to sustain her burden of proof in this case, plaintiff's claim of gender discrimination under Title VII must be DENIED, and a judgment must be entered in favor of the defendant.

Judgment for Harding Academy of Memphis.

The issue in the following case is whether a club designed to provide positive role models for teenage girls may bar single pregnant workers. The employee in this case was dismissed because of her pregnancy. The club maintained that it was justified in doing so.

CASE

Chambers v. Omaha Girls Club, Inc.

840 F.2d 583 (8th Cir. 1988)

LAY, Chief Judge

The Omaha Girls Club's termination of its arts and crafts teacher because of her pregnancy is the most blatant form of sex discrimination that can exist. In my judgment the Girls Club's pregnancy-based discrimination constitutes a per se violation of Title VII of the Civil Rights Act of 1964. The proffered reasons for the discharge of Crystal Chambers are entirely inconsistent with Congress' avowed intent to "ensure that working women are protected against *all* forms of employment discrimination" and with its "unmistakable reaffirmation that sex discrimination includes discrimination based on pregnancy."

The action of the Girls Club is contrary to the letter of the law under the Pregnancy Discrimination Act of 1978 (PDA), the spirit of equal treatment for pregnant women intended by Congress under that Act, and decisions both of this court and of the Supreme Court of the United States.

The district court found that Chambers "was fired solely because of her pregnancy," but did not discuss the enactment of the PDA in 1978. Even prior to passage of the PDA such a finding was sufficient in this circuit to establish a prima facie violation of Title VII.

The district court found that the Girls Club had articulated a neutral reason for its rule barring single pregnant workers: to provide positive role models for the teenagers with whom the Girls Club worked. The court then shifted the burden back to the plaintiff to show that "the rule was a pretext for discriminating against *black women or single black women.*" The difficulty I have with this analysis is that when a court finds as a fact, as the district court did, that a plaintiff was fired "solely" because of membership in a protected class, the inquiry should be ended, unless the employer can establish that non-membership in the protected class is a BFOQ. There can be no issue of pretext—whether an alleged nondiscriminatory reason masks a discriminatory reason—when the employer openly admits the reason for the discharge was solely because of the employee's membership in a protected class. The issue of pretext is not involved. When this occurs we mistakenly substitute our judgment for that of the district court and attempt to make such judgment under standards the district court did not even consider.

In its discussion of Chambers's disparate *impact* claim, the district court stated that because the Girls Club "met its burden on the basis of business necessity, it was not necessary to determine

whether the evidence would satisfy a BFOQ, although presumably it would." Nonetheless the panel decides, based on the district court's findings with respect to the business necessity defense, that a BFOQ was shown. The Girls Club raised the business necessity defense to Chambers's *race* discrimination claim, however, which was not based on the disparate impact of the Girls Club role model rule on blacks. I respectfully submit that a business necessity defense to a race-based disparate impact claim is simply not equivalent to a BFOQ defense to a sex-based disparate treatment claim; the factual findings relevant to one defense are not necessarily relevant to or sufficient to sustain the other defense.

The BFOQ defense in a pregnancy discrimination case thus invokes only an extremely narrow inquiry: (1) what are the requirements of the *particular* job in question; and (2) is there objective and compelling proof that the excluded woman is unable to perform the duties that constitute the essence of that job because of her pregnancy.

The PDA and its legislative history contain numerous indications that Congress intended pregnancy to be a relevant consideration in an employer's decision to fire a worker only when the pregnancy affects the woman's physical capabilities such that the employer would fire *anyone* who was similarly physically affected. The language of the PDA itself suggests that Congress so intended:

The terms "because of sex" or "on the basis of sex" include, but are not limited to, because of or on the basis of pregnancy, childbirth, or *related medical conditions;* and women *affected by* pregnancy, childbirth, or related medical conditions shall be treated the same for all employment-related purposes, including receipt of benefits under fringe benefit programs, as other persons not so affected *but similar in their ability or inability to work.* Its use of the terms "related medical conditions" and "affected by" suggests that Congress thought of pregnancy as a physical condition that, like gender, is unrelated to job capabilities except in the narrowest of circumstances.

Moreover, by requiring employers to treat pregnant employees the same as other employees "not so affected but similar in their ability or inability to work," Congress must have been referring to *physical* ability to work; there is no other ability-to-work basis on which all pregnant women as a class can be compared to all non-pregnant persons. Congress clearly stated that pregnant women must be treated the same as those similarly situated, which presupposes that there are other workers who are in some sense similarly situated. Yet by treating pregnancy as a distasteful component of a negative "role model" rather than as a physical condition that may or may not affect one's ability to work, the employer here has relegated pregnant women to a class by themselves, incapable of being "similarly situated" to anyone. Such segregation is exactly the type of invidious discrimination that Congress intended to eradicate when it enacted the PDA.

As one commentator has stated:

"Accidents of the body," such as one's female sex and thus one's capacity to become pregnant, are not to be criteria for differentiation. Instead all employees, regardless of bodily differences, shall be judged on their ability to perform on the job. That the cause of disability is pregnancy becomes, like one's race or eye color, irrelevant to how one is treated.

Judgment for Chambers.

FETAL PROTECTION POLICIES

Companies that research, manufacture, warehouse, transport, and use hazardous chemicals and toxic waste are concerned from a liability standpoint about the effect these chemicals may have on their workers, particularly female workers in their childbearing years. While no adult is immune from the harmful effects of hazardous chemicals and toxic waste upon them, exposure of a fetus to toxic waste could result in deformities, diseases, brain dysfunction and cancer. The fetus's future quality of life may be severely jeopardized.

From an ethical viewpoint, companies should not want this to happen. From a liability perspective, companies do not want to become embroiled in expensive, time-consuming lawsuits that they will not win and that will result in a public-relations nightmare. To resolve this dilemma, fetus protection policies have been adopted by certain companies, which prohibit women in their childbearing years from working in an environment with hazardous chemicals and toxic waste. This places an economic burden on women who cannot find another position paying the same wages. Some companies will arrange transfers, but often the compensation is lower or without the benefit of overtime. This arrangement is not an adequate accommodation. Women claim that this action is discriminatory because their childbearing state has no impact on their job performance and therefore should not be a reason for exclusion.

In *United Auto Workers v. Johnson Controls, Inc.*, the Supreme Court ruled that fetal protection policies were a form of gender discrimination. This decision places companies in a catch-22 situation. If they exclude women, they are guilty of sex discrimination. If they permit women to work and their offspring are born defective or with a life-threatening illness, they will be held strictly liable for the injuries. A possible benefit could occur if exposure to the hazardous chemicals and toxic waste is minimized or eliminated as a result of the development of protective equipment and gear or the modification of the plant and working environment.

If that solution is impossible or not economically feasible, companies will either close down the plants or move them offshore where there will be no resulting liability for damage to the fetus. While the latter may be unethical, it is a realistic and practical solution. In any event, both actions will result in a loss of jobs for all workers, something that the women were initially trying to guard against.

The issue in the next case is whether a female worker whose position was eliminated while on family leave can claim sexual discrimination. Her employer claims that her department was restructured because of budgetary constraints.

CASE

Pearlstein v. Staten Island University Hosp.

886 F.Supp. 260 (E.D.N.Y. 1995)

SEYBERT, District Judge.

In this action, plaintiff, Janet Pearlstein, alleges that her former employer, Staten Island University Hospital (the "Hospital") discriminated against her on the basis of gender in violation of Title VII of the Civil Rights Act of 1964, by eliminating her managerial position in the budget and reimbursement department of the Hospital's finance division. The Hospital claims that Pearlstein's position was eliminated because of budgetary problems and in connection with a consolidation and restructuring of the Hospital's finance division following the merger between Staten Island Hospital and Richmond Memorial Hospital (the "Merger").

Currently before the Court is the Hospital's motion for summary judgment.

Background

Pearlstein began working at the Hospital in June 1988 as Budget Manager. Pearlstein's responsibilities involved making recommendations on the Hopsital's budget and budget process. She was initially responsible for supervising one employee, a statistical clerk. Pearlstein acknowledged in her deposition testimony that her position was at the

lowest rung of the managerial ladder within the Hospital's finance division.

Until January 1989, Pearlstein reported to Dennis Hill, Director of Budget and Reimbursement. As a result of the Merger, in January 1989, Pearlstein began reporting to Lee Amato, the former Director of Budget at Richmond Memorial Hospital. Amato, in turn, reported to Hill. According to Hill's deposition testimony, one other woman, Laura Thompson, who prior to the Merger worked at the Richmond Memorial Hospital, continued to work in a managerial capacity within the budget and reimbursement department after the Merger.

In August 1989, Pearlstein informed Amato that she had decided to adopt a child that was to be born sometime in late September 1989. Pearlstein requested that Amato grant her an unpaid four-month leave to commence after the adoption. Pearlstein testified that she had requested this unpaid leave after concluding, through informal discussions with various colleagues at the Hospital and reading a Hospital manual, the title of which she could not recall, that such leave was available to all of the Hospital women employees. According to Pearlstein, Amato congratulated her after hearing the news and told her that she was free to take the leave.

On October 3, 1989, Pearlstein telephoned Amato at home and informed him that because her adopted child was in the process being born, her leave of absence would begin immediately. Pearlstein indicated that "he said that was fine. And that when I returned home after, you know, picking up my child, to come to the hospital and sign forms." It was Pearlstein's understanding that she would resume her position once her leave ended.

Pearlstein went to the Hospital on October 20, 1989, to sign the requisite forms and was informed by Amato that her leave had been approved and was asked when she would return to work. Pearlstein stated that she "would like the four month leave. February 5th I would like to return. He said, "that's fine." Until January 1990, Pearlstein did not again discuss her leave with her supervisors.

Hill testified at his deposition that Amato informed him in mid-August 1989 that Amato had granted Pearlstein a leave of absence to care for the child she was in the process of adopting. Upon hearing this plan, Hill had been "happy" for Pearlstein "because she was trying for so long to have a child."

Pearlstein appears to have commenced her leave at a time when the Hospital's finance division was in a state of flux. Hill claims that in July 1989, he had contacted the Hospital's personnel department to discuss the effects of the Merger on the budget and reimbursement department. Hill asserts that he was concerned abut the overlapping responsibilities among his managers, Amato, Pearlstein and Thompson. The personnel department according to Hill, responded that his concerns regarding overlap were valid and would need to be addressed in the future. According to a memorandum, dated January 28, 1990, prepared by Hill (the "January 1990 Memorandum"), Pearlstein's role was specifically considered at the July 1989 meeting; "it was obvious that she no longer functioned in a managerial capacity (but her salary continued at a manager's level). It was agreed that a salary adjustment would not be made at the time, and that any appropriate adjustment would be made by reducing future pay increases."

In December 1989 and January 1990, the Hospital allegedly discovered that the effect of the Merger would cause a budgetary shortfall for 1990. Hill testified in his deposition that the Hospital's president instructed the vice president of each area to "achieve a dollar budget reduction" to address this anticipated budgetary shortfall.

Hill decided in the middle of January 1990, that Pearlstein's position would be the one to be downgraded. On January 22, 1990, while she was still on leave, Pearlstein received a telephone call from Hill informing her that for budgetary reasons, her position was being eliminated. Hill stated that since Pearlstein's "skills were so good," he wanted to offer her a non-managerial position as a financial analyst at the Hospital, earning thirty percent less income. Pearlstein did not accept his job offer.

Pearlstein has simply failed to adduce any factual dispute that, viewed in a light most favorable to her, raises a material issue for trial on whether the Hospital's claimed business reasons for downgrading Pearlstein's position were a pretext for discrimination.

In so concluding, the Court is mindful that summary judgment is ordinarily inappropriate in an employment discrimination suit where an individual's intent and state of mind are implicated.

Judgment for S.I. University Hospital.

The following case addresses the question of whether an employee's termination was based on her pregnancy. The employer argued that it was based on her competency. She retorted that it was a pretext used to disguise the discriminatory intent of her employer.

CASE

Hansen v. Dean Witter Reynolds, Inc.

887 F.Supp. 669 (S.D.N.Y. 1995)

BAER, District Judge.

Plaintiff Michele Hansen brought this action under Title VII of the Civil Rights Act of 1964, The Pregnancy Discrimination Act, 42 U.S.C. #2000e (k), and the New York Human Rights Law, claiming sex and pregnancy discrimination by her former employer, defendant Dean Witter Reynolds, Inc. ("Dean Witter") in the termination of her employment as Dean Witter's Assistant Vice President/Intermediate Mortgage-Backed "Repo" Trader.

I find that plaintiff has failed to establish that (1) Dean Witter terminated her on the basis of her sex and/or her pregnancy, or that (2) Dean Witter's reasons for terminating her employment were pretextual. Plaintiff's complaint must therefore be dismissed.

The Law

Relevant Statutes

Title VII of the Civil Rights Act of 1964 42 U.S.C. #2000e-2(a) (1), provides that it is unlawful for "an employer to fail or refuse to hire or to discharge any individual . . . with respect to his or her compensation, terms, conditions or privileges of employment, because of such individual's race, color, religion, sex or national origin." In 1978, pregnancy discrimination was also expressly prohibited as constituting impermissible discrimination on the basis of sex. The New York State equivalent of the federal Title VII protections are found in the New York Human Rights Law.

One manner of establishing a prima facie case of sex discrimination under Title VII involves plaintiff showing that she was treated less favorably than comparable male employees in circumstances from which a gender based motive could be inferred.

Once plaintiff has established her prima facie case, the burden shifts to the defendant to show that unlawful discrimination did not cause the subject's employment action. If the employer has articulated a legitimate reason for the challenged employment decision, plaintiff must establish that the proffered reason is a pretext for discrimination.

The ultimate burden of persuasion, as always, rests with the plaintiff to persuade the factfinder that the defendant intentionally discriminated against her. This may be accomplished "either directly by persuading the court that a discriminatory reason more likely motivated the employer or indirectly by showing that the employer's proffered explanation is unworthy of credence."

At trial, plaintiff's claim that her discharge from Dean Witter resulted from sex and pregnancy discrimination relied heavily on Dean Witter's decision to retain Melvin Relova, a man, on its TFU desk at the time of plaintiff's discharge. Plaintiff attempted in her case-in-chief to show that Relova was less qualified than she, and therefore, that her termination from Dean Witter must have been discriminatory. For the reasons stated below, I find plaintiff's argument unpersuasive.

At the outset, I find that Hansen has not put forth sufficient evidence of pregnancy discrimination. Plaintiff proffered as evidence of her pregnancy discrimination claim isolated statements made by Ian Berstein, a Dean Witter manager, about how difficult it was to raise children in New

York. I find credible Bernstein's assertion that these comments were conversational in nature. His testimony included the fact that he himself had twins. I can find nothing in Berstein's testimony to suggest that his comments evidenced a discriminatory attitude toward pregnant women in that workplace. This is made especially clear by juxtaposing Bernstein's comments with Dean Witter's consistent policy that permitted pregnant employees to retain their position at Dean Witter following their pregnancies, including plaintiff herself following her 1987 pregnancy. While Dean Witter's treatment of other pregnant women, as well as Hansen in 1987, cannot preclude a finding of discrimination in the instant case, it does appear inconsistent with plaintiff's claim and therefore militates against that finding. I turn now to Hansen's sex discrimination claim.

Bernstein testified that Relova was the best qualified to staff the TFU desk. He based that assessment on "having worked with those individuals for several years in the capital markets area, as well as having supervised them for a period of time." Bernstein testified that his assessment was also based on reviews from the sales force that were generally much more favorable towards Melvyn's. . . .

In view of the findings, I conclude that plaintiff has not met her burden of proving that sex and/or pregnancy discrimination caused her termination. The record contains ample testimony supporting Dean Witter's position that Relova was better qualified for the position than Hansen. Indeed, the law provides that, in discrimination actions, the court is not to second-guess the defendant's judgment; the factfinder should not assess "whether the employer's decision was erroneous or even rational, so long as the employer's actions were not taken for a discriminatory reason."

Conclusion

For the reasons stated above, I find that plaintiff has failed to satisfy her burden of proof that Dean Witter's decision to retain Melvyn Relova and terminate plaintiff was motivated by the plaintiff's sex and/or pregnancy. The complaint is dismissed.

Judgment for Dean Witter.

In the following case, an employer terminated an employee because at the time of her interview she knew she was pregnant and withheld that fact.

CASE

Lysak v. Seiler Corp.

614 N.E.2d 991 (Mass. 1993)

O'CONNOR, Justice.

The plaintiff, Patricia Lysak, states in her complaint that her employer, the defendant, The Seiler Corporation, terminated her employment because she was pregnant, and that therefore the termination violated the prohibition against discrimination in employment because of sex.

We summarize the evidence relevant to the first two issues, beginning with the plaintiff's testimony. The plaintiff testified that, after being interviewed on February 20, 1987, by William Zammer, the defendant's president, she was employed by the defendant as its marketing director beginning March 23, 1987. On April 24, 1987, she told Zammer that she was pregnant. Zammer was extremely upset by that revelation. He told her that the situation was "untenable" and that she could not continue in the position for which she had been employed. He said that he felt "personally betrayed." Zammer told her that she had lied to him about being career oriented. She denied that she had lied. On the Monday following April 24, the plaintiff proposed to Zammer that her employee status be terminated and that, instead, she be considered an independent contractor. The plaintiff and defendant then entered into such a relationship which lasted until the middle of July, 1987.

According to the plaintiff's testimony, when Zammer interviewed her for employment on February 10, 1987, Zammer and she did not discuss any plans she might have had with regard to either having or not having more children. The plaintiff was pregnant at the time of her interview with Zammer and, because of positive laboratory tests and her doctor's confirmation, she knew at that time she was pregnant.

Zammer's testimony in substance was that, when he and the plaintiff first met on February 20, 1987, she told him, without any solicitation by him, that her husband stayed home and took care of their two children with the help of an au pair and that "she was not planning on having any more kids." Zammer's testimony was that he would have hired the plaintiff if he had known she was pregnant, but, because she told him, without being asked, that she had no intention of having more children and that was a lie, he felt betrayed. Zammer testified that on the Monday following the April 24 disclosure of her pregnancy, the plaintiff told him that she had made a mistake, that she had lied to him and wanted to make it up to him. According to his testimony, Zammer told the plaintiff that she had lied to him and he would not be able to trust her anymore. Nevertheless, he accepted her proposal that she and the defendant would enter into an independent contractor relationship because the defendant had some unfinished projects that needed prompt completion and she could complete them.

The plaintiff argues that, "accepting the defendant's version of the facts," that is, that Zammer discharged the plaintiff for giving unsolicited false information about whether she was pregnant, Zammer, and therefore the defendant, violated the law by discharging the plaintiff, at least constructively, on April 24, 1987. Therefore, the plaintiff argues, the discharge cannot stand.

A rule that bars an employer from discharging an employee because of the employee's false responses to the employer's unlawful inquiries, does not bar a discharge due to unsolicited, volunteered, false statements made by the employee.

Here there was no evidence, binding on the defendant, that unlawful inquiries had been made. Therefore, the evidence warranted the jury's verdict that the defendant's discharge of the plaintiff was lawful, and the plaintiff was not entitled to a directed verdict.

Judgment for Seiler Corp.

Pregnancy disability must not be viewed any differently than any other disability.

The question in the next case is whether protection is afforded against pregnancy discrimination under the state statute.

Badih v. Myers

43 Cal.Rptr.2d 229 (Cal.App. 1 Dist. 1995)

DOSSEE, Associate Justice.

On June 25, 1990, Badih filed a complaint against Myers alleging, among other things, that Myers had discriminated against her on the basis of race and pregnancy. The complaint also alleged that Badih had attempted to file a complaint with the Department of Fair Employment and Housing (FEHA) but that the department had refused to accept the complaint because Myers employed less than five people.

At trial, Badih gave the following testimony: In January 1987, Badih, a recent immigrant from the West African nation of Sierra Leone, began working as a medical assistant in the offices of Myers, a medical doctor. About nine months later, she started dating Constantine Kalaveras. Myers, who disapproved of interracial relationships, referred to Kalaveras as "the White guy."

In December 1988, Badih married Kalaveras. When Badih told Myers about the marriage, "he slapped on the table, stood up, and started yelling and hollering about what a mistake I've made, how much I'm going to regret this, and how disappointed he is in me, that he's never seen an African that . . . came to this country and started, you know, doing things I did, you know, hanging—marrying my husband and all that, having a White boyfriend and finally marrying him. And he gave me long lectures how marriages like that don't last and how they end up in tragedy and it's very bad, especially if children get involved and all that, and he just got so upset."

On September 6, 1989, Badih told Myers that she was pregnant. According to Badih, Myers replied, "'I just can't believe you. I just don't know what to say to you anymore. It seems like everything I ever told you just went right in vain. First you introduce me to this White guy, and then you marry him, and then you're having his baby. What's next? I can't take this anymore. If you told me you were going to get married and have babies, I wouldn't have hired you in the first place. I need an office girl when I need her, not a person that has responsibilities the way you do now. And . . . I am just so sorry, but I don't think I can take this anymore. You're going to have to go.'" Badih asked Myers whether he was serious. He told her that he was and that her last day would be September 15. On September 13, Myers threatened to call security if Badih did not leave immediately. Badih complied.

Myers denied that he had fired Badih because she was pregnant. According to Myers, Badih quit her job.

Following its deliberations, the jury found that Myers had not terminated Badih's employment on the basis of race but that he had terminated her employment on the basis of pregnancy. The jury awarded $20,226 in damages to Badih. The trial curt subsequently granted Badih's motion for attorney fees. Myers has filed timely notices of appeal from both the judgment and the attorney fees order.

Badih argues that pregnancy discrimination in employment is a form of sex discrimination and, as such, is prohibited not only by the FEHA but also by article I, section 8 of the California Constitution. For the reasons discussed below, we agree.

The question of whether pregnancy discrimination in employment is a form of sex discrimination is not without controversy. In *Geduldig v. Aiello* the United States Supreme Court, in the context of the equal protection clause of the United States Constitution, concluded that "while it is true that only women can become pregnant, it does not follow that every legislative classification concerning pregnancy is a sex-based classification. . . . Normal pregnancy is an objectively identifiable physical condition with unique characteristics. Absent a showing that distinctions involving pregnancy are mere pretexts designed to effect an invidious discrimination against the members of one sex or the other, lawmakers are constitutionally free to include or exclude pregnancy from the coverage of legislation such as this on any reasonable basis, just as with respect to any other physical condition. The lack of identity between the excluded disability pregnancy and gender as such under this insurance program becomes clear upon the most cursory analysis. The program divides potential recipients into two groups—pregnant women and non-pregnant persons. While the first group is exclusively female, the second includes members of both sexes. The fiscal and actuarial benefits of the program thus accrue to members of both sexes." In *General Electric Co. v. Gilbert,* the court extended the reasoning of *Geduldig* to employment discrimination cases brought under Title VII of the Civil Rights Act of 1964.

Both the California Legislature and the United States Congress reacted swiftly to the *Gilbert* decision. In 1978, the California Legislature amended the Fair Employment Practices Act (later recodified as the FEHA) to add a provision specifically prohibiting pregnancy discrimination in employment. The provision states that it "shall not be construed to affect any other provision of law relating to sex discrimination or pregnancy." Also in 1978, the United States Congress amended Title VII to provide that "the terms 'because of sex' or 'on the basis of sex' include, but are not limited to, because of or on the basis of pregnancy, childbirth, or related medical conditions." "When Congress amended Title VII in 1978, it unambiguously expressed its disapproval of both the holding and the reasoning of the Court in the *Gilbert* decision."

With this background in mind, we turn to the question at hand—namely, whether pregnancy discrimination is a form of sex discrimination under article I, section 8 of the California Constitution.

In short, we conclude that pregnancy discrimination is a form of sex discrimination under article I, section 8 of the California Constitution. Since article I, section 8 expresses a fundamental public policy against sex discrimination in employment, Badih was properly allowed to maintain her cause of action for wrongful discharge in contravention of public policy.

Judgment for Badih.

In the next case, an employer attempted to prohibit fertile woman from the workplace to avoid damage to fetuses. Female employees claimed this policy was an attempt to discriminate against pregnant women and women who potentially could become pregnant.

CASE

International Union, United Automobile, Aerospace and Agricultural Implement Workers of America, UAW v. Johnson Controls, Inc.

499 U.S. 187 (1991)

JUSTICE BLACKMUN delivered the opinion of the Court.

In this case we are concerned with an employer's genderbased fetal-protection policy. May an employer exclude a fertile female employee from certain jobs because of its concern for the health of the fetus the woman might conceive?

Before the Civil Rights Act of 1964, became law, Johnson Controls did not employ any woman in a battery-manufacturing job. In June 1977, however, it announced its first official policy concerning its employment of women in lead-exposure work:

"Protection of the health of the unborn child is the immediate and direct responsibility of the prospective parents. While the medical profession and the company can support them in the exercise of this responsibility, it cannot assume it for them without simultaneously infringing their rights as persons."

I

". . . Since not all women who can become mothers wish to become mothers (or will become mothers), it would appear to be illegal discrimination to treat all who are capable of pregnancy as though they will become pregnant."

Consistent with that view, Johnson Controls "stopped short of excluding women capable of bearing children from lead exposure," but emphasized that a woman who expected to have a child should not choose a job in which she would have such exposure. The company also required a woman who wished to be considered for employment to sign a statement that she had been advised of the risk of having a child while she was exposed to lead. The statement informed the woman that although there was evidence "that women exposed to lead have a higher rate of abortion," this evidence was "not as clear . . . as the relationship between cigarette smoking and cancer," but that it was, "medically speaking, just good sense not to run that risk if you want children and do not want to expose the unborn child to risk, however small. . . ."

Five years later, in 1982, Johnson Controls shifted from a policy of warning to a policy of exclusion. Between 1979 and 1983, eight employees became pregnant while maintaining blood lead levels in excess of 30 micrograms per deciliter. This appeared to be the critical level noted by the Occupational Health and Safety Administration (OSHA) for a worker who was planning to have a family. The company responded by announcing a broad exclusion of women from jobs that exposed them to lead: " . . . It is Johnson Controls' policy that women who are pregnant or who are capable of bearing children will not be placed into jobs involving lead exposure or which could expose them to lead through the exercise of job bidding, bumping, transfer or promotion rights."

The policy defined "women . . . capable of bearing children" as "all women except those whose inability to bear children is medically documented." It further stated that an unacceptable work station was one where, "over the past year," an employee had recorded a blood lead level of more than 30 micrograms per deciliter or the work site had yielded an air sample containing a lead level in excess of 30 micrograms per cubic meter.

II

In April 1984, petitioners filed in the United States District Court for the Eastern District of Wisconsin a class action challenging Johnson Controls' fetal-protection policy as sex discrimination that violated Title VII of the Civil Rights Act of 1964. Among the individual plaintiffs were petitioners Mary Craig, who had chosen to be sterilized in order to avoid losing her job, Elsie Nason, a 50-year-old divorcee, who had suffered a loss in compensation when she was transferred out of a job where she was exposed to lead, and Donald Penney, who had been denied a request for a leave of absence for the purpose of lowering his lead level because he intended to become a father. Upon stipulation of the parties, the District Court certified a class consisting of "all past, present and future production and maintenance employees" in United Auto Workers bargaining units at nine of Johnson Controls' plants "who have been and continue to be affected by the employer's Fetal Protection Policy implemented in 1982."

The District Court granted summary judgment for defendant-respondent Johnson Controls. Applying a three-part business necessity defense derived from fetal-protection cases in the Courts of Appeals for the Fourth and Eleventh Circuits, the District Court concluded that while "there is a disagreement among the experts regarding the effect of lead on the fetus," the hazard to the fetus through exposure to lead was established by "a considerable body of opinion"; that although "expert opinion has been provided which holds that lead also affects the reproductive abilities of men and women . . . and that these effects are as great as the effects of exposure of the fetus . . . a great body of experts are of the opinion that the fetus is more vulnerable to levels of lead that would not affect adults"; and that petitioners had "failed to establish that there is an acceptable alternative policy which would protect the fetus." The court stated that, in view of this disposition of the business necessity defense, it did not "have to undertake a bona fide occupational qualification's (BFOQ) analysis."

The Court of Appeals for the Seventh Circuit, sitting en banc, affirmed the summary judgment by a 7-to-4 vote. The majority held that the proper standard for evaluating the fetal-protection policy was the defense of business necessity; that Johnson Controls was entitled to summary judgment under that defense; and that even if the proper standard was a BFOQ, Johnson Controls still was entitled to summary judgment.

The Court of Appeals, first reviewed fetal-protection opinions from the Eleventh and Fourth Circuits. Those opinions established the three-step business necessity inquiry: whether there is a substantial health risk to the fetus; whether transmission of the hazard to the fetus occurs only through women; and whether there is a less discriminatory alternative equally capable of preventing the health hazard to the fetus. The Court of Appeals agreed with the Eleventh and Fourth Circuits that "the components of the business necessity defense the courts of appeals and the EEOC have utilized in fetal protection cases balance the interests of the employer, the employee and the unborn child in a manner consistent with Title VII." The court further noted that, under *Wards Cove Packing Co. v. Atonio,* the burden of persuasion remained on the plaintiff in challenging a business necessity defense, and—unlike the Fourth and Eleventh Circuits—it thus imposed the burden on the plaintiffs for all three steps.

Applying this business necessity defense, the Court of Appeals ruled that Johnson Controls should prevail. Specifically, the court concluded that there was no genuine issue of material fact about the substantial health-risk factor because the parties agreed that there was a substantial risk to a fetus from lead exposure. The Court of Appeals also concluded that, unlike the evidence of risk to the fetus from the mother's exposure, the evidence of risk from the father's exposure, which petitioners presented, "is, at best, speculative and unconvincing."

The en banc majority ruled that industrial safety is part of the essence of respondent's business, and that the fetal-protection policy is reasonably necessary to further that concern.

III

The bias in Johnson Controls' policy is obvious. Fertile men, but not fertile women, are given a choice as to whether they wish to risk their reproductive health for a particular job. Section 703 (a) of the Civil Rights Act of 1964, 42 U.S.C. 2000e-2(a), prohibits sexbased classifications in terms and conditions of employment, in hiring and discharging decisions, and in other employment decisions that adversely affect an employee's status. Respondent's fetal-protection policy explicitly discriminates against women on the basis of their sex. The policy excludes women with childbearing capacity from lead-exposed jobs and so creates a facial classification based on gender. Respondent assumes as much in its brief before this Court.

First, Johnson Controls' policy classifies on the basis of gender and childbearing capacity, rather than fertility alone. Respondent does not seek to protect the unconceived children of all its employees. Despite evidence in the record about the debilitating effect of lead exposure on the male reproductive system, Johnson Controls is concerned only with the harms that may befall the unborn offspring of its female employees.

Our conclusion is bolstered by the Pregnancy Discrimination Act of 1978 (PDA), Congress explicitly provided that, for purposes of Title VII, discrimination "on the basis of sex" includes discrimination "because of or on the basis of pregnancy, childbirth, or related medical conditions." "The Pregnancy Discrimination Act has now made clear that, for all Title VII purposes, discrimination based on a woman's pregnancy is, on its face, discrimination because of her sex." In its use of the words "capable of bearing children' in the 1982 policy statement as the criterion for exclusion, Johnson Controls explicitly classifies on the basis of potential for pregnancy. Under the PDA, such a classification must be regarded, for Title VII purposes, in the same light as explicit sex discrimination. Respondent has chosen to treat all its female employees as potentially pregnant; that choice evinces discrimination on the basis of sex.

We concluded above that Johnson Controls' policy is not neutral because it does not apply to the reproductive capacity of the company's male employees in the same way as it applies to that of the females. Moreover, the absence of a malevolent motive does not convert a facially discriminatory policy into a neutral policy with a discriminatory effect. Whether an employment practice involves disparate treatment through explicit facial discrimination does not depend on why the employer discriminates but rather on the explicit terms of the discrimination.

In sum, Johnson Controls' policy "does not pass the simple test of whether the evidence shows 'treatment of a person in a manner which but for that person's sex would be different.'" We hold that Johnson Controls' fetal-protection policy is sex discrimination forbidden under Title VII unless respondent can establish that sex is a "bona fide occupational qualification."

IV

Under Title VII, an employer may discriminate on the basis of "religion, sex, or national origin in those certain instances where religion, sex, or national origin is a bona fide occupational qualification reasonably necessary to the normal operation of that particular business or enterprise." 42 U.S. C. 2000e-2 (e) (1). We therefore turn to the question whether Johnson Controls' fetal-protection policy is one of those "certain instances" that come within the BFOQ exception.

The BFOQ defense is written narrowly, and this Court has read it narrowly.

The wording of the BFOQ defense contains several terms of restriction that indicate that the exception reaches only special situations. The statute thus limits the situations in which discrimination is permissible to "certain instances" where sex discrimination is "reasonably necessary" to the "normal operation" of the "particular" business. Each one of these terms—certain, normal, particular—prevents the use of general subjective standards and favors an objective, verifiable requirement. But the most telling term is "occupational"; this indicates that these objective, verifiable requirements must concern job-related skills and aptitudes.

The unconceived fetuses of Johnson Controls' female employees, however, are neither customers nor third parties whose safety is essential to the business of battery manufacturing. No one can disregard the possibility of injury to future children; the BFOQ, however, is not so broad that it transforms this deep social concern into an essential aspect of batterymaking.

Our case law, therefore, makes clear that the safety exception is limited to instances in which sex or pregnancy actually interferes with the employee's ability to perform the job. This approach is consistent with the language of the BFOQ provision itself, for it suggests that permissible distinctions based on sex must relate to ability to perform the duties of the job. Johnson Controls suggests, however, that we expand the exception to allow fetal-protection policies that mandate particular standards for pregnant or fertile women. We decline to do so. Such an expansion contradicts not only the language of the BFOQ and the narrowness of its exception but the plain language and history of the Pregnancy Discrimination Act.

The PDA's amendment to Title VII contains a BFOQ standard of its own: unless pregnant employees differ from others "in their ability or inability to work," they must be "treated the same" as other employees "for all employment related purposes." 42 U.S.C. 2000e(k). This language clearly sets forth Congress' remedy for discrimination on the basis of pregnancy and potential pregnancy. Women who are either pregnant or potentially pregnant must be treated like others "similar in their ability . . . to work." In other words, women as capable of doing their jobs as their male counterparts may not be forced to choose between having a child and having a job.

We conclude that the language of both the BFOQ provision and the PDA which amended it, as well as the legislative history and the case law, prohibit an employer from discriminating against a woman because of her capacity to become pregnant unless her reproductive potential prevents her from performing the duties of her job.

V

We have no difficulty concluding that Johnson Controls cannot establish a BFOQ. Fertile women, as far as appears in the record, participate in the manufacture of batteries as efficiently as anyone else. Johnson Controls' professed moral and ethical concerns about the welfare of the next generation do not suffice to establish a BFOQ of female sterility. Decisions about the welfare of future children must be left to the parents who conceive, bear, support, and raise them rather than to the employers who hire those parents. Congress has mandated this choice through Title VII, as amended by the Pregnancy Discrimination Act. Johnson Controls has attempted to exclude women because of their reproductive capacity. Title VII and the PDA simply do not allow a woman's dismissal because of her failure to submit to sterilization.

VI

Our holding today that Title VII, as so amended, forbids sex-specific fetal-protection policies is neither remarkable nor unprecedented. Concern for a woman's existing or potential offspring historically has been the excuse for denying women equal employment opportunities. Congress in the PDA prohibited discrimination on the basis of a woman's ability to become pregnant. We do no more than hold that the Pregnancy Discrimination Act means what it says.

It is no more appropriate for the courts than it is for individual employers to decide whether a woman's reproductive role is more important to herself and her family than her economic role. Congress has left this choice to the woman as hers to make.

The judgment of the Court of Appeals is reversed and the case is remanded for further proceedings consistent with this opinion.

It is so ordered.
Judgment for UAW.

Some employers have instituted pre-natal counseling programs to give medical and emotional assistance. This reduces absenteeism, minimizes complications during the pregnancy and otherwise helps a woman to work longer and more productively during the pregnancy.

With employer sponsored programs, women are learning morning sickness and fatigue are common ailments to pregnant women. They are adjusting their work days to perform their most important tasks at the time of the day when they are most likely going to feel well.

Some companies have nurses and counselors on call to respond to their pregnant employees' needs. The results of these programs mean better health for pregnant women employees and their babies and minimal loss of employee efficiency. Some employers are contributing a portion of the increased savings to more comprehensive obstetrics care coverage.

The plight of pregnant women and mothers with small children which in past times had been neglected, has now received the attention it deserves. Attitudes concerning their employment capability are changing with time. Whereas before it can be said that they needed the companies, as the labor shortage increases, it is turning out that companies need them. The greatest thing that can happen to these women is to be needed, wanted, and employed.

REVIEW QUESTIONS

1. Explain the significance of the Family Medical Leave Act.
2. What are the eligibility requirements?
3. For what duration may family or medical leave be taken?
4. Define serious health conditions.
5. Is the employee entitled to health benefits while on leave?
6. What percentage of women return to the job within one year of giving birth?
7. Is pregnancy a disability?
8. Explain the significance of the Pregnancy Disability Act.
9. With whom should pregnant women file complaints of discrimination?
10. Can pregnancy ever be considered a bona fide occupational qualification?
11. A temporarily disabled male employee sought to receive the same treatment afforded to a female temporarily disabled by pregnancy. His claim was not meritorious. He claimed reverse discrimination. What was the result? *Newport News Shipbuilding & Dry Dock Co. v. EEOC,* 962 U.S. 669 (1983)

12. Gilbert, who was pregnant, sued General Electric, claiming that it discriminated against pregnant women by excluding pregnancy from its disability coverage. General Electric's reason was that its disability coverage was intended to apply evenly to both sexes. What was the result? *General Electric Co. v. Gilbert,* 429 U.S. 125 (1976)
13. The EEOC brought suit against the Newport News Shipbuilding & Dry Dock Co. for discriminating against its male employees. Newport News provided less coverage for the pregnant spouses of male employees than for pregnant female employees. What was the result? *Newport News Shipbuilding & Dry Dock Co. v. Equal Employment Opportunity Commission,* 462 U.S. 669 (1983)
14. After expiration of her pregnancy disability leave, an employee requested further leave for child care, specifically breast feeding. Her employer denied her request. She sued, claiming sexual discrimination due to her pregnancy. What was the result? *Barrash v. Bowen,* 846 F.2d 927 (4th Cir. 1988)
15. Phillips, who was pregnant, was discharged from Martin Marrietta Corp. because she was not married. May the corporation pass judgment on her morality? What was the result? *Phillips v. Martin Marrietta Corp.,* 400 U.S. 542 (1971)
16. If an employer attempted to judge the morality of women employees, could it discriminate against unwed mothers?
17. In the case on pp. 318, should an employer have to accommodate a pregnant worker even though the accommodation is disruptive to the workplace?
18. In the case on pp. 324, must an applicant disclose the fact that she is pregnant?
19. Is it acceptable for an employer to ask all female applicants if they are pregnant?
20. In the case on pp. 308 is there any justifiable reason to deny a pregnant employee maternity leave?

Family and Medical Leave Act
29 U.S.C. 2601–2654

Sec. 101. Definitions.

(2) ELIGIBLE EMPLOYEE.
(A) IN GENERAL.—The term "eligible employee" means an employee who has been employed—
(i) for at least 12 months by the employer with respect to whom leave was requested under section 102; and
(ii) for at least 1,250 hours of service with such employer during the previous 12-month period.

(5) EMPLOYMENT BENEFITS.—The term "employment benefits" means all benefits provided or made available to employees by an employer, including group life insurance, health insurance, disability insurance, sick leave, annual leave, educational benefits, and pensions, regardless of whether such benefits are provided by a practice or written policy of an employer or through an "employee benefit plan," as defined in section 3(3) of the Employee Retirement Income Security Act of 1974.

(11) SERIOUS HEALTH CONDITION.—The term "serious health condition" means an illness, injury, impairment, or physical or mental condition that involves—
(A) inpatient care in a hospital, hospice, or residential medical care facility; or

(B) continuing treatment by a health care provider.

(12) SON OR DAUGHTER.—The term "son or daughter" means a biological, adopted, or foster child, a stepchild, a legal ward, or a person standing in loco parentis, who is—

(A) under 18 years of age; or

(B) 18 years of age or older and incapable of self-care because of a mental or physical disability.

(13) SPOUSE.—The term "spouse" means a husband or wife, as the case may be.

Sec. 102. Leave Requirement.

(a) IN GENERAL.—

(1) ENTITLEMENT TO LEAVE.—Subject to section 103, an eligible employee shall be entitled to a total of 12 workweeks of leave during any 12-month period for one or more of the following:

(A) Because of the birth of a son or daughter of the employee and in order to care for such son or daughter.

(B) Because of the placement of a son or daughter with the employee for adoption or foster care.

(C) In order to care for the spouse, or a son, daughter, or parent, of the employee, if such spouse, son, daughter, or parent has a serious health condition.

(D) Because of a serious health condition that makes the employee unable to perform the functions of the position of such employee.

(2) EXPIRATION OF ENTITLEMENT.—The entitlement to leave under subparagraphs (A) and (B) of paragraph (1) for a birth of placement of a son or daughter shall expire at the end of the 12-month period beginning on the date of such birth or placement.

(b) LEAVE TAKEN INTERMITTENTLY OR ON A REDUCED LEAVE SCHEDULE.—

(1) IN GENERAL.—Leave under subparagraph (A) or (B) of subsection (a)(1) shall not be taken by an employee intermittently or on a reduced leave schedule unless the employee and the employer of the employee agree otherwise.

(2) ALTERNATIVE POSITION.—If an employee requests intermittent leave, or leave on a reduced leave schedule, under subparagraph (C) or (D) of subsection (a)(1), that is foreseeable based on planned medical treatment, the employer may require such employee to transfer temporarily to an available alternative position offered by the employer for which the employee is qualified and that—

(A) has equivalent pay and benefits; and

(B) better accommodates recurring periods of leave than the regular employment position of the employee.

(c) UNPAID LEAVE PERMITTED.—Except as provided in subsection (d), leave granted under subsection (a) may consist of unpaid leave.

(d) RELATIONSHIP TO PAID LEAVE.—

(1) UNPAID LEAVE.—If an employer provides paid leave for fewer than 12 workweeks, the additional weeks of leave necessary to attain the 12 workweeks of leave required under this title may be provided without compensation.

(2) SUBSTITUTION OF PAID LEAVE.—

(A) IN GENERAL.—An eligible employee may elect, or an employer may require the employee, to substitute any of the accrued paid vacation leave, personal leave, or medical or sick leave of the employee for the leave provided.

(e) FORESEEABLE LEAVE.—

(1) REQUIREMENT OF NOTICE.—In any case in which the necessity for leave under subparagraph (A) or (B) of subsection (a)(1) is foreseeable based on an expected birth or placement, the employee shall provide the employer with not less than 30 days' notice, before the date the leave is to begin, of the employee's intention to take leave under such subparagraph, except that if the date of the birth or placement requires leave to begin in less than 30 days, the employee shall provide such notice as is practicable.

(2) DUTIES OF EMPLOYEE.—In any case in which the necessity for leave under subparagraph (C) or (D) of subsection

(a)(1) is foreseeable based on planned medical treatment, the employee—

(A) shall make a reasonable effort to schedule the treatment so as not to disrupt unduly the operations of the employer, subject to the approval of the health care provider of the employee or the health care provider of the son, daughter, spouse, or parent of the employee, as appropriate; and

(B) shall provide the employer with not less than 30 days' notice, before the date the leave is to begin, of the employee's intention to take leave under such subparagraph, except that if the date of the treatment requires leave to begin in less than 30 days, the employee shall provide such notice as is practicable.

(f) SPOUSES EMPLOYED BY THE SAME EMPLOYER—In any case in which a husband and wife entitled to leave under subsection (a) are employed by the same employer, the aggregate number of workweeks of leave to which both may be entitled may be limited to 12 workweeks during any 12-month period, if such leave is taken—

(1) under subparagraph (A) or (B) of subsection (a)(1); or

(2) to care for a sick parent under subparagraph (C) of such subsection.

Sec. 103. Certification.

(a) IN GENERAL.–An employer may require that a request for leave under subparagraph (C) or (D) of section 102 (a)(1) be supported by a certification issued by the health care provider of the eligible employee or of the son, daughter, spouse, or parent of the employee, as appropriate. The employee shall provide, in a timely manner, a copy of such certification to the employer.

(b) SUFFICIENT CERTIFICATION.–Certification provided under subsection (a) shall be sufficient if it states—

(1) the date on which the serious health condition commenced;

(2) the probable duration of the condition;

(3) the appropriate medical facts within the knowledge of the health care provider regarding the condition;

(4)(A) for purposes of leave under section 102(a)(1)(C), a statement that the eligible employee is needed to care for the son, daughter, spouse, or parent and an estimate of the amount of time that such employee is needed to care for the son, daughter, spouse, or parent; and

(B) for purposes of leave under section 102(a)(1)(D), a statement that the employee is unable to perform the functions of the position of the employee;

(5) in the case of certification for intermittent leave, or leave on a reduced leave schedule, for planned medical treatment, the dates on which such treatment is expected to be given and the duration of such treatment;

(6) in the case of certification for intermittent leave, or leave on a reduced leave schedule, under section 102(a)(1)(D), a statement of the medical necessity for the intermittent leave or leave on a reduced leave schedule, and the expected duration of the intermittent leave or reduced leave schedule; and

(7) in the case of certification for intermittent leave, or leave on a reduced leave schedule, under section 102(a)(1)(C), a statement of the employee's intermittent leave or leave on a reduced leave schedule is necessary for the care of the son, daughter, parent, or spouse who has a serious health condition, or will assist in their recovery, and the expected duration and schedule of the intermittent leave or reduced leave schedule.

(c) SECOND OPINION.—

(1) IN GENERAL.—In any case in which the employer has reason to doubt the validity of the certification provided under subsection (a) for leave under subparagraph (C) or (D) of section 102(a)(1), the employer may require, at the expense of the employer, that the eligible employee obtain the opinion of a second health care provider designated or approved by the employer concerning any information certified under subsection (b) for such leave.

(d) RESOLUTION OF CONFLICTING OPINIONS.—

(1) IN GENERAL.—In any case in which the second opinion described in subsection (c) differs from the opinion in the original certification provided under subsection (a), the employer may require, at the expense of the employer, that the employee obtain the opinion of a third health care provider designated or approved jointly by the employer and the employee concerning the information certified under subsection (b).

(2) FINALITY.—The opinion of the third health care provider concerning the information certified under subsection (b) shall be considered to be final and shall be binding on the employer and the employee.

Sec. 104. Employment and Benefits Protection.

(a) RESTORATION TO POSITION.—

(1) IN GENERAL.—Except as provided in subsection (b), any eligible employee who takes leave under section 102 for the intended purpose of the leave shall be entitled, on return from such leave—

(A) to be restored by the employer to the position of employment held by the employee when the leave commenced; or

(B) to be restored to an equivalent position with equivalent employment benefits, pay, and other terms and conditions of employment.

(2) LOSS OF BENEFITS.—The taking of leave under section 102 shall not result in the loss of any employment benefits accrued prior to the date on which the leave commenced.

(3) LIMITATIONS.—Nothing in this section shall be construed to entitle any restored employee to—

(A) the accrual of any seniority or employment benefits during any period of leave; or

(B) any right, benefit, or position of employment other than any right, benefit, or position to which the employee would have been entitled had the employee not taken the leave.

(b) EXEMPTION CONCERNING CERTAIN HIGHLY COMPENSATED EMPLOYEES.—

(1) DENIAL OF RESTORATION.—An employer may deny restoration under subsection (a) to any eligible employee described in paragraph (2) if—

(A) such denial is necessary to prevent substantial and grievous economic injury to the operations of the employer;

(c) MAINTENANCE OF HEALTH BENEFITS.—

(1) COVERAGE.—Except as provided in paragraph (2), during any period that an eligible employee takes leave under section 102, the employer shall maintain coverage under any "group health plan" (as defined in section 5000(b)(1) of the Internal Revenue Code of 1986) for the duration of such leave at the level and under the conditions coverage would have been provided if the employee had continued in employment continuously for the duration of such leave.

(2) FAILURE TO RETURN FROM LEAVE.—The employer may recover the premium that the employer paid for maintaining coverage for the employee under such group health plan during any period of unpaid leave under section 102.

CHAPTER 14
Sexual Orientation

INTRODUCTION

The Civil Rights Act does not prohibit employers from refusing to hire or subsequently firing someone because he or she is a homosexual. Although there is no federal law, state and local laws do exist in select jurisdictions. The term most commonly used is sexual orientation. Connecticut, Hawaii, Massachusetts, New Jersey, and Wisconsin prohibit discrimination based on sexual orientation by both public and private employers. California, Minnesota, New Mexico, New York, Ohio, Pennsylvania, Rhode Island, and Washington have an executive order issued by the Governor making it unlawful for the government to discriminate on the basis of sexual orientation. Many cities also disallow discrimination, but only a few of them extend it to employment.

There is also no federal law protecting transsexuals and those undertaking gender corrective surgery.

Available Protection

Gays and lesbians working pursuant to employment contracts or employee handbooks may be protected by a clause in the agreement requiring that an employee may be discharged only for cause. In such a case, sexual orientation would not qualify as cause, and the homosexual employee could not be terminated. Some courts have overruled the dismissal based on public policy considerations. Other courts have stated that dismissing an individual because of sexual orientation violates the implied covenant of good faith and fair dealing which exists between employer and employee.

The issue in the next case is whether an amendment overriding a city ordinance protecting sexual orientation is unconstitutional.

CASE *Equality Foundation v. City of Cincinnati*

54 F.3d 261 (6th Cir. 1995)

KRUPANSKY, Circuit Judge.

On March 13, 1991, the Cincinnati City Council (the "Council) enacted ordinance No. 79-1991, commonly known as the "Equal Employment Opportunity Ordinance." This measure provided that the City could not discriminate in its own hiring practices on the basis of classification factors such as race, color, sex, handicap, religion, national or ethnic origin, age, sexual orientation, HIV status, Appalachian regional ancestry, and marital status.

Subsequently, Council on November 25, 1992 adopted Ordinance No. 490-1992 (commonly referred to as the "Human Rights Ordinance") which prohibited, among other things, private discrimination in employment, housing, or public accommodation for reasons of sexual orientation. The opening paragraph of the Human Rights Ordinance expressed the purpose of the legislation as:

> PROHIBITING unlawful discriminatory practices in the City of Cincinnati based on race, gender, age, color, religion, disability status, sexual orientation, marital status, or ethnic, national or Appalachian regional origin, in employment, housing, and public accommodations by ordaining Chapter 914, Cincinnati Municipal Code.

Among other things, the new law created complaint and hearing procedures for purported victims of sexual orientation discrimination and exposed offenders to potential civil and criminal penalties.

ERNSR was organized for the purpose of eliminating special legal protection accorded to persons based upon their sexual orientation pursuant to the Human Rights Ordinance. ERNSR campaigned to rescind the Human Rights Ordinance by enacting a proposed City Charter amendment (Issue 3), which was to be submitted directly to the voters on the November 2, 1993 local ballot. On July 6, 1993, plaintiff Equality Foundation of Greater Cincinnati, Inc. ("Equality Foundation") was incorporated by the opponents, of the ERNSR agenda. A vigorous political contest between ERNSR and Equality Foundation, involving aggressive campaigning by both sides and high media exposure, ensued over Issue 3.

The ERNSR-sponsored proposed charter amendment ultimately appeared on the November 2, 1993 ballot as:

> NO SPECIAL CLASS STATUS MAY BE GRANTED BASED UPON SEXUAL ORIENTATION CONDUCT OR RELATIONSHIPS.
>
> The City of Cincinnati and its various Boards and Commissions may not enact, adopt, enforce or administer any ordinance, regulation, rule or policy which provides that homosexual, lesbian, or bisexual orientation, status, conduct, or relationship constitutes, entitles, or otherwise provides a person with the basis to have any claim of minority or protected status, quota preference or other preferential treatment. This provision of the City Charter shall in all respects be self-executing. Any ordinance, regulation, rule or policy enacted before this amendment is adopted that violates the foregoing prohibition shall be null and void and of no force or effect.

Issue 3 passed by a popular vote of approximately 62% in favor and 38% opposed and became Amendment XII to the Cincinnati City Charter.

On November 8, 1993, plaintiffs Equality Foundation, several individual homosexuals (Richard Buchanan, Chad Bush, Edwin Greene, Rita Mathis, and Roger Asterino), and Housing Opportunities Made Equal, Inc. ("H.O.M.E.") (a housing rights organization), filed a complaint against

the City under 42 U.S.C. 1983 which alleged that their constitutional rights had been, or would potentially be, violated by the adoption of Issue 3, and sought temporary and permanent injunctive relief, a declaration that the Amendment was unconstitutional, and an award of costs (including attorneys' fees). It concluded that the Amendment infringed the plaintiffs' purported "fundamental right to equal access to the political process," as well as First Amendment rights of free speech and association and the right to petition the government for redress of grievances, which violations of constitutional rights subjected the Amendment to a "strict scrutiny" constitutional evaluation. Additionally, the district court posited that, because homosexuals collectively comprise a "quasi-suspect class," the Amendment was alternatively reviewable under the intermediate "heightened scrutiny" constitutional standard. The constitutional guarantee of equal protection insulates citizens only from unlawfully discriminatory state action; it constructs no barrier against private discrimination, irrespective of the degree of wrongfulness of such private discrimination (1972). The Equal Protection Clause of the Fourteenth Amendment to the United States Constitution did not compel the City of Cincinnati to enact legislation to protect homosexuals from discrimination, and accordingly the City, through its ordinary legislative processes, was at liberty to rescind any previous enactments which had fashioned such safeguards. Accordingly, the mere repeal of certain sections of the Human Rights Ordinance which had previously protected homosexuals, lesbians, and bisexuals was not itself constitutionally assailable. However, the district court ruled that the Amendment not only nullified the previously-enacted special legal protection for homosexuals; rather, it assertedly prevented a distinct class of citizens from exercising certain equal protection and First Amendment rights in the future, which, in the lower court's analysis, triggered constitutional review of the Amendment. In declaring this novel ruling, the lower court in the instant case misconstrued *Bowers v. Hardwick,* wherein the Court mandated that homosexuals possess no fundamental right to engage in homosexual conduct and consequently that conduct could be criminalized. The Bowers Court further directed that the courts should resist tailoring novel fundamental rights. Since *Bowers,* every circuit court which has addressed the issue has decreed that homosexuals are entitled to no special constitutional protection, as either a suspect or a quasi-suspect class, because the conduct which places them in that class is not a constitutionally protected categorization. The trial court found that gays, lesbians, and bisexuals are not identified by any particular conduct; to the contrary, they are distinguished by their "sexual orientation," which references an innate and involuntary state of being and set of drives. From this perspective, the Amendment uniquely affected individuals belonging to a discrete segment of society on the basis of their status as persons oriented towards a particular sexual attraction or lifestyle.

Assuming arguendo the truth of the scientific theory that sexual orientation is a "characteristic beyond the control of the individual" as found by the trial court, the reality remains that no law can successfully be drafted that is calculated to burden or penalize, or to benefit or protect, an unidentifiable group or class of individuals whose identity is defined by subjective and unapparent characteristics such as innate desires, drives, and thoughts. Those persons having a homosexual "orientation" simply do not, as such, comprise an identifiable class. Many homosexuals successfully conceal their orientation. Because homosexuals generally are not identifiable "on sight" unless they elect to be so identifiable by conduct (such as public displays of homosexual affection or self-proclamation of homosexual tendencies), they cannot constitute a suspect class or a quasi-suspect class because "they do not necessarily exhibit obvious, immutable, or distinguishing characteristics that define them as a discrete group."

Therefore, *Bowers v. Hardwick* and its progeny command that, as a matter of law, gays, lesbians, and bisexuals cannot constitute either a "suspect class" or a "quasi-suspect class," and, accordingly, the district court's application of the intermediate heightened scrutiny standard to the constitutional analysis of the Amendment was erroneous.

The lower court also invalidated the Amendment by theorizing that it was unconstitutionally vague, because it affected only special legal protection for "gays, lesbians and bisexuals," whereas the Human Rights Ordinance had erstwhile protected all persons based upon their sexual orientation. The district court found that plaintiff H.O.M.E. and other private employers in the City were confronted by a hiring dilemma, a result of a purported ambiguity inherent in the Amendment. Initially, it is noted that plaintiff H.O.M.E. is without standing to assert its argument because it has suffered no actual or imminent injury by the implementation of the Amendment, nor do its assertions present a case in controversy. Rather, H.O.M.E. has merely asserted an abstract hypothetical scenario and conjectured that it was unable to determine if the employment of a homosexual, lesbian, or bisexual because of his or her sexual orientation would be civilly or criminally actionable under the Human Rights Ordinance as anti-heterosexual discrimination. Moreover, even if H.O.M.E. had standing below, the vagueness issue has been rendered moot by Council's March 8, 1995 amendment to the Human Right Ordinance (per Ordinance No. 66-1995), which struck all references to "sexual orientation" from the legislation. At the present time, the City's municipal ordinances provide no protection against private discrimination to any citizen by reason of sexual orientation, irrespective of whether that orientation is heterosexual, homosexual, lesbian, or bisexual.

Accordingly, the judgment below in favor of the plaintiffs is hereby REVERSED.
Judgment for the City of Cincinnati.

In the case that follows, a municipality granted special protection for sexual orientation. This action was in direct contravention of a state statute. The issue is whether both laws may coexist.

CASE

deParrie v. State

893 P.2d 541 (OR. App. 1995)

DEITS, Presiding Judge.

These are appeals by the plaintiffs in two consolidated declaratory judgment actions that were brought, respectively, by plaintiff deParrie and by plaintiffs Mahon, Neet, Graham and No Special Rights Committee, PAC. In both actions, the plaintiffs sought a declaration that ORS 659.165 is invalid. That statute provides:

> "(1) A political subdivision of the state may not enact or enforce any charter provision, ordinance, resolution or policy granting special rights, privileges or treatment to any citizen or group of citizens on account of sexual orientation, or enact or enforce any charter provision, ordinance, resolution or policy that singles out citizens or groups of citizens on account of sexual orientation.

We turn to the merits of plaintiffs' appeal. Their principal argument is that ORS 659.165 is not a "valid preemptive statute" and that it cannot be used, consistently with the Home Rule Amendments to the Oregon Constitution, to prevent "municipalities from establishing substantive policy on the issue of sexual orientation."

Plaintiffs state that, "until the legislature establishes statewide standards on the issue of sexual orientation, it is without authority to preclude the local governments from establishing their own."

We do not agree that, in order to rise to the level of a policy choice, a statute must regulate particular persons or subjects in either a positive or negative manner; it is just as much a substantive policy of the state if the legislature prohibits any regulation of particular persons or matters, or defines the extent to which they may be regulated, as if the legislature itself regulates the persons or matters in a particular manner. In both situations, the legislature has established a state policy concerning the regulation of a subject. To the extent that plaintiffs' argument is that the statute fails to establish a state policy because it does not say enough, we again disagree.

We conclude that ORS 659.165 validly and effectively preempts local legislation of the kind that it declares. Such local legislation is ipso facto in conflict with the statute, because the statute prohibits the legislation. For the same reason, the defined local legislation "cannot operate concurrently" with the statute. It is also clear that "the legislature meant its law to be exclusive"; the entire purpose of the statute is exclusionary.

As the emphasis we have added to plaintiffs' text shows, their argument is misfocused. We might agree that the legislature cannot prevent the people of the state as a whole from exercising initiative and referendum rights to enact or reject state statutes. However, that is not what ORS 659.165 does. It preempts the enactment or enforcement of certain local legislation. Its preemptive effect does and may apply to all local legislation on the subject, whether it is adopted by the local legislative body or the local voters.

Judgment for the State.

The case that follows addresses the question of whether a female who has undergone gender corrective surgery is entitled to protection against discrimination.

CASE

Wood v. C. G. Studios, Inc.

660 F.Supp. 176 (E.D.Pa 1987)

O'NEILL, District Judge.

Plaintiff Wilma Wood instituted this suit in the Court of Common Pleas claiming that defendant C. G. Studios discriminated against her on the basis of sex in violation of Section 5 of the Pennsylvania Human Relations Act (PHRA). Specifically, she claims that defendant failed to promote her and terminated her employment solely because it learned that she had undergone surgery to correct her hermaphroditic condition prior to working for defendant. Plaintiff also alleges that she has exhausted her administrative remedies. Defendant removed the case to this court on the basis of diversity of citizenship.

Defendant moves for summary judgment; a response and a reply have been filed. I will grant the motion because I predict that the Supreme Court of Pennsylvania would find, as a matter of law, that discrimination on the basis of sex under Section 5(a) of the PHRA.2 does not include gender-corrective surgery.

Section 5(a) of the Act Provides:

> It shall be unlawful discriminatory practice, unless based upon a bona fide occupational qualification . . .:
>
> For any employer, because of the race, color, religious creed, ancestry, age, handicap or disability of any individual to refuse to hire or employ, or to bar or to discharge from employment such individual, or to otherwise discriminate against such individual with respect to compensation, hire, tenure, terms, conditions or privileges of employment, if the individual is the best able or most competent to perform the services required. . . .

No Pennsylvania Court has addressed the issue of whether discrimination against a person who has undergone gender-corrective surgery could expose an employer to liability for sex discrimination under the PHRA.

The case law under the PHRA evaluates sex discrimination in terms of discrimination against women because of their status as females. The cases cited by the parties involve discrimination due to stereotypic concepts about a woman's ability to perform a job or due to a condition common to women alone.

There is no showing that the Act was intended to remedy discrimination against individuals because they have undergone gender-corrective surgery. In the absnce of such a showing, I cannot conclude that the Supreme Court of Pennsylvania would give the term "sex" as used in the Act anything anything but its plain meaning.

The Title VII cases unanimously hold that Title VII does not extend to transsexuals nor to those undergoing sexual conversion surgery, and that the term "sex" should be given its traditional meaning.

Plaintifff argues that the PHRA is a remedial statute and should be liberally construed. Remedial statutes, however, should be liberally construed only to achieve their purpose. Plaintiff has not provided this Court with any evidence that the PHRA purpose includes remedying discrimination against people because they have undergone gender-corrective surgery.

Judgment for C. G. Studios.

The following case addresses the question of whether a male transsexual may come to work dressed like a female. The employer argued that a transsexual is not a member of a protected class.

CASE *James v. Ranch Mart Hardware, Inc.*

881 F.Supp. 478 (D. Kan. 1995)

VRATIL, District Judge.

Barbara Renee James, an anatomically male transsexual, alleges sex discrimination under Title VII of the Civil Rights Act of 1991, and the Kansas Act Against Discrimination (KAAD). More specifically, plaintiff claims that Ranch Mart Hardware, Inc. ("Ranch Mart"), terminated her employment under circumstances in which "a similarly situated male, living and working full time as a male," would not have been terminated.

The undisputed facts are as follows:

On September 1, 1992, Ranch Mart hired Glenn Wayne James as a sales clerk in its electrical department. James M. Bays, the store manager who hired James, made no inquiry regarding the applicant's sexual orientation and had no knowledge before August 19, 1993, that James was a transsexual. From September 1, 1992, through August 19, 1993, James worked in the Ranch Mart hardware store "as a man," using the name Glenn Wayne James. James did not wear women's clothing, a wig or makeup.

James was not scheduled to work on August 19, 1993. On that date, however, James went to the store to speak with Bays. James told Bays that she wanted to start dressing and trying to appear as a woman and to use the name Barbara Renee James. James also told Bays that she wanted to wear a wig and makeup to work. James does not recall telling Bays what her dress would be, but Bays remembers James saying that she wanted to wear a dress to work.

In response to James's statements, Bays told her that he preferred that James not come to work in a wig and makeup and that he did not want James wearing a dress at the store. When James protested, Bays agreed to discuss the matter with Vic Regnier, the president of Ranch Mart, and get back in touch with James. James apparently assumed that Bays would call her on August 20, 1993, to report the outcome of that discussion.

Bays talked to Regnier on August 19, 1993, and they agreed to make no final decision until James appeared for work the next day, so they could see what James was wearing and decide whether it was appropriate for work in a hardware store. Bays did not call James to report this decision.

James was scheduled to work on August 20 and 21, 1993, but did not report to work, call in, or inquire why she had not heard from Bays. As a result, as of August 21, 1993, Ranch Mart assumed that James had quit her job without notice. Ranch Mart subsequently terminated James' employment for the stated reason that James "did not show up for scheduled work shift."

The Court has previously determined that James cannot state an actionable claim under Title VII or the KAAD for employment discrimination based upon transsexualism. To proceed on her claim that Ranch Mart terminated her employment when it would not have terminated "a similarly situated female, living and working full time as a male," James must establish a prima facie case of employment discrimination. The four elements of a prima facie employment discrimination case are (1) plaintiff must be a member of a protected class, (2) plaintiff must have been discharged, (3) plaintiff must have been qualified, and (4) plaintiff must show that non-class members in the same or similar circumstances were treated more favorably.

The first element presents the defeating hurdle for plaintiff. If plaintiff claims that Ranch Mart discriminated against her as a male, then this case must be viewed in the reverse discrimination context. As such, the first element becomes a question whether the plaintiff has shown the "existence of background circumstances which support the suspicion that the defendant is that unusual employer who discriminates against the majority." James makes no allegations and provides no facts to support any assertion that Ranch Mart discriminates against males. Thus, under this reverse discrimination analysis, James has failed to show membership in a protected class under Title VII.

Thus, regardless of whether James can prevail on the three remaining elements of the prima facie case, she fails to demonstrate the existence of the first element. Because James fails to meet this primary burden, Ranch Mart is entitled to summary judgment.

Judgment for Ranch Mart.

A woman discharged because she is a lesbian may argue that her sexual orientation was a mere pretext. The real reason for her dismissal was because of her gender. Arguing gender discrimination places a lesbian in a protected class, but she will be protected only as far as her womanhood is the issue and not her homosexuality. Gays and lesbians have been trying to have sex discrimination enlarged to encompass sexual orientation, but so far most courts and legislatures do not agree.

Homosexuals who have the AIDS virus or other sexually transmitted disease will be protected under the Americans with Disabilities Act because they are operating under a disability. Homosexuals who are promoting gay rights may not be discharged in some states for espousing their political beliefs.

Gays and lesbians have been fired for flaunting their relationships. While this may sound egregious, it is no different from a heterosexual speaking about his or her amorous relationship. Treatment should be similar. If heterosexuals may display pictures of loved ones, so should homosexuals. Buttons espousing political beliefs such as "Support Gay Rights" or "It's OK to Be Gay" may be disallowed if the company has a policy disallowing the visible expression of political viewpoints at the workplace.

The issue in the next case is whether a male employee may have long hair and wear facial jewelry. The employee argued that the company's imposition was discriminatory. The company claimed it had the right to uphold its image.

CASE

Lockhart v. Louisiana-Pacific Corp.

795 P2d 602 (OR.App. 1990)

RICHARDSON, Presiding Judge.

Plaintiff was discharged by Louisiana-Pacific Corporation (employer), after he refused to comply with the requirement of a dress and grooming rule that male employees not wear facial jewelry while on the job. The rule allows female employees to wear jewelry that is not "unusual or overly-large." Plaintiff contends that the rule is sexually discriminatory, and that he was discharged for "resisting" the discriminatory policy. He brought this action for wrongful discharge against his employer and for interference with contractual relations against his supervisor, Montel Work (Work). The trial court dismissed the wrongful discharge claim for failure to state a claim and allowed Work's motion for summary judgment on the interference claim. Plaintiff appeals and assigns error to both rulings. We affirm.

> "The recent federal cases hold that a private employer's promulgation and enforcement of reasonable grooming regulations that restrict the hair length of male employees only is not forbidden by the sex discrimination provisions of the federal act. Only those distinctions between the sexes which are based on immutable, unalterable, or constitutionally protected personal characteristies are forbidden.
>
> ". . . The federal statute was never intended to prohibit sex-based distinctions inherent in a private employer's personal grooming code for employees which do not have a significant effect on employment and which can be changed easily by the employee. . . . The enforcement of a reasonable hair length policy is permissible since such a policy is not used to inhibit equal access to employment opportunities between males and females, is not an employer's attempt to deny employment to a particular sex, and is not a significant employment advantage to either sex."

Perhaps no facet of business life is more important than a company's place in public estimation. That the image created by its employees dealing with the public when on company assignment affects its relations is so well known that we may take judicial notice of an employer's proper desire to achieve favorable acceptance. Good grooming regulations reflect a company's policy in our highly competitive business environment. Reasonable requirements in furtherance of that policy are an aspect of managerial responsibility.

Congress has said that no exercise of that responsibility may result in discriminatory deprivation of equal opportunity because of immutable race, national origin, color, or sex classification.

It is not a purpose of the federal statute to accommodate a male employee's desire to wear his hair longer than a private employer's appearance policy allows.

It is unnecessary in this case for us to address the full sweep of the Washington court's reasoning. Plaintiff advances the argument that employer may not prohibit him from wearing an earring, if it allows female employees to wear jewelry. As his argument is cast, plaintiff cannot demonstrate impermissible discrimination unless every difference in dress or grooming requirements for men and women under an employer's rules is impermissibly discriminatory. We reject that argument. The trial court was correct in dismissing the wrongful discharge claim.

Judgment for Louisiana-Pacific Corp.

Homosexual Partners

Currently, gays and lesbians do not have the right to include their partners under their health coverage. Since homosexual marriages are not legally sanctioned (Hawaii is in the process of allowing this), partners are considered mere friends who are not qualified for coverage. Family leave policies for sickness and death do not extend to gays and lesbians.

Employment Perspective

Bruce Wagner's gay partner, Paul, has passed away. Bruce asks for time off to attend Paul's wake and funeral. The firm is amenable as long as Bruce uses his personal days or takes a leave without pay. Bruce argues that if he were married, he would be entitled to leave with pay. The company asserts that neither it nor state law recognizes homosexual marriages. Does Bruce have any recourse? No! Sexual orientation is not included under the Family Leave Act. ◆

Federal Government's Policy

The federal government's treatment of homosexuals is divisive. Some agencies discriminate, while others do not. The Civil Service Commission was charged with actively implementing the Equal Employment Opportunity Act of 1972. On December 21, 1973, the Commission issued a directive in its Civil Service Bulletin to supervisors in the employ of the federal government regarding the treatment of homosexuals. It provided, that with respect to employment no action should be taken against a person because he or she is a homosexual.

The military has long had a policy of refusing to enlist homosexuals. Early in his tenure as president, Bill Clinton took an opposing viewpoint to the military's rigidness on the exclusion of gays. After being adjudicated in federal court, the ban on gays was lifted to the extent that the military will not inquire into the sexual preference of enlisted persons nor will it discharge someone who is gay on that basis alone. But if the homosexual engages in any overt acts ranging from hand holding to sexual conduct, the homosexual will be discharged from the military.

Professional license requirements often mandate good moral character as a criteria for acceptance. This often barred homosexuals from being admitted to a practice. Over time this obstacle has fallen into disuse because homosexual behavior is not evidence of a person's lack of morality. Furthermore, sexual orientation has nothing to do with the practice of a trade or profession.

Employment Perspective

Wilson Fredericks, who is gay, has just learned he has passed the bar exam. He is given an appointment before members of the character and fitness committee. During the interview, one member asks Wilson about his sexual orientation. Wilson refuses to answer on the grounds of his right to privacy. Has Wilson addressed this matter appropriately? Yes! Wilson's homosexuality is a private matter. The fact that he prefers men to women does not mean he is unethical and therefore any less qualified to practice law. ◆

Teaching in Schools

Perhaps the most heated debate is over whether gays and lesbians should be allowed to teach in the public school system and work in day care centers. The fear persists among many that gays and lesbians will indoctrinate the children into the homosexual way of life and possibly persuade children into having homosexual acts with them. First, teachers must submit a plan book detailing their course content for each day. This must parallel the course curriculum. If a teacher substantially deviates from this requirement, appropriate disciplinary measures may be taken. The fact that a homosexual teacher may interject subtle references of the benefits of an alternative lifestyle is a given. However, there is no evidence that these remarks, if made, are enough to change a child's sexual orientation involuntarily. Second, homosexuality is not synonymous with pedophilia. Homosexuals usually engage in relationships with other adults, not little children. Being a homosexual is not indicative of being a pedafile. Within the pedafile constituency exist both homosexual and heterosexual adults. Allowing a homosexual to work in a day care center is no more dangerous for fear of pedophilia than allowing a heterosexual to work there. Pedophilia is a sickness unrelated to sexual orientation.

The important criterion for a teacher or a day care worker is job performance capability. A teacher or day care worker should be dismissed if the person is unfit to teach or unfit to exhibit care and concern, not on the basis of having chosen an alternative lifestyle. In most cultures, one dominant party has ruled; that party has been men. Where there have been different races, religions, and national origins present, the group having the greatest wealth, military strength, or political power is in control. In the United States, white Anglo Saxon Protestant (WASP) men have long held the power.

The next case deals with denial of employment as a public school teacher to a man because of his sexual tendencies.

Jantz v. Muci

759 F.Supp. 1543 (D.Kan. 1991)

KELLY, District Judge.

Plaintiff Vernon Jantz has brought the present action under 42 U.S.C. 1983 alleging a violation of his right to equal protection. The plaintiff alleges that he was denied by the defendant, then school principal Cleofas Muci, employment as a public school teacher on the basis of Muci's perception that Jantz had "homosexual tendencies."

Jantz graduated from high school in Newton, Kansas in 1963. He graduated cum laude from Wichita State University, receiving a bachelor's degree from Wichita State University in 1972 and a master's degree in 1978. After serving in the United States Air Force, Jantz completed course work in secondary education at Western New Mexico State University, and obtained a New Mexico secondary school teaching permit in 1985.

During the 1985–86 school year, Jantz taught social studies in the New Mexico schools. Jantz and his wife moved to Wichita, Kansas in the summer of 1986. Obtaining Kansas certification in September, 1986, Jantz took employment with Unified School District No. 259 and began substitute teaching for the district in early 1987. Jantz substituted at several middle and elementary schools in the district, including Wichita North High School.

During this time, Jantz did no coaching. In his interviews with school administrators, including an interview conducted by a Wichita North administrative officer on behalf of Muci, Jantz did not volunteer to perform coaching activities. By the same token, Jantz was not asked whether he was able and willing to assume coaching responsibilities. Jantz, who had experience in basketball, baseball, soccer, and tennis, was able to coach, and would have done so had he been asked.

In May, 1987, Jantz contacted the district's Director of Secondary Personnel, Frank Crawford, and inquired about the possibility of obtaining a teacher's position for the 1987–88 school year. Despite his talk with Crawford, it remained uncertain whether there were any openings for the upcoming school year. Jantz interviewed at Wichita South and at Wichita North (with associate principal Milford Johnson). However, as it turned out, no positions were open for the 1987–88 school year at the schools where Jantz interviewed. As with the previous year, Jantz provided substitute teaching services during the 1987–88 school year.

Jantz met with Crawford's successor, Jane Ware, in February, 1988. Due to the upcoming merger of ninth grade students into the Wichita high schools, a combined social studies teacher and coach position was created at Wichita North for the 1989 school year. Jantz applied for the position.

The contentions of fact presented by the parties establish that the principals of the individual schools in the district exercise de facto the predominant role in hiring decisions, with some input by the district personnel office. The principal usually conducts the job interview with any applicant and his determination is normally decisive.

Jantz's application was turned down and Matthew Silverthorne was selected to fill the new position. The parties dispute the reason for this decision by Wichita North's principal, Cleofas Muci. Muci was principal of Wichita North for the 1986–87 and 1987–88 school years. Muci retired in November, 1988.

According to Muci, he hired Silverthorne because he was the best candidate. Silverthorne had student taught and coached at Wichita North. In Muci's opinion, Silverthorne had done a good job while coaching. Silverthorne was certified to teach social studies (with the exception of world geography, in which he had only a provisional certification).

Jantz disputes this version of the decision to hire Silverthorne. Jantz cites the testimony of Sharon Fredin (Muci's secretary) and William

Jenkins (the coordinator of social studies at Wichita North). Fredin has acknowledged in her deposition that during the 1987–88 school year she "made the offhand comment" to Muci that Jantz reminded her of her husband, whom she believed to be a homosexual. Jenkins has testified that when he asked why Jantz was not hired for the new position, Muci told him it was because of Jantz's "homosexual tendencies."

After being denied the social sciences position at Wichita North, Jantz worked during the 1989–90 school year as a (half-time) social studies teacher and a (half-time) facilitator for gifted students at the middle school. Jantz currently is employed full-time as a facilitator for gifted students at Hadley Intermediate School. Jantz is a 45-year-old white male. He is married with two children.

In *Bowers v. Hardwick,* the Supreme Court held that the due process clause of the Fourteenth Amendment does not prohibit the states from criminalizing homosexual sodomy. That case, cited by defendant Muci, is not directly relevant here. The Bowers Court only addressed the respondent's claim that the Georgia statute was a violation of due process; equal protection was not an issue. The case presented the limited issue of whether homosexual conduct could be regulated by the states. Whether a state or its agents may discriminate among citizens on the basis of their sexual orientation was not at issue.

The distinction between conduct and orientation is both proper and useful in analyzing the constitutional rights of homosexuals. Due process, which was at issue in *Bowers,* serves as a limitation of majoritarian restrictions of traditionally favored and sanctioned activities and rights; it necessarily focuses on historical practice and tradition. Equal protection, on the other hand, protects disadvantaged groups of individuals from governmental discrimination, even where the discrimination is enshrined in a deep historical tradition. Bowers merely established that homosexual conduct was not a recognized historical liberty. The case does not deal with the issue of whether societal bigotry against private homosexual orientation or tendencies legitimizes governmental discrimination against homosexuals under equal protection.

The strength of the historical tradition of discrimination against homosexuals documented by the Supreme Court in Bowers, while supporting the denial of the due process claim in that case, in fact supports the view that governmental discrimination on the basis of sexual orientation may represent a violation of equal protection considerations. It is perfectly consistent to say that homosexual sodomy is not a practice so deeply rooted in our traditions as to merit due process protection, and at the same time to say, for example, that because homosexuals have historically been subject to invidious discrimination, laws which burden homosexuals as a class should be subjected to heightened scrutiny under the equal protection clause. Indeed, the two propositions may be considered complementary: In all probability, homosexuality is not considered a deeply-rooted part of our traditions precisely because homosexuals have historically been subjected to invidious discrimination.

Bowers, however, provides no bar to the use of heightened scrutiny when analyzing governmental discrimination based upon sexual orientation. However, in identifying which governmental classifications require heightened scrutiny analysis, the Supreme Court, in a series of cases, has identified several considerations which are relevant. The discrimination must be invidious and unjustifiable, that is, discrimination based upon an obvious, immutable, or distinguishing trait which frequently bears no relation to ability to perform or contribute to society. A second factor is whether the class historically has suffered from purposeful discrimination. Third and finally, the class must lack the political power necessary to obtain protection from the political branches of government.

According to that information, sexual orientation (whether homosexual or heterosexual) is generally not subject to conscious change. Sexual orientation becomes fixed during early childhood, "it is not a matter of conscious or controllable choice." If the government began to discriminate against heterosexuals, how many heterosexuals "would find it easy not only to abstain from heterosexual activity but also shift the object of their desires to persons of the same sex?"

Aside from the available scientific evidence, which strongly supports the view that sexual orientation is not easily mutable, complete and absolute immutability simply is not a prerequisite for suspect classification. Race, gender, alienage, and illegitimacy can all be changed, yet discrimination on the basis of any of these categories compels heightened scrutiny by the courts. Aliens may obtain citizenship, gender may be altered by surgery, lighter-skinned blacks may pass as white. Discrimination on the basis of race would not become permissible merely because a future scientific advance permits the change in pigmentation.

While traits such as race, gender, or sexual orientation may be altered or concealed, that change can only occur at a prohibitive cost to the average individual. Immutability therefore defines traits which are central, defining traits of personhood, which may be altered only at the expense of significant damage to the individual's sense of self.

In this context, classification on the basis of orientation fulfills the concern that the identifying trait of the class be immutable. Sexual orientation is a trait which is not subject to voluntary control or change. More importantly, to discriminate against individuals who accept their given sexual orientation and refuse to alter that orientation to conform to societal norms does significant violence to a central and defining character of those individuals.

Discrimination on the basis of sexual orientation is invidious. In addition to the immutable nature of the trait, homosexual individuals have been and are the subject of incorrect stereotyping. Homosexual orientation "implies no impairment in judgment, stability, reliability or general social or vocational capabilities." Nor does homosexual orientation alone impair job performance, including the job of teaching in public schools.

Yet homosexuals remain the subject of significant and virulent stereotyping in modern society. Homosexuals are believed to be effeminate (if gay) or masculine (if lesbian), they are believed to proselytize children to homosexuality or indeed seek out children to molest, they are believed to be mentally ill; stereotypes which are all demonstrably false. In truth, the sexual orientation of the vast majority of homosexuals is not identifiable on the basis of mannerism alone. Homosexuals are no more likely to molest children than are heterosexuals. "The National Association for Mental Health, the American Psychiatric Association, and the Surgeon General now agree that homosexuality, in and of itself, is not a mental illness."

Widespread discrimination against homosexuals exists in both public and private employment. Homosexuals must also face discrimination in many other facets of modern life. In finding jobs, securing housing, in nearly every aspect of social existence, discrimination on the basis of sexual orientation has been a persistent facet of life in America. The prejudice against homosexuals is "so severe and pervasive that homosexuals are often forced to hide their identities as homosexuals." Unfortunately, the deep-seated societal prejudice against homosexuals also evidences itself in widespread violence against homosexuals. One study has found that homosexuals probably face victimization more frequently than any other minority group. Law enforcement officials report that violence against homosexuals is both significant, and, perhaps due to the AIDS epidemic, increasing. "Unfortunately, very little legislation protects gay men and lesbians from discrimination in the private sector. No federal statute bars discrimination by private citizens or organizations on the basis of sexual orientation. Nor do the states provide such protection: only Wisconsin has a comprehensive statute barring such discrimination in employment." The Harvard study concludes that discrimination against homosexuals is pervasive, and recent changes in the law too inadequate to provide adequate protection. Unless more is done, the study found, "gay men and lesbians will remain unable to conduct their lives free from discrimination."

The existence of isolated, local anti-discrimination successes is insufficient to deprive homosexuals of the status of a suspect classification. Compare the situation with that of blacks, who clearly constitute a suspect category for equal protection purposes. Blacks are protected by three federal constitutional amendments, major federal Civil Right Acts as well as anti-discrimination laws in 48 of the states. By that comparison, and by absolute standards as well, homosexuals are politically powerless.

In reality, homosexuals face severe limitations on their ability to protect their interest by means of the political process. As Justice Brennan has observed, "because of the immediate and severe opprobrium often manifested against homosexuals once so identified publicly, members of this group are particularly powerless to pursue their rights openly in the political arena."

There are several factors which limit effective political action by homosexuals. Due to the harsh penalties imposed by society on persons identified as homosexual, many homosexual persons conceal their sexual orientation. Silence, however, has its cost. It may allow a given individual to escape from the discrimination, abuse, and even violence which is often directed at homosexuals, but it ensures that homosexuals as a group are unheard politically. Moreover, the prejudice that compels many homosexuals to refrain from open political activity also limits access to political power in other ways. By diminishing contact between the heterosexual majority and avowed homosexuals, the majority loses any perspective on concerns in the homosexual community and is deprived of the resulting sensitivity to those concerns. Politicians seeking to limit the impact of anti-homosexual prejudices through legislation are themselves the target of prejudice.

There is, the court believes, no way to analyze the present issue under the guidelines set down by the Supreme Court and reach any conclusion other than that discrimination based on sexual orientation is inherently suspect. Sexual orientation is not a matter of choice; it is a central and defining aspect of the personality of every individual. Homosexuals have been and remain the subject of invidious discrimination. No other identifiable minority group faces the dilemma dealt with every day by the homosexual community—the combination of active and virulent prejudice with the lack of an effective political voice. Only by abandoning the established tests of suspectness, and retreating to some other formulation is it possible to achieve some other result. This court cannot join in such a retreat. Accordingly, the court finds that a governmental classification based on an individual's sexual orientation is inherently suspect.

Judgment for Jantz.

Comparison to Other Discrimination Victims

Over time, significant inroads have been made by Jews and Catholics and others with European ancestry. All of them are white males. It is difficult, at times, to determine religion or national origin by someone's demeanor. Intermarriage has also resulted in less homogeneous groups. The distinction for women and minorities remains because it cannot be disguised. Racial and gender differences are obvious. Although age, pregnancy, and disabilities are often obvious, sexual orientation may not be so. It can be through the displaying of overt acts such as exhibiting feminine mannerisms and speech, cross dressing, hand holding, and other characteristics of the opposite sex. For the most part, homosexuality is not readily identifiable unless the individual chooses to speak about it. Many gays and lesbians want their lifestyles to be tolerated to the point where people will not be shocked to learn of their choice, snide remarks and jokes will not be made, and discrimination will not take place. Is this asking too much? No!

The prejudices of the white male should not have a deleterious effect on the rights of others, who for some particular reason are different because of their gender, race, religion, age, disability, pregnancy, sexual orientation, personality, hobbies, standard of living, social connections, or vices (drinking, smoking, gambling). Tolerance of differences should be preached. In diversity there is strength. Economic livelihood through the deprivation of employment opportunities should not be affected. Job qualifications and performance should rule. All other unrelated suspect classifications should not be considered. It is time for individuals to be judged on the merits of what they do rather than on the personal characteristics they cannot change.

In the case following, an employee was discharged from his position when the employer learned he was a homosexual. The employee claimed that action violated his right to equal protection and due process.

Kelley v. Vaughn

760 F.Supp. 161 (W.D.Mo.1991)

BARTLETT, District Judge.

Plaintiff names Frank Vaughn, Food Service manager at the Western Missouri Correctional Center, as defendant in this action. According to plaintiff, defendant removed plaintiff from his job as a bakery worker at the Western Missouri Correctional Center solely because of the fact that plaintiff is a homosexual. Plaintiff asserts that this action was discriminatory and that it infringed upon his personal liberty. For relief, plaintiff seeks $50,000.00 in damages.

Plaintiff apparently bases his claim on an alleged violation of Title VII of the Civil Rights Act of 1964, which prohibits employers from discriminating against an individual because of his or her sex. However, the term "sex" as it is used in the Act refers to gender, not to sexual orientation. Because homosexuality pertains to sexual preference, and not to gender, "Title VII does not prohibit discrimination against homosexuals."

Plaintiff, along with his complaint, attached a copy of a letter he wrote regarding his termination from his job. In that letter, plaintiff asserts that removal from the Bakery Crew amounts to "an unconstitutional infringement upon his personal liberty." In granting plaintiff's claims a liberal construction, the Court considers the possibility that plaintiff is attempting to allege that he had a protected interest in his job in the bakery and that defendant violated his due process rights when he removed plaintiff from the job.

Plaintiff, however, has no right to be assigned to a particular job. Further, the expectation of keeping a particular job in prison is not a property or liberty interest entitled to due process protection. Because plaintiff had no protected interest in his job in the Prison bakery, denial of that job does not constitute a violation of due process.

The complaint by plaintiff is further subject to analysis under the equal protection clause of the Fourteenth Amendment. For example, regardless of any liberty or property interest in his position as a bakery worker if plaintiff were to be removed from the position because of his race, or prisoner animosity based on race, a constitutional violation would be patent. Whether claims of discrimination because of homosexual orientation will support a valid equal protection claim is a subject of some current debate.

The New Hampshire Supreme Court held that practicing homosexuals could validly be excluded prospectively as adoptive parents or foster parents but could not be validly excluded from operating day care or child care agencies. Such exclusion was held to violate the equal protection clause. Since plaintiff in this case denies "any overt or covert homosexual activities on my part" he would appear to have a distinctly nonfrivolous claim of arbitrary discrimination if the state action of which he complains occurred in the manner alleged.

Although plaintiff appears to have no statutory claims or due process claims that would survive scrutiny for legal frivolousness, his equal protection claim authorizes further processing of this case.

Judgment for Kelley in part.

In the following case, a homosexual was terminated for discussing the details of his homosexual relationships. He claimed he was treated differently because he was a homosexual. The company argued that this behavior was inappropriate behavior regardless of sexual orientation.

CASE

Darrell N. Williamson v. A.G. Edwards and Sons, Inc.

876 F. 2d 69 (8th Cir. 1989)

ARNOLD, BOWMAN, and MAGILL, Circuit Judges.

Darrell Williamson, a black male, appeals from the district court's order granting summary judgment to A.G. Edwards and Sons, Inc. (Edwards), and Bruce Morgan, his former supervisor at Edwards, on Williamson's claim that they discharged him on the basis of his race, in violation of Title VII. We affirm.

Williamson worked for Edwards from November 1979 until May 1985 when he was discharged because of his disruptive and inappropriate conduct at work. In his one-count amended complaint, Williamson alleged that Morgan had falsely accused him of disrupting the workflow by continuing to discuss the details of his homosexual lifestyle in the workplace and harassing another employee, and that white employees who behaved as Williamson did were not disciplined. The district court granted summary judgment to Edwards finding that Williamson's complaint and deposition testimony clearly indicated Williamson believed he had been treated differently because of his homosexuality and not his race. Title VII does not prohibit discrimination against homosexuals.

Although Williamson stated in his deposition that he believed that he was treated differently because he was black, he failed to allege facts sufficient to establish that other similarly situated white employees were treated differently. He did not claim that the other white, alleged homosexuals behaved as he did (openly discussed their sex lives while at work), but only compared his behavior in that regard to the behavior of other heterosexuals. Although he alleged he was reprimanded for wearing makeup at work while the two other alleged white homosexuals were only reprimanded for wearing jewelry, there is no indication in the record that the other men wore any makeup.

Accordingly, we affirm.
Judgment for A. G. Edwards.

A strong argument has been made to grant homosexuals Title VII protection under gender discrimination because they have the right to work. Equal employment opportunities should not be denied to them, as it is not denied to single and married heterosexuals who sleep around. Sexual orientation is a private matter that is not job related. As long as conduct such as hand holding, kissing, touching, and incessantly preaching the virtues of homosexuality is not displayed on the job, an employee's private affinity for members of his or her gender should be tolerated. A gay or lesbian should be held to the same standards as a so-called straight male or female, no more, no less.

Acceptance or Tolerance

Acceptance of gays and lesbians may never take place, but tolerance must. Acceptance means confirming a personal conviction in the person in question. Tolerance means keeping any personal hostility to oneself and refraining from causing harm to the individual because of his or her difference. This applies to race, religion, gender, national origin, age, pregnancy and disability as well. We cannot delude ourselves into thinking someday everyone will accept everyone else. There have been a lot of somedays that have come and gone. Personal prejudices and traditions stand in the way. They have been instilled from generation to generation in family life, the community, the educational system, and the media. Personal prejudices exist on both sides. There are many minorities and people of foreign extraction who despise whites. Many women have hostile feelings toward men. Many claim justification because of past atrocities. Many white males feel resentful because of what they perceive to be favorable dispositions given to others.

CONCLUSION

The bottom line is there will never come a day where there will be complete acceptance. Some feel we are losing ground rather than gaining it. After Rodney King and O.J. Simpson, it may be true in the racial arena. The practical solution is to mandate tolerance. Society would like you to love everybody, but society cannot make you. However, society can require you to tolerate everyone. In your mind, if you choose to hate someone, that is up to you. It is subjective, and although society may try, society cannot enforce that because it is your state of mind. But any objective manifestation of your state of mind which results in harm to another can be disciplined. Society can judge people's objective actions, and it should where it results in unfair treatment of another. Political correctness is an example of this. People who are politically correct may hate their neighbor, but they do not show it. They keep their prejudices to themselves or amongst people who have the same feelings. Politically correct people do not offend anyone. They tolerate the behavior of others. Whether they accept it or not, will never be known. Society may have a higher goal acceptance, but realistically, it should be looking to achieve removal of discrimination from the workplace and everyday life.

REVIEW QUESTIONS

1. Is the Civil Rights Act applicable to homosexuals?
2. Are there any laws prohibiting discrimination against gays and lesbians?
3. Why is sexual-orientation discrimination not covered under gender discrimination?
4. Is it ethical to discriminate against people of alternative lifestyles?
5. Can a homosexual wear a button saying "Support Gay Rights" at the workplace?
6. Are there any homosexuals protected against discrimination?
7. Do Family Medical Leave policies extend to homosexual partners?
8. What is the policy with regard to gays and lesbians in the military?
9. Should gays and lesbians be allowed to teach in the schools?
10. Can a homosexual be denied a professional license because he or she is lacking good moral character?
11. A gay stenographer whose job transcribing presidential speeches and press conferences was terminated when the government revoked his White House security clearance. The

government asserted he was a "national security risk" and barred him from access to the White House. What was the result?

12. Plaintiffs' first amendment complaint alleges only a single cause of action: sex discrimination. This complaint alleges the following:

> Supervisors Jennings and Daniel, and other coemployees of Plaintiffs, in an open and notorious manner, engaged in the sexual harassment of plaintiffs by means of writing, drawing, and explicitly discussing homosexual acts, excrement, urine, and other topics in a depraved manner which created for Plaintiffs a harmful and oppressive work environment and which materially interfered with plaintiffs' ability to perform their work-related duties. Jennings's and Daniel's depraved comments and conduct were done openly, and Jennings's and others' drawings were posted openly and near his office.

What was the result? *Fox v. Sierra Development Co.,* 876 F.Supp.1169–D.Nev. (1995)

13. Two issues were addressed in this particular case: first, whether homosexuals could qualify as adoptive parents, and second, whether homosexuals could operate a day care center. What result did the court arrive at? *Opinion of the Justices,* 530 A.2d 21 (1987)

14. Holloway sued Arthur Andersen & Co. claiming that it discriminated against her because she was having an operation to change her sex. What was the result? *Holloway v. Arthur Andersen & Co.,* 566 F.2d 659, (9th Cir. 1977)

15. Carreno complained that his coworkers were harassing him because of his sexual orientation. He claimed that he was afforded protection from this situation under Title VII. What was the result? *Carreno v. Local Union No. 226, International Brotherhood of Electrical Workers,* 54 FEP 81 (D. Kan. 1990)

16. Ethically, should homosexuals be protected against discrimination under Title VII? Refer to the case on pp. 351.

17. In the case on pp. 341, should transsexuals be entitled to dress as they please?

18. In the case on pp. 342, was the employee treated fairly?

19. In the case on pp. 344, should a company be allowed to dictate what jewelry its male and female employees may wear?

20. In the case on pp. 347, is it ethical for a school to refuse to hire a homosexual as a teacher?

CHAPTER 15 Religious Discrimination

INTRODUCTION

The First Amendment to the United States Constitution provides for freedom of religion. It also states that Congress shall not establish a national religion, thus insuring the right of individuals to engage in whatever religious practices they wish. These practices must not, however, violate other laws such as criminal laws prohibiting sacrificial offerings. The First Amendment applies directly to the federal government and to the states through the Fourteenth Amendment.

While the Constitution protects individuals from governmental infringement, Title VII protects them from employment discrimination. Religious affiliation is one of the classes protected under Title VII from invidious discrimination. Employers may not refuse to hire an individual because he or she is a member of a particular religion.

Employment Perspective

Herman Tuffle, an atheist, is the owner of bookstores called "The Classics." Shamus O'Neill applies for a position in the bookstore. During the course of the interview, Shamus mentions that one of the priests of his parish saw the Classic's employment advertisement in the local paper. Herman, who never questioned Shamus about his religion, refused to hire him. Shamus, uncertain as to why he was not hired, relates the story to one of his friends. The friend tells him that Herman is a confirmed atheist. Shamus files a claim with the EEOC. Will he win? Yes! As long as Shamus was otherwise qualified for the position, Herman will have no valid defense for refusing to hire him. What if Herman had hired him and then, upon learning of Shamus's religious affiliation, terminated him? The result would be the same. ◆

ACCOMMODATING RELIGIOUS BELIEFS

To require an employer to accommodate an employee's religious beliefs, the employee must first explain to the employer what his or her religious beliefs are and how they are being compromised by the employer because of the task at hand. The employer must acquiesce if such accommodation would not cause the employer undue hardship, compromise the rights of others, or does not require more than minimal cost. If the employee resigns or is terminated for failing to perform the job because of religious beliefs, then the question of religious discrimination will be decided on the basis of the criteria of reasonable accommodation.

The following case addresses the question of whether a company must accommodate an employee's religious belief that would violate the terms of the collective bargaining agreement. The religious belief prohibited work from sundown on Friday to sundown on Saturday. The collective bargaining agreement provided that shift assignments would be determined by seniority.

981 F.2d 336 (8th Cir.1992)

BEAM, Circuit Judge.

Jesse Cook was employed on the assembly line at Chrysler's St. Louis plants from 1976 until 1986, when he was terminated for excessive absences. Cook is a Seventh Day Adventist. His religious beliefs prohibit work from sundown Friday to sundown Saturday. The terms and conditions of Cook's employment are determined in part by a national collective bargaining agreement between Chrysler and the International Union, United Automobile, Aerospace and Agricultural Implement Workers of America (UAW or Union). This national agreement is supplemented by local agreements between Chrysler and the UAW local representing employees at each Chrysler plant. Under the agreement applicable to Cook, seniority is determined on a plant-by-plant basis and seniority at a plant prevails over seniority with the corporation. Shift assignments at the St. Louis plants are determined by seniority.

Cook was laid-off at Chrysler St. Louis Assembly Plant I and was later offered a position at St. Louis Assembly Plant II, with a loss of seniority. Because he had no seniority at Plant II, he was placed on the evening shift, which requires that he work on Friday nights. He could have retained his seniority if he had remained on lay-off until recalled to Plant I.

The collective bargaining agreement provides a negotiated no-fault absenteeism policy, known as the Uniform Attendance Procedure. The policy deals with excessive and chronic absenteeism and provides a six-step system of progressive discipline and also provides grievance and arbitration procedures. Any employee absent more than twenty percent of his regularly scheduled time is subject to discharge. In addition, the local agreement at Plant II was amended in 1985 to address the particular problem of Friday night absenteeism. Under the amended system, known as the "excused in advance system" or "book procedure," employees could sign up in a book for an excused day off on a first-come, first-serve basis. Fridays are most sought for excused absences.

After his transfer to Plant II in January, 1986, Cook informed his supervisor of the need for accommodation of his religious beliefs. Cook proposed a shift change, working on a Sunday instead of a Friday, or a flexible schedule. His supervisor contacted the union shop steward and the labor relations supervisor in an effort to find an accommodation. Cook missed work every Friday night and was late every Saturday night. He was disciplined after his sixth and seventh absences, pursuant to the six-step procedure for discipline, but was not disciplined for eight subsequent absences while Chrysler and the UAW investigated his request. He was then informed that Chrysler could not accommodate him by changing his shift. Cook continued to miss work on Fridays and was eventually terminated.

Cook brought suit against Chrysler and the UAW (collectively, "defendants") in district court under Title VII of the Civil Rights Act of 1964. He alleged he was terminated by Chrysler on the basis of his religion and also alleged that the Union failed to represent him on the basis of his religion. The district court entered judgment for defendants after a bench trial. The district court found that Chrysler's efforts to accommodate Cook satisfied the requirements of Title VII and that the Union had not breached any duties to Cook.

. . . First, accommodating Cook would compromise other employees' contractual rights as secured by the collective bargaining agreement. The collective bargaining agreement provides both a system for determining seniority and an absenteeism policy. Efforts to accommodate Cook would violate the terms of the collective bargaining agreement and contravene the "book" procedures.

The record shows that Chrysler approached the Union and tried to find a way to accommodate Cook. The Union was not willing to grant Cook a change of shift out of line with seniority. Chrysler's efforts satisfied the requirements of Title VII in view of the obstacles presented by the collective bargaining agreement.

With respect to the Union, its refusal to waive or modify the collective bargaining agreement's seniority provisions do not constitute unlawful discrimination.

Judgment for Chrysler.

Many claims of religious discrimination relate to religious observance. Employers have a duty to make reasonable accommodations for the employee as long as it does not present an undue hardship for the employer.

Employment Perspective

John Edwards, a Catholic, is employed as an intern at Bay Ridge Hospital. At times, John must be physically present at the hospital for thirty-six hours. When this occurs mid-Saturday to Sunday evening, it conflicts with John's religious belief of attending Mass. When John informs the hospital, his plea is ignored. Is the hospital guilty of religious discrimination? Yes! Bay Ridge Hospital could make a reasonable accommodation for John to allow him one hour to attend Mass, either on Saturday evening or on Sunday. This provision does not present an undue hardship to the hospital which could either rearrange his work hours or give him a one-hour break.

Suppose that the hospital is able to rearrange John's work hours to allow him to have all Saturday evenings off. Some time ago, the Catholic Church permitted its members to attend a service after 4:00 p.m. on Saturdays to fulfill the Sunday obligation. John insists that he must attend Mass on Sunday because that is the way he was raised. He does not accept this Saturday night exception. Has Bay Ridge Hospital made a reasonable accommodation? Yes! After John advised Bay Ridge Hospital that he was a Catholic, it worked out a schedule to permit him to attend Mass on Saturday afternoon or evening, which is acceptable to the Catholic Church. John is being unreasonable in insisting that he be permitted to attend Mass on Sunday. He is asking for an exception on religious grounds that is not required by the religion itself. ◆

Employment Perspective

Sidney Green, who is Jewish, responds to an advertisement for a position as a manager in a Food King store. During the interview, Sidney is informed that the position is for weekend work. Sidney tells Food King that his religion does not permit him to work on Saturdays. Food King says that that is the only position open and the hours cannot be altered with the weekday manager. Sidney argues that the advertisement did not specify weekend work and files a religious discrimination claim with the EEOC. Will he win? No! The advertisement does not have to specify every detail of the job. Sidney asked for an accommodation, and Food King recounted that the accommodation would impose an undue hardship on it because it would leave no managerial coverage for Saturdays. Sidney claims that once Food King learned he was Jewish, it informed him that the position was for weekend work, knowing that he would have to decline because of his religious beliefs. If Sidney could prove this, he would win. But there is no evidence that Food King knew Sidney was Jewish when it told him that the opening was for a weekend job. Under the facts as stated, Sidney's claim would most likely fail. ◆

In the case that follows, an employee in a skin care salon asked for a day off without pay to observe a religious holiday. The employer refused to accommodate the employee, citing the busy schedule on that day as a business necessity.

CASE

E.E.O.C. v. Ilona of Hungary, Inc.

885 F.Supp. 1111 (N.D. Ill. 1995)

LEFKOW, Judge.

On October 12, 1990, Lyudmila Tomilina ("Tomilina") filed with the EEOC a timely Charge of Discrimination, alleging that defendant had discriminated against her because of her religion in violation of Title VII.

On October 17, 1990, Alina Gulkhovsky ("Glukhovsky") filed with the EEOC a timely Charge of Discrimination alleging that defendant had discriminated against her because of her religion in violation of Title VII.

Following an investigation, a reasonable cause finding and unsuccessful conciliation efforts with respect to Tomilina's and Glukhovsky's charges, the EEOC filed this action on October 5, 1992.

In 1990, Ilona of Hungary was owned by George and Ilona Meszaros (the "Meszaroses"); in

1990, George Meszaros was owner and chairman of defendant; in 1990, Ilona Meszaros was owner and president of defendant; in 1990, Ilona Meszaros's two children also owned a portion of the stock of defendant.

Ilona of Hungary is engaged in the business of providing skin care services to the public through commercial salons; not only does Ilona of Hungary serve the conventional "beauty" market, it also treats clients for skin care problems on referral from physicians. Ilona of Hungary also manufactures, uses, and sells a proprietary line of skin and nail care products.

In the beauty and skin care business generally, and for the Chicago Salon in particular, Saturday was the busiest day of the week, when the most revenue was generated.

On or about August 4, 1989, Tomilina began to work for defendant as a manicurist at the Chicago salon. The employer-employee relationship was in all significant respects mutually satisfactory throughout.

Between approximately September 12 and September 15, 1990, Tomilina requested of Theresa Gold, the manager of defendant's Chicago salon, that Tomilina be permitted to take off from work on Saturday, September 29, 1990, to observe Yom Kippur.

Yom Kippur is, according to the witnesses, one of the highest holy days in the Jewish faith. A faithful adherent of the Jewish religion refrains from work on Yom Kippur.

In requesting Yom Kippur off from work, Tomilina did not ask and did not expect to be paid for that day.

At the time, Ilona of Hungary employed three manicurists, two of whom were Jewish. At the time Tomilina made her request, one of the other manicurists, Sophie Kapmar, had also asked for Yom Kippur off but had agreed to work when Gold indicated she could not have the day off.

At the time she requested Yom Kippur off, Tomilina sincerely believed that she should not work on Yom Kippur because of her religion.

When Tomilina made her request to observe Yom Kippur, neither Gold nor the Meszaroses questioned the sincerity of Tomilina's religious beliefs, not did they express any such doubt.

Gold vaguely recalled that she had checked the appointment book and noted that Tomilina had four to seven clients booked. Gold told Tomilina that she would check with the Meszaroses.

Gold testified that she contacted the Meszaroses, informing them of Tomilina's request and that Tomilina was already partially booked for September 29. The Meszaroses instructed Gold to deny the request.

Gold testified that she informed Tomilina that her request was denied. Tomilina testified that she was never told her request had been denied.

After defendant learned that Tomilina needed Yom Kippur 1990 off from work, neither Gold nor any other member of defendant's management considered or offered any accommodation to allow Tomilina to take one day off from work to observe the religious holiday, and defendant did nothing to attempt to accommodate Tomilina's request, such as to attempt to reschedule any appointments which may have been booked for Tomilina to another date or another manicurist.

After informing Tomilina that she could not have the day off, Gold expected Tomilina to work on September 29 and she continued to book appointments for Tomilina for that day.

On Saturday, September 29, 1990, Tomilina observed Yom Kippur and did not report to work.

Tomilina took her regular days off from work on Sunday, September 30, and Monday, October 1, 1990. She returned to work on Tuesday, October 2, 1990, the first date after Yom Kippur on which she was scheduled to work.

Tomilina worked October 2, 1990, through October 6, 1990, as scheduled, during which time Gold never advised Tomilina that she had violated any company policy by failing to report to work on September 29, 1990.

At the close of business on Saturday, October 6, 1990, Gold called Tomilina into her office and informed Tomilina that the Meszaroses had decided to terminate her employment because she had not come to work on September 29, 1990.

On October 6, 1990, when Tomilina was discharged by defendant, neither Gold nor any other member of defendant's management ever told Tomilina that she was terminated because the company could not afford to allow her to be off from work on a Saturday.

At the time defendant terminated Tomilina, no member of defendant's management doubted the sincerity of Tomilina's religious beliefs.

Defendant replaced Tomilina one month after she was fired.

In or about November, 1982, Glukhovsky began to work for defendant as an esthetician at defendants' Chicago facility.

At some time shortly before Tomilina's request, on or about September 13, 1990, Glukhovsky requested that she be permitted to take off from work on Saturday, September 29, 1990, to observe Yom Kippur.

In requesting Yom Kippur off from work, Glukhovsky did not ask and did not expect to be paid for that day.

At the time, Ilona of Hungary employed five estheticians of whom only Glukhovsky was Jewish.

On or about September 13, 1990, when Glukhovsky made her request to Gold for time off on September 29 to observe Yom Kippur, Gold did not question the sincerity of Glukhovsky's religious beliefs.

Both Gold and the Meszaroses conceded that at the time of Glukhovsky's request they had no basis for doubting the sincerity of Glukhovsky's request for time off from work on Yom Kippur, 1990, and did not question her sincerity.

At the time she requested Yom Kippur off in September, 1990, Glukhovsky, in fact, intended to observe the holy day in keeping with the tenets of her Jewish faith.

Glukhovsky testified credibly that although she had not practiced her faith in the past years, in recent years she has sincerely believed her religion requires that she refrain from work on Yom Kippur. She testified that her faith has become more important to her life as the result of observing that religion had helped her husband grieve his mother's death, her desire that her son grow up in a religious community, and her husband's family, which is very religious, coming to live in Chicago. This progression is corroborated to an extent by evidence that Glukhovsky worked on Yom Kippur through 1987, but did not in 1988, 1989, or 1990. Glukhovsky's testimony about the sincerity of her religious beliefs is credible.

When Glukhovsky made her request to Gold to be off from work to observe Yom Kippur on September 29, 1990, Gold told Glukhovsky that she could not approve her request without first consulting with the Meszaroses.

Gold testified that after Glukhovsky's request, she checked the appointment book and noted that Glukhovsky was partially booked for Saturday, September 29. Gold believed that if Glukhovsky was already partially booked, she would be fully booked by September 29. Other estheticians were also partially booked. Gold testified that she informed Glukhovsky that, based on the amount of clients booked and the nature of her request, she probably could not have the day off but would check with headquarters.

On or about September 20, 1990, Gold told Glukhovsky that the Meszaroses had decided that she could not take Yom Kippur off.

Glukhovsky testified that when Gold informed her that her request for time off from work to observe Yom Kippur on September 29, 1990, had been denied, she asked Gold whether or not she had stressed to the Meszaroses the importance of the Yom Kippur holiday to her; she asked Gold whether she could speak to the Meszaroses directly the next time Gold communicated with the owners so that she could personally stress the importance of the holiday to them; and she told Gold not to book any clients for her because she was not going to report to work on Yom Kippur. Glukhovsky testified that Gold even advised her to call in sick so as to avoid a confrontation on the issue. Gold denied all of these statements.

Gold testified that she expected Glukhovsky to come to work on September 29. The absence record for that day, prepared by Gold, reflects, however, that Glukhovsky's absence was "expected in advance." The court finds that it is likely that Glukhovsky did inform Gold that, despite the Meszaroses' denial of her request, she would not come to work on Yom Kippur, but that Gold, being "between a rock and a hard place", followed her employer's direction and continued to book appointments as if Glukhovsky would come to work. The court credits Glukhovsky's testimony concerning her conversations with Gold.

After defendant learned that Glukhovsky needed Yom Kippur 1990 off from work, neither Gold nor any other member of defendant's management considered or offered any accommodation to allow Glukhovsky to observe the religious holiday, and defendant did nothing to attempt to accommodate Glukhovsky's request. For example, between the time of Glukhovsky's request, and September

29, 1990, defendant did not attempt to reschedule any appointments which may have been booked for Glukhovsky to another date or another esthetician, and did not attempt to avoid scheduling appointments for Glukhovsky for September 29.

On Saturday, September 29, 1990, Glukhovsky observed Yom Kippur and did not report to work.

Glukhovsky took her regular days off from work on Sunday, September 30, 1990, and Monday, October 1, 1990.

Glukhovsky returned to work on Tuesday, October 2, 1990, the first date after Yom Kippur on which she was scheduled to work.

Glukhovsky worked through October 6, 1990, during which time Gold never advised Glukhovsky that she had violated any company policy by failing to report to work on September 29, 1990.

The Meszaroses made a decision to terminate Glukhovsky and instructed Gold to fire her.

At the close of business on Saturday, October 6, 1990, Gold called Glukhovsky into Gold's office and informed Glukhovsky that the company had decided to terminate her employment because she did not work on September 29, 1990.

On October 6, 1990, when Glukhovsky was discharged by defendant, neither Gold nor any other member of defendant's management told Glukhovsky that she was terminated because the company could not afford to allow her to be off on a Saturday.

At the time defendant terminated Glukhovsky, no member of defendant's management doubted the sincerity of Glukhovsky's religious beliefs.

The defendant did not replace Glukhovsky until June, 1991.

On September 29, Gold was required to accommodate Ilona of Hungary's customers who had been scheduled for Tomilina and Glukhovsky. Some of the customers were seen by other manicurists or estheticians; some may have rescheduled and some may have left disappointed, even angry, that Ilona of Hungary had not been able to keep their appointments. There are no records, however, and no one could identify anyone who was turned away. At the least, the unplanned absence of two of the service employees made the day more difficult for coworkers and for the manager.

Ilona of Hungary's assertion that September 29 was an exceptionally busy day is not borne out by the evidence. Notably, it was Yom Kippur, which likely eliminated some of the clientele for that day. Otherwise, there was nothing remarkable about the day, such as an upcoming holiday, that would have made it a particularly busy Saturday.

According to financial records of Ilona of Hungary, an exceptionally busy day occurred on August 25 when the revenue from estheticians was $3,065. The revenue from estheticians on September 29 was $1,742. The preceding Saturday, it was $1,640, and the Saturday following, $1,526. The revenue from manicurists on September 29 was $622. The preceding Saturday, it was $705 and the following, $535. These figures suggest that September 29 revenues were essentially normal.

Similarly, Ilona of Hungary has asserted that Tomilina had committed sufficient work violations that she would have been fired anyhow. This is not credible where Ilona of Hungary concedes that Tomilina had a loyal customer base, indeed, "the largest following of clients." The assertion that Tomilina was headed for termination apart from the September 29 incident is simply not credible.

Title VII prohibits an employer from discriminating against an employee, with respect to terms, conditions or privileges of employment, because of the employee's religion, 42 U.S.C. 2000e-2(a)(1), unless the employer can show that "he is unable to reasonably accommodate an employee's or prospective employee's religious observation or practice without undue hardship on the conduct of the employer's business." 2000eJ). In a curious use of language, 2000eJ) recites that "The term 'religion' includes all aspects of religious observance and practice, as well as belief, unless an employer demonstrates that he is unable to reasonably accommodate an employee's . . . religious observance or practice without undue hardship on the conduct of the employer's business." This section has been interpreted to mean "that an employer, short of 'undue hardship,' is required to make 'reasonable accommodations' to the 'religious needs of its employees.'" The courts have described the prime facie case of religious discrimination as requiring a plaintiff to show that (1) the discharged employee's practices were religious; (2) the employee called the religious practice to the attention of the employer;

and (3) the religious practice was the basis for the discharge.

EEOC has demonstrated that Tomilina and Glukhovsky requested a day off for observance of a sincerely held religious practice, that defendant denied their requests without any attempt to accommodate their religious practice, and that defendant fired them after they chose to miss work rather than forgo their religious observance. Defendant has disputed the sincerity of Glukhovsky's religious belief, but, as indicated in the Findings of Fact, the court has resolved this issue in favor of EEOC and found her beliefs to be sincere. Defendant has also suggested that it did accommodate Tomalina and Glukhovsky by offering them another day off, but because Yom Kippur is not a moveable day, this was no accommodation at all.

With regard to Tomilina, the court stated that she is entitled to an award of back pay for wages and vacation pay lost as a result of the events at issue in the amount of $3,240, plus prejudgment interest. ("Prejudgment interest is an element of complete compensation and a normal incident of relief under Title VII."). Tomilina does not seek reinstatement.

Concerning Glukhovsky, as the Finding of Facts indicate, the court finds that Glukhovsky would not have left her job voluntarily at Ilona of Hungary and is thus entitled to an award of back pay for the entire period, including benefits. This amount must, however, be reduced by the amount of Glukhovsky's interim earnings from her businesses. Glukhovsky is also entitled to prejudgment interest.

Glukhovsky is also entitled to reinstatement to all benefits of her employment on the same terms as existed on September 29, 1990, and as would have inured to her had she remained to the present. Glukhovsky is entitled to "front pay" from the date of judgment until the date the offer of reinstatement is presented and thereafter until Glukhovsky should be allowed to return to work. If the offer is outstanding for 14 days and is not accepted, it may be withdrawn and the order for front pay shall be void.

Concerning the injunction, the court agrees with EEOC that an injunction is proper which shall permanently restrain defendant from discriminating against employees on the basis of their religion. In cases presenting abundant evidence of consistent past discrimination, injunctive relief is mandatory absent clear and convincing proof that there is no reasonable probability of further noncompliance with the law. Although the court has no evidence of prior incidents such as these, where in response to the events at issue here, the defendant withdrew its employment manual which provided a policy of accommodation an injunction is appropriate. EEOC is also entitled to monitoring provisions it requests for a three-year period, as follows:

Ilona of Hungary, Inc., shall report to the EEOC every six (6) months regarding its employees' requests for time off, including:

a. identity of employee making the request;
b. position of employee making the request;
c. location of facility which employs the requesting employee;
d. nature of the employee's request;
e. whether the request was granted or denied;
f. identity of person(s) who made the decision to grant or deny the request; and
g. if the request is denied, all efforts made to accommodate the request and the reasons for the denial.

The EEOC is awarded its costs incurred in this action.

Judgment for EEOC.

BONA FIDE OCCUPATIONAL QUALIFICATION

Religious organizations are permitted to discriminate as long as the position relates to the promotion of the religion. Religious belief is considered a Bona Fide Occupational Qualification.

Employment Perspective

John's Lutheran Church has a position available as administrative assistant to the minister. MaryBeth Luciano, a Catholic, is refused the position because she is not Lutheran. Is this religious discrimination? No! St. John's Lutheran may discriminate in favor of its own parishioners because the position is involved with the operation of the Church. ◆

Employment Perspective

Mount Franklin United Methodist Church runs a summer soccer camp for children aged six through twelve. It is open to children of all faiths. Al Kaplan, who is Jewish, applies for the position of soccer instructor. Al played four years as starting forward for the state university and he is well qualified. Mount Franklin refuses to hire Al because he is not Methodist. Al claims that religious beliefs are not a bona fide occupational qualification of a soccer instructor. Who would win? Most likely Al! The determination would hinge upon whether Mount Franklin is trying to promote the Methodist Religion to young children through their participation in the soccer camp. As the camp is open to children of all faiths, this is not the case. ◆

The term *religion* refers to religious practice as well as religious belief. There is often a conflict as to whether a group qualifies as a religion or is secular in nature. One test to apply would be to find whether its members belong to an organized religion in addition to the group.

Employment Perspective

During an interview for a supervisory position in the auto plant of Prestige Motors, Tom Westfield, the applicant, was asked whether he could start to work the evening shift every Tuesday night. Tom responded that on Tuesday nights, he was obligated to attend a Ku Klux Klan meeting but that he would be available every other evening. Tom was rejected because he was unavailable on Tuesday nights. Tom filed a claim with the EEOC under Title VII, claiming that Prestige would not make a reasonable accommodation for his religious practices. Prestige argued that the Ku Klux Klan is not a religious organization. Will Tom win? No! The Ku Klux Klan has been determined to be a political rather than a religious organization and that as such no accommodation has to be made. ◆

Religious practices that require its members to wear certain clothing or to groom themselves in certain ways are protected unless they present an undue hardship to the employer.

In the next case, a worker wore a button having controversial religious overtones. The employer prohibited her from wearing the button. She cited religious discrimination, claiming that she was not reasonably accommodated.

CASE *Wilson v. U.S. West Communications*

58 F.3d 1337 (8th Cir. 1995)

JOHN R. GIBSON, Senior Circuit Judge.

Christine L. Wilson appeals from judgment entered in favor of U.S. West Communications on her religious discrimination claim under Title VII of the Civil Rights Act of 1964. Wilson's wearing of a graphic anti-abortion button caused immediate and emotional reactions from co-workers, and U.S. West asked Wilson to cover the button during work. She refused, and U.S. West ultimately fired her.

Wilson worked for U.S. West for nearly 20 years before U.S. West transferred her to another location as an information specialist assisting U.S. West engineers in making and keeping records of the location of telephone cables. This facility had no dress code.

In late July 1990, Wilson, a Roman Catholic, made a religious vow that she would wear an anti-abortion button "until there was an end to abortion or until she could no longer fight the fight." The button was two inches in diameter and showed a color photograph of an eighteen to twenty-week old fetus. The button also contained the phrases "Stop Abortion," and "They're Forgetting Someone." Wilson chose this particular button because she wanted to be an instrument of God like the Virgin Mary. She believed that the Virgin Mary would have chosen this particular button. She wore the button at all times, unless she was sleeping or bathing. She believed that if she took off the button she would compromise her vow and lose her soul.

Wilson began wearing the button to work in August 1990. Another information specialist asked Wilson not to wear the button to a class she was teaching. Wilson explained her religious vow and refused to stop wearing the button. The button caused disruptions at work. Employees gathered to talk about the button. U.S. West identified Wilson's wearing of the button as a "time robbing" problem. Wilson acknowledged that the button caused a great deal of disruption. A union representative told Wilson's supervisor, Mary Jo Jensen, that some employees threatened to walk off their jobs because of the button. Wilson's co-workers testified that they found the button offensive and disturbing for "very personal reasons," such as infertility problems, miscarriage, and death of a premature infant, unrelated to any stance on abortion or religion.

In early August 1990, Wilson met with her supervisors, Jensen and Gail Klein, five times. Jensen and Klein are also Roman Catholics against abortion. Jensen and Klein told Wilson of co-workers' complaints about the button and an anti-abortion T-shirt Wilson wore which also depicted a fetus. Jensen and Klein told Wilson that her co-workers were uncomfortable and upset and that some were refusing to do their work. Klein noted a 40 percent decline in the productivity of the information specialists since Wilson began wearing the button. Wilson told her supervisors that she should not be singled out for wearing the button because the company had no dress code. She explained that she "just wanted to do [her] job," and suggested that co-workers offended by the button should be asked not to look at it. Klein and Jensen offered Wilson three options: (1) wear the button only in her work cubicle, leaving the button in the cubicle when she moved around the office; (2) cover the button while at work; or (3) wear a different button with the same message but without the photograph. Wilson responded that she could neither cover nor remove the button because it would break her promise to God to wear the button and be a "living witness." She suggested that management tell the other information specialists to "sit at their desk[s] and do the job U.S. West was paying them to do."

On August 22, 1990, Wilson met with Klein, Jensen, and the union's chief steward. During the meeting, Klein again told Wilson that she could either wear the button only in her cubicle or cover the button. Klein explained that, if Wilson continued to wear the button to work, she would be sent home until she could come to work wearing proper attire.

In an August 27, 1990 letter, Klein reiterated Wilson's three options. He added that Wilson could use accrued personal and vacation time instead of reporting to work. Wilson filed suit but later dismissed the action when U.S. West agreed to allow her to return to work and wear the button pending an investigation by the Nebraska Equal Opportunity Commission.

Wilson returned to work on September 18, 1990, and disruptions resumed. Information specialists refused to go to group meetings with Wilson present. The employees complained that the button made them uneasy. Two employees filed grievances based on Wilson's button. Employees accused Jensen of harassment for not resolving the button issue to their satisfaction. Eventually, U.S. West told Wilson not to report to work wearing anything depicting a fetus, including the button or the T-shirt. U.S. West told Wilson again that she could cover or replace the button or wear it only in her cubicle. U.S. West sent Wilson home when she returned to work wearing the button and fired her for missing work unexcused for three consecutive days. Wilson sued U.S. West, claiming that her firing constituted religious discrimination.

An employee establishes a prima facie case of religious discrimination by showing that: (1) the employee has a bona fide religious belief that conflicts with an employment requirement; (2) the employee informed the employer of this belief; (3) the employee was disciplined for failing to comply with the conflicting employment requirement. The parties stipulated that Wilson's "religious beliefs were sincerely held," and the district court ruled that Wilson made a prima facie case of religious discrimination. The court then considered whether U.S. West could defeat Wilson's claim by demonstrating that it offered Wilson a reasonable accommodation. An employer is required to "reasonably accommodate" the religious beliefs or practices of employees unless doing so would cause the employer undue hardship.

The court considered the three offered accommodations and concluded that requiring Wilson to leave the button in her cubicle or to replace the button were not accommodations of Wilson's sincerely held religious beliefs because: (1) removing the button at work violated Wilson's vow to wear the button at all times; and (2) replacing the button prohibited Wilson from wearing the particular button encompassed by her vow. However, the court concluded that requiring Wilson to cover the button while at work was a reasonable accommodation. The court based this determination on its factual finding that Wilson's vow did not require her to be a living witness. The court reasoned that covering the button while at work complied with Wilson's vow but also reduced office turmoil. The court also concluded that, even if Wilson's vow required her to be a living witness, U.S. West could not reasonably accommodate Wilson's religious beliefs without undue hardship. The court entered judgment for U.S. West, and Wilson appeals.

The employer violates the statute unless it "demonstrates that [it] is unable to reasonably accommodate . . . an employee's . . . religious observance or practice without undue hardship on the conduct of the employer's business." When the employer reasonably accommodates the employee's religious beliefs, the statutory inquiry ends. The employer need not show that the employee's proposed accommodations would cause an undue hardship. Undue hardship is at issue "only where the employer claims that it is unable to offer any reasonable accommodation without such hardship." Because we hold that U.S. West offered Wilson a reasonable accommodation, our inquiry ends, we need not consider Wilson's argument that her suggested accommodations would not cause undue hardship.

We recognize that this case typifies workplace conflicts which result when employees hold strong views about emotionally charged issues. We reiterate that Title VII does not require an employer to allow an employee to impose his religious views on others. The employer is only required to reasonably accommodate an employee's religious views.

We affirm the district court's judgment.
Judgment for U.S. West Communications.

Employment Perspective

Morris Gold was hired as a teller for Mid-Island Savings Bank. He wore his yarmulke for work the first day and was told to remove it as it was not proper attire. Because he refused, he was terminated. Morris filed a claim with the EEOC, stating that it was a recognized religious practice of the Jewish faith. Will he win? Yes! The practice of wearing a yarmulke is protected as it does not present an undue hardship to the employer. ◆

In the following case, an employee selected the town in which he wished to relocate on the basis of its having an active religious community of his faith. His employer objected because it was too far from the place of employment. The first issue is whether an employee's residence may be determined by an employer. The second is, if so, then may an exception be carried out to accommodate this employee because of his religious beliefs.

CASE

Vetter v. Farmland Industries, Inc.

884 F.Supp. 1287 (N.D. Iowa 1995)

BENNETT, District Judge.

The summary judgment record reveals that the following facts are undisputed: Vetter and his wife are adherents of the Jewish faith. Although Mrs. Vetter had been born into the Jewish faith, Vetter had converted to Judaism in a ceremony only about four months prior to Vetter's employment with Farmland. Prior to his employment with Farmland, Vetter and his family were living in Muscatine, Iowa, a town without a significant Jewish community. While living in Muscatine, the Vetters travelled approximately thirty miles to attend regular religious services. Farmland is an agricultural products company that sells supplies to the farming community. Farmland is a corporation owned by its member farm cooperatives. In its Webster City trade area, Farmland works with United Co-op, a member farm cooperative, to sell farming supplies to farmers in the area.

Vetter applied for a job with Farmland as a Livestock Production Specialist (LPS) in July of 1992. The principal job duties of an LPS are to work in conjunction with the management of the assigned cooperative to sell Farmland livestock feed and animal health products within the cooperative's trade territory. Vetter had an initial telephone interview with George Gleckler, Farmland's Area Feed Sales Manager. In-person interviews with Farmland officials followed in early and mid-August.

Vetter's mid-August interview was with Gleckler, Dave Engstrom, who was Farmland's LPS Supervisor, Al Jorth, the General Manager for the United Co-op, and Ken Bever, a Supervisor for the United Co-op. During this interview, Mr. Jorth asked how soon Vetter could start, and also asked about Vetter's interest in purchasing or renting housing. Mr. Jorth suggested that rental housing would be difficult to find. Following the interview, in a separate conversation, Gleckler informed Vetter that he "could live where he could find a house," which Vetter understood to mean anywhere within a reasonable distance of Webster City. The evening following the interview, Vetter and his wife drove around Webster City for approximately forty-five minutes looking for appropriate housing.

Gleckler offered Vetter the job in Webster City by telephone on August 21, 1992. In a follow-up telephone call on August 24, Vetter indicated that they had been looking for housing in Ames, approximately 35 miles from Webster City, because it had an active synagogue. Gleckler responded that Ames might be "a little far," but that he would check on it. Later that evening, Gleckler called Vetter back to inform him that he had found out that there was a synagogue in Fort Dodge, Iowa. Vetter began working for Farmland on September 1, 1992, by attending a sales meeting in Des Moines, at which he again raised the issue of living in Ames with Gleckler. Gleckler reiterated that he thought that Ames would not be acceptable. Again during meetings in Kansas City on September 9th and 10th, 1992, Vetter discussed the possibility of living in Ames with Terry Allen, Farmland's regional Feed Manager. Allen also indicated that Ames would not be an acceptable place for Vetter to live. Gleckler and Allen suggested that Vetter look further in Webster City and Fort Dodge. The Vetters rejected Fort Dodge after learning that the synagogue there was essentially "inactive," providing services only every few months, and that there was no Jewish community of significant size or activity. The Vetters also considered the only housing they had found in Webster City that was large enough to accommodate their whole family inadequate on the grounds that they believed it was in a government subsidized complex for which they would not qualify and which they did not think was adequate.

On September 21, 1992, Gleckler told Vetter that the had learned that Vetter was planning to rent housing in Ames. Vetter explained that he had put a small deposit on one residence in Ames. Vetter was therefore terminated effective September 21, 1992. Vetter asserts that he was not given any reason for his termination at the time he was discharged. The employee separation form filled out by Terry Allen has checked as the reason for discharge "other," and in the space provided for explanation "Relocation within trade territory was condition of employment. Employee refused to locate as required." Gleckler, Vetter's supervisor, testified in deposition that Vetter was terminated for "insubordination." In answer to interrogatories from Vetter, Farmland identified as the reason for his discharge that Vetter "apparently was not willing to live within the trade territory he was responsible for servicing after having been informed as to the requirement and after having agreed to do so."

There are a number of factual disputes raised by the Parties, some of which are material to disposition of this case. A key dispute in this matter is whether Farmland officials ever specifically told Vetter that Ames was an unacceptable place for him to live. Farmland asserts that Vetter was told on a number of occasions that Ames would not be acceptable. Vetter asserts that he was never told Ames was unacceptable, just that various people doubted that it would be acceptable, and that every time he raised the issue, it was apparent that Farmland officials preferred that he live closer to Webster City, because he was encouraged to keep looking in the surrounding area.

Juxtaposed to this dispute over the genuineness of Farmland's interest in where Vetter lives is the dispute of the parties over whether Vetter's desire to live in Ames was based on his religious beliefs or merely on personal preference. Vetter has provided the affidavit of Rabbi Stanley Herrnan, who affirms that "living in an active Jewish community with an active synagogue is essential to the sustenance of one's faith as a Jew, so much so it rises to the level of being a niitzvah (Jewish law)." However, Farmland points out that Vetter formerly lived in a community that had no such active Jewish community, and the court observes that a great many Jews in this area of the country do not live in such an "active Jewish community."

The parties also dispute the availability and definition of "suitable" housing in the Webster City trade area. Vetter has found little housing of any kind available either for sale or rent in Webster City, Vetter said that he doubted that his family would be qualified for housing suggested by Farmland because it was government subsidized. Vetter admits that he considered the housing complex in question otherwise unacceptable for personal reasons. Farmland asserts that Vetter was unduly selective in his definition of suitable housing and made inadequate efforts to find housing within the trade territory.

Vetter's complaint alleges discrimination on the basis of religion on two theories. First, Vetter alleges that he was subjected to disparate treatment, because other LPSs have been allowed to live either outside of their trade areas or at greater distances from cooperatives that they serve than he would have been if allowed to live in Ames, and further that other LPSs were not terminated, whereas he was, for desiring to live or living outside of their trade areas. Second, Vetter alleges that Farmland refused to make reasonable accommodations to his religious observances or practices by refusing to allow him to live in Ames, or to allow him to live in Webster City while his family lived in Ames. The court will consider whether Farmland is entitled to summary judgment on either of these claims.

A disparate treatment case based on religion requires the plaintiff to show that he or she is, or was, treated less favorably than others because of the plaintiff's religion. Thus, the plaintiff in a disparate case based on religion must prove he or she is a member of a protected class and must compare his or her treatment to that of a similarly situated member of a non-protected class in his complaint.

Vetter argues that Farmland refused to make reasonable accommodations to his religious beliefs because Farmland refused to consider his suggestion that he maintain a residence for himself in Webster City while his family lived in Ames. Vetter has since argued that he also suggested as a reasonable accommodation that he bear any additional costs of his travel to his trade area that might result if he and his family were to live in Ames. Farmland argues that nothing about Vetter's religion required him to live in Ames, or outside of the trade area, therefore it was under no obligation to provide any accommodation. Farmland has also, at least implicitly, suggested that by pointing out that Fort Dodge had a synagogue and that Vetter could live there, they offered a reasonable accommodation.

To reiterate, Vetter must make the following prima facie showing in support of his claim of failure to accommodate his religion: (1) Vetter has a bona fide belief that compliance with an employment requirement is contrary to his religious faith; (2) Vetter informed Farmland about the conflict; and (3) Vetter asserts that a religious belief is incompatible with a requirement of employment. On this issue: Vetter was a recent convert to Judaism, and his children were endeavoring to pursue religious training in that faith. Thus, the growth of the family's faith during the period in question is uncontradicted. Because Vetter was a recent convert to Judaism, the court finds that his prior conduct in Muscatine is of little relevance to the question of the sincerity of his belief in a need to live in a Jewish community. To the extent that is relevant, the court finds that Vetter's uncontradicted testimony is that even had Vetter not taken the job with Farmland, they would have attempted to move to the Quad Cities area, because of its active Jewish community. Their evidence, again uncontroverted, is that their plans to move to the Quad Cities for this reason before Vetter was offered the job with Farmland were thwarted by floods in the area. Furthermore, the sincerity of Vetter's belief is reinforced by his conduct of asserting the belief in the face of opposition from his employer, and in his offers to provide for that belief at some personal cost in his offers either to pay for extra travel costs or to live in Webster City while his family lives in Ames. Thus, the court finds as a matter of law that Vetter's religious beliefs in question here were indeed sincerely held. As to the third element, there is no dispute that Vetter was discharged because of noncompliance with the employment requirement that he live within his trade area. Vetter has established at least a genuine issue of material fact in each element of his prima facie case of disparate treatment because of religion and on the question of whether Farmland's proffered legitimate reason for his discharge is pretextual. The court concludes that the elements of a prima facie case of disparate treatment because of religion are as follows: (1) the plaintiff was a member of a protected class because of the plaintiff's religious affiliation or beliefs; (2) the employee informed the employer of his or her religious beliefs; (3) the plaintiff was qualified for the position; (4) despite plaintiff's qualifications, the plaintiff was fired or denied an employment benefit; and (5) similarly situated employees, outside of the plaintiff's protected class were treated differently or there is other evidence giving rise to an inference of discrimination.

Examining these elements in this light the court finds that there is no significant dispute that Vetter was a member of a protected class on the basis of his adherence to the Jewish faith, he informed his employer of his adherence to that faith, he was qualified for the position in which he was employed, and he was fired from that position. Vetter has generated a genuine issue of material fact to go with the final element of his prima facie case because, although he was hired and fired essentially by the same person, there is no presumption that the termination was not discriminatory, because it was only after he was hired that Farmland officials learned of his religious affiliation, and because of evidence of more favorable treatment of similarly situated LPSs who were not members of his faith.

Judgment for Vetter.

Employment Perspective

Mustafa Darey, a Rastafarian, wore his hair in dreadlocks. When he was hired by Faster Food Service, he was told he would have to cut them. He refused. Mustafa filed a claim with the EEOC citing the wearing of dreadlocks were part of his religion. Faster Food maintained it was unsanitary in violation of Health Department regulations. Will Mustafa prevail? It may be possible to accommodate Mustafa by having him enclose his hair in a plastic cap. If Mustafa refuses, then his religious practice will be overridden for public health reasons. ◆

FIRST AMENDMENT PROTECTION

The First Amendment to the United States Constitution addresses religion in two respects. First, it prohibits the government from establishing a national religion. Freedom from religious persecution is an important reason why many immigrants came to this country. Permitting people the freedom to choose how, when, and where to worship is an important consideration in this country. Allowing others to discriminate because of religion not only compromises this First Amendment right but also promotes the economic advantages of belonging to one religion. The latter factor violates the Establishment Clause.

In the case that follows, an employee who acted as an interpreter for deaf students refused to convey certain foul language that she found objectionable to her religious beliefs. Her employer refused to accommodate her practice, arguing that all language must be interpreted. She may not act as a censor.

CASE

Sedalia School Dist. v. Com'n on Human Rights

843 S.W.2d 928 (Mo.App. W.D. 1992)

LOWENSTEIN, Chief Judge.

The facts as found show that Mary E. Schumaker, a member of the United Pentecostal Church, was employed by the District as an interpreter and tutor for deaf students. During her three prior years employment she worked at an elementary school a year and then at a middle school for two years. In those positions, she either modified language she found objectionable, or informed students that the speaker had cursed or used "bad language." Schumaker would not take God's name in vain nor use everyday swear words. She interpreted the line in *Gone With the Wind,* "Frankly my dear, I don't give a damn," as "Frankly, I don't care." During a film shown in science class about an erupting volcano, a man who wouldn't get off the mountain "was using bad language," and Schumaker "didn't interpret it."

The District then set up an advisory committee of deaf students' parents and teachers to develop guidelines for interpreters. The committee procured a copy of the guidelines of the Registry for Interpreters of the Deaf (R.I.D.), a nationally recognized organization, and after deliberation, adopted the guidelines. Set out below is a portion of the R.I.D. guidelines important to this case. The advisory committee felt it was necessary for deaf students to develop socially, and that students should receive exact information and make their own judgments. Interpreter/transliterators are not editors and must transmit everything the same way as it was intended. This is especially difficult when the interpreter disagrees with what is being said or feels uncomfortable when profanity is being used. Interpreters/transliterators must remember that they are not at all responsible for what is said, only for conveying it accurately. If the Interpreter/transliterator's own feelings interfere with rendering the message accurately, he/she shall withdraw from the situation.

Before the guidelines were formally adopted, Schumaker told District personnel, she couldn't interpret "everything," due to her religious convictions against using "bad language"; never has anyone questioned the genuineness of Schumaker's religious beliefs.

The District board then adopted the committee's guidelines, including the requirement of literal word for word interpretation to the deaf students. When it came to contract time, Schumacher wrote on her contract "(1) I request to go to primary level, and (2) I request parents tell their child they are cursing or using bad language." Her feeling was that there would be fewer obscene words used at the primary school. However, the District, due to Schumacher's 22 years of signing experience, wanted to use her at the higher grade level rather than in primary levels, where other interpreters were better suited to work. Because she would not work at the District's high school under the new guidelines, she was terminated. This court reviews the Commission's conclusion that the District failed to accommodate her religious beliefs by making no attempt to put her in a grade school, or acceding to her proviso of being able to talk to the students' parents about her non-literal interpretations. This is accomplished when the plaintiff demonstrates (1) a bona-fide belief that compliance with the District's requirement would be contrary to her religious belief, (2) the employer was so notified, and, (3) the employee was discharged for failing to comply with the requirement. Schumaker and the Commission made such a case. Although not binding on the Commission, the Chief Hearing Examiner for the Commission decided in favor of the District. The Commission decided otherwise in its Decision and Order, and found telling the fact that the District did not utilize the R.I.D. guideline language allowing the interpreter to withdraw from the situation if their own feelings interfered with an accurate message being conveyed. This court must decide "whether Commission, after detached consideration of all the evidence before it, could reasonably have made the findings and order whether the decision is arbitrary, capricious, unreasonable or an abuse of discretion.

Requiring a literal translation of classroom conversation is not an unreasonable guideline. Neither Schumaker nor the Commission could articulate what her religious beliefs were, other than that she did not want to use or repeat any words which she found offensive. Neither could they reasonably define what words were included in her personal taboo but this would have made the District entirely beholden to Schumaker in making ad hoc decisions about which words to translate.

The District should not be required to subject itself to a potentially arbitrary administration of its policy. Due to the virtual impossibility of accommodating Schumaker's religious beliefs, no further meetings or attempts to negotiate with her would have netted a satisfactory compromise. To require the District to assign a specific teacher to an area where a compromising situation might arise is unreasonable. Requiring a shuffling of other interpreters in and out of a classroom on an ad hoc basis would disrupt attempts to educate. Moving interpreters into classrooms where their abilities and experience are either under-used or over-taxed is unreasonable. Similarly, having an interpreter pre-censor work with parents would create an ill-advised policy, and would be subject to the same definitional problem previously mentioned—there being no information as to what words or in what context those words would offend the employee. Hardship and more than a de minimis cost are demonstrated by the District.

The District's regulation requiring literal translation was reasonable as a legitimate means of giving students social and educational skills and awareness, and was applied here without discrimination.

Judgment for Sedalia School District.

The First Amendment also promotes the freedom to associate. If a person chooses to associate socially only with members of his or her own religion that is a protected choice. Employment, however, is not social; it is economic. It is unfair for an employer to choose its employees on the basis of their religious preference. How is this characteristic job-related? It is not. Employers should respect the right of employees to worship as they please on their own time, and if possible, should reasonably accommodate their employees to enable them to do so.

CONCLUSION

Employers should not pry into the personal lives of their employees any more than they would like their employees seeking personal information about them or their top executives. If everyone converted to a particular religion, their job performance would not therefore improve. Thus, employers have no right to discriminate because of religion.

Employers need only consider global trade. It would be a foolish thought for an employer to trade only with countries having the same religion as the employer. More so, if an employer establishes a subsidiary overseas or otherwise employs foreign people to work on its behalf, it would be nearly impossible to discriminate on the basis of religion, race, or national origin. Religious discrimination is rendered impracticable in a global employment. The same philosophy should apply domestically. The practice of any form of discrimination weakens the employer by narrowing the pool of qualified candidates available for the job.

REVIEW QUESTIONS

1. Define religious discrimination.
2. Explain the significance of the First Amendment with respect to religious discrimination.
3. Define reasonable accommodation for religious observances.
4. Can an employer refuse to accommodate an employee's religious belief because it imposes a hardship?

5. How can an employer discern whether a group to which an employee claims membership qualifies as a religion?
6. Can religious belief qualify as a bona fide occupational qualification?
7. May an employee dress in his or her religious garb at work?
8. Must an employer allow the wearing of a button saying "Stop Abortion Now"?
9. Is religious grooming an acceptable practice in the workplace?
10. May an employer question the authenticity and genuineness of an employee's religion?
11. An airline employee requested to be absent from work every Saturday. Since the airline was open twenty-four hours every day, the job had to be filled at all times. The airline argued that it would incur extra costs to accommodate the employee's religious observance and to do so would create an undue economic hardship. Hardison, the employee, claimed that the airline's failure to acquiesce constituted religious discrimination. What was the result? (*Trans World Airlines, Inc. v. Hardison,* 432 U.S.63, 1977).
12. Plaintiff has brought suit under 42 U.S.C. 1983, contending that Defendants deprived him of his civil rights by offering Christian prayers at university-sponsored functions that he is required to attend. Plaintiff also complains that Defendant Onwubiko holds Bible study classes at the Engineering School. Plaintiff alleges that the promotion of these religious activities in such a manner violates the Establishment Clause of the First Amendment. He further contends that requiring students and faculty to attend such events violates their rights under the Free Exercise Clause of the First Amendment. What was the result? *Chaudmuri v. State of Tennessee,* 886 F.Supp. 1374 (M.D. Tenn. 1995).
13. Mary Myers is a Seventh Day Adventist who abstains from work on the Sabbath, from sundown on Friday to sundown on Saturday. In June 1988 she was hired by the TA as a bus operator trainee. After completing six weeks of Monday-through-Friday training, she selected the East New York Depot as her assignment, and Wednesday and Thursday as her regular days off. Her first choice was Friday and Saturday, but those more popular off-days were already preempted by employees more senior to her. When Myers presented a request for special consideration on religious grounds, petitioner Transit Workers Union ("TWU") objected to any such accommodations on the ground that it would violate the seniority rules in the collective bargaining agreement. What was the result? *N.Y. City Transit v. State Exec. Dept.,* 627 N.Y.S.2d 360 (A.D. 1 Dept. 1995).
14. Plaintiff claimed that his supervisor was anti-Semitic. He said that the supervisor had a subjective bias against Jews and made disparaging remarks about them. When asked specifically what those remarks were, plaintiff could not recount them. What was the result? *Meiri v. Dacon,* 759 F.2d 989 (2nd Cir. 1985).
15. An action was brought by two members of the Native American Church, who had been denied unemployment compensation by the State of Oregon. Compensation had been denied because the two workers had been discharged by their private employer for "misconduct." The "misconduct" was the ingestion of peyote at a religious ceremony. Oregon law made the possession of peyote a crime and provided no exception for religious use. The two church members claimed that the denial of unemployment benefits on that ground violated their First Amendment right to free exercise of their religion. Was this an act of religious discrimination? *Employment Division, Dept. of Human Resources of Oregon v. Smith,* 494 U.S. 872 (1990).
16. In the case on pp. 356, should religious beliefs be accorded reasonable accommodation in the workplace?

17. Was the case on pp. 369 decided ethically?
18. In the case on pp. 358, was the employer unreasonable in refusing to give the employee the day off?
19. In the case on pp. 366 should an employer be allowed to dictate where an employee lives in regard to his or her proximity to the workplace?
20. In the case on pp. 364, should employees be allowed to express their religious beliefs through the wearing of buttons at the workplace?

First Amendment to the Constitution of the United States of America

AMENDMENT I (1791)

Congress shall make no law respecting an establishment of religion, or prohibiting the free exercise thereof; or abridging the freedom of speech, or the press, or the right of the people peaceably to assemble, and to petition the Government for a redress of grievances.

CHAPTER 16

National Origin

Individuals are protected from discrimination based on national origin under Title VII of the Civil Service Rights Act and the Immigration Reform and Control Act of 1986. National origin refers to a person's roots, that is, the country in which the person or the person's ancestors were born. The four-step test for national origin discrimination is as follows:

1. Employee belongs to the protected class.
2. Employee wanted to retain or obtain the position.
3. Employee was terminated or applicant was refused employment.
4. Termination or refusal to hire occurred because of employee's or applicant's national origin.

Employment Perspective

Manolo Fuentes is a Spanish-American; his ancestors came from Spain. When Manolo applies for a position as a stockbroker with Bull and Bear after graduating at the top of his university class, he is offered a job in the mail room. When he questions this offer, a manager from Bull and Bear informs him that "this is where you Puerto Ricans belong." Manolo corrects Bull and Bear about his heritage, but the manager retorts, "You are all the same." Manolo argues that it should not matter whether he is from Spain, Puerto Rico, Latin America, or Mexico and that he should be judged on the basis of his qualifications, not regional or ethnic stereotypes. Will Manolo win? Yes! Offering a person a low level position solely because he or she is from Spain, Puerto Rico, Latin America, or Mexico is in violation of Title VII's prohibition against national origin discrimination. ◆

The following case addresses the question of whether an employee's dismissal was due to her national origin or to her inability to acclimate herself to the newly computerized quality control system. The employee argued that her supervisor and coworkers made ethnic slurs. The issue is whether her national origin was the reason for her discharge.

CASE

Hong v. Children's Memorial Hosp.

993 F.2d 1257 (7th Cir. 1993)

KANNE, Judge.

Children's Memorial Hospital hired Hong in November 1968 as a medical technologist in the hospital's Clinical Chemical Laboratory. As a technologist, Ms. Hong conducted tests on patient specimens in accordance with hospital procedures and quality control control measures. She worked part-time until October 15, 1976, when she was made a full-time medical technologist or "Medical Technologist II." In April 1981, as the result of an across-the-board salary adjustment applicable to all medical technologists working in the laboratory, Ms. Hong's employment classification was changed to that of a "Medical Technologist III." From 1976 until her discharge in October 1987, Ms. Hong's immediate supervisor was Marina Barrientos. As one of her responsibilities, Ms. Barrientos conducted annual performance appraisals of Ms. Hong's work. The record shows that, prior to 1985, these reviews were generally favorable. Dr. Frederick Smith, Division Head of the Department of Clinical Pathology at Children's Memorial Hospital, supervised the Clinical Chemistry Laboratory, but did not participate in either annual evaluations of medical technologists or informal disciplinary matters.

Beginning in early 1986, the hospital commenced an internal evaluation of its laboratory operations for the purpose of upgrading equipment and technology, and improving overall performance. In addition to installing more modern instrumentation, Dr. Smith implemented a computerized quality control system for use in specimen testing. All medical technologists received training in the new procedures and on the new instruments.

In 1985, 1986, and 1987, Ms. Hong's annual performance evaluation scores steadily declined. Among other things, she was cited for excessive absenteeism, failure to perform assigned tasks in a timely manner, failure to identify instrument malfunctions during testing procedures, failure to report test results to her supervisors, failure to maintain laboratory inventory, and failure to follow the laboratory's quality control and management procedures. In addition, from February 1986 to July 1987, Ms. Hong was issued seven formal written disciplinary notices for deficiencies in her work and uncooperative behavior. Two of these reports resulted in probationary periods of two and three months; a third resulted in a two-day suspension. She also received informal counseling from her superiors, including additional training on the new quality control instruments.

On March 5, 1987, Dr. Smith sent Ms. Hong a memorandum informing her of the two month probation mentioned above and explaining that unless her performance on the job improved to an acceptable level during that period she would be discharged. Months later, on October 20 after yet another formal disciplinary notice, Dr. Smith sent Ms. Hong a memorandum stating that her term of employment in the Clinical Chemistry

Laboratory was at an end. The memo indicated that staff are obliged to conduct laboratory work reliably and quickly for the benefit of patients and that Ms. Hong's poor performance record over the previous year and a half was simply unsatisfactory. She was encouraged to seek other suitable positions within the hospital, and was advised of her right to file an internal grievance. She did file a grievance, and received a hearing before a committee composed of hospital management and staff. The committee affirmed Dr. Smith's decision. Ms. Hong then brought this suit in federal district court, averring that Children's Memorial Hospital had wrongfully discharged her from its employ because of her Korean ancestry in violation of Title VII of the 1964 Civil Rights Act. According to the plaintiff, Dr. Smith told her brother-in-law that Ms. Hong "should move back to Korea." Second, the plaintiff claims that her supervisor, Marina Barrientos, told her repeatedly at work to "learn to speak English" despite the absence of evidence that the plaintiff spoke anything other than English. Finally, the plaintiff claims that she was singled out for disciplinary action, and that non-Korean medical technologists with comparable annual evaluation scores were not discharged. This evidence of disparate treatment, the plaintiff submits, demonstrates that the hospital's stated reason for discharging her was pretextual. The critical issue is whether she was performing well in her job at the time of her termination.

In the Clinical Chemistry Laboratory, Medical Technologists receive annual written evaluations as scored on a range from 100 points (quality and quantity of work is marginal) to 400 points (quality and quantity of work is consistently exceptional). A score of 200 denotes competency, while a score of 300 "exceeds expectations."

In 1985, the plaintiff received a total evaluation score of 230 and had no disciplinary notices in her file. The following year she received a score of 225 and in 1987, a score of 140. The only technologist with an annual score comparatively close to the plaintiff's 1987 score of 140, was Iqbal Mohammed, who received a score of 185. The plaintiff points to this, in her words "less than adequate score," the two disciplinary notices issued to Ms. Mohammed that year and the fact that Ms. Mohammed was not discharged as proof of disparate treatment.

Children's Memorial Hospital is in a better position than this court to assess the relative qualifications of its employees and to determine when an employee's performance is so deficient as to potentially compromise the level of care to which patients are entitled. In 1987, Ms. Mohammed had a higher evaluation score and half as many disciplinary notices as the plaintiff. That the hospital did not discharge Ms. Mohammed as well as the plaintiff is hardly evidence of disparate treatment. Rather it appears to be a business decision within the defendant's sound discretion.

Such is not the case here. The record leaves us with the firm impression that the plaintiff's troubles on the job had far more to do with learning the laboratory's new computerized quality control system than contending with acts of invidious discrimination by her supervisors. We conclude that the plaintiff's proffer of Ms. Barrientos' remarks is insufficient to stave off summary judgment.

As part of her prima facie case of intentional discrimination under Title VII, the plaintiff has failed to establish that she performed her job well enough to meet her employer's legitimate expectations. Likewise the evidence she presents in an effort to show that national origin was a factor in the hospital's decision to terminate her is insufficient to avert summary adjudication. Accordingly, the district court's grant of summary judgment in favor of Children's Memorial Hospital is affirmed.

Judgment for Children's Memorial Hospital.

In the following case, a Hispanic male applied for a position on three separate occasions. He met the qualifications, but each time the employer hired a white person. The Hispanic male alleged that he would have been hired except for his national origin.

CASE Sanchez v. Philip Morris, Inc.

992 F.2d 244 (10th Cir. 1993)

SETH, Circuit Judge.

Appellee Raul C. Sanchez filed an action against Philip Morris, Inc. ("Philip Morris") and Ralph Rayburn alleging reverse gender and national origin discrimination in violation of Title VII of the federal Civil Rights Acts, as well as violations of Oklahoma public policy.

The dispositive facts in this case are essentially undisputed. Mr. Rayburn is a division manager for Philip Morris and is authorized to hire entry level sales personnel. On three different occasions, Appellee, a Hispanic male, applied for an entry level sales position with Philip Morris. The minimum requirements for such a position are that an applicant be at least twenty-one years old and possess a valid driver's license. Although Appellee satisfied these minimum requirements, the Appellants hired one Caucasian male and two Caucasian females for the three sales positions.

Mr. Rayburn testified that he was impressed with and interested in hiring Appellee after interviewing Appellee for the first sales position. Although Mr. Rayburn did not hire Appellee, he retained Appellee's application for future consideration. Thereafter, a second sales position became available in another division of Philip Morris, managed by Mr. Lay. Mr. Rayburn forwarded Appellee's application to Mr. Lay, and together they interviewed Appellee for the position. Mr. Lay was not impressed with Appellee, and Mr. Rayburn conceded that Appellee's second interview was not as good as the first. Again Appellee was not hired, but his application was retained. Appellee was not interviewed for the third sales position for which another applicant, Loraine Smoot, was hired by Mr. Rayburn. While it is clear from the record that Appellee was in fact considered for three positions to which he applied, other applicants were hired because according to the Appellants they were better qualified.

At trial, Appellee proffered evidence to establish a prima facie case of disparate treatment in a failure to hire context by showing that he was a member of a protected class, that he was qualified for the sales positions, and that of the three people actually hired none were Hispanic and two were women.

In order to rebut the inference of intentional discrimination created by Appellee's prima facie case, the Appellants' witnesses testified that they always hire the best qualified applicant and that Appellee was not the best qualified for any of the three positions. The district court found this to be a facially nondiscriminatory reason explaining Appellants' failure to hire Appellee.

However, the court observed as to the third opening that Appellee was more qualified than Loraine Smoot who was hired, and therefore the Appellants' "assertion that the selected applicant was the best person for the position was not the true reason for their hiring decision but was merely a pretext for discrimination" in violation of Title VII.

The district court's finding the Appellee was better qualified than Loraine Smoot was based on its comparison of their educational and occupational backgrounds, which we will briefly summarize. Appellee possessed a two-year college degree as well as over twelve years of experience in the food industry with increasing levels of responsibility from stock clerk for a supermarket to the manager/owner of a convenience store. Appellee's various jobs furnished him with experience in marketing, retail sales, accounting, and hiring, firing and supervision of employees. On the other hand, prior to applying for the sales position with Philip Morris, Loraine Smoot had been a school secretary for thirteen years. As the school's secretary, she was responsible for fund raising activities, record keeping and communicating with virtually everyone related to the school. She also had worked contemporaneously as a part-time sales person for a department store for seven years.

Consequently, with respect to the Title VII liability dispute before this court, we are left with a single issue of whether the Appellee adduced sufficient evidence to warrant a determination that the Appellants intentionally discriminated against Appellee based on gender or national origin by hiring Loraine Smoot.

We emphasize that the plaintiff in a Title VII case must prove that intent to discriminate based upon plaintiff's protected class characteristics was the determining factor for the allegedly illegal employment decision. Because the prima facie case only creates an inference of unlawful discrimination, some evidence that the articulated legitimate business reason for the decision was pretextual does not compel the conclusion that the employer intentionally discriminated. If a plaintiff successfully proves that the defendant's reasons are not worthy of credence, the plaintiff must still prove that the true motive for the employment decision violates Title VII.

The ultimate finding of whether there was intentional discrimination against a protected class is a question of fact.

On appeal, Appellants urge the extreme position that their articulated legitimate reason for not hiring Appellee, i.e., that they hire the best qualified applicant, invokes the business judgment rule, thereby necessarily precluding the district court from comparing the relative qualifications of the Appellee and Loraine Smoot. Such a position is untenable because it would severely limit Title VII by divesting courts of their power to determine if a defendant, who offers this type of business justification, is trying to cover up a gross disparity which could be one of several factors in a discriminatory action. The reality of the entire situation must be examined. However, Appellants correctly observe that district courts are not in the position of determining whether a business decision was good or bad. Title VII is not violated by the exercise of erroneous or even illogical business judgment. An employer's business judgment is relevant only insofar as it relates to the motivation of the employer with respect to the allegedly illegal conduct. Therefore, the district court in the case before us was empowered to compare the qualifications of Appellee and Loraine Smoot within the above limitations.

Throughout this case, the Appellee has attempted to prove intentional discrimination by comparing his "objective" job qualifications with those of Loraine Smoot. The Appellee insists that because he was so much more qualified than Loraine Smoot, the Appellants' articulated reason is a pretext for intentional discrimination as above considered. It is conceivable that a plaintiff in a case such as this could be so overwhelmingly better qualified than another applicant that on this evidence alone a trial court could properly find pretext and intent to discriminate. However, the facts in the record do not suggest this was such a case. There was a difference in the qualifications of the two applicants here concerned. There was a difference in their experiences. The trial court stated that the successful applicant was "not nearly as well qualified." We must assume that the company employees who did the hiring knew what particular qualifications and experiences were necessary. The trial court did not suggest that the difference in "qualifications" was the equivalent of discrimination. Again the court made no findings of discrimination. Instead it considered that its findings of differences in qualifications was in itself sufficient to support a judgment for Appellee. This cannot be.

The trial court in a previous hiring held that there the successful applicant, not Appellee, was the better qualified and that determined the outcome. As noted above, we are not in the business of determining whether an employer acted prudently or imprudently in its hiring decisions. Consequently, even if we were to agree that the Appellants exercised poor business judgment in hiring the lesser qualified Loraine Smoot, the district court's conclusions do not follow as the evidence at most demonstrated an application of what might be poor business judgment. Therefore, we must conclude that the district court must have erroneously substituted its own business judgment for that of the Appellants in finding that the Appellants' articulated justification was pretextual.

Furthermore, assuming that Appellants' articulated reason was pretextual, there is insufficient evidence they intended to discriminate in violation of Title VII. Appellee attempted to prove intentional discrimination with circumstantial evidence. However, there were no facts produced at trial which would constitute circumstantial evidence of intentional discrimination. This is demonstrated by the fact that the district court did not find unlawful discrimination. Rather, there was a consistent and affirmative showing of a determination that the Appellee failed to prove that his not being hired was motivated by an intent to unlawfully discriminate, as opposed to a mere mistake, favoritism or some other reason. We therefore hold that the district court erred by imposing Title VII liability on the Appellants under both the reverse gender and national origin theories.

Judgment for Philip Morris.

The next case deals with an individual employed by a pharmacy who manipulated pricing for her own aggrandizement. After she was terminated for this action, she claimed that the discharge was a pretext to mask the company's discriminatory intent.

CASE

Jean v. Walgreen Co.

887 F.Supp. 1007 (N.D. Ill. 1994)

HART, District Judge.

Elma Jean began her employment with Walgreen in 1977 as an "extra board," or relief, pharmacist, filling in as needed at Walgreen stores within the Chicago area. She later moved into a "registered pharmacist" position, working exclusively at one location. At some later point, Jean served both as an assistant store manager and a store pharmacist. Walgreen promoted her to "chief pharmacist" for its Markham, Illinois, store in 1981. In 1988, the title of her position changed to "pharmacy manager."

For her first ten years as chief pharmacist/pharmacy manager, Jean was supervised by Clarence Gaines. Audrey Neely replaced Gaines in January or February of 1991. On March 6, 1991, Jean attended a mandatory pharmacy managers' meeting, but was not paid for her attendance. Believing that non-Haitian pharmacy managers were paid, she filed a claim with the Equal Employment Opportunity Commission ("EEOC") alleging discrimination based on national origin. There is no evidence that anyone at Walgreen ever mentioned the complaint to Jean.

Walgreen pharmacies make use of a computerized inventory, ordering, and pricing system that automatically calculates employee and physician discounts. Pharmacy employees are authorized to enter drug prices manually, or override a price, only when a drug must be specially ordered because it is unavailable from Walgreen's warehouse. In December of 1991, Neely discovered that Jean had used the override system to enter lower prices for over-the-counter children's medicine she had purchased for her son. Neely also discovered that Jean had used the override system to order drugs for Dr. Alix Charles that were available in the warehouse, but could be ordered from an outside supplier at a cheaper price. Plaintiff purchased these drugs as a gift for the relief effort in Haiti.

Count II of Jean's complaint alleges that Walgreen illegally terminated her because of her national origin. Under Title VII, to establish a prima facie case of national origin discrimination, Jean must show (1) she is a member of a protected class; (2) she was doing her work well enough to meet her employer's legitimate expectations; (3) despite her satisfactory performance, she was discharged; and (4) the employer sought a replacement for her. Walgreen does not dispute that Jean is a member of a protected class, or that her position was filled by a non-Haitian. Walgreen argues, however, that Jean cannot establish that her performance was satisfactory prior to her termination because she was dishonest and violated company policies. Thus, to meet her initial burden, Jean must show that she was performing satisfactorily in her job at the time of her discharge.

An occasional or sporadic use of a slur directed at an employee's national origin is generally insufficient to support a Title VII claim. This is true even when the remarks are made by a decision-maker, unless the Plaintiff can show that the remark is related to the decision process. Plaintiff shows no such connection.

Plaintiff relies upon mere allegations, conclusory statements and assertions of belief rather than admissible facts; the evidence presented does not raise a genuine dispute on the question of intentional discrimination. Plaintiff fails to provide any evidence from which a reasonable jury could conclude that Walgreen intentionally discriminated against her.

Plaintiff's Section 1981 claims are based solely on national origin. Claims founded on that status are not cognizable under Section 1981, which is designed to remedy discrimination based on race or ethnicity.

Judgment for Walgreen.

Not only is discrimination against a person for his or her own national origin prohibited, but the issue can also be raised by a person who is discriminated against because of

1. his or her spouse's national origin;
2. membership in an association of a particular national origin;
3. attendance at a school or religious institution identified with people of a specific national origin;
4. or the association of his or her name with persons of a particular national origin.

The Immigration Reform and Control Act requires that employers discern whether their employees are citizens or immigrants. If they are immigrants, the employer must verify the documentation of the employee to determine whether he or she has legal immigration status.

A passport, Certificate of U.S. citizenship, a Certificate of Naturalization or a resident alien card is sufficient. A Social Security Card, or Certificate of U.S. Birth when combined with a driver's license is also appropriate. The employer must photocopy these documents for verification. The individual must attest that either he or she is a U.S. citizen or an alien lawfully admitted for permanent residence.

IMMIGRATION REFORM AND CONTROL ACT

The Immigration Reform and Control Act of 1986, which applies to employers with four or more employees, prohibits discrimination for national origin or for citizenship when the latter is an alien lawfully admitted for permanent residence. Whereas Title VII affords no protection against discrimination for citizenship or against employers of four to fourteen employees, the Immigration and Control Act does. However, The Immigration and Control Act makes no provision for disparate impact that occurs unintentionally, as does Title VII. Intent to discriminate is mandated by the Immigration and Control Act. The Immigration Reform and Control Act has been amended by the Immigration Act of 1990.

The next case deals with a religious organization which refuses to verify an alien employee's immigration documentation. Its reasoning is that it will not refuse to help anyone in need. The issue is whether religious beliefs take precedence over the provisions of the Immigration Reform and Control Act.

CASE

American Friends Service Committee v. Thornburgh

941 F.2d 808 (9th Cir. 1991)

CANBY, Circuit Judge.

The American Friends Service Committee appeals the district court's dismissal of its suit for injunctive and declaratory relief. AFSC alleges that its free exercise of religion is violated by the "employer sanction" provisions of the Immigration Reform and Control Act. Those provisions require, generally, that employers verify the legal immigration status of their employees. The district court dismissed the action for failure to state a claim.

Background

The AFSC is a Quaker organization, whose activities include charitable and relief work. The employer sanction provisions of IRCA apply to the AFSC's employment of approximately 400 persons. Those provisions prohibit an employer from hiring, or continuing to employ, an alien who the employer knows is not authorized to work in the United States. IRCA also requires an employer to attest that it has verified the legality of an alien's immigration status by examining documents which evidence identity and work authorization. Failure to comply with these provisions can result in civil and criminal sanctions.

AFSC has not complied with these provisions of IRCA because it believes that to do so would violate the religious beliefs and practices of its members. Those beliefs require that AFSC and its members "welcome—that they help and not show hostility to—the sojourner, the stranger, the poor, and the dispossessed in their midst." Thus AFSC contends that it can neither discharge brothers and sisters whose religious beliefs preclude their producing proof of secular work authorization, nor refuse human beings work—thus depriving them of the means to feed and clothe themselves and their children—simply because they may be strangers in our land.

The district court granted the government's motion to dismiss for failure to state a claim. The district court ruled that plaintiffs are unable to state a claim under both the "wholly irrational" or "compelling interest standards." Specifically, the court finds that, assuming IRCA has a substantial impact upon plaintiff's interests, plaintiff's interests cannot overcome the government's interest in immigration control as a matter of law. The Court indicated that such free exercise claims must fail "if prohibiting the exercise of religion . . . is not the object of the law but merely the incidental effect of a generally applicable and otherwise valid provision. . . ."

The present case falls squarely within the rule. There is no allegation, nor does AFSC contend, that IRCA's employer sanction provisions are directed at religious beliefs or the exercise of religion. "IRCA neither regulates religious beliefs nor burdens acts because of the religious expression or motivation." Nor does AFSC assert, in this case, any defect in IRCA other than its infringement of AFSC's free exercise of religion. Thus, for purposes of the analysis required, IRCA is a "valid and neutral law of general applicability."

Judgment for Thornburgh.

The Immigration Reform and Control Act applies to foreign and domestic companies who employ people within the United States. It has no application to American workers who are employed by foreign or domestic companies abroad.

The following case addresses the question of whether Title VII's protection against discrimination because of national origin applies to those American citizens who are working for American companies abroad.

CASE

Equal Employment Opportunity Commission v. Arabian American Oil Company and ARAMCO Services Company

Ali Boureslan v. Arabian American Oil Company and ARAMCO Services Company

111 S.Ct. 1227 (1991)

Chief Justice REHNQUIST delivered the opinion of the Court.

These cases present the issue whether Title VII applies extraterritorially to regulate the employment practices of United States employers who employ United States citizens abroad. The United States Court of Appeals for the Fifth Circuit held that it does not, and we agree with that conclusion.

Petitioner Boureslan is a naturalized United States citizen who was born in Lebanon. The respondents are two Delaware corporations, Arabian American Oil Company (ARAMCO), and its subsidiary, ARAMCO Service Company (ASC). Aramco's principal place of business is Dhahran, Saudi Arabia, and it is licensed to do business in Texas. ASC's principal place of business is Houston, Texas.

In 1979, Boureslan was hired by ASC as a cost engineer in Houston. A year later he was transferred, at his request, to work for ARAMCO in Saudi Arabia. Boureslan remained with ARAMCO in Saudi Arabia until he was discharged in 1984. After filing a charge of discrimination with the Equal Employment Opportunity Commission (EEOC), he instituted this suit in the United States District Court for the Southern District of Texas against ARAMCO and ASC. He sought relief under both state law and Title VII of the Civil Rights Act of 1964, 42 U.S.C. 2000a–2000h6, on the ground that he was harassed and ultimately discharged by respondents on account of his race, religion, and national origin.

Respondents filed a motion for summary judgment on the ground that the District Court lacked subject matter jurisdiction over Boureslan's claim because the protections of Title VII do not extend to United States citizens employed abroad by American employers. The District Court agreed, and dismissed Boureslan's Title VII claim. . . .

Both parties concede, as they must, that Congress has the authority to enforce its laws beyond the territorial boundaries of the United States. Whether Congress has in fact exercised that authority in this case is a matter of statutory construction. It is our task to determine whether Congress intended the protections of Title VII to apply to United States citizens employed by American employers outside of the United States.

It is a long-standing principle of American law "that legislation of Congress, unless a contrary intent appears, is meant to apply only within the territorial jurisdiction of the United States." This "canon of construction . . . is a valid approach whereby unexpressed congressional intent may be ascertained." It serves to protect against unintended clashes between our laws and those of other nations which could result in international discord.

In applying this rule of construction, we look to see whether "language in the relevant act gives any indication of a congressional purpose to extend its coverage beyond places over which the United States has sovereignty or has some measure of legislative control." We assume that Congress legislates against the backdrop of the presumption against extraterritoriality. Therefore, unless there is "the affirmative intention of the Congress clearly expressed," we must presume it "is primarily concerned with domestic conditions."

Title VII prohibits various discriminatory employment practices based on an individual's race, color, religion, sex, or national origin. See 42 U.S.C. 2000e-2, 2000e-3. An employer is subject to Title VII if it has employed 15 or more employees for a specified period and is "engaged in an industry affecting commerce." An industry affecting commerce is "any activity, business, or industry in commerce or in which a labor dispute would hinder or obstruct commerce or the free flow of commerce and includes any activity or industry 'affecting commerce' within the meaning of the Labor-Management Reporting and Disclosure Act of 1959. (LMRDA) (42 U.S.C. 2000e(h). "Commerce," in turn, is defined as "trade, traffic, commerce, transportation, transmission, or communication among the several States; or between a State and any place outside thereof; or within the District of Columbia, or a possession of the United States; or between points in the same State but through a point outside thereof." (See 42 U.S.C. 2000e(g).

Petitioners argue that by its plain language, Title VII's "broad jurisdictional language" reveals Congress's intent to extend the statute's protections to employment discrimination anywhere in the world by a U.S. employer who affects trade "between a State and any place outside thereof." More precisely, they assert that since Title VII defines "States" to include States, the District of Columbia, and specified territories, the clause "between a State and any place outside thereof" must be referring to areas beyond the territorial limit of the United States.

Similarly, Congress failed to provide any mechanisms for overseas enforcement of Title VII. For instance, the statute's venue provisions, U.S.C. 2000e-5(f)(3), are ill-suited for extraterritorial application as they provide for venue only in a judicial district in the state where certain matters related to the employer occurred or were located. And the limited investigative authority provided for the EEOC, permitting the Commission only to issue subpoenas for witnesses and documents from "anyplace in the United States or any Territory or possession thereof," U.S.C. 2000e-9, suggests that Congress did not intend for the statute to apply abroad.

It is also reasonable to conclude that had Congress intended Title VII to apply overseas, it would have addressed the subject of conflicts with foreign laws and procedures. In amending the Age Discrimination in Employment Act of 1967, (ADEA), to apply abroad, Congress specifically addressed potential conflicts with foreign law by providing that it is not unlawful for an employer to take any action prohibited by the ADEA "where such practices involve an employee in a workplace in a foreign country, and compliance with the ADEA would cause such employer . . . to violate the laws of the country in which such workplace is located." Title VII, by contrast, fails to address conflicts with the laws of other nations.

Our conclusion today is buttressed by the fact that "when it desires to do so, Congress knows how to place the high seas within the jurisdictional reach of a statute." Congress's awareness of the need to make a clear statement that a statute applies overseas is amply demonstrated by the numerous occasions on which it has expressly legislated the extraterritorial application of a statute. Finally, the EEOC, as one of the two federal agencies with primary responsibility for enforcing Title VII, argues that we should defer to its "consistent" construction of Title VII, first formally expressed in a statement issued after oral argument but before the Fifth Circuit's initial decision in this case, "to apply to discrimination against American citizens outside the United States." Citing a 1975 letter from the EEOC's General Counsel, 1983 testimony by its Chairman, and a 1985 decision by the Commission, it argues that its consistent administrative interpretations "reinforce" the conclusion that Congress intended Title VII to apply abroad.

In *General Electric Co. v. Gilbert,* we addressed the proper deference to be afforded the EEOC's guidelines. Recognizing that "Congress, in enacting Title VII, did not confer upon the EEOC authority to promulgate rules or regulations," we held that the level of deference afforded "will depend upon the thoroughness evident in its consideration, the validity of its reasoning, its consistency with earlier and later pronouncements, and all those factors which give it power to persuade, if lacking power to control."

The EEOC's interpretation does not fare well under these standards. As an initial matter, the position taken by the Commission "contradicts the position which it had enunciated at an earlier date, closer to the enactment of the governing statute." The Commission's early pronouncements on the issue supported the conclusion that the statute was limited to domestic application. ("Title VII . . . protects all individuals, both citizen and noncitizens, domiciled or residing in the United States, against discrimination on the basis of race, color, religion, sex, or national origin.") While the Commission later intimated that the statute applied abroad, this position was not expressly reflected in its policy guidelines until some 24 years after the passage of the statute. The EEOC offers no basis in its experience for the change. The EEOC's interpretation of the statute here thus has been neither contemporaneous with its enactment nor consistent since the statute came into law. As discussed above, it also lacks support in the plain language of the statute. While we do not wholly discount the weight to be given to the 1988 guideline, its persuasive value is limited. We are of the view that, even when considered in combination with petitioners' other arguments, the EEOC's interpretation is insufficiently weighty to overcome the presumption against extraterritorial application.

Petitioners have failed to present sufficient affirmative evidence that Congress intended Title VII to apply abroad. Accordingly, the judgment of the Court of Appeals is

Affirmed.
Judgment for ARAMCO.

Employment Perspective

The law firm of Knapp and Schultz have twelve employees. Knapp and Schultz makes it their policy never to hire anyone who is not a U.S. citizen. Prasait Theesowatt, a permanent resident alien from Thailand, applies for a job with Knapp and Schultz, only to be informed of their policy. Prasait claims that Knapp and Schultz are in violation of the Immigration Reform and Control Act. Is he correct? Yes! The Immigration Reform and Control Act prohibits discrimination against permanent resident aliens and applies to employers with at least four employees. ◆

Discriminating against people who are not citizens is permissible under the Civil Rights Act, but not under the Immigration Reform and Control Act if they have a Certificate of Naturalization or a resident alien card.

In the next case, the issue is whether an employer can discriminate against someone who is not a citizen. The applicant, a Mexican, claimed that the protection afforded National Origin encompasses citizenship.

Espinoza v. Farah Manufacturing Company

462 F.2d 1331 (1972)

CLARK, Circuit Judge.

This appeal requires us to decide which practices Congress intended to prohibit when it made it unlawful for an employee "to fail or refuse to hire . . . any individual . . . because of such individual's . . . national origin." More precisely, we must determine whether the words "national origin" should be read to mean or at least include, "citizenship." Since we conclude they should not; that none of the reasons offered for doing so will withstand close analysis; that this is one of those cases where Congress should be taken at its words; and that, put simply, "national origin" means exactly and only that, we reverse the judgment below.

The material facts are clear and undisputed. Cecilia Espinoza, plaintiff appellee in this cause, is a lawfully admitted resident alien living in San Antonio, Texas with her citizen husband. In July 1969 she was refused employment at the San Antonio division of Farah Manufacturing Company, defendant appellant, because she was not a United States citizen. This refusal was based upon a longstanding policy of the company, established by its founder for security reasons. The merits of such a policy are not at issue here, but rather we examine the company's right to enforce it in light of Title VII of the Civil Rights Act of 1964.

Subsequent to Farah's refusal of employment, Espinoza filed a charge with the Equal Employment Opportunity Commission, alleging that Farah had discriminated against her on the basis of her national origin—which is Mexican—in violation of Title VII. After making findings of fact, the EEOC, under provisions of the Act, authorized Espinoza to bring suit in federal court since no administrative solution to the complaint was forthcoming.

The EEOC Regional Director found, and the parties have never contested, that Espinoza was not denied employment because she is Spanish surnamed. Indeed, the district judge found that "persons of Mexican ancestry made up more than 92% of defendant's total employees, 96% of its San Antonio employees, and 97% of the people doing the work for which plaintiff applied." The judge concluded that there was *no discrimination on the basis of ancestry or ethnic background.* Thus, this is not a case wherein an employer has feigned adherence to a policy which is no more than a subterfuge designed to conceal a brand of discrimination the Act prohibits. The record before us makes it unquestionable that Espinoza was denied an opportunity for employment because she lacks United States citizenship, and for no other reason.

Espinoza was not denied a job because of her Spanish surname, her Mexican heritage, her foreign ancestry, her own or her parents' birthplace—all of which characteristics she shared with the vast majority of Farah's employees. Rather she was refused employment—irrespective of what her national origin may have been—because she had not acquired United States citizenship. Neither the language of the Act, nor its history, nor the specific facts of this case persuade us that such a refusal has been condemned by Congress.

It avails Espinoza naught to argue that by denying her relief we thwart the Act's general purpose of bringing to every man and woman in this country the opportunity to "provide decently for one's family in a job or profession for which he or she qualifies and chooses." Laudable though this objective may be, we have not the authority to declare unlawful any and all activities that might impede its effectuation. Quite obviously, a great host of arbitrary and discriminatory employment practices, far too numerous to mention, remain unchecked and unhampered by the Act. We hold that refusal to hire non-citizens is one of them. Though the general policy of the Act doubtless was to halt arbitrary employment practices, through the unmistakable words of the Act's actual text Congress has offered its conception of the specific spheres in which this general policy is to operate, and thereby has necessarily limited the policy's outreach.

As a person within this country's jurisdiction, Espinoza is unquestionably protected against discrimination based upon race, color, religion, sex, or national origin. Having found no persuasive reasoning to upset the ordinary meaning of the last of these five prohibitions, we conclude that Espinoza was not entitled to relief and that the summary judgment granted in her behalf must be

Reversed.
Judgment for Farah Manufacturing.

In the case that follows, the issue is whether the employee was discharged for failing to perform the essential functions of the job or whether the discharge was due to the employee's national origin.

CASE

Falczynski v. Amoco Oil Co.

533 N.W.2d 226 (Iowa 1995)

McGIVERIN, Chief Justice.

Danuta Falczynski brought this action against her former employer, Amoco Oil Company, claiming national origin discrimination, and breach of contract of employment.

Plaintiff, Danuta Falczynski, immigrated to the United States from her native Poland in 1984.

In June 1988 the defendant, Amoco Oil Company (Amoco), hired Falczynski as a non-exempt or hourly employee to work in the general ledger section of its accounting department as an accounting clerk. She worked in this capacity for Amoco for almost two years and received two "satisfactory" performance evaluations.

In spite of these ratings, Falczynski's skill level was not what Amoco expected, and she had difficulty getting her work completed in a timely fashion. Recognizing this, some of Amoco's supervisors decided she could do better at repetitive work, and, accordingly, on April 30, 1990 transferred her to the capital investment section of Amoco's accounting department to perform computer data entry work. In doing so, Amoco made an exception in order to allow the plaintiff to remain at her then current pay and benefit level.

Feeling she was qualified to perform accounting work, Falczynski was not happy with the transfer. She was also unhappy with her new supervisor, Helen Rode. She described Rode as a tough and demanding supervisor who was mean to her and other minorities. At one time in 1990, Falczynski and another Amoco employee of Laotian background went to the human resources department and lodged a complaint against Rode. Although neither employee reported instances of Rode making overt references to their national origin nor examples of Rode's specific behavior, they stated that they felt that they were treated differently than other nonforeign-born Amoco employees.

Besides plaintiff's alleged problems with her immediate supervisor Rode, she also had problems with her health. In 1989, she began experiencing problems with her lungs.

On September 10, 1990, at which time Falczynski had twelve "occasions" of absences, she received and signed a written warning letter from Rode. Through the letter Rode informed Falczynski that time away from work would have to be made up in order to avoid further "occasions" of absence. The letter further advised her that failure to follow the letter's instructions could be grounds for immediate termination.

After Falczynski received the warning letter she accrued two more "occasions" of absence, making a total of fourteen for the year. Amoco then terminated Falczynski on October 16, 1990. Amoco's stated reason for the termination was Falczynski's violation of its attendance policy.

Following her termination, Falczynski brought against Amoco claims of national origin discrimination under the Iowa civil rights statute and under Title VII of the Civil Rights Act of 1964. These law action claims were tried to the court without a jury. The trial court dismissed all of the claims, generally concluding that Amoco terminated Falczynski's employment because of her excessive absenteeism in violation of its policy rather than because of her national origin or any disability, and that policies were not sufficiently definite to create an offer of continued employment.

Plaintiff first contends that her former employer, defendant Amoco, terminated her employment with it for the discriminatory reason of her Polish origin. The plaintiff bases her national origin discrimination claims on the Iowa civil rights act. Among other things, these statutes prohibit any person from discriminating in employment against any employee because of national origin. The trial court correctly set out the elements of a prima facie case of national origin discrimination based on discriminatory treatment. To establish a prima facie case of discrimination for an existing employee/employer relationship, the plaintiff must show by a preponderance of the evidence that: (1) she belongs to a protected group; (2) she was qualified to retain the job; (3) she was terminated; and (4) it is more likely than not that the termination was based on an impermissible consideration, in this case national origin.

Substantial evidence supports the court's conclusion that Plaintiff was not qualified to retain her position with Amoco because she violated Amoco's attendance policy and that it was not more likely that Plaintiff's termination was based on her Polish origin than on her excessive absenteeism in violation of Amoco's attendance policy.

In order to determine whether a person is qualified for a given job in the context of a national origin discrimination case, the fact finder must decide whether the plaintiff can perform the essential functions of the job. The "essential functions" of the job are those that "bear more than a marginal relationship to the job at issue." If the plaintiff proves she can perform the essential functions of the job, then she is qualified.

Substantial evidence supports the trial court's determination that Falczynski's excessive absenteeism prevented her from performing the essential functions of her computer data entry job with Amoco.

Judgment for Amoco Oil.

In the next case, an applicant was denied a position at a pizza franchise after an in-person interview. The applicant claimed that the denial was due to his national origin because others were hired after he had applied. The issue is whether the franchisor or the franchisee is ultimately responsible for the discriminatory acts.

Bahadirli v. Domino's Pizza

873 F.Supp. 1528 (M.D.Ala. 1995)

Albritton, District Judge.

On April 12, 1993, Mehrnet Bahadirli sought employment as a pizza delivery person at the Westgate Parkway store, a Domino's pizza franchise in Dothan, Alabama. According to the plaintiff, he visited the store and was told that he was well qualified for the position, but he never received word regarding the job. The plaintiff alleges that on his return to the store around April 25, 1993, he was told that he would not receive the position. According to the plaintiff, in the interim four other individuals were hired at the Westgate Parkway store.

Clarkfinn asserts that plaintiff returned to the store after approximately one month from his initial visit to inquire as to the status of his application. According to Clarkfinn, plaintiff was told that the application had been misfiled, that the Westgate Parkway store did not have any openings, but perhaps another location in Dothan did. Defendants allege that they contacted another store and that plaintiff said that he would pick up an application there.

Bahadirli contends that on learning he would not be hired, he went directly home and asked his wife to call the shop and inquire about employment. Plaintiff alleges his wife was offered a position over the phone.

As stated above, both Clark and Clarkfinn have filed Motions to Dismiss. Clarkfinn is the corporate entity that owns the Domino's Pizza franchise at issue here. Mr. Clark owns 75% of Clarkfinn's stock and serves as the corporation's president.

Until very recently, Eleventh Circuit law was very clear in holding that Title VII claims against a person in his individual capacity were "inappropriate." Accordingly, Clark may not be sued in his individual capacity. As stated above, in order to make out a case, plaintiff must show the plaintiff is of different nationality, plaintiff applied for a position, was qualified for that position; that the plaintiff was rejected for the position despite his qualifications; and that the defendant continued to accept applications for the position following the rejection of the plaintiff.

However, in addition to establishing a prima facie case, the plaintiff must show that the defendants named are properly before the court on these claims. Domino's argues that it is entitled to summary judgment on plaintiff's Title VII claims because it is not the employer in this case. The defendant Reams contends that he cannot be sued under Title VII in his individual capacity and that, because the employer is named in the suit, naming him in his official capacity is repetitive. The court agrees with the argument of both Domino's and Reams.

Reams is the individual who served as manager at the Domino's franchise that plaintiff is suing. According to plaintiff, Reams turned him down for a position at the Westgate Parkway store because of plaintiff's national origin. Reams no longer works for Clarkfinn.

Plaintiff admits that Reams cannot be sued in his individual capacity, but argues that the court should not grant summary judgment as to Reams in his official capacity. The Court disagrees. As stated above, a suit under Title VII brought against an employee as agent of the employer is properly regarded as a suit against the employer. Domino's contends that it did not have control over the day to day operations or over hiring and firing that would allow a finding of liability should Bahadirli prove his claim. In support of its argument, Domino's has submitted affidavits from Linda Popevich, a Divisional Vice President of Franchise Services for Domino's. According to these affidavits, the Westgate Parkway store was, and is, a franchise, operated by an independent contractor—Clarkfinn. Popevich also avers that "persons who work at a store operated by a franchisee, including the Westgate Parkway Store, are employees of the Franchisee Clarkfinn and not DPI Domino's." In her supplemental affidavit, Popevich stated that Domino's has no knowledge of individuals who apply for positions at Domino's franchises. In this case, the plaintiff has presented no evidence that the defendant Domino's had any control over the employees' day to day activities, or control over hiring and firing at the Westgate Parkway store. Accordingly, Domino's Motion for Summary Judgment is due to be granted.

Judgment for Domino's.

CONCLUSION

The United States of America is a melting pot and is probably the most integrated country in the world. America derives its strength from the attributes of a population diverse in culture and tradition. Excluding individuals because of their national origin goes against the grain of American heritage; individuals should be judged only on the basis of their merit. Most immigrants have taken their lumps upon entering this country. One hundred years ago, the Irish and Germans were not well received. Seventy-five years ago, the Italians and Polish were resented. Twenty-five years ago, the Spanish and Latin Americans were not wanted. Today, Indians and Koreans are looked upon with contempt.

Many Americans want immigration laws tightened up to the point of restricting most nonwhite immigrants. What these Americans are forgetting is the work ethic that their ancestors brought with them in building the infrastructure that exists today. Most immigrants are not freeloaders but rather are people seeking opportunities to put their talents to work to build a future for their families and themselves, a goal that everyone should encourage.

Immigrants are often used to perform the routine ministerial tasks that Americans refuse to do. Hard labor, assembly line factory work, janitorial maintenance, and gas pumping are a few occupations serviced by a significant number of immigrants. On the other side of the coin, as immigrants mesh themselves into our society and have children, those children will eventually compete with Americans for better-paying positions. Also, as the population grows, pollution and garbage increases proportionately. Development causes overuse of the land, natural resources, and water; erosion occurs, disease proliferates, and quality of life deteriorates. For America to maintain a sustainable quality of life, immigration cannot run rampant. In areas of technology, communications, and product development, our innovation is unparalleled, but in purifying our air, water, and food supply, we are underachievers. Therefore, the number of people that can adequately be supported by America's vital resources is an issue to be seriously considered.

This problem pertains to the number of immigrants in the future. For those immigrants already here, America should embrace them into our society and encourage them to utilize their talents to their greatest potential for the benefit of all of us. Discrimination against immigrants serves no purpose, since they rarely leave involuntarily; it serves only to delay their inevitable amalgamation into American employment and society.

Thoughtful planning with regard to supporting future immigrants with the vital resources available to us is an intelligent policy, but purposeful discrimination against the ones among us is not. They should be treated as our own.

REVIEW QUESTIONS

1. Define national origin discrimination.
2. Explain the significance of the Immigration Reform and Control Act.
3. Can a person claim to be discriminated against because of his or her spouse's national origin?
4. Does discrimination because of membership in an association of a particular national origin qualify as national origin discrimination?
5. When a student is discriminated against because he or she is attending a school of a particular national origin, does Title VII apply?
6. Does the Civil Rights Act extend to a person's claiming discrimination because his or her surname is associated with a particular national origin?
7. Can an employer discriminate against someone on the basis of the person's lacking United States citizenship?
8. Does the Immigration Reform and Control Act apply to all employers?
9. Can national origin ever be considered a bona fide occupational qualification?
10. Must an employee be 100 percent of a particular national origin to qualify for protection under Title VII?
11. Rys once heard Lehman say that Adolf Hitler did not finish his job because he did not kill all the Polish and Jewish people. Lehman also said that he should shove those people into the ovens. Lehman once saw a woman having lunch and asked her what were "all those dumb Polacks" doing in the hallway. When Lehman fired the crew, Rys complained that Palka should be present. Lehman then said that he would fire "that dumb Polack, too." Are these events sufficient to constitute a claim for national origin discrimination? *ISS Intern. Service v. Human Rights Commission,* 651 N.E.2d 592 (Ill. App. 1 Dist. 1995)
12. Cruz alleged as follows in her EEOC complaint: Respondent stated that "since my employment with him I have been unable to get a decent letter out of my typewriter." Respondent stated that this might be attributed to her language barrier. In these circumstances, Cruz charged Ecolab with unlawful discrimination "by denying the equal terms, conditions and privileges of employment and terminating me because of my national origin." When editing letters typed for Vice President Mosh by Cruz, Mosh would on occasion comment "that plaintiff did not understand English because she was Puerto Rican." What was the result? *Cruz v. Ecolab* 817 F.Supp. 388 (S.D. N.Y. 1993)
13. To reduce costs, Philippine Airlines (PAL) closed ten of its U.S. District Sales offices. Nine managers were discharged as follows: four non-Filipinos, two Filipinos, and three U.S. citizens of Filipino origin. Two non-Filipinos sued PAL, claiming reverse discrimination on the basis of national origin. What was the result? *Lemnitzer v. Philippine Airlines, Inc.,* 816 F.Supp. 1441 (N.D. Cal. 1992)
14. The Immigration Reform and Control Act (IRCA) requires employers to verify the legal immigration status of their employees. Catholic nuns challenged the civil and criminal

sanctions for noncompliance. Their reasoning is their belief that they cannot refuse to aid their fellow brothers and sisters. To comply with this statute would mean they would have to do so. What was the result? *Inter-community Center for Justice and Peace v. INS*, 910 F.2d 42 (2nd Cir. 1990)

15. A Chinese and an African-American, both employees of Spun Steak Co. complained that two Hispanic coworkers made abusive racial remarks about them. Spun Steak adopted a rule permitting only the English language to be used at work. Buitrago and Garcia, the alleged harassers, claimed that an English-language-only rule was an act of discrimination perpetrated by the company against them because of their national origin. What was the result? *Garcia v. Spun Steak Co.*, 988 F.2d 1980 (9th Cir. 1993)

16. In the case on pp. 377, is the scenario presented prevalent in our world today?

17. Was the case on pp. 381 decided ethically?

18. In the case on pp. 382, should Title VII be extended to cover American citizens working abroad?

19. In the case on pp. 386, was the plaintiff treated in an ethical manner?

20. In the case on pp. 388, should a franchisor be responsible for the unethical conduct of the franchisee?

Immigration Reform and Control Act of 1986
8 U.S.C. 1324 (a) (b)

1324(a) UNLAWFUL EMPLOYMENT OF ALIENS

(a) Making employment of unauthorized aliens unlawful

(1) In general

It is unlawful for a person or other entity—

(A) to hire, or to recruit or refer for a fee, for employment in the United States an alien knowing the alien is an unauthorized alien with respect to such employment, or

(B) to hire for employment in the United States an individual without complying with the requirements if the person or entity is an agricultural employer, or farm labor contractor.

(2) Continuing employment

It is unlawful for a person or other entity, after hiring an alien for employment in accordance with paragraph (1) to continue to employ the alien in the United States knowing the alien is (or has become) an unauthorized alien with respect to such employment.

(3) Defense

A person or entity that establishes that it has complied in good faith with the requirements of subsection (b) of this section with respect to the hiring, recruiting, or referral for employment of an alien in the United States has established an affirmative defense that the person or entity has not violated paragraph (1)(A) with respect to such hiring, recruiting, or referral.

(4) Use of labor through contract

For purposes of this section, a person or other entity who uses a contract, subcontract, or exchange, entered into, renegotiated, or extended after the date of the enactment of this section, obtained the labor of an alien in the United States knowing that the alien is an unauthorized alien (as defined in subsection) with respect to performing such labor, shall be considered to have hired the alien for employment in the

United States in violation of paragraph (1)(A).

(b) Employment verification system

The requirements referred to in paragraphs (1)(B) and (3) of subsection (a) of this section are, in the case of a person or other entity hiring, recruiting, or referring an individual for employment in the United States, the requirements specified in the following three paragraphs:

(1) Attestation after examination of documentation

(A) In general

The person or entity must attest, under penalty of perjury and on a form designated or established by the Attorney General by regulation, that it has verified that the individual is not an unauthorized alien by examining—

(i) a document described in subparagraph (B), or

(ii) a document described in subparagraph (C) and a document described in subparagraph (D).

A person or entity has complied with the requirement of this paragraph with respect to examination of a document if the document reasonably appears on its face to be genuine. If an individual provides a document or combination of documents that reasonably appears on its face to be genuine and that is sufficient to meet the requirements of the first sentence of this paragraph, nothing in this paragraph shall be construed as requiring the person or entity to solicit the production of any other document or as requiring the individual to produce such another document.

(B) Documents establishing both employment authorization and identity

A document described in this subparagraph is an individual's—

(i) United States passport;

(ii) certificate of United States citizenship

(iii) certificate of naturalization;

(iv) unexpired foreign passport, if the passport has an appropriate, unexpired endorsement of the Attorney General authorizing the individual's employment in the United States; or

(v) resident alien card or other alien registration card, if the card—

(I) contains a photograph of the individual or such other personal identifying information relating to the individual as the Attorney General finds, by regulation, sufficient for purposes of this subsection, and

(II) is evidence of authorization of employment in the United States.

(C) Documents evidencing employment authorization

A document described in this subparagraph is an individual's—

(i) social security account number card (other than such a card which specifies in the face that the issuance of the card does not authorize employment in the United States);

(ii) certificate of birth in the United States or establishing United States nationality at birth, which certificate the Attorney General finds, by regulation, to be acceptable for purposes of this section; or

(iii) other documentation evidencing authorization of employment in the United States which the Attorney General finds, by regulation, to be acceptable for purposes of this section.

(D) Documents establishing identity of individual

A document described in this subparagraph is an individual—

(i) driver's license or similar document issued for the purpose of identification by a State, if it contains a photograph of the individual or such other personal identifying information relating to the individual as the Attorney General finds, by regulation, sufficient for purposes of this section; or

(ii) in the case of individuals under 16 years of age or in a State which does not provide for issuance of an identification document (other than a driver's license) referred to in clause (i), documentation of personal identity of such other type as the Attorney General finds, by regulation, provides a reliable means of identification.

(2) Individual attestation of employment authorization

The individual must attest, under penalty of perjury on the form designated or established for purposes of paragraph (1), that the individual is a citizen or national of the United States, or an alien who is authorized under this chapter or by the Attorney General to be hired, recruited, or referred for such employment.

(3) Retention of verification form

After completion of such form in accordance with paragraphs (1) and (2) the person or entity must retain the form and make it available for inspection by officers of the Service, the Special Counsel for Immigration-Related Unfair Employment Practices, or the Department of Labor during a period beginning on the date of the hiring, recruiting, or referral of the individual and ending—

(A) in the case of the recruiting or referral for a fee (without hiring) of an individual, three years after the date of the recruiting or referral, and

(B) in the case of the hiring of an individual—

(i) three years after the date of such hiring, or

(ii) one year after the date the individual's employment is terminated, whichever is later.

(B) UNFAIR IMMIGRATION-RELATED EMPLOYMENT PRACTICES

(a) Prohibition of discrimination based on national origin or citizenship status

(1) General rule

It is an unfair immigration-related employment practice for a person or other entity to discriminate against any individual (other than an unauthorized alien) with respect to the hiring, or recruitment of referral for a fee, of the individual for employment or the discharging of the individual from employment—

(A) because of such individual's national origin, or

(B) in the case of a protected individual's citizenship status.

(2) Exceptions

Paragraph (1) shall not apply to—

(A) a person or other entity that employs three or fewer employees,

(B) a person's or entity's discrimination because of an individual's national origin if the discrimination with respect to that person or entity and that individual is covered under section 2000e-2 of Title 42.

(3) Definition of protected individual

As used in paragraph (1), the term "protected individual" means an individual who—

(A) is a citizen or national of the United States, or

(B) is an alien who is lawfully admitted for permanent residence.

CHAPTER 17 Age Discrimination

AGE DISCRIMINATION IN EMPLOYMENT ACT

The Age Discrimination in Employment Act of 1967 (ADEA) was enacted to promote the employment of individuals over 40 years of age. Later, it was amended to discontinue mandatory retirement thereby shifting the requirement for employment from age to ability. There is an exception, which is that companies can force executives in high policy-making positions to retire.

Employment Perspective

Lawrence Wright is the chief financial officer for Code Blue Medical Supplies, Inc. Miriam Hodges is a quality control analyst. Both will be seventy in March. Code Blue has a policy of compulsory retirement at age seventy. Will Lawrence and Miriam both have to retire? Under the ADEA, Miriam can continue to work as long as she is able to do the job. Lawrence will be forced to retire as CFO because he is a high policy-making executive. However, he will not be prevented from doing consulting work for the company. ◆

The issue in the next case is whether an employee was discharged for doing business with the competition. The employee maintained that that reasoning was a pretext to disguise the real reason for the discharge: age.

Hazen Paper Company, et al. v. Walter F. Biggins

113 S.Ct. 1701 (1993)

Justice O'CONNOR delivered the opinion of the Court.

In this case we clarify the standards for liability and liquidated damages under the Age Discrimination in Employment Act of 1967 (ADEA).

Petitioner Hazen Paper Company manufactures coated, laminated, and printed paper and paperboard. The company is owned and operated by two cousins, petitioners Robert Hazen and Thomas N. Hazen. The Hazens hired respondent Walter F. Biggins as their technical director in 1977. They fired him in 1986, when he was 62 years old.

Respondent brought suit against petitioners in the United States District Court for the District of Massachusetts, alleging a violation of the ADEA. He claimed that age had been a determinative factor in petitioners' decision to fire him. Petitioners contested this claim, asserting instead that respondent had been fired for doing business with competitors of Hazen Paper. The case was tried before a jury, which rendered a verdict for respondent on his ADEA claim and . . . found that petitioners—willfully—violated the statute.

The United States Court of Appeals for the First Circuit affirmed judgment for respondent on both the ADEA and ERISA counts, and reversed judgment notwithstanding the verdict for petitioners as to "willfulness."

We now clarify that there is no disparate treatment under the ADEA when the factor motivating the employer is some feature other than the employee's age.

We long have distinguished between "disparate treatment" and "disparate impact" theories of employment discrimination.

"Disparate treatment" . . . is the most easily understood type of discrimination. The employer simply treats some people less favorably than others because of their race, color, religion or other protected characteristics. Proof of discriminatory motive is critical, although it can in some situations be inferred from the mere fact of differences in treatment. . . .

"Claims that stress 'disparate impact' by contrast involve employment practices that are facially neutral in their treatment of different groups but that in fact fall more harshly on one group than another and cannot be justified by business necessity. Proof of discriminatory motive . . . is not required under a disparate-impact theory." The disparate treatment theory is of course available under the ADEA, as the language of that statute makes clear. "It shall be unlawful for an employer . . . to fail or refuse to hire or to discharge any individual or otherwise discriminate against any individual with respect to his compensation, terms, conditions, or privileges of employment, because of such individual's age."

In a disparate treatment case, liability depends on whether the protected trait (under the ADEA, age) actually motivated the employer's decision. The employer may have relied upon a formal, facially discriminatory policy requiring adverse treatment of employees with that trait. Or the employer may have been motivated by the protected trait on an ad hoc, informal basis. Whatever the employer's decisionmaking process, a disparate treatment claim cannot succeed unless the employee's protected trait actually played a role in that process and had a determinative influence on the outcome.

Disparate treatment, thus defined, captures the essence of what Congress sought to prohibit in the ADEA. It is the very essence of age discrimination for an older employee to be fired because the employer believes that productivity and competence decline with old age. As we explained in *EEOC v. Wyoming,* Congress' promulgation of the ADEA was prompted by its concern that older workers were being deprived of employment on the basis of inaccurate and stigmatizing stereotypes.

"Although age discrimination rarely was based on the sort of animus motivating some other forms of discrimination, it was based in large part on stereotypes unsupported by objective fact. . . . Moreover, the available empirical evidence demonstrated that arbitrary age lines were in fact generally unfounded and that, as an overall matter, the performance of older workers was at least as good as that of younger workers."

Thus the ADEA commands that "employers are to evaluate older employees . . . on their merits and not their age." The employer cannot rely on age as a proxy for an employee's remaining characteristics, such as productivity, but must instead focus on those factors directly.

Yet a decision by the company to fire an older employee solely because he has nine-plus years of service and therefore is "close to vesting" would not constitute discriminatory treatment on the basis of age. The prohibited stereotype ("Older employees are likely to be less productive") would not have figured in this decision, and the attendant stigma would not ensue. The decision would not be the result of an inaccurate and denigrating generalization about age, but would rather represent an accurate judgment about the employee that he indeed is "close to vesting."

We also address the second question: the meaning of "willful" in 7(b) of the ADEA, which provides for liquidated damages in the case of a "willful" violation.

A violation of the Act would be "willful" if the employer knew or showed reckless disregard for the matter of whether its conduct was prohibited by the ADEA.

The ADEA . . . provides for liquidated damages where the violation was "willful."

We therefore reaffirm that the Thurston definition of "willful" that the employer either knew or showed reckless disregard for the matter of whether its conduct was prohibited by the statute—applies to all disparate treatment cases under the ADEA. Once a "willful" violation has been shown, the employee need not additionally demonstrate that the employer's conduct was outrageous, or provide direct evidence of the employer's motivation, or prove that age was the predominant rather than a determinative factor in the employment decision.

The judgment of the Court of Appeals is vacated and the case is remanded for further proceedings consistent with this opinion.

Judgment for Biggins.

Discrimination Requirements

The initial test for determining age discrimination has four prongs:

1. Employee was qualified.
2. Employee was terminated.
3. Employee was a member of a protected class.
4. Employee was replaced by someone younger or was otherwise discharged because of age.

The employer must then provide a legitimate nondiscriminatory reason for the discharge. After satisfying this burden, the employee must prove that the employer's reasoning was false and that the real reason was to discriminate.

The issue in the next case is whether the poor evaluations received by the employee were purposely given as a pretext to mask the employer's true intent of age discrimination.

CASE

Martin v. Ryder Distributions Resources, Inc.

811 F.Supp. 658 (1992)

MOORE, Judge.

The following case concerns a fifty-three-year old employee who was terminated due to poor performance. He alleged that his evaluations were purposely lowered to effectuate his dismissal and that the underlying reason was his age.

Ryder Systems, Inc. is a holding company located in Miami, Florida with a number of operating subsidiaries providing highway transportation services, aviation services and insurance management services. Ryder Truck Rental, Inc. ("RTR"), is a subsidiary of Ryder System and the largest of a group of companies which make up the Vehicle Leasing and Services Division of Ryder System ("VLSD"). RTR provides full service leasing and short-term rental of trucks, tractors, and trailers throughout the United States. Ryder Distribution Resources, Inc., ("RDR"), is a subsidiary of RTR and one of the VLSD companies. RDR provides contract carriages throughout the country.

Plaintiff, Kirk Martin, was hired by RTR on September 19, 1962. From 1982 until June, 1985, Martin was a vice-president of RTR, responsible for the Birmingham, Alabama, region, one of the eighteen regions at RTR. In 1985, RTR consolidated various regions and as a result the Birmingham region was closed. Martin transferred to RDR, where he was a Group Director. During his tenure at RDR, the chief operating officer of RDR was Paul Levering and the person to whom Martin directly reported was Willard Eaves.

On April 1, 1988, at the age of 53, Martin was terminated from his position at RDR. On December 2, 1988, Martin filed this claim under the Age Discrimination in Employment Act of 1967 ("ADEA"). The complaint alleges that RDR, RTR and Ryder System (hereafter collectively referred to as "Ryder"), willfully violated the ADEA. Martin alleges that no reason was given for his termination; that he had never been reprimanded, counseled, or disciplined in any way during his employment; that his evaluations were always "satisfactory"; and that he met all of the goals and objectives set by Ryder. Martin also alleges that after his termination Levering directed Eaves to lower Martin's performance to a level below satisfactory as a pretext for Martin's termination.

In ADEA cases, the plaintiff has the ultimate burden of proving that age was a determining factor in the employer's decision to terminate his employment. Initially, the plaintiff must establish a prima facie case of age discrimination. Once the plaintiff satisfies this initial burden, a rebuttable inference of discrimination is created and the burden shifts to the defendant to articulate a legitimate nondiscriminatory reason for dismissing the plaintiff. If the defendant succeeds in rebutting the inference of discrimination, the plaintiff must prove by a preponderance of the evidence that the articulated reason is merely a pretext for a discriminatory discharge.

The initial test to determine Age Discrimination has four prongs:

1. that he is a member of the protected group;
2. that adverse employment action has been taken against him (e.g., discharge, demotion or failure to hire);
3. that he was replaced by a person outside the protected group; and
4. that he was qualified for the position for which he was rejected.

The record indicates that Martin can show the first, second and fourth prongs of the test: (1) he was 53 years old, (2) he was discharged, and (4) he was qualified for the job. However, because Martin was replaced by another age-protected employee, the Court must scrutinize Martin's ability to satisfy the third prong of the test.

Martin shows that this replacement was ten years younger. Although a plaintiff may establish the third prong of the test by showing that he was replaced by a substantially younger employee, Martin's ten year differential, standing alone, is insufficient to satisfy Martin's burden with respect to the third prong. However, considering the circumstances of this case in the light most favorable to the plaintiff, the Court finds that Martin has established a prima facie case under the *McDonnell Douglas* test.

Martin does not adduce any statistical evidence of a pattern and practice of age discrimination. Instead, he alleges that Levering's "good old boys" and "old-fashioned" comments show that Ryder had a pattern and practice of discrimination. However, as previously discussed, these comments are not direct evidence of discrimination. These comments merely refer to characteristics of individuals and are not associated with increasing age. Therefore, Martin has failed to put forth any evidence of a pattern and practice of discrimination and cannot establish a prima facie case under this alternative.

This Court finds that Martin has established a prima facie case of discrimination under the McDonnell Douglas test. The analysis must now determine whether the defendants respond with sufficient rebuttal evidence.

Once a prima facie case of discrimination is established, the burden shifts to the defendant to articulate a legitimate, nondiscriminatory reason for discharging the plaintiff. Ryder asserts that Martin was discharged because of a poor performance evaluation in 1986, rated in the lowest 20% of all executives, that his rating in 1987 was in the lowest 2%, that the overall performance of his Group deteriorated each year, and that in 1987 he failed on the company's objectives in 62% of his accounts. Further, Ryder claims that Willard Eaves, Martin's direct supervisor, was not satisfied with his work.

The Court finds these are legitimate, nondiscriminatory reasons for Martin's discharge and, based thereon, Ryder has met its burden. Once the defendant succeeds in rebutting the inference of discrimination, the plaintiff must prove by a preponderance of the evidence that the articulated reason is merely a pretext for a discriminatory discharge. Martin may show pretext by "either directly persuading the court that a discriminatory reason more likely motivated the employer or indirectly by showing that the employer's proffered explanation is unworthy of credence." Martin contends that he has met his burden or created a material issue of fact by showing that: (1) Levering directed Eaves to lower his performance evaluation without reason, against Eaves' will and as a pretext for his firing and (2) that his performance evaluations were unfair and incorrect.

Martin does not contest his 1986 evaluation, nor the deteriorating performance of his group, nor the failure to meet the objectives of a majority of his accounts.

In light of Ryder's substantial evidence of its dissatisfaction with Martin's performance, the direct contradiction of Levering's alleged actions, and the insufficiency of the Scarpa affidavit, this Court concludes that a jury could not reasonably find by a preponderance of the evidence that Ryder's legitimate, nondiscriminatory reasons for dismissing Martin are unworthy of belief or that a discriminatory reason more likely motivated Ryder. Accordingly, defendant's motion for summary judgment should be granted.

Judgment for Ryder.

Mandatory Retirement

The mandatory retirement age was originally sixty-five. In 1978, it was adjusted to seventy, and more recently, it has been extinguished. Age discrimination can begin at forty.

Employment Perspective

Big Mac Kowalski is the quarterback for the Raleigh Rainbows. In the past year, he was ranked among the upper half of all quarterbacks in the league. Before the beginning of the season, Chubby Shelten, coach of the Rainbows, informs Kowalski that he is being discharged. Chubby explains that the team will be committing itself to younger players and that the younger players would prefer someone of similar age to be quarterback rather than an old man whom they cannot relate to. Kowalski is thirty-eight years of age. He sues the Rainbows for age discrimination. Will he score? No. Big Mac is under forty. The protection of the Age Discrimination in Employment Act does not apply to him. Big Mac will become an armchair quarterback. ◆

The following case addresses the question of whether an employee who has retired and is collecting a pension may return to work. The employer refused to allow the employee to return. The employee claimed that this is an act of age discrimination.

CASE

E.E.O.C. v. Local 350, Plumbers and Pipefitters

982 F.2d 1305 (9th Cir. 1992)

FLETCHER, Circuit Judge.

Local 350 represents pipefitters and plumbers in Northern Nevada and parts of California. Together with industry employers, Local 350 operates a hiring hall. The hiring dispatcher keeps four "out of work lists," with different qualifications and priorities, from which members are hired. At issue in this case is list number 1, the "out of work list," reserved for persons who have been employed for at least 4,000 hours or more during the five years immediately preceding placement on the list. The dispatcher sends members out to jobs in the order in which they signed up.

Donald Pilot, a member of Local 350, retired in 1983. After retirement, he paid retired members' dues. In 1984, he decided to return to work, and signed onto the out of work list. Local 350 removed his name from the list, stating he was not eligible. In a letter dated April 20, 1984, Local 350 informed Pilot that, "as a retiree, having applied for and been granted pension, you are not presently eligible for dispatch through the UA Local 350 Hiring Hall." Local 350 informed Pilot that to be eligible to sign up for referral, he would have to cease receiving his pension.

In December, 1987, Pilot filed a discrimination charge with the Nevada Equal Rights Commission and the EEOC. In June, 1989, the EEOC filed an action under the Age Discrimination in Employment Act ("ADEA"), on behalf of Pilot and similarly situated union members, seeking equitable relief, back-pay, and liquidated damages. In May, 1990, the district court granted summary judgment in favor of Local 350.

Does the statute of limitations bar the EEOC's action?

While the district court granted summary judgment on the merits, Local 350 argues that its decision can be affirmed on the ground that the statute of limitations bars the EEOC's action. A suit alleging a violation of the ADEA must be brought within two years after the cause of action accrues; if "willful" violation is at issue, the statute of limitations is three years. Local 350 contends that Pilot was required to file suit within two, or, arguably at most three, years after Local 350 removed his name from the list in April.

To enforce the ADEA, the EEOC may seek injunctive relief, as provided in 29 U.S.C. 217, or may seek damages on behalf of an injured individual. In its suit, the EEOC sought both types of relief from Local 350.

With regard to injunctive relief, the EEOC need not rely on a charge by an individual to bring suit. "The EEOC's role in combating age discrimination is not dependent on the filing of a charge; the agency may receive information concerning alleged violations of the ADEA 'from any source,' and it has independent authority to investigate age discrimination."

Thus, the EEOC was required to file suit within two (or three) years of the last date the challenged policy was in place. As the challenged policy remains in effect to this day, the EEOC's claim for injunctive relief is timely.

The EEOC's suit also asked that Local 350 be ordered to "make whole" Donald Pilot and similarly situated union members through payment of backpay and liquidated damages.

The EEOC also argues that Pilot can obtain monetary relief from the date he was first refused listing because Local 350's policy constitutes a "continuing violation" of the ADEA.

"Under the continuing violation doctrine, 'a systematic policy of discrimination is actionable even if some or all of the events evidencing its inception occurred prior to the limitations period.'" The doctrine is applied because "'the continuing system of discrimination operates against the employee and violates his or her rights up to a point in time that falls within the applicable limitations period.'" When the doctrine is applicable, "no part of a continuing violation *which persists into the period within which suit is allowed* is time-barred."

Here, Local 350's allegedly discriminatory policy was in effect when Pilot first encountered it in 1984, and remains in force today. Thus, under the continuing violation doctrine, relief for Pilot is not barred.

The EEOC claims that Local 350's policy violates 29 U.S.C. 623(c)(2) because it discriminates against older workers.

Section 623(c)(2) provides:

> It shall be unlawful for a labor organization . . . (2) to limit, segregate, or classify its membership, or fail or refuse to refer for employment any individual, in any way which would deprive or tend to deprive any individual of employment opportunities, or would limit such employment opportunities or otherwise adversely affect his status as an employee or as an applicant for employment, because of such individual's age.
>
> "An employer discriminates 'because of' age whenever age is 'but for' cause of discrimination."

Under this analysis, Local 350's policy discriminates on the basis of age. On its face, it discriminates only against retired employees; however, only employees 55 or older are eligible to retire. There is thus a very close connection between age and the factor on which discrimination is based.

Local 350 argues that the policy is not discriminatory because the "but for" cause of discrimination is not the retiree's age, but his voluntary decision to retire and remain retired.

Moreover, the very "choice" Local 350 identifies is discriminatory. Only retired, older employees need decide whether to remain retired and forego alternative sources of income while they seek work as pipefitters; younger workers need not choose between receiving unemployment benefits or holding another job and placing their name on Local 350's list. Younger employees who have "chosen" not to work as pipefitters for some time for whatever reason are not penalized in the same way as retired workers.

Thus, Local 350's policy violates Section 623(c)(2) because it refuses to refer certain employees for work on the basis of a factor very closely related to age. Because the policy discourages retired employees from seeking to return to the workforce, it frustrates the ADEA's goal of promoting the employment of older persons based on their ability rather than age.

Was Local 350's policy based on "reasonable factors other than age."

Local 350 proposes several additional factors cited by Local 350 business manager George Foster in his declaration. It argues that it needs to preserve work opportunities for its members. It suggests that a flood of retirees returning to work would result in long periods of unemployment for non-retired members who would otherwise get work. However, it is hard to see why Local 350's management of employment opportunities should be carried out by requiring retirees to forego their pensions before being allowed to sign up for work. Once again, the proposed factor seems to embody the very discrimination that is the subject of this suit. If preventing retirees from reentering the working force is the rationale (which it could not be, under the ADEA), no retirees should be allowed to sign up. Moreover, as the EEOC notes, the Local had fewer than 130 retired members in 1990 and since 1981 only a handful have sought to return to work.

Because neither the reason proposed by the district court nor the justifications presented by Local 350 satisfy the requirements, we find the district court erred in concluding that this defense protected Local 350's policy. We thus reverse the grant of summary judgment in favor of Local 350.

Judgment for EEOC.

Damages

Damages recoverable for age discrimination include reinstatement, back pay, differential in pay due to seniority, and pension-benefit contributions. Where the employer's motivation for discharge was intentional, double lost wages may be assessed as a form of liquidated damages. Interest and attorney's fees may also be awarded at the discretion of the court.

A victim of age discrimination must file a claim with the EEOC within two years of the incident. This statute of limitations is extended to three years if the employer acted with intent. After filing with the EEOC, the complainant may proceed in State or Federal Court himself or herself. It is possible for two corresponding suits, one brought by the EEOC and the other brought by the complainant, to take place at the same time.

Under Title VII, a separate suit may be commenced only when EEOC's determination is not to proceed. If the complaining party has not yet filed a separate suit and the EEOC has decided not to pursue the claim, the complainant has ninety days to bring a lawsuit from the receipt of the said notice.

In the following case, a woman over forty years of age was discharged. She claimed age discrimination. Her employer complained of her unsatisfactory work. The issue is whether the employer's reason for the discharge was false and that the real reason was purposely to discriminate against her.

CASE

Zelewski v. American Federal Sav. Bank

811 F.Supp. 456 (D.Minn. 1993)

DOTY, Judge.

On May 4, 1990, plaintiff requested a one-year leave of absence for health reasons. In addition to her lung condition, plaintiff had been suffering from depression since 1987, had been on anti-depressants since 1988 and had been suffering from rheumatoid arthritis since 1989. The bank again granted plaintiff's request, combining the maximum disability leave, vacation time, sick leave and personnel leave available to permit the requested leave of absence. Plaintiff began her leave on May 21, 1990.

Prior to her leave of absence, plaintiff reported to dependent Steven P. Worwa, who became president of the bank in February 1989. Plaintiff claims that after Worwa became president, the bank instituted a program of eliminating employees over 40 years of age and replacing them with younger employees. In support of that contention, plaintiff identifies various bank employees over 40 who either resigned or were terminated, for a variety of reasons, after 1989. Plaintiff, however, fails to identify any younger employees who have allegedly replaced those older employees.

Based on the foregoing, plaintiff asserts age discrimination claims under the Age Discrimination and Employment Act ("ADEA").

Plaintiff filed a charge of age discrimination with the Equal Employment Opportunity Commission ("EEOC") on August 2, 1991. Under the ADEA, a plaintiff is required to file a charge with the EEOC "within 300 days after the alleged unlawful practice occurred." Thus, plaintiff's age discrimination claim is barred to the extent that it is premised on acts which occurred 300 days before the filing of her charge, that is, before October 4, 1990.

Plaintiff began her leave of absence on May 21, 1990. To support her age discrimination claims, she alleges only one discriminatory act occurring after that time, that the bank failed to send her various internal memoranda. All of the other acts on which plaintiff relies occurred before she began her her leave, and more than one year before plaintiff filed her charge with the EEOC. Plaintiff nonetheless argues that her age discrimination claims are timely because she did not fully experience the physical or emotional effects of the challenged acts until much later, and thus the limitation periods did not begin to run until she fully felt such effects.

The court rejects plaintiff's contention. In determining when a statute of limitations begins to run, "the proper focus is upon the time of the discriminatory acts, not upon the time at which the consequences of the acts became most painful."

Moreover, although the bank wanted plaintiff to return to work after her leave ended, she failed to do so because of her health and proffers no evidence that her failure to return involves some discriminatory act. As discussed more fully, the only act of alleged discrimination occurring after plaintiff began her leave, that the bank failed to send her various internal memoranda, is insufficient to raise an inference of age discrimination.

In summary, the court concludes that plaintiff's age discrimination claim fails because all of plaintiff's allegations of age discrimination . . . are barred by the applicable statutes of limitations.

Judgment for American Federal Savings Bank.

The case that follows addresses the argument of whether individuals with different employment experiences regarding potential age discrimination claims may band together in a class action suit.

CASE *Mooney v. Aramco Services Co.*

54 F.3d 1207 (5th Cir. 1995)

DUHE, Circuit Judge.

Appellants are eighty-five former managerial and skilled employees terminated under Aramco's "Manpower Control Program" during 1984–87. In 1987, Robert Mooney, William Holcomb and John Marcum filed their representative complaint alleging unlawful termination in violation of the Age Discrimination Employment Act (ADEA).

The specific circumstances of termination alleged by Plaintiffs are equally diverse. Deposition testimony from the respective Plaintiffs reveals a wide range of claims and theories of recovery, including: discriminatory selection for RIF (reduction in force), forced retirement, replacement with younger, American, Saudi, or Muslim employees, and Aramco's refusal to transfer Plaintiffs to other departments. Some

Plaintiffs allege that Aramco should have "bumped" other employees to create open positions for them. Still others claim that Aramco "retaliated" against them by refusing to rehire them after they complained of discriminatory treatment.

In view of the hodgepodge of claims and allegations, it is clear that the defenses available to Aramco are just about as disparate as the Plaintiffs themselves. Moreover, Aramco, as a defendant in an ADEA action, is entitled to articulate "legitimate, nondiscriminatory reasons for the employees' reaction, including "reasonable factors other than age" ("RFOA"). The court's evaluation of Aramco's defenses inevitably will require presentation of evidence unique to each individual plaintiff. Third, the evidence submitted by Aramco indicates that there existed no single company-wide reduction in force ("RIF"). As reflected in the affidavits of Aramco officers and supervisors, the downsizing of the Aramco work force was implemented on a highly decentralized level by local management. In contrast to the cases relied upon by Plaintiffs, wherein the common thread unifying Plaintiffs' claims was a company-wide action executed by a relatively small number of supervisors within a short time period, in the instant case it appears that "the elections for individual terminations were made by hundreds of different supervisors in separate departments with differing constraints and objectives, based upon considerations of various skills, performance factors, and business needs in each of five years."

These facts, and the absence of any controverting evidence submitted by Plaintiffs, lead the Court to conclude that Aramco's surplussing decisions were made in a manner similar to that in *Lusardi:* between 1984 and 1988, Aramco experienced not one, but well over 297 separate RIFs.

The facts developed at this time indicate that it would be difficult, if not impossible, to identify as many as two or three of more than 130 potential Plaintiffs who could be said to be "similarly situated" within the meaning of the ADEA statute. Moreover, Plaintiffs themselves have made no attempt to identify a smaller group of individuals who might comprise a "similarly situated" sub-class for ADEA purposes.

Other than the global allegations of Plaintiffs that the ADEA was violated, that they were formerly Aramco employees, and that they were in the protected age group over forty, there is no real commonality among the named Plaintiffs.

For numerous reasons, including (1) the widely disparate factual, employment, and discharge histories of the individual Plaintiffs; (2) the variety of particular, differing, and sometimes unique defenses available to Aramco in contesting the varied and disparate claims of 130 or more former employees; and (3) fairness and procedural considerations, the Court concludes that Plaintiffs are not "similarly situated" within the meaning of Section 16(b) of the ADEA.

In general, a plaintiff can prove age discrimination in two ways. A plaintiff can prove discriminatory animus by direct evidence or by an indirect or inferential method of proof. Discrimination can be shown indirectly by following the "pretext" method of proof set out in *McDonnell Douglas Corp. v. Green.* "The shifting burdens of proof set forth in *McDonnell Douglas* are designed to assure that the 'plaintiff has his day in court despite the unavailability of direct evidence.' "

If, however, plaintiff produces direct evidence of discrimination, the *McDonnell Douglas* test is "inapplicable." The *Price Waterhouse* mixed-motives theory of discrimination comes into play where direct evidence of discrimination is presented, but the employer asserts that the same adverse employment decision would have been made regardless of discrimination. Although Price Waterhouse can be characterized as a method to prove discrimination, the mixed-motives theory is probably best viewed as a defense for an employer.

As we have noted previously, "one cannot take legal action in ADEA cases unless one has filed an administrative charge in cases arising in Texas, within 300 days of the last act of discrimination." However, "the federal courts now universally hold that an individual who has not filed an administrative charge can opt-in to a suit filed by any similarly situated plaintiff under certain conditions." This so-called "single filing rule" generally allows a plaintiff, who did not file an EEOC charge, to piggyback on the EEOC complaint filed by another person who is similarly situated. In this case, all of the named Trial Plaintiffs filed an individual EEOC charge, but failed to include an ex gratia claim. Trial Plaintiffs now attempt to rely on the ex gratia claim contained in the individual EEOC charge of Robert Olson, a named plaintiff who was not included in the group of Trial Plaintiffs. Whether the single filing rule can be used by someone who actually filed an EEOC charge to append an additional claim appears to be a matter of first impression.

"It is uncontroversial that the 'single filing rule' is not limited to class actions but also can permit a plaintiff to join individual ADEA actions if the named Plaintiff filed a timely administrative charge to permit 'piggybacking' by the joining plaintiff." Two conditions must be satisfied. First, the person attempting to piggyback must be similarly situated to the person who actually filed the EEOC charge. Second, the charge must provide notice of the collective or classwide nature of the charge. There is no dispute that Olson's EEOC charge contained language purporting to make the ex gratia claim class-wide, however, that does not end our inquiry.

The policy behind the single filing rule is that, it would be wasteful, if not vain, for numerous employees, all with the same grievance, to have to process many identical complaints with the EEOC." As long as the EEOC and the company are aware of the nature and scope of the allegations, the purposes behind the filing requirement are satisfied and no injustice or contravention of congressional intent occurs by allowing piggybacking. However, where the party wishing to piggyback has filed his own EEOC charge, policy cuts the other way.

Once the charge is filed, unless it is permissibly modified, the EEOC and the employer are entitled to rely on the allegations contained therein. To allow a plaintiff to file an EEOC charge, file suit upon that charge and then, at the eleventh hour, when the statute of limitations has run, to amend his complaint in reliance on the charge of another belies the policies behind the single filing rule and controverts congressional intent. The employee, by failing to assert a particular allegation in his charge, has necessarily excluded himself from the class of persons purportedly covered by the charge of another. As a result, the EEOC and the employer are given no notice and no opportunity to remedy his complaint. He is bound by the parameters of his own EEOC charge, and cannot subsequently utilize the single filing rule to avoid the statute of limitations. Because the single filing rule was inapplicable, the district court Properly denied Trial Plaintiffs' motion for leave to amend.

For the reasons set forth herein, we affirm the orders and rulings of the district court.

Judgment for Aramco Services Co.

In the case that follows, the questions presented were whether the age discrimination claim was barred because the employment expired according to the duration specified in the contract and if not, whether the claim still fails because it was not timely filed.

CASE

Ode v. Omtvedt

883 F.Supp. 1308 (D. Neb. 1995)

KOPF, District Judge.

I find and conclude that Defendants' motion for summary judgment should be granted because there are no material facts genuinely in dispute and because (1) Ode's ADEA claim is barred because (a) he failed to file a timely EEOC charge within 300 days of the date of the alleged unlawful action, and (b) Ode has failed in his burden proof to establish a jury question on his entitlement to equitable tolling of the 300-day time period; (2) there was no due process violation since Ode had no property interest in continued employment; and (3) even if the reasons for nonrenewal of Ode's contract were false and pretextual, the contract was not breached because it unambiguously provided for expiration on a date certain and did not require renewal if Defendants gave timely notice of nonrenewal (which they did), recognizing that the contract also unambiguously provided that Defendants need not have cause for nonrenewal.

Plaintiff Arthur H. Ode, Jr., is an adult citizen of the United States and currently resides in Milwaukee, Wisconsin. Ode holds a Ph.D. in public administration, with undergraduate degrees in botany.

Defendant University of Nebraska-Lincoln (UNL) is a public university established by the State of Nebraska which provides higher education and has been organized pursuant to the laws of the State of Nebraska.

Defendant Irvin T. Omtvedt was employed by UNL as the vice chancellor and as vice president for agriculture and natural resources throughout the University of Nebraska system during the period that Dr. Ode was employed at UNL.

Dr. Ode was hired by Dr. Omtvedt to be the director of the Nebraska State Arboretum (NSA) in 1988. Dr. Ode began his employment on July 1, 1988. Dr. Ode held a "special appointment" as a member of the "academic-administrative staff." The category of "academic-administrative staff" includes:

all faculty and such administrative officers as the Board may designate. The faculty of the University of Nebraska includes all persons holding the academic rank of assistant instructor and above, or formally approved equivalent ranks. The bylaws provide that a "special appointment" will terminate:

in accordance with the time stated in the appointment to the position or in the written contract, and, if no time is stated in the appointment to the position or in the written contract, the appointment may be terminated by either party giving the other at least 90 days notice of the date of termination. Such appointments may also be terminated by the University for adequate cause, disability, bona fide discontinuance of a program or department, or extraordinary circumstances because of financial exigencies.

When Dr. Ode was initially hired by Dr. Omtvedt, Dr. Ode was placed in a "nontenured" position. In June, 1990, Dr. Ode and Dr. Omtvedt negotiated a written contract of employment which is exhibit 6 in the Ode deposition. The pertinent portions of that contract of employment are as follows:

> **Section 1. Term of Contract; Extension.** The term of this Contract shall be for a period of three (3) years beginning on the 1st day of July, 1990, and expiring at midnight on the 30th day of June, 1993. Thereafter this Contract shall be automatically extended for two (2) additional years; provided, that the University may terminate this contract without cause as of July 1 of any year by giving Dr. Ode at least 12 months advance written notice of such termination. . . .
>
> **Section 3. Professional Staff Appointment Status, Fringe Benefits, and Terms and Conditions of Employment.** (a) The professional staff appointment status of Dr. Ode pursuant to this Contract shall be an all-year, full-time special appointment as a member of the Academic-Administrative staff of the University of Nebraska-Lincoln. He shall receive all of the fringe benefits of employment received by other members of the Academic-Administrative staff on all-year appointments.
>
> (b) Dr. Ode's employment shall be subject to (1) the terms and conditions of employment for members of the Academic-Administrative staff as provided in Chapter III of the Bylaws of the board of Regents and (2) the rights and responsibilities of the Professional staff as provided in Chapter IV of the Bylaws of Board of Regents.
>
> (c) Without limiting the generality of the provisions of subsection (b) of this section, Dr. Ode's employment may be terminated by the Board during the term of this contract or any extension thereof for adequate cause, disability, bona fide discontinuance of the Nebraska Statewide Arboretum as a program of the University, or extraordinary circumstances because of financial exigencies.

Dr. Ode alleges that he was appointed as a graduate faculty member at UNL. Dr. Ode was given "courtesy" faculty appointments in two academic departments at UNL, horticulture and forestry, which gave him certain privileges in those departments. He admits he was not a tenured faculty member and was never placed on a track which could lead to tenure, even though he twice requested to be placed on a tenure-leading track. Under the Regents' bylaws, the term "special appointments" includes faculty appointments which are "courtesy appointments." In his evaluation, Dr. Omtvedt made a number of critical comments about Dr. Ode's performance and concluded by saying:

> This is the first time I have personally evaluated you since you got established in the position, but the feedback I received clearly indicates you need to provide stronger, more aggressive responsible leadership for NSA. There are many people who are anxious to help and are capable, but you are going to have to provide the leadership.

Dr. Omtvedt went over the evaluation with Dr. Ode at their meeting and they talked about the various points in the evaluation.

On June 11, 1992, Dr. Omtvedt notified Dr. Ode that he had decided to terminate Dr. Ode as director of the NSA. Dr. Omtvedt met with Dr. Ode that day and gave him a letter advising him of Dr. Omtvedt's decision. The letter states in pertinent part:

As you know, your current contract as Director of the Nebraska Statewide Arboretum and Curator of the University of Nebraska Arboretum expires on June 30, 1993. After carefully evaluating the wide range of input I received from the Administrative Council, NSA Board members, NSA staff, and some NSA members, I regret to inform you that we are not in a position to renew or extend your contract beyond June 30, 1993.

As soon as he received the notice of termination Dr. Ode concluded that he was the victim of age discrimination.

With the information in his possession when he received the notice of nonrenewal, Ode could have reasonably asserted to the EEOC that (a) his contract was not being renewed; (b) he was in a protected class; (c) according to his employer's evaluations he had performed his job satisfactorily in the past, save for the last evaluation received immediately prior to nonrenewal of his contract; (d) his employer was purportedly restructuring the job he was performing, while endeavoring to hire someone to perform that restructured job at a substantially reduced wage; and (e) as a consequence of these facts, he believed he was the target of age discrimination.

This information clearly constituted a sufficient charge under the EEOC guidelines. Indeed, EEOC regulations provide that a charge is adequate if it simply names prospective respondent and generally describes the discriminatory act. In summary, because the record is undisputed that at the time he received the notice of nonrenewal, Ode possessed facts which alerted him to the possibility that he had been discriminated because of age, and because he also possessed facts sufficient for an EEOC charge, Ode cannot excuse the tardy filing of his charge on grounds that he did not know that a younger man would be hired.

Judgment for Omtevdt.

Employment Perspective

Myrtle Eldridge has been working for Marvin Wilson as his personal secretary for thirty-five years. Their employer is Seacrest Shipping. Marvin retired recently. His replacement is Buddy Johnson, who is twenty-seven. After one look at Myrtle, he has decided that he would prefer someone who is more youthful. Buddy replaces Myrtle with Rhonda, a twenty-two-year-old whose office skills barely measure up to Myrtle's. Myrtle files a claim with EEOC. Before its determination, she sues Seacrest Shipping in State Court. Seacrest argues that her suit cannot be brought until the EEOC determination has been made, as in Title VII cases. Are they correct? No! After the filing of the EEOC claim, Myrtle is free to pursue her own suit in State Court, unlike under Title VII, which requires an EEOC dismissal before suing. With regard to the issue in her case, Seacrest claims that incompatibility was the reason why Buddy wanted her replaced. Is this a sufficient reason? No! Since Buddy had Myrtle dismissed immediately, there is no basis on which to draw a conclusion of incompatibility. Myrtle will win and will be reinstated in the secretarial position. Naturally, it would be ludicrous for Buddy and Myrtle to work together, given the EEOC investigation and the lawsuit. Myrtle will be entitled to double back pay. The doubling is a form of liquidated damages because Buddy's actions were intentional: he did not want her because of her age. In addition, she will receive compensation for lost benefits, loss of seniority, and possibly attorney fees and interest. ◆

The following case addresses the question of whether an employee is precluded from commencing a court action because he is required to arbitrate according to a securities registration application that he had signed.

CASE

Gilmer v. Interstate/Johnson Lane Corp.

111 S.Ct. 1647 (1991)

Justice WHITE delivered the opinion of the Court.

The question presented in this case is whether a claim under the Age Discrimination in Employment Act of 1967 (ADEA), can be subjected to compulsory arbitration pursuant to an arbitration agreement in a securities registration application. The Court of Appeals held that it could, and we affirm.

Respondent Interstate/Johnson Lane Corporation (Interstate) hired petitioner Robert Gilmer as a Manager of Financial Services in May 1981. As required by his employment, Gilmer registered as a securities representative with several stock exchanges, including the New York Stock Exchange (NYSE). His registration application, entitled "Uniform Application for Securities Industry Registration or Transfer," provided, among other things, that Gilmer "agreed to arbitrate any dispute, claim or controversy" arising between him and Interstate "that is required to be arbitrated under the rules, constitutions or by-laws of the organizations with which I register." Of relevance to this case, NYSE Rule 347 provides for arbitration of "any controversy between a registered representative and any member or member organization arising out of the employment or termination of employment of such registered representative."

Interstate terminated Gilmer's employment in 1987, at which time Gilmer was 62 years of age. After first filing an age discrimination charge with the Equal Employment Opportunity Commission (EEOC), Gilmer subsequently brought suit in the United States District Court for the Western District of North Carolina, alleging that Interstate had discharged him because of his age, in violation of the ADEA. In response to Gilmer's complaint, Interstate filed in the District Court a motion to compel arbitration of the ADEA claim. In its motion, Interstate relied upon the arbitration agreement in Gilmer's registration application, as well as the Federal Arbitration Act (FAA).

The FAA was originally enacted in 1925, and then reenacted and codified in 1947 as Title 9 of the United States Code. Its purpose was to reverse the longstanding judicial hostility to arbitration agreements that had existed at English common law and had been adopted by American courts, and to place arbitration agreements upon the same footing as other contracts. Its primary substantive provision states that "a written provision in any maritime transaction or a contract evidencing a transaction involving commerce to settle by arbitration a controversy thereafter arising out of such contract or transaction . . . shall be valid, irrevocable, and enforceable, save upon such grounds as exist at law or in equity for the revocation of any contract."

Although all statutory claims may not be appropriate for arbitration, "having made the bargain to arbitrate, the party should be held to it unless Congress itself has evinced an intention to preclude a waiver of judicial remedies for the statutory rights at issue."

Gilmer concedes that nothing in the text of the ADEA or its legislative history explicitly precludes arbitration. He argues, however, that compulsory arbitration of ADEA claims pursuant to arbitration agreements would be inconsistent with the statutory framework and purposes of the ADEA. Like the Court of Appeals, we disagree.

Congress enacted the ADEA in 1967 "to promote employment of older persons based on their ability rather than age; to prohibit arbitrary age discrimination in employment; and to help employers and workers find ways of meeting problems arising from the impact of age on employment." To achieve those goals, the ADEA, among other things, makes it unlawful for an employer "to fail or refuse to hire or to discharge any individual or otherwise discriminate against any individual with respect to his compensation, terms, conditions, or privileges of employment, because of such individual's age." This proscription is enforced both by private suits and by the EEOC. In order for an aggrieved individual to bring suit under the ADEA, he or she must first file a charge with the EEOC and then wait at least 60 days. An individual's right to sue is extinguished, however, if the EEOC institutes an action against the employer. Before the EEOC can bring such an action, though, it must "attempt to eliminate the discriminatory practice or practices alleged, and to effect voluntary compliance with the requirements of this chapter through informal methods of conciliation, conference, and persuasion."

As Gilmer contends, the ADEA is designed not only to address individual grievances, but also to further important social policies. We do not perceive any inherent inconsistency between those policies, however, and enforcing agreements to arbitrate age discrimination claims. It is true that arbitration focuses on specific disputes between the parties involved. The same can be said, however, of judicial resolution of claims. Both of these dispute resolution mechanisms nevertheless also can further broader social purposes. The Sherman Act, the Securities Exchange Act of 1934, RICO, and the Securities Act of 1933 all are designed to advance important public policies, but, as noted above, claims under those statutes are appropriate for arbitration. "So long as the prospective litigant effectively may vindicate his or her statutory cause of action in the arbitral forum, the statute will continue to serve both its remedial and deterrent function."

We also are unpersuaded by the argument that arbitration will undermine the role of the EEOC in enforcing the ADEA. An individual ADEA claimant subject to an arbitration agreement will still be free to file a charge with the EEOC, even though the claimant is not able to institute a private judicial action. Indeed, Gilmer filed a charge with the EEOC in this case. In any event, the EEOC's role in combating age discrimination is not dependent on the filing of a charge; the agency may receive information concerning alleged violations of the ADEA "from any source," and it has independent authority to investigate age discrimination. Moreover, nothing in the ADEA indicates that Congress intended that the EEOC be involved in all employment disputes. Such disputes can be settled, for example, without any EEOC involvement. Finally, the mere involvement of an administrative agency in the enforcement of a statute is not sufficient to preclude arbitration.

Gilmer first speculates that arbitration panels will be biased. However, "we decline to indulge the presumption that the parties and arbitral body conducting a proceeding will be unable or unwilling to retain competent, conscientious and impartial arbitrators." In any event, we note that the NYSE arbitration rules, which are applicable to the dispute in this case, provide protections against biased panels. The rules require, for example, that the parties be informed of the employment histories of the arbitrators, and that they be allowed to make further inquiries into the arbitrators' backgrounds.

Gilmer also complains that the discovery allowed in arbitration is more limited than in the federal courts, which he contends will make it difficult to prove discrimination. It is unlikely, however, that age discrimination claims require more extensive discovery than other claims that we have found to be arbitrable, such as RICO and antitrust claims.

A further alleged deficiency of arbitration is that arbitrators often will not issue written opinions, resulting, Gilmer contends, in a lack of public knowledge of employers' discriminatory policies, an inability to obtain effective appellate review, and a stifling of the development of the law. The NYSE rules, however, do require that all arbitration awards be in writing, and that the awards contain the names of the parties, a summary of the issues in controversy, and a description of the award issued.

It is also argued that arbitration procedures cannot adequately further the purposes of the ADEA because they do not provide for broad equitable relief and class actions. As the court below noted, however, arbitrators do have the power to fashion equitable relief. Indeed, the NYSE rules applicable here do not restrict the types of relief an arbitrator may award, but merely refer to "damages and/or other relief."

We conclude that Gilmer has not met his burden of showing that Congress, in enacting the ADEA, intended to preclude arbitration of claims under that Act. Accordingly, the judgment of the Court of Appeals is

Affirmed.
Judgment for Interstate/Johnson Lane Corp.

Employer's Justification for Layoffs

Many firms lay off older workers for financial reasons. They can save money by replacing older workers with young workers, who are willing to do the same work for an entry level salary. For layoffs not to be in violation of the Age Discrimination in Employment Act, they must be made across the board.

Employment Perspective

Michael Ryan has worked as a driver for Yukon Bus Company for thirty-five years. He is sixty-two years old; his salary is $47,000. Ryan is laid off and then replaced by twenty-two-year-old Jude West. West is paid $25,000. Ryan sues, citing age discrimination. Does he win? Yes! Unless Yukon can show cause, then it intentionally terminated Ryan because of his age and correspondingly higher salary. Ryan will be entitled to back pay, loss of pension benefits, as well as liquidated damages in the form of doubling the back pay that is owed. ◆

Retirement Packages

Forcing older employees to accept retirement packages is another form of age discrimination. Retirement must not be mandatory; otherwise, the employer will be in violation of the Act. The retirement package must be accepted voluntarily, without coercion.

In the next case, the issue is whether economic factors dictated the company's decision to downsize or whether they serve as a pretext for the company to discriminate.

Jones v. UNISYS Corp.

54 F.3d 624 (10th Cir. 1995)

LOGAN, Circuit Judge.

The district court found that plaintiffs failed to establish a prima facie case of age discrimination because they did not produce evidence from which a factfinder might reasonably conclude that Unisys made employment decisions with intent to discriminate on the basis of age. Alternatively, the district court found that plaintiffs failed to raise a genuine issue of material fact as to whether Unisys' proffered explanation was pretextual. We assume, for purposes of this opinion, that plaintiffs established a prima facie case of age discrimination. Therefore, we proceed to the district court's determination that Unisys provided evidence of legitimate, nondiscriminatory reasons for the decisions.

The district court summarized the reasons for laying off plaintiffs: Unisys was losing billions of dollars, facing economic disaster, and had to implement drastic cost-cutting measures. The district court thus found that Unisys articulated a legitimate nondiscriminatory reason for the reduction in force. We agree. Although the district court did not specifically address the reasons Unisys offered for its decisions to lay off or deny transfers to specific plaintiffs, the record reveals that Unisys articulated legitimate nondiscriminatory reasons for these decisions.

Of the sixty-three employees at the distribution center, forty-nine were laid off, one voluntarily retired, eight were transferred, and four were retained by the residual shipping and receiving group. Nineteen of the plaintiffs, all but Cole, were laid off from the Salt Lake distribution center. Unisys articulated legitimate nondiscriminatory reasons for retaining the four employees in the residual group.

Cole was laid off from the procurement group which was reduced from thirteen to five employees. Unisys produced evidence that his buying and contract negotiation skills and other qualifications did not meet the needs of the group as well as the five employees retained.

Many of the plaintiffs also asserted that decisions to transfer younger employees was evidence of age discrimination. However, only six plaintiffs applied for transfer; thus we need address only their situation.

Plaintiff Duncan requested a transfer to the defense division in Salt Lake only, but did not demonstrate she was qualified for the position to which she sought to be transferred. She made out no prima facie case of age discrimination on the adverse transfer decision. Cantrell did not identify specific jobs to which he claims he should have been transferred nor present evidence he was qualified for such jobs. Thus, we need not consider whether Unisys presented legitimate reasons for not transferring these plaintiffs because the burden of production never shifted to Unisys as to these individuals.

Plaintiffs Hall, Jones, Lowther, and Sturgeon each asserted that their transfers to San Jose engineer positions were denied because of age discrimination. Assuming plaintiffs produced evidence that younger employees were given those jobs for which plaintiffs arguably were qualified, Unisys articulated legitimate nondiscriminatory reasons for granting those transfers.

Plaintiff Duncan requested a transfer to the defense division in Salt Lake only, but did not demonstrate she was qualified for the position to which she sought to be transferred. She made out no prima facie case of age discrimination on the adverse transfer decision. Cantrell did not identify specific jobs to which he claims he should have been transferred nor present evidence he was qualified for such jobs. Thus, we need not consider whether Unisys presented legitimate reasons for not transferring these plaintiffs because the burden of production never shifted to Unisys as to these individuals.

Because Unisys produced evidence of legitimate reasons for the challenged decisions, plaintiffs then had the burden to produce evidence of age discrimination or to show that the reasons given were a pretext for age discrimination.

Plaintiffs utterly failed to show direct evidence of age discrimination: they offer the "telling" statistic that "historically, 33.3% of the employees within the protected class were terminated in any given reduction in force. In the 1991 reduction in force which affected the plaintiffs, 62.5% of the employees in the protected class were terminated." However, as Unisys outlined in the 1991 layoffs a slightly higher percentage of employees outside the protected age group were terminated compared with those in the protected group. Indeed, the percentage of employees in the age group before and after the reduction force was almost the same—about sixty-nine percent. Statistics taken in isolation are generally not probative of age discrimination, and the statistics here do not support a finding of intent to discriminate.

The only other purported case of age discrimination was a double heresay comment by a Unisys employee responsible for job posting, that "It's about time we unloaded some of this old driftwood." This stray remark by someone not in a decision-making position does not establish intent to discriminate. Further, plaintiffs admitted they had not experienced negative treatment or discriminatory remarks based on age before the challenged decisions.

Because plaintiffs failed to produce direct evidence of intent to discriminate we have carefully reviewed the record for rebuttal evidence on which a finder of fact could conclude that Unisys' explanations for the challenged decisions were actually a pretext for age discrimination. "A plaintiff demonstrates pretext by showing either 'that a discriminatory reason more likely motivated the employer or . . . that the employer's proffered explanation is unworthy of credence.'" Plaintiff need not disprove defendant's reasons or demonstrate that age was the factor motivating the decision, but they "must show that age actually played a role in the employees decision-making process had a determinative influence" on the decision. In opposing summary judgment a plaintiff must be given an opportunity to show by competent evidence that the presumably valid reasons for the layoffs were really a pretext for a discriminatory decision. In evaluating plaintiffs' evidence, we must determine whether the evidence interpreted in the light most favorable to the plaintiffs "could persuade a reasonable jury that the employer had discriminated against the plaintiffs." If no material facts are in dispute concerning the pretextuality of defendants' actions, summary judgment is appropriate.

As the district court pointed out, plaintiffs conceded that "Unisys was facing an economic disaster," and that economic problems were "an adequate reason to declare a reduction in force." Thus, plaintiffs do not appear to argue that the reduction in force itself was a pretext for discrimination. Rather, plaintiffs argued that Unisys' failure to use the historical seniority-based layoff approach showed an intent to discriminate. The district court correctly found that a change of policy from seniority-based to skills-based evaluations does not establish pretext. Failure to base layoffs on seniority is not necessarily related. The district court also stated that "Unisys had a written policy of skills-based layoffs which plaintiffs concede is age-neutral."

Plaintiffs also alleged, however, that the policy of skills-based layoffs was not consistently followed and that the transfer decisions were improperly based on age. Plaintiffs failed to counter Unisys' evidence supporting the legitimacy of the reasons supporting the challenged layoffs. Summary judgment for Unisys on the ADEA claims was appropriate.

Affirmed.
Judgment for Unisys.

In the following case, an employee was denied a promotion because of the relocation of an office. The employee claimed the denial was because of her age. The employer argued that a transfer was offered to the employee, but it was refused.

Conroy v. Anchor Sav. Bank, FSB.

CASE

810 F.Supp 42 (E.D.N.Y. 1993)

JOHNSON, District Judge.

Plaintiff Lucille Conroy ("Conroy") brings this action under the Age Discrimination in Employment Act ("ADEA"). Conroy began her employment with Anchor on January 5, 1970 as a key punch operator in the Compubank Department. In 1976, she became the Senior Clerk of the Archives Department, and in 1982, Supervisor of the Records Management Department. Her final promotion to Senior Supervisor of the Records Management Department occurred in 1986.

The Records Management Department processed and stored the raw data generated by the Bank's branches in Long Island, New Jersey, Florida, and Georgia. After the records were processed into microfilm and microfiche, the Records Management Department distributed them to the branches or sent them to Albion, New York, for long-term storage.

When Conroy began working at the Records Management Department in 1986, the department headquarters were located in Bay Ridge, Brooklyn. In October 1987, as part of an intensive effort to diminish expenses, Anchor relocated the majority of the records management functions, including permanent storage, to a new records center in Albion, New York. This relocation required that ten positions be transferred from Bay Ridge to Albion. The Bay Ridge office, thereafter consisting of three full-time employees, remained as the clearing center and was responsible for the verification of all microfiche and microfilm. This office checked the accuracy of the processed information and ultimately forwarded the information to Albion for long-term storage. Anchor retained the Bay Ridge office because of its proximity to Anchor's computer center in Wayne, New Jersey.

The following employees remained at the Bay Ridge Office: Conroy, age 56, Senior Supervisor; Arlene Wilson, age 56, Department Specialist; and Guyatri Kissoon, age 34, Department Clerk. Conroy was responsible for performing the aforementioned duties as well as supervising the work of Ms. Wilson and Ms. Kissoon. Wilson and Kissoon checked the accuracy of the information on the microfilm and microfiche by comparing it with the original raw data of Anchor's departments. Afterwards, they distributed the processed information to their respective departments or to Albion. Kissoon, however, also prepared statistical computer reports and the typewritten work for the department. The Bay Ridge Records Management Department answered to Donald Cowan of the Albion office.

In late 1989, Robert Moore, the Vice President of Security for Anchor, in accordance with Anchor's plan to diminish expenses, requested a report from Cowan regarding the cost-effectiveness of transferring the Bay Ridge functions to Albion. Cowan submitted a proposal, dated January 19, 1990, recommending that Anchor transfer Bay Ridge branch of the Records Management Department to Albion to eliminate the cost of overhead in the Bay Ridge office and the duplication of certain verification duties in both offices. Cowan also suggested that Conroy, Wilson, and Kissoon be transferred to Albion to continue to perform their assigned duties. This proposal specifically stated that Conroy play a supervisory role at Albion. Additionally, the report included an organizational chart of the proposed consolidated office in Albion that listed Conroy as well as her subordinates in their present position. Cowan also recommended that the transfer take place in the middle of March of 1990.

Upon reviewing the report, Moore decided to implement Cowan's proposal of consolidating the entire Records Management Department in Albion. He proceeded to make a written recommendation of the department transfer to his immediate supervisor, Patricia Dawley, Executive Vice President and Secretary of Anchor, gain emphasizing the goal of cost-effectiveness. Dawley soon approved said recommendation.

Moore then contacted John Coughlin, First Vice President, Human Resources, and Sharon Taylor, Assistant Vice President, regarding the announcement and implementation of the consolidation. Anchor implemented the following policy on relocating a position or a department. First action, Plaintiff succeeds in making out a prima facie case. First, Conroy clearly falls within the age group protected by ADEA because she was 56 years old at the time of her termination. Second, the position of Department Specialist was filled by an employee twenty-two years younger than Conroy. Third, Conroy has made a showing sufficient to establish that she was qualified for the position. The Department Specialist position required personal computer knowledge, including knowledge of Data Base III, Lotus 1-2-3, and Multi Mate software as well as excellent typing skills, in her affidavit, Conroy avers that she had full knowledge of personal computers, Database III, and Lotus 1-2-3 because she had taught herself how to use them by means of in-house tapes. Conroy also testified at her deposition that she was familiar with Lotus 1-2-3 but "had no reason to use it in the department." She also knew how to do data entry on Database III.

Based on the foregoing, the Court finds that Conroy has succeeded in establishing a prima facie case, a causative or a determinative factor in deciding whether the plaintiff should be employed. On this motion for summary judgment, the evidence must create a genuine issue of fact as to Anchor's proffered reasons or as to a discriminatory motive. Based upon the record, the court fails to find anything creating a genuine issue of fact that anyone was motivated by a discriminatory purpose.

In relocating the Records Management Department, Anchor offered Conroy, Kissoon and Wilson several alternatives in compliance with the bank's policy of providing options to employees affected by transfers. Anchor offered all three employees the following option: transfers to Albion. Having demonstrated an absence of evidence to support Conroy's claim that Anchor's proffered reasons are pretextual, Anchor is entitled to summary judgment.

Judgment for Anchor Savings Bank.

The next case presents the question of whether an employee who accepts early retirement because of intolerable working conditions may claim age discrimination.

CASE

Stetson v. NYNEX Service Co.

995 F.2d 355 (2nd Cir. 1993)

CARTER, Circuit Judge.

NSC was a centralized support company owned by two NYNEX subsidiaries including New York Telephone ("Telco"). Stetson was employed by Telco for some 20 years beginning in 1966. In 1986, he went to work for NSC, where he remained until he formally elected to take early retirement effective in May 1990. The following description consists largely of facts admitted by

Stetson in connection with defendants' motion for summary judgment.

In 1986, Stetson, then 53 years old, spoke to his contemporary and longtime friend Raymond Burke, who was NYNEX's Executive Vice President and General Counsel, about the availability of legal positions in NYNEX subsidiaries other than Telco. Burke arranged an interview for Stetson with Saul Fisher, Vice President, Secretary, and General Counsel of NSC, and Fisher hired Stetson as a "fourth-level attorney" to handle general legal issues. Prior to taking that position, Stetson was aware that Fisher had a reputation for being a "taskmaster," and that "nobody wanted to be a Service Company lawyer."

During 1986 and part of 1987, Stetson's performance with NSC was apparently satisfactory. For his 1986 performance, he received a $2,300 salary increase, raising his base salary to $93,000, plus a "Team Award" of $10,200, and an "Exceptional Merit Award" of $3,000.

In the summer of 1987, however, Fisher received complaints from attorneys at Telco in regard to the quality of certain contracts.

Stetson also received feedback from Fisher at weekly staff meetings, during which each of the attorneys would report on significant matters they were handling. Fisher would ask questions, make suggestions, and sometimes give critical feedback. All of the attenders were subject to this process and had their work critiqued from time to time. Stetson felt that in late 1988 into 1989, Fisher was unduly critical of Stetson's work.

In his semi-annual personnel review in October 1988, Stetson told Fisher he was unhappy with the work he was doing and wanted more substantial projects to supplement his day-to-day assignments. Thereafter, Fisher suggested that Stetson begin to attend the bi-weekly staff meetings of Mary McDermott. McDermott, hired as a fourth-level attorney in late 1987 and promoted to the fifth-level position of "general attorney" in 1988, handled regulatory and marketing work. Stetson attended her meetings but did not volunteer for any of her work.

In February 1989, Fisher reviewed Stetson's 1988 work performance and advised Stetson that his work was sloppy and not thorough. Fisher was also critical of Stetson's failure to keep him informed of work Stetson was performing. Fisher decided that Stetson would receive a Team Award of $15,400, but no increase in his base salary and no Exceptional Merit Award.

During the first seven months of 1989, Fisher assigned various projects to Stetson. Fisher viewed these projects as important; Stetson did not. From August 1989 until December 1989, non-management employees of NYNEX engaged in a strike; most management-level employees, including Stetson, had special strike-duty assignments that took them out of their usual offices. Stetson had an assignment on Long Island, and during that time he had little or no contact with Fisher. From December 1989 until his annual performance review in March 1990, Stetson did not ask either Fisher or McDermott for any assignments.

In late December 1989, NYNEX announced to the employees in its various companies a voluntary Special Retirement Incentive ("SRI") program for management-level employees who were eligible for pensions. Approximately 11,000 employees were eligible to participate in the program, which would enable them to retire voluntarily between January 1 and May 31, 1990, with enhanced pension benefits.

On January 12, 1990, Stetson went to see Burke, stating that he was unhappy with Fisher and seeking Burke's advice and assistance. Stetson expected that because Burke was a friend he would get Stetson another job in a NYNEX company. In March 1989, however, NYNEX had established a formal transfer process for filling attorney vacancies in the legal departments of its various units. At this January 1990 meeting, Burke refused to get Stetson a new job. Burke said Stetson had three options: continue to work at NSC, use the formal transfer process to seek a job in another NYNEX unit, or apply for early retirement under the SRI. According to Stetson, Burke said, "Don't you feel like you have slowed down? I know I have."

Other than the January 12, 1990, discussion, Stetson never discussed retirement with Burke. Nor did Stetson at any time discuss the issue of retirement or the SRI with Fisher. At no time during Stetson's employment did Fisher ever threaten, either expressly or impliedly, that Stetson's employment would be terminated. On March 21, 1990, Stetson submitted his application for early retirement under the SRI.

During this meeting, Stetson did not disclose his intention to take early retirement within

a few months. After Fisher learned of Stetson's March 21 application, he sent Stetson a letter dated May 24, 1990, inviting Stetson to rescind his retirement decision and remain with NSC. Burke, by letter dated May 21, had likewise advised Stetson that he was free to remain employed by NSC. Stetson informed Fisher that he was not interested. He retired effective May 31.

In August 1990, Stetson commenced the present action, alleging that his early retirement decision was not voluntary but rather was a response to intolerable working conditions. He asserted that NYNEX and NSC executives had been pressured to force employees to participate in the early retirement plan, and that Fisher and Burke imposed the intolerable working conditions on him solely because of his age and with the intent of forcing him to retire. He alleged that his retirement was thus the result of a constructive discharge in violation of the ADEA and New York's Human Rights Law ("HRL").

In sum, a claim of constructive discharge must be dismissed as a matter of law unless the evidence is sufficient to permit a rational trier of fact to infer that the employer deliberately created working conditions that were "'so difficult or unpleasant that a reasonable person in the employee's shoes would have felt compelled to resign.'"

In the present case, though Stetson was dissatisfied with his assignments, with the criticisms of his work, and apparently with his compensation, the record falls far short of reflecting working conditions so difficult or unpleasant as to permit an inference that a reasonable person in Stetson's position would believe he was forced to resign. Fisher had indeed lived up to his advance reputation as a tough taskmaster; he received complaints about Stetson's work, reviewed that work, and was critical of it; he was also critical of other work done by Stetson. The nature of Stetson's assignments and the criticisms of the quality of his work caused Stetson to become dissatisfied with NSC barely a year after he was employed there, and he decided in 1987 that he wanted to leave. Yet Stetson did not feel compelled to resign in 1987; given the record, he could not reasonably have felt at that time that he had no alternative but to resign; and the record does not show any change in Stetson's working conditions thereafter that could have caused a reasonable person in his position to conclude that he was forced to resign in 1990. After 1987, Fisher had continued to give Stetson assignments; in response to Stetson's complaints that his assignments were mundane, Fisher had Stetson attend meetings of a group dealing with other types of matters. Fisher never reduced Stetson's rank or salary; rather, he granted Stetson a raise, or a team bonus, or an individual merit bonus, or some combination thereof, for every year that Stetson was employed by NSC, with variations in the awards tied to Stetson's work performance.

Fisher never mentioned retirement to Stetson and never either expressly or impliedly suggested that Stetson's employment would be terminated. When Stetson sought out his old friend Burke for help in getting a new NYNEX job, Burke told him that one of his options, along with the options of early retirement and finding his own new NYNEX position, was to stay with NSC. Though early retirement with special benefits became available in 1990 through the SRI plan, there was no evidence that the plan was other than entirely voluntary or that executives of NYNEX or NSC were under pressure to force eligible employees to take early retirement. When Stetson eventually opted for early retirement, both Burke and Fisher urged him to stay with NSC.

Thus, the undisputed facts show that Stetson's working conditions were essentially the same from late 1987 until he applied for early retirement in 1990. Stetson does not even remotely suggest that he was constructively discharged prior to 1990. Instead, he argues that Burke's 1990 refusal to find him a new job within NYNEX, suggesting that he remain employed by NSC, constituted a constructive discharge from NSC.

Judgment for NYNEX.

The issue in the following case is whether an employer who has discharged all of its employees at a particular plant can be guilty of age discrimination.

CASE

McCann v. Texas City Refining, Inc.

984 F.2d 667 (5th Cir. 1993)

PER CURIAM.

In the summer of 1989, Blanche Hickman and Jo Ann McCann lost their jobs. Hickman and McCann had been working at a refinery owned by Texas City Refining, Inc. (TCR). When that refinery was sold to Hill Petroleum, Inc. (Hill), Hickman and McCann were not offered jobs by the new owners. Subsequently Hickman and McCann sued Hill, TCR, and TCR's parent corporations (collectively Agway) for violations of the Age Discrimination in Employment Act (ADEA). At trial, the jury found that Hill was guilty of willful age discrimination against Hickman; however, the jury found that McCann had not been a victim of age discrimination. As to the issues raised by Hickman and McCann, we hold that the district court did not err either in denying Hickman prejudgment interest on the award of backpay or in holding that McCann's complaint failed to state a cause of action against TCR and Agway.

On June 30, 1988, Hill Petroleum purchased and took over the refining facility owned by TCR in Texas City, Texas. Hill restructured the work force and hired back approximately 300 of the 450 employees of TCR. All positions filled by Hill were staffed with former TCR employees. As a part of this restructuring, Hickman was laid off and her position as shift clerk was filled by younger employees, and McCann's position as a confidential secretary and personnel administrator was eliminated. Both Hickman and McCann had been long-time employees of TCR and were within the protected class of the ADEA.

Both Hickman and McCann filed suit against Hill, TCR, and Agway, alleging that the defendants had violated the ADEA. After concluding that the remaining ADEA claims failed to state a cause of action against TCR and Agway, the district court dismissed those defendants. The plaintiffs later filed several motions to amend their complaint to add a pendant state-law claim of "tortious interference with employment contract" against TCR and Agway. The district court, however, denied the motions to amend, concluding that the amended complaints were subject to dismissal in the same manner as the original complaint. The ADEA makes it unlawful for any employer "to fail or refuse to hire or to discharge any individual or otherwise discriminate against any individual with respect to his compensation, terms, conditions, or privileges of employment, because of such individual's age." McCann's complaint fails to allege any actions by TCR or Agway that would violate the ADEA. TCR was the former employer of McCann. However, it cannot be said that TCR discharged McCann because of her age; TCR sold the refinery and discharged everyone. In reality, the sole act of discrimination asserted by McCann's complaint was Hill's refusal to hire her. Although it is true that courts will bend over backwards to avoid granting a 12(b)(6) motion to dismiss, here McCann simply did not allege any facts that could possibly support her ADEA claim against TCR and Agway.

Texas law does recognize a cause of action for tortious interference with an employment contract. The first element of such a claim, however, is the existence of an employment contract. McCann's proposed amended complaint does not allege that McCann was ever hired by Hill. It should be obvious to all that TCR and Agway could not possibly have interfered with an employment contract that never existed. Therefore, since McCann's proposed amended complaint also failed to state a claim against TCR or Agway, it was not error for the district court to refuse to allow McCann to amend her complaint.

Judgment for Texas City Refining.

Employment Perspective

Mildred Greene is fifty-eight years old. Her employer, Suds & Bubbles, a soap manufacturer, has offered her an attractive retirement package. Mildred, who has no family, would rather continue working in public relations, where she is able to meet new people. Suds & Bubbles informs Mildred that if she does not retire, she will be transferred to back-office bookkeeping work, where she will not be able to interact with anyone. Mildred files a claim with the EEOC and later brings an action in state court. Will she win? Of course! There is no reasonable basis for transferring her. The prospect of a transfer is being used as a threat to force her to retire. ◆

The following case addresses the issue of whether an employee's claim of age discrimination can be subjected to arbitration. The securities registration application that the employee signed contains a provision requiring all disputes to be subject to arbitration. The employee argued that the law does not permit a waiver of judicial forum in Age Discrimination in Employment Act proceedings.

Frey v. State of Cal.

982 F.2d 399 (9th Cir. 1993)

LEAVY, Judge.

Archer Frey was a commissioned officer in the California National Guard on State Active Duty. He served in the State Guard from 1971 until 1991, when he was terminated under the authority of section 167, which contains a provision for mandatory retirement at age 60 for state active duty commissioned officers of the California National Guard who can no longer be called into active federal service. Frey's retirement from active service at age sixty comports with the mandatory retirement age for reserve officers of the United States Army below the rank of major general.

In 1985, because he had attained 30 years of commissioned service, Frey lost federal recognition, the effect being that he ceased to be a member of the National Guard of the United States (Army National Guard). From 1985 until his mandatory retirement, Frey served only as a military officer in the California National Guard. His job title during all relevant periods was Chief Engineering Branch, and his rank at retirement was Colonel. Frey never served on active duty in the regular United States Army.

Frey's loss of federal recognition meant he could no longer be called into active federal service. Notwithstanding the loss of federal recognition, as a member of the California National Guard on state active duty, Frey was subject to being called to duty 24 hours a day, seven days a week; he had no entitlement to compensatory time off; he was required to meet the same physical standards as prescribed for federally recognized National Guard members; and he wore a military uniform while on duty. Frey was exempt from the requirements of state civil service. His pay and allowances were determined in accordance with those of officers of the United States Army. Discipline, if necessary, was determined according to the Federal Uniform Code of Military Justice, and he was subject to reassignment at will to any duty, or being called into active service in case of war, insurrection, rebellion, invasion, tumult, riot, breach of the peace, public calamity, catastrophe, or other emergency.

Prior to his sixtieth birthday, the State informed Frey that it intended to discharge him at the end of April 1991, under the authority of section 167. In response, Frey filed this action alleging four claims and seeking a declaration that the ADEA applies to him and section 167 violates the ADEA. The complaint also alleged that section 167 directly conflicts with the provisions of the ADEA, thereby violating the Supremacy Clause of the United States Constitution. In addition, he sought damages for the alleged age discrimination and a preliminary injunction to restrain the State defendants from forcing him to retire pending the outcome of this action. The district court denied his request for preliminary injunction relief, and Frey did not appeal from that denial.

The State then moved to dismiss for failure to state a claim. In granting the State's motion, the district court held that the military departments of the states, when taking actions affecting uniformed active duty officers of the state national guard, are not included within the definition of "employer" as that term is defined under the ADEA. The court went on to conclude that because this was a state employment action, taken under a state statute, it could not be preempted by federal law. Frey filed a timely appeal from the district court's dismissal.

Section 623(a) provides in relevant part that: "it shall be unlawful for an employer (1) to fail or refuse to hire or to discharge any individual . . . because of such individual's age. . . ." The term "employer" is defined by the ADEA to include "a State or political subdivision of a State." Similarly, section 633(a) extended the ADEA to protect federal employees as well. Finally, section 630(f) of the ADEA defines the term "employee" as follows:

> An individual employed by an employer except that the term "employee" shall not include any person elected to public office in any State or political subdivision of any State by the qualified voters thereof, or any person chosen by such officer to be on such officer's personal staff, or an appointee on the policy making level or an immediate adviser with respect to the exercise of the constitutional or legal powers of the office. The exemption set forth in the preceding sentence shall not include employees subject to the civil service laws of a state government, governmental agency, or political subdivision. . . .

Although, in 1986, Congress amended the ADEA in order to exempt state firefighters and law enforcement officers from the Act, no such exemption was provided for state military personnel.

> "The special status of the military has required, the Constitution has contemplated, Congress has created, and this Court has long recognized two systems of justice, to some extent parallel: one for civilians and one for military personnel."

The policy considerations that preclude us from applying the ADEA to the federal military in the absence of a clear congressional directive similarly precludes the application of the ADEA to the state militia based solely upon the loss of federal recognition, when Congress has not expressly so directed. As the district court recognized:

> It is most unlikely that Congress intended to permit the federal military to discharge plaintiff because of his age, but to prohibit state military officials from acting in accordance simply because plaintiff has lost federal recognition. . . . The deference and restraint the courts apply to military questions is just as appropriate to the state militia as to the Army National Guard.

Under these circumstances, Frey's loss of federal recognition alone cannot justify this court according less deference to the state militia than to the National Guard of the United States. There is no indication from Congress, either in the ADEA or its legislative history, to suggest that the Act should apply to the state military departments. Due to the special status of the military, we hold that Congress' failure to expressly include the states' military departments within the definition of employer demonstrates an intent to exclude the military departments of the states from the ADEA. The judgment of the district court is affirmed.

Judgment for the State of California.

The following case addresses the question of whether older workers can be discharged in a reduction of the workforce. The employees who were dismissed argued that the layoff is just a pretext for intentionally downsizing the number of older workers.

CASE

Garner v. Arvin Industries, Inc.

885 F.Supp. 1254 (E.D.Mo. 1995)

LIMBAUGH, District Judge.

Plaintiff has filed this age discrimination action alleging that she was terminated from her position, as part of a reduction-in-force (RIF), on the basis of her age. She alleges that her employment termination was in violation of the Age Discrimination in Employment Act (ADEA).

Plaintiff had been employed by the defendant beginning in 1975. Early in her employment, she had been a union-employee working as a dispatcher. Approximately, the last ten years of her employment had been as a non-union employee working in the maintenance area of the Engineering Department as a clerk.

Defendant Arvin Industries is comprised of several divisions, including the Arvin North American Automotive Division. The Arvin North American Automotive Division had a production facility in Dexter, Missouri. Plaintiff was employed, during the relevant time-period, at this production facility in Dexter, Missouri.

The Dexter plant produces automobile exhaust systems: mufflers, tailpipes, manifolds, and catalytic converters. These products are original automobile equipment sold directly to the automobile manufacturers for installation in new cars. During the relevant time-period approximately 65% of the defendant's products were sold to General Motors, the remaining 35% sold to Ford and Toyota. During the relevant time-period, defendant employed approximately 750 persons at its Dexter facility.

In 1991 defendant instituted a division-wide RIF (reduction in force) necessitated by negative economic conditions in the automobile industry. In August 1991, Phil Davis (Dexter plant manager) attended a division-wide meeting of defendant's automotive plant managers at defendant's headquarters in Indiana. He, along with other plant managers, was told that a division-wide RIF was to be implemented immediately for cost reasons. Davis was instructed to reduce twenty (20) non-union salaried positions at the Dexter facility. Although he was not given specific instructions or criteria regarding the selections for the RIF, he was told that the elimination of these positions would be permanent. The plant managers were given nine (9) days to prepare a list of eliminated positions to be submitted to defendant's headquarter's personnel.

Upon returning to Dexter, Davis held a staff meeting with his six (6) department heads to announce the RIF. Attending this meeting, along with others, was Robert Willis, the Dexter plant engineering manager. Davis instructed his staff that because the people selected for the RIF would not be replaced "they needed to select people who would affect the operation of the plant the least." Since he had only been at the plant approximately eighteen (18) months, Davis gave full responsibility to the department heads to make the selections because "they knew the people better . . . they had to run their department, and they have to know who they need to have to do the job, and so they selected the people."

At the time of the RIF, plaintiff's department head was Robert Willis. Two people reported directly to Willis: Tom Holt, the maintenance general foreman; and Phil LeBeau, the chief project engineer. Plaintiff reported directly to Holt, the other two clerks (Nora Hardin and Resa Foushee) reported directly to LeBeau. Including Holt and LeBeau, a total of seventeen people were under Willis' supervision. At the time of the RIF, Willis was age 50, Holt was age 46, and plaintiff was age 58. Only two other employees under Willis' supervision were over age 50.

At the time of the RIF, plaintiff's primary duties consisted of entering work orders into the defendant's computer system, reading air-compressor meters, general office filing, running errands into Dexter, maintaining a "return goods" list and issuing notices of same, printing out open work orders, and answering the telephone. She performed all of these tasks satisfactorily.

The Dexter RIF resulted in the elimination of nineteen (19) non-union salaried positions. Of these 19 positions, five (5) persons were placed in "bargaining unit positions." Thus, a total of fourteen (14) positions were permanently eliminated. Plaintiff's position was selected as one of the 19 positions eliminated by the RIF. She was one of the three (3) oldest employees in Willis' department. All three of these employees lost their jobs in the RIF.

Of the fourteen (14) terminated employees, eight (8) were under the age of forty (40); while six (6) were over the age forty (40). Of the six over the age of 40, three (3) were over the age of 50.

Holt submitted plaintiff's name to Willis for consideration. Willis gave final approval for plaintiff's employment termination. Plaintiff was given personal notice of her selection for termination by Holt and Willis. She was offered the opportunity to return to a "bargaining unit position" but she declined the offer.

Final approval of the plaintiff's termination, as well as of the other thirteen (13) employees at the Dexter facility, was made after Richard Hendricks, defendant's divisional Vice-President for Human Resources, evaluated the Dexter facility's proposed RIF list for impact upon employees over the age of forty (40). He determined that the average age of salaried and non-exempt employees at the Dexter facility would actually increase slightly, i.e., increase average age to age 40, after the proposed RIF.

Plaintiff contends that out of the fourteen (14) persons selected for permanent employment termination, three (3), including herself, were over the age of fifty (50). She further contends that her job duties were assumed by a younger employee, Resa Foushee. Defendant contends that plaintiff's statistical pool is too small to support her contention of discrimination, that in fact more employees under the age of 40 were let go than those over the age of 40, and that plaintiff's job responsibilities were distributed among several of defendant's employees.

However, on the morning in question, plaintiff avers that Holt was sitting at her desk and that when he saw her standing, "he jumped up out of his seat and said, 'Here sit down,' and I said to go ahead and finish. He said 'I'm not too old to stand.'"

Assuming that the statement was made, the Court finds no evidence to support plaintiff's contention that the remark was discriminatory and reflected an age-bias on the part of Holt. No reasonable juror could conclude, as plaintiff does, that this comment implied that Garner was too old to stand; rather it makes light of Holt's ability to stand. The comment is simply too vague to create a reasonable inference of age discrimination.

Judgment for Arvin Industries.

Comparative Treatment of the Elderly

In many cultures, the elderly are looked upon as having much wisdom and are revered. In the United States, the elderly were often forced into retirement unless they were executives or politicians. Although under the Age Discrimination in Employment Act, mandatory retirement is gone, certain prejudices remain. Some prejudices are understandable in economic terms. For example, the performance of routine office work by a person with twenty-four years' seniority making a salary of $42,000 could easily be replaced by a young person for a salary of $28,000. With age often comes seniority, and with seniority often comes greater wages and benefits and sometimes greater knowledge. While in telecommunications and software development, that may not be so, in many other cases it is. To automatically discount an older worker's skill, knowledge, and experience would not be prudent because it would not be utilizing the talents of all American workers.

The following case addresses the question of whether an older employee was terminated because of his age, with his work then reassigned to younger employees.

CASE *Kern v. Kollsman*

885 F.Supp. 335 (D.N.H. 1995)

DIVINE, Senior District Judge.

Kollsman is a defense, avionics and medical equipment manufacturer with its principal place of business located in Merrimack, New Hampshire. Plaintiff, having attained a masters degree in electrical engineering, was originally hired by Kollsman on July 18, 1966, to fill the position of Principal Engineer, Electronics. In 1977, plaintiff was promoted to Project Engineer, and in 1978 to Program Manager, a position he held until 1990. In 1990, plaintiff was transferred from Engineering to Marketing, where he was employed as a Manager of International Marketing. On April 8, 1993, Kern, then 60 years of age and earning an annual salary of $79,542, was terminated by Kollsman after nearly 27 years of continuous employment.

"Kollsman's business has traditionally been in the defense area," with the military systems division comprising approximately "70 percent" of all business. Due to a variety of reasons, both global and domestic, "it became clear that defense expenditures around the world would decline and that the defense business would become more difficult."

As an alleged result of such reduced defense expenditures, Kollsman experienced a 50 percent drop in sales between 1990 and 1992, posting a loss of over $23 million in 1991.

Consistent with such decreasing sales, defendant began to reduce the number of Kollsman employees in order to save the business and save jobs. . . ." Between November 1989 and April 1993, when Kern was terminated, Kollsman reduced its work force by approximately 1100 employees on five separate occasions. It was understood by Kollsman employees, and Kern in particular, that the reason for such reductions was declining sales in the defense business.

Despite such fiscal belt-tightening, sales and prospective orders "in the military area for 1993 were way behind budget."

Determining that further cuts in manufacturing and engineering were no longer feasible, Ronald Wright, President of Kollsman, targeted marketing as the area for further appropriate downsizing. Wright then asked Charles Bernhardt, Vice President of Marketing and Kern's direct supervisor, to prepare a list of individuals recommended for elimination.

Bernhardt returned to Wright with a list of five individuals whose average age was 57.2. Wright agreed with Bernhardt in part, but chose to keep two of the five—Herb Sandberg, then aged 69, and Al Friedrich, then age 65—since they "both performed important functions for Kollsman." Kern claims that he was not dismissed pursuant to a reduction in force because many of his previous responsibilities were not eliminated with his position, but rather were allocated to younger employees. Such a redistribution of responsibilities, Kern argues, proves that his position was not "eliminated" and thus Kollsman's purported work force reduction is merely a pretext for age discrimination. In the alternative, Kern argues that his position was subject to a job combination rather than a job elimination and, as such, a peer ranking should have been performed. The failure of Kollsman to conduct such a ranking, according to Kern, is further evidence of discriminatory animus.

Discriminatory Pretext

Kern initially proffers the following deposition testimony of Bernhardt to establish pretext:

> Q. In terms of the thinking that went into deciding who to put on the layoff list, was their impact on the payroll a consideration?
>
> A. Yeah.
>
> Q. . . . A person's cost to the company was figured by reference not only to his salary, but by reference to other things, as well; would you agree?
>
> A. That's correct.
>
> Q. Okay. And some of those other things would be his employee benefits?
>
> A. Yes.
>
> Q. Secretary?
>
> A. Yes.
>
> Q. Expense accounts?
>
> A. Yes.
>
> Q. Going back to the employee benefits, how close they'd be to retirement, that is when the pension would have to be paid?
>
> A. I would assume that's a consideration, because under the new laws, you have to reserve for that type of thing.
>
> And I think that is a factor, and it could be a very large factor.
>
> Q. And in terms of the pensions, Kollsman had a so-called defined benefit.
>
> A. Yes.
>
> Q. Defined benefit type of plan; is that correct?
>
> A. Yes, that's correct.
>
> Q. And the longer a person served at Kollsman, the higher his pension benefits would be once he retired?
>
> A. That's correct.

However, the mere reference to a correlation between pension and age, standing alone, is insufficient to sustain plaintiff's burden of demonstrating pretext.

Plaintiff contends that on several occasions defendants promulgated literature which either expressly or implicitly served to modify his status as an at-will employee. More specifically, Kern asserts that, based on alleged oral and written representations from Kollsman, he developed "an expectation of continued employment unless the application of peer ranking procedures and other objective criteria indicated that my termination was warranted." Defendant's employment handbook contains the following disclaimer:

> EMPLOYMENT-AT-WILL STATEMENT
>
> It is understood that nothing contained in the employment application, in the granting of an interview, or in this handbook is intended to create an employment contract between Kollsman and the individual either for employment or for providing any benefit. It is understood that no employment guarantee is binding upon Kollsman unless the terms and conditions are specified in writing. If an employment relationship is established, it is understood that the employee has the right to terminate his/her employment at any time and that Kollsman retains a similar right.

Defendant asserts that the clear meaning of said disclaimer is that it "did not alter the at-will relationship of the parties. It created no employment contract."

This conclusion, however, does not end the matter. Kern further submits that certain documents promulgated by Kollsman regarding reduction in force procedures lack any disclaiming language, can be found to be contractual promise equivalents, and are thus valid and enforceable modifications to his at-will status.

Plaintiff's case similarly rests on too frail or thin a reed. The court therefore finds and rules that plaintiff's breach of express or implied contract claim based on materials promulgated by his employer is insufficient as a matter of law. In consequence thereof, defendant's motion for summary judgment with respect to said breach of contract claim must be and is herewith granted.

Judgment for Kollsman.

The issue in the following case is whether age discrimination exists when one employee is chosen over a more experienced one.

CASE *Deaver v. Texas Commerce Bank, N.A.*

886 F.Supp. 578 (E.D. Tex. 1995)

SCHELL, Judge.

Martha Deaver is a white female who was born in 1934. She began working for First City Bank of Beaumont in 1952. Over the next forty years, she continued to work for First City. During this time, she was promoted several times and her salary grew proportionately.

In the early 1990's, First City Bank experienced financial difficulty and was taken over by the FDIC. Subsequently, First City Bank of Beaumont was sold to Texas Commerce Bank on February 24, 1993. During this transition period, Texas Commerce formed Transition Management Services Company, a wholly owned subsidiary of Texas Commerce, to employ the former employees of First City until First City was fully absorbed into Texas Commerce Bank.

During this interim period, Texas Commerce Bank overhauled the entire First City Bank of Beaumont and terminated many First City employees. Along with the other discharged First City employees, Texas Commerce also terminated Plaintiff. Plaintiff alleges that she was wrongfully terminated because of her age and gender. Thus, Plaintiff brings this suit against Texas Commerce Bank and Transition Management Services Company under Title VII of the Civil Rights Act of 1964 and the Texas Commission on Human Rights Act.

In response to Plaintiff's suit, Defendants argue that Plaintiff was terminated because of her unsatisfactory job performance, her poor attitude, and job duplication. Additionally, Defendants claim that there is no evidence of age or gender discrimination and seek a summary judgment against Plaintiff's claims.

In proceeding with an ADEA Title VII case, a court must follow a three-step procedural analysis. First, plaintiff is required to make a prima facie case. "Generally to establish a prima facie case, plaintiff need only make a very minimal showing." To fashion a prima facie case, a plaintiff must demonstrate that:

(1) she was discharged;
(2) she was qualified for the position;
(3) she was within the protected class at the time of discharge; and
(4) she was either
 (i) replaced by someone outside the protected class,
 (ii) replaced by someone younger, or
 (iii) otherwise discharged because of age.

And a Title VII claim has a substantially similar prima facie case:

(1) she was discharged;
(2) she was qualified for the position;
(3) she was a female; and
(4) she was replaced by a man.

If a plaintiff can vivify a prima facie case, a presumption of discrimination arises.

Once a presumption of discrimination arises, a defendant may only rebut the presumption "by articulating a legitimate, nondiscriminatory reason for the discharge." "'A defendant must clearly set forth, through the introduction of admissible evidence,' reasons for its actions which, if believed by the trier of fact would support a finding that unlawful discrimination was not the cause of the employment action." An employer only has to set forth a lawful termination, regardless of the reason.

If a defendant satisfies the second step, the burden of production returns to plaintiff. A plaintiff must prove that defendant's reasons for discharge were pretexts for discrimination. "But a reason cannot be proved to be a pretext for discrimination unless it is shown both that the reason was false, and that discrimination was the real reason." Thus, in making this inquiry, "it's not enough . . . to disbelieve the employer, the factfinder must believe the plaintiff's explanation of intentional discrimination."

In resolving Defendants' motion for summary judgment, this court is concerned with this third step in the analysis. Plaintiff has satisfied the first step for the ADEA and Title VII claims: Plaintiff was discharged; Plaintiff was qualified for the position; Plaintiff was over forty (was a female), so she was within the protected class at the time of discharge; and, Plaintiff was replaced by someone younger (a man). The second step was also satisfied by Defendants. In response to Plaintiff's prima facie showing, Defendants assert that Plaintiff was fired due to job duplication, inadequate performance, and an unsatisfactory attitude. These reasons are sufficient to satisfy defendants' burden of production. Therefore, this court must decide whether the record supports summary judgment for the defendants on the third step. As previously mentioned, under the third step, a plaintiff must prove (1) that the defendants' reasons for discharge were false and (2) that discrimination was the real reason for discharge.

Clearly, Plaintiff has established a genuine issue of fact with regard to the first prong of the third step. Nevertheless, Plaintiff has failed to establish a genuine issue with regard to the second prong of the third step. Under the second prong, Plaintiff must prove that age and gender discrimination were the real reasons for her discharge. Plaintiff claims that there is enough evidence in the record for the jury to infer that her age and gender were the real reasons behind her discharge. Specifically, Plaintiff argues that the implausibility of Defendants' reasons is enough to state a genuine issue of material fact.

None of this evidence is sufficient to create a genuine issue of fact. Plaintiff claims that she was a better employee and more qualified than her replacement. These assertions that she is more qualified than her replacement because she has worked in the banking industry longer than her replacement are not particularly persuasive. Clearly, these statements are Plaintiff's own personal beliefs. It will always be arguable that one is a better worker or more suited to a particular position. But that is a decision for an employer to make. The ADEA and Title VII are not vehicles to question or evaluate personnel moves, which although legal, may have been the result of poor business judgment. These statutes were not "intended to transform the courts into personnel managers"; rather, the ADEA and Title VII are safeguards against discrimination.

While Plaintiff has raised an issue as to whether Defendants' reasons were false, Plaintiff's subjective belief that she was the victim of discrimination is legally insufficient for a trier of fact to conclude that age or gender were factors in her termination. Therefore, Defendants are entitled to summary judgment on Plaintiff's ADEA and Title VII claims.

Judgment for Texas Commerce Bank.

CONCLUSION

In years gone by, most people worked either until they became disabled or until they died. Disabled workers were usually cared for by family members. There was no such thing as retirement unless a person was independently wealthy and could therefore live off the income from his or her investments. With the advent of Social Security, those aged sixty-five years or older are entitled to a small amount of income. As pensions became more prevalent, workers were guaranteed a defined benefit. The income from Social Security and the pension enabled people to survive after mandatory retirement. How well they survived depended upon the size of their pension and of their investment income. Pensions remained fixed because they were not adjusted for inflation. Social Security recipients received cost-of-living adjustments. Investment income has a built-in guard against inflation.

As life expectancies increased, the majority of Americans now live beyond sixty-five. Surreptitiously prohibiting people from continuing to work because of their age when they are perfectly capable of doing so is discriminatory. The purpose of the Age Discrimination in Employment Act is to dispel this conduct and to give free access to the workplace to those people over the age of sixty-five. Workers will be able to continue in their present job or to seek new employment elsewhere, thus broadening the pool of workers for companies to select from. As was stated, many older workers have special skills, knowledge, and experience. The freedom to employ these people is certainly a bonus for employers, especially those involved in the growing competitiveness of the global marketplace.

REVIEW QUESTIONS

1. What is the significance of the Age Discrimination in Employment Act?
2. At what age may an employee claim age discrimination?
3. Is there a mandatory retirement age?
4. Are there any exceptions?
5. Is an advertisement which specifies "recent college graduate" discriminatory?
6. Can age be considered a bona fide occupational qualification?
7. What must be the determining factor in the dismissal of an older worker?
8. Can a young person who is not hired because of his or her youth, claim age discrimination?
9. Does the Civil Rights Act encompass those discriminated against because of age?
10. In many cultures, age is a sign of wisdom. Why is that not generally the case in the United States?
11. The plaintiff was a federally recognized officer in the California National Guard. Because of his federal recognition, he was also a member of the Army National Guard. Claiming that he was wrongfully denied a promotion, the plaintiff sued the state and federal national guards, claiming age discrimination under the ADEA. Section 633a of the ADEA, applicable to federal agencies, uses language identical to that in Title VII; namely, discrimination against "employees . . . in military departments as defined in 102 of Title 5" is prohibited. What was the result? *Helm v. California,* 722 F.2d 507 (9th Cir. 1983)
12. At the time of his termination, Naas then age sixty (60), was employed as a "Senior Systems Consulting Analyst." On October 29, 1991, Naas timely filed a Charge of Discrimination with the Equal Employment Opportunity Commission, alleging that his termination violated the Age Discrimination in Employment Act (ADEA), 29 U.S.C. 621. Thereafter, plaintiff filed a complaint in this Court against Westinghouse, alleging violation of the ADEA. What was the result? *Naas v. Westinghouse Elec. Corp,* 818 F.Supp. 874 (W.D.Pa. 1993)

13. When Borden closed a plant, it gave severance pay to all of the plant's employees except for those eligible for retirement benefits. Those employees claimed Borden discriminated against them because of their age in denying them severance pay. What was the result? *EEOC v. Borden's Inc.*, 724 F.2d 1390 (9th Cir. 1984)
14. Gilmer filed an age discrimination lawsuit against Interstate/Johnson Lane Corp. The company argued that all employment matters were subject to arbitration. Gilmer retorted that an ADEA claim was exempt from that requirement. What was the result? *Gilmer v. Interstate/Johnson Lane Corp.*, 111 S.Ct 1647 (1991)
15. Must the EEOC be involved in all employment disputes regarding age discrimination? *Coventry v. United States Steel Corp.*, 856 F.2d 514 (3rd Cir. 1988)
16. In the case on p. 423, what would the employer's motivation be for discharging the plaintiff solely because of her age?
17. In the case on p. 413, is it possible to claim age discrimination even though the individual opted for early retirement?
18. Is it ethical for a supervisor to discharge an employee, when he or she knows that the employer's motivation is age?
19. Was age truly the motivating factor in the decision in the case on pp. 412?
20. In the case on p. 410, are economic factors a justifiable defense to a suit based on age discrimination?

Age Discrimination in Employment Act of 1967

STATEMENT OF FINDINGS AND PURPOSE

Sec. 2 (a) The Congress Hereby Finds and Declares That—

(1) in the face of rising productivity and affluence, older workers find themselves disadvantaged in their efforts to retain employment, and especially to regain employment when displaced from jobs;

(2) the setting of arbitrary age limits regardless of potential for job performance has become common practice, and certain otherwise desirable practices may work to the disadvantage of older persons;

(3) the incidence of unemployment, especially long-term unemployment with resultant deterioration of skill, morale, and employer acceptability is, relative to the younger ages, high among older workers; their numbers are great and growing; and their employment problems have grave consequences;

(4) the existence in industries affecting commerce of arbitrary discrimination in employment because of age burdens commerce and the free flow of goods in commerce.

(b) It is therefore the purpose of this Act to promote employment of older persons based on their ability rather than their age; to prohibit arbitrary age discrimination in employment; to help employers and workers find ways of meeting problems arising from impact of age on employment.

Sec. 4 Prohibition of Age Discrimination

(a) It shall be unlawful for an employer—

(1) to fail or refuse to hire or to discharge any individual or otherwise discriminate against any individual with respect to his

compensation, terms, conditions, or privileges of employment, because of such individual's age;
(2) to limit, segregate, or classify his employees in any way which would deprive or tend to deprive any individual of employment opportunities or otherwise adversely affect his status as an employee, because of such individual's age; or
(3) to reduce the wage rate of any employee in order to comply with this chapter.

(b) It shall be unlawful for an employment agency to fail or refuse to refer for employment, or otherwise to discriminate against, any individual because of such individual's age or to classify or refer for employment any individual on the basis of such individual's age.

(c) It shall be unlawful for a labor organization—
(1) to exclude or to expel from its membership, or otherwise to discriminate against, any individual because of his age;
(2) to limit, segregate, or classify its membership, or to classify or fail or refuse to refer for employment any individual, in any way which would deprive or would tend to deprive any individual of employment opportunities, or would limit such employment opportunities or otherwise adversely affect his status as an employee or as an applicant for employment, because of such an individual's age;
(3) to cause or attempt to cause an employer to discriminate against an individual in violation of this section.

(d) It shall be unlawful for an employer to discriminate against any of his employees or applicants for employment, for an employment agency to discriminate against an individual, or for a labor organization to discriminate against any member thereof or applicant for membership, because such individual, member or applicant for membership has opposed any practice made unlawful by this section, or because such individual, member or applicant for membership has made a charge, testified, assisted, or participated in any manner in an investigation, proceeding, or litigation under this chapter.

(e) It shall be unlawful for an employer, labor organization, or employment agency to print or publish, or cause to be printed or published, any notice or advertisement relating to employment by such an employer or membership in or any classification or referral for employment by such a labor organization, or relating to any classification or referral for employment by such an employment agency, indicating any preference, limitation, specification, or discrimination, based on age.

(f) It shall not be unlawful for an employer, employment agency, or labor organization—
(1) to take any action otherwise prohibited under subsections (a), (b), (c), or (e) of this section where age is a bona fide occupational qualification reasonably necessary to the normal operation of the particular business, or where the differentiation is based on reasonable factors other than age, or where such practices involve an employee in a workplace in a foreign country, and compliance with such subsections would cause such employer, or a corporation controlled by such employer, to violate the laws of the country in which such workplace is located;

(h) (1) If an employer controls a corporation whose place of incorporation is in a foreign country, any practice by such corporation prohibited under this section shall be presumed to be such practice by such employer.
(2) The prohibitions of this section shall not apply where the employer is a foreign person not controlled by an American employer.

LIMITATION

Sec. 12 (a) The prohibitions in this chapter shall be limited to individuals who are at least 40 years of age.

(c)(1) Nothing in this chapter shall be construed to prohibit compulsory retirement of any employee who has attained 65 years of age, and who, for the two-year period immediately before retirement, is employed in a bona fide executive or high policymaking position, if such employee is entitled to an immediate nonforfeitable annual retirement benefit from a pension, profitsharing, savings, or deferred compensation plan, or any combination of such plans, of the employer of such employee, which equals, in aggregate, at least $44,000.

(d) Nothing in this Act shall be construed to prohibit compulsory retirement of any employee who has attained 70 years of age, and who is serving under a contract of unlimited tenure (or similar arrangement providing an unlimited tenure) at an institution of higher education (as defined by section 1141(a) of Title 20).

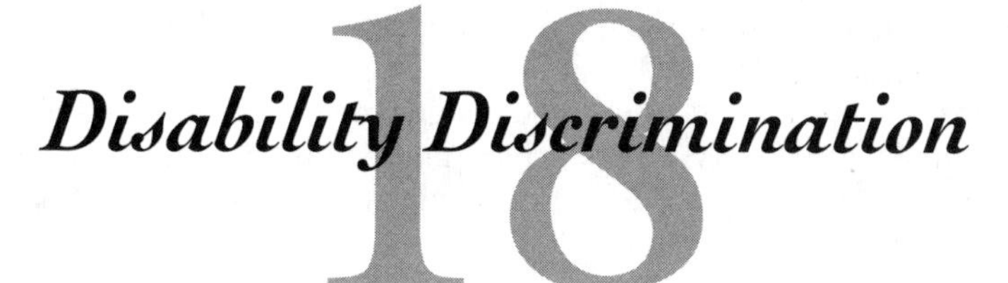

CHAPTER 18 Disability Discrimination

DISCRIMINATING AGAINST THE DISABLED

In 1990, Congress passed the Americans with Disabilities Act (ADA). The ADA has a profound effect on the many millions of Americans who live with some type of disability. The Americans with Disabilities Act (ADA) requires employers with fifteen or more employees to refrain from discriminating against any individual who has an impairment that limits major life activities, such as an impairment to sight, speech, hearing, walking, and learning. Also included are people with cancer, heart conditions, AIDS, and disfigurement, as well as people recovering from substance abuse.

The four largest categories of disabilities are physical (prosthetic, wheelchair, carpal tunnel), disease (heart, lung, cancer, AIDS), sensory (sight, speech, hearing) and mental (retarded, emotionally disabled, chemical dependency). The examples given are not all inclusive. Physical and disease represent a much larger proportion than sensory or mental.

REASONABLE ACCOMMODATIONS

The ADA requires employers to make reasonable accommodations to enable the disabled to work. This includes making the worksite accessible, modifying equipment, and changing work schedules. Those businesses providing a service to the public must make their establishments accessible to the handicapped. This includes, but is not limited to stores, restaurants, hotels, museums, theatres, historical landmarks, visitor centers, sports arenas, health and fitness facilities and night clubs. The disabled person must be qualified to do the job; that is, he or she must be able to perform the

essential function with reasonable accommodation. The ADA was not designed to force employers to hire disabled workers who were not qualified. The qualifications required, however, must be necessary to do the job. If someone is more qualified than the disabled individual, the employer is not required to give the disabled individual preferential treatment.

The issue in the next case is whether an employee's injury qualifies as a disability. The employee, who is a truck driver, injured his shoulder. The company refused to place him on disability because it claimed that his injury was not debilitating.

CASE

Mowat v. Transportation Unlimited, Inc.

984 F.2d 230 (8th Cir. 1992)

HENLEY, Senior Circuit Judge.

Mowat began working as a delivery truck driver for Transportation Unlimited in February 1983. In November 1985, Mowat injured his shoulder while on the job. After Mowat's shoulder surgery and several months of physical therapy, Transportation Unlimited fired Mowat in July 1986, stating that Mowat could no longer perform his duties as a driver. Mowat sued Transportation Unlimited under the Iowa Civil Rights Act (the Act), invoking the federal court's diversity jurisdiction. Mowat claimed that he had a "disability" as deimed by the Act and that he had been terminated in violation of the Act. The district court granted Transportation Unlimited's motion for summery judgment, finding that Mowat did not have a disability and therefore was not entitled to protection under the Act.

There is little factual dispute as to the extent of Mowat's shoulder injury. As a result of the injury, Mowat is essentially unable to lift objects above shoulder height. Transportation Unlimited contends it terminated Mowat because his duties as a deliver truck driver included lifting objects over his head. Mowat was terminated in July 1986, and since January 1987 has been almost continuously employed as a truck driver. The district court, relying on Probasco, found that Mowat's shoulder injury did not amount to a disability under the Act. We see no error in this ruling.

There is no evidence that Mowat's shoulder injury is "generally debilitating," nor is there any evidence that the injury prevents Mowat from working as a truck driver.

Mowat also argues that because Transportation Unlimited "perceived" him as being disabled, he is disabled under the Act. He cites several sections of the Iowa Administrative Code to support his argument. This argument, which was rejected by the Iowa Supreme Court is without merit.

The district court's grant of summary judgment is affirmed.
Judgment for Transportation Unlimited.

In the next case, an employee who had claimed to be totally disabled asked for a temporary, part-time employment accommodation, but this was refused. The employee was terminated for failure to return to work. He claimed disability discrimination for a failure to accommodate reasonably his clinical depression.

CASE

August v. Offices Unlimited, Inc.

981 F.2d 576 (1st Cir. 1992)

CAMPBELL, Judge.

August worked as an office furniture salesman for Offices Unlimited, Inc. (OUI) and its predecessor company since 1966. He began experiencing symptoms of clinical depression in late 1988. In September 1988, August went to his internist, Dr. Martin Vogel, for a routine physical examination. At this visit, August told Dr. Vogel that he felt distressed because of a number of personal and family problems, including the fact that his pay from OUI had been cut by fifty percent.

On February 14, 1989, August visited Dr. Vogel again. August asked the doctor to write a letter to OUI recommending that August be given a month's leave of absence from work. August later presented this letter to OUI management. Dr. Vogel's letter stated that August "has been severely distressed with resultant weight loss, fatigue and weakness. It is most desirable that he have a month's leave from work to avoid continued stress. During this time he will receive therapy in hopes that on his return he can better compensate."

At a February 1989 meeting with OUI management August requested a one-month leave of absence. OUI responded to this request by offering August a six-week paid leave. August preferred to continue working another month until April 1st because the weather would be better then. OUI initially agreed to the April 1st start, but later asked August to leave on March 27, 1989, because of complaints OUI had received from one of August's customers. Before leaving, August met with OUI sales personnel to arrange for his accounts to be covered by other sales representatives while he was away.

In early May, August contacted Mel Goldberg, his supervisor at OUI, to notify him that he would not be able to return to work on May 8, 1989, the scheduled end of the leave period. August also sent Goldberg a letter from Dr. Stanley Wallace, a psychiatrist. Dr. Wallace's letter dated May 3, 1989, stated that August "is currently under my care for treatment of his Major Depression. He has shown significant improvement in his condition but has not yet fully recovered. My estimation is that he will require another two to four weeks before complete recovery is achieved." Goldberg told August that he could take an additional two weeks off, until May 22, 1989, but that the time would count as vacation.

At August's request, he met with Goldberg and Marilyn Campbell, OUI's Director of Administration, on May 11, 1989. According to August's deposition, at the meeting he told the OUI officials that he expected to feel ready to return to work by May 22. When asked whether 100 percent better, August replied, "I don't know if I'm 100 percent until I start working." Goldberg told August that the company would expect "110 percent" from him and that August was "going to be under a lot more pressure than he was prior to leaving." August was advised that business conditions were worsening, that fewer sales representatives were available to handle customer accounts, and that he would be assigned different accounts when he returned. August says he asked if he could "come back on a part-time basis" and if he "could miss the first couple of sales meetings because the sales meetings were in the morning" when he experienced side effects of the antidepressant medication. Goldberg refused both requests. Ms. Campbell suggested that if August continued to feel unable to work, he should consider applying for disability benefits under the company's insurance plan.

August claims the May 11 meeting so distressed him as to reactivate his depression. On May 12, 1989, August made out and executed a claim application under the company's disability plan. In the signed application, August asserted that he had been totally continuously disabled since March 24, 1989. August also wrote on the form that he did not know when he would be able to resume work. An attending physician's statement attached to the application, complete by Dr.

Wallace, verified that August had been totally disabled since March 1989 and that is was unknown when he could resume part-time or full-time work.

In a letter dated May 18, 1989, August's attorney notified OUI that August had filed for disability benefits. In that letter the attorney stated that "the commencement date of Mr. August's disability was March 27, 1989." The letter made no mention of when August would return to OUI. Four days later, August's attorney wrote to Goldberg again, maintaining that August had not resigned from OUI and that it was his "intention to return to his employment with OUI upon the conclusion of his disability." Again, August's attorney did not indicate when August might return.

On May 22, 1989, the end of the second leave of absence, August did not report for work. On May 25, 1989, Campbell, on OUI's behalf, sent August a letter informing him that his employment with OUI was terminated effective June 1, 1989, because "it is certainly unclear when and if you will be able to return to work." The letter explained that OUI could not continue to have other sales representatives temporarily cover August's accounts because "continuity of staff managing account business is, as you know, critical in our industry." Except for the termination letter, there is no evidence of any communication between August and OUI on or after May 22, 1989.

August renewed his claim for disability benefits in December 1989, February 1990, April 1990, and June 1990. Each signed application stated that he had been totally and continuously disabled since late March 1989, the day he began his first leave of absence from OUI. Attached to each application was a statement from Dr. Wallace, verifying the fact that August had been totally disabled since March 1989. Regarding the handicapped discrimination claim, the court found that August was not "a qualified handicapped person" and that, even if he was, OUI had made all necessary reasonable accommodations to his handicap.

Having conceded that he was totally disabled at all relevant times, August cannot now establish that he was a "qualified handicapped person" and thus cannot make the prima facie case required to prevail on his claim. Summary judgment in favor of OUI was proper because there are no genuine issues of material fact as to whether August could have performed his job if his handicap had been accommodated.

The district court also granted summary judgment on the handicapped discrimination claim on the ground that OUI made the required reasonable accommodation to August.

Judgment for OUI.

Employment Perspective

Lisa Conroy applied for a position as a paralegal with the law firm of Moran, Holochwost, and Mullins. Lisa is a paraplegic confined to a wheelchair. The firm is located on the second floor of an office building with no elevator. The firm employs eighteen individuals. What must the law firm do? The law firm has to refuse to hire Lisa. Existing businesses are not required to install elevators. If the law firm occupied the first floor as well, it would be required to make a reasonable accommodation for Lisa on the first floor. If the law firm was going to construct its own office building, an elevator would be required if the building was three stories or more.

If the law firm was located on the first floor but had two steps inside and a bathroom entrance that was not wide enough for a wheelchair, what would the law firm have to do? It would have to install a ramp and make the bathroom entrance wider. These are modifications that are reasonable. To do otherwise would be to refuse to hire Lisa solely because her disability. ◆

The issue in the following case is whether an individual who became handicapped and as a result was reasonably accommodated with light-duty work, can be

demoted in rank. The employer argued that the employee's function now qualified as a lower position than the one he previously held and that as a consequence he should be paid accordingly. The employee claimed that such action would be discriminatory against the disabled.

CASE

Gaither v. Anne Arundel County

618 A.2d 244 (Md. App. 1993)

MOTZ, Judge.

Appellant, Alfred Gaither, has been employed by appellee, Anne Arundel County (County), for many years. In 1989, Gaither was demoted from a grade 14 position, senior water plant operator, to a grade 9 position, utilities maintenance worker. On appeal, the Personnel Board of Anne Arundel County (Board) rejected Gaither's claim of handicap discrimination and upheld his demotion; the Circuit Court for Anne Arundel County (Rushworth, J.) affirmed that decision.

In 1978, while classified as a water plant operator in the Department of Utilities, Gaither was injured in a job-related automobile accident and sustained injuries to his neck and back. Found to have a 12 1/2% permanent disability by the Workers' Compensation Commission, Gaither returned to work but was placed on "light duty" status. In 1985 Gaither was reinjured on the job. As a result of this second accident, the Workers' Compensation Commission determined that Gaither suffered an additional 21% permanent disability. After this second accident and until 1989, Gaither again returned to work in the same "light duty" status.

In 1988, in response to scheduling problems, the Chief of the Bureau of Operations for the County Department of Utilities requested that the Personnel Department conduct desk audits for ten Utilities employees on "light duty" assignment. Gaither held one of these positions. The audits were designed "to identify specifically what . . . roles employees were filling . . . and to determine from that what the proper grading of each position would be." As part of this desk audit, Gaither was asked to complete a job description form. On the form, Gaither listed his responsibilities as well as the amount of time he spent performing each duty. From the job description form as well as an on-site inspection of Gaither's performance by a personnel analyst, the Personnel Department determined that Gaither was not performing the duties of a water plant operator and, subsequently, decided that his position should be reclassified to a utilities maintenance worker at pay grade 9.

In June of 1989, Gaither was informed of the result of the desk audit. Gaither was given 60 days to search for another position in the County. When Gaither did not submit an application for another position, he was given the choice of accepting a demotion to utilities maintenance worker or being terminated. In August 1989, Gaither accepted the position of utilities maintenance worker with a corresponding decrease in salary of approximately $5,000 per year. Thereafter, Gaither challenged the reclassification and filed a grievance with the Board.

The County, in fact, proved that it offered Gaither numerous additional accommodations consistent with Maryland law on the "reasonable accommodation" of handicapped workers. The County adopted fair, reasonable physical standards for water plant operators "adapted to the actual requirements of . . . employment." These were used in evaluating not only Gaither's ability to do the job but that of all other water operators. Thus, the physical standards were not used "to arbitrarily eliminate" him from consideration. The County engaged in a "re-analysis" of the job specifications to "fully consider" Gaither's needs. Moreover, when this analysis was initiated, Gaither's supervisor offered him a transfer to a water plant operator position at the Arnold Plant because in this southern Anne Arundel County facility the physical requirements were less onerous than in other plants. Gaither refused this offer because of "extra traveling." Instead, Gaither indicated that "he felt that he could physically perform the duties of a water plant operator in the northern region." His supervisors then agreed to draw up a list of physical duties of the job and send that list to Gaither's own physician to determine if Gaither could perform those duties or could undergo work hardening training to enable him to complete these duties. Only after Gaither's physician, Dr. Chang, unequivocally opined that Gaither could not perform most of these physical duties did the County determine that Gaither was not medically released for work hardening and would have to be transferred to another position. All of this evidence supports the Board's finding. . . .

Judgment for Anne Arundel County Affirmed.

Employment Perspective

Patricia Krakowski is fifty-two years old. She applied for a position as a high school history teacher with the Monroe Township Academy. Although her credentials were superior, she was passed over for a younger applicant. Patricia had had a cancerous kidney removed. The Academy feared that she might be a candidate for dialysis, which could cause its health costs to increase. Since the Academy was operating within a tight budget, Patricia posed a potential financial risk that it did not want to take. Has Patricia been discriminated against? Yes! Were it not for her disability, Patricia would have been hired. The Academy must give Patricia the position or reimburse her until she finds another suitable one. ◆

The following case addresses the issue of whether an employer can question a prospective employee about whether he or she ever received workers' compensation and for what type of injury it was given. On an employment application, the employee was not forthcoming about his prior employment-related back injury. After he was hired, he sustained further back injuries. Must the new employer pay him although he lied on the job application?

CASE

Huisenga v. Opus Corp.

494 N.W.2d 469 (Minn. 1992)

TOMLJANOVICH, Justice.

On April 19, 1986, while employed as a carpenter by Opus Corporation, Lonnie Huisenga injured his lower back. Because of this injury, he underwent a lumbar decompression on November 7, 1986, for removal of a herniated disc and release of subarticular stenosis. After the surgery, he had behind-the-knee tightness and a sore back. He was rated as having a 9 per-

cent permanent partial disability of the whole body.

Huisenga returned to work at Opus in March 1987. At first, he did only light-duty work, but in a month or so, he was back to full duties. After returning to full time work, he was more careful about how he lifted and did not lift large pieces of sheetrock by himself. He left Opus in 1987 to enter an alcohol treatment program.

From June 1988 until the spring of 1989, Huisenga worked for two construction companies, doing lighter work than he had at Opus. In May 1989, Huisenga inquired of Lund Martin Construction Company to see if it might have work for him. He was told that a carpentry job was available and that he could begin the next day. When Huisenga reported to work, he was given a form entitled "Pre-Employment Health Questionnaire" to complete. The form sought information about, among other things, whether Huisenga had ever had a back injury, whether he had ever received workers' compensation benefits, whether he had ever made a workers' compensation claim for a hernia, a slipped disc, a strain or sprain of his back or shoulder, and whether any former workers' compensation claim established a medical permanency. Huisenga answered "no" to each of these questions.

Because of work activities in February of 1991, Huisenga again sustained an injury to his back. He filed a workers' compensation claim. The compensation judge found that his prior employment had contributed to 65 percent of his temporary disability, medical and hospital expenses, and need for rehabilitation. He attributed the remaining 35 percent of the expenses to Lund Martin. The compensation judge did not award Huisenga benefits for Lund Martin's share, ruling that it did not need to pay them because Huisenga had not responded truthfully to the questions on the medical questionnaire.

It is unfair employment practice for an employer to discriminate against a person with respect to hiring because of a disability. The Minnesota Health Reform Act (MHRA) prohibits an employer from making inquiries about an employee's disabilities before a job offer has been made.

We believe the Pre-Employment Questionnaire was not designed to ferret out only those disabilities which would hamper the applicant from doing the essential functions of the job. One inquiry made on the questionnaire was whether the employee had ever had a back injury. We believe this inquiry was too broad; clearly it was not calculated to discern only those back injuries which would impact an employee's ability to perform the tasks of a carpenter. Having a functional back is necessary in order to perform the work of a carpenter—having a back that has never been injured is not. We also believe that it would be unsuitable for us to declare an arbitrary time period about which employers may ask questions. The critical inquiry is whether the inquiries are tailored to test the employee's present abilities or disabilities, not past health history regardless of remoteness.

Lund Martin's inquiries regarding prior workers' compensation claims of an employee or applicant also stray from the mark. We do not see how asking if an employee or applicant has ever received workers' compensation benefits can survive the requirement of the MHRA. A person could have been previously injured in the workplace in a fashion completely irrelevant to the requirements for the job in question. Yet the questionnaire clearly asks an applicant or employee to divulge information regarding not only the claims which go to the essence of the job, but also those which do not. Probing into the health history and disabilities of an applicant or employee in this fashion is not permitted under the MHRA unless the inquiries are tailored to the requirements of the job in question. The general nature of the question indicates that no such tailoring effort was made here.

The questionnaire also asked if any former workers' compensation claim established a medical permanency. Again this inquiry goes too far. An employee or applicant could have suffered a permanent medical disability from another job which would not affect his or her ability to do the carpentry work at issue in this case. This inquiry is not restricted to only those permanent disabilities essential to the job and is thus improper under the MHRA.

The questionnaire also asked if the employee or applicant had ever made a workers' compensation claim for hernia, slipped disc, or a sprain of the back or shoulder. This question comes closer to complying with the requirements of the MHRA. The injuries listed are the exact types of injuries which might prevent a carpenter from adequately performing the tasks of carpentry. Again, however, the fact that the question probes into the entire health history of the employee or applicant causes the question to run afoul of the requirements of the MHRA. It seems to us that a workers' compensation claim for a strain of the shoulder in the distant past is not relevant to the present ability of an employee or applicant to do the job.

For the above reasons, we conclude that Lund Martin's questions violated the MHRA. Because Lund Martin's questions were not adequately tailored, it must pay the portion of workers' compensation benefits attributable to it.

We reverse and remand
to the compensation judge.
Judgment for Huisenga.

THE FUTURE FOR DISABLED WORKERS

With the increase in information service type positions, the computer and the telephone become great equalizers for the disabled. Couple this with the decline in the number of young people entering the job market, and the future for disabled workers looks promising. Disabled individuals represent the largest pool of potential workers. This is but another group of productive and dedicated workers, whose abilities have remained untapped. They will prove to be useful resources to many companies in the future and will integrate themselves into the work force similar to those other groups who had previously been unwanted. McDonald's McJobs program hires individuals with mental and physical disabilities. It began in the early 1980's and has proven to be a sound business solution to McDonald's need for dedicated and loyal employees with low turnover ratio.

In the case that follows, two school-van drivers were demoted because of their diabetes. They proposed carrying snacks and self-administered blood tests. The school district claimed that this action would not overcome the substantial risk of harm if they continued driving. The issue is whether their request amounts to a reasonable accommodation.

CASE

Wood v. Omaha School Dist.

985 F.2d 437 (8th Cir. 1993)

BEAM, Circuit Judge.

Audry Wood and Ella Mae Whitcomb appeal the district court's grant of summary judgment against them in their action for handicap discrimination in employment under the Rehabilitation Act.

Wood and Whitcomb are diabetics who worked as school van drivers for the School District of Omaha. In May 1986, the School District of Omaha, the Department of Motor Vehicles and the Nebraska Department of Education ("defendants") modified policies with respect to the li-

censing of school van drivers. The new rules required Wood and Whitcomb to undergo physical examinations and required their doctors to certify them as qualified under the Department of Transportation regulations. Because Wood and Whitcomb's treating physicians indicated that they were treated with insulin to control diabetes, the Department of Motor Vehicles refused to consider their applications. The School District then demoted Wood and Whitcomb to positions as van aides, at lower rates of pay. Wood and Whitcomb are Type II diabetics who require insulin to lower their blood sugar levels.

The federal regulations and corresponding state rules address the concern that insulin-using diabetic drivers are subject to hypoglycemia. Hypoglycemic episodes increase the potential for involvement in an accident. Wood and Whitcomb contend that they are at low risk because they are Type II diabetics, are obese, and have a history of high blood sugar. They propose that any risk can be obviated by a self-test of their blood sugar levels before driving and at four hour intervals thereafter. They also propose they be allowed to carry a snack to elevate their blood sugar if necessary.

The only issue for resolution in this case is whether reasonable accommodations by defendants would allow Wood and Whitcomb to perform their jobs in spite of their handicaps. Defendants proffer the affidavits of Dr. Duckworth, who states that "any diabetic treated with insulin is at risk for developing hypoglycemia, a condition of low blood glucose concentrations," the onset of which "can be sudden and may not be perceived by the diabetic."

Wood and Whitcomb submit the affidavit of Dr. Ratner, who states that "neither plaintiff should be considered a high risk to experience hypoglycemia on the job and that the proposed accommodation would eliminate any significant or appreciable risk to the employer . . . while driving a school van."

Wood and Whitcomb have met their burden by proposing that defendants allow them to conduct self blood test and to carry snacks.

An accommodation is unreasonable if it would necessitate modification of the essential nature of the program or place undue burdens on the employer. The district court found that the proposal by Wood and Whitcomb would not eliminate the actual substantial risk. . . .

Viewing the evidence in the light most favorable to Wood and Whitcomb, as we must, this court is unable to affirm the district court. The fact that the burden is on defendants to prove that the accommodation is not reasonable strengthens our holding.

Accordingly, we reverse.
Judgment for Wood and Whitcomb.

CONCLUSION

The percentage of disabled workers who are unemployed is much greater than that of the general population. Public access and specific job accommodations have gone a long way to aid the gainful employment of many of the disabled. Encouraging a change in the mind set of employers remains a formidable task. Many employers view disabled applicants as inferior to others. They represent an additional worry employers do not need. However, with reasonable accommodation, many disabled employees have proven to work as effectively as other workers because their handicap has been alleviated. They are operating on a level playing surface with the rest of the work population.

REVIEW QUESTIONS

1. Explain the importance of the American with Disabilities Act of 1990.
2. What is the significance of the Rehabilitation Act of 1973?

3. Define disability.
4. Are disabled people covered under Title VII?
5. Explain the changes made to better accommodate the disabled in our society.
6. What types of reasonable accommodations have to be made for the disabled employee?
7. Can a disability ever preclude employment because it is considered a bona fide occupational qualification?
8. When can a request for disability accommodation be denied?
9. Are alcoholism and drug addiction disabilities?
10. How should the employer deal with these conditions?
11. A worker suffered from a knee injury that prevented him from working for several days in July. He requested reassignment to a position having a lighter workload. The company refused, claiming that the injury was only temporary. What was the result?
12. Aucutt claimed that Six Flags refused to accommodate his handicap by reassigning him to a less stressful position. Six Flags argued that high blood pressure and coronary artery disease do not qualify Aucutt as being handicapped. What was the result? *Aucutt v. Six Flags Over Mid America,* 869 F.Supp. 736 (E.D. Mo. 1994)
13. Paegle injured his back on two occasions, the second of which necessitated light-duty work status for nearly one year. He requested an accommodation but was refused by his employer. Is this disability discrimination? *Paegle v. Department of Interior,* 813 F.Supp. 61 (D.D.C. 1993)
14. In November 1987, a worker became ill and had gallbladder surgery. She did not work from November 16, 1987, through February 1, 1988. On February 3, 1988, after returning to her position with the Election Board, she reinjured her back because of continued heavy lifting. Upon the advice of a medical doctor, plaintiff did not work for two days. Upon her return to work she requested a transfer to a job with lighter duties. No transfer was offered. What was the result?
15. In July 1993, the plaintiff was diagnosed as having high blood pressure. His treating physician, Dr. Edmund Miller, stated that he authorized the plaintiff to remain out of work for nearly the entire month of July while his body adjusted to his high blood pressure medication. During this time, the plaintiff failed to report directly to his supervisor at Bryant Foods regarding his condition. After one of the supervisors reported seeing the plaintiff's car parked at his shop during the lunch hour, two members of management drove to the plaintiff's shop, whereupon they found the plaintiff standing in the hot sun, appearing to supervise work on automobiles. When the plaintiff returned to work on July 27, he was placed on 90 days probation for failing to communicate properly with his supervisor as to his medical condition and for working at his shop when he was supposedly unable to work at Bryant Foods. The plaintiff returned to work on August 11, after an absence of five working days, with a medical excuse for only one day. The defendant fired the plaintiff, effective August 12, 1993. The stated reason for the plaintiff's discharge was his failure to provide a doctor's excuse for the days he missed and his false statement about his medical treatment. Is this a violation of the ADA? *Oswalt v. Sara Lee Corp.,* 889 F.Supp. 253 (N.D. Miss. 1995)
16. In the case on p. 433, is it ethical to demote an employee who has become disabled?
17. In the case on p. 436, what are the limits to which an employer must go in order reasonably to accommodate an employee?

18. In the case on p. 431, is the request for part-time work unreasonable when an employee becomes disabled?

19. In the case on p. 430, how severe would the plaintiff's injury have had to be to qualify as disabled?

20. Are the accommodations public establishments have been forced to make under the ADA reasonable or an undue burden?

Americans with Disabilities Act of 1990

Sec. 1. Short Title; Table of Contents.

(a) Short Title.—This Act may be cited as the "Americans with Disabilities Act of 1990."

(b) Table of Contents.—The table of contents is as follows:

Sec. 1. Short title; table of contents.
Sec. 2. Findings and purposes.
Sec. 3. Definitions.

Title I—Employment

Sec. 101. Definitions.
Sec. 102. Discrimination.
Sec. 103. Defenses.
Sec. 104. Illegal use of drugs and alcohol.
Sec. 105. Posting notices.
Sec. 106. Regulations.
Sec. 107. Enforcement.
Sec. 108. Effective date.

Sec. 2. Findings and Purposes.

(a) Findings.—The Congress finds that—

(1) some 43,000,000 Americans have one or more physical or mental disabilities, and this number is increasing as the population as a whole is growing older;

(2) historically, society has tended to isolate and segregate individuals with disabilities, and, despite some improvements, such forms of discrimination against individuals with disabilities continue to be a serious and pervasive social problem;

(3) discrimination against individuals with disabilities persists in such critical areas as employment, housing, public accommodations, education, transportation, communication, recreation, institutionalization, health services, voting, and access to public services;

(4) unlike individuals who have experienced discrimination on the basis of race, color, sex, national origin, religion, or age, individuals who have experienced discrimination on the basis of disability have often had no legal recourse to redress such discrimination;

(5) individuals with disabilities continually encounter various forms of discrimination, including outright intentional exclusion, the discriminatory effects of architectural, transportation, and communication barriers, overprotective rules and policies, failure to make modifications to existing facilities and practices, exclusionary qualification standards and criteria, segregation, and relegation to lesser services, programs, activities, benefits, jobs, or other opportunities;

(6) census data, national polls, and other studies have documented that people with disabilities, as a group, occupy an inferior status in our society, and are severely disadvantaged socially, vocationally, economically, and educationally;

(7) individuals with disabilities are a discrete and insular minority who have been faced with restrictions and limitations, subjected to a history of purposeful unequal treatment, and relegated to a position of political powerlessness in our society, based on characteristics that are beyond the control of such individuals and resulting

from stereotypic assumptions not truly indicative of the individual ability of such individuals to participate in, and contribute to, society;

(8) the Nation's proper goals regarding individuals with disabilities are to assure equality of opportunity, full participation, independent living, and economic self-sufficiency for such individuals; and

(9) the continuing existence of unfair and unnecessary discrimination and prejudice denies people with disabilities the opportunity to compete on an equal basis and to pursue those opportunities for which our free society is justifiably famous, and costs the United State billions of dollars in unnecessary expenses resulting from dependency and nonproductivity.

(a) Purpose—It is the purpose of this Act—

(1) to provide a clear and comprehensive national mandate for the elimination of discrimination against individuals with disabilities;

(2) to provide clear, strong, consistent, enforceable standards addressing discrimination against individuals with disabilities;

(3) to ensure that the Federal Government plays a central role in enforcing the standards established in this Act on behalf of individuals with disabilities; and

(4) to invoke the sweep of congressional authority, including the power to enforce the fourteenth amendment and to regulate commerce, in order to address the major areas of discrimination faced day-to-day by people with disabilities.

Sec. 3. Definitions.

As used in this Act:

(1) Auxiliary aids and services.—The term "auxiliary aids and services" includes—

(A) qualified interpreters or other effective methods of making orally delivered materials available to individuals with hearing impairments;

(B) qualified readers, taped texts, or other effective methods of making visually delivered materials available to individuals with visual impairments;

(C) acquisition or modification of equipment or devices; and

(D) other similar services and actions.

(2) Disability.—The term "disability" means, with respect to an individual—

(A) a physical or mental impairment that substantially limits one or more of the major life activities of such individual;

(B) a record of such an impairment; or

(C) being regarded as having such an impairment.

(3) State. The term "State" means each of the several States, the District of Columbia, the Commonwealth of Puerto Rico, Guam, American Samoa, the Virgin Islands, the Trust Territory of the Pacific Islands, and the Commonwealth of the Northern Mariana Islands.

Sec. 101. Definitions.

As used in this title:

(1) Commission.—The term "Commission" means the Equal Employment Opportunity Commission established by section 705 of the Civil Rights Act of 1964 (42 U.S.C. 2000e-4).

(2) Covered entity.—The term "covered entity" means employer, employment agency, labor organization, or joint labor-management committee.

(3) Direct threat.—The term "direct threat" means a significant risk to the health or safety of others that cannot be eliminated by reasonable accommodation.

(4) Employee.—The term "employee" means an individual employed by an employer.

(5) Employer.—

(A) In general.—The term "employer" means a person engaged in an industry affecting commerce who has 15 or more employees for each working day in each of 20 or more calendar weeks in the current or preceding calendar year, and any agent of such person, except that, for two years following the effective date of this title, an employer means a person engaged in an industry affecting commerce who has 25 or more employees for each working day in each of 20 or more calendar weeks in the current or preceding year, and any agent of such person.

(B) Exceptions.—The term "employer" does not include—

(i) the United States, a corporation wholly owned by the government of the United States, or an Indian tribe; or

(ii) a bona fide private membership club (other than a labor organization) that is exempt from taxation under section 501(c) of the Internal Revenue Code of 1986.

(6) Illegal use of drugs.—

(A) In general.—The term "illegal use of drugs" means the use of drugs, the possession or distribution of which is unlawful under the Controlled Substances Act (21 U.S.C. 812). Such term does not include the use of a drug taken under supervision by a licensed health care professional, or other uses authorized by the Controlled Substances Act or other provisions of Federal law.

(B) Drugs.—The term "drug" means a controlled substance, as defined in schedules I through V of section 202 of the Controlled Substances Act.

(7) Person, etc.—The terms "person," "labor organization," "employment agency," "commerce," and "industry affecting commerce," shall have the same meaning given such terms in section 701 of the Civil Rights Act of 1964 (42 U.S.C. 2000e).

(8) Qualified individual with a disability.—The term "qualified individual with a disability" means an individual with a disability who, with or without reasonable accommodation, can perform the essential functions of the employment position that such individual holds or desires. For the purposes of this title, consideration shall be given to the employer's judgment as to what functions of a job are essential, and if an employer has prepared a written description before advertising or interviewing applicants for the job, this description shall be considered evidence of the essential functions of the job.

(9) Reasonable accommodation.—The term "reasonable accommodation" may include—

(A) making existing facilities used by employees readily accessible to and usable by individuals with disabilities; and

(B) job restructuring, part-time or modified work schedules, reassignment to a vacant position, acquisition or modification of equipment or devices, appropriate adjustment or modifications of examinations, training materials or policies, the provision of qualified readers or interpreters, and other similar accommodations for individuals with disabilities.

(10) Undue hardship.—

(A) In general.—The term "undue hardship" means an action requiring significant difficulty or expense, when considered in light of the factors set forth in subparagraph (B).

(B) Factors to be considered.—In determining whether an accommodation would impose an undue hardship on a covered entity, factors to be considered include—

(i) the nature and cost of the accommodation needed under this Act;

(ii) the overall financial resources of the facility or facilities involved in the provision of the reasonable accommodations; the number of persons employed at such facility; the effect on expenses and resources, or the impact otherwise of such accommodation upon the operation of the facility;

(iii) the overall financial resources of the covered entity; the overall size of the business of a covered entity with respect to the number of its employees; the number, type, and location of its facilities; and

(iv) the type of operation or operations of the covered entity, including the composition, structure, and functions of the workforce of such entity; the geographic separateness, administrative, or fiscal relationship of the facility or facilities in question to the covered entity.

Sec. 102. Discrimination.

(a) General Rule.—No covered entity shall discriminate against a qualified individual with a disability because of the disability of such individual in regard to job application procedures, the hiring, advancement, or discharge of employees, employee compensation, job training, and other terms, conditions, and privileges of employment.

(b) Construction.—As used in subsection (a), the term "discriminate" includes—

(1) limiting, segregating, or classifying a job applicant or employee in a way that adversely affects the opportunities or status of such applicant or employee because of the disability of such applicant or employee;

(2) participating in a contractual or other arrangement or relationship that has the effect of subjecting a covered entity's qualified applicant or employee with a disability to the discrimination prohibited by this title (such relationship includes a relationship with an employment or referral agency, labor union, an organization providing fringe benefits to an employee of the covered entity, or an organization providing training and apprenticeship programs);

(3) utilizing standards, criteria, or methods of administration—

(A) that have the effect of discrimination on the basis of disability; or

(B) that perpetuate the discrimination of others who are subject to common administrative control;

(4) excluding or otherwise denying equal jobs or benefits to a qualified individual because of the known disability of an individual with whom the qualified individual is known to have a relationship or association;

(5)(A) not making reasonable accommodations to the known physical or mental limitations of an otherwise qualified individual with a disability who is an applicant or employee, unless such covered entity can demonstrate that the accommodation would impose an undue hardship on the operation of the business of such covered entity; or

(B) denying employment opportunities to a job applicant or employee who is an otherwise qualified individual with a disability, if such denial is based on the need of such covered entity to make reasonable accommodation to the physical or mental impairments of the employee or applicant;

(6) using qualification standards, employment tests or other selection criteria that screen out or tend to screen out an individual with a disability or a class of individuals with disabilities unless the standard, test or other selection criteria, as used by the covered entity, is shown to be job-related for the position in question and is consistent with business necessity; and

(7) failing to select and administer tests concerning employment in the most effective manner to ensure that, when such test is administered to a job applicant or employee who has a disability that impairs sensory, manual, or speaking skills, such test results accurately reflect the skills, aptitude, or whatever other factor of such applicant or employee that such test purports to measure, rather than reflecting the impaired sensory, manual, or speaking skills of such employee or applicant (except where such skills are the factors that the test purports to measure).

(c) Medical Examinations and Inquiries.—

(1) In general.—The prohibition against discrimination as referred to in subsection (a) shall include medical examinations and inquiries.

(2)Preemployment.—

(A) Prohibited examination or inquiry.—Except as provided in paragraph (3), a covered entity shall not conduct a medical examination or make inquiries of a job applicant as to whether such applicant is an individual with a disability or as to the nature or severity of such disability.

(B) Acceptable inquiry.—A covered entity may make preemployment inquiries into the ability of an applicant to perform job-related functions.

(3) Employment entrance examination.—A covered entity may require a medical examination after an offer of employment has been made to a job applicant and prior to the commencement of the employment duties of such applicant, and may condition an offer of employment on the results of such examination, if—

(A) all entering employees are subjected to such an examination regardless of disability;

(B) information obtained regarding the medical condition or history of the applicant is collected and maintained on separate forms and in separate medical files and is treated as a confidential medical record, except that—

(i) supervisors and managers may be informed regarding necessary restrictions on the work or duties of the employee and necessary accommodations;

(ii) first aid and safety personnel may be informed, when appropriate, if the disability might require emergency treatment; and

(iii) government officials investigating compliance with this Act shall be provided relevant information on request; and

(C) the results of such examination are used only in accordance with this title.

(4) Examination and inquiry.—

(A) Prohibited examinations and inquiries.—A covered entity shall not require a medical examination and shall not make inquiries of an employee as to whether such employee is an individual with a disability or as to the nature of severity of the disability, unless such examination or inquiry is shown to be job-related and consistent with business necessity.

(B) Acceptable examinations and inquiries.—A covered entity may conduct voluntary medical examinations, including voluntary medical histories, which are part of an employee health program available to employees at that work site. A covered entity may make inquiries into the ability of an employee to perform job-related functions.

(C) Requirement.—Information obtained under subparagraph (B) regarding the medical condition or history of any employee are subject to the requirements of subparagraphs (B) and (C) of paragraph (3).

Sec. 103. Defenses.

(a) In General.—It may be a defense to a charge of discrimination under this Act that an alleged application of qualification standards, tests, or selection criteria that screen out or tend to screen out or otherwise deny a job or benefit to an individual with a disability has been shown to be job-related and consistent with business necessity, and such performance cannot be accomplished by reasonable accommodations, as required under this title.

(b) Qualification Standards.—The term "qualification standards" may include a requirement that an individual shall not pose a direct threat to the health or safety of other individuals in the workplace.

(c) Religious Entities.—

(1) In general.—This title shall not prohibit a religious corporation, association, educational institution, or society from giving preference in employment to individuals of a particular religion to perform work connected with the carrying on by such corporation, association, educational institution, or society of its activities.

(2) Religious tenets requirements.—Under this title, a religious organization may require that all applicants and employees conform to the religious tenets of such organization.

(d) List of Infectious and Communicable Diseases.—

(1) In general.—The Secretary of Health and Human Services, not later than 6 months after the date of enactment of this Act, shall—

(A) review all infectious and communicable diseases which may be transmitted through handling the food supply;

(B) publish a list of infectious and communicable diseases which are transmitted through handling the food supply;

(C) publish the methods by which such diseases are transmitted; and

(D) widely disseminate such information regarding the list of diseases and their modes of transmissibility to the general public.

Such list shall be updated annually.

(2) Applications.—In any case in which an individual has an infectious or communicable disease that is transmitted to others through the handling of food, that is in-

cluded on the list developed by the Secretary of Health and Human Services under paragraph (1), and which cannot be eliminated by reasonable accommodation, a covered entity may refuse to assign or continue to assign such individual to a job involving food handling.

(3) Construction.—Nothing in this Act shall be construed to preempt, modify, or amend any State, county, or local law, ordinance, or regulation applicable to food handling which is designed to protect the public health from individuals who pose a significant risk to the health or safety of others, which cannot be eliminated by reasonable accommodation, pursuant to the list of infectious or communicable diseases and the modes of transmissibility published by the Secretary of Health and Human Services.

Sec. 104. Illegal Use of Drugs and Alcohol.

(a) Qualified Individual With a Disability.—For purposes of this title, the term "qualified individual with a disability" shall not include any employee or applicant who is currently engaging in the illegal use of drugs, when the covered entity acts on the basis of such use.

(b) Rules of Construction.—Nothing in subsection (a) shall be construed to exclude as a qualified individual with a disability an individual who—

(1) has successfully completed a supervised drug rehabilitation program and is no longer engaging in the illegal use of drugs, or has otherwise been rehabilitated successfully and is no longer engaging in such use;

(2) is participating in a supervised rehabilitation program and is no longer engaging in such use; or

(3) is erroneously regarded as engaging in such use, but is not engaging in such use; except that it shall not be a violation of this Act for a covered entity to adopt or administer reasonable policies or procedures, including but not limited to drug testing, designed to ensure that an individual described in paragraph (1) or (2) is no longer engaging in the illegal use of drugs.

(c) Authority of Covered Entity.—A covered entity—

(1) may prohibit the illegal use of drugs and the use of alcohol at the workplace by all employees;

(2) may require that employees shall not be under the influence of alcohol or be engaging in the illegal use of drugs at the workplace;

(3) may require that employees behave in conformance with the requirements established under the Drug-Free Workplace Act of 1988 (41 U.S.C. 701 et seq.);

(4) may hold an employee who engages in the illegal use of drugs or who is an alcoholic to the same qualification standards for employment or job performance and behavior that such entity holds other employees, even if any unsatisfactory performance or behavior is related to the drug use or alcoholism of such employee; and

(5) may, with respect to Federal regulations regarding alcohol and the illegal use of drugs, require that—

(A) employees comply with the standards established in such regulations of the Department of Defense, if the employees of the covered entity are employed in an industry subject to such regulations, including complying with regulations (if any) that apply to employment in sensitive positions in such an industry, in the case of employees of the covered entity who are employed in such positions (as defined in the regulations of the Department of Defense);

(B) employees comply with the standards established in such regulations of the Nuclear Regulatory Commission, if the employees of the covered entity are employed in an industry subject to such regulations, including complying with regulations (if any) that apply to employment in sensitive positions in such an industry, in the case of employees of the covered entity who are employed in such positions (as defined in the regulations of the Nuclear Regulatory Commission); and

(C) employees comply with the standards established in such regulations of the Department of Transportation, if the employees of the covered entity are employed in a transportation industry subject to such regulations, including complying with such regulations (if any) that apply to employment in sensitive positions in such an industry, in the case of employees of the covered entity who are employed in such positions (as defined in the regulations of the Department of Transportation).

(d) Drug Testing.—
(1) In general.—For purposes of this title, a test to determine the illegal use of drugs shall not be considered a medical examination.
(2) Construction.—Nothing in this title shall be construed to encourage, prohibit, or authorize the conducting of drug testing for the illegal use of drugs by job applicants or employees or making employment decisions based on such test results.

(e) Transportation Employees.—Nothing in this title shall be construed to encourage, prohibit, restrict, or authorize the otherwise lawful exercise by entities subject to the jurisdiction of the Department of Transportation of authority to—
(1) test employees of such entities in, and applicants for, positions involving safety-sensitive duties for all illegal use of drugs and for on-duty impairment by alcohol; and
(2) remove such persons who test positive for illegal use of drugs and on-duty impairment by alcohol pursuant to paragraph (1) from safety-sensitive duties in implementing subsection (c).

Sec. 105. Posting Notices.

Every employer, employment agency, labor organization, or joint labor-management committee covered under this title shall post notices in an accessible format to applicants, employees, and members describing the applicable provisions of this Act, in the manner prescribed by section 711 of the Civil Rights Act of 1964 (42 U.S.C. 2000e-10).

Sec. 106. Regulations.

Not later than 1 year after the date of enactment of this Act, the Commission shall issue regulations in an accessible format to carry out this title in accordance with subchapter II of chapter 5 of title 5, United States Code.

Sec. 107. Enforcement.

(a) Powers, Remedies, and Procedures.—The powers, remedies, and procedures set forth in sections 705, 706, 707, 709, and 710 of the Civil Rights Act of 1964 (42 U.S.C. 2000e-4, 2000e-5, 2000e-6, 2000e-8, and 2000e-9) shall be the powers, remedies, and procedures this title provides to the Commission, to the Attorney General, or to any person alleging discrimination on the basis of disability in violation of any provision of this Act, or regulations promulgated under section 106, concerning employment.

(b) Coordination.—The agencies with enforcement authority for actions which allege employment discrimination under this title and under the Rehabilitation Act of 1973 shall develop procedures to ensure that administrative complaints filed under this title and under the Rehabilitation Act of 1973 are dealt with in a manner that avoids duplication of effort and prevents imposition of inconsistent or conflicting standards for the same requirements under this title and the Rehabilitation Act of 1973. The Commission, the Attorney General, and the Office of Federal Contract Compliance Programs shall establish such coordinating mechanisms (similar to provisions contained in the joint regulations promulgated by the Commission and the Attorney General at part 42 of title 28 and part 1691 of title 29, Code of Federal Regulations, and the Memorandum of Understanding between the Commission and the Office of Federal Contract Compliance Programs dated January 16, 1981 (46 Fed. Reg. 7435, January 23, 1981)) in regulations implementing this title and Rehabilitation Act of 1973 not later than 18 months after the date of enactment of this Act.

Sec. 108. Effective Date.

This title shall become effective 24 months after the date of enactment.

CHAPTER 19

AIDS Discrimination

Employers' concerns are many with regard to AIDS. Whenever an employee is questioned concerning whether he or she has the disease or whenever that information is related to other employees, an invasion of privacy may occur. If an assertion is made that an employee is suffering from the AIDS virus turns out to be unfounded, defamation may occur. If an employee is refused employment because he or she has the AIDS virus, employment discrimination may be asserted. When an existing employee who is capable of working is discharged because he or she has the AIDS virus, a violation of the Federal Rehabilitation Act, Americans with Disabilities Act or state law protecting the handicapped may result. Under the circumstances, how can an employer maintain harmony in the workplace? Employers must develop policies regarding the treatment afforded existing AIDS employees regarding the fringe benefits given, including absences, dental care and medical benefits, alternative work location, and reassurance of support by the company. Applicants for positions who have AIDS must be treated on an equal basis. As long as an AIDS victim is capable of performing the work, he or she should be treated no differently from any other employee. Employers are encouraged to develop an educational program designed to ease the fears of coworkers who worry about catching the virus. The key is successful planning. Companies who have no known existing cases of AIDS should plan now because, according to the Center for Disease Control's projections, the number of AIDS cases will continue to increase.

WORKERS WITH CONTAGIOUS DISEASES

The Question of Disclosure

The word *AIDS* has become synonymous with the word *fear,* and nowhere has this fear of AIDS been more pervasive than in the workplace. This fear results in problems for all concerned parties: AIDS victims, coworkers, and employers.

To disclose or not to disclose—that has been the question for AIDS employees. Disclosure may be necessary to obtain excessive absences and to explain poor performance on the job which may result from a weakened physical condition. Although an AIDS victim has little choice, disclosure has generally compounded the problems. Once notified, many employers have fired or coaxed AIDS employees into leaving quietly, promising to retain confidentiality not to tell the world. Many panic-stricken fellow employees react negatively upon learning the news. They refuse to share drinking fountains, pens, telephones, and toilets. There are even some who refuse to breathe the same air as an AIDS victim in a confined work environment. As a result, AIDS employees become isolated in much the same way as did lepers. However, unlike leprosy, AIDS cannot be transmitted through touching or any of the other unfounded ways which are responsible for the mass hysteria in the workplace. AIDS is communicable, but only through the exchange of body fluids, which allow for the AIDS virus to enter the bloodstream. AIDS cannot be transmitted by casual contact because the AIDS virus dies shortly after it is exposed to the air.

Just as the defense system of the United States is vital to the security of this country, protecting us from invasion by foreign enemies, so, too, is the immune system of every person vital to the person's existence and well-being by fighting infections and diseases. AIDS is the Acquired Immune Deficiency Syndrome. It is a disorder of the immune system that renders it defenseless. With the body's defense system unable to battle viruses, infection and disease can spread, consuming the entire body and resulting in death. AIDS does not kill, but it makes a person easy prey for opportunistic infections such as pneumonia.

The Sources

The AIDS virus has been found in various body fluids: semen, vaginal secretions, blood, saliva, tears, urine, breast milk, and spinal fluid, as well as bone marrow. However, to date, only through semen, vaginal secretions, and blood has the disease been transmitted. The AIDS virus can exist for only a very short time (seconds) once exposed to air. It is not like leprosy. Therefore, AIDS cannot be transmitted through touching, breathing the same air, or using the same toilets, drinking fountains, telephones, or pens. AIDS is communicable, but only through the exchange of body fluids, which allow for the AIDS virus to enter the bloodstream.

Preventative Planning

Preventative planning will diminish the worry over lawsuits involving discrimination, defamation, and invasion of privacy. It will also bolster the company's public image concerning the treatment of a life-threatening disease. Planning is the key. Developing a sound AIDS policy now will prepare companies for the AIDS cases that are sure to follow.

A company's first priority is to protect the privacy of an AIDS victim, thus shielding itself from an invasion of privacy or defamation suit. Employees should be encouraged, but not required, to inform their managers of their affliction with AIDS. By advocating that AIDS employees should discuss their illness with the human resource department, AIDS employees are assured that medical benefits and other accommodations, such as flexible work hours, may be arranged. The company may also place AIDS victims in contact with community groups that are concerned with the welfare of AIDS victims and that provide counseling or medical assistance.

The implementation by companies of effective planning and educational programming will result in more humane treatment of AIDS victims. Employees base their objections to AIDS victims on the principles of agency law. The maintenance of safe working conditions is another obligation placed on the principal; otherwise the principal may be liable for the harm resulting to an agent. The National Labor Relations Act permits employees to act together for their mutual protection. In addition, employees fearful of AIDS argue for the displacement of AIDS employees under the Occupational Safety and Health Act (OSHA), which requires workplaces to be free of hazards that could result in death or serious injury. Although lawsuits based on these acts would probably be resolved in favor of the AIDS victims, complications in labor relations arise because of a lack of clarity and decisiveness in the law.

The Insurance Dilemma

The average claim on an insurance policy held by AIDS victims greatly exceeds the norm. Since current premium income is not sufficient to meet claims, insurance companies fear going bankrupt. It is difficult for insurers to estimate the risk without proper testing to determine whether a prospective applicant has the AIDS virus.

The American Council on Life Insurance contends that those who test positive for the AIDS antibody are twenty times more likely to die within the next five years. Furthermore, they argue that AIDS victims take out huge amounts of life insurance after being diagnosed with the AIDS virus. If an insurance company cannot set a premium equivalent to the risk that it underwrites, it will go bankrupt. Balancing the interests of the insurance companies is the need for AIDS victims to be able to obtain insurance coverage. The question is, who is to bear the brunt of the cost: the AIDS victim or all policyholders together?

Testing for AIDS

The main criticism of testing is the availability of a reliable test and the legal dilemma of whether a person should be subjected to such a test. The Center for Disease Control decided not to require AIDS testing as a public health measure in March 1987. The reasoning employed was that it constituted an invasion of privacy in that even a positive result did not mean a person would develop AIDS. For the same reasons, employers are advised not to test their employees for AIDS.

Protecting AIDS Victims

AIDS employees who become debilitated resign when they can no longer perform their function rather than be ridiculed. These victims often join the ranks of the unemployed which will place a financial burden on society as the number of people afflicted with the AIDS virus grows.

AIDS employees can stay and fight, rather than resign. The recourse available to assist AIDS employees in their fight against discrimination is the ADA. The Americans with Disabilities Act of 1990 prohibits discrimination against a person with a major life impairment. AIDS certainly qualifies as one.

The following case was the first one which decided that AIDS is a handicap under a state anti-discrimination statute.

CASE

Shuttleworth v. Broward County Office

No. 85-0624
Florida Commission on Human Relations (1985)

The Florida Human Rights Act of 1977 embraces the handicapped as one of the classifications against which an employer may not discriminate. The question of whether AIDS would be included as a handicap was resolved by the Florida Commission on Human Relations in December 1985 in the case of *Shuttleworth v. Broward County Office of Budget and Management Policy.* Mr. Shuttleworth, a public employee of Broward County, was discharged when it was discovered he contracted AIDS (acquired immune deficiency syndrome). Shuttleworth was in the employ of the county for sixteen months when he was dismissed. His work performance had been satisfactory during this duration. The County's defense centered around its unwillingness to assume the risk of a co-worker contracting AIDS from Shuttleworth in the workplace.

Broward County based their reasoning on an article entitled *AIDS—Information and Procedural Guidelines for Providing Health and Social Services to Persons with AIDS.* This article acknowledged that the medical community does not believe AIDS can be transmitted through casual contact, however, it stated that individuals in certain high risk groups including pregnant women and persons receiving chemotherapy should not be exposed to AIDS patients. The Florida Commission on Human Relations resolved that only those with transmissible opportunistic infections place co-workers at risk. Furthermore, the Commission stated that Broward County offered no proof that Shuttleworth had a transmissible opportunistic infection when it fired him.

Section 760.10 of the Florida Human Rights Act of 1977, paragraph 1, provides in part: "It is an unlawful employment practice for an employer: (a) To discharge . . . any individual . . . because of such individual's . . . handicap. . . .

In determining whether the term handicap encompassed AIDS victims, the Florida Commission on Human Relations determined the term handicap should be defined by common usage. "A person with a handicap does not enjoy, in some manner, the full and normal use of his sensory, mental or physical faculties." The Florida Commission on Human Relations decided, "Based upon the plain meaning of the term handicap and the medical evidence presented, an individual with acquired immune deficiency syndrome is within the coverage of the Human Rights Act of 1977 in that such individual does not enjoy . . . normal use of his sensory, mental or physical faculties."

Section 760, 10, paragraph (8) Florida Statutes (Florida Human Rights Act) provides: "Notwithstanding any other provision of this section, it is not an unlawful employment practice for an employer . . . to: (a) Take or fail to take any action on the basis of . . . handicap . . . in those certain instances in which . . . absence of a particular handicap . . . is a bona fide occupational qualification reasonable necessary for the performance of the particular employment to which such action or inaction is related."

In interpreting the phrase "bona fide occupational qualification," the Florida First District Court of Appeals in *School Board of Pineallas County v. Rateau* stated that the defense of risk of future injury must be substantial. The employer's conclusion that the risk of injury is substantial must be supported by evidence which indicates that the employer had a reasonable basis for its assessment of the risk of injury or death to establish the bona fide occupational qualification.

The Florida Commission on Human Relations concluded there was no reasonable basis to support Broward County's conclusion that Shuttleworth posed a substantial risk of future injury to his co-workers by retaining Shuttleworth in its employ.

Subsequently, Shuttleworth brought a discrimination claim in the Southern District Court of Florida which was settled in December 1986. The terms of the settlement were payment of $196,000 to Shuttleworth and reinstatement as an employee of Broward County.

Decision for Shuttleworth.

In the following case, an employee sued for discrimination and invasion of privacy when his employer informed his co-workers he had AIDS.

CASE

Cronan v. New England Telephone

No. 80332 Mass Sup.Ct. (Suffolk Cty 1986)

Paul Cronan was a repair technician for the New England Telephone Company. He was in their employ since 1973. In May 1985, Cronan requested permission on two separate occasions to leave work for one and a half hours for medical appointments. His supervisor, O'Brien, granted both requests. However, on a third occasion, O'Brien demanded to know the details of Cronan's medical problems, assuring confidentiality even though he received a note from a physician stating that Cronan was under medical care. Cronan acquiesced to O'Brien's demands and revealed he had ARC (AIDS Related Complex). Cronan explained the difference between AIDS and ARC to O'Brien, ARC being the less serious of the two.

O'Brien informed his superiors, who when notified placed Cronan on disability. According to Cronan, the company officials assembled Cronan's coworkers, some of whom threatened to lynch him if he returned to work. In August 1985, Cronan attempted to contact his supervisor to inform him of his desire to return to work, but his calls were never answered. In September 1985, Cronan was hospitalized and, after undergoing extensive blood tests, was diagnosed as having AIDS. Subsequently, Cronan filed a lawsuit in the Massachusetts Superior Court of Suffolk County claiming breach of privacy, employment discrimination, and violation of civil rights.

New England Telephone's strategy was to move the case from state court to the U.S. District Court of Massachusetts claiming that state court's jurisdiction was preempted by Section 301 of the Labor Management Relations Act of 1947. District Judge Skinner held, "Since the privacy claim asserted in Count I need not be resolved through contractual interpretation of the Agreement, and since a right to privacy is exactly the type of individual right that need not be subject to collective processes and is independent of private agreements, I conclude that Count I is not preempted by Section 301." Judge Skinner also decided that discrimination is a violation of civil rights. Cronan's motion to remand the case back to the Massachusetts Superior Court of Suffolk County was granted.

In Superior Court, New England Telephone moved to dismiss each of Cronan's allegations. In denying New England Telephone's motions, the Court discussed each one at length. Concerning the invasion of privacy, Cronan contended that the company's act of forcing him to disclose information regarding his personal state of health and thereafter disseminating this information to other employees was not necessary to protect its legitimate business interests.

Under Massachusetts General Laws, it is stated, "A person shall have a right against unreasonable substantial or serious interference with his privacy."

The Supreme Judicial Court of Massachusetts in *Bratt v. International Business Machines* set forth the standard with regard to the disclosure of medical information under the above statute. The Court stated, "In determining whether there is a violation, it is necessary to balance the employer's legitimate business interest in obtaining and publishing the information against the substantiality of the intrusion on the employee's privacy resulting from the disclosure." The Superior Court concluded that the allegations set forth by Cronan met this standard and that there is a triable issue of fact to be resolved.

Concerning the employment discrimination claim, Cronan argued that New England Telephone would not allow him to return to work because he was handicapped and that a reasonable accommodation on their part would not have placed an undue burden on them. New England Telephone contended that neither ARC nor AIDS is tantamount to a handicap as defined in Massachusetts General Laws where it stated that it is not lawful for any employer, personally or through an agent, to . . . discriminate against, because of his handicap, any person alleging to be a qualified handicapped person, capable of performing the essential functions of the position involved with reasonable accommodation unless the employer can demonstrate the accommodation required to be made to the physical or mental limitations of the person would impose an undue hardship to the employer's business.

With reference to the above statute, the Supreme Judicial Court of Massachusetts has decided that, "the primary responsibility to determine the scope of the statute has been entrusted to the MCAD, not the courts." The Massachusetts Commission Against Discrimination (MCAD) has concluded that AIDS victims are handicapped and therefore entitled to protection under the anti-discrimination statute. The Superior Court, acceding to the Supreme Judicial Court's mandate, states that deference should be given to the opinion of the Massachusetts Commission Against Discrimination. The motion to dismiss with regard to Cronan's employment discrimination claim was not granted.

New England also argued in the alternative that if Cronan was considered handicapped, to accommodate him would be an undue burden. The Superior Court stated, "that the burden of whether the accommodation requested is unreasonable is on the employer." Massachusetts General Laws stipulate the employer must "demonstrate that the accommodation required to be made to the physical or mental limitations of the person would impose an undue hardship to the employer's business." New England Telephone's assertions were not supported by sufficient evidence to meet the statute's criteria.

Finally, with regard to the issue of civil rights violation, threats, intimidation, or coercion are required. New England Telephone claims that no company officials made any threats, and if any employees did they made them outside the scope of employment. A principal is liable for the acts of his or her agents if these acts were committed during the scope of employment which may be defined as relating to the business at hand. The Superior Court concluded it was a genuine factual issue as to who in the company made the threats and as to whether they were made in the discharge of official duties.

Subsequently this case was settled out of court with Cronan being allowed to return to work in October, 1986. When they learned of Cronan's reinstatement, his co-workers requested that they receive their assignments outside to avoid close contact with Cronan in a confined setting. New England refused and seventy-five percent of the workers walked off the job. The company quickly assembled three physicians who convinced the workers that the AIDS virus could not be transmitted through casual contact with Cronan. The reaction to Cronan's return and the subsequent education and return of his co-workers is proof that fear of AIDS is caused by false rumor and ignorance of the facts and that proper and timely education given before mass hysteria develops will help to maintain harmony in the workplace.

Judgment for Cronan.

The next case deals with a company who refused to allow an employee with AIDS to resume working. Their inquiries concerning whether AIDS was contagious were met with continued medical reassurances that AIDS could not be contracted from casual contact at the workplace.

Dept. of Fair Employment and Housing v. Raytheon Co.

No. FEP 83-84 L1-031p (1987)

John Chadbourne was hired by the Raytheon Company in 1980. Chadbourne worked as a Quality Control Analyst in an office shared with five co-workers. His work required him to come into casual contact with many other employees throughout the plant.

In December, 1983, Chadbourne was diagnosed as having AIDS by Doctor Hosea and subsequently released into his care. Patricia Heyble, the nurse in charge of medical services for the division of Raytheon for which Chadbourne worked, requested medical documentation concerning Chadbourne's condition. She received a letter from Dr. Hosea's associate stating Chadbourne had AIDS. Ms. Heyble contacted Dr. Donald, a medical consultant to Raytheon. He, in turn, contacted Dr. Juels, Director of Communicable Disease Control for Santa Barbara County. Dr. Juels toured the Raytheon plant and viewed Chadbourne's work environment. He concluded that Chadbourne's co-workers would not be at risk of contracting AIDS from him through contact in the workplace. Dr. Juels offered the training services of the Santa Barbara Department of Public Health to educate Raytheon's employees about AIDS.

After receiving a letter from Dr. Hosea in mid-January stating Chadbourne was physically able to return to work, Raytheon postponed Chadbourne's reinstatement to gather more information. Ms. Heyble contacted Dr. Kenneth Kastro of the Center for Disease Control in Atlanta, who advised her of the Center's position with regard to AIDS. AIDS is communicable only through the exchange of blood and body fluids not through casual contact in the workplace.

Even with the affirmation of Raytheon's Medical Director, Dr. Stephen Alphas, regarding permission for Chadbourne to return to work, Raytheon decided to stall his comeback attempt, postponing reinstatement in 1984 from February 6 to February 26, March 3, June 15 and then indefinitely. By August, 1984, the effects of AIDS had overtaken Chadbourne precluding him from working again. He died five months later. His estate filed a complaint with the Department of Fair Employment and Housing who instituted an action on the estate's behalf with the Fair Employment and Housing Commission of the State of California for back pay, compensatory damages for pain and suffering, and punitive damages for the malicious and deliberate harm.

Raytheon's first argument was that Section 503 of the Rehabilitation Act of 1973 preempted the physical handicap provisions of the Fair Employment and Housing Act. The Fair Employment and Housing Commission rejected this argument stating it lacked either express or implicit Congressional intent to preempt.

Raytheon's second argument stated that AIDS does not constitute a physical handicap as defined in the Fair Employment and Housing Act. The Commission disagreed stating the California Supreme Court mandated a broad interpretation of the term physical handicap when it defined physical handicap as any physical condition that has a disabling effect making it difficult to achieve. The California Supreme Court expanded the definition further by including physical conditions which disable in the future, but show no present signs of disability. Based on this reasoning, the California Fair Employment and Housing Commission decided, "Under this standard there can be no doubt that AIDS does constitute a physical handicap. It is plainly a physical condition of the body. And while AIDS does not impair Chadbourne's physical ability to do his job until long after he was first excluded from it by respondent, there was not simply a possibility but a tragic certainty that the condition would at some time in the future seriously impair his physical ability and ultimately kill him. AIDS thus falls squarely within the physical handicap coverage of the Act."

In assessing Raytheon's liability, the Commission resolved, "There is no dispute that respondent discriminated against Chadbourne "because of . . . physical handicap" within the meaning of the Act. . . . There is no question here that Chadbourne's AIDS was the sole reason that respondent denied him reinstatement to his job, and we therefore determine that respondent discriminated against him under the Act."

Raytheon then attempted to justify the discrimination, claiming reinstating Chadbourne would endanger the health and safety of his co-workers. The burden of proving this rests with Raytheon and cannot be shifted to the Department of Fair Employment and Housing. The Commission concluded,". . . . The great weight of the evidence demonstrates that Chadbourne would not have endangered the health or safety of his co-workers any more than would an employee without AIDS."

The California Fair Employment and Housing Commission awarded back pay to Chadbourne's estate, but refused to grant both compensatory damages for emotional distress and suffering and punitive damages for malicious and deliberate harm claiming, "The unique circumstances of this case, however, convince us that an award of compensatory damages would not be appropriate here. We fully recognize that Chadbourne suffered significant emotional injury as a result of respondent's actions. . . . But we also recognize that respondent took these actions in early 1984, in a state of considerable uncertainty, and we therefore believe that we cannot, in fairness, order respondent to pay compensatory damages in this case."

Concerning the punitive damages, the Commission decided that Raytheon knew there was no risk of harm to Chadbourne's co-workers based on the opinions of the medical experts they consulted which was affirmed by their own Director of Medicine as well as other medical personnel. In light of this, the Commission believed that Raytheon read into these statements an uncertainty which did not exist. However, the Commission concluded, "We cannot find that this misreading of the medical evidence was malicious. . . . Respondent was surely aware of the devastating effect this exclusion would have on a man already beleaguered by an illness that promised him only an early and difficult death. But in view of the atmosphere of anxiety and uncertainty that existed in early 1984 and the lack of precedent, we do not believe that respondents's misinterpretation of the information it received was intended to vex, injure, harass or annoy Chadbourne or was undertaken in conscious disregard of his right to return to work. We therefore decline to order an award of punitive damages. . . ."

The Commission cautioned that they may not be so lenient with future employees who come before them for unlawfully discharging AIDS employees especially after the publication of this decision. The Commission hoped that their decision would have the effect of deterring employers from discriminating against AIDS employees in the future. The Commission admitted though, that the deterrent may be undermined by limiting liability to back pay and by the fact that the AIDS employee may die before the case is resolved and a remedy is awarded. For this reason, the Commission urged the Department of Fair Employment and Housing to seek injunctive relief for future deposed AIDS employees who wish to be reinstated to their former positions. This suggestion makes sense because it addresses the immediate concern of the AIDS victim; employment with related medical benefits. Back pay with interest payable to the deceased estate may vindicate the AIDS employee but does not resolve his or her immediate financial problems.

Decision for Dept. of Fair Employment and Housing.

This particular case deals with the issue of whether an employer can discriminate against a person with a contagious disease or whether that person is considered disabled.

School Board of Nassau County, Florida, and Craig Marsh v. Gene H. Arline

CASE

107 S.Ct. 1123 (1987)

Justice BRENNAN.

Section 504 of the Rehabilitation Act of 1973 prohibits discrimination against the handicapped. The question presented here is whether a person having a contagious disease may be considered handicapped with Section 504 of the Rehabilitation Act. Gene Arline first contracted tuberculosis when she was a teenager in 1957. After that the disease was in remission for twenty years until she suffered three relapses in 1977 and 1978. At this point she was an elementary school teacher in Nassau County, Florida and had been so from 1966 until 1979 when she was dismissed by the School Board because of her reoccurring relapses of tuberculosis.

The District Court concluded that Arline was not a handicapped person within Section 504. It is "difficult . . . to conceive that Congress intended contagious diseases to be included within the definition of a handicapped person." The Court of Appeals disagreed stating, "persons with contagious diseases are within the coverage of Section 504." The United States Supreme Court affirmed declaring that Congress addressed the widespread problem of discrimination against those who are handicapped through Section 504, which is an anti-discrimination provision modeled after Title VII of the Civil Rights Act of 1964.

Section 504 of the Rehabilitation Act states in part, "No otherwise qualified handicapped individual in the United States, as defined in section 706(7) of this title, shall, solely by reason of his handicap, be excluded from participation in, be denied the benefits of, or be subjected to discrimination under any program or activity receiving Federal Financial assistance. . . ."

This definition was expanded in 1974 by Congress: "Any person who (i) has a physical or mental impairment which substantially limits one or more of such person's major life activities, (ii) has a record of such an impairment, or (iii) is regarded as having such an impairment."

The reference to subsection (iii), the United States Supreme Court in *Southeastern Community College v. Davis,* resolved that it was Congress' intent to prohibit discrimination against "a person who has a record of, or is regarded as having an impairment may at present have no actual incapacity at all." Arline's hospitalization for tuberculosis in 1957 establishes that she has a "record of such an impairment" within the meaning of Section 504 and is therefore handicapped.

The United States Supreme Court decided that both Arline's physical impairment, and its contagiousness resulted from the same underlying condition, tuberculosis. The two cannot be distinguished as argued by the Nassau County School Board. To do so, would permit the employer to justify discrimination by raising the distinction. Congress did not intend such a result. In fact, Congress is as concerned about the effects of the impairment on others as it is about the effects on the individual. That is why Congress amended the definition of the handicapped to embrace those individuals who are regarded as having a physical or mental impairment. In doing so, Congress acknowledged that the mounting rumors and fear about disability and disease are as handicapping as the actual impairments themselves.

The United States Supreme Court reached its decision on March 3, 1987 when it held that a person suffering from a contagious disease, (tuberculosis) is handicapped under Section 504 of the Rehabilitation Act of 1973. The Court stated, "The fact that some persons who have contagious diseases may pose a serious health threat to others under certain circumstances does not justify excluding from the coverage of the Act all persons with actual or perceived contagious diseases. Such exclusion would mean that those accused of being contagious would never have the opportunity to have their condition evaluated in light of medical evidence and a determination made as to whether they were otherwise qualified. Rather, they would be vulnerable to discrimination on the basis of mythology—precisely the type of injury Congress sought to prevent. We conclude that the fact that a person with a record of a physical impairment is also contagious does not suffice to remove that person from coverage under Section 504."

As to whether Arline is qualified to continue teaching elementary school children, this issue was remanded to the District Court for further findings of fact as to the duration and severity of Arline's condition, the probability that she will transmit the disease, whether Arline was contagious at the time she was discharged, and whether the School Board could have reasonably accommodated her. In making medical inquiries, the court should defer to the reasonable medical judgments of public health officials.

The Supreme Court opinion prevents employers from setting themselves up as judges defining what diseases are contagious. Justice Brennan, the senior justice who authored the opinion was joined by Justices White, Marshall, Blackman, Powell, Stevens, and O'Connor. Chief Justice Rehnquist and Justice Scalia dissented because they felt the decision went beyond Congress' intent when it passed the Rehabilitation Act.

Although the *Arline* case does not focus on AIDS discrimination, many believe lawsuits will be resolved in favor of AIDS employees. This is based on the reasoning that AIDS is a disabling illness and based on current medical opinion AIDS is not contagious on casual contact, unlike tuberculosis which may be.

The bottom line appears to be that an employer cannot justify discrimination by contending it was the contagious nature of the disease and not the disabling effect which resulted in a handicapped employee's dismissal. If an individual has been or is now impaired, or is regarded as being impaired then it matters not whether the impairment which has substantially curtailed his or her activities was caused by the actual or perceived contagiousness or the actual or perceived disabling effect. Therefore, the fact that AIDS is contagious in certain respects does not mean that AIDS employees who are suffering from the disabling effects can be discriminated against solely on the reasoning that AIDS is contagious.

Judgment for Arline.

A MODEL FOR A COMPANY POLICY ON AIDS

Employers should take heed to educate themselves concerning the legal and medical issues and then develop a company policy to deal with AIDS employees incorporating an educational program such as the one set forth below.

1. Equal treatment will be accorded to AIDS employees with regard to their right to work and to seek promotion and raises and their right to be protected from discrimination and harassment by managers and co-workers.
2. An employee suspected of having AIDS will not be approached and no statement will be made regarding the suspected illness to co-workers. This guards against an invasion of privacy suit as well as a defamation action should the hunch turn out to be false.
3. A well-informed human resource staff will be provided which will be trained in dealing with all aspects of the AIDS dilemma. AIDS employees will be encouraged to confide in the human resource staff. The staff will help AIDS victims cope with unfriendly co-workers and protect the victim from harassment and/or discrimination through education and then disciplinary action, if necessary. The human resource staff will explore the possibility of flexible work hours or permitting the AIDS victim to work at home through a computer terminal and modem. The future course of the AIDS virus will be discussed with the AIDS employee by explaining the medical and disability benefits available. A

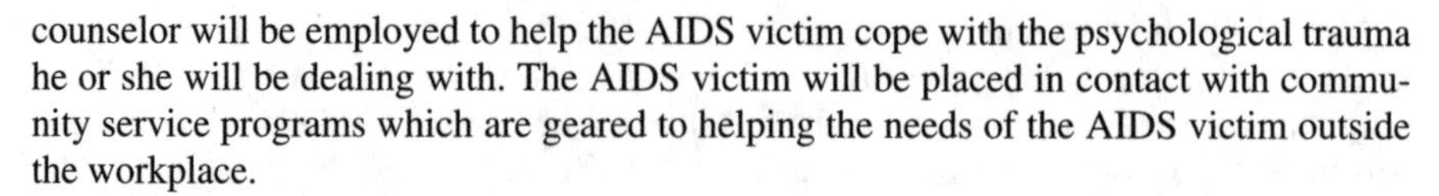
counselor will be employed to help the AIDS victim cope with the psychological trauma he or she will be dealing with. The AIDS victim will be placed in contact with community service programs which are geared to helping the needs of the AIDS victim outside the workplace.

4. Confidentiality will be extended to information received by the company from the AIDS employee. This information will not be placed in the AIDS employee's personnel file, but may be documented in the employee's medical file with consent. This procedure guards against an invasion of privacy.
5. An educational program will be implemented consisting of booklets and other printed information on the causes of AIDS, working with AIDS or with someone who has AIDS. Seminars may be set up where a physician and psychologist are invited to discuss the physical and emotional consequences of AIDS and how to deal with them. The theory behind the program will be to create a comfortable atmosphere in which both AIDS employees and their co-workers can function productively.
6. Co-workers will be educated and counseled to dispel their fear of catching the AIDS virus from casual contact. An employee's refusal to work with an AIDS victim will not be given preferential treatment beyond the normal request for a transfer.
7. Those employees who hold positions of leadership in the community will be encouraged to espouse their concern for the need for AIDS awareness.
8. An employer's right to dismiss an AIDS employee is restricted to evaluating the employee's caliber of work. If the quality of the AIDS victim's work has suffered due to excessive absences and/or a weakened physical condition, the employer may legally exclude the employee from the workplace by placing him or her on disability. Prior to this, the employer will sit down with the AIDS victim and discuss the health benefits the company will provide.

REVIEW QUESTIONS

1. Define AIDS.
2. Is AIDS a contagious disease?
3. Can a person having a contagious disease be discriminated against?
4. Is AIDS considered to be a disability?
5. Can a co-worker refuse to work with an AIDS employee?
6. Do the co-workers have the right to know if an employee has AIDS?
7. If management discloses that an employee has AIDS, what recourse does the AIDS employee have?
8. Is harassing an AIDS employee actionable?
9. If false rumors are spread stating that an employee has AIDS, on what principle of law would the employee sue?
10. Can AIDS ever be considered a bona fide occupational qualification?
11. Chalk, a teacher, was removed from the classroom once the school learned that she tested positive for AIDS. Chalk argued that the disease is not communicable. What was the result? *Chalk v. U.S. District Court,* 840 F.2d 701 (9th Cir. 1988)

12. Ronald Senter tested HIV positive in May 1986. In March 1991, he was diagnosed with AIDS. He died in January 1993. As owner of Car Parts Distribution Center, Senter participated in the Automotive Wholesaler's Association of New England Health Benefits Plan (Association). In October 1990, the Association amended its plan to limit the amount a person with AIDS could collect to $25,000. All other illnesses remained capped at $1 million. Senter contended that the Association limited its AIDS benefits after he began submitting claims in 1989. He felt this action amounted to discrimination based on his disability. What was the result? *Car Parts Distribution Center, Inc. v. Automotive Wholesaler's Association,* 37 F.3d 112 (1st Cir. 1994)

13. The Eastern Nebraska Community Office of Retardation instituted a mandatory policy of AIDS testing for all its employees. Glover argued that the testing was an invasion of privacy. What was the result? *Glover v. Nebraska Community Office of Retardation,* 867 F.2d 461 (8th Cir. 1989)

14. The law firm of Kohn, Nast & Graf searched the office of one of its employees, Doe, and found a letter from an AIDS organization discussing his condition. Is this an invasion of privacy? *Doe, Esquire, v. Kohn, Nast, & Graft, P.C.,* 862 F.Supp. 1310 (E.D. Pa. 1994)

15. Leckelt was a male hospital nurse. After he had undergone an HIV test, the hospital insisted that he disclose the result. Leckelt refused. The hospital fired him because his refusal prevented the hospital from having the information it felt necessary to insure the safety of its patients and staff. Leckelt claimed that he was discriminated against because of the perception that he might be HIV positive. What was the result? *Leckelt v. Board of Commissioners,* 909 F.2d 820 (5th Cir. 1990)

16. Referring to the case on pp. 449, should people with AIDS be classified as victims deserving of accommodation, or should they be treated as alcoholics and drug addicts who are responsible for their actions?

17. In the case on pp. 450, should the tort of invasion of privacy have been extended to AIDS victims?

18. In the case on pp. 452, if a decision could not be reached concerning whether AIDS was contagious, would the decision have been different?

19. In the case on pp. 454, if Arline has AIDS, would the decision have been the same?

20. Is it ethical to spend so much money on research for one illness—AIDS—rather than spreading the money around?

Rehabilitation Act of 1973

Sec. 706 Definitions.

For the purposes of this chapter:

(7) (A) Except as otherwise provided in subparagraph (B), the term "individual with handicaps" means any individual who (i) has a physical or mental disability which for such individual constitutes or results in a substantial handicap to employment and (ii) can reasonably be expected to benefit in terms of employability from vocational rehabilitation services.

(B) Subject to the second sentence of this subparagraph, the term "individual with handicaps" means any person who (i) has a physical or mental impairment which substantially limits one or more of such person's major life activities, (ii) has a record of such an impairment, or (iii) is regarded as having such an impairment. For the purposes of section 793 of this title as such section relates to employment, such term does not include any individual who is an alcoholic or drug abuser whose current use of alcohol or drugs prevents such individual from performing the duties of the job in question or whose employment, by reason of such current alcohol or drug abuse, would constitute a direct threat to property or the safety of others.

(C)(i) For purposes of title V, the term "individual with handicaps" does not include an individual who is currently engaging in the illegal use of drugs, when a covered entity acts on the basis of such use.

Sec. 791 (501) Employment of Handicapped Individuals.

(b) Federal agencies; affirmative action program plans

Each department, agency, and instrumentality (including the United States Postal Service and the Postal Rate Commission) in the executive branch shall, within one hundred and eight days after September 26, 1973, submit to the Office of Personnel Management and to the Committee an affirmative action program plan for the hiring, placement, and advancement of individuals with handicaps in such department, agency, or instrumentality. Such plan shall include a description of the extent to which and methods whereby the special needs of employees with handicaps are being met.

Sec. 793 (503) Employment Under Federal Contracts.

(a) Amount of contracts or subcontracts; provision for employment and advancement of qualified individuals with handicaps; regulations

Any contract in excess of $2,500 entered into by any Federal department or agency for the procurement of personal property and nonpersonal services (including construction) for the United States shall contain a provision requiring that, in employing persons to carryout such contract the party contracting with the United States shall take affirmative action to employ and advance in employment qualified individuals with handicaps as defined in section 706(7) of this title.

PART IV

Employment Regulation

CHAPTER 20 Labor Law

HISTORY

In the 1800s, the working class was divided by race, religion, gender, national origin, politics, and skill. These are the same concerns that survived for more than one hundred years and are only now being addressed. In the mid-1800s, the beginnings of an attempt to organize among skilled laborers took place.

The northern United States had no tradition of feudalism or aristocracy. There was a movement toward industrial and urban dominance similar to what already existed in England. The southern United States exhibited some of these tendencies, but not to the extent as in Europe. In 1850, in the United States 20 percent of the labor was in manufacturing and 64 percent in agriculture. In comparison, England had 22 percent of its labor force in agriculture and 43 percent in manufacturing, mining, and construction. In England, 61 percent of the population lived in urban areas compared with 15 percent in the United States.

In 1860, there were 4 million slaves in the south and 385,000 slave owners out of 12.3 million people in fifteen states embracing slavery. Because of the excessive control over slaves by their owners, it was hard for the slaves to achieve any form of independence. The Southerners who did not own slaves often lived on the fringes of the market economy, and their main goal was sustenance.

Artisans, such as weavers, shoemakers, and framework knitters proliferated in the manufacturing field. By the middle of the 1800s, they were the largest component of manufacturing workers and ranked third behind agricultural workers and domestic servants.

In the early 1800s, the head of the household was the individual who monitored the work of a small group of family members devoted to the production of a single product such as clothing, shoes, etc. As the 1800s rolled on, specialty merchants undertook the manufacturing component, to the dismay of the household artisans. Approaching 1850, the movement continued as retail merchants abandoned their shops in favor of concentrating on wholesale production.

Wholesale manufacturers prospered as a result of their hiring of cheap labor and the exploitation of the common laborer. Their profits came at the expense of the common laborer, thus leading to a revolt among laborers in 1860 in the form of a strike.

Women's work consisted of attending to the common chores of the household, raising the children, tending gardens, and sewing clothing and linens. A number engaged in piecemeal work derived from spinning, weaving, and the like. Although the work was essential, the value placed on women's work was low. Their identity was defined in terms of their families, with only 15 percent working outside the home. Many of the women who worked found employment in the garment industry. They were overworked, underpayed, lived in poverty, and had no job security. New York became the London of America, with sweatshops proliferating. Also, young women were employed as domestic servants and were thus provided with food and shelter. Women suffered from low wages, dependency status, low stature, and female subordination. Many women worked in isolation so that there was no opportunity to organize. Also, their employers were a multitude of small businesses with no common link.

In the early 1800s, men worked as carpenters and bricklayers, and as tailors and leather workers. Later there was a movement to larger, machineless factories and then to machine factories and workshops of all sizes. Skilled artisans suffered as larger concerns hired unskilled workers. As a result, wages were depressed, hours of work increased, and job security diminished.

UNIONS

The first unions were organized during the economic depression of the 1820s. The unions were against excessive taxation, prison labor as competition, and debtors' prisons. Unions stood for public schools and mechanics' liens, which tie up assets of those who refuse to pay their bills. Unions became politically active in their fight to limit the workday to ten hours. They argued that the government, instead of protecting the poor and middle-class workers, protected the upper class, employers, and management by allowing them to maintain and at times increase their economic advantage.

In 1833, the general trade union was formed from 20 to 30 percent of Manhattan's workforce. Skilled and unskilled workers became members. By 1836, two-thirds of New York City workers and 15 percent of the entire American labor force were union members. Strikes were the unions' main weapon against employers. Strikes involved women as well as men—female bookbinders as well as male shoemakers. The general trade union admitted women to membership. Many other trade unions did not extend membership to women and blacks. Non admittance into unions impeded any rise in economic stature and public recognition of women and blacks.

Their work in a low paying non union trade reinforced their meager standard of living, which resulted in their continued economic dependence on men and whites respectively.

In the 1830s as employers gained wealth, employees and artisans, now known as independent contractors, remained poor. Occupational solidarity was fostered. Unions were stronger in urban arenas, but the economic depression hurt unions as wages were lowered and unemployment increased. Ugly race riots developed in the 1830s and 1840s. This tension fueled racism, ignited violence, and increased unskilled job competition between blacks and whites. Skilled white craftsmen were replaced by immigrant and black laborers. As a result, ethnic and religious discrimination became pervasive.

The Democratic party was formed with workers as its constituents. Tammany Hall is an example at the local level of New York; it was a political machine run by Boss Tweed. Boss Tweed and his Tammany Hall cronies fell because of the eight-hour-day protest strike of 1872. The eight-hour-day was instituted temporarily pursuant to the eight-hour bill for government workers in 1868. It was ineffective because of the lack of enforcement provisions and clauses permitting longer hours by mutual agreement between employers and employees.

In 1868, Tweed accepted an eight-hour mandate from the New York state legislature. In 1871, the stonecutters called an eight-hour-day strike along with eight thousand sympathizers, demanding enforcement of the legislature's ruling. In 1872, there was a massive rise of labor and a decline of Tweed's hold on a hundred thousand workers. He fell out of power, and the eight-hour day was achieved for the moment.

In the meantime, employers used subordinate labor to squeeze profit margins through mechanization, division of labor, task simplification, mass production, and increased competition. Employers exercised greater control over semiskilled and unskilled labor. There was an increased concentration in economic power among large capitalized corporations. With it came both a greater movement toward urban areas, where people worked in close proximity, and the growth of the white-collar worker, who provided a service.

Agriculture, which contained 64 percent of the workforce in 1850, contained only 38 percent in 1900 and now contains a miniscule 3.9 percent. The beginning of the twentieth century marked the arrival of immigrants from southern and eastern Europe, whereas before northern and central European immigrants provided the bulk of the labor force. The Industrial Age from 1840 to 1890 left an indelible mark on America, predominantly after the Civil War. As corporations grew larger, antiunionism sentiment mounted. Employers used immigrant labor for their seven-day operations. Manual operations decreased with the increase in the use of automated machinery, much like today as the computer decreases the need for manual office labor.

The depression of the 1870s reinforced class structure and division. Strikes became more violent. On May 1, 1866, May Day protest marches were held across the country in support of union recognition and wage increases. Between 1870 and 1890, the Knights of Labor recruited two or three million members. They favored arbitration to striking. Their membership was based on factory workers and was open to blacks and women, but not to the Chinese. By 1886, there were 60,000 blacks and 65,000 women, each group representing about 10 percent of the union membership.

After the depression of the 1870s, corporate mergers began. From 1879 to 1893, horizontal mergers took place, that is, mergers between companies performing the same business operation. From 1898 to 1904, vertical combinations flourished with the integration of suppliers with manufacturers, manufacturers with wholesalers and in some instances manufacturers with retailers. Giant corporations monopolized key businesses, such as oil, tobacco, steel, and sugar. The year 1911 marked a setback for large monopolistic companies with the breakup of Standard Oil, but this deterrence did not last long. In the 1920s mergers resumed. The 1980s and mid-1990s has seen a resurgence of merger mania, but now the rationale is to enable American-based companies to be more competitive in the global business environment.

Conspiracies and force were used to break strikes. In the 1860s and 1870s, unions were local, lacking a national power base. Workers were divided by religion, race, ethnicity, politics, and class. Employers used this situation to divide them. The ignorance of workers refusing to unite because of their differences made it easier for employers to maintain the upper hand.

In 1870, domestic servants were the largest occupational group. Class supremacy ruled. Women tried to organize, but they were barred from unions. In 1868, Susan B. Anthony started the Working Women's Association, but it failed.

When unions called a strike, employers used black workers as strikebreakers. The white workers organized the Ku Klux Klan to instill fear into those black workers who took union jobs.

The American Federation of Labor leaders and their workers opposed immigration for economic rather than ethnic or racial motives; they were afraid of losing their jobs. The advent of railways, buses, and streetcars enabled the middle class to move to the suburbs. The 1920s were prosperous years for many, but the final year in the decade of the roaring twenties marked the beginning of the longest depression in United States history.

NATIONAL LABOR RELATIONS ACT

The National Labor Relations Act (NLRA) was enacted in 1935 to insure the right of employees to organize and participate in unions without fear of reprisals from employers.

The Civil War helped people overcome prejudices within their ranks. Catholics fought alongside Protestants in the North, and slave owners and those against slavery fought together in the South. This effect was short-lived, though, and certainly did not radiate out to the rest of the population.

In 1886, Debs' Knights of Labor and Gompers's AFL tried to form the United Labor Party to gain political clout. The movement failed. While it had some success in small towns, it came and went quickly.

The high level of employer opposition together with military, political, and judicial backing made recognition difficult for unions.

One of the most famous strikes occurred in 1890. The Homestead strike was called in response to wage reduction and open shop. A twenty-week lockout ensued. Sixty workers were wounded, and nine workers and seven Pinkerton guards were killed. The town was occupied by eight thousand Pennsylvania National Guardsmen. Strikebreakers were brought in to open the steel mills.

Chief Judge Payton declared that the union advisory committee did "unlawfully, falsely, maliciously and traitorously conjure, imagine and intend to raise and levy war, insurrection and rebellion against the Commonwealth of Pennsylvania."

In 1894, a strike against the Pullman Railway Carriage workshop sidelined twenty-five thousand railway cars. Disruption of interstate commerce was legal grounds for terminating a boycott, so an injunction ordered the strikers back to work. Troups numbering twelve thousand went to Chicago to confront workers. Hundreds were injured, and many died. The Knights of Labor union leader, Eugene Debs, was arrested. Debs asked for a sympathy strike from the AFL. Samuel Gompers, its leader, declined to strike and issued a call for all workers to immediately return to work. The strike was not successful and was a major setback for the unions.

AFL

In 1886, the American Federation of Labor (AFL) was founded by Samuel Gompers. It was an outgrowth of the Federation of Organized Trades and Labor Unions of 1881. The AFL survived the depression of 1893 to 1897. After the depression, from 1893 to 1897, the Knights of Labor appeared and faded out. Gompers faced a formidable foe in the Sherman Antitrust Act. Instead of being used against large corporations, it was used against unions to break them up, as they were held to be in violation of the Sherman Act. By 1903, it had two million members. By 1918, membership increased 50 percent to 3 million. The AFL did not try for social transformation as had the Knights of Labor; its goals were home ownership, job security, and decent wages. The AFL's intent was to organize collectively to safeguard mutual interests. The AFL's strategy was to accommodate corporate America by rising with it instead of against it. The Knights of Labor paid the price for its unrealistic process of a power struggle.

In 1909, the AFL developed political interests to support Democratic candidates. The AFL did not approve of the confrontational tactics used in the Homestead and Pullman strikes. Therefore, it adopted a more civilized approach than doing battle. The AFL lobbied for the Clayton Act of 1914 to reduce federal use of injunctions in labor disputes. The Clayton Act provided, " . . . Labor of human beings is not a community or article of commerce. . . ." The federal government wanted to consult with Samuel Gompers to provide mediation in industrial conflicts. Union's involvement in the World War I effort earned them state approval. Gompers fought for a reduction in hours worked per day. He said, "We have secured the eight-hour workday not only as a basic principle but as a fact." Gompers opposed racism and advocated equal pay for blacks and women.

In 1903, the Women's Trade Union League was formed with the aim of recruiting women into the AFL. In 1909, women called a strike against the New York garment industry. Other strikes ensued during the years 1912 through 1922, including the W. Lawrence Textile Strike.

Socialists had solid support in the AFL until 1920, when the attraction of the Democratic party reduced the Socialist party's influence in the AFL. Meantime, the Socialist Labor Party, created in 1877 became a force from 1901 to 1912. It had strong support because it opposed the greed and power of the corporations. In 1912, the Socialist Labor Party had 118,000 members and provided 6.9 percent of the presidential vote that year. Corporations' antisocialism drives were stymied when labor shifted its support to the Democrats. The Democrats had greater influence and political clout and did not have the negative attributes connected with socialism.

The AFL, which had represented predominantly white skilled workers, now embraced all workers, with its support for the eight-hour day.

In 1916, the eight-hour-day situation resurfaced. To head off a national railway strike, Congress passed an eight-hour bill. The year 1916 set a record for the number of strikes.

Employers battled unions by bringing in strikebreakers between 1916 and 1922; 1.5 million to 4 million workers went on strike each of those years. An abundance of employment gave workers the confidence to strike. Union membership doubled from 2.6 million in 1915 to 5.1 million in 1920. Recent immigrants, numbering 396,000, made up 7.8 percent of the total membership. Immigrants were united and determined to fight. Still, most attempts at organizing a union failed. Key industrial sectors were without unions. This failure was attributed to the power of corporate America with their political, judicial, and military connections.

The 1929 depression led to widespread unemployment, poverty, and insecurity. In the 1920s, wages and salaries rose 45 percent. Rural isolation ended with the mass production of the automobile, which gave people independence. Agricultural workers suffered with the influx of illegal Mexican workers. In 1929, 35 to 40 percent of all non-farm-workers were poor. Between 1930 and 1934, one million farms were repossessed.

To diminish the appeal of unions and to build up loyalty, companies reduced turnover and promoted security, reliability, and efficiency through the establishment of employee representatives, stock purchase programs, evening classes, old age benefits, and time off with pay for illness, family deaths, and holidays.

Collective bargaining failed to be achieved in the 1920s. As a result, union workers took action. However, the courts ruled against them by issuing injunctions against strikers, outlawing secondary boycotts, and restricting peaceful protests. Open shop practices of hiring nonunion workers flourished; companies also brought in unskilled labor to act as strikebreakers. Active union members were blacklisted in the coal industry, meaning that no company would hire them. Unemployment, which had reached a low of 1.6 percent in 1929, skyrocketed to 25.2 percent in the mid-1930s. Popular protests against unemployment ensued. The growth of the Communist party began. If traditional leadership did not respond to the needs of the workers, they would turn to radicals for support.

As a result, the following measures were passed: social security, unemployment insurance, minimum wage and hour requirements, prohibition against child labor, and the right of workers to unionize and collectively bargain. Initially these measures did not have legislative enforcement. They were defeated by the companies, but workers saw a glimmer of light. Many strikes resulted with regard to the conflict over labor supply. Closed shops were legitimized. Wages increased. Unions reorganized.

CIO

The Congress for Industrial Organization (CIO) organized auto, steel, and electrical workers. The CIO broke down barriers of race and class. By 1940, the CIO had 4 million members.

Arbitration

In the second half of the nineteenth century, railroad employees in the United States formed brotherhoods, i.e., forerunners of unions. They exercised their collective strength through a series of strikes. In response to this, the Arbitration Act of 1888 was enacted. It prevented voluntary mediation between employers and employees, and it also set up an investigative board to discern the reason for the strike. However, the board did not have the power to impose its decision upon the parties. The merits of arbitration were soon recognized as being an inexpensive and expeditious method to resolve disputes, but enforcement of arbitration decisions was not forthcoming for a long time. The Erdman Act of 1898 provided for federal intervention in labor disputes of industries vital to the United States through the use of a federal mediator. The weakness of this Act is the reliance on voluntary enforcement of the arbitrator's determination.

SHERMAN ACT

Back in the early 1900s, monopolistic companies totally dominated labor. This trend was accepted more in Great Britain than in America, where it led to some unrest. Wage differences widened between skilled and unskilled workers. Employers exhibited a weak sense of responsibility and began to hoard their wealth. Single women worked, while married women stayed home.

The Sherman Antitrust Act, enacted in 1890, was initially applied to any activity, which interrupted the free flow of commerce. The term "every business combination" came into use to include the unions. Whereas citizens had hoped that the Sherman Act would be used to lessen the power of monopolies, instead it became a tool for big business to use against its employees.

The Clayton Act enacted in 1914, with good intent toward labor, exacerbated the problem by strengthening the application of the Sherman Act against labor. Whereas before, applications for injunctive relief rested only with the federal courts, under the Clayton Act employers themselves could file an application against their employees.

The language of Sections 6 and 20 of the Clayton Act seemed to invalidate the use of injunctive relief under the Sherman Act with regard to labor. Section 6 provided that employees' work is not goods available in commerce and that labor unions and their members are not illegal combinations acting in restraint of free trade. Section 20 went on to provide that injunctive relief is not to be granted in a labor dispute unless damage to property was intended. The language could not be clearer that Congress's intent was that the Sherman Act and its remedy of injunctive relief should not apply to labor. However, the courts carved many exceptions by claiming the Clayton Act does not apply to individuals who strike because they are no longer employees, to union organizers because they are not employees, and to employees who sign yellow-dog contracts.

Yellow Dog Contract

A yellow-dog contract is a stipulation mandated by the employer that the employee will not join a union as a condition of continued employment. Yellow-dog contracts were upheld by the courts in strict opposition to the legal principle of interference with contractual business relations, which is an actionable tort, meaning that an individual can sue for money damages. In any event, this doctrine was overlooked and yellow-dog contracts were in effect until the passage of the Railway Labor Act of 1926 and the Federal Anti-Injunction Act of 1932.

RAILWAY LABOR ACT

The Railway Labor Act of 1926 outlawed yellow-dog contracts by prohibiting an agreement of nonunion membership as a condition to employment. It strengthened the right of unions to strike as long as the work stoppage and related protest were peaceful. The Act instituted the National Mediation Board (NMB) to encourage voluntary mediation between management and labor. If no resolution could be reached, then the NMB would propose binding arbitration. If agreed, both sides would be bound by its decision.

NORRIS LAGUARDIA ACT

This activity against labor continued until 1932, when the Federal Anti-Injunctive Act, more commonly known as the Norris LaGuardia Act, was passed. Its first section relieved federal courts of the power to grant injunctions in labor disputes, with limited exceptions, thus marking the end of the use of the Sherman and Clayton Acts' injunctive relief against labor.

In 1935, with the passage of the NLRA, also known as the Wagner Act, unions organized with the power of enforcement. Certified bargaining agreements were forthcoming. Company attempts at domination were stymied with the creation of the National Labor Relations Board, with investigatory and enforcement power being placed at its discretion.

THE FUTURE FOR UNIONS

The struggle waged by unions was certainly profitable for their members. From the 1940s until recently, skilled laborers have enjoyed a relatively high standard of living. However, many businesses have now taken advantage of lower living costs and cheaper office space outside the United States. With the emergence of the General Agreement of Tariffs and Treaties (GATT) and the North American Free Trade Agreement (NAFTA), more jobs especially those in manufacturing, are moving to Mexico and overseas. The power of the unions has been crippled. In the past, unions were a major political force in the Democratic party. Now that is no longer true. Ironically, it was Democratic President Bill Clinton who signed off on the GATT, which signaled the death knell for the unions.

In the global marketplace, comparative advantage will prevail. If goods can be manufactured somewhere cheaper while suffering no loss in quality, then a company will move its operation there, and high-paying union jobs will be lost. The result will be the lowering of the standard of living for skilled, semiskilled, and unskilled laborers. The same phenomenon is happening even in the service sector with regard to certain data entry positions. Communications and computers are making this trend possi-

ble. Location is no longer a key factor. As a result, American office workers are working harder, lunch hours have been given up, longer hours are becoming the norm, and taking work home or coming into the office on weekends is commonplace. Workers had believed that using the computer to link their office with their home would cut their commuting time to three days a week. Instead, the office worker will still work a standard five-day week at the office. The computer link will enable the worker to work at home in the evenings and on the weekend.

Office workers and laborers are also being forced continually to reeducate and retrain themselves. Developing skills that cannot be easily and efficiently replicated overseas is vital to keeping one's job and maintaining a comfortable standard of living.

The following case addresses a number of issues; first, whether the statute of limitations is halted while a union member pursues a union remedy. Second, whether a six-month statute of limitations applies to an unfair labor practice claim. Third, whether the union breached its duty of fair representation. Fourth, whether the company breached the collective bargaining agreement by discharging her because of her race and her filing for workers' compensation.

CASE

Robinson v. Central Brass Mfg. Co.

818 F.Supp. 207 (N.D. Ohio 1991)

WHITE, Judge.

The Plaintiff alleges that the defendant Central Brass Manufacturing Company (Company) breached its collective bargaining agreement and that the defendant International Union, United Automobile, Aerospace and Agriculture Workers of America Local No. 1996 (Union) breached its duty of fair representation concerning plaintiff's discharge from employment. She also claims she was discharged because of her race and that she was terminated for filing a workers' compensation claim. The defendant Company filed a motion for summary judgment arguing that the plaintiff's Labor, Title VII and state claims are barred by the statute of limitations and the plaintiff has not stated a cause of action.

The United States Supreme Court held in *Del Costello v. International Brotherhood of Teamsters,* that claims for breach of contract against an employer and breach of duty of fair representation against a union are subject to the six month statute of limitations applicable to unfair labor practice claims under Section 10(b) of the National Labor Relations Act. The action accrues when the plaintiff discovers or in the exercise of reasonable diligence should have discovered the acts constituting the violation. It has been held that the six month statute of limitations is tolled during the time when internal union remedies are being pursued.

Plaintiff states that she received a letter from the Union informing her that the Bargaining Committee decided that her grievance had no merit and should not be advanced to arbitration and that she had the right to appeal this decision under the Local No. 1196 By-Laws, Article 16. Article 16 of the By-Laws provides:

> Section 1—Any member of this Local Union shall have the right to appeal.
>
> Section 2—Any member of the Local Union after first having exhausted every appeal step within the Local Union, may appeal from any action, decision or penalty to the International Executive Board and to the International

> Convention. However, the decision of the Local Union must be complied with and shall remain in effect until reversed or modified.
>
> Section 3—In no case shall a member appeal to a court or governmental agency for redress until he has exhausted his rights of appeal under the laws of the International Union and the By-Laws of this Local Union. Any violation thereof shall be cause for summary suspension or expulsion by the International Executive Board insofar as imposition of any such penalty is not inconsistent with any applicable laws.

Plaintiff appealed as instructed. A hearing was held in May, 1990. As of the present time, plaintiff has not received notice of a decision of her appeal.

The grievance procedure in the collective bargaining agreement provides in paragraph g,

> "In the event a grievance is not filed or processed within the time limits set forth in Paragraphs a, b, c, e, and f above, it shall be barred from further processing in the grievance and arbitration procedures."

Plaintiff's next step in the grievance procedure would have been pursuant to paragraph f requiring that arbitration must be requested within 10 working days from the Company's written answer in paragraph e. In other words the Union told the plaintiff her grievance was terminated as far as the Union was concerned but she could appeal this decision if she desired. However, the provision of the collective bargaining agreement bars her from processing her grievance any further.

Clayton v. International Union, United Automobile, Aerospace and Agricultural Implement Workers of America, dealt with the issue of the requirement of exhaustion of union remedies as prerequisite to filing a lawsuit. The Court held that where an internal union appeals procedure cannot result in reactivation of the employee's grievance or an award of complete relief, such as reinstatement, exhaustion will not be required with respect to a suit against the employer or the Union. In *Clayton,* the Court was asked to require exhaustion of internal union procedures. The procedures were created by the union and were not bargained for by the employer and union and were not mentioned in the collective bargaining agreement. The same facts apply to the case at bar. The Court in *Clayton* ruled that requiring exhaustion under those circumstances would be futile. The Court also disagreed with the union's argument that even if exhaustion is not required with respect to the employer it should be required with respect to union remedies. Since the plaintiff was suing the employer as well as the union, exhaustion should not be required because the Court would have to resolve two undesirable alternatives. If it stayed the action against the employer while the internal union appeals were being resolved it would actually be requiring exhaustion with respect to the employer, a result the Court ruled would violate national policy. If it permitted the action to proceed against the employer and tolled the statute of limitations as to the union until the union procedures had been exhausted, there could be two suits based on the same facts proceeding at different paces. So the Court decided the best procedure would be to allow the 301 action to proceed against the employer and the Union despite the plaintiff's failure to exhaust internal union remedies.

Based on *Clayton,* defendant Company argues that plaintiff did not have to exhaust her internal union remedies and should have filed her 301 action within six months of the time she received notice that the Union would not pursue her grievance.

The Court in *Smith v. Expert Automation, Inc.,* used the *Clayton* case as guidance in holding that the six months statute of limitations in a hybrid Labor Management Relation Act case is not tolled during the resolution of optional internal union proceedings. The Court noted that common sense suggests that the limitations period should not be tolled when a plaintiff can decide whether to exercise optional union remedies. It was reasoned that if this were allowed a plaintiff could opt for an internal union procedure insufficient to conclude in complete relief, and depending on the outcome, either relitigate the entire dispute or simply seek a judicial determination of the issue omitted from the union proceeding. This would be contrary to the public policy of favoring speedy resolution of labor disputes.

As previously stated, plaintiff's Union appeal could not have resulted in reinstatement of her grievance or reinstatement to her job. The letter she received from the Union informing her that her grievance would not be advanced to arbitration advised that she may appeal that decision under the Union By-Laws. The appeal was optional, not mandatory. The statute of limitations was not tolled. Therefore, the Company's motion to dismiss the 301 claim is granted.

The plaintiff has not responded to defendant's remaining arguments. Title VII requires that an action be filed with the federal court within 90 days from receipt of the notice of right to sue from the EEOC. This is not a jurisdictional prerequisite to filing a suit, but is analogous to a statute of limitations which is subject to waiver, estoppel and equitable tolling. Plaintiff has not argued that the statute of limitations is tolled or that equitable estoppel applies as to her Title VII claim. The evidence before the Court shows that defendant received notice of right to sue in February, 1990. Plaintiff should have received notice about that time. The action was filed October 24, 1990. In order to have filed within 90 days from the receipt of the notice of right to sue, the notice must have been received after July 26, 1990. Plaintiff is silent in this regard despite having benefit of defendant's argument and also failed to answer a request for admission on this question. Plaintiff could not claim to be relying on Article 16 of the By-Laws because she filed her EEOC charge in February, 1990 after she received the notice of right to appeal the denial of her grievance that concluded the letter warning her not to appeal to a government agency while her appeal was pending. Also, the Title VII case is a separate claim to which the Article 16 provisions have no application.

Plaintiff's fourth cause of action alleges that plaintiff was wrongfully terminated for filing a workers' compensation claim in violation of Ohio Revised Code Section 4123.90. Ohio Revised Code Section 4123.90 provides in pertinent part:

> "No employer shall discharge . . . or take any punitive action against any employee because the employee filed a claim or instituted, pursued or testified in any proceedings under the workers' compensation act for an injury or occupational disease which occurred in the course of or arising out of his employment with that employer. Any such employee may file an action in the common pleas court of the county of such employment. . . . The action shall be forever barred unless filed within one hundred eighty days immediately following the discharge . . . or punitive action taken, and no action may be instituted or maintained unless the employer has received written notice of a claimed violation of this paragraph within the ninety days immediately following the discharge . . . or punitive action taken."

Defendant has never received the required notice, nor was the action filed within 180 days from the date of discharge. Therefore, summary judgment must be granted on the state pendent claim.

A cause of action for race discrimination under 42 U.S.C. 1981 was also included. The United States Supreme Court in *Patterson v. McLean Credit Union,* held that 1981 protects the right to make and enforce contracts. But the right to make contracts extends only to the formation of a contract and not to problems that may arise during the employment. Section 1981 also protects against efforts to impede access to the Courts or obstruct nonjudicial methods of adjudicating disputes. Plaintiff's claim involves conduct after the formation of the employment relationship. It does not involve the impediment of access to the Courts. Plaintiff has not stated the existence of any nonjudicial remedies. The complaint alleges discharge on account of race. Discharge occurs after the formation of a contract and is not protected by 1981. Discriminatory treatment after one is employed also occurs after the formation of a contract. Plaintiff has not alleged failure to promote her on a account of race.

Accordingly the Company's motion for summary judgment is granted as to all of plaintiff's claims against it.

It is is ordered.
Judgment for Central Brass Mfg.

The issue in the next case is whether a company worker who is paid by a union to organize a chapter at the company forgoes his status as an employee under the National Labor Relations Act.

CASE

National Labor Relations Board v. Town & Country Electric, Inc., and Ameristaff Personnel Contractors, Ltd.

116 S.Ct. 450 (1995)

JUSTICE BREYER delivered the opinion of the Court.

Can a worker be a company's "employee," within the terms of the National Labor Relations Act, if, at the same time, a union pays that worker to help the union organize the company? We agree with the National Labor Relations Board that the answer is "yes."

The relevant background is the following: Town & Country Electric, Inc., a nonunion electrical contractor, wanted to hire several licensed Minnesota electricians for construction work in Minnesota. Town & Country (through an employment agency) advertised for job applicants, but it refused to interview 10 of 11 union applicants (including two professional union staff) who responded to the advertisement. Its employment agency hired the one union applicant whom Town & Country interviewed, but he was dismissed after only a few days on the job.

The members of the Union (the International Brotherhood of Electrical Workers, Locals 292 and 343) filed a complaint with the National Labor Relations Board claiming that Town & Country and the employment agency had refused to interview (or retain) them because of their union membership. An administrative law judge ruled in favor of the Union members, and the Board affirmed that ruling.

In the course of its decision, the Board determined that all 11 job applicants (including the two Union officials and the one member briefly hired) were "employees" as the Act defines that word. The Board recognized that under well-established law, it made no difference that the 10 members who were simply applicants were never hired. (statutory word "employee" includes job applicants, for otherwise the Act's prohibition of "discrimination in regard to hire" would "serve no function"). Neither, in the Board's view, did it matter (with respect to the meaning of the word "employee") that the Union members intended to try to organize the company if they secured the advertised jobs, nor that the Union would pay them while they set about their organizing. The Board then rejected the company's fact-based explanations for its refusals to interview or to retain these 11 "employees" and held that the company had committed "unfair labor practices" by discriminating on the basis of union membership.

The United States Court of Appeals for the Eighth Circuit reversed the Board. It held that the Board had incorrectly interpreted the statutory word "employee." In the court's view, that key word does not cover (and therefore the Act does not protect from antiunion discrimination) those who work for a company while a union simultaneously pays them to organize that company. For this threshold reason the court refused to enforce the Board's order.

Because other Circuits have interpreted the word "employee" differently, (paid union organizers can be "employees" protected by the Act); we granted certiorari. We now resolve the conflict in the Board's favor.

The National Labor Relations Act seeks to improve labor relations (eliminate the causes of

certain substantial obstructions to the free flow of commerce) in large part by granting specific sets of rights to employers and to employees. This case grows out of a controversy about rights that the Act grants to "employees," namely, rights "to self-organization, to form, join, or assist labor organizations, to bargain collectively . . . and to engage in other concerted activities for the purpose of collective bargaining or other mutual aid or protection." We granted certiorari to decide only that part of the controversy that focuses upon the meaning of the word "employee," a key term in the statute, since these rights belong only to those workers who qualify as "employees" as that term is defined in the Act.

The relevant statutory language is the following:

> "The term 'employee' shall include any employee, and shall not be limited to the employees of a particular employer, unless this subchapter explicitly states otherwise, and shall include any individual whose work has ceased as a consequence of, or in connection with, any current labor dispute or because of any unfair labor practice, and who has not obtained any other regular and substantially equivalent employment, but shall not include any individual employed as an agricultural laborer, or in the domestic service of any family or person at his home, or any individual employed by his parent or spouse, or any individual having the status of an independent contractor, or any individual employed as a supervisor, or any individual employed by an employer subject to the Railway Labor Act, as amended from time to time, or by any other person who is not an employer as herein defined."
>
> We must specifically decide whether the Board may lawfully interpret this language to include company workers who are also paid union organizers.

Finally, at least one other provision of the 1947 Labor Management Relations Act seems specifically to contemplate the possibility that a company's employee might also work for a union. This provision forbids an employer (say, the company) from making payments to a person employed by a union, but simultaneously exempts from that ban wages paid by the company to "any . . . employee of a labor organization, who is also an employee" of the company. If *Town & Country* is right, there would not seem to be many (or any) human beings to which this last phrase could apply.

If a paid union organizer might quit, leaving a company employer in the lurch, so too might an unpaid organizer, or a worker who has found a better job, or one whose family wants to move elsewhere. And if an overly zealous union organizer might hurt the company through unlawful acts, so might another unpaid zealot (who may know less about the law), or a dissatisfied worker (who may lack an outlet for his grievances). This does not mean they are not "employees."

Further, the law offers alternative remedies for Town & Country's concerns, short of excluding paid or unpaid union organizers from all protection under the Act. For example, a company disturbed by legal but undesirable activity, such as quitting without notice, can offer its employees fixed-term contracts, rather than hiring them "at will" as in the case before us; or it can negotiate with its workers for a notice period. A company faced with unlawful (or possibly lawful) activity can discipline or dismiss the worker, file a complaint with the Board, or notify law enforcement authorities (arsonist who is also union member is still an "employee," but may be discharged) (worker who was intoxicated while on duty, "came to work when he chose and . . . left the plant and his shift as he pleased," and utterly failed to perform his assigned duties, is still an "employee" protected under the Act). And, of course, an employer may as a rule limit the access of nonemployee union organizers to company property.

This is not to say that the law treats paid union organizers like other company employees in every labor law context. For instance, the Board states that, at least sometimes, a paid organizer may not share a sufficient "community of interest" with other employees (as to wages, hours, and working conditions) to warrant inclusion in the same bargaining unit (some confidential workers, although "employees," may be excluded from bargaining unit). We need not decide this matter. Nor do we express any view about any of the other matters Town & Country raised before the Court of Appeals, such as whether or not Town & Country's conduct (in refusing to interview, or to retain, "employees" who were on the union's payroll) amounted to an unfair labor practice. We hold only that the Board's construction of the word "employee" is lawful; that term does not exclude paid union organizers.

For these reasons the judgment of the Court of Appeals is vacated, and the case is remanded for further proceedings consistent with this opinion.

Judgment for NLRB.

In the next case, six employees were discharged after signing union authorization cards. They claim that the company's action of mass firing was antiunion and constituted an unfair labor practice.

CASE

Davis Supermarkets, Inc. v. N.L.R.B.

2 F.3d 1162 (D. C. Cir. 1993)

MIKVA, Judge.

Davis Supermarkets, a family-owned corporation engaged in the retail grocery business, owns and operates a supermarket in Greensburg, Pennsylvania, and a supermarket in Hempfield Township, Pennsylvania. The Greensburg store has been open for approximately thirty years. The United Steelworkers of America ("Steelworkers") has represented the Greensburg employees throughout the period relevant to this case. The Hempfield store opened in 1984. When the events giving rise to this case commenced in 1986, the Hempfield employees were unrepresented.

In March 1986, Local 23 launched a concerted organizing campaign in the Hempfield store, which employed more than one hundred men and women. Over the next few months, Donald Porter, an organizer for Local 23, met with various employees on and off the store's premises, urging them to sign authorization cards for Local 23. Some of the employees that he successfully recruited solicited authorization cards from other employees.

By April 19, 1986, a total of thirteen employees had signed authorization cards for Local 23. On that day, the Company summarily laid off eight workers, six of whom had signed authorization cards: Debra Defibaugh, Charlene Garris, Lance Good, Jennifer Hilty, Sharlene Shotts, and Sonia Welsh. In May, the Company fired or constructively fired two other employees who had signed cards, Larry Miller and Charles Miscovich. In July, the Company constructively discharged Linda Kunkle, who had also signed a card for Local 23.

On May 1, at two separate meetings with various employees of the Hempfield store, Bob Davis, the chairman of the Company's board of directors, told the assembled workers that he wanted them to sign authorization cards for the Steelworkers. After one of the meetings, a Steelworkers' representative from the Greensburg store and an official of that union handed out Steelworkers' contracts and authorization cards to the employees. Following the other meeting, two Steelworkers' representatives from the Greensburg facility distributed Steelworkers' contracts and cards.

Despite the Company's anti-Local 23 actions, Local 23 concluded that it had attained majority support among the Hempfield store's employees and issued a continuing request for bargaining on May 13, 1986. By May 24, 58 out of 109 employees had signed authorization cards for Local 23, and Local 23 had therefore actually achieved majority status. An election was scheduled for July 25. On July 22, however, Local 23, fearing a loss of support, requested cancellation of the election. This request was granted.

Meanwhile, a dispute raged between the Company and Local 23 pickets who were marching on the premises of the Hempfield store to protest unfair labor practices. On May 23, the Company filed a civil trespass suit in state court against the pickets and on May 28, acquired an injunction enjoining them from entering the store grounds and limiting them to three pickets at each parking lot entrance. On June 2, Local 23 filed a charge with the Board, alleging that the Company had unlawfully prevented them from picketing in the parking lot. On July 25, the NLRB's General Counsel issued a complaint alleging that the Company had violated section 8(a) (1) by denying Local 23 access to the premises and by maintaining the civil trespass suit.

In late July, Local 23 resumed picketing and some pickets distributed handbills to customers in the parking lot. The Company threatened them with arrest and, on August 2, a sheriff's deputy presented the pickets with a document indicating that they were not allowed in the parking lot. In late November, a number of laid-off employees of the Hempfield store resumed picketing on the sidewalk in front of the facility. The Company, despite the issuance of the General Counsel's complaint, obtained a court order from the state court requiring Local 23 and the pickets to show cause why they should not be held in contempt for violating the terms of the May 28 injunction.

Overall, between June 1986 and December 1987, the General Counsel filed four complaints that collectively alleged that the Company firings were motivated by anti-union animus, satisfied under the mass discharge theory. The employer can only overcome the showing of anti-union motivation by establishing, by a preponderance of the evidence, that "the discharge would have occurred in any event and for valid reasons."

The Board properly found that the Company failed to meet this burden. The Company proffered allegedly valid reasons why each of the six employees was fired on April 19. The Board confidently rejected all of these explanations as inconsistent and implausible. "Under the substantial evidence standard of 5 U.S.C. 706(2) (E), our function is to determine only whether the agency could fairly and reasonably find the facts as it did." Because the Board's findings were clearly reasonable, we see no basis for overturning its conclusions. We therefore uphold the Board's determination that the six April 19 layoffs constituted unfair labor practices in violation of section 8(a) (1) and 8(a) (3) of the Act.

Judgment for NLRB.

In the following case, a black civil association picketed a local butcher shop until the shop employed a black resident. The store requested a black butcher from the union. The civic association continued its protest, claiming that the black butcher was not a neighborhood resident. The store requested an injunction to stop the protest.

Stoller et al. v. Citizens' Civic Affairs Committee, Inc., et al.

19 N.Y.S. 2d 597
(Sup.Ct. Kings Cty. 1940)

DALY, Justice.

This is an application for an injunction enjoining and restraining the defendants from picketing the plaintiffs' store with signs and handbills distributed to the public, calculated and intended to persuade patrons from patronizing the plaintiffs' store.

The plaintiffs conduct a butcher store in a neighborhood populated largely by people of the Negro race. On or about the 27th day of February, 1940, and continuing up to the present, the defendants Eugenia Wright and Alexander Clayborn and other persons alleged to be members of the codefendant Citizens' Civic Affairs Committee, Inc., visited the plaintiffs' store and place of business and demanded that the plaintiffs employ Negroes from the members of said Citizens' Civic Affairs Committee, Inc. In their store, the plaintiffs employ a butcher who is a member in good standing of the Meat Cutters Union, Local 342, American Federation of Labor. After having pointed out to the defendants that it was impossible to breach their existing agreement with the union, the plaintiffs went to the union officials, and asked the union officials to give them a man from the union, who was a Negro, to work as a butcher in their place of business. The union officials complied with this request and the plaintiffs have an employee at the present time, working in the store in question, who is of the Negro race and a member of the Meat Cutters local. From the affidavit of Eugenia Wright, the only objection the Citizens' Civic Affairs Committee seem to have is that the plaintiffs have not employed in their store a member of the Negro race who is a resident in the neighborhood and a member of the defendant Committee. In other words, this is not a case involving racial discrimination. Moreover, on or about March 2, 1940, the picket line was called off when the plaintiff Stoller told the defendant Eugenia Wright that if she had a butcher, he would put one right to work. However, she furnished her own son who had not the slightest experience in the butcher trade.

Upon all the facts in this case presented by the affidavits of both sides, I find that there is no labor dispute existing between the plaintiffs and the defendants. I therefore grant the motion of the plaintiffs for a temporary injunction restraining the defendants from picketing and distributing handbills and carrying signs calculated to interfere with patrons and members of the public seeking to patronize plaintiffs' store. Settle order on two days' notice. Bond fixed in the sum of $500.

Judgment for Stoller.

The following case addresses the dispute between two unions as to which union should be certified as the sole collective bargaining agent for the company's employees.

CASE

Euclid Candy of New York, Inc. v. Summa et al.

19 N.Y.S. 2d 382 (Sup. Ct. Kings Cty. 1940)

DALY, Justice.

The plaintiff moves to enjoin the officers and members of the Candy and Confectionary Workers Union, Local No. 452, Greater New York A. F. of L., from calling or continuing a strike against plaintiff, picketing its premises, interfering with its business, officers, employees and customers, and for other relief.

Originally, there was a controversy between two unions, namely, the union against which relief is sought herein, which hereafter will be referred to as Local 452, and Independent Confectionary Workers Union, which hereafter will be referred to as the Independent Union, as to which should be the sole collective bargaining agent for plaintiff's employees. By an agreement dated February 15, 1940, to which the plaintiff and the two unions were parties, it was agreed that an election be held under the auspices of the National Labor Relations Board for the purpose of certifying the sole collective bargaining representative for the plaintiff's employees. It was there also provided that the union which the National Labor Relations Board certifies shall be recognized as the sole bargaining representative for plaintiff's employees, and that the two unions would exchange assurances of no strikes of one against the other during the term of the contract to be entered into between the plaintiff and the union certified. On February 21, 1940, said agreement was modified to the effect that the contract to be entered into by the certified union and the plaintiff should provide for a closed shop, to wit, "that all employees of Euclid will be required, during the period of said contract to become members of the Union certified as the bargaining agency." On February 29, 1940, an election was held by secret ballot, and the National Labor Relations Board certified that the Independent Union had been designated by plaintiff's employees as their sole collective bargaining agency. Thereupon the plaintiff entered into negotiations with the union so certified, and an agreement was made and executed, dated March 6, 1940. This contract, in accordance with the closed shop provision of the agreement dated February 21, 1940, provided that "All employees excepting clerical workers, etc., shall be members of the Union. Each employee who is not now a member of the Union shall be required to join the Union within one week from the date of the execution of this agreement; and Euclid agrees that it will continue in its employ only members of the Union in good standing." In accordance with the terms of this contract, the following notice was posted on the bulletin board:

> "Under the terms of the contract entered into on March 6th, 1940, with the Independent Confectionary Workers Union all employees of the Euclid who are not members of the above union are required to join on or before March 13, 1940.
>
> "Please take further notice, that on March 14th, 1940, all employees will be required to show that they are members of the Independent Confectionary Workers Union, in good standing, before being permitted to report for work.
>
> The Management"

Some thirty-one employees, members of Local 452, refused to comply and went out on strike and began to picket the premises.

Upon this application the Independent Union has appeared and joined the plaintiff in its prayer for relief. It has filed an answer containing a cross-complaint against Local 452, in which it prays for injunctive relief restraining the local from unlawfully attempting to induce plaintiff to breach its aforesaid contract, and for other relief.

Although in the course of the oral argument counsel for Local 452 conceded that in this controversy no labor dispute was involved, he nevertheless contends in his memorandum that the instant controversy is a labor dispute. Notwithstanding the broad language of the statute in defining a labor dispute, the controversy existing between the parties herein does not, in the court's opinion, come within the purview of said statute. There was a labor dispute prior to the certification by the National Labor Relations Board. This certification, following an election duly held by that Board pursuant to the agreements above referred to brought that labor dispute to a conclusion. It would be anomalous, under these circumstances, to say that the labor dispute still exists merely because a minority of employees, apparently dissatisfied with the result (the National Labor certification), is unwilling to abide by the will of the majority. There being no labor dispute, the sole purpose of the minority union would seem to be to induce the breach of the contract which the certified union entered into with the plaintiff, and which contained the provision for a closed shop, pursuant to the agreement entered into by both unions prior to the election. The plaintiff has thus been placed in a dilemma. If it accedes to the demand of the minority union it breaches its contract with the certified union. If it attempts to abide by the terms of said contract, as it did in the instant case, it has a strike on its hands, and picketing and the other activities that go with it. It seems to the court that since the picketing by the minority union is, in effect, an attempt to force the breach of the agreement which was entered into under the circumstances above described, this court of equity should prevent the irreparable injury which flows therefrom.

Judgment for Euclid Candy.

REVIEW QUESTIONS

1. Why did workers have so much difficulty organizing?
2. How was the Sherman Antitrust Act used against workers?
3. When was the first union formed?
4. What is beneficial about unions?
5. How has the GATT and NAFTA affected unions?
6. Why did unions switch their political support from the Labor Party to the Democratic Party?
7. Why was the American Federation of Labor successful?
8. Explain the significance of the Homestead strike.
9. Define yellow-dog contract.
10. Explain the function of the National Labor Relations Board.
11. The Florida Industrial Commission refused to pay unemployment benefits to an employee in accordance with state law because he filed an unfair labor practice charge with the National Labor Relations Board against the Commission. How should the conflict between state law and federal labor law be resolved? *Nash v. Florida Industrial Commission,* 389 U.S. 235 (1967)
12. The City of Los Angeles refused to renew a franchise until the company's labor dispute was resolved. The company argued that this was an unfair labor practice. What was the result? *Golden State Transit Corp. v. City of Los Angeles,* 493 U.S. 103 (1989)
13. A public employer required an employee to contribute to an ideological cause that the employee opposed. This requirement was a condition to maintaining the job as a public

educator. Is this a violation of the First Amendment? *Torcaso v. Watkins,* 367 U.S. 488 (1961)

14. Is a union shop legal? A union shop mandates that the employer hire only union members. *Railway Employees v. Hanson,* 351 U.S. 225 (1956)

15. Employees who were required to join the union objected to charges relating to union publications, conventions, and social functions, not because those activities were inherently expressive or ideological in nature, but purely because they were sponsored by the union. What was the result? *Ellis v. Railway Clerks,* 466 U.S. 435 (1984)

16. Was the decision in the case on pp. 473 decided in an ethical manner?

17. In the case on pp. 472 can an individual be paid as a union representative without forgoing his rights under the NLRA?

18. In the case on pp. 474, were the company's actions ethical?

19. In the case on pp. 476, how far should the union have to go to appease the local residents?

20. In the case on pp. 477, did the minority union act ethically?

Clayton Antitrust Act of 1914 38 Stat. 730 (1914), as amended, 15 U.S.C. 15, 17, 26 (1970), 29 U.S.C. 52 (1970)

Sec. 6. That the labor of a human being is not a commodity or article of commerce. Nothing contained in the antitrust laws shall be construed to forbid the existence and operation of labor, agricultural, or horticultural organizations, instituted for the purposes of mutual help, and not having capital stock or conducted for profit, or to forbid or restrain individual members of such organizations from lawfully carrying out the legitimate objects thereof; nor shall such organizations, or the members thereof, be held or construed to be illegal combinations or conspiracies in restraint of trade, under the antitrust laws.

Sec. 20. That no restraining order or injunction shall be granted by any court of the United States, or a judge or judges thereof, in any case between an employer and employees, or between employers and employees, or between employees, or between persons employed and persons seeking employment, involving, or growing out of, a dispute concerning terms and conditions of employment, unless necessary to prevent irreparable injury to property, or to a property right, of the party making the application, for which injury there is no adequate remedy at law, and such property or property right must be described with particularity in the application, which must be in writing and sworn to by the applicant or by his agent or attorney.

And no such restraining order or injunction shall prohibit any person or persons, whether singly or in concert, from terminating any relation of employment, or from ceasing to perform any work or labor, or from recommending, advising, or persuading others by peaceful means so to do; or from attending at any place where any such person or persons may lawfully be, for the purpose of peacefully obtaining or communicating information, or from peacefully persuading any person to work or to abstain from working; or from ceasing to patronize or to employ any party to such dispute, or from recommending, advising, or persuading others by peaceful and lawful means so to do; or from paying or giving to, or withholding from, any person engaged in such dispute, any strike benefits or other moneys or things of value; or from peaceably assembling in lawful manner, and for lawful purposes; or from doing any act or thing which might lawfully be done in the absence of such dispute by any party thereto; nor shall any of the acts specified in this paragraph be considered or held to be violations of any law of the United States.

Norris LaGuardia Act 47 Stat. 70 (1932), 29 U.S.C. 101-15 (1970)

Sec. 1. Issuance of Restraining Orders and Injunctions; Limitation; Public Policy.

No court of the United States, as herein defined, shall have jurisdiction to issue any restraining order or temporary or permanent injunction in a case involving or growing out of a labor dispute, except in a strict conformity with the provisions of this Act; nor shall any such restraining order or temporary or permanent injunction be issued contrary to the public policy declared in this Act.

Sec. 2. Public Policy in Labor Matters Declared.

In the interpretation of this Act and in determining the jurisdiction and authority of the courts of the United States, as such jurisdiction and authority are defined and limited, the public policy of the United States is hereby declared as follows:

Whereas under prevailing economic conditions, developed with the aid of governmental authority for owners of property to organize in the corporate and other forms of ownership association, the individual unorganized worker is commonly helpless to exercise actual liberty of contract and to protect his freedom of labor, and thereby to obtain acceptable terms and conditions of his employment, and that he shall be free from the interference, restraint, or coercion of employers of labor, or their agents, in the designation of such representatives or in self organization or in other concerted activities for the purpose of collective bargaining or other mutual aid or protection; therefore, the following definitions of and limitations upon the jurisdiction and authority of the courts of the United States are enacted.

Sec. 3. Nonenforceability of Undertakings in Conflict with Public Policy; "Yellow Dog" Contracts.

Any undertaking or promise, such as is described in this section, or any other undertaking or promise in conflict with public policy declared in section 2 of this Act is hereby declared to be contrary to the public policy of the United States, shall not be enforceable in any court of the United States and shall not afford any basis for the granting of legal or equitable relief by any such court, including specifically the following:

Every undertaking or promise hereafter made, whether written or oral, express or implied, constituting or contained in any contract or agreement of hiring or employment between any individual, firm, company, association, corporation, and any employee or prospective employee of the same, whereby

(a) Either party to such contract or agreement undertakes or promises not to join, become, or remain a member of any labor organization or of any employer organization; or

(b) Either party to such contract or agreement undertakes or promises that he will withdraw from employment relation in the event that he joins, becomes, or remains a member of any labor organization or of any employer organization.

Sec. 4. Enumeration of Specific Acts Not Subject to Restraining Orders or Injunctions.

No court of the United States shall have jurisdiction to issue any restraining order or temporary or permanent injunction in any case involving or growing out of any labor dispute to prohibit any person or persons participating or interested in such dispute (as these terms are herein defined) from doing, whether singly or in concert, any of the following acts:

(a) Ceasing or refusing to perform any work or to remain in any relation of employment;

(b) Becoming or remaining a member of any labor organization or of any employer organization, regardless of any such undertaking or promise as is described in section 3 of this Act;

(c) Paying or giving to, or withholding from, any person participating or interested in such labor dispute, any strike or unemployment benefits or insurance, or other moneys or things of value;

(d) By all lawful means aiding any person participating or interested in any labor dispute who is being proceeded against in, or is prosecuting, any action or suit in any court of the United States or of any State;

(e) Giving publicity to the existence of, or the facts involved in any labor dispute, whether by advertising, speaking, patrolling or by any other method not involving fraud or violence;

(f) Assembling peaceably to act or to organize to act in promotion of their interests in a labor dispute;

(g) Advising or notifying any person of an intention to do any of the acts heretofore specified;

(h) Agreeing with other persons to do or not to do any of the acts heretofore specified; and

(i) Advising, urging, or otherwise causing or inducing without fraud or violence the acts heretofore specified, regardless of any such undertaking or promise as is described in section 3 of this Act.

Sec. 5. Doing in Concert of Certain Acts as Constituting Unlawful Combination or Conspiracy Subjecting Person to Injunctive Remedies.

No court of the United States shall have jurisdiction to issue a restraining order or temporary or permanent injunction upon the ground that any of the persons participating or interested in a labor dispute constitute or are engaged in an unlawful combination or conspiracy because of the doing in concert of the acts enumerated in section 4 of this Act.

Sec. 6. Responsibility of Officers and Members of Associations or their Organizations for Unlawful Acts of the Individual, Officers, Members, and Agents.

No officer or member of any association or organization, and no association or organization participating or interested in a labor dispute, shall be held responsible or liable in any court of the United States for the unlawful acts of individual officers, members, or agents, except upon clear proof of actual participation in, or actual authorization of, such acts, or of ratification of such acts after actual knowledge thereof.

Sec. 7. Issuance of Injunctions in Labor Disputes; Hearings; Findings of Court; Notice to Affected Persons; Temporary Restraining Order; Undertakings.

No court of the United States shall have jurisdiction to issue a temporary or permanent injunction in any case involving or growing out of a labor dispute, as herein defined, except after hearing the testimony of witnesses in open court (with opportunity for cross-examination) in support of the allegations of a complaint made under oath, and testimony in opposition thereto, if offered, and except after findings of fact by the court, to the effect—

(a) That unlawful acts have been threatened and will be committed unless restrained or have been committed and will be continued unless restrained, but no injunction or temporary restraining order shall be issued on account of any threat or unlawful act or actually authorizing or ratifying the same after actual knowledge thereof;

(b) That substantial and irreparable injury to complainants's property will follow;

(c) That as to each item of relief granted greater injury will be inflicted upon complainant by the denial of relief than will be inflicted upon defendants by the granting of relief;

(d) That complainant has no adequate remedy at law; and

(e) That the public officers charged with the duty to protect complainant's property are unable or unwilling to furnish adequate protection.

Sec. 13. Definitions of Terms and Words Used in Chapter.

When used in this Act, and for the purposes of this Act—

(a) A case shall be held to involve or to grow out of a labor dispute when the case involves persons who are engaged in the same industry, trade, craft, or occupation; or have direct or indirect interests therein; or who are employees of the same employer; or who are members of the same or are an affiliated organization of employers or employees; whether such dispute is (1) between one or more employers or associations of employers and one or more employees or associations of employees; (2) between one or more employers or associations of employers and one or more employers or association of employers; or (3) between one or more employees or associations of employees and one or more employees or associations of employees; or when the case involves any conflicting or competing interests in a "labor dispute" (as hereinafter defined) of "persons participating or interested" therein (as hereinafter defined).

(b) A person or association shall be held to be a person participating or interested in a labor dispute if relief is sought against him or it, and if he or it is engaged in the same industry, trade, craft, or occupation in which such dispute occurs, or has a direct or indirect interest therein, or is a member, officer, or agent of any association composed in whole or in part of employers or employees engaged in such industry, trade, craft, or occupation.

(c) The term "labor dispute" includes any controversy concerning terms conditions of employment, or concerning the association or representation of persons in negotiating, fixing, maintaining, changing, or seeking to arrange terms or conditions of employment, regardless of whether or not the disputants stand in the proximate relation of employer and employee.

Sherman Antitrust Act, 26 Stat. 209 (1890), as amended, 15 U.S.C. 1-7 (1970)

Sec. 1. Every contract, combination in the form of trust or otherwise, or conspiracy, in restraint of trade or commerce among the several States, or with foreign nations, is hereby declared to be illegal. . . . Every person who shall make any contract or engage in any combination or conspiracy hereby declared to be illegal shall be deemed guilty of a misdemeanor, and on conviction thereof, shall be punished by fine not exceeding fifty thousand dollars, or by imprisonment not exceeding one year, or by both said punishments, in the discretion of the court.

CHAPTER 21

Collective Bargaining

INTRODUCTION

Collective bargaining is the negotiation process undertaken by a union on behalf of its members with the management of an organization with the intent of entering into a contract after the resolution of labor issues. The contract, known as the *collective bargaining agreement,* is binding on all union members. The advantage of collective bargaining is that the union has greater bargaining strength than an individual employee would have in attempting to negotiate the best possible deal.

Key Terms

The key terms to be negotiated in a collective bargaining agreement include full time wages, minimum number of hours required for full time status, overtime pay, vacation time, personal days, pension benefits, health care coverage for the employees and their dependents, description and classification of jobs, work schedules, rules regarding employee behavior, cost of living adjustments in pay, determination of promotion, policy termination committee to handle grievances, and procedure for arbitration to handle contract disputes.

The following case addresses the question of whether a nonunion employee must pay union dues as a condition of his employment. The nonunion employee claimed his constitutional rights would be violated by the collective bargaining unit's service fee.

CASE

James P. Lehnert v. Ferris Faculty Association

500 U.S. 507 (1991)

JUSTICE BLACKMUN, Judge.

This case presents issues concerning the constitutional limitations, if any, upon the payment, required as a condition of employment, of dues by a nonmember to a union in the public sector.

Michigan's Public Employment Relations Act (Act), provides that a duly selected union shall serve as the exclusive collective-bargaining representative of public employees in a particular bargaining unit. The Act, which applies to faculty members of a public educational institution in Michigan, permits a union and a government employer to enter into an "agency shop" arrangement under which employees within the bargaining unit who decline to become members of the union are compelled to pay a "service fee" to the union. Respondent Ferris Faculty Association (FFA), an affiliate of the Michigan Education Association (MEA) and the National Education Association (NEA), serves, pursuant to this provision, as the exclusive bargaining representative of the faculty of Ferris State College in Big Rapids, Mich. Ferris is a public institution established under the Michigan Constitution and is funded by the State. Since 1975, the FFA and Ferris have entered into successive collective-bargaining agreements containing agency-shop provisions. Those agreements were the fruit of negotiations between the FFA and respondent Board of Control, the governing body of Ferris.

Subsequent to this Court's decision in *Abood v. Detroit Board of Education,* in which the Court upheld the constitutionality of the Michigan agency-shop provision and outlined permissible uses of the compelled fee by public-employee unions, Ferris proposed, and the FFA agreed to, the agency-shop arrangement at issue here. That agreement required all employees in the bargaining unit who did not belong to the FFA to pay a service fee equivalent to the amount of dues required of a union member. Of the $284.00 service fee for 1981–1982, the period at issue, $24.80 went to the FFA, $211.20 to the MEA, and $48.00 to the NEA.

Petitioners were members of the Ferris faculty during the period in question and objected to certain uses by the unions of their service fees. Petitioners instituted this action, in the United States District Court for the Western District of Michigan, claiming that the use of their fees for purposes other than negotiating and administering a collective-bargaining agreement with the Board of Control violated rights secured to them by the First and Fourteenth Amendments of the United States Constitution. Petitioners also claimed that the procedures implemented by the unions to determine and collect service fees were inadequate.

The Court of Appeals, with one judge dissenting in large part, affirmed. After reviewing this Court's cases in the area, the court concluded that each of the challenged activities was sufficiently related to the unions' duties as the exclusive bargaining representative of petitioners' unit to justify compelling petitioners to assist in subsidizing it. The dissenting judge concurred with respect to convention expenses but disagreed with the majority's resolution of the other items challenged. Because of the importance of the issues, we granted certiorari.

It was not until the decision in *Abood* that this Court addressed the constitutionality of union-security provisions in the public-employment context. There, the Court upheld the same Michigan statute which is before us today against a facial First Amendment challenge. At the same time, it determined that the claim that a union has utilized an individual agency-shop agreement to force dissenting employees to subsidize ideological activities could establish, upon a proper showing, a First Amendment violation. In so doing, the Court set out several important propositions:

First, it recognized that "to compel employees financially to support their collective-bargaining representative has an impact upon their First Amendment interests." Unions traditionally have aligned themselves with a wide range of social, political, and ideological viewpoints, any number of which might bring vigorous disapproval from individual employees. To force employees to contribute, albeit indirectly, to the promotion of such positions implicates core First Amendment concerns. "The right of freedom of thought protected by the First Amendment against state action includes both the right to speak freely and the right to refrain from speaking at all".

Second, the Court in *Abood* determined that, as in the private sector, compulsory affiliation with, or monetary support of, a public-employment union does not, without more, violate the First Amendment rights of public employees. Similarly, an employee's free speech rights are not unconstitutionally burdened because the employee opposes positions taken by a union in its capacity as collective-bargaining representative. "The judgment clearly made in Hanson and Street is that such interference as exists is constitutionally justified by the legislative assessment of the important contribution of the union shop to the system of labor relations established by Congress."

In this connection, the Court indicated that the considerations that justify the union shop in the private context—the desirability of labor peace and eliminating "free riders"—are equally important in the public-sector workplace. Consequently, the use of dissenters' assessments "for the purposes of collective bargaining, contract administration, and grievance adjustment," approved under the RLA, is equally permissible when authorized by a State vis-a-vis its own workers.

Third, the Court established that the constitutional principles that prevent a State from conditioning public employment upon association with a political party, or upon professed religious allegiance, similarly prohibit a public employer "from requiring an employee to contribute to the support of an ideological cause he may oppose as a condition of holding a job" as a public educator.

The Court in *Abood* did not attempt to draw a precise line between permissible assessments for public-sector collective-bargaining activities and prohibited assessments for ideological activities.

We therefore conclude that a local bargaining representative may charge objecting employees for their pro rata share of the costs associated with otherwise chargeable activities of its state and national affiliates, even if those activities were not performed for the direct benefit of the objecting employees' bargaining unit. This conclusion, however, does not serve to grant a local union carte blanche to expend dissenters' dollars for bargaining activities wholly unrelated to the employees in their unit. The union surely may not, for example, charge objecting employees for a direct donation or interest-free loan to an unrelated bargaining unit for the purpose of promoting employee rights or unionism generally. Further, a contribution by a local union to its parent that is not part of the local's responsibilities as an affiliate but is in the nature of a charitable donation would not be chargeable to dissenters. There must be some indication that the payment is for services that may ultimately enure to the benefit of the members of the local union by virtue of their membership in the parent organization. And, as always, the union bears the burden of proving the proportion of chargeable expenses to total expenses. We conclude merely that the union need not demonstrate a direct and tangible impact upon the dissenting employee's unit.

Judgment for Ferris Faculty Association.

The issue in the next case is whether the National Labor Relations Board can define bargaining units in a hospital according to its general rules or whether it must make a separate decision in regard to each unit.

American Hospital Association v. National Labor Relations Board

CASE

499 U.S. 606 (1991)

JUSTICE STEVENS delivered the opinion of the Court.

For the first time since the National Labor Relations Board was established in 1935, the Board has promulgated a substantive rule defining the employee units appropriate for collective bargaining in a particular line of commerce. The rule is applicable to acute care hospitals and provides, with three exceptions, that eight and only eight units shall be appropriate in any such hospital. The three exceptions are for cases that present extraordinary circumstances, cases in which nonconforming units already exist, and cases in which labor organizations seek to combine two or more of the eight specified units. The extraordinary circumstances exception applies automatically to hospitals in which the eight unit rule will produce a unit of five or fewer employees.

Petitioner, American Hospital Association, brought this action challenging the facial validity of the rule on three grounds: First, petitioner argues that Section 9(b) of the National Labor Relations Act requires the Board to make a separate bargaining unit determination "in each case" and therefore prohibits the Board from using general rules to define bargaining units; second, petitioner contends that the rule that the Board has formulated violates a congressional admonition to the Board to avoid the undue proliferation of bargaining units in the health care industry; and, finally, petitioner maintains that the rule is arbitrary and capricious.

The United States District Court for the Northern District of Illinois agreed with petitioner's second argument and enjoined enforcement of the rule. The Court of Appeals found no merit in any of the three arguments and reversed. Because of the importance of the case, we granted certiorari. We now affirm.

Petitioner's first argument is a general challenge to the Board's rulemaking authority in connection with bargaining unit determinations based on the terms of the National Labor Relations Act (NLRA), as originally enacted in 1935. In the NLRA Congress made the legislative finding that the "inequality of bargaining power" between unorganized employees and corporate employers had adversely affected commerce and declared it to be the policy of the United States to mitigate or eliminate those adverse effects "by encouraging the practice and procedure of collective bargaining and by protecting the exercise by workers of full freedom of association, self-organization, and designation of representatives of their own choosing, for the purpose of negotiating the terms and conditions of their employment or other mutual aid or protection." The central purpose of the Act was to protect and facilitate employees' opportunity to organize unions to represent them in collective-bargaining negotiations.

Sections 3, 4, and 5 of the Act created the Board and generally described its powers. Section 6 granted the Board the "authority from time to time to make, amend, and rescind . . . such rules and regulations as may be necessary to carry out the provisions" of the Act. This grant was unquestionably sufficient to authorize the rule at issue in this case unless limited by some other provision in the Act.

Petitioner argues that Section 9(b) provides such a limitation because this section requires the Board to determine the appropriate bargaining unit "in each case." We are not persuaded. Petitioner would have us put more weight on these three words than they can reasonably carry.

Section 9(a) of the Act provides that the representative "designated or selected for the purposes of collective bargaining by the majority of the employees in a unit appropriate for such purposes" shall be the exclusive bargaining representative for all the employees in that unit. This section, read in light of the policy of the Act, implies that the initiative in selecting an appropriate unit resides with the employees. Moreover, the language suggests that employees may seek to organize "a unit" that is "appropriate"—not necessarily the single most appropriate unit. Thus, one union might seek to represent all of the employees in a particular plant, those in a particular craft, or perhaps just a portion thereof.

Given the obvious potential for disagreement concerning the appropriateness of the unit selected by the union seeking recognition by the employer—disagreements that might involve rival unions claiming jurisdiction over contested segments of the work force as well as disagreements between management and labor—Section 9(b) authorizes the Board to decide whether the designated unit is appropriate. Section 9(b) provides:

> "The Board shall decide in each case whether, in order to insure to employees the full benefit of their right to self-organization and to collective bargaining, and otherwise to effectuate the policies of this Act, the unit appropriate for the purposes of collective bargaining shall be the employer unit, craft unit, plant unit, or subdivision thereof."

The more natural reading of these three words is simply to indicate that whenever there is a disagreement about the appropriateness of a unit, the Board shall resolve the dispute. Under this reading, the words "in each case" are synonymous with "whenever necessary" or "in any case in which there is a dispute." Congress chose not to enact a general rule that would require plant unions, craft unions or industry-wide unions for every employer in every line of commerce, but also chose not to leave the decision up to employees or employers alone. Instead, the decision "in each case" in which a dispute arises is to be made by the Board.

In resolving such a dispute, the Board's decision is presumably to be guided not simply by the basic policy of the Act but also by the rules that the Board develops to circumscribe and to guide its discretion either in the process of case-by-case adjudication or by the exercise of its rulemaking authority. The requirement that the Board exercise its discretion in every disputed case cannot fairly or logically be read to command the Board to exercise standardless discretion in each case. As a noted scholar on administrative law has observed:

> "The mandate to decide 'in each case' does not prevent the Board from supplanting the original discretionary chaos with some degree of order, and the principal instruments for regularizing the system of deciding 'in each case' are classifications, rules, principles, and precedents. Sensible men could not refuse to use such instruments and a sensible Congress would not expect them to."

In sum, we believe that the meaning of Section 9(b)'s mandate that the Board decide the appropriate bargaining unit "in each case" is clear and contrary to the meaning advanced by petitioner. Even if we could find any ambiguity in Section 9(b) after employing the traditional tools of statutory construction, we would still defer to the Board's reasonable interpretation of the statutory text. We thus conclude that Section 9(b) does not limit the Board's rulemaking authority under Section 6.

Judgment for NLRB.

In the case that follows, a company required employees who intended on transferring to its new plant to pass a test. When only a few employees passed the test, the employer filled its slots from nonunion individuals. The employees claimed that this action was in breach of the collective bargaining agreement.

The company negotiated a plant-closing agreement with its employees. The agreement provided for transfer opportunities to its new plant. When the employees applied for the transfer, they were required to take a test. This was not provided for in the agreement. The employees maintained that the test was not job-related.

CASE

Jones v. Pepsi Cola Bottling Co., Inc.

822 F.Supp. 396 (E.D. Mich. 1993)

FEIKENS, District Judge.

Plaintiffs, approximately sixty-four former unionized employees of Pepsi who worked in the production department at Pepsi's now defunct Exeter Avenue plant in Detroit, were represented by Local 337, and the terms and conditions of their employment were governed by a collective bargaining agreement ("CBA") between Pepsi and Local 337. In 1989, Pepsi announced its intention to close the Exeter plant and build a new plant in the City of Detroit to be known as the Detroit Distribution and Production Center ("DPC"). According to plaintiffs, Pepsi sought from the Detroit City Council a twelve-year $6 million property tax abatement; as inducement for such abatement, Pepsi promised that seventy employees, many of whom are plaintiffs in this case, would be transferred from the Exeter Avenue facility to the new plant.

As operations at the Exeter Avenue plant came to a halt, Pepsi and Local 33 negotiated a plant closing agreement regarding the terms and conditions which would govern the closure of the plant. Employees who were not transferred to the new facility or another Pepsi facility were laid off in February 1991. Some of the plaintiffs were among the employees who did not transfer to a different facility and some of them were laid off.

In order to apply for work at the new assembly plant, Exeter Avenue production employees were required to pass a written test. Plaintiffs say Pepsi imposed this requirement only on Exeter Avenue production employees; no such transfer prerequisite was imposed on any other bargaining unit employees. Approximately 75% of the production employees at the Exeter Avenue plant were black with high seniority. Approximately 10% were female with high seniority. Approximately 16% were over 40 with high seniority. Approximately 50% were unmarried. Plaintiffs say a written test did not measure in any way an employee's abilities or qualifications to perform production jobs in the new plant.

Those Exeter Avenue production employees who achieved the minimum cut-off score on the written test underwent Group Assessment Exercises which plaintiffs say were nothing more than subjective interviews irrelevant to the ability of the employees to perform production jobs. Only four Exeter Avenue production employees achieved a passing score on the Group Assessment Exercise, all of whom were white males with seniority of less than ten years. These four white males were given production jobs at the new facility. Pepsi filled the remaining production jobs at the new facility with new hires who had never worked for Pepsi before and who were not represented by the Teamsters Union. Plaintiffs claim they were all qualified to perform the production work at the new facility.

Specifically, in Court I, plaintiffs claim a breach of the CBA by Pepsi and a breach of Local 337's duty of fair representation because plaintiffs' preferential hiring rights as set forth in Article XXXII of the CBA were allegedly violated. Plaintiffs claim Local 337 violated section 8(b) (1) (A) of the National Labor Relations Act ("NLRA"). Count II alleges a breach of duty of fair representation by Local 337 because Local 337 did not submit the plant closing agreement to a vote of the membership as allegedly required by Local 337's bylaws. Plaintiffs claim the plant closing agreement amended the CBA and therefore the members were entitled to vote on it. Plaintiffs say this breach of duty to fairly represent them under section 9(a) of NLRA, amounts to a violation under section 8(b) (1) (A) of NLRA. Count III alleges the same actions in Count II; Count III claims that such actions amount to a breach of section 411(a) (1) of the Labor Management Reporting and Disclosure Act ("LMRDA").

In the case at hand, it is true that plaintiffs' attorney was not allowed to actively participate in the grievance proceedings. The grievants were represented by their union's attorney. However, I have already found above that Local 337 has not breached its duty of fair representation. Further, a union's good faith decision regarding the evidence it will present in an arbitration cannot amount to a breach of the duty, even if the union's decision proves to have been mistaken.

Further, plaintiffs request that Count I not be dismissed before they have a chance to conduct discovery; they say such discovery could lead to evidence supporting allegations of a conspiracy between the defendants to deprive plaintiffs of their jobs. According to plaintiffs, such a conspiracy might demonstrate the arbitration was tainted and thus breathe new life into Count I. Plaintiffs are simply asking this court to allow them to conduct a fishing expedition. Plaintiffs have no proof at this time of any kind of conspiracy to affect the arbitrator's decision. I will not allow plaintiffs to engage in such abusive discovery. Thus, Counts I claims against both defendants are dismissed.

Defendant Local 337 argues that these counts must be dismissed as well. These counts center on plaintiffs' contention that Local 337 was obligated by its bylaws to submit the plant closing agreement it negotiated for its members at the Exeter Avenue plant in December 1990 to a vote of those members. Plaintiffs contend section 26 of Local 337's bylaws privileged them to vote on all collective bargaining agreements affecting them and that a plant closing agreement should be considered a collective bargaining agreement within the meaning of the bylaw. Section 26 provides in part:

> Whenever a Collective Bargaining Agreement is about to be negotiated, modified, or extended at the request of this Local Union, the President shall call a meeting at which the membership shall determine and authorize bargaining demands to be made. Proposed Collective Bargaining Agreements or amendments thereto shall be submitted by the Secretary Treasurer of the Joint Council and Area Conference, as required by the Area Conference bylaws, for approval before submission to the employer. . . . Ratification of agreements or amendments shall be subject to vote in the same manner as provided for in connection with bargaining demands as set forth in Section 26(a), or in the case of area wide or conference wide agreements in accordance with the constitution and rules adopted by such bargaining group.

Plaintiffs concede that bylaw section 26 does not list plant closing agreements among the requirements which required ratification. Nonetheless, plaintiffs argue the plant closing agreement is an amendment to the CBA, and section 26 requires ratification of amendments to the CBA.

Thus, despite all of plaintiffs' examples, the plant closing agreement does not amend the CBA. Indeed, Local 337 and Pepsi never intended the plant closing agreement to amend the CBA. Paragraph 21 of the plant closing agreement states:

> The provisions of this Agreement do not vary or contradict the terms of the Contract [CBA]. To the extent this Agreement covers matters that are also covered by the Contract, it sets forth the mutual understanding of the parties as to the meaning of the Contract.

Nevertheless plaintiffs argue that even if the closing agreement did not modify employees' rights under the CBA, the union's relinquishment of its continuing obligation to represent Pepsi production employees in Detroit was a matter that plaintiffs had a right to approve or reject as a matter of law.

Local 337 did not suddenly say it was no longer going to represent the production employees at the Exeter Avenue facility. Instead, these employees represented by Local 337 were losing their jobs. There was simply no one left for Local 337 to represent. This is why Local 337's status as bargaining unit agent ceased.

Judgment for Pepsi.

The next case deals with the issue of whether a proposed ban on smoking should be compelled by the Federal Labor Relations Authority or should be bargained for with the local union chapters. The Department of Health and Human Services has sought the mandate, while the Federal Labor Relations Authority has argued for collective bargaining.

CASE

Dept. of Health & Human Serv. v. FLRA

920 F.2d 45 (D.C. Cir. 1990)

SILBERMAN, Circuit Judge.

The Department of Health and Human Services (HHS) seeks review of a decision by the Federal Labor Relations Authority rejecting HHS's assertion of a compelling need for an agency-wide ban on smoking within HHS facility and ordering HHS to bargain with local chapters of the National Treasury Employees Union (NTEU) regarding the agency's smoking regulations. The FLRA asks this court to enforce its bargaining order. We reject HHS's petition for review and grant the FLRA's cross-petition for enforcement of its bargaining order.

In May of 1987 HHS announced that it was creating a smoke-free working environment in all HHS facilities and in August of that year it issued personnel regulations implementing the smoking ban. Three local chapters of the NTEU attempted to negotiate over the policy, presenting proposals to accommodate smokers by establishing designated smoking areas within HHS facilities. Their proposals were consistent with the government-wide regulation issued by the General Services Administration (GSA), which calls for agencies to accommodate the needs of smokers by creating "smoking areas" that "do not impinge on the health of those who do not smoke," and instruct agencies to honor their collective bargaining obligations, but allows an agency, in its discretion, to implement more stringent smoking regulations. HHS maintained, however, that the smoking ban was nonnegotiable under Title VII of the Civil Service Reform Act of 1978, commonly known as the Federal Service Labor-Management Relations Act (FSLMRA), because it fell within the compelling need exception to the duty to bargain. Each of the three bargaining units filed negotiability appeals with the FLRA. The appeals were consolidated for decision.

HHS argued before the Authority that a complete ban on smoking in the workplace was essential to the performance of its mission to educate the public about the dangers of smoking. The agency claimed that it could not effectively persuade private-sector employers to create smoke-free work environments if it did not do so itself. Its credibility would be jeopardized, HHS claimed, unless it were free to set an example by creating for its own employees the healthiest working environment possible without being subject to the lengthy and uncertain collective bargaining process. Moreover, in light of the Surgeon General's 1986 report on the harmful effects of environmental tobacco smoke (ETS) and the difficulties of confining ETS so as not to endanger nonsmokers, such a ban was, in the agency's view, necessary to protect employees' health.

The FLRA determined that HHS had failed to meet its burden of demonstrating that a smoking ban in all HHS facilities was essential to the agency's mission within the meaning of the statute's and its implementing regulations. The Authority thought that a complete smoke-free working environment in all HHS buildings, while helpful or desirable as an aid to HHS's advocacy role, was not essential to the agency's mission of "performing research and informing the public on the hazards of smoking."

In any event, we do not dispute, and we do not understand the FLRA to dispute, that all agencies are legitimately concerned with their employees' health. It is hard to see how it can be argued, however, that HHS's concern for its employees can be qualitatively different from that of other government agencies. Its health-based argument is consequently a collateral attack on the government-wide GSA regulation referred to above. That regulation, it will be recalled, governs smoking in federal buildings and requires that agencies accommodate the needs of smokers where feasible. Although an agency has discretion to "establish more stringent guidelines," the GSA regulation instructs the agency to "meet its collective bargaining obligation." And to the extent that the GSA regulation gives HHS discretion regarding its smoking policy, HHS is obligated by the FSLMRA "to exercise that discrimination through negotiation." With this backdrop, we think HHS has no basis to quarrel with the FLRA's refusal to designate a regulation prohibiting bargaining over smoking on HHS premises as arising out of "compelling need" because of concern with its employees' health. It would appear that HHS's quarrel is instead with the Administration.

Accordingly, the petition for review is denied and the cross-petition is granted.

Judgment for the Federal Labor Relations Authority.

Purpose

Collective bargaining serves a useful purpose in allowing management to negotiate with one union rather than the hundreds or thousands of individual employees that the union represents. In most cases, it is an expeditious and inexpensive method of resolving labor issues.

In the following case, an employer did not give an employee her severance pay upon discharge. The state labor commissioner argued that the employee's right to pursue this is governed by a collective bargaining agreement that provides for arbitration. The employee retorted that the collective bargaining agreement is overridden by state law.

CASE

Karen Livadas v. Victoria Bradshaw, California Labor Commissioner

114 S.Ct. 2068 (1994)

Justice SOUTER delivered the opinion of the Court.

California law requires employers to pay all wages due immediately upon an employee's discharge, imposes a penalty for refusal to pay promptly, precludes any private contractual waiver of these minimum labor standards, and places responsibility for enforcing these provisions on the State Commissioner of Labor (Commissioner or Labor Commissioner), ostensibly for the benefit of all employees. Respondent, the Labor Commissioner, has construed a further provision of state law as barring enforcement of these wage and penalty claims on behalf of individuals like petitioner, whose terms and conditions of employment are governed by a collective-bargaining agreement containing an arbitration clause. We hold that federal law pre-empts this policy, as abridging the exercise of such employees' rights under the National Labor Relations Act (NLRA or Act), and that redress for this unlawful refusal to enforce may be had under 42 U.S.C. 1983.

Until her discharge on January 2, 1990, petitioner Karen Livadas worked as a grocery clerk in a Vallejo, California, Safeway supermarket. The terms and conditions of her employment were subject to a collective-bargaining agreement between Safeway and Livadas's union, Local 373 of the United Food and Commercial Workers, AFL-CIO. Unexceptionally, the agreement provided that "disputes as to the interpretation or application of the agreement," including grievances arising from allegedly unjust discharge or suspension, would be subject to binding arbitration. When notified of her discharge, Livadas demanded immediate payment of wages owed her, as guaranteed to all California workers by state law, but her store manager refused, referring to the company practice of making such payments by check mailed from a central corporate payroll office. On January 5, 1990, Livadas received a check from Safeway, in the full amount owed for her work through January 2.

On January 9, 1990, Livadas filed a claim against Safeway with the California Division of Labor Standards Enforcement (DLSE or Division), asserting that under 203 of the Labor Code the company was liable to her for a sum equal to three days' wages, as a penalty for the delay between discharge and the date when payment was in fact received. Livadas requested the Commissioner to enforce the claim.

By an apparently standard form letter dated February 7, 1990, the Division notified Livadas that it would take no action on her complaint:

> "It is our understanding that the employees working for Safeway are covered by a collective bargaining agreement which contains an arbitration clause. The provisions of Labor Code Section 229 preclude this Division from adjudicating any dispute concerning the interpretation or application of any collective bargaining agreement containing an arbitration clause."
>
> "Labor Code Section 203 requires that the wages continue at the 'same rate' until paid. In order to establish what the 'same rate' was, it is necessary to look to the collective bargaining agreement and 'apply' that agreement. The courts have pointed out that such an application is exactly what the provisions of Labor Code 229 prohibit."

The only issue raised by Livadas's claim, whether Safeway "willfully failed to pay" her wages promptly upon severance, was a question of state law, entirely independent of any understanding embodied in the collective-bargaining agreement between the union and the employer. There is no indication that there was a "dispute" in this case over the amount of the penalty to which Livadas would be entitled. When liability is governed by independent state law, the mere need to "look to" the collective-bargaining agreement for damage computation is no reason to hold the state law claim defeated.

Beyond the simple need to refer to bargained-for wage rates in computing the penalty, the collective-bargaining agreement is irrelevant to the dispute (if any) between Livadas and Safeway.

The right Livadas asserts, to complete the collective-bargaining process and agree to an arbitration clause, is, if not provided in so many words in the NLRA, at least imminent in its structure. Finding no cause for special caution here, we hold that Livadas's claim is properly brought under U.S.C. 1983.

In an effort to give wide berth to federal labor law and policy, the Commissioner declines to enforce union-represented employees' claims rooted in unwaivable rights ostensibly secured by state law to all employees, without regard to whether the claims are valid under state law or pre-empted by LMRA 301. Federal labor law does not require such a heavy-handed policy, and, indeed, cannot permit it. We do not suggest here that the NLRA automatically defeats all state action taking any account of the collective-bargaining process or every state law distinguishing union-represented employees from others. It is enough that we find the Commissioner's policy to have such direct and detrimental effects on the federal statutory rights of employees that it must be pre-empted. The judgment of the Court of Appeals for the Ninth Circuit is accordingly reversed.

Judgment for Livadas.

Unlawful Practices

Where there is a valid collective bargaining agreement, it would be an unlawful practice to compromise employees' contracted rights, such as seniority and shift preference, in order to accommodate the religious beliefs of a particular employee. This would present an undue hardship for the employer.

Employment Perspective

Mitchell Feldstein, an Orthodox Jew, has been employed at the Giant Motors Lexington Kentucky plant where he has seniority. Mitchell is granted a transfer to the Flint, Michigan, plant. According to the collective bargaining agreement, seniority is determined by years at the plant, not at the company. At Flint, Mitchell, having no seniority, is required to work Saturdays. Mitchell asserts that this requirement is against his religious beliefs. Giant Motors refuses to accommodate him, claiming undue hardship in that the accommodation will compromise the seniority rights of other employees as determined by the collective bargaining agreement. Mitchell is subsequently discharged for excessive absenteeism on Saturdays. Mitchell files an EEOC claim for religious discrimination. Will he be successful? No! To accommodate Mitchell would be a breach of the collective bargaining agreement and an unlawful employment practice. It is an undue hardship for Giant Motors. ◆

In the following case, a dispute arose after the expiration of a collective bargaining agreement. The issue is whether the parties to the contract intended any of its provisions to be binding beyond the expiration of the contract.

CASE

Litton Financial Printing Division, A Division of Litton Business Systems, Inc. v. National Labor Relations Board

501 U.S. 190 (1991)

Justice KENNEDY delivered the opinion of the Court.

This case requires us to determine whether a dispute over layoffs which occurred well after expiration of a collective-bargaining agreement must be said to arise under the agreement despite its expiration. The question arises in the context of charges brought by the National Labor Relations Board (Board) alleging an unfair labor practice in violation of Sections 8(a) (1) and (5) of the National Labor Relations Act (NLRA).

Petitioner Litton operated a check printing plant in Santa Clara, California. The plant utilized both cold-type and hot-type printing processes. Printing Specialties & Paper Products Union No. 777, Affiliated with District Council No. 1 (Union), represented the production employees at the plant. The Union and Litton entered into a collective-bargaining agreement which, with extensions, remained in effect until October 3, 1979. Section 19 of the Agreement is a broad arbitration provision:

> "Differences that may arise between the parties hereto regarding this Agreement and any alleged violations of the Agreement, the construction to be placed on any clause or clauses of the Agreement shall be determined by arbitration in the manner hereinafter set forth."

Section 21 of the Agreement sets forth a two-step grievance procedure, at the conclusion of which, if a grievance cannot be resolved, the matter may be submitted for binding arbitration.

Soon before the Agreement was to expire, an employee sought decertification of the Union. The Board conducted an election on August 17, 1979, in which the Union prevailed by a vote of 28 to 27. On July 2, 1980, after much postelection legal maneuvering, the Board issued a decision to certify the Union. No contract negotiations occurred during this period of uncertainty over the Union's status.

Litton decided to test the Board's certification decision by refusing to bargain with the Union. The Board rejected Litton's position and found its refusal to bargain an unfair labor practice. Meanwhile, Litton had decided to eliminate its cold-type operation at the plant, and in late August and early September of 1980, laid off 10 of the 42 persons working in the plant at that time. The laid off employees worked either primarily or exclusively with the cold-type operation, and included six of the eleven most senior employees in the plant. The layoffs occurred without any notice to the Union.

The Union filed identical grievances on behalf of each laid off employee, claiming a violation of the Agreement, which had provided that "in case of layoffs, lengths of continuous service will be the determining factor if other things such as aptitude and ability are equal." Litton refused to submit to the grievance and arbitration procedure or to negotiate over the decision to lay off the employees, and took a position later interpreted by the Board as a refusal to arbitrate under any and all circumstances. It offered instead to negotiate concerning the effects of the layoffs.

On November 24, 1980, the General Counsel for the Board issued a complaint alleging that Litton's refusal to process the grievances amounted to an unfair labor practice within the meaning of Sections 8(a) (1) and (5) of the NLRA. On September 4, 1981, an Administrative Law Judge found that Litton had violated the NLRA by failing to process the grievances. The Administrative Law Judge went on to state that if the grievances remained unresolved at the conclusion of the grievance process, Litton could not refuse to submit them to arbitration. The Administrative Law Judge held also that Litton violated Sections 8(a) (1) and (5) when it bypassed the Union and paid severance wages directly to the 10 laid off employees, and Litton did not contest that determination in further proceedings.

Although the Board refused to order arbitration, it did order Litton to process the grievances through the two-step grievance procedure, to bargain with the Union over the layoffs, and to provide a limited backpay remedy.

The Board sought enforcement of its order, and both the Union and Litton petitioned for review.

Sections 8(a) (5) and 8(d) of the NLRA require an employer to bargain "in good faith with respect to wages, hours, and other terms and conditions of employment." The Board has taken the position that it is difficult to bargain if, during negotiations, an employer is free to alter the very terms and conditions that are the subject of those negotiations. The Board has determined, with our acceptance, that an employer commits an unfair labor practice if, without bargaining to impasse, it effects a unilateral change of an existing term or condition of employment.

Whether or not a company is bound to arbitrate, as well as what issues it must arbitrate, is a matter to be determined by the court, and a party cannot be forced to "arbitrate the arbitrability issue." We acknowledge that where an effective bargaining agreement exists between the parties, and the agreement contains a broad arbitration clause, "there is a presumption of arbitrability in the sense that 'an order to arbitrate the particular grievance should not be denied unless it may be said with positive assurance that the arbitration clause is not susceptible of an interpretation that covers the asserted dispute.'" But we refuse to apply that presumption wholesale in the context of an expired bargaining agreement, for to do so would make limitless the contractual obligation to arbitrate. Although "doubts should be resolved in favor of coverage," we must determine whether the parties agreed to arbitrate this dispute, and we cannot avoid that duty because it requires us to interpret a provision of a bargaining agreement.

We apply these principles to the layoff grievances in the present case. The layoffs took place almost one year after the Agreement had expired. It follows that the grievances are arbitrable only if they involve rights which accrued or vested under the Agreement, or rights which carried over after expiration of the Agreement, not as legally imposed terms and conditions of employment but as continuing obligations under the contract.

The contractual right at issue, that "in case of layoffs, lengths of continuous service will be the determining factor if other things such as aptitude and ability are equal," involves a residual element of seniority. Seniority provisions, the Union argues, "create a form of earned advantage, accumulated over time, that can be understood as a special form of deferred compensation for time already worked." Leaving aside the question whether a provision requiring all layoffs to proceed in inverse order of seniority would support an analogy to the severance pay at issue, which has been viewed as a form of deferred compensation, the layoff provision here cannot be so construed, and cannot be said to create a right that vested or accrued during the term of the Agreement, or a contractual obligation that carries over after expiration.

The order of layoffs under the Agreement was to be determined primarily with reference to "other factors such as aptitude and ability." Only where all such factors were equal was the employer required to look to seniority. Here, any arbitration proceeding would of necessity focus upon whether aptitude and ability—and any unenumerated "other factors"—were equal long after the Agreement had expired, as of the date of the decision to lay employees off and in light of Litton's decision to close down its cold-type printing operation.

The important point is that factors such as aptitude and ability do not remain constant, but change over time. They cannot be said to vest or accrue or be understood as a form of deferred compensation. Specific aptitudes and abilities can either improve or atrophy. And the importance of any particular skill in this equation varies with the requirements of the employer's business at any given time. Aptitude and ability cannot be measured on some universal scale, but only by matching an employee to the requirements of an employer's business at that time. We cannot infer an intent on the part of the contracting parties to freeze any particular order of layoff or vest any contractual right as of the Agreement's expiration.

V

For the reasons stated, we reverse the judgment of the Court of Appeals to the extent that the Court of Appeals refused to enforce the Board's order in its entirety and remanded the cause for further proceedings.

Judgment for NLRB.

REVIEW QUESTIONS

1. Define collective bargaining.
2. What is a collective bargaining agreement?
3. Is a collective bargaining agreement binding on all union members?
4. Explain the terms in the agreement.
5. What is the method for dispute resolution?
6. Explain the purpose served by collective bargaining.
7. Give an example of when contract rights secured through collective bargaining conflict with civil rights.

8. How is this conflict resolved?
9. Explain the advantage of collective bargaining from an employer's perspective.
10. What is the law which secured the right of workers to bargain collectively?
11. A union used member's dues in supporting litigation not directly for the benefit of the collective bargaining group. The union argued that litigation was the most effective form of political association. What was the result? *NAACP v. Button,* 371 U.S. 415 (1963)
12. Is it permissible for a union to collect dues from a nonunion employee? *Abood v. Detroit Board of Education,* 431 U.S. 209 (1977)
13. A union subsidized lobbying and other political activity that was related to its collective bargaining duties. Those nonunion members objected to their dues being used for these purposes. What was the result? *Robinson v. New Jersey,* 741 F.2d 598 (Third Circuit 1984)
14. Employees who were forced to join the Railway Labor Association complained that the union was spending part of their dues for political campaign contributions. The employees who did not believe in the union's cause resented those expenditures and asserted that all of their dues should go to further the collective bargaining process. What was the result? *Railway Clerks v. Allen,* 373 U.S. 113 (1983)
15. The Las Vegas Culinary Workers Union brought suit against Royal Center, Inc., with regard to pension benefits. Royal Center argued that only those rights already accrued or vested as of the date of termination are within the scope of arbitration as defined by the collective bargaining agreement. The union claimed that this was too restrictive. What was the result? *Local Joint Executive Board of Las Vegas Culinary Workers Union, Local 226 v. Royal Center, Inc.,* 796 F.2d 1159 (9th Cir. 1986)
16. In the case on pp. 489, was the company's actions ethical?
17. In the case on pp. 492, should a big deal have been made over a check that arrived three days late?
18. In the case on pp. 494, can provisions of a collective bargaining agreement survive its termination?
19. Referring to the case on pp. 491, is a ban on smoking in the workplace ethical?
20. In the case on pp. 485, is it ethical to compel a nonunion member to pay union dues as a condition of his or her employment?

National Labor Relations Act of 1935
29 U.S.C. 15

FINDING AND POLICIES

Section 1. The denial by some employers of the right of employees to organize and the refusal by some employers to accept the procedure of collective bargaining lead to strikes and other forms of industrial strife or unrest, which have the intent or the necessary effect of burdening or obstructing commerce by (a) impairing the efficiency, safety, or operation of the instrumentalities of commerce; (b) occurring in the current of commerce; (c) materially affecting, restraining, or controlling the flow of raw materials or manufactured or processed goods from or into the channels of commerce, or the prices of such materials or goods in commerce; or (d) causing diminution of employment and wages in such volume as substantially to impair or disrupt the market for goods flowing from or into the channels of commerce.

The inequality of bargaining power between employees who do not possess full freedom of association or actual liberty of contract, and employers who are organized in the corporate or other forms of ownership association substantially burdens and affects the flow of commerce, and tends to aggravate recurrent business depressions, by depressing wage rates and the purchasing power of wage earners in industry and by preventing the stabilization of competitive wage rates and working conditions within and between industries.

Experience has proved that protection by law of the right of employees to organize and bargain collectively safeguards commerce from injury, impairment, or interruption, and promotes the flow of commerce by removing certain recognized sources of industrial strife and unrest, by encouraging practices fundamental to the friendly adjustment of industrial disputes arising out of differences as to wages, hours, or other working conditions, and by restoring equality of bargaining power between employers and employees.

Experience has further demonstrated that certain practices by some labor organizations, their offices and members have the intent or the necessary effect of burdening or obstructing commerce by preventing the free flow of goods in such commerce through strikes and other forms of industrial unrest or through concerted activities which impair the interest of the public in the free flow of such commerce. The elimination of such practices is a necessary condition to the assurance of the rights herein guaranteed.

It is hereby declared to be the policy of the United States to eliminate the causes of certain substantial obstructions to the free flow of commerce and to mitigate and eliminate these obstructions when they have occurred by encouraging the practice and procedure of collective bargaining and by protecting the exercise by workers of full freedom of association, self-organization, and designation of representatives of their own choosing, for the purpose of negotiating the terms and conditions of their employment or other mutual aid or protection.

NATIONAL LABOR RELATIONS BOARD

Section 3. (a) The National Labor Relations Board (hereinafter called the "Board") created by this Act prior to its amendment by the Labor Management Relations Act, 1947, is hereby continued as an agency of the United States, except that the Board shall consist of five instead of three members, appointed by the President by and with the advice and consent of the Senate.

RIGHTS OF EMPLOYEES

Section 7. Employees shall have the right to self-organization to form, join, or assist labor organizations, to bargain collectively through representatives of their own choosing, and to engage in other concerted activities for the purpose of collective bargaining or other mutual aid or protection, and shall also have the right to refrain from any or all of such activities except to the extent that such right may be affected by an agreement requiring membership in a labor organization as a condition of employment as authorized in section 8(a) (3).

UNFAIR LABOR PRACTICES

Section 8. (a) It shall be an unfair labor practice for an employer—

(1) to interfere with, restrain, or coerce employees in the exercise of the rights guaranteed in section 7;

(2) to dominate or interfere within the formation or administration of any labor organization or contribute financial or other support to it: *Provided,* That subject to rules and regulations made and published by the Board pursuant to section 6, an employer shall not be prohibited from permitting employees to confer with him during working hours without loss of time or pay;
(3) by discrimination in regard to hire or tenure of employment or any term or condition of employment to encourage or discourage membership in any labor organization;
(4) to discharge or otherwise discriminate against an employee because he has filed charges or given testimony under this Act;
(5) to refuse to bargain collectively with the representatives of his employees, subject to the provisions of section 9(a).
(b) It shall be an unfair labor practice for a labor organization or its agents—
(1) to restrain or coerce (A) employees in the exercise of the rights guaranteed in section 7;
(2) to cause or attempt to cause an employer to discriminate against an employee;
(3) to refuse to bargain collectively with an employer, provided it is the representative of his employees subject to the provisions of section 9(a);
(4) (i) to engage in, or to induce or encourage any individual employed by any person engaged in commerce or in an industry affecting commerce to engage in, a strike or a refusal in the course of his employment to use, manufacture, process, transport, or otherwise handle or work on any goods, articles, materials, or commodities or to perform any services; or (ii) to threaten, coerce, or restrain any person engaged in commerce or in an industry affecting commerce, where in either case an object thereof is:

(A) forcing or requiring any employer or self-employed person to join any labor or employer organization or to enter into any agreement;

(B) forcing or requiring any person to cease using, selling, handling, transporting, or otherwise dealing in the products of any other producer, processor, or manufacturer, or to cease doing business with any other person, or forcing or requiring any other employer to recognize or bargain with a labor organization as the representative of such employees under the provisions of section 9;

(C) forcing or requiring any employer to recognize or bargain with a particular labor organization as the representative of his employees if any other labor organization has been certified as the representative of such employees under the provisions of section 9;

(D) forcing or requiring any employer to assign particular work to employees in a particular labor organization or in a particular trade, craft, or class rather than to employees in another labor organization or in another trade, craft, or class, unless such employer is failing to conform to an order or certification of the Board determining the bargaining representative for employees performing such work;

(5) to require of employees covered by an agreement authorized under subsection (a)(3) the payment, as a condition precedent to becoming a member of such organization, of a fee in an amount which the Board finds excessive or discriminatory under all the circumstances;
(6) to cause or attempt to cause an employer to pay or deliver or agree to pay or deliver any money or other thing of value, in the nature of an exaction, for services which are not performed or not to be performed; and
(7) to picket or cause to be picketed, or threaten to picket or cause to be picketed, any employer where an object thereof is forcing or requiring an employer to recognize or bargain with a labor organization as the representative of his employees, or forcing or requiring the employees of an employer to accept or select such labor organization as their collective bargaining representative.

REPRESENTATIVES AND ELECTIONS

Section 9. (a) Representatives designated or selected for the purpose of collective bargaining by the majority of the employees in a unit appropriate for such purposes, shall be the exclusive representatives of all the employees in such unit for the purpose of collective bargaining in respect to rates of pay, wages, hours of employment, or other conditions of employment.

Section 19. Any employee who is a member of and adheres to established and traditional tenets or teachings of a bona fide religion, body, or sect which has historically held conscientious objections to joining or financially supporting labor organizations shall not be required to join or financially support any labor organization as a condition of employment; except that such employee may be required in a contract between such employees' employer and a labor organization in lieu of periodic dues and initiation fees, to pay sums equal to such dues and initiation fees to a nonreligious, nonlabor organization charitable fund exempt from taxation under section 501(c)(3) of title 26, chosen by such employee from a list of at least three such funds, designated in such contract or if the contract fails to designate such funds, then to any such fund chosen by the employee.

CHAPTER 22 Wage and Hour Regulation

FAIR LABOR STANDARDS ACT

In 1938, Congress enacted the Fair Labor Standards Act to regulate both the minimum compensation that could be given to a worker on an hourly basis and the maximum number of hours an employee could be required to work before being compensated at an overtime rate of one and one-half times the normal rate of pay. The minimum wage has risen through the years but is not indexed to the cost of living. Since October 1, 1996, the minimum wage rate was $4.75. On September 1, 1997, the minimum wage will be increased to $5.15. The maximum number of hours before the overtime is required is forty hours per work week. The regular rate of pay, which is used to determine the maximum wage, may include the reasonable cost of room, board, and other facilities; gifts; bonuses; days compensated for vacation, illness, or personal reasons; reimbursed expenses for meals, lodging, and travel expenses; contributions toward pensions; premiums for life, disability, and health insurance; and extra compensation for work performed on a Saturday or Sunday.

Employment Perspective

Brittany Robinson works at the Baked Cake Shop in Vernon. She is a full-time employee who works Wednesday through Sunday, eight hours a day. Brittany's gross pay per week is $190.00. The Baked Cake pays $6.50 per hour on Saturday and Sunday. Is the Baked Shop in violation of the minimum wage law established in the Fair Labor Standard Act? Yes! The extra compensation Brittany received for Saturday and

Sunday work cannot be used in determining the regular rate of hourly pay. Subtracting her Saturday and Sunday wages of $104 ($6.50 per hour times sixteen hours), Brittany is paid $86.00 for the twenty-four hours of work. This amounts to $3.58 per hour, which is below the minimum wage. ◆

In the following case, the question is whether wages are considered unpaid under the Fair Labor Standards Act if they are paid late. Here, there were no funds appropriated for wages because there was no state budget.

1 F.3d 1537 (9th Cir. 1993)

RYMER, Circuit Judge.

This appeal requires us to decide whether California violated the minimum wage provisions of the Fair Labor Standards Act ("FLSA"), by paying wages 14–15 days late because there was no state budget, and thus no funds appropriated for the payment of salaries, on payday. The district court granted a summary judgment declaring that the failure to issue paychecks promptly when due violated the FLSA. We agree, and hold that under the FLSA wages are "unpaid" unless they are paid on the employees' regular payday.

Payday in this case—July 16, 1990—came and went without highway maintenance workers employed by the State of California Department of Transportation being issued their pay checks. California was undergoing one of its perennial rites, the budget impasse. In 1990, State law prohibited the release of paychecks until a budget was approved by the Legislature and signed by the Governor. That didn't happen until July 28, when the budget passed the Legislature, and July 31, when then Governor Deukmejian signed it into law. The payroll was met on July 30 and 31, 14–15 days late.

William Biggs represents a class of highway maintenance workers who brought suit against the Governor, Treasurer, Controller, and the Transportation Director (collectively "state officials"). The class seeks injunctive and declaratory relief, liquidated damages, and prejudgment interest on the account and delay of receiving wages.

State officials now appeal the district court's October 3, 1991 order, raising two issues: whether the FLSA contains an implicit requirement that wages be paid promptly, and if so, does it violate the State of California's Tenth Amendment sovereignty.

The FLSA requires that an employer pay each employee a minimum wage set by the Act. Section 206 (b) mandates that "every employer shall pay" employees the minimum wage if "in any work week the employee is engaged in commerce."

State officials correctly point out that the FLSA does not in terms say that a minimum wage must be paid promptly. It simply says that employers "shall pay" a minimum wage. However, in construing the FLSA, we must be mindful of the directive that it is to be liberally construed to apply to the furthest reaches consistent with Congressional direction.

This case requires us to consider the obligation to pay in light of the statutory scheme as a whole. The FLSA provides for the recovery of unpaid minimum wages, unpaid overtime compensation, and liquidated damages; and has its own statute of limitations for private enforcement.

These provisions necessarily assume that wages are due at some point, and thereafter become unpaid.

We start with 206 (b). It directs every employer to pay the minimum wage. The obligation kicks in once an employee has done covered work in any workweek. To us, "shall pay" plainly connotes shall make a payment. If a payday has passed without payment, an employer cannot have met his obligation to "pay."

Section 216 (b) then provides that an employer who violates 206 is liable to the affected employees "in the amount of their unpaid minimum wages, or their unpaid overtime compensation . . . and in an additional equal amount as liquidated damages." Unless there is a due date after which minimum wage has become unpaid, imposing liability for both unpaid minimum wages and liquidated damages would be meaningless.

The statute must therefore contemplate a time at which 206 is violated, or, put another way, when minimum wages become "unpaid." "Unpaid minimum wages" have to be "unpaid" as of some distinct point, otherwise courts could not compute the amount of liquidated damages. If an employee had a right to recover only at the point of nonpayment (as opposed to late payment), but the period of limitations began running as of the employees' payday, the statute would start running before an employee had a right to recover. That cannot be correct.

State officials do not explain when or how "late payments" metamorphose into "nonpayment" such that the Act is violated and the employer is exposed to liability for unpaid minimum wages and additional compensation by way of liquidated damages. Likewise, it is unclear on their theory how many paychecks an employee has to miss before filing suit, being able to show a violation, and recovering liquidated damages or prejudgment interest. Nor do we agree with their suggestion that a rule that paychecks are due on payday unfairly penalizes employers who happen to be late in paying their employees. An employer who acts in good faith is not subject to liquidated damages. While the employer remains obligated to pay overdue wages and is subject to prejudgment interest on the unpaid wages in the event of litigation, this result properly deters employers from "gambling on evading the Act" as they could if the remedy were only liability of the amount originally due.

Thus, state officials' argument for why the absence of an explicit prompt payment obligation means that wages need not be paid promptly without enhanced compensation by way of liquidated damages or prejudgment interest, is unpersuasive.

We therefore hold that state officials' failure to issue the class's paychecks promptly when due violates the FLSA. Paychecks are due on payday after that the minimum wage is "unpaid."

Judgment for Biggs.

Employment Perspective

Hector Jiminez is a Mexican farmworker in Southern California. Pine Valley Farm pays Hector $3.50 per hour throughout the year and then makes up the difference between that rate and the minimum wage rate at the end of the year. Is Pine Valley in violation of the minimum wage standard? Yes! The minimum wage is determined on the basis of each work week. The year-end payment must be looked on as extra compensation or a bonus and may not be factored in. Pine Valley is in violation of the minimum wage requirement. The first week it paid Hector at the rate of $3.50 per hour. Pine Valley is not given a grace period of an entire year to make up the difference. ◆

In the next case, the issue is whether a state labor agency can automatically give its employees time off in lieu of overtime pay when the employees have designated a union representative to bargain for them.

CASE

Lynwood Moreau v. Johnny Klevenhagen, Sheriff, Harris County, Texas

113 S.Ct. 1905 (1993)

Justice STEVENS delivered the opinion of the Court.

The Fair Labor Standards Act (FLSA or Act) generally requires employers to pay their employees for overtime work at a rate of one and a half times the employees' regular wages. In 1985, Congress amended the FLSA to provide a limited exception to this rule for state and local governmental agencies. Under the Fair Labor Standards Amendments of 1985 (1985 Amendments), public employers may compensate employees who work overtime with extra time off instead of overtime pay in certain circumstances. The question in this case is whether a public employer in a State that prohibits public sector collective bargaining may take advantage of that exception when its employees have designated a union representative.

Because the text of the Amendments provides the framework for our entire analysis, we quote the most relevant portion at the outset. Subsection 7(o) (2) (A) states:

> "(2) A public agency may provide compensatory time [in lieu of overtime pay] only—
>
> –(A) pursuant to—
>
> –(i) applicable provisions of a collective bargaining agreement, memorandum of understanding, or any other agreement between the public agency and representatives of such employees; or
>
> –(ii) in the case of employees not covered by subclause (i), an agreement or understanding arrived at between the employer and employee before the performance of the work. . . ."

Petitioners are a group of employees who sought, unsuccessfully, to negotiate a collective FLSA compensatory time agreement by way of a designated representative. The narrow question dispositive here is whether petitioners are employees not covered by subclause (i) within the meaning of subclause (ii), so that their employer may provide compensatory time pursuant to individual agreements under the second subclause.

Congress enacted the FLSA in 1938 to establish nationwide minimum wage and maximum hours standards. Section 7 of the Act encourages compliance with maximum hours standards by providing that employees generally must be paid on a time-and-one-half basis for all hours worked in excess of 40 per week.

Amendments to the Act in 1966 and 1974 extended its coverage to most public employers, and gave rise to a series of cases questioning the power of Congress to regulate the compensation of state and local employees. Following our decision in *Garcia v. San Antonio Metropolitan Transit Authority,* upholding that power, the Department of Labor (DOL) announced that it would hold public employers to the standards of the Act effective April 15, 1985.

In response to the Garcia decision and the DOL announcement, both Houses of Congress held hearings and considered legislation designed to ameliorate the burdens associated with necessary changes in public employment practices. The projected financial costs of coming into compliance with the FLSA—particularly the overtime provisions—were specifically identified as a matter of grave concern to many States and localities. The statutory provision at issue in this case is the product of those deliberations.

In its Report recommending enactment of the 1985 Amendments, the Senate Committee on Labor and Human Resources explained that the new subsection 7(o) would allow public employers to compensate for overtime hours with compensatory time off, or "comp time," in lieu of overtime pay, so long as certain conditions were met: the provision of comp time must be at the premium rate of not less than one and one-half hours per hour of overtime work, and must be pursuant to an agreement reached prior to performance of the work. With respect to the nature of the necessary agreement, the issue raised in this case, the Committee stated: "Where employees have a recognized representative, the agreement or understanding must be between that representative and the employer, either through collective bargaining or through a memorandum of understanding or other type of agreement."

The Secretary of Labor explained:

> "The Department believes that the proposed rule accurately reflects the statutory requirement that a CBA [collective bargaining agreement], memorandum of understanding or other agreement be reached between the public agency and the representative of the employees where the employees have designated a representative. Where the employees do not have a representative, the agreement must be between the employer and the individual employees. The Department recognizes that there is a wide variety of State law that may be pertinent in this area. It is the Department's intention that the question of whether employees have a representative for purposes of FLSA section 7(o) shall be determined in accordance with State or local law and practices."

Petitioner Moreau is the president of the Harris County Deputy Sheriffs Union, representing approximately 400 deputy sheriffs in this action against the County and its sheriff, respondent Klevenhagen. For several years, the Union has represented Harris County deputy sheriffs in various matters, such as processing grievances and handling workers' compensation claims, but it is prohibited by Texas law from entering into a collective-bargaining agreement with the County. Accordingly, the terms and conditions of petitioners' employment are included in individual form agreements signed by each employee. These agreements incorporate by reference the County's regulations providing that deputies shall receive one and one-half hours of compensatory time for each hour of overtime work.

Petitioners filed this action in 1986, alleging, that the County violated the Act by paying for overtime work with comp time, rather than overtime pay, absent an agreement with their representative authorizing the substitution. Petitioners contended that they were "covered" by subclause (i) of subsection 7(o) (2) (A) by virtue of their union representation, and that the County therefore was precluded from providing comp time pursuant to individual agreements (or pre-existing practice) under subclause (ii).

At least one proposition is not in dispute. Subclause (ii) authorizes individual comp time agreements only "in the case of employees not covered by subclause (i)." Our task, therefore, is to identify the class of "employees" covered by subclause (i). This task is complicated by the fact that subclause (i) does not purport to define a category of employees, as the reference in subclause (ii) suggests it would. Instead, it describes only a category of agreements—those that (a) are bargained with an employee representative, and (b) authorize the use of comp time.

The most plausible reading of the phrase "employees . . . covered by subclause (i)" is, in our view, neither of the extreme alternatives described above. Rather, the phrase is most sensibly read as referring to employees who have designated a representative with the authority to negotiate and agree with their employer on "applicable provisions of a collective bargaining agreement" authorizing the use of comp time. This reading accords significance to both the focus on the word "agreement" in subclause (i) and the focus on "employees" in subclause (ii). It is also true to the hierarchy embodied in subsection 7(o), which favors subclause (i) agreements over individual agreements by limiting use of the latter to cases in which the former are unavailable.

Thus, under both the statute and the DOL regulations, employees are "covered" by subclause (i) when they designate a representative who lawfully may bargain collectively on their behalf—under the statute, because such authority is necessary to reach the kind of "agreement" described in subclause (i), and under the regulation, because such authority is a condition of "representative" status for subclause (i) purposes. Because we construe the statute and regulation in harmony, we need not comment further on petitioners' argument that the Secretary's interpretation of the 1985 Amendments is entitled to special deference.

Petitioners in this case did not have a representative authorized by law to enter into an agreement with their employer providing for use of comp time under subclause (i). Accordingly, they were "not covered by subclause (i)," and subclause (ii) authorized the individual agreements challenged in this litigation.

The judgment of the Court of Appeals is affirmed.

Judgment for Klevenhagen.

Employment Perspective

Angela Montalbano is a Floral Arranger for Violets and Roses Flower Shop. She is a full-time employee. During Valentine's Day week Angela worked fifty hours, and the following week Angela worked thirty hours. Angela is paid every two weeks. In her paycheck, she was compensated at her regular rate of pay for eighty hours. Is Violets And Roses in violation of the overtime pay provision of the maximum hours requirement of the Fair Labor Standards Act? Yes! Each workweek must be looked at unto itself. One cannot offset against the other. The fact that Violets and Roses does not have enough work for Angela the week following Valentine's Day is immaterial. Angela is entitled to the hours of overtime pay for Valentine's week at the rate of one and one-half times the regular rate of pay. In the second week Angela will receive her regular rate of pay for thirty hours unless she was hired with the proviso that she would be guaranteed a forty-hour work week. Then she must be paid for the additional hours even if there is no work to do. ◆

Overtime pay is not required when the employee is receiving up to ten hours per week of remedial education that is not specific job training. Overtime would be required in excess of the ten hours if this remediation is mandated by the company. If it were a voluntary after-work program, no pay at all would be required.

Employment Perspective

Rufus Buttonwod is an employee at Maple Woods Convention Center. At times, Rufus is asked to fill in as a customer service representative. Rufus's grammar is poor. Maple Woods provides him with remedial tutoring one hour per day, in addition to his normal eight hour day. Rufus's attendance is mandatory. He is paid at his regular rate for forty-five hours. Is Maple Woods adhering to the provisions of the maximum-hour laws? Yes! The five hours' remediation is compensable at the regular rate of pay. ◆

In the case that follows, police officers' overtime pay was calculated on the basis of a different number of hours from other city workers. The city argued that as long as all police officers were treated equally, the formula was acceptable. The officers complained that it violated the Fair Labor Standards Act in that one class of employees was treated differently from the others.

CASE *Marie v. City of New Orleans*

612 So.2d 244 (La. App. 4 Cir. 1992)

LOBRAND, Judge.

The Civil Service Commission and the City have violated the Louisiana Constitution by discriminating against plaintiffs in the computation of overtime pay. The factual thrust of their assertion is that police officers are treated differently than other civil service employees because police officers must work 171 hours within 28 days before overtime begins, whereas other civil service employees begin overtime after working 40 hours a week.

The Commission and the City argue that the mandates of the Fair Labor Standards Act, preempts state law and alternatively, even if this court finds that pre-emption is not applicable, there is no violation of the Louisiana Constitution under the facts as pleaded.

Article 10, section 10 (A) (1) of the Louisiana Constitution requires every Civil Service Commission to adopt a uniform pay plan. "A major intent and purpose of Civil Service is to insure uniformity among employees covered thereby, to the end that such employees in a particular class will enjoy equal and uniform rights with others in the same class regardless of the department, agency, board or commission in which they may be employed." Variations in pay schedules between employees in the same classification violates the Constitutional requirement of a uniform pay plan. Thus, it is a fundamental notion that employees who perform equal work should receive equal pay and classifications that have no rational basis for difference in treatment will not support pay differentials.

In 1985, the U.S. Supreme Court held that the minimum wage and overtime obligations of the Fair Labor Standards Act (FLSA) were applicable to state and local governmental employees. The court expressly held that the Congressional legislation adopted pursuant to the Commerce Clause which regulates employees' minimum wage and hours does not violate any Tenth Amendment immunity enjoyed by the States. In response to that decision, Congress amended the FLSA to provide for compensatory time off for public employees in lieu of overtime pay. Subsection k of Section 7 of FLSA (29 U.S.C. 207(k)) provides a method of computing maximum hours for firefighters and police officers that is different than the forty hour per week maximum of subsection (a). That is, the maximum hours firefighters and police officers must work before overtime pay is required (either cash or compensatory time) is predicated on a work period of 28 consecutive days, rather than a regular work week. Thus FLSA provides for a different treatment of police officers and firefighters presumably because of the nature of their duties.

In the instant case appellants have not alleged that the Commission's implementation of the 28 day, 171 hour overtime standard is violative of FLSA, only that it violates the Louisiana Constitutional requirement of a uniform pay plan. Thus the first issue for our determination is whether the Civil Service Commission's compliance with FLSA's provisions pre-empt any State requirement for uniformity.

Garcia v. Metropolitan Transit Authority resolved the issue of whether forcing state and local governments to comply with the FLSA infringed upon the sovereign immunity doctrine of the Tenth Amendment of the U.S. Constitution. That decision specifically held that "affording employees the protection of the wage and hour provisions of FLSA contravened no affirmative limit on Congress' power under the Commerce Clause." The question of pre-empting a conflicting state law was not at issue. Preemption occurs where compliance with both federal and state law is, in effect, physically impossible and when the federal legislation implicitly acts as barrier to state regulation.

Here, we find that the pre-emption doctrine is inapplicable. While it is true that public employees are not subject to FLSA, compliance with that act does not necessarily require the Commission to violate its uniform pay plan mandate. At this juncture of the case we cannot say that compliance with both Federal and State law is impossible. Even though subsection K allows different treatment for computing maximum hours for fire and police officers, it does not mandate that governmental employers follow its provisions in order to be in compliance.

We find merit, however, in the City's alternative argument that the Constitutional mandate of a uniform pay plan requires uniform pay for like classes. That is, uniform pay arguments are only applicable when members of the same civil service class are paid differently. There is no prohibition against computing different overtime pay for different classes. As we have previously noted, the intent of Civil Service is to insure uniformity in pay among employees who are similarly situated, i.e. of the same classification. Appellants' allegations consistently asserted that they are subject to disparate treatment because other civil service employees are treated differently. Assuming their allegations are true, appellants have no remedy because the Commission's uniform pay obligation extends only to those employees within the same classification. Merely alleging treatment different from other civil service employees does not afford a remedy for discrimination. For that reason appellants fail to state a cause of action for discriminatory treatment. Accordingly, we affirm the trial court.

AFFIRMED.
Judgment for City of New Orleans.

The following case addresses the question of whether an employee who is "on call" should be compensated for those hours in excess of forty hours per week at the overtime rate. The employees argued they could not effectively use the waiting time for their own personal purposes.

Casserly v. State

844 P.2d 1275 (Colo. App. 1992)

METZER, Judge.

Plaintiffs were employed as physician assistants at the State Correctional Facility at Canon City, Colorado. Each plaintiff was assigned to a single facility for full-time duties requiring not less than 40 hours per week. In addition, on a rotating basis, each plaintiff was required to provide emergency medical services to inmates after regular working hours. Plaintiffs were compensated at one and one-half their regular rate of pay for those hours they were physically present at a facility responding to a call.

Before November 1988, plaintiffs were not paid for the time spent waiting for calls. After that time, defendants paid plaintiffs at a rate of $1.75 per hour as "on-call" pay.

During on-call periods, plaintiffs were required to respond to any of seven facilities covering an 8-mile radius within 20 minutes of receiving a call for services (if they determined that the call necessitated a physical response to a facility

and could not be handled by telephone). The number and frequency of calls received during any on-call shift were not predictable.

The need to respond immediately to medical calls required plaintiffs to maintain a constant state of readiness. They did not engage in recreational activities during these hours, nor did they use this time for their own personal purposes. Plaintiffs testified that they did not shower, walk for recreation, cook meals, eat in restaurants, entertain guests, perform yard work, or attend sporting events during their on-call hours. Some plaintiffs rented motel rooms in Canon City in order to meet the response time requirements rather than going home during these shifts.

Plaintiffs claimed their time spent waiting for calls constituted hours worked pursuant to the Federal Fair Labor Standards Act (FLSA), and that they should be compensated at a rate of time and one-half for all hours spent on-call in excess of their regular 40 hours per week.

Plaintiffs filed a formal grievance with defendants in March 1988 for overtime pay and supplied copes of state fiscal rules incorporating the provisions of the FLSA and affidavits detailing the restrictions imposed upon their lives while on call. The grievance was denied.

Thereafter, plaintiffs commenced this action, alleging violations of the FLSA and breach of contract. The trial court entered summary judgment in favor of defendants and dismissed the contract claim. The FLSA claims were tried to the court, which entered judgment in favor of plaintiffs. It awarded damages of one and one-half times plaintiffs' hourly rate for on-call time from May 1, 1987, based on application of a two-year statute of limitations for non-wilful violations of the FLSA. Defendants appeal the liability determination; plaintiffs cross-appeal the damages awarded. We will address only those issues raised in the parties' opening briefs.

Defendants assert that, in March 1988, the Department of Corrections officials and the plaintiffs had agreed that time spent waiting for calls would be compensated at $1.75 per hour, and time spent when plaintiffs physically traveled to a facility responding to a call would be compensated at time and one-half. Thus, they argue the trial court erred in refusing to consider the impact of this agreement on plaintiffs' FLSA claims.

The FLSA's overtime requirement has two purposes: 1) to encourage employers to hire additional workers rather than employ fewer workers for longer hours, and 2) to compensate employees who do work overtime for the burden of having to do so. The Act "forbids pay plans that have the effect of reducing the pay for overtime to less than one-half times the employees' regular rate, even though the plans may be acceptable to the employees involved."

Given the nature of the demands on the plaintiffs during their waiting time, we conclude, as did the trial court, that any agreement to pay them $1.75 per hour (well below their average salary of nearly $18 per hour) would be contrary to the purpose of the FLSA and thus would violate public policy.

The FLSA requires the payment of time and one-half of an employee's regular rate of pay for each hour worked in excess of 40 hours in any workweek.

"An employee who is required to remain on call on the employer's premises or so close thereto that he cannot use the time effectively for his own purposes is working while 'on call.' Whether 'waiting time' is 'working time' depends on the particular case and is a question of fact to be resolved by the trial court."

The test is whether the time is spent predominantly for the employer's benefit, the employee is 'engaged to be waiting,' and is entitled to compensation.

There is overwhelming evidence in the record demonstrating that waiting time was not spent in ways the plaintiffs would have chosen had they been free to do so. Hence, we will not disturb the trial court's finding that the plaintiffs could not use the time effectively for their own purposes and, thus, were "working" for purposes of the FLSA.

The portion of the judgment finding defendants liable is affirmed.
Judgment for Casserly.

Exemptions

Certain employees are exempted from the minimum wage and the maximum hour requirements. These include executives, administrators, professionals, salespeople, elementary and secondary schoolteachers, domestic helpers who reside in the household, baby-sitters, and people who provide companionship and care to the elderly. Camp counselors are also exempted if the camp is not in operation for more than seven months in the calendar year.

Employment Perspective

Tiffany O'Toole works as a camp counselor for three months each summer at Camp Fooey. The camp operates thirteen weeks each year. She often works eight hours a day, seven days a week. Tiffany is paid a flat rate of $3,000 plus room and board, which has a reasonable value of $1,000. Is Camp Fooey in violation of the minimum wage and maximum hour requirement? No! Camp counselors are exempt even though Tiffany's cumulative compensation of $4,000 is less than the $4,284.80 minimum wage including overtime required by the Fair Labor Standards Act. The $4,284.80 figure is arrived at as follows: 13 weeks times 40 hours times $5.15 equals $2,678.00 plus 13 weeks times 16 hours (Saturday and Sunday) times $7.725 equals $1,606.80 for a total of $4,284.80. ◆

There are many exceptions to the maximum hours requirement. A few of which include domestic helpers, taxicar drivers and movie theater employees.

Employment Perspective

Myrtle Dover is a domestic helper who resides with the Remingtons. At times, she works in excess of eight-hour days and always works on Saturdays and Sundays unless the family is vacationing. Myrtle is paid a set fee each week in accordance with the minimum wage law, but she is not paid overtime. Are the Remingtons in violation of the maximum hour laws? No! There is an exception for domestic helpers. ◆

The issue in the next case is whether a city mass transit system is exempt from the Fair Labor Standards Act because it is involved with intrastate commercial activity.

CASE *Garcia v. San Antonio Metro. Transit Auth.*

469 U.S. 528 (1984)

Justice BLACKMUN delivered the opinion of the Court.

In the present cases, a Federal District Court concluded that municipal ownership and operation of a mass-transit system is a traditional governmental function and thus, under *National League of Cities,* is exempt from obligations imposed by the FLSA (Fair Labor Standards Act). Faced with the identical question, three Federal Courts of Appeals and one state appellate court have reached the opposite conclusions.

Appellees have not argued that San Antonio Metro. Transit Authority (SAMTA) is immune from regulation under the FLSA on the ground that it is a local transit system engaged in intrastate commercial activity. In a practical sense, SAMTA's operations might well be characterized as "local." Nonetheless, it long has been settled that Congress' authority under the Commerce Clause extends to intrastate economic activities that affect interstate commerce. Were SAMTA a privately owned and operated enterprise, it could not credibly argue that Congress exceeded the bounds of its Commerce Clause powers in prescribing minimum wages and overtime rates for SAMTA's employees. Any constitutional exemption from the requirements of the FLSA therefore must rest on SAMTA's status as a governmental entity rather than on the "local" nature of its operations.

Under that summary, four conditions must be satisfied before a state activity may be deemed immune from a particular federal regulation under the Commerce Clause. First, it is said that the federal statute at issue must regulate "the 'State as States.'" Second, the statute must "address matters that are indisputably 'attributes of state sovereignty.'" Third, state compliance with federal obligation must "directly impair the States' ability 'to structure integral operations in areas of traditional government functions.'" Finally, the relation of state and federal interests must not be such that "the nature of the federal interest . . . justifies state submission."

As far as the present cases are concerned, then, we need go no further than to state that we perceive nothing in the overtime and minimum wage requirements of the FLSA, as applied to SAMTA, that is destructive of state sovereignty of any constitutional provision. SAMTA faces nothing more than the same minimum wage and overtime sanctions that hundreds of thousands of other employers, public as well as private, have to meet.

This analysis makes it clear that Congress' action in affording SAMTA employees the protection of the wage and hour provisions of the FLSA contravened no affirmative limit on Congress' power under the Commerce Clause. The judgment of the District Court therefore must be reversed.

Judgment for Garcia.

CHILD LABOR

Children who are at least sixteen years of age may work in any occupation as long as it has not been deemed hazardous by the Secretary of Labor. Children who are fourteen or fifteen years of age shall not be permitted to work in manufacturing, mining, and other occupations that interfere with their schooling and/or their health and well-being. Children under fourteen are not permitted to work unless it is for their parents or approved by the court for entertainment or athletic contracts.

Employment Perspective

Robby Landry, who is seventeen, was hired by Major Waste Materials Corp. to load hazardous and radioactive containers for shipment. Is this permissible? No! The transport of hazardous and radioactive waste is a dangerous activity. Therefore, children may not work in this occupation. ◆

Employment Perspective

Lawrence Connery is an attorney with his own practice. He employs his twelve-year-old daughter, Tiffany, to work for him two hours after school each day. Her responsibilities include photocopying, stapling, dusting, and making coffee. Is this permissible? Yes! Parents may employ the services of their children as long as it is not in a hazardous occupation. ◆

Employment Perspective

Michele Goldsmith is a fourteen-year-old freshman at Richmond Hill High. She works the 2-to-10 shifts at Foodway three days a week. In order to get to work on time, she has to cut her last class, which because of a rotating schedule, changes each day, and is not particularly noticeable. Is this permissible? No! The Fair Labor Standards Act would prohibit Michele's current employment because it interferes with her schooling in that it forces her to leave school early and leaves her no time to do her homework. ◆

Employment Perspective

Cindy Masterson is a four-year-old model of children's clothes. She also performs in a television commercial occasionally and is employed by various manufacturers and retail clothing stores. Is this employment permissible? Yes! Cindy's contracts must be court-approved. If the court determines this action is in Cindy's best interest, she will be allowed to perform. ◆

REVIEW QUESTIONS

1. Explain the significance of the Fair Labor Standards Act.
2. Is the current minimum wage adequate?
3. Explain the purpose of the minimum wage law.
4. What is the rule regarding maximum hours and overtime?
5. Why is there a need to cap the number of hours worked?
6. Explain the child labor laws.
7. What are the exceptions to the child labor laws?
8. Explain what would happen if there was no Fair Labor Standards Act.
9. Is it ethical to employ illegal immigrants at a wage below the minimum?
10. What effect will the GATT (General Agreement on Tariffs and Treaties) and NAFTA (North American Free Trade Agreement) have on wage and hour regulation?

11. O'Neil accepted a delayed payment of wages from his employer. The employer, Brooklyn Savings Bank, argued that O'Neil's action constituted a waiver of his right to receive liquidated damages. What was the result? *Brooklyn Savings Bank v. O'Neil,* 324 U.S. 697 (1945)

12. Usery argued that the National League of Cities violated the minimum-wage and overtime provisions of the Fair Labor Standards Act. The National League of Cities argued that Congress was not empowered through the Commerce Clause to enforce the minimum wage and overtime provisions against the States in areas of traditional government functions. Usery retorted with the opposite. What was the result? *National League of Cities v. Usery,* 426 U.S. 833 (1976)

13. The Michigan Window Cleaning Company entered into a collective bargaining agreement with its employees providing for 44 hours of regular wage per week. Martino, an employee, claimed that this agreement was entered into in violation of the Fair Labor Standards Act providing for maximum hours before payment of overtime. What was the result? *Martino v. Michigan Window Cleaning Company,* 327 U.S. 173 (1945)

14. What is the test to determine whether an employee is on the job and entitled to compensation? *Armour & Co. v. Wantock,* 323 U.S. 126 (1994)

15. Mireles, an employee for Frio Foods, was required to be on call. Frio Foods refused to compensate him for this time. Mireles brought suit, alleging that he was entitled to be paid wages for time on call according to the Fair Labor Standards Act. What was the result? *Armour & Co. v. Wantock,* 323 U.S. 126 (1994)

16. Skidmore was required by his employer, Swift Co., to be "on call." His hours exceeded the 40-hour-workweek. Skidmore was not paid overtime. Swift argued Skidmore was not entitled to compensation. Whether "waiting time" is "working time" depends on the particular case and is a question of fact to be resolved by the trial court. The FLSA requires the payment of time and one-half of an employee's regular rate of pay for each hour worked in excess of 40 hours in any workweek. What was the result? *Skidmore v. Swift Co.,* 323 U.S. 134 (1994)

17. Was the case on pp. 508 decided ethically?

18. In the case on pp. 511, should there be any exceptions to the FLSA?

19. In the case on pp. 502, is the lack of a state budget sufficient excuse for nonpayment of wages?

20. In the case on pp. 507 was it ethical to calculate the police officer's overtime pay according to a different method?

Fair Labor Standards Act of 1938

Sec. 202 Congressional Finding and Declaration of Policy.

(a) The Congress has found that the existence, in industries engaged in commerce or in the production of goods for commerce, of labor condition detrimental to the maintainance of the minimum standard of living necessary for health, efficiency, and general well-being of workers (1) causes commerce and the channels and instrumentalities of commerce to be used to spread and perpetuate such labor conditions among the workers of the several States; (2) burdens commerce and the free flow of goods in commerce; (3) constitutes an unfair method of competition in commerce; (4) leads to labor disputes burdening and obstructing commerce and the free flow of goods in commerce; and (5) interferes with the orderly and fair free marketing of goods in commerce. The Congress further finds that the employment of persons in domestic service in households affect commerce.

Sec. 206 Minimum Wage.

(a) Employees engaged in commerce; home workers in Puerto Rico and Virgin Islands; employees in American Samoa; seamen on American vessels; agricultural employees

Every employer shall pay to each of his employees who in any work week is engaged in commerce or in the production of good for commerce, or is employed in an enterprise engaged in commerce or in the production of goods for commerce, wages at the following rates:

(1) except as otherwise provided in this section, not less than $3.35 an hour during the period ending March 31, 1990, not less than $3.80 an hour during the year beginning April 1, 1990, and not less than $4.25 an hour after March 31, 1991;

(Section 206(d) of the Fair Labor Standards Act is more familiarly known as the Equal Pay Act)

(d) (1) No employer having employees subject to any provisions of this section shall discriminate. within any establishment in which such employees are employed, between employees on the basis of sex by paying wages to employees of the opposite sex in such establishment for equal work on jobs the performance of which requires equal skill, effort, and responsibility, and which are performed under similar working conditions, except where such payment is made pursuant to (i) a seniority system; (ii) a merit system; (iii) a system which measures earnings by quantity or quality of production; or (iv) a differential based on any other factor than sex: Provided, That an employer who is paying a wage rate differential in violation of this subsection shall not, in order to comply with the provisions of this subsection, reduce the wage rate of any employee.

(2) No labor organization, or its agents, representing employees of an employer having employees subject to any provisions of this section shall cause or attempt to cause such an employer to discriminate against an employee in violation of paragraph (1) of this subsection.

(3) For purposes of administration and enforcement, any amounts of money owing to any employee which have been withheld in violation of this subsection shall be deemed to be unpaid minimum wages or unpaid overtime compensation under this chapter.

(4) As used in this subsection, the term "labor organization" means any organization of any kind, or any agency or employee representation committee or plan, in which employees participate and which exists for the purpose, in whole or in part, of dealing with employers concerning grievances,

labor disputes, wages, rates of pay, hours of employment, or conditions of work.

Sec. 207 Maximum Hours.

(a) Employees engaged in interstate commerce; additional applicability to employees pursuant to subsequent amendatory provisions

(1) Except as otherwise provided in this section, no employer shall employ any of his employees who in any workweek is engaged in commerce or production of goods for commerce, or is employed in an enterprise engaged in commerce or in the production of goods for commerce, for a workweek longer than forty hours unless such employee receives compensation for his employment in excess of the hours such as maximum workweek.

Sec. 212 Child Labor Provisions.

(c) Oppressive child labor

No employer shall employ an oppressive child labor in commerce or in the production of goods for commerce or in any enterprise engaged in commerce or in the production of goods for commerce.

Sec. 213 Exemptions.

(a) Minimum wage and maximum hour requirements

The provisions of section 206 (except subsection (d) in the case of paragraph (1) of this subsection) and section 207 of this title shall nor apply with respect to—

(1) any employee employed in a bona fide executive, administrative, or professional capacity (including any employed in the capacity of academic administrative personnel or teacher in elementary or secondary schools), or in the capacity of outside salesman (as such terms are defined and delimited from time to time by regulations of the Secretary, subject to the provisions of subchapter II of chapter 5 of title 5, except that an employee of a retail or service establishment shall not be excluded from the definition of employee employed in a bona fide executive or administrative capacity because of the number of hours in his workweek which he devotes to activities not directly or closely related to the performance of executive or administrative activities, if less than 40 percent of his hours worked in the workweek are devoted to such activities).

(c) Child labor requirements

(1) Except as provided in section 212 of this title relating to child labor shall not apply to any employee employed in agriculture outside of school hours for the school district where such employee is living while he is so employed, if such employee—

(A) is less than twelve years of age and (i) is employed by his parent, or by a person standing in the place of his parent, on a farm owned or operated by such parent or person, or (ii) is employed, with the consent of his parent or person standing in the place of his parent, on a farm, none of the employees of which are required to be paid at the wage rate prescribed by this title,

(B) is twelve or thirteen years of age and (i) such employment is with the consent of his parent or person standing in the place of his parent, or (ii) his parents or such person is employed on the same farm as such employee, or

(C) is fourteen years of age or older.

(2) The provisions of section 212 of this title relating to child labor shall apply to an employee below the age of sixteen employed in agriculture in an occupation that the Secretary of Labor finds and declares to be particularly hazardous for the employment of children below the age of sixteen, except where such employee is employed by his parent or by a person standing in the place of his parent on a farm owned or operated by such parent or person.

(3) The provisions of section 212 of this title relating to child labor shall not apply to any child employed as an actor or performer in motion pictures or theatrical productions, or in radio or television productions.

CHAPTER 23

Occupational Safety and Health Act

INTRODUCTION

The Occupational Safety and Health Act of 1970 (OSHAct) was designed to set forth a standard which would provide for the safety and health of employees while on the job. Employers are required to provide a place of employment free of occupational hazards. Employees are required to follow rules and regulations established to promote their safety and to use equipment designed to insure their safety.

ADMINISTRATIVE AGENCIES

OSHAct created three administrative agencies. The first is the Occupational Safety and Health Administration, also known as OSHA. Its purpose is to set health and safety standards and see to it that these standards are implemented by employers through plant and office inspections. If an employer is in violation, OSHA seeks corrective action voluntarily by the employer through a hearing conducted by the Occupational Safety and Health Review Commission (OSHRC). If OSHRC rules against an employer, it may impose fines or other penalties against the employer. The employer has the right of appeal to the Circuit Court. OSHRC is the enforcement arm created by the Occupational Safety and Health Act. Finally, the National Institute of Occupational Safety and Health (NIOSH) was created to conduct research and make health and safety recommendations to OSHA for consideration.

The Occupational Safety and Health Act (OSHAct) was enacted to reduce safety and health hazards, thereby preventing injuries, loss of wages, lost production, and incurrence of medical and disability expenses. Employees must be provided with a safe environment free of toxic substances, asbestos dust, and cotton dust. Precautions must be taken for first aid, eye and face protection, and safety at excavation sites to prevent cave-ins. Employees must be accorded a work environment with adequate lighting, ventilation, and heat, as well as tools and equipment that are in proper working order. The Department of Labor has the right to inspect the work environment to insure adherence to the OSHA requirements. The Occupational Safety and Health Review Commission is the initial review body for violations of the act.

SECRETARY OF LABOR

The addition of or deletion of occupational health and safety standards are promulgated by the Secretary of Labor. Interested parties may submit written comments regarding a proposal. If the Secretary reiterates a proposal, an objection can be entered and a hearing held, after which the Secretary will submit the final document.

In establishing standards, the Secretary of Labor must set forth standards to prevent employees from suffering substantial harm to their health even if the employee worked at this job for most of his or her adult life. The Secretary of Labor must rely on research and experiments to establish reliable standards, which will be set forth objectively. The specific actions and the desired results must be set forth.

Employees may request a temporary variance from the Secretary of Labor if they do not have the technical know-how or materials and/or equipment needed to comply or the plant or equipment cannot be altered by the required date. Employers must make every effort to comply as soon as possible. The time limit is one year, which can be renewed twice.

Although it was thought that employers would have enough incentive to ensure a safe working environment because of the absolute liability imposed upon them under Worker's Compensation, Congress did not feel employers were doing all that they could do, so they created OSHAct.

Before OSHAct was enacted, most employees who were injured on the job were not successful in suing their employers if they were injured by a coworker, were negligent themselves, or were held to have assumed the risk. This situation was not a sufficient impetus for employers to improve the workplace, knowing that they would not have to compensate most employees for their injuries. The purpose of OSHAct was to insure that employees would not sustain the injuries in the first place.

Employers are required to comply with certain mandates of the Department of Labor regarding safety and health. Furthermore, the employment environment must be a safe and healthy place in which to work without hazards.

PERMANENT STANDARDS

Permanent standards are the standards originally introduced when OSHA was created as well as standards promulgated thereafter. The latter are referred to as National Consensus Standards. When OSHA develops a new standard, it is published in the *Federal Register*. The public, especially employees, has thirty days to request a hearing. If requested, notice of a public hearing will be made. After the hearing, OSHA must publish the standard incorporating the changes, if any, and the date of its commencement, within sixty days. The Secretary of Labor must explain the need for the new standard, or else it will be null and void. He or she may delay the date of its commencement. In one case, a delay of four years was imposed. An employer may file an appeal in the Circuit Court of Appeals within sixty days from OSHA's final announcement. If there is an appeal, the Secretary of Labor must demonstrate for the Court that the standard mitigates a significant health risk. If the Circuit Court is convinced that the Secretary of Labor has provided sufficient evidence, the standard will become permanent.

Employment Perspective

Veggie King has just begun irradiating fruits and vegetables for a longer shelf life. OSHA has promulgated a standard that all workers who are subjected to the low levels of radiation used on the fruits and vegetables must wear radiation-proof jumpsuits and headwear. These suits are very expensive. Veggie King asks for a hearing, but OSHA's final determination is unchanged. On appeal before Circuit Court, Veggie King proclaims that low levels of radiation have no impact on humans. The Secretary of Labor counters that studies have shown that subjecting a human to low levels of radiation for twenty years or longer will cause cancer. What is the likely result? If the Circuit Court believes that the studies introduced by the Secretary of Labor have merit, then the standard of requiring radiation-protective garments will become permanent. ◆

The occupational safety and health standard requires the employer to adopt appropriate practices necessary to insure that the place of employment is a safe and healthy environment.

The national consensus standard is an occupational safety and health standard designated by the Secretary of Labor after its formulation by a nationally recognized safety and/or health organization which has conducted hearings.

Inspections

Inspections of business premises and records may be made during working hours and at other times deemed reasonable by OSHA compliance officers. The employees and the employer may be questioned privately. Record-keeping relating to occupational accidents and illnesses is required and must be produced upon demand. Exposure of employees to toxic chemicals must be documented. Employees have the right of free access to the documents relating to their exposure. If the level exceeds the occupational safety and health standard, the employer must immediately notify the employee and take corrective action. If the employees believe a standard is being violated, they may notify the Secretary of Labor in writing. If the Secretary determines that there is a viable issue, he or she will authorize an investigation.

Citations and Penalties

If an employer has committed a violation, an OSHA director will issue a citation, which will describe the particulars as well as reference to the occupational safety and health standard that the Secretary believes has been violated. The employer, upon receipt, has fifteen business days to contest the citation, or it will become a final order not subject to judicial review.

If the employer fails to correct the violation of a safety and health standard, a penalty will be assessed against the employer. The employer has fifteen days to object to the penalty. Otherwise, it will become a final order not subject to judicial review.

Penalties may be assessed between $5,000 and $70,000 for each violation of an occupational safety and health standard. These penalties may be made in increments of up to $7,000 per day per violation. Payment for these penalties shall be made to the Secretary of Labor and deposited in the U.S. Treasury.

With regard to any issues of occupational safety and health not addressed by the Secretary of Labor, the individual states are free to develop their own standards.

If an employer timely contests the citation or penalty, the matter is referred to the Occupational Safety and Health Review Commission, which is an administrative agency composed of three commissioners, each of whom has been appointed by the President. The Secretary of Labor has the burden of proving that the employer violated an OSHA standard, in a hearing heard before an administrative law judge. The judge's decision is then given to the Commission, which has the option of reviewing it.

The commission may render its own decision or else allow the administrative law judge's decision to be final. An appeal may be made in either case within sixty days from the Commission's decision to the Federal Circuit Court of Appeals.

There are no specific standards set forth in the Occupational Safety and Health Act itself. OSHA was empowered to adopt existing standards and to develop new ones as conditions warrant.

Employment Perspective

Stan Meyers was installing aluminum siding on a house, working on a platform twenty-two feet high. The platform was flat and had no guardrails. An OSHA standard requires guardrails to be installed on all platforms that are ten feet or higher above the ground. Stan has asked his employer to install guardrails, without success. Finally, Stan notifies OSHA, which sends a compliance officer to the work site. The compliance officer investigates and makes a determination that there is a violation of the OSHA standard regarding guardrails. The OSHA director then issues a citation. Must the employer install the guardrails? Yes! ◆

EMERGENCY STANDARDS

The Secretary of Labor has the power to institute health and safety standards for OSHA. These standards may be emergency or permanent.

Emergency standards are imposed where an immediate concern for the health and safety of workers has just arisen and needs to be addressed in an expeditious manner. Emergency standards are effective for only six months. The Secretary of Labor must explain what the emergency is and then follow regular procedures to have the standard become permanent, if it is believed that the problem will continue to exist.

Employment Perspective

Pesto, Inc. created a new cleanser for industrial ovens. When workers began to use the cleanser, they felt a burning sensation on the hands and face. It was discovered that the product contained a caustic acid that would burn exposed areas of the skin that came into proximity of its fumes. What recourse is available? Through the Secretary of Labor, an emergency standard can be imposed, requiring breathing ventilators and appropriate gloves, uniforms, and masks to guard against the caustic effects of the acid in the oven cleanser. ◆

The next case deals with a conflict between the Secretary of Labor and the Occupational Safety and Health Review Commission over the power of interpret OSHA.

CASE

Lynn Martin, Secretary of Labor v. Occupational Safety and Health Review Commission

499 U.S. 144 (1991)

Justice MARSHALL delivered the opinion of the Court Per Curiam.

In this case, we consider the question to whom should a reviewing court defer when the Secretary of Labor and the Occupational Safety and Health Review Commission furnish reasonable but conflicting interpretations of an ambiguous regulation promulgated by the Secretary under the Occupational Safety and Health Act of 1970. The Court of Appeals concluded that it should defer to the Commission's interpretation under such circumstances. We reverse.

The Occupational Safety and Health Act of 1970 (OSH Act or Act) establishes a comprehensive regulatory scheme designed "to assure so far as possible . . . safe and healthful working conditions" for "every working man and woman in the Nation." To achieve this objective, the Act assigns distinct regulatory tasks to two independent administrative actors: the Secretary of Labor (Secretary); and the Occupational Safety and Health Review Commission (Commission), a three-member board appointed by the President with the advice and consent of the Senate.

The Act charges the Secretary with responsibility for setting and enforcing workplace health and safety standards. The Secretary establishes these standards through the exercise of rulemaking powers. If the Secretary (or the Secretary's designate) determines upon investigation that an employer is failing to comply with such a standard, the Secretary is authorized to issue a citation and to assess the employer a monetary penalty.

The Commission is assigned to "carry out adjudicatory functions" under the Act. If an employer wishes to contest a citation, the Commission must afford the employer an evidentiary hearing and "thereafter issue an order, based on findings of fact, affirming, modifying, or vacating the Secretary's citation or proposed penalty."

Initial decisions are made by an administrative law judge (ALJ), whose ruling becomes the order of the Commission unless the Commission grants discretionary review. Both the employer and the Secretary have the right to seek review of an adverse Commission order in the court of appeals, which must treat as "conclusive" Commission findings of fact that are "supported by substantial evidence."

This case arises from the Secretary's effort to enforce compliance with OSH Act standards relating to coke-oven emissions. Promulgated pursuant to the Secretary's rulemaking powers, these standards establish maximum permissible emissions levels and require the use of employee respirators in certain circumstances. An investigation by one of the Secretary's compliance officers revealed that respondent CF&I Steel Corporation (CF&I) had equipped 28 of its employees with respirators that failed an "atmospheric test" designed to determine whether a respirator provides a sufficiently tight fit to protect its wearer from carcinogenic emissions. As a result of being equipped with these loose-fitting respirators, some employees were exposed to coke-oven emissions exceeding the regulatory limit. Based on these findings, the compliance officer issued a citation to CF&I and assessed it a $10,000 penalty which requires an employer to "institute a respiratory protection program in accordance with OSHAct." CF&I contested the citation.

The ALJ sided with the Secretary, but the full Commission subsequently granted review and vacated the citation. In the Commission's view, the "respiratory protection program" expressly requires only that an employer train employees in the proper use of respirators. The obligation to assure proper fit of an individual employee's respirator, the Commission noted, was expressly stated in another regulation. Reasoning, that the Secretary's interpretation of Section 1910.1029(g) (3) would render Section 1910.1029(g) (4) superfluous, the Commission concluded that the facts alleged in the citation and found by the ALJ did not establish a violation of Section 1910.1029(g) (3). Because Section 1910.1029(g) (3) was the only asserted basis for liability, the Commission vacated the citation.

The Secretary petitioned for review in the Court of Appeals for the Tenth Circuit, which affirmed the Commission's order. The court concluded that the relevant regulations were ambiguous as to the employer's obligation to assure proper fit of an employee's respirator. The court thus framed the issue before it as whose reasonable interpretation of the regulations, the Secretary's or the Commission's, merited the court's deference. The court held that the Commission's interpretation was entitled to deference under such circumstances, reasoning that Congress had intended to delegate to the Commission "the normal complement of adjudicative powers possessed by traditional administrative agencies" and that "such an adjudicative function necessarily encompasses the power to 'declare' the law." Although the court determined that it would "certainly be possible to reach an alternate interpretation of the ambiguous regulatory language," the court nonetheless concluded that the Commission's interpretation was a reasonable one. The court therefore deferred to the Commission's interpretation without assessing the reasonableness of the Secretary's competing view.

The Secretary thereafter petitioned this Court for a writ of certiorari. We granted the petition in order to resolve a conflict among the Circuits on the question whether a reviewing court should defer to the Secretary or to the Commission when these actors furnish reasonable but conflicting interpretations of an ambiguous regulation under the OSH Act.

It is well established "that an agency's construction of its own regulations is entitled to substantial deference." In situations in which "the meaning of regulatory language is not free from doubt," the reviewing court should give effect to the agency's interpretation so long as it is "reasonable," that is, so long as the interpretation "sensibly conforms to the purpose and wording of the regulations." Because applying an agency's regulation to complex or changing circumstances calls upon the agency's unique expertise and policymaking prerogatives, we presume that the power authoritatively to interpret its own regulations is a component of the agency's delegated lawmaking powers. The question before us in this case is to which administrative actor—the Secretary or the Commission—did Congress delegate this "interpretive" lawmaking power under the OSH Act.

To put this question in perspective, it is necessary to take account of the unusual regulatory structure established by the Act. Under most regulatory schemes, rulemaking, enforcement, and adjudicative powers are combined in a single administrative authority. Under the OSH Act, however, Congress separated enforcement and rulemaking powers from adjudicative powers, assigning these respective functions to two independent administrative authorities. The purpose of this "split enforcement" structure was to achieve a greater separation of functions than exists within the traditional "unitary" agency, which under the Administrative Procedure Act (APA) generally must divide enforcement and adjudication between separate personnel.

Although the Act does not expressly address the issue, we now infer from the structure and history of the statute, that the power to render authoritative interpretations of OSH Act regulations is a "necessary adjunct" of the Secretary's powers to promulgate and to enforce national health and safety standards. The Secretary enjoys readily identifiable structural advantages over the Commission in rendering authoritative interpretations of OSH Act regulations. Because the Secretary promulgates these standards, the Secretary is in a better position than is the Commission to reconstruct the purpose of the regulations in question. Moreover, by virtue of the Secretary's statutory role as enforcer, the Secretary comes into contact with a much greater number of regulatory problems than does the Commission, which encounters only those regulatory episodes resulting in contested citations.

Consequently, we think the more plausible inference is that Congress intended to delegate to the Commission the type of nonpolicymaking adjudicatory powers typically exercised by a court in the agency-review context. Under this conception of adjudication, the Commission is authorized to review the Secretary's interpretations only for consistency with the regulatory language and for reasonableness. In addition, of course, Congress expressly charged the Commission with making authoritative findings of fact and with applying the Secretary's standards to those facts in making a decision.

We emphasize the narrowness of our holding. We deal in this case only with the division of powers between the Secretary and the Commission under the OSH Act. We conclude from the available indicia of legislative intent that Congress did not intend to sever the power authoritatively to interpret OSH Act regulations from the Secretary's power to promulgate and enforce them.

In addition, although we hold that a reviewing court may not prefer the reasonable interpretations of the Commission to the reasonable interpretations of the Secretary, we emphasize that the reviewing court should defer to the Secretary only if the Secretary's interpretation is reasonable. The Secretary's interpretation of an ambiguous regulation is subject to the same standard of substantive review as any other exercise of delegated lawmaking power.

The judgment of the Court of Appeals is reversed, and the case is remanded for further proceedings consistent with this opinion.

It is so ordered.
Judgment for Lynn Martin,
Secretary of Labor.

PARTIAL AND PERMANENT DISABILITY

Over ten thousand workers die on the job each year. In the vicinity of one hundred thousand workers are permanently disabled. Permanent disability means that the worker is unable to work again and has suffered a serious physical impairment. Over two million workers are partially disabled, meaning that they have missed one or more days from work as a result of the work-related injury. All together, approximately two and one half million workers suffer some form of disabling injury each year. In addition, in excess of six million more suffer minor injuries for which no time is taken off from work.

In the following case, the issue is whether the Secretary of Labor has acted reasonably in promulgating standards of entitlement to benefits for coal miners under the Black Lung Benefits Act.

CASE

Harriet Pauley, survivor of John C. Pauley v. Bethenergy Mines, Inc.

501 U.S. 680 (1991)

JUSTICE BLACKMUN delivered the opinion of the Court.

The black lung benefits program, created by Congress, was to be administered first by the Social Security Administration (SSA) under the auspices of the then-existent Department of Health, Education, and Welfare (HEW), and later by the Department of Labor (DOL). Congress authorized these Departments, during their respective tenures, to adopt interim regulations governing the adjudication of claims for black lung benefits, but constrained the Secretary of Labor by providing that the DOL regulations "shall not be more restrictive than" HEW's. This litigation calls upon us to determine whether the Secretary of Labor has complied with that constraint.

I

A

The black lung benefits program was enacted originally as Title IV of the Federal Coal Mine Health and Safety Act of 1969 (FCMHSA), to provide benefits for miners totally disabled due at least in part to pneumoconiosis arising out of coal mine employment, and to the dependents and survivors of such miners.

B

Dissatisfied with the increasing backlog of unadjudicated claims and the relatively high rate of claim denials resulting from the application of the HEW permanent regulations, Congress in 1972 amended FCMSHA and redesignated Title IV of that Act as the Black Lung Benefits Act of 1972.

The Secretary of Labor, pursuant to this authorization, adopted interim regulations governing the adjudication of part C claims. These regulations differ significantly from the HEW interim regulations. The DOL regulations include two presumption provisions similar to the two presumption provisions in the HEW interim regulations. To invoke the presumption of eligibility under these two provisions, however, a claimant need not prove that the "impairment . . . arose out of coal mine employment," as was required under the HEW interim regulations.

In addition, the DOL interim regulations add three methods of invoking the presumption of eligibility not included in the HEW interim regulations. Specifically, under the DOL regulations, a claimant can invoke the presumption of total disability due to pneumoconiosis by submitting blood gas studies that demonstrate the presence of an impairment in the transfer of oxygen from the lung alveoli to the blood; by submitting other medical evidence establishing the presence of a totally disabling respiratory or pulmonary impairment; or, in the case of a deceased miner for whom no medical evidence is available, by submitting a survivor's affidavit demonstrating such a disability.

Finally, the DOL interim regulations provide four methods for rebutting the presumptions. Two of the rebuttal provisions mimic those in the HEW regulations, permitting rebuttal upon a showing that the miner is performing or is able to perform his coal mining or comparable work. The other two rebuttal provisions are at issue in these cases. Under these provisions, a presumption of total disability due to pneumoconiosis can be rebutted if "the evidence establishes that the total disability or death of the miner did not arise in whole or in part out of coal mine employment," or "if the evidence establishes that the miner does not, or did not, have pneumoconiosis."

II

The cases before us present the question whether the DOL's interim regulations are "more restrictive than" the HEW's interim regulations by virtue of the third and fourth rebuttal provisions, and therefore are inconsistent with the agency's statutory authority. The Court of Appeals for the Third Circuit concluded that the DOL interim regulations were not more restrictive. John Pauley, the now deceased husband of petitioner Harriet Pauley, filed a claim for black lung benefits on April 21, 1978, after he had worked 30 years in the underground mines of Pennsylvania. Pauley stopped working soon after he filed his claim for benefits. At a formal hearing on November 5, 1987, the Administrative Law Judge (ALJ) found that Pauley had begun to experience shortness of breath, coughing, and fatigue in 1974, and that those symptoms had gradually worsened, causing him to leave his job in the mines. The ALJ also found that Pauley had arthritis requiring several medications daily, had suffered a stroke in January 1987, and had smoked cigarettes for 34 years until he stopped in 1974.

Because respondent BethEnergy did not contest the presence of coal workers' pneumoconiosis, the ALJ found that the presumption had been invoked. Turning to the rebuttal evidence, the judge concluded that Pauley was not engaged in his usual coal mine work or comparable and gainful work, and that Pauley was totally disabled from returning to coal mining or comparable employment. The judge then weighed the evidence submitted and determined that respondent BethEnergy had sustained its burden of establishing that pneumoconiosis was not a contributing factor in Pauley's total disability and, accordingly, that his disability did not "arise in whole or in part out of coal mine employment."

Having determined that Pauley was not entitled to receive black lung benefits under the DOL interim regulations, the ALJ felt constrained by Third Circuit precedent to apply the HEW interim regulations to Pauley's claim. He first concluded that respondent BethEnergy's concession that Pauley had pneumoconiosis arising out of coal mining employment was sufficient to invoke the presumption of total disability due to pneumoconiosis. Because the evidence demonstrated Pauley's inability to work, and the statute precluded rebuttal of the presumption by "showing that the claimant's total disability is unrelated to his coal mine employment," the judge found that BethEnergy could not carry its burden on rebuttal, and that Pauley was entitled to benefits.

After the ALJ denied its motion for reconsideration, BethEnergy appealed unsuccessfully to the Benefits Review Board. It then sought review in the Court of Appeals for the Third Circuit. That court reversed. It pointed out that the decisions of the ALJ and the Benefits Review Board created "two disturbing circumstances." First, the court found it to be "surely extraordinary," that a determination that Pauley was totally disabled from causes unrelated to pneumoconiosis, which was sufficient to rebut the presumption, would preclude respondent BethEnergy from rebutting the presumption. Second, the court considered it to be "outcome determinative" that the purpose of the Benefits Act is to provide benefits to miners totally disabled at least in part due to pneumoconiosis if the disability arises out of coal mine employment, and that the ALJ had made unchallenged findings that Pauley's disability did not arise even in part out of such employment. The court found it to be "perfectly evident that no set of regulations under the Benefits Act may provide that a claimant who is statutorily barred from recovery may nevertheless recover."

III

We turn to the statutory text that provides that "criteria applied by the Secretary of Labor . . . shall not be more restrictive than the criteria applicable" under the interim HEW regulations. Specifically, we must determine whether the third and fourth rebuttal provisions in the DOL regulations render the DOL regulations more restrictive than were the HEW regulations. These provisions permit rebuttal of the presumption of eligibility upon a showing that the miner's disability did not arise in whole or in part out of coal mine employment or that the miner does not have pneumoconiosis.

The Senate Committee on Human Resources stated:

> "It is the Committee's belief that the Secretary of Labor should have sufficient statutory authority . . . to establish eligibility criteria. . . . It is intended that pursuant to this authority the Secretary of Labor will make every effort to incorporate within his regulations . . . to the extent feasible the advances made by medical science in the diagnosis and treatment of

pneumoconiosis . . . since the promulgation in 1972 of the Secretary of HEW's medical eligibility criteria."

Finally, we do not accept the implicit premise of this argument: that the Secretary cannot prevail unless she is able to demonstrate that her interpretation of the HEW interim regulations comports with HEW's contemporaneous interpretation of those regulations. As is stated above, the Secretary's interpretation of HEW's interim regulations is entitled to deference so long as it is reasonable. An interpretation that harmonizes an agency's regulations with their authorizing statute is presumptively reasonable, and claimants have not persuaded us that the presumption is unfounded in this case.

IV

We conclude that the Secretary of Labor has not acted unreasonably, or inconsistently with the Black Lung Benefits Act, in promulgating interim regulations that permit the presumption of entitlement to black lung benefits to be rebutted with evidence demonstrating that the miner does not, or did not, have pneumoconiosis or that the miner's disability does not, or did not, arise out of coal mine employment. Accordingly, we affirm the judgment of the Third Circuit in No. 89-1714. The judgments of the Fourth Circuit in No. 90-113 and No. 90-114 are reversed, and those cases are remanded for further proceedings consistent with this opinion. No costs are allowed in any of these cases.

Judgment for BethEnergy Mines.

In about half of the cases, manually handling an object or falling is the cause. Other major types of injuries include being struck by falling or moving objects; machinery-related injuries; motor-vehicle and other types of vehicle-induced injuries; stepping on or striking against objects; the use of hand tools, elevators, hoists, or conveyors; and being in the proximity of electric heat and explosives. Motor-vehicle accidents and falling account for a significant portion of fatalities.

Ancillary Expenses

There are numerous ancillary expenses which must be absorbed by an employer when a worker is injured on the job. At the time of the injury, other employees and their supervisors may have stopped working to assist their injured coworker or to view and discuss the event. This constitutes a loss of working time. If the injured worker suffered a temporary disability and remained out from work for a short duration, the injured employee would still be entitled to wages, and the employer would have to bear the corresponding loss of productivity. When the injury is permanent or death results, the costs for these losses are substantial. A replacement will have to be hired, and the cost of his or her training must be recognized. The time devoted to investigatory questioning about the accident is time lost for supervisors and coworkers. There is the cost to repair or replace the equipment and/or premises involved in the incident. Another consideration is the time taken for the repair or replacement that may have resulted in a partial work stoppage for those dependent on that equipment or access to the premises in question. The loss of productivity caused by the accident could result in overtime needed to facilitate a return to status quo. These ancillary costs may on occasion exceed the payments made on behalf of the insured worker.

There are two criteria which must be satisfied before an employer is held to be in violation of OSH Act. The first criterion is that the employer did not provide a workplace free from recognized hazards. A hazard is considered recognized when the employer either knew of it or should have known of it because the hazard is of the type that is understood throughout the industry. The second is that the hazard is likely to cause serious harm or death to the employees. When the Secretary of Labor brings an action against an employer, he or she must set forth the OSHA standard held to be violated. Standards vary among the four designated industries: general, maritime, construction, and agriculture. The Secretary must describe how, when, and where the violation took place and whether the employer knew or should have known of it, as well as the proximity of the employees to the hazard. The proximity requirement does not suggest that an employee must have been injured by the hazard, only that the potential for injury exists because the employee was in the vicinity of the hazard.

Employment Perspective

The Boxer is a company that manufactures and recycles cardboard boxes. A mechanical forklift is used to carry and stack the flattened boxes. OSHA requires that all motorized vehicles emit a beeping sound when they are in reverse. Forklift 17's beeper is not functional, but the forklift is still being used until Friday when the repair is scheduled. On Wednesday morning, Ryan Madison has just turned a corner and is now walking in the aisle when forklift 17, operating in reverse, just misses hitting him. Is the Boxer in violation? Yes! The Boxer knew of the violation, because forklift 17 was scheduled for repair; an employee, Ryan Madison, was in proximity of the recognized hazard; and the potential for an injury to occur existed. ◆

Employer Defenses

The greater hazard defense is applicable where the imposition of a safety standard while remedying one hazard actually has caused a greater hazard in its place. The employer should request a variance for noncompliance; otherwise, the employer's excuse for not adhering to the safety standard may be denied.

Employment Perspective

Assume that during roadway construction, orange cones must be laid for a quarter mile before the construction work commences, and, furthermore, a flag-waver must stand by the first cone to wave off oncoming traffic. On days when there is fog, snow, or heavy rain, poor visibility makes it difficult for drivers to see the flag-waver. Does this situation pose a greater hazard? Yes! The imposition of this safety standard on clear days makes sense, but on days of poor visibility it exposes the flag-waver to a greater hazard than those workers one-quarter mile down the road. A variance should be requested for days when there is inclement weather. ◆

In the following case, women were excluded from the workplace. The company argued the level of lead in the manufacturing process could cause harm to the fetus of a pregnant woman. The level of lead had exceeded the critical level prescribed by OSHA for workers planning on having a family.

CASE

International Union, United Automobile, Aerospace and Agricultural Implement Workers of America, UAW v. Johnson Controls, Inc.

499 U.S. 187 (1991)

JUSTICE BLACKMUN delivered the opinion of the Court.

Respondent Johnson Controls, Inc., manufactures batteries. In the manufacturing process, the element lead is a primary ingredient. Occupational exposure to lead entails health risks, including the risk of harm to any fetus carried by a female employee.

In 1982, Johnson Controls shifted from a policy of warning to a policy of exclusion. Between 1979 and 1983, eight employees became pregnant while maintaining blood lead levels in excess of 30 micrograms per deciliter. This appeared to be the critical level noted by the Occupational Health and Safety Administration (OSHA) for a worker who was planning to have a family. The company responded by announcing a broad exclusion of women from jobs that exposed them to lead:

. . .

". . . It is Johnson Controls' policy that women who are pregnant or who are capable of bearing children will not be placed into jobs involving lead exposure or which could expose them to lead through the exercise of job bidding, bumping, transfer or promotion rights."

The policy defined "women . . . capable of bearing children" as "all women except those whose inability to bear children is medically documented." It further stated that an unacceptable work station was one where, "over the past year," an employee had recorded a blood lead level of more than 30 micrograms per deciliter or the work site had yielded an air sample containing a lead level in excess of 30 micrograms per cubic meter.

. . .

A word about tort liability and the increased cost of fertile women in the workplace is perhaps necessary. One of the dissenting judges in this case expressed concern about an employer's tort liability and concluded that liability for a potential injury to a fetus is a social cost that Title VII does not require a company to ignore. It is correct to say that Title VII does not prevent the employer from having a conscience. The statute, however, does prevent sex-specific fetal-protection policies. These two aspects of Title VII do not conflict.

More than 40 States currently recognize a right to recover for a prenatal injury based either on negligence or on wrongful death. According to Johnson Controls, however, the company complies with the lead standard developed by OSHA and warns its female employees about the damaging effects of lead. It is worth noting that OSHA gave the problem of lead lengthy consideration and concluded that "there is no basis whatsoever for the claim that women of childbearing age should be excluded from the workplace in order to protect the fetus or the course of pregnancy." Instead, OSHA established a series of mandatory protections which, taken together, "should effectively minimize any risk to the fetus and newborn child." Without negligence, it would be difficult for a court to find liability on the part of the employer. If, under general tort principles, Title VII bans sex-specific fetal-protection policies, the employer fully informs the woman of the risk, and the employer has not acted negligently, the basis for holding an employer liable seems remote at best.

If state tort law furthers discrimination in the workplace and prevents employers from hiring women who are capable of manufacturing the product as efficiently as men, then it will impede the accomplishment of Congress' goals in enacting Title VII. Because Johnson Controls has not argued that it faces any costs from tort liability, not to mention crippling ones, the pre-emption question is not before us. We therefore say no more than that the concurrence's speculation appears unfounded as well as premature.

The tort-liability argument reduces to two equally unpersuasive propositions. First, Johnson Controls attempts to solve the problem of reproductive health hazards by resorting to an exclusionary policy. Title VII plainly forbids illegal sex discrimination as a method of diverting attention from an employer's obligation to police the workplace. Second, the spectre of an award of damages reflects a fear that hiring fertile women will cost more. The extra cost of employing members of one sex, however, does not provide an affirmative Title VII defense for a discriminatory refusal to hire members of that gender. Indeed, in passing the PDA, Congress considered at length the considerable cost of providing equal treatment of pregnancy and related conditions, but made the "decision to forbid special treatment of pregnancy despite the social costs associated therewith."

. . .

We, of course, are not presented with, nor do we decide, a case in which costs would be so prohibitive as to threaten the survival of the employer's business. We merely reiterate our prior holdings that the incremental cost of hiring women cannot justify discriminating against them.

The judgment of the Court of Appeals is reversed and the case is remanded for further proceedings consistent with this opinion.

It is so ordered.
Judgment for UAW.

Another defense exists where compliance with the safety standard requires a device that is not available on the market. Finally, an employee's negligence or refusal to comply with an OSHA safety standard does not justify the employer's inaction. The employer will still be held in violation.

The following case addresses the question of whether a State Hazardous Waste Laborers Licensing Act must yield to the Occupational Safety and Health Act when they are in conflict.

CASE

Mary Gade, Director, Illinois Environmental Protection Agency v. National Solid Wastes Management Association

509 U.S. 88 (1992)

JUSTICE O'CONNOR.

In 1988, the Illinois General Assembly enacted the Hazardous Waste Crane and Hoisting Equipment Operators Licensing Act, and the Hazardous Waste Laborers Licensing Act, (together, licensing acts). The stated purpose of the acts is both "to promote job safety" and "to protect life, limb and property." In this case, we consider whether these "dual impact" statutes, which protect both workers and the general public, are preempted by the federal Occupational Safety and Health Act of 1970, (OSH Act), and the standards promulgated thereunder by the Occupational Safety and Health Administration (OSHA).

The OSH Act authorizes the Secretary of Labor to promulgate federal occupational safety and health standards. In the Superfund Amendments and Reauthorization Act of 1986 (SARA), Congress directed the Secretary of Labor to "promulgate standards for the health and safety protection of employees engaged in hazardous waste operations" pursuant to her authority under the OSH Act. In relevant part, SARA requires the Secretary to establish standards for the initial and routine training of workers who handle hazardous wastes.

In response to this congressional directive, OSHA, to which the Secretary has delegated certain of her statutory responsibilities, promulgated regulations on "Hazardous Waste Operations and Emergency Response," including detailed regulations on worker training requirements. The OSHA regulations require, among other things, that workers engaged in an activity that may expose them to hazardous wastes receive a minimum of 40 hours of instruction off the site, and a minimum of three days actual field experience under the supervision of a trained supervisor. Workers who are on the site only occasionally or who are working in areas that have been determined to be under the permissible exposure limits must complete at least 24 hours of off-site instruction and one day of actual field experience. On-site managers and supervisors directly responsible for hazardous waste operations must receive the same initial training as general employees, plus at least eight additional hours of specialized training on various health and safety programs. Employees and supervisors are required to receive eight hours of refresher training annually. Those who have satisfied the training and field experience requirement receive a written certification; uncertified workers are prohibited from engaging in hazardous waste operations.

In 1988, while OSHA's interim hazardous waste regulations were in effect, the State of Illinois enacted the licensing acts at issue here. The laws are designated as acts "in relation to environmental protection," and their stated aim is to protect both employees and the general public by licensing hazardous waste equipment operators and laborers working at certain facilities. Both acts require a license applicant to provide a certified record of at least 40 hours of training under an approved program conducted within Illinois, to pass a written examination, and to complete an annual refresher course of at least eight hours of instruction. In addition, applicants for a hazardous waste crane operator's license must submit "a certified record showing operation of equipment used in hazardous waste handling for a minimum of 4,000 hours." Employees who work without the proper license, and employers who knowingly permit an unlicensed employee to work, are subject to escalating fines for each offense.

The respondent in this case, National Solid Waste Management Association (the Association), is a national trade association of businesses that remove, transport, dispose, and handle waste material, including hazardous waste. The Association's members are subject to the OSH Act and OSHA regulations, and are therefore required to train, qualify, and certify their hazardous waste remediation workers. For hazardous waste operations conducted in Illinois, certain of the workers employed by the Association's members are also required to obtain licenses pursuant to the Illinois licensing acts. Thus, for example, some of the Association's members must ensure that their employees receive not only the three days of field experience required for certification under the OSHA regulations, but also the 500 days of experience (4,000 hours) required for licensing under the state statutes.

The Association sought to enjoin Illinois Environmental Protection Agency (IEPA) from enforcing the Illinois licensing acts, claiming that the acts were pre-empted by the OSH Act and OSHA regulations and that they violated the Commerce Clause of the United States Constitution.

"The question whether a certain state action is pre-empted by federal law is one of congressional intent. The purpose of Congress is the ultimate touchstone."

In the OSH Act, Congress endeavored "to assure so far as possible every working man and woman in the Nation safe and healthful working conditions." To that end, Congress authorized the Secretary of Labor to set mandatory occupational safety and health standards applicable to all businesses affecting interstate commerce, and thereby brought the Federal Government into a field that traditionally had been occupied by the States. Federal regulation of the workplace was not intended to be all-encompassing, however. First, Congress expressly saved two areas from federal pre-emption. Section 4(b) (4) of the OSH Act states that the Act does not "supersede or in any manner affect any workmen's compensation law or . . . enlarge or diminish or affect in any other manner the common law or statutory rights, duties, or liabilities of employers and employees under any law with respect to injuries, diseases, or death of employees arising out of, or in the course of, employment." Section 18(a) provides that the Act does not "prevent any State agency or court from asserting jurisdiction under State law over any occupational safety or health issue with respect to which no federal standard is in effect."

Congress not only reserved certain areas to state regulation, but it also, in 18(b) of the Act, gave the States the option of pre-empting federal regulation entirely. That section provides:

> "Submission of State plan for development and enforcement of State standards to preempt applicable Federal standards."
>
> "Any State which, at any time, desires to assume responsibility for development and enforcement therein of occupational safety and health standards relating to any occupational safety or health issue with respect to which a Federal standard has been promulgated by the Secretary under the OSH Act shall submit a State plan for the development of such standards and their enforcement."

About half the States have received the Secretary's approval for their own state plans as described in this provision. Illinois is not among them.

Looking at the provisions of 18 as a whole, we conclude that the OSH Act precludes any state regulation of an occupational safety or health issue with respect to which a federal standard has been established, unless a state plan has been submitted and approved pursuant to 18(b). Our review of the Act persuades us that Congress sought to promote occupational safety and health while at the same time avoiding duplicative, and possibly counterproductive, regulation. It thus established a system of uniform federal occupational health and safety standards, but gave States the option of pre-empting federal regulations by developing their own occupational safety and health programs. In addition, Congress offered the States substantial federal grant monies to assist them in developing their own programs. To allow a State selectively to "supplement," certain federal regulations with ostensibly nonconflicting standards would be inconsistent with this federal scheme of establishing uniform federal standards, on the one hand, and encouraging States to assume full responsibility for development and enforcement of their own OSH programs, on the other.

The OSH Act defines an "occupational safety and health standard" as "a standard which requires conditions, or the adoption or use of one or more practices, means, methods, operations, or processes, reasonably necessary or appropriate to provide safe or healthful employment and places of employment." Any state law requirement designed to promote health and safety in the workplace falls neatly within the Act's definition of an "occupational safety and health standard." Clearly, under this definition, a state law that expressly declares a legislative purpose of regulating occupational health and safety would, in the absence of an approved state plan, be pre-empted by an OSHA standard regulating the same subject matter.

We recognize that "the States have a compelling interest in the practice of professions within their boundaries, and that as part of their power to protect the public health, safety, and other valid interests they have broad power to establish standards for licensing practitioners and regulating the practice of professions." But under the Supremacy Clause, from which our pre-emption doctrine is derived, "any state law, however clearly within a State's acknowledged power, which interferes with or is contrary to federal law, must yield" ("even state regulation designed to protect vital state interests must give way to paramount federal legislation"). We therefore reject petitioner's argument that the State's interest in licensing various occupations can save from OSH Act pre-emption those provisions that directly and substantially affect workplace safety.

The judgment of the Court of Appeals is hereby Affirmed.
Judgment for National Solid Wastes Management Association.

An employer is required to provide its employees with a safe working environment. Inherent in this requirement is the employer's duty to inspect and maintain the working environment. An employer breaches its duty when it knew or should have known of a workplace hazard and failed either to correct the defect or notify its employees of it.

In the next case, an employee fell through a trap door covering a manhole and sustained a back injury. The employee sued for failure to maintain a safe working environment.

Sinclair v. Long Island R.R.

985 F.2d 74 (2nd Cir. 1993)

MCLAUGHLIN, Circuit Judge.

In 1986, while walking in a dark train tunnel, Sinclair fell over a depression in a bent trap door covering a manhole. Sinclair immediately experienced "sharp low back pains" and could not stand straight or walk normally. He was out of work for almost three weeks, during which time he was treated and examined twice by a private physician and three times by LIRR physicians.

Sinclair returned to work but, during 1987, was often given light duty because of his back pain. From July to December 1987, while continuing to work, Sinclair was treated by a chiropractor. At Sinclair's request, LIRR then placed him on its own "Work Hardening" program, a physical therapy regimen, which he attended three times a week through January 1988. Between February 1988 (when he left the program) and July 1988, Sinclair did not receive any treatment for his back.

On July 5, 1988, Sinclair was lifting a 120-pound third-rail drill with two co-workers when he felt back pain. According to Sinclair, this was no sharper or different than the pain he felt constantly since 1986. He immediately stopped working and reported this incident to a LIRR supervisor. From July 7, 1988 until early 1989, an orthopedist treated Sinclair with medication, physical therapy, and a back brace. Sinclair continued to work and to visit the LIRR Medical Department when he was unable to work.

In February 1989, a neurosurgeon began treating Sinclair. From March 1989 to November 1989, Sinclair did not work, but did attend physical therapy three times a week. At the direction of LIRR physicians, Sinclair stopped that therapy and resumed the "Work Hardening" program. In November 1989, the LIRR instructed Sinclair to return to work, which he did, working from November 1989 to June 1990.

In May 1990, a Magnetic Resonance Image test ordered by his neurosurgeon revealed a herniated disc and Sinclair underwent a laminectomy on August 30, 1990. Except for a two-week attempt in June 1991, Sinclair never worked after June 1990 but again engaged in physical therapy and attended the "Work Hardening" program. At the time of his March 1992 trial, Sinclair was still employed by LIRR and receiving sick pay.

Sinclair commenced this FELA (Fair Employment Labor Authority) action in September 1989, alleging a single theory of liability: the LIRR breached its duty to exercise reasonable care in providing a safe workplace. The claim was limited to the September 1986 incident with the manhole cover, and the parties agree that, as a matter of law, the LIRR was not liable for any negligence relevant to the third-rail drill accident of July 5, 1988.

The only unsafe condition alleged in his complaint was the defective condition of the manhole cover of which Sinclair claimed the LIRR had notice. We have held that "FELA is not an insurance program." Rather, it makes railroads liable to employees who suffer "injury or death resulting in whole or in part from the negligence of . . . the carrier, or by reason of any defect or insufficiency, due to its negligence, in its . . . roadbed . . . or other equipment." The Act requires an employer to provide its employees with a reasonably safe work place to work, and this includes the duty to maintain and inspect work areas. The scope of this ongoing duty is clear: "An employer breaches its duty to provide a safe workplace when it knows or should know of a potential hazard in the workplace, yet fails to exercise reasonable care to inform and protect its employees."

FELA does not make an employer liable for workplace inquiries and, therefore, requires that "claimants must at least offer some evidence that would support a finding of negligence."

Here, Sinclair introduced several photographs of the bent trap door to demonstrate its defective condition. The pictures were taken shortly after the accident, and having examined them, we conclude that a jury could reasonably infer from them that the condition had existed long enough to impart constructive, if not actual, notice of the defect.

Because Sinclair is not totally disabled, the district court should have focused the instruction on the impairment of Sinclair's earning capacity and, more precisely, on the differential between what he could earn, with his disability, and what Sinclair would have earned were he not disabled. The LIRR would be free to introduce testimony about the types of employment that Sinclair, though disabled, could reasonably engage in, and the jury would then be instructed to reduce its award by these anticipated earnings if it found this testimony credible.

Judgment for LIRR.

An employer is not an insurer of the employee's safety. Liability attaches when the employer had a better understanding of the hazards to be anticipated. However, the employer's liability ceases when the employee's knowledge of the hazard is at least the equivalent of the employer's.

REVIEW QUESTIONS

1. Explain the significance of the OSH Act.
2. Who is responsible for establishing OSHA standards?
3. If an employer is unable to comply with an OSHA standard, what alternative is available to it?
4. Absent OSH Act, what should provide employers with enough incentive to insure a safe working environment?
5. Explain the purpose of the Occupational Safety and Health Administration.
6. May OSHA representatives inspect an employer's place of business?
7. Explain the purpose of the National Institute of Occupational Safety and Health.
8. What kind of record-keeping is mandated by OSHA?
9. Explain National Consensus Standards.
10. What is the procedure once a determination has been made that an employer is in violation of OSHA standards?

11. Is an employer an insurer of an employee's safety? *Stinnett v. Buchele,* 598 S.W.2d 469 (KY. App. 1980)

12. The Occupational Safety and Health Review Commission issued a citation for the purpose of an administrative adjudication. The Secretary of Labor vacated the citation. Who will prevail? *Cuyahoga Valley R. R. Co. v. United Transp. Union,* 474 U.S. 3 (1985)

13. At issue is whether OSHA preempts all state laws regarding regulation of worker health and safety or only those state laws in direct conflict with it. What was the result? *National Solid Wastes Management Association v. Killian,* 918 F.2d 671 (1990)

14. OWCP, the Court of Appeals for the Fourth Circuit, struck down the DOL interim regulations. John Taylor, a respondent in No. 90-113, applied for black lung benefits in 1976, after having worked for almost twelve years as a coal loader and roof bolter in underground coal mines. The Administrative Law Judge found that Taylor properly had invoked the presumption of eligibility for benefits under MDRV 727.203 (a) (3), based on qualifying arterial blood gas studies demonstrating an impairment in the transfer of oxygen from his lungs to his blood. The ALJ then proceeded to weigh the rebuttal evidence, consisting of negative X-ray evidence, nonqualifying ventilatory study scores, and several medical reports submitted respectively by Taylor and by his employer, petitioner Clinchfield Coal Company. In light of this evidence, the ALJ concluded that Taylor neither suffered from pneumoconiosis nor was totally disabled. Rather, the evidence demonstrated that Taylor suffered from chronic bronchitis caused by thirty years of cigarette smoking and obesity. The Benefits Review Board affirmed, concluding that the ALJ's decision was supported by substantial evidence. Section 410.416 (a) provides: "If a miner was employed for 10 years or more in the Nation's coal mines, and is suffering or suffered from pneumoconiosis, it will be presumed, in the absence of persuasive evidence to the contrary, that the pneumoconiosis arose out of such employment." What was the result? *Clinchfield Coal Co. v. Director, Office of Workers' Compensation Programs, U.S. Dept. of Labor,* 501 U.S. 680 (1991)

15. Albert Dayton, a respondent in No. 90-114, applied for black lung benefits in 1979, after having worked as a coal miner for 17 years. The ALJ found that Dayton invoked the presumption of eligibility based on ventilatory test scores showing a chronic pulmonary condition. The judge then determined that petitioner Consolidated Coal Company had successfully rebutted the presumption under 15 727.203 (b) (2) and (4) by demonstrating that Dayton did not have pneumoconiosis and, in any event, that Dayton's pulmonary impairment was not totally disabling. The Benefits Review Board affirmed, concluding that the medical evidence demonstrated that Dayton's pulmonary condition was unrelated to coal and dust exposure, but was instead secondary to his smoking and "other ailments," and that the ALJ had correctly concluded that Consolidation had rebutted the presumption. *Consolidation Coal Co. v. Director, Office of Workers' Compensation Programs,* U.S. Dept. of Labor, 501 U.S. 680 (1991)

16. Is the burden and cost of compliance with OSHA standards justified by the injuries and lives saved?

17. In the case on pp. 520, who should the appropriate party be in interpreting OSHA?

18. Was the case on pp. 523 decided in an ethical manner?

19. In the case on pp. 527, how should a decision ethically be made when compliance with OSHA standards perpetrates discrimination against women?

20. In the case on pp. 528, should OSHA take precedence in all conflicts with state law?

Occupational Safety and Health Act of 1970

DEFINITIONS

Sec. 3. (652) For the purposes of this Act—

(8) The term "occupational safety and health standard" means a standard which requires conditions, or the adoption or use of one or more practices, means, methods, operations, or processes, reasonably necessary or appropriate to provide safe or healthful employment and places of employment.

(9) The term "national consensus standard" means any occupational safety and health standard or modification thereof which (1) has been adopted and promulgated by a nationally recognized standards-producing organization under procedures whereby it can be determined by the Secretary that persons interested and affected by the scope or provisions of the standard have reached substantial agreement on its adoption, (2) was formulated in a manner which afforded an opportunity for diverse views to be considered and (3) has been designated as such a standard by the Secretary, after consultation with other appropriate Federal agencies.

(10) The term "established Federal standard" means any operative occupational safety and health standard established by any agency of the United States and presently in effect, or contained in any Act of Congress in force on the date of enactment of this Act.

DUTIES

Sec. 5. (654) (a) Each employer—

(1) shall furnish to each of his employees employment and a place of employment which are free from recognized hazards that are causing or are likely to cause death or serious physical harm to his employees;

(2) shall comply with occupational safety and health standards promulgated under this Act.

(3) Each employee shall comply with the occupational safety and health standards and all rules, regulations, and orders issued pursuant to this Act which are applicable to his own actions and conduct.

OCCUPATIONAL SAFETY AND HEALTH STANDARDS

Sec. 6. (655) (a) Without regard to chapter 5 of title 5, United States Code, or to the other subsections of this section, the Secretary shall, as soon as practicable during the period beginning with the effective date of this Act and ending two years after such date, by rule promulgate as an occupational safety or health standard any national consensus standard, and any established Federal standard, unless he determines that the promulgation of such a standard would not result in improved safety or health for specifically designated employees. In the event of a conflict among any such standards, the Secretary shall promulgate the standard which assures the greatest protection of the safety or health of the affected employees.

(5) The Secretary, in promulgating standards dealing with toxic materials or harmful physical agents under this subsection, shall set the standard which most adequately assures, to the extent feasible, on the basis of the best available evidence, that no employee will suffer material impairment of health or functional capacity even if such employee has regular exposure to the hazard dealt with by such standard for the period of his working life. Development of standards under this subsection shall be based upon research, demonstrations, experiments, and such other information as may be appropriate. In addition to the attainment of the highest degree of health and safety protection for the employee, other

considerations shall be the latest available scientific data in the field, the feasibility of the standards, and experience gained under this and other health and safety laws. Whenever practicable, the standard promulgated shall be expressed in terms of objective criteria and of the performance desired.

(7) Any standard promulgated under this subsection shall prescribe the use of labels or other appropriate forms of warning as are necessary to insure that employees are apprised of all hazards to which they are exposed, relevant symptoms and appropriate emergency treatment, and proper conditions and precautions of safe use or exposure. Where appropriate, such standards shall also prescribe suitable protective equipment and control or technological procedures to be used in connection with such hazards and shall provide for monitoring or measuring employee exposure at such locations and intervals, and in such manner as may be necessary for the protection of employees. In addition, where appropriate, any such standard shall prescribe the type and frequency of medical examinations or other tests which shall be made available, by the employer or at his cost, to employees exposed to such hazards in order to most effectively determine whether the health of such employees is adversely affected by such exposure.

INSPECTIONS, INVESTIGATIONS, AND RECORDKEEPING

Sec. 8. (657) (a) In order to carry out the purposes of this Act, the Secretary, upon presenting appropriate credentials to the owner, operator, or agent in charge, is authorized—

(1) to enter without delay and at reasonable times any factory, plant, establishment, construction site, or other area, workplace or environment where work is performed by an employee of an employer; and

(2) to inspect and investigate during regular working hours and at other reasonable times, and within reasonable limits and in a reasonable manner, any such place of employment and all pertinent conditions, structures, machines, apparatus, devices, equipment, and materials therein, and to question privately any such employer, owner, operator, agent, or employee.

(f) (1) Any employees or representative of employees who believe that a violation of a safety or health standard exists that threatens physical harm, or that an imminent danger exists, may request an inspection by giving notice to the Secretary or his authorized representative of such violation or danger.

THE OCCUPATIONAL SAFETY AND HEALTH REVIEW COMMISSION

Sec. 12. (661) (a) The Occupational Safety and Health Review Commission is hereby established. The Commission shall be composed of three members who shall be appointed by the President, by and with the advice and consent of the Senate, from among persons who by reason of training, education, or experience are qualified to carry out the functions of the Commission under this Act. The President shall designate one of the members of the Commission to serve as Chairman.

PENALTIES

Sec. 17. (666) (a) Any employer who willfully or repeatedly violates the requirements of section 5 of this Act, any standard, rule, or order promulgated pursuant to section 6 of this Act, or regulations prescribed pursuant to this Act, may be assessed a civil penalty of not more than $70,000 for each violation, but not less than $5,000 for each willful violation.

CHAPTER 24 Workers' Compensation

PURPOSE

In return for absolute liability for injury or death, employers are immune from lawsuits for unintentional torts when an injury occurs on the job but the employer is liable without regard to fault. It makes no difference whether the negligent act was committed on the part of the employee, employer, or coworker. The term *injury* also includes diseases that occur in the workplace, such as lung-related diseases from asbestos.

Workers Compensation affords employers and employees the following benefits. Employers save the time and expense of defending a lawsuit. Employees, in turn, receive immediate medical benefits, continued wage earnings, retraining, and death or disfigurement benefits, if applicable.

REPORTING A CLAIM

An employee must report an injury to his or her employer and then file a claim with the Workers' Compensation Board.

In the following case, the question is whether a psychological condition qualifies as a permanent disability. The employer claimed that only physical injuries meet the test.

Bingham Memorial Hosp. v. Special Indemnity Fund

842 P.2d 273 (Idaho 1992)

BAKES, Chief Justice.

The Industrial Commission (Commission) found Amanda Dance (claimant) permanently and totally disabled under the odd-lot doctrine and apportioned liability for the claimant's benefits between the Industrial Special Indemnity Fund (ISIF) and Bingham Memorial Hospital (Hospital) and its surety the State Insurance Fund. ISIF appeals from the Commission's apportionment contending that the Commission erred in considering the claimant's pre-existing pain because the pain was derived from a psychological condition which is not a pre-existing permanent *physical* impairment under the Idaho Code I.C. 72–332. The ISIF argues that the pain caused by the claimant's psyche should be treated as a personal circumstance and therefore a nonmedical factor, not as a pre-existing permanent physical impairment.

The claimant in this case has a lengthy medical history both preceding and following her industrial accident at the Bingham Memorial Hospital on March 25, 1985. At the time of her hearing before the Industrial Commission she has been diagnosed as suffering from the following conditions: degenerative arthritis of the lumbar spine; cervical and lumbar strain aggravating previous arthritic conditions; thoracic strain; degenerative changes of the lumbar spine, especially at L4–5; acute lumbosacral spine strain and possible myofascial syndrome with the claimant complaining of low-back pain radiating into her left leg; mild osteoporosis; and advanced degenerative disc disease. The Commission found the claimant to be totally and permanently disabled and apportioned the responsibility for income benefits amounting to 15% of the whole person to the employer-surety, and responsibility for the remainder of the benefits to ISIF.

ISIF moved for reconsideration arguing that the Commission's apportionment was incorrect because there was no physical manifestation of the claimant's pre-existing psychological impairment. The ISIF argued that the permanent physical impairment ratings of Dr. Mott, which was relied upon by the Commission, "contained a psychological component" which has not been previously diagnosed. The ISIF argued that I.C. 72–332, which determines the ISIF's liability, limits the commission's consideration of pre-accident impairments to "physical" impairments, and that psychological problems do not qualify. Therefore, the ISIF argued that the commission erred in accepting Dr. Mott's opinion that 85% of the claimant's impairment was from her preexisting condition because Dr. Mott testified that a majority of that impairment was psychologically caused, rather than physically caused.

> **I.C. 72–332. Payment for second injuries from industrial special indemnity account—** (1) if an employee who has a permanent physical impairment from any cause or origin, incurs a subsequent disability by an injury or occupational disease arising out of and in the course of his employment, and by reason of the combined effects of both the pre-existing impairment and the subsequent injury or occupational disease or by reason of the aggravation and acceleration of the pre-existing impairment suffers total and permanent disability, the employer and surety shall be liable for payment of compensation benefits only for the disability caused by the injury or occupational disease, including scheduled and unscheduled permanent disabilities, and the injured employee shall be compensated for the remainder of his income benefits out of the industrial special indemnity account.
>
> (2) "permanent physical impairment" is as defined in section 72–422, Idaho Code, provided, however, as used in this section such impairment must be a permanent condition, whether congenial or due to injury or disease,

of such seriousness as to constitute a hindrance or obstacle to obtaining employment or to obtaining re-employment if the claimant should become employed. This shall be interpreted subjectively as to the particular employee involved, however, the mere fact that the claimant is employed at the time of the subsequent injury shall not create a presumption that the preexisting permanent physical impairment was not of such seriousness as to constitute such hindrance or obstacle to obtaining employment.

I.C. 72–422. Permanent impairment.—"Permanent impairment" is any anatomic or functional abnormality or loss after maximal medical rehabilitation has been achieved and which abnormality or loss, medically, is considered stable or nonprogressive at the time of evaluation. Permanent impairment is a basic consideration in the evaluation of permanent disability, and is a contributing factor to, but not necessarily an indication of, the entire extent of permanent disability.

This Court addresses the question of whether pain can constitute a physical impairment: Pain can produce "functional . . . loss" under I.C. 72–422. Because it relates to functional loss, *pain is a medical factor to be considered in determining impairment itself.*

Pain, whether physically or psychologically caused can produce a functional impairment, such as the Commission found in the present case. This Court has stated that:

The physical symptoms indirectly caused by psychological illness might come within the definition of physical impairment, preexisting or otherwise.

Although the Court did acknowledge that it felt compelled by the plain language of the statute to conclude that a personality disorder lacking any bodily symptoms could not serve as a pre-existing physical impairment, the Commission found in this case that the claimant *did* have bodily symptoms of pain which were evident and therefore there was evidence of a "permanent pre-existing physical impairment."

The record in this case demonstrates that the claimant suffered from pain due to the physical condition of her lower back as well as her psychological problems. The deposition of the physicians treating the claimant prior to her March 25, 1985, accident all make reference to pain and its impairment of the claimant's movements.

Dr. Mott in his opinion stated that the pain of the claimant was an actual part of her *physical impairment.* Accordingly the Commission did not err in its decision finding that 85% of the claimant's total impairment resulted from her preexisting condition because there was evidence of an actual physical impairment which was both anatomical and psychologically caused. We hold that the Commission did not err in its interpretation of I.C. 72–332 as applied to the evidence in this case.

The order of the Industrial Commission is affirmed.
Judgment for Bingham Memorial Hospital.

Employment Perspective

Peter Hallmark worked at Freedom Printing Press. One day, Sam Houseman, a coworker caught his hand in a press. When Peter attempted to extricate Sam from his peril, Peter banged his head on the press and suffered a bad head injury that resulted in his death. Peter's widow filed a claim with the Workers' Compensation Board for Peter's wrongful death. Sam filed a claim for the injury to his hand. Will they be successful? Yes! Fault is not at issue here. Peter may have been contributorily negligent. Sam may have been contributorily negligent in jamming his hand. Freedom may have been negligent if the machine was not functioning properly. All that matters is that

the injuries occurred on the job. Freedom is liable for the medical expenses, loss of wages, death benefits, and a possible benefit for disfigurement depending on the severity of the injury to Sam's hand. ◆

Employment Perspective

Tom Woodstock was working on the third floor of a new office building. While walking along a beam, his attention was distracted when two waitresses came out of the Masters Restaurant across the street. Tom slipped off the beam and fell thirty feet. As a result, he became quadraplegic. Tom filed a claim with the Workers' Compensation Board for permanent disability. His employer, Build-Rite claimed that Tom should have watched where he was walking. Will Tom recover? Yes! Although Tom was clearly negligent, he will recover because his injury occurred on the job. ◆

Employment Perspective

Sidney Wood was cleaning debris off the railroad tracks that are owned and operated by Northwest Railway System. Billy Thomas, a teenager, threw a rock that hit Sidney on the head. Sidney suffered a concussion and blurred vision and was out of work for one month. He filed a workers' compensation claim. Northwest Railway claimed that only the perpetrator of this intentional tort can be held liable. Is Northwest correct? No! Sidney was injured on the job. Northwest Railway is liable for medical expenses and lost wages. This situation does not preclude Sidney from suing Billy for pain and suffering for the intentional tort of battery or from pressing criminal charges against him for assault. ◆

Employment Perspective

Herman Munsun worked for the West Virginia Coal Mining Company for thirty years. At fifty-one years of age, while still employed, Herman was diagnosed with black lung disease. He filed a claim under workers' compensation for a work-related disease. West Virginia Coal disputed the claim, asserting it was not conclusive that Herman contracted the disease while on the job. Will Herman be successful? Yes! Expert opinion is on the side of Herman because of the multitude of case histories. West Virginia Coal Mining Company will probably be liable. ◆

Employment Perspective

P's and Q's Grammar School has discovered that its building is laced with asbestos. An asbestos removal firm has estimated the cost of removal at $175,000. School administrators decide to have Oscar Clark, their maintenance man, do the work over the summer. Oscar is not particularly knowledgeable about what asbestos is and how properly to remove it. Oscar works all summer on the job, without proper clothing or equipment. Seventeen years later, he is diagnosed with lung cancer. He sues P's and Q's Grammar School in court, claiming that the school administrators intentionally exposed him to asbestos, knowing its harmful effects. Will Oscar win? Yes! ◆

ORIGINATION OF WORKERS' COMPENSATION

Workers' compensation originated under the Master/Servant Doctrine where a master was liable for the death or injury of his servant. Master/Servant evolved into Employer/Employee. Originally the liability of the employer was not absolute. If the employee was contributorily negligent, assumed the risk, or was injured by another employee, he or she would be barred from recovery. As employee issues gained importance, those roadblocks to recovery were removed and the employer's negligence became absolute.

The issue addressed in the next case is whether an employee's voluntary exposure of himself to danger that results in an injury is a bar to recovery of workers' compensation. The employee argued that the employer is absolutely liable.

Farmer v. Heard

Ky. App. 844 S.W.2d 425 (1993)

SCHRODER, Judge.

The Material facts in this case are not in dispute. Alfred Farmer, appellant ("Farmer"), commenced this tort action in Warren Circuit Court against his employer, Maurice Heard ("Heard"). Heard, appellee, is a self-employed farmer who operates his own farm. Farmer was employed and worked on Heard's farm from November 1, 1988 through June 1, 1989. During his seven-month employment, Farmer's job involved feeding and moving hogs, which included loading and unloading a feed wagon on a daily basis.

The day before the accident, Farmer had left the feed wagon attached to a tractor to be automatically loaded with feed during the evening. The following morning, June 1, 1989, Farmer returned to find the wagon loaded but unhitched from the tractor. A co-employee, Mr. Bratcher, while attempting to hitch the wagon to the tractor, stuck the tongue of the wagon with the tractor draw bar causing the wagon to tip backward and rest on its back end in a stationary position.

In an attempt to set the wagon upright, Farmer climbed onto the tongue as Mr. Bratcher was lifting from the back of the wagon, but they were unable to set the wagon upright. As Mr. Farmer started to climb down from the tongue of the wagon, he slipped and fell, injuring his knee. Farmer's primary contention was that Heard had a duty to instruct his employees not to disconnect the tractor from the feed wagon when it was loaded. The lower court granted summary judgment to Heard.

In the case at bar, it is uncontroverted that Heard was not on the premises when the incident occurred, was not operating the tractor which caused the wagon to tip backward, nor did he instruct Farmer to climb upon the tongue of the wagon. Farmer also was familiar with the wagon, and stated that the wagon was in good working order and had no defects. More importantly, however, the evidence shows Farmer was not injured when the wagon tipped backward, but rather as Farmer concedes, it was his voluntary act that led to his fall and resulting injuries. Consequently, we

believe it was Farmer, not his employer, Heard, who was in a better position to appreciate that if he slipped and fell from the stationary feed wagon, an injury might result.

We further agree with the lower court that an unhooked wagon or a wagon in an upturned position does not present any hidden danger, but even if it did, since any danger was obvious under the facts of this case, Heard cannot be held liable since Farmer voluntarily exposed himself to such danger. Accordingly, we conclude Heard did not breach any duty and cannot be held responsible for an injury resulting from Farmer's voluntary action which created his own hazard.

Judgment for Heard.

WORKERS' COMPENSATION BOARD

The social purpose of workers' compensation were to provide injured workers with support and medical treatment expeditiously and to provide an incentive to employers to create and maintain a safe working environment for their employees.

The Workers' Compensation Board is administered by the state. Each employer must carry its own workers' compensation insurance unless it is a self-insurer.

Insurance companies assess premiums on the basis of the number of claims that are made. There has been an abuse of the system by some lawyers and physicians. Certain lawyers steer individuals with skeptical claims to physicians who will always diagnose a work-related injury. In deciding whether to pay, insurance companies have to weigh the investigation and litigation expenses against the cost of the settlement. Employers should consult with their insurers before a settlement to assess whether the claim is bogus and what the potential pubic relations ramifications are. Employers are concerned with keeping premiums low. Litigating bogus claims may result in fewer doubtful claims in the future.

Employers often do not want to hire people who have a condition that could be aggravated on the job, for they fear an almost certain workers' compensation claim in the future. If an individual is not hired because of his or her physical condition and he or she could perform the job at the present time, the person may file a claim with the EEOC for violation of the Americans with Disabilities Act (ADA).

Employment Perspective

Susan Hampton is a registered nurse. She applies for a position with the Midway Hospital. While Susan is undergoing a physical exam, it is discovered that she suffered a lower back strain. Midway refuses to hire Susan, although she can do the job required. Susan files a claim with the EEOC, alleging a violation of the ADA. Midway claims that eventually Susan will reinjure her back and file a workers' compensation claim. Will Susan win? Yes! Midway is discriminating against Susan for a past disability. Although the odds may favor a reinjury, this is discrimination. There is no way for Midway to guard against a future workers' compensation claim by Susan if she reinjures her back. ◆

Employment Perspective

Ken Warren delivers groceries for Foodway. His main hobby is playing racquetball. One night, Ken is late for a match and forgoes his usual preplay routine. During the intensive match, Ken injures his groin muscle. Ken will be out of work for at least six weeks. The next day he files a workers' compensation claim, alleging that the injury resulted from carrying two heavy packages up the flights of stairs to Thelma Johnson's apartment, one of the previous day's deliveries. Foodway does not believe Ken. North Star Insurance wants to settle the claim. What should Foodway do? It should insist that North Star investigate by speaking to his racquetball partners and by questioning how he could play at night if he suffered such a painful injury earlier during the day. This investigation will keep costs down and discourage other employees from submitting fraudulent claims. ◆

FALSE REPRESENTATIONS

A worker who makes a false representation with regard to his or her physical or mental state of health will be prevented from recouping compensation if the following are true: the representation was made intentionally; reliance was justifiably placed on the representation; the representation influenced the employer in the hiring of the employee; and the resulting injury is of the same condition as the one falsely represented. The burden of proving this is on the employer.

EMPLOYER DEFENSES

During the Industrial Age many workers labored under the most deplorable conditions, such as lack of heat, lighting, ventilation, and having to use unsafe equipment and machinery. Workers for the most part assumed the risk of injury. Recovering damages for loss of earnings, medical expenses, and pain and suffering was rare. The employee suffered not only an injury but possibly the loss of his or her job as well for non-performance. Coworkers were afraid to testify for fear of employer retaliation. Even worse than that was the courts' allowance of the legal defenses of the fellow servant negligence and assumption of risk. The fellow servant rule prohibited an employee from suing the employer when the injury occurred because of the negligence of a coworker. The employer's deep pocket was immune from liability. The injured employee's only recourse was to sue the coworker.

When a worker is injured, the employer sustains an economic loss due to the nonproduction of the worker. The employer must absorb this loss. The employee's entitlement to compensation depends on whether the injury was in the scope of employment. If the employer provides health and disability benefits, this will compensate the employee for medical expenses and loss of earnings while temporarily or partially disabled because of an injury or illness which occurred outside the scope of employment. The employee must make up the difference.

In the next case, a minor who left work during a night shift because of illness was assaulted. The question is whether the employer is responsible for promising the parents that the minor would not be allowed to leave during the night shift. The company argued that the assault falls outside the scope of employment.

CASE

Slagle v. White Castle Systems, Inc.

607 N.E.2d 45 (Ohio App. 10 Dist. 1992)

PETREE, Judge.

Ty Slagle was sixteen years of age when he applied for a job at a nearby White Castle restaurant. In addition to working weekday afternoons, Ty planned to work the night shift, 11:00 p.m. to 7:00 a.m., on Fridays and Saturdays. Concerned with their son's safety, Ty's parents discussed his proposed working hours with Marge Whittaker, a White Castle supervisor. During that conversation, Whittaker allegedly assured them that Ty would not be allowed to leave the restaurant during the night shift. With this understanding, Ty began working at White Castle in October 1986. Although he usually walked to work for his afternoon shifts, his parent arranged transportation for the night shifts. On January 10, 1987, Ty was scheduled to work from 11:00 p.m. to 7:00 a.m. Several hours into the shift, Ty began to feel ill. At 3:15 a.m., he received the manager's permission to leave work early. Although he was offered a ride by several co-workers, Ty chose to walk home instead. Several blocks from the restaurant, Ty was robbed and assaulted by unknown assailants.

Employers who comply with the Workers' Compensation Act are immune from damages for any injury sustained by an employee in the course of and arising out of the employment relationship. Likewise, an injury is compensable if it is "received in the course of, and arising out of, the injured employee's employment." Thus, the tests for compensability and immunity are the same. If an unintentional injury is compensable under Workers' Compensation Act, then the employer will be immune from any suit claiming damages for that injury.

The requirement that a compensable injury be received in the course of, and arising out of, the injured employee's employment is a conjunctive one. Each of the two elements must be satisfied before a claim will be allowed. As the defendant points out, the latter element is satisfied in this case by the very nature of the plaintiff's claims. An injury arises out of the employment when there is a casual connection between the injury and the employment.

To be compensated under the Workers' Compensation Act, an injury which arises out of the employment must also be sustained during the course of employment. This element refers to the time, place and circumstances of the injury. For employees with a fixed and limited place of employment, the course of employment is typically restricted to activities occurring on the employer's premises or within the immediate adjacent "zone of employment." Injuries occurring on the employer's premises are generally sustained in the course of employment. But injuries sustained while traveling to and from a fixed place of employment are not generally compensable because time spent commuting is considered a private activity, not one undertaken in the service of the employer.

Recognizing that Ty's injuries were not compensable under the general rule, the trial court relied on an exception to that rule fashioned by the Supreme Court in *Littlefield.* In that case, the court held that an injury sustained while commuting to and from a fixed place of employment was compensable if the employment created a special hazard of risk. "The special hazard rule applies where: (1) 'but for' the employment, the employee would not have been at the location where the injury occurred, and (2) the risk is distinctive in nature or quantitatively greater than the risk common to the public." In *Littlefield,* the Supreme Court held that the risk of making a left turn from a busy street into the employer's plant was a special hazard under the rule. However, in a more recent case, the Supreme Court has retreated somewhat from the board rule announced in *Littlefield.* In *Robatin,* the court was confronted with a set of facts indistinguishable from those in *Littlefield.* Nevertheless, the court held that these facts did not establish a special hazard because the risk encountered in making a left turn on a busy street is no greater than the risk encountered by the general public. Concluding that *Littlefield* was an incorrect application of the law to the facts of the case, the court overruled *Littlefield* to the extent that it conflicted with the *Robatin* opinion.

Although the special hazard rule apparently survived the court's later opinion in *Robatin,* we think that the trial court incorrectly applied the rule to the facts of this case. The applicability of the special hazard rule typically turns on the second prong—whether the risk is distinctive in nature or quantitatively greater than the risk encountered by the general public. The risk of criminal assault on a public street, like the risk of traffic accidents, is shared equally by all citizens. Even before *Robatin,* we held that risks occurring late at night are not quantitatively different from those encountered by the general public. The same may be said for "high crime areas." These are risks encountered by the public at large, not work risks distinctive to a given employment.

The trial court held that the risk of criminal assault was quantitatively greater for Ty than for the general public due to Ty's status as a minor. Even if we were to accept this somewhat doubtful proposition as true, the trial court's approach improperly shifts the focus from the nature of the risk to the characteristics of the person injured. A special hazard under *Littlefield* and *Robatin* is a work-related condition or risk which is distinctive in nature or quantitatively greater than the risks common to the general public. The existence of such a risk does not depend upon the individual characteristics of the employee injured. It depends, instead upon the nature of the risk or condition and whether that risk is greater for employees than it is for members of the general public. Ty's minority at the time in question has no impact upon this analysis. Because White Castle employees are no more susceptible to criminal assaults than members of the general public walking down the street, the special hazard rule does not apply. As Ty's injury was not sustained in the course of employment, the injury is not compensable and defendant is not entitled to immunity.

Judgment for White Castle.

When the injury occurs on the job and is within the scope of employment, the employee may seek retribution from the employer's workers' compensation plan.

The next case deals with an injury to a teacher arising out of a faculty/student basketball game. Being present on the court or in the stands was required of each teacher. The teacher claimed that the game was work-related and filed for workers' compensation for the injury sustained during that game.

CASE *Highlands Cty. School v. Savage*

609 So.2d 133 (Fla. App. 1 Dist. 1992)

WOLF, Judge.

Highlands County School Board and McCreary Corporation (E/C), appeal from a final order of the judge of compensation claims (JCC) determining that the injury sustained by claimant, Rosalie Savage, was compensable. The E/C asserted that the JCC erred in finding that claimant's injury while participating in a basketball game was a result of an incident of her employment, and therefore, compensable. We find that the basketball game during which claimant was injured constituted part of her employment rather than social or recreational activity and is, therefore, compensable.

The facts are undisputed. The claimant, a teacher at Sebring Middle School, was injured in December 1990 during a basketball game between the teachers and students. The game was an annual charity event. The game occurred during regular school hours, and the teachers received their regular salary. The teachers were required to participate in the game, either as a spectator or a player. No benefit or detriment resulted from a teacher's decision to play or to act as a spectator.

The claimant's claim for benefits to cover the injury sustained in the faculty basketball game was denied by the E/C, on the grounds that the recreational or social activity was not an expressly required incident of employment nor did it produce a benefit to the employer beyond improvement in employee health and morale. The JCC found, following a June 7, 1991, hearing, that the claimant's participation was an incident of her employment and, therefore, compensable.

The E/C's main argument on appeal is that the JCC erred in finding the accident to be compensable in light of section 440.092(1), Florida Statutes (1991), where there was no proof that playing in the basketball games was expressly required as an incident of employment. Section 440.092(1) was created in 1990 and was in effect on December 21, 1990, the date of the claimant's injury. The statute provides as follows:

> Recreational or social activities are not compensable unless such recreational or social activities are an expressly required incident of employment and produce a substantial direct benefit to the employer beyond improvement in employee health and morale that is common to all kinds of recreation and social life.

Prior to the adoption of the statute, the law concerning compensability of recreational and social activities was as follows:

> Social activities . . . are deemed to be in the course and scope of employment when *any one* of the following criteria are met: (1) They occur on the premises during a lunch or recreation period as a regular incident of the employment; or (2) the employer, by expressly or impliedly requiring participation, or by making the activity part of the services of an employee, brings the activity within the orbit of the employment; or (3) the employer derives substantial direct benefits from the activity beyond the intangible value of improvement in employee health and morale that is common to all kinds of recreation and social life.

It appears that the statutory change was enacted to avoid compensability in situations where the activity in question was neither part of the job duties of an individual or expressly required by the employer. There is nothing in the statute as adopted which would indicate a desire to preclude compensation where a person was injured in conducting actual job duties. Thus, the JCC did not ignore the requirement for a finding of an "express incident of employment" as argued by the E/C. As a matter of fact, the JCC specifically found that the activity in which the claimant was injured was *not* social and recreational but was a regular incident of her employment. This finding is supported by competent substantial evidence; therefore, the E/C's reliance on the statute to deny benefits was inappropriate.

Even if the JCC had found that the facts of this case are controlled by section 440.092 (1), there would be record support for finding of both "an expressly required incident of employment" *and* "a substantial direct benefit to the employer beyond improvement in employee health and morale" as required by the statute. It was uncontradicted that the basketball game was a school activity which required attendance of both students and faculty. Teachers were expressly required to participate in the basketball game in some manner. The event was a part of developing community awareness by requiring students to participate in a community service project. The order of the JCC is affirmed.

Judgment for Savage.

Temporarily debilitating injuries are paid according to a schedule of benefits that determines the amount of compensation given during each pay period and its duration. Once the time limit has been reached, payments cease. The benefit to both the employer and the employee is the time and expense saved by not engaging in litigation. Also, employees do not have to lay out money for medical expenses and to wonder how they will support themselves until the case is tried or a settlement is reached.

The issue in the following case concerns whether an employee is permanently disabled or permanently partially disabled. The former means that the employee can perform no work. The latter means that the employee may be precluded from performing her present job but can function at other types of work.

Tee v. Albertsons, Inc.

842 P.2d 3774 (Or. 1992)

PETERSON, Justice.

Here, an injured worker has been found capable of part-time work in an occupation, but her earnings would be approximately one-third of her pre-injury wages. She claims that her earnings are so greatly reduced as to entitle her to a permanent total disability (PTD) award. ORS 656 206(1) (a) provides:

> "'Permanent total disability' means the loss, including preexisting disability, of use or function of any scheduled or unscheduled portion of the body which permanently incapacitates the worker from regularly performing work at a gainful and suitable occupation. As used in this section, a suitable occupation is one which the worker has the ability and the training or experience to perform, or an occupation which the worker is able to perform after rehabilitation."

Claimant contends that the occupation that she had been found capable of performing part-time does not constitute a "gainful" occupation. She asserts: "The maximum earnings claimant could make post-injury without training is less than one-third of what she earned pre-injury. This disparity between pre-injury and post-injury salary establishes that the jobs which the Board found claimant could perform, as a matter of law, do not constitute gainful employment."

Claimaint, while working as a meat wrapper, suffered a back injury. Thereafter, claimant's back condition worsened, and she underwent a lumbar laminectomy and diskectomy, left L4–5 and L5–S1 with an L4 through sacrum fusion. Claimant achieved a good result and returned to work in April 1981 without significant problems. In October 1984, while working for Albertson's, Inc. (employer), a self-insured employer, claimant slipped and almost fell, causing low back and bilateral leg symptoms. Claimant was off work for a brief period of time and then returned to work for three months, but was unable to continue. Claimant has not worked since mid-March 1985.

Before her October 1984 injury, claimant worked a 40-hour week at an hourly rate of pay of $10.90. Her gross weekly pay was $436. The record contains evidence that telemarketing and hotel/motel inspection jobs pay $4.75 and $4.00 per hour, respectively, and that claimant could earn from $80 to $142.50 per week for such part-time work. As a part-time hotel/motel inspector or telemarketer, claimant's earnings would be as little as 18.3 percent of her pre-injury weekly wage (20 hours work at $4 per hour), but no more than 32.7 percent of her pre-injury weekly wage (30 hours at $4.75 per hour).

The referee concluded that claimant was not capable of regularly performing work at a gainful and suitable occupation and thus was entitled to PTD benefits. The Workers' Compensation Board (Board) reversed that part of the referee's order, concluding that claimant was "employable without training as a telemarketer and hotel/motel inspector" and that such work was available. Claimant does not contest that finding. The Board concluded that claimant was entitled to an award of 75 percent unscheduled permanent partial disability. The Court of Appeals, with one judge dissenting, affirmed. We modify the decision of the Court of Appeals and remand the case to the Board.

ORS 656.206(1) defines PTD as a loss "which permanently incapacitates the worker from regularly performing work at a *gainful* and *suitable* occupation." The word "occupation" is modified by both "gainful" and "suitable." The term "suitable occupation" is defined in ORS 656.206(1) (a) as "one which the worker has the ability and the training or experience to perform, or an occupation which the worker is able to perform after rehabilitation." The term "gainful occupation" is not defined by statute or rule. The decision in this case turns on the meaning of the term "gainful occupation" contained in the definition of PTD in ORS 656.206(1) (a) of the Workers' Compensation Law.

In ascertaining the meaning of "gainful occupation," we follow the methodology summarized in *Springfield Education Assn. v. School District.* In Springfield, this court discussed the allocation between administrative agencies and courts of responsibility for giving specific meaning to statutory terms. The opinion divided statutory terms into three classes, each of which conveys to the agency different responsibilities for definition. The first class, terms of precise meaning, requires the agency only to apply the terms to the facts. The second class, inexact terms, comprises a complete expression of legislative policy and requires the agency to interpret the legislature's meaning, either by rule or by decision in a contested case. The third class, terms of delegation, is incomplete legislation that the agency is authorized to complete, by making rules within the range of discretion established by the statutes.

The term "gainful occupation" is ORS 656.206(1) (a) is a statutory term within the second class described in Springfield. That is, it is a statutory term that embodies a complete expression of legislative meaning, even though its exact meaning is not necessarily obvious. To determine the intended meaning of an inexact statutory term, this court "looks to extrinsic indicators such as the context of the statutory term, legislative history, a cornucopia of rules of construction, and its own intuitive sense of the meaning which legislators probably intended to communicate by use of the particular word or phrase." The ultimate inquiry is what the legislature intended by using the term. The determination of the meaning of a statutory term is one of law, ultimately for the court. Thus, the inquiry in this case is: What did the legislature intend by using the word "gainful?"

Claimant makes several arguments in support of her contention that a "gainful" occupation, is one that pays a wage comparable to the worker's pre-injury wage. First, she contends that the court, in interpreting the word "gainful," should adopt the statutory definition of "suitable employment" found in ORS 656.340(6) (b) (B) (iii), a definition that is used to determine whether an injured worker is entitled to vocational assistance, and that incorporates comparability of pre-injury and post-injury wages. Under ORS 656.340, an injured worker who is not able to obtain "suitable employment" may be entitled to vocational assistance, at the expense of the insurer or self-insured employer, to enable the worker to achieve "a wage as close as possible to the worker's wage at the time of injury."

"Suitable employment' is defined, in part, as "employment that produces a wage within 20 percent of that currently being paid for employment which was the worker's regular employment."

Claimant next argues that the court should interpret the term "gainful" as the equivalent of "suitable." Claimant contends that not requiring comparability of wages is contrary to the purpose for which the Workers' Compensation Law was enacted. Claimant asserts that denying her PTD benefits because she is capable of regular part-time, low-paying employment is not consistent with the objective of returning "the injured worker physically and economically to a self-sufficient status in an expeditious manner and to the greatest extent practicable."

There are two flaws in that argument. One is that it gives no weight to the significant difference between the specific goal of vocational assistance—which is to "return the worker to employment which is as close as possible to the worker's regular employment at a wage as close as possible to the worker's wage at the time of injury," and the broader goal of the Worker's Compensation Law—which is "to restore the injured worker physically and economically to a self-sufficient status." Second, claimant's argument discounts the different roles played by the PTD benefits statute and the vocational assistance statute and virtually ignores the existence and role of the statute providing for permanent partial disability (PPD) benefits, in achieving the declared objectives of the Workers' Compensation Law.

An award of PTD or PPD benefits aims to compensate an injured worker for permanently lost earning capacity, thereby promoting the goal of returning the worker to economical self-sufficiency. An injured worker who is incapable of regularly working at a gainful and suitable occupation is entitled to PTD benefits. An injured worker who is not permanently totally disabled, but suffers from an unscheduled PPD, is entitled to compensation for that portion of earning capacity permanently lost as a result of a compensable injury. PPD benefits aim to compensate the worker who is capable of regular work, but whose earning capacity has been diminished permanently as a result of injury.

Vocational assistance, on the other hand, aims to ameliorate lost earning capacity by retraining. It promotes the general goal of self-sufficiency by assisting permanently disabled workers to achieve wages comparable to their pre-injury wages. If vocational assistance is successful, the injured worker's status may be re-evaluated to allow for a reduction in the extent or for the complete elimination of permanent disability benefits. (Insurers must re-examine PTD claims every two years); (awards of PTD and unscheduled PPD benefits shall be subject to periodic examination and adjustment). Because vocational assistance serves a different purpose than that served by PTD and PPD benefits, there is no sound reason for interpreting the term "gainful" as equivalent to "suitable."

Claimant relies on *Harris v. SAIF,* which also concerned eligibility for PTD benefits. There, the court determined that an injured worker who earned substantial income on real estate investments still could be entitled to PTD benefits, because the criterion for PTD is not income, but employability. The court stated the test as follows: "The determination of PTD status does not turn upon whether the claimant has money-earning capacity, but rather upon whether the claimant is currently employable or able to sell his services on a regular basis in a hypothetically normal labor market."

The claimant's active, albeit irregular, participation in his real estates investment activities, and his ability thereby to earn income did not mean that he was no longer permanently totally disabled.

Requiring post-injury employment to produce a wage comparable to a worker's pre-injury wage, in order to be "gainful," would judicially overrule, at least in part, the statutory provision for unscheduled PPD. According to claimant's argument, any worker with a permanent disability who is not capable of post-injury employment that would produce 80 percent of the wages paid for the worker's pre-injury employment would be entitled to PTD benefits. PPD benefits thus would be limited to workers whose earning capacity was diminished less than 20 percent as a result of an unscheduled permanent disability. There is nothing in the PPD statute that indicates it is so limited. The legislature has created a system that compensates unscheduled PPD on the basis of its permanent effect on earning capacity. The decision to compensate injured workers for unscheduled PPD reflects a policy choice that such workers should be required to earn that portion of their income that they are capable of earning in regular employment. PPD benefits are for injured workers who are permanently partially disabled.

Having rejected claimant's contentions concerning the meaning of "gainful occupation," our "ultimate task is to discern and apply the legislature's intended meaning." As stated, ORS 656.206(1) (a) itself defines a "suitable occupation" as "one which the worker has the ability and the training or experience to perform, or an occupation which the worker is able to perform after rehabilitation." The definition of "suitable occupation" concerns work that the worker is capable of performing, irrespective of the remuneration received for the work. What is the worker capable of doing? By contrast, the term "gainful occupation" concerns remuneration; it relates to the earning that the worker can obtain by working at a "suitable occupation." The plain and ordinary meaning of "gainful" is "profitable, lucrative: gainful employment." The term "gainful occupation" contained in the definition of PTD means profitable remuneration.

The Board found that "both the telemarketing job and the hotel/motel room inspectress jobs were gainful and suitable employments for claimant." It then "concludes that claimant is not permanently and totally disabled" and awarded claimant an unscheduled permanently disability of 75 percent. The Board did not have the benefit of this opinion in deciding whether claimant's part-time employment was for profitable remuneration. Its decision was not made in light of the meaning of "gainful occupation" contained in this opinion. Because this is the first decision of this court interpreting the meaning of "gainful occupation" and because the Board is the appropriate body to apply the meaning of "gainful occupation" under the facts of this case in performing its fact-finding function, it is appropriate to remand this case to the Board for further consideration in light of this opinion.

Therefore, the decision of the Court of Appeals is modified, and this case is remanded to the Workers' Compensation Board for further consideration.

Judgment for Albertsons.

Workers' Compensation is a form of no-fault insurance. Under most workers' compensation plans, medical expenses for on-the-job injuries resulting in permanent disability or death will be fully covered, and disability payments for loss of earnings will be payable for life at a fixed rate, i.e., two-thirds of the wage earned at the time the employee was disabled. In cases of death, benefits will be paid to the surviving spouse until remarriage or death and to any children until they reach the age of majority.

In the following case, the issue concerns whether the employee's disability is permanent. The employee argued that he is unable to do light work without interruption and that he could not find suitable employment elsewhere. The company claimed that the employee's contentions are unfounded.

CASE

Asplundh Tree Expert Co. v. Challis

609 So.2d 135 (Fla. App. 1 Dist. 1992)

WEBSTER, Judge.

In this workers' compensation case, the employer and servicing agent seek review of an order which holds that claimant is permanently and totally disabled. They contend that the record does not contain competent substantial evidence to support that holding.

"To establish entitlement to permanent total disability benefits, . . . the claimant must show either that he is unable to do light work uninterruptedly due to physical limitations, or that he has conducted a lengthy, exhaustive job search which has proved to be futile." In this case, nobody, including claimant, testified that claimant is "unable to do light work uninterruptedly due to physical limitations." The only medical evidence presented was to the effect that, although claimant was not suited for "the general heavy construction job market," there were "many work activities within his limitations." Claimant was not to lift more than twenty-five pounds. However, "he could bend with some moderate regularity," as long as he avoided "the extremes of heavy manual labor."

The judge of compensation claims concluded that claimant was "not physically capable of engaging in gainful employment on a full time basis, and that he had met his burden . . . in that he is not able uninterruptedly to do even light work due to physical limitations and restrictions." He based this conclusion on claimant's age (52), work history (principally unskilled, relatively heavy, manual labor), limited education (8 years) and physical limitations and restrictions. However, there is no evidence in the record to suggest that this combination of factors effectively eliminated all types of employment within claimant's capacity and qualifications. Accordingly, the conclusion that claimant "is not able uninterruptedly to do even light work due to physical limitations and restrictions" is not supported by competent substantial evidence.

The judge of compensation claims also concluded that claimant had "performed an adequate and good faith job search," and "that any further job search would be futile." These conclusions were likewise based upon claimant's age, work history, limited education and physical limitations and restrictions. Again, we conclude that there is no competent substantial evidence in the record to support the conclusions.

The evidence regarding the length and intensity of claimant's job search was, to say the least, vague and general. Claimant was laid off by the employer in October 1990. In November 1990, claimant began doing a job search. He inquired "at about six to eight places every two weeks." However, he listed some the "places" two or three times. Claimant was told at all of the "places" where he inquired either that they were not hiring, or that they were "laying off" or "shutting down." Nobody told claimant that he would not be hired because of his injuries.

In March 1991, claimant was offered another job by the employer. He worked for parts of three days before concluding that he was unable to perform tasks, which he had been told would involve light duty but did not. Claimant testified that, after he stopped working for the employer in March 1991, he "kept on looking for work." However, in response to more specific questions, claimant was able to recall only one "place" where had gone looking for employment between March 1991 and the hearing in September 1991. We do not believe that, under any reasonable construction of this evidence, one can conclude that claimant's job search qualified as either "lengthy" or "exhaustive."

The record does not contain competent substantial evidence to support the conclusion that claimant is permanently and totally disabled. Accordingly, we reverse.

Judgment for Asplundh Tree Expert Co.

Injured workers may also seek compensation for pain and suffering. An employee must file an accident report at the time of the injury, and if the injury results in a disability, then a workers' compensation claim must also be filed with the insurance company administering the plan. Some states administer the plan themselves. In other jurisdictions, the employer may choose a private carrier or may self-insure. After an award is made, the employee will be notified. If the employee is not satisfied with the amount given, he or she may appeal to the state workers' compensation board. If the board affirms the award, the employee may appeal the decision in court. This will result in legal fees, court costs, and the loss of time. However, it may be a necessary evil when an award is unjustifiably deficient.

The following case addresses the issue of whether an employee who was waiting for an opening to return to work after a long illness had a duty to mitigate damages by seeking substitute work elsewhere.

CASE

Huffman v. Ace Elec. Co., Inc.

883 F.Supp. 1469 (D. Kan. 1995)

NEWMAN, Judge.

Plaintiff was employed by the defendant in its production plant in Columbus, Kansas, on March 17, 1981, and continued her employment until she was terminated on September 18, 1992. Prior to her termination, plaintiff was employed as a parts assembler. There is no dispute but that plaintiff's work for the defendant had, at all times, been satisfactorily performed. Throughout her employment plaintiff had suffered various work-related injuries and other medical conditions for which she was off work for periods of time. However, until May 23, 1990, plaintiff had not filed a workers' compensation claim. Commencing in 1986 or 1987, plaintiff began suffering certain pulmonary problems for which she received medical treatment. She was off work for substantial periods of time, but returned to work in August 1988, after several months of absence. During this period, her leave was considered medical leave unrelated to her employment and she received temporary disability payments under the employer's disability policy at the rate of $125.00 per week.

In November 1989, plaintiff developed a persistent cough. On December 5, 1989, she consulted her personal physician, Rick L. Scacewater, M.D., who advised her not to return to work for approximately two weeks. This leave was further extended and plaintiff returned to work on January 22, 1990, with a release properly executed by her physician. After several days, plaintiff's cough reoccurred and on January 29, 1990, plaintiff left work and went to the company physician, R.L. Andreasen, M.D., who took her off work. She again saw Dr. Andreasen on February 9, 1990, and repetitively thereafter. He recommended that she remain off work for an indefinite period and that she consult with an industrial specialist. On February 19, 1990, Dr. Andreasen noted that he was then waiting for defendant to notify him as to a lung specialist, after consulting with Gallagher Bassett, the claims adjusting firm who handled defendant's workers' compensation claims.

On March 20, 1990, the defendant filed an Employer's Report of Accident with the Workers' Compensation Director, noting that Dr. Andreasen, the company physician, had advised plaintiff that her cough might be work related. Plaintiff's medical records were sent to the defendant by Dr. Andreasen on March 22, 1990, with multiple notations that he was waiting on defendant to select a consulting physician. On April 11, 1990, plaintiff was referred by Dr. Andreasen to Dr. Harold W. Barkman, a pulmonary specialist, for consultation. Plaintiff saw Dr. Barkman on April 18, 1990, who opined that plaintiff had a work-related cough. Dr. Barkman recommended that plaintiff not return to the "specific environment" in which she had previously worked, and suggested that she might be moved, administratively, to another area of the plant. His recommendations were communicated to Dr. Andreasen by letter dated April 19, 1990.

Plaintiff contacted the defendant about returning to work numerous times between February and April 1990. Each time, plaintiff was told that she would be required to produce a physician's release prior to returning to work. In May 1990, plaintiff again contacted the defendant concerning her return to work. She was advised that prior to returning to work she would be required to have a physician's release by the company doctor. Since Dr. Andreasen had left Columbus, Kansas, and was no longer available to handle matters for the defendant, plaintiff was told that it would be necessary for the defendant to contact Gallagher Bassett concerning the assignment of a new physician to examine her on defendant's behalf. Plaintiff was also told that the Gallagher Basset claims adjuster who had previously handled her claim had left the company and that a new adjuster would be designated. Defendant advised plaintiff that, as a result of these changes, it would be at least 45–60 days before a physician could be designated to examine her to determine her ability to return to work. Plaintiff was told that she did not need to contact the defendant again, but that the defendant would contact her when a new physician had been designated.

On May 23, 1990, plaintiff filed a claim for workers' compensation which has been contested by defendant and had remained unresolved at the time of trial. Plaintiff did not return to work due to the defendant's instructions and the company policy requiring the plaintiff be released to return to work after examination by the company physician. Plaintiff remained off work until her employment was terminated on September 18, 1992.

At all times during plaintiff's employment, the defendant had a written policy related to medical leave which was contained in an employee handbook distributed to employees at the time of their employment. It provided for a maximum allowable medical leave of twelve months. It further provided that the company may require its employees to submit to an examination other than the one selected by the employee and to submit a written release from a physician before returning to work. Employees returning to work after a six-month absence would be reinstated into any open position for which the employee was qualified. This policy was consistently applied prior to plaintiff's termination as related to only non-work-related injuries or illnesses. Employees who were off work due to work-related injuries or illnesses were not terminated. Rather, when employees had disabilities due to work-related illness or injury, defendant made every effort to accommodate their physical limitations and find suitable work for them within their restrictions. Plaintiff was aware of this policy.

Policy No. ERP-22 related to long-term absences provides:

> I. POLICY
>
> Any employee who is absent for a period greater than twelve (12) consecutive months shall be separated from the company. This pol-

icy covers non-occupational illness or injury, occupational illness or injury, personal leave and layoffs due to reduction in force.

II. PROCEDURE

An employee in any of these circumstances shall upon maintaining inactive status for twelve (12) consecutive months be separated at the end of that period.

If an employee absent for any of the above reasons fails to fulfill the requirements for maintaining inactive status, termination shall take place after a waiting of three (3) consecutive working days without notification or proof that the terms of the leave have not been observed. Example: Working during authorized leave without the company's approval.

Policy No. ERP-20 related to medical leave provides:

III. LIMITS

The total continuous absence shall not exceed a period of time greater than the period of full-time, permanent employment or twelve (12) months whichever is the lesser.

IV. PROCEDURES

A. Planned absences

The Employee Relations Department shall be responsible for monitoring the employee's continued ability to perform their assignments via observation and written advisories from the employee's attending physician.

The employee bears sole responsibility for providing the company with a completed attending physician's statement. This statement is required to commence the leave and to extend a leave for additional periods of time as mandated by the attending physician.

The leave and any extension of authorized leave may be granted with proper documentation of need for periods of sixty (60) days or shorter at the discretion of the Employee Relations Manager.

An employee must satisfy a two-part test to establish the defense of failure to mitigate: (1) that the damages could have been avoided, i.e., that suitable positions were available which plaintiff could have discovered and for which the plaintiff was qualified; and (2) that the plaintiff failed to use reasonable care and diligence in seeking such positions. The employer must satisfy both prongs of the test. To prevail on a mitigation defense, the defendant must show that there was reasonable likelihood that plaintiff might have found comparable work if he had exercised reasonable diligence. Reasonable efforts are determined by the economic climate, the worker's skill, qualifications, age, and personal limitations.

It is undisputed that plaintiff did not seek other employment. The defendant offered want ads in various newspapers available to plaintiff commencing on September 18, 1992, and continuing through January 16, 1994, reflecting available employment for manufacturing and clerical positions. While there were numerous clerical positions available prior to January 9, 1993, which required computer skills, which plaintiff did not then have, only one full-time general manufacturing position was advertised. Thereafter, manufacturing positions were regularly advertised.

The court finds that plaintiff failed to use reasonable care and diligence in seeking employment and that most of her economic damages could possibly have been avoided had she attempted to look for work. Although defendant has not established that plaintiff would have been employed had she applied, defendant has established that positions were available for which plaintiff was qualified after January 9, 1993. Plaintiff may well have had some difficulty in obtaining employment due to her age, physical condition, and the circumstances of the termination of her employment had she made an effort to locate employment. However, her claim that she was embarrassed that she had been fired and consequently could not bring herself to admit such to prospective employers does not excuse her failure to attempt to mitigate her damages. Plaintiff may not recover for economic damages incurred after January 1993.

The court finds that plaintiff has suffered economic damages in the amount of $5,670.00, which represents the eighteen week period from termination to the date when regular manufacturing positions were reasonably available to her.

Judgment for Huffman.

The issue in the case that follows is whether the determination of eligibility for survivor and disability benefits was correctly made by the Secretary of Veterans Affairs. Agent Orange was not deemed to be the cause of several cancers that Vietnam veterans were diagnosed with. The soldiers claimed that the determination was not valid. While not directly related to workers' compensation, the decision regarding payment of survivor and disability benefits to Vietnam veterans is an interesting case study.

CASE

Lefevre, Hill, Rada and Veldman v. Secretary, Department of Veterans Affairs

66 F.3d 1191 (Fed. Cir. 1995)

FRIEDMAN, Senior Circuit Judge.

The issue on the merits is the validity of the determination of the Secretary of Veterans Affairs, pursuant to the Agent Orange Act of 1991, (the 1991 Act), not to create a presumption that prostate cancer, liver cancer, and nose cancer are connected to exposure to herbicides in Vietnam, which would be applied in determining eligibility for disability and survivor's benefits. The Secretary contends that under the 1991 Act we do not have jurisdiction to review his determination. We hold that we have jurisdiction, and affirm his determination.

In 1984, Congress recognized that it would be virtually impossible to determine on a case-by-case basis whether exposure to herbicides in Vietnam caused a disease in a particular veteran. It therefore decided to require the Secretary to create or reject a presumption-of-service connection for particular diseases, based upon the statistical probability of such connection, as reflected in scientific studies of the relationship between those diseases and exposure to herbicides and the incidence of those diseases in person and animals subject to herbicide exposure.

By 1991 Congress had concluded that the Secretary's administration of the 1984 Act had created doubt about the way the Act was being applied. A Senate Committee report on the 1991 Act stated:

> A number of reviews of the scientific literature on the effects of exposure to dioxin have been carried out under contract with VA and published by VA pursuant to the mandate in the 1984 Act. . . . General acceptance of these reviews has been impaired because of concern that VA may have exerted influence on their content. Although the Committee does not share such a concern, it nevertheless recognizes that the perception of a possibility of some taint does exist and cannot be dismissed out of hand. Other than these reviews, the Committee is unaware of any other unified analysis of the results obtained from studies on the effects of dioxin exposure or of any up-to-date analysis.

Congress therefore enacted the 1991 Act to provide a review, by an entity completely independent of VA, that will yield unified compilation and analysis of the results from the various scientific studies.

The 1991 Act directed the Secretary to seek to enter into an agreement with the National

Academy of Science (the Academy or NAS), an independent non-profit, non-governmental scientific organization, under which the Academy would "review and summarize the scientific evidence and assess the strength thereof, concerning the association between exposure to an herbicide used in support of military operations in Vietnam," and "each disease suspected to be associated with such exposure."

The Academy summarized the extent of the evidence of association between herbicide exposure and 31 specific health problems by placing each disease in one of four categories. The first category, diseases for which the scientific evidence constituted "Sufficient Evidence of an Association." "Between Specific Health Problems and Exposure to Herbicides," contained five diseases, none of which is at issue in this case. The second category was:

> Limited/Suggestive Evidence of an Association: Evidence is suggestive of an association between herbicides and the outcome but is limited because chance, bias, and confounding could not be ruled out with confidence.

The Report placed three types of cancer in this category, one of which, prostate cancer, is at issue here.

The third category was:

> Inadequate/Insufficient Evidence to Determine Whether an Association Exists: The available studies are insufficient quality, consistency, or statistical power to permit a conclusion regarding the presence or absence of an association.

The Report placed 20 diseases in this category. Two of them—hepatobiliary (liver) and nasal/nasopharyngeal (nose) cancer—are at issue here.

The task force made recommendations based on the Academy's conclusions. It endorsed the Secretary's decision that the five diseases that the Academy placed in its first category ("Sufficient Evidence of an Association") "also meet the standard for a positive finding under the statute, i.e., the credible evidence for an association is equal to or outweighs the credible evidence against an association." The task force spent substantial time on the three types of cancer that the Academy placed in the second category ("Limited/Suggestive Evidence of an Association"). The task force concluded that two of those cancers (respiratory cancers and multiple myeloma) met the statutory standard and recommended the establishment of a presumption of service connection for them. It concluded, however, that prostate cancer did not meet the statutory standard and recommended not establishing a presumption of service connection for it. The task force concluded that none of the diseases that the Academy placed in the third category ("Inadequate/Insufficient Evidence of an Association"), which included liver and nose cancer, met the statutory standard, and recommended not to establish a presumption of service connection for them.

The Secretary adopted the task force's recommendations. He explained his reasons for denying a presumption of service connection for most of the diseases, including the three here at issue. The Secretary discussed the scientific reports, both pro and con, upon which he based his decision. The Secretary requested that the Academy "focus particularly on the evidence regarding prostate cancer and peripheral neuropathy in its next review."

The four petitioners are a Vietnam veteran who has prostate cancer and three widows of Vietnam veterans who died of liver or nose cancer. They allege that the veterans' exposure to herbicides in Vietnam caused the cancers. The veteran has a claim for disability compensation pending before the Department of Veterans Affairs. The three widows have pending their claims for dependency and indemnity compensation. The petition for review asserts that the Secretary's denial of a presumption for the three types of cancer "will cause the VA imminently to deny their claims for compensation."

The petition for review challenges the Secretary's determination "insofar as it determines not to allow veterans presumptive service connection, based on herbicide exposure in Vietnam, for prostate cancer, hepatobiliary cancers and nasal/nasopharyngeal cancer". The petitioners' brief asserts that the Secretary's denial of a "positive association" between those three types of cancers and exposure to herbicides in Vietnam was arbitrary, capricious and contrary to law.

Our role, however, "is not to substitute our judgment for that of the" Secretary. Instead, we consider whether the Secretary has "examined the relevant facts and articulated an adequate explanation for his action including a rational connection between the facts found and the choice made . . . and whether the decision was based on a consideration of the relevant factors and whether there has been a clear error of judgment." The Secretary's decision refusing to establish a presumption of service connection for the three cancers must stand.

The Secretary did not uncritically accept or merely rubber-stamp the Academy's factual findings. Instead, he carefully reviewed the evidentiary bases for them, recognizing the strengths and weaknesses of the underlying scientific studies that the Academy discussed. As the Academy had urged, he did not view the report's categorization of the disease according to the strength of statistical association "as recommendations regarding DVA policy." Instead of merely applying the presumption to whole categories, the DVA task force, and then the Secretary, examined each disease to determine if it met the statutory standard. "The task force spent a great deal of time focusing on" the disease in the Academy's second category, Limited/Suggestive Evidence of an Association, and determined that two of those diseases, respiratory cancers and multiple myeloma, met the standard, whereas prostate cancer did not. The Secretary followed this recommendation, thus demonstrating independent judgment by recognizing that the Academy's factual conclusions did not equate to the ultimate decision entrusted to him.

Affirmed.
Judgment for Secretary,
Department of Veterans Affairs.

REVIEW QUESTIONS

1. Define workers' compensation.
2. Before workers' compensation, what procedure was followed when an employee was injured?
3. What defenses were available before workers' compensation that are no longer applicable?
4. Are there any instances in which an employer is not liable for an injured employee?
5. Explain the advantages of workers' compensation.
6. Define the fellow servant rule.
7. Who administers workers' compensation claims?
8. Prior to workers' compensation, why were employees afraid to testify?
9. Explain the benefits that an employee who suffers a temporary disability is entitled to.
10. What factor will determine an employer's liability?
11. Harris put in a claim for permanent total disability (PTD) benefits. His employer questioned his qualifications because Harris earns substantial monies from real estate investments. The issue is whether the requirement is income or employability. What was the result? *Harris v. SAIF* 642 P.2d 1147 (1982)
12. Kunze was criminally assaulted on the way home from work. Kunze claimed that this situation was within the scope of employment and filed a claim for workers' compensation. The employer argued that it was no longer responsible once the employees had left for home. What was the result? *Kunze v. Columbus Police Dept.,* 600 N.E.2d. 697 (1991)

13. Robatin made a left turn from a busy intersection into the employer's plant. Robatin claimed this "turn" qualified him for workers' compensation under the special hazard rule. The employer argued that this risk was similar to risks encountered by the public in general. What was the result? *MTD Products, Inc. v. Robatin,* 572 N.E.2d 661 (1991)

14. Taylor slipped and fell on the steps of a silo where decomposed silage had been allowed to accumulate. Taylor filed a workers' compensation claim. The employer argued that it was not negligent and therefore is not an insurer of the employee's safety. What was the result? *Taylor v. Kennedy,* 700 S.W.2d 415 (1985)

15. Cory Grote, 16 years old, was a high school rodeo champion. After receiving permission from Bruce Bushnell, foreman, he was allowed to visit his brother Brad, at Joy Ranch, a division of Meyers. During his visit, Cory helped Brad release twelve colts into a corral. One of the colts, known to the ranchers to be uncontrollable, kicked Cory, causing him to have a skull fracture. Cory sued the ranch, claiming that the ranch was negligent in not informing him of the colt's dangerous propensities. Does Cory qualify for workers' compensation? *Grote v. Meyers Land and Cattle Co.,* 485 N.W.2d 748 (Neb. 1992)

16. In the case on pp. 537, do psychological illnesses qualify as permanent disabilities?

17. In the case on pp. 540, is an employer absolutely liable for an employee's injuries when the employee has voluntarily exposed himself to danger?

18. In the case on pp. 545, the teacher could have opted to view the game instead of to participate in it. Are her actions voluntary?

19. In the case on pp. 551, how is a decision regarding permanent disability arrived at?

20. In the case on pp. 551, why should an employee have to attempt to find another job while he is waiting for an opening at his old place of employment?

CHAPTER 25

Employment Retirement Income Security Act

INTRODUCTION

The Employees Retirement Income Security Act of 1974 (ERISA) divides employee benefit plans into pension plans and welfare plans. Pension plans provide income for retirement. Welfare plans include, but are not limited to, medical and insurance benefits.

DEFINED BENEFIT PLAN

Originally, pension plans provided a defined benefit based on the employee's salary and the number of years of service. The determination of the "employee's salary" may be based on an average over more than one year. The amount determined to be paid will be fixed for the remainder of the retiree's life. This amount, which may be generous on the date of retirement, may become seriously eroded after many years. While providing a larger percentage of a retiree's income initially, this will gradually decrease in comparison with social security and investment income, which will move to some extent with inflation.

DEFINED CONTRIBUTION PLAN

A more popular type of pension is the defined contribution plan. The income generated at retirement is not guaranteed as in the defined benefit plan. Rather, it depends on the contribution made on the employee's part. The employer may also contribute to this plan. The amount of the employer's contribution may be conditioned on the

employee's contribution, or it may be independent. A positive element of this plan is that the payment upon retirement either may be fixed or may vary with the investments in the employee's retirement plan.

Profit-sharing plans provide for employer contributions based on a formula or at the discretion of the employer.

Eligibility

An employee must be twenty-one years of age and have worked one year with the employer before becoming eligible to participate in that employer's pension plan.

The following case addresses the issue of whether an insurance agent is an employee and, if so, must forfeit his retirement benefits if he violates a restrictive covenant. The restrictive covenant was designed to prohibit the employee from working for competitors in the same vicinity for a period of one year.

CASE

Nationwide Mutual Insurance Company v. Robert T. Darden

112 S.Ct. 1344 (1992)

Justice SOUTER delivered the opinion of the Court.

In this case we construe the term "employee" as it appears in 3(6) of the Employee Retirement Income Security Act of 1974 (ERISA), 29 U.S.C. 1002(6), and read it to incorporate traditional agency law criteria for identifying master-servant relationships.

From 1962 through 1980, respondent Robert Darden operated an insurance agency according to the terms of several contracts he signed with petitioners Nationwide Mutual Insurance Co., et al. Darden promised to sell only Nationwide insurance policies, and, in exchange, Nationwide agreed to pay him commissions on his sales and enroll him in a company retirement scheme called the "Agent's Security Compensation Plan" (Plan). The Plan consisted of two different programs: the "Deferred Compensation Incentive Credit Plan," under which Nationwide annually credited an agent's retirement account with a sum based on his business performance, and the "Extended Earnings Plan," under which Nationwide paid an agent, upon retirement or termination, a sum equal to the total of his policy renewal fees for the previous 12 months.

Such were the contractual terms. However, Darden would forfeit his entitlement to the Plan's benefits if, within a year of his termination and 25 miles of his prior business location, he sold insurance for Nationwide's competitors. The contracts also disqualified him from receiving those benefits if, after he stopped representing Nationwide, he ever induced a Nationwide policyholder to cancel one of its policies.

In November 1980, Nationwide exercised its contractual right to end its relationship with Darden. A month later, Darden became an independent insurance agent and, doing business from his old office, sold insurance policies for several of Nationwide's competitors. The company reacted with the charge that his new business activities disqualified him from receiving the Plan benefits to which he would have been entitled otherwise. Darden then sued for the benefits, which he claimed were nonforfeitable because he was already vested under the terms of ERISA. 29 U.S.C. 1053(a).

Darden brought his action under 29 U.S.C. 1132(a), which enables a benefit plan "participant" to enforce the substantive provisions of ERISA. The Act elsewhere defines "participant" as "any employee or former employee of an employer . . . who is or may become eligible to receive a benefit of any type from an employee benefit plan. . . ." 1002(7). Thus, Darden's ERISA claim can succeed only if he was Nationwide's "employee," a term the Act defines as "any individual employed by an employer." 1002(6).

It was on this point that the District Court granted summary judgment to Nationwide. After applying common-law agency principles, the court found that 'the total factual context' of Mr. Darden's relationship with Nationwide shows that he was an independent contractor and not an employee."

The United States Court of Appeals for the Fourth Circuit reversed. After observing that "Darden most probably would not qualify as an employee" under traditional principles of agency law, it found the traditional definition inconsistent with the 'declared policy and purposes.' It therefore held that an ERISA plaintiff can qualify as an "employee" simply by showing "(1) that he had a reasonable expectation that he would receive pension benefits, (2) that he relied on this expectation, and (3) that he lacked the economic bargaining power to contract out of [benefit plan] forfeiture provisions." The court remanded the case to the District Court, which then found that Darden had been Nationwide's "employee" under the standard set by the Court of Appeals. The Court of Appeals affirmed.

In due course, Nationwide filed a petition for certiorari, which we granted on October 15, 1991. We now reverse.

ERISA's nominal definition of "employee" as "any individual employed by an employer," is completely circular and explains nothing. As for the rest of the Act, Darden does not cite, and we do not find, any provision either giving specific guidance on the term's meaning or suggesting that construing it to incorporate traditional agency law principles would thwart the congressional design or lead to absurd results. Thus, we adopt a common-law test for determining who qualifies as an "employee" under ERISA, a test we most recently summarized in Reid:

> "In determining whether a hired party is an employee under the general common law of agency, we consider the hiring party's right to control the manner and means by which the product is accomplished. Among the other factors relevant to this inquiry are the skill required; the source of the instrumentalities and tools; the location of the work; the duration of the relationship between the parties; whether the hiring party has the right to assign additional projects to the hired party; the extent of the hired party's discretion over when and how long to work; the method of payment; the hired party's role in hiring and paying assistants; whether the work is part of the regular business of the hiring party; whether the hiring party is in business; the provision of employee benefits; and the tax treatment of the hired party."

Quite apart from its inconsistency with our precedents, the Fourth Circuit's analysis reveals an approach infected with circularity and unable to furnish predictable results. Applying the first element of its test, which ostensibly enquires into an employee's "expectations," the Court of Appeals concluded that Nationwide had "created a reasonable expectation on the 'employees' part that benefits would be paid to them in the future," by establishing "a comprehensive retirement benefits program for its insurance agents." The court thought it was simply irrelevant that the forfeiture clause in Darden's contract "limited" his expectation of receiving pension benefits, since "it is precisely that sort of employer-imposed condition on the employee's anticipations that Congress intended to outlaw with the enactment of ERISA." Thus, the Fourth Circuit's test would turn not on a claimant's actual "expectations," which the court effectively deemed inconsequential, but on his statutory entitlement to relief, which itself depends on his very status as an "employee." This begs the question.

This circularity infects the test's second prong as well, which considers the extent to which a claimant has relied on his "expectation" of benefits by "remaining for 'long years,' or a substantial period of time, in the 'employer's' service, and by foregoing other significant means of providing for his retirement." While this enquiry is ostensibly factual, we have seen already that one of its objects may not be: to the extent that actual "expectations" are (as in Darden's case) unnecessary to relief, the nature of a claimant's required "reliance" is left unclear. Moreover, any enquiry into "reliance," whatever it might entail, could apparently lead to different results for claimants holding identical jobs and enrolled in identical plans. Because, for example, Darden failed to make much independent provision for his retirement, he satisfied the "reliance" prong of the Fourth Circuit's test, whereas a more provident colleague who signed exactly the same contracts, but saved for a rainy day, might not.

Any such approach would severely compromise the capacity of companies like Nationwide to figure out who their "employees" are and what, by extension, their pension-fund obligations will be. To be sure, the traditional agency law criteria offer no paradigm of determinacy. But their application generally turns on factual variables within an employer's knowledge, thus permitting categorical judgments about the "employee" status of claimants with similar job descriptions. Agency law principles comport, moreover, with our recent precedents and with the common understanding, reflected in those precedents, of the difference between an employee and an independent contractor.

While the Court of Appeals noted that "Darden most probably would not qualify as an employee" under traditional agency law principles, it did not actually decide that issue. We therefore reverse and remand the case to that court for proceedings consistent with this opinion.

Judgment for Nationwide.

Vesting

Vesting occurs when the employee acquires the right to the contribution made on his or her behalf by the employer. An employee may be partially or fully vested. An employee becomes partially vested if beginning in the third year, the plan provides for 20 percent vesting for each of the next five years. In that way, by the end of the seventh year, the employee will be completely vested. This means that all contributions made by the employer belong to the employee. Vesting applies only to the employer's contribution. When the employee contributes his or her own money in a defined contribution plan, it always belongs to the employee.

Employment Perspective

Tanya Redding worked as a customer service representative for the Fifth Avenue Fund. After four years she left for another company. During that period, Fifth Avenue contributed $5,000 to Tanya's pension fund. The plan called for a graduated method of vesting. Tanya is 40 percent vested after the fourth year. After the fifth year, she will be entitled to 60 percent of the employer's contributions, and after the seventh year, 100 percent. If the pension is a defined contribution plan, the contributions she makes herself will always belong to her. How much will Tanya be entitled to when she leaves? The amount is $2,000. ◆

In the following case, an employee was laid off four months before he was vested. The company cited economic reasons. The employee retorted that he was laid off to preclude him from obtaining the company portion of the contributions paid in for his retirement.

Ingersoll-Rand Company v. Perry McClendon

CASE

494 U.S. 133 (1990)

Justice O'CONNOR.

This case presents the question whether the Employee Retirement Income Security Act of 1974 (ERISA), pre-empts a state common law claim that an employee was unlawfully discharged to prevent his attainment of benefits under a plan covered by ERISA.

Petitioner Ingersoll-Rand employed respondent Perry McClendon as a salesman and distributor of construction equipment. In 1981, after McClendon had worked for the company for nine years and eight months, the company fired him citing a companywide reduction in force. McClendon sued the company in Texas state court, alleging that his pension would have vested in another four months and that a principal reason for his termination was the company's desire to avoid making contributions to his pension fund. McClendon did not realize that pursuant to applicable regulations, (break-in-service regulation), he had already been credited with sufficient service to vest his pension under the plan's 10-year requirement. McClendon sought compensatory and punitive damages under various tort and contract theories; he did not assert any cause of action under ERISA. After a period of discovery, the company moved for, and obtained, summary judgment on all claims. The State Court of Appeals affirmed, holding that McClendon's employment was terminable at will.

In a 5 to 4 decision, the Texas Supreme Court reversed and remanded for trial. The majority reasoned that notwithstanding the traditional employment-at-will doctrine, public policy imposes certain limitations upon an employer's power to discharge at-will employees. The majority concluded that "the state has an interest in protecting employees' interests in pension plans." As support the court noted that "the very passage of ERISA demonstrates the great significance attached to income security for retirement purposes." Accordingly, the court held that under Texas law a plaintiff could recover in a wrongful discharge action if he established that "the principal reason for his termination was the employer's desire to avoid contributing to or paying benefits under the employee's pension fund." The court noted that federal courts had held similar claims pre-empted by ERISA, but distinguished the present case on the basis that McClendon was "not seeking lost pension benefits but was instead seeking future lost wages, mental anguish and punitive damages as a result of the wrongful discharge."

Because this issue has divided state and federal courts, we granted certiorari, and now reverse.

"ERISA is a comprehensive statute designed to promote the interests of employees and their beneficiaries in employee benefit plans." "The statute imposes participation, funding, and vesting requirements on pension plans. It also sets various uniform standards, including rules concerning reporting, disclosure, and fiduciary responsibility, for both pension and welfare plans." As part of this closely integrated regulatory system Congress included various safeguards to preclude abuse and "to completely secure the rights and expectations brought into being by this landmark reform legislation." Prominent among these safeguards are three provisions of particular relevance to this case: ERISA's broad pre-emption provision; a provision which proscribes interference with rights protected by ERISA; and a "'carefully integrated'" civil enforcement scheme that "is one of the essential tools for accomplishing the stated purposes of ERISA."

We must decide whether these provisions, singly or in combination, pre-empt the cause of action at issue in this case. "The question whether a certain state action is preempted by federal law is one of congressional intent. 'The purpose of Congress is the ultimate touchstone.'"

Here, the existence of a pension plan is a critical factor in establishing liability under the State's wrongful discharge law. As a result, this cause of action relates not merely to pension benefits, but to the essence of the pension plan itself.

We have no difficulty in concluding that the cause of action which the Texas Supreme Court recognized here—a claim that the employer wrongfully terminated plaintiff primarily because of the employer's desire to avoid contributing to or paying benefits under the employee's pension fund—"relates to" an ERISA-covered plan, and, is therefore pre-empted.

Thus, in order to prevail, a plaintiff must plead, and the court must find, that an ERISA plan exists and the employer had a pension-defeating motive in terminating the employment.

The conclusion that the cause of action in this case is preempted is supported by our understanding of the purposes of that provision. 29 U.S.C. 1144 was intended to ensure that plans and plan sponsors would be subject to a uniform body of benefit law; the goal was to minimize the administrative and financial burden of complying with conflicting directives among States or between States and the Federal Government. Otherwise, the inefficiencies created could work to the detriment of plan beneficiaries. Allowing state based actions like the one at issue here would subject plans and plan sponsors to burdens not unlike those that Congress sought to foreclose. Particularly disruptive is the potential for conflict in substantive law. It is foreseeable that state courts, exercising their common law powers, might develop different substantive standards applicable to the same employer conduct, requiring the tailoring of plans and employer conduct to the peculiarities of the law of each jurisdiction. Such an outcome is fundamentally at odds with the goal of uniformity that Congress sought to implement.

Even if there were no express pre-emption in this case, the Texas cause of action would be pre-empted because it conflicts directly with an ERISA cause of action. McClendon's claim falls squarely within the ambit of ERISA 29 U.S.C. 1140, which provides:

> "It shall be unlawful for any person to discharge, fine, suspend, expel, discipline, or discriminate against a participant or beneficiary for exercising any right to which he is entitled under the provisions of an employee benefit plan . . . or for the purpose of interfering with the attainment of any right to which such participant may become entitled under the plan. . . ."

By its terms MDRV 510 protects plan participants from termination motivated by an employer's desire to prevent a pension from vesting. Congress viewed this section as a crucial part of ERISA because, without it, employers would be able to circumvent the provision of promised benefits. We have no doubt that this claim is prototypical of the kind Congress intended to cover.

We rely on this same evidence in concluding that the requirements of conflict pre-emption are satisfied in this case. Unquestionably, the Texas cause of action purports to provide a remedy for the violation of a right expressly guaranteed by and exclusively enforced by ERISA. Accordingly we hold that "'[w]hen it is clear or may fairly be assumed that the activities which a State purports to regulate are protected" by ERISA, "due regard for the federal enactment requires that state jurisdiction must yield.'"

The judgment of the Texas Supreme Court is reversed.

Judgment for Ingersoll Rand Company.

An alternative to the graduated method of vesting is complete vesting after five years. Before the fifth year, if the employer terminates the employee or if the employee resigns, the employee is not entitled to any of the contributions made on the employee's behalf by the employer.

Employment Perspective

Mary Lou Shelby is an editor for Book World Publishing. Book World subscribes to complete vesting after five years. Two months prior to her fifth anniversary on the job, Mary Lou is terminated. Is she entitled to any part of her employer's contributions? No! Those contributions will revert back to the employer. Had she survived the fifth year, all of the contributions would have been hers. ◆

When an employee becomes vested, he or she has the right to the employer's contributions but does not have access until he or she retires.

In the following case, a sixty-two-year-old worker was terminated prior to earning vesting rights. The issue is whether his age is germane with regard to determining whether the company violated ERISA.

CASE

Hazen Paper Company v. Walter F. Biggins

113 S.Ct. 1701 (1993)

JUSTICE O'CONNOR delivered the opinion of the Court.

I

The Hazens hired respondent Walter F. Biggins as their technical director in 1977. They fired him in 1986, when he was 62 years old.

Respondent brought suit against petitioners in the United States District Court for the District of Massachusetts. . . . The case was tried before a jury, which found violations of the Employee Retirement Income Security Act of 1974 (ERISA).

An appeal ensued. The United States Court of Appeals for the First Circuit affirmed judgment for respondent on the ERISA counts. . . .

In affirming the judgments of liability, the Court of Appeals relied heavily on the evidence that petitioners had fired respondent in order to prevent his pension benefits from vesting. That evidence, as construed most favorably to respondent by the court, showed that the Hazen Paper pension plan had a 10-year vesting period and that respondent would have reached the 10-year mark had he worked "a few more weeks" after being fired. There was also testimony that petitioners had offered to retain respondent as a consultant to Hazen Paper, in which capacity he would not have been entitled to receive pension benefits. The Court of Appeals found this evidence of pension interference to be sufficient for ERISA liability, and also gave it considerable emphasis in upholding ADEA liability. After summarizing all the testimony tending to show age discrimination, the court stated:

> "Based on the foregoing evidence, the jury could reasonably have found that Thomas Hazen decided to fire respondent before his pension rights vested and used the confidentiality agreement that petitioners had asked respondent to sign as a means to that end. The jury could also have reasonably found that age was inextricably intertwined with the decision to fire respondent. If it were not for respondent's age, sixty-two, his pension rights would not have been within a hairbreadth of vesting. Respondent was fifty-two years old when he was hired; his pension rights vested in ten years."

Because age and years of service are analytically distinct, an employer can take account of one while ignoring the other, and thus it is incorrect to say that a decision based on years of service is necessarily "age-based."

The instant case is illustrative. Under the Hazen Paper pension plan, as construed by the Court of Appeals, an employee's pension benefits vest after the employee completes 10 years of service with the company. Perhaps it is true that older employees of Hazen Paper are more likely to be "close to vesting" than younger employees. Yet a decision by the company to fire an older employee solely because he has nine-plus years of service and therefore is "close to vesting" would not constitute discriminatory treatment. . . .

The judgment of the Court of Appeals is vacated and the case is remanded for further proceedings consistent with this opinion.

Judgment for Hazen Paper Company.

PURPOSE

ERISA was introduced in response to unfair practices by employers. Numerous pension funds were underfunded. Therefore, when an employee retired, there was no guarantee that the money would be there for his or her pension. This situation occurred often in companies that went out of business. ERISA imposed minimum funding standards in response to this problem. Companies also had peculiar rules regarding age and years of service as the following examples will illustrate.

Employment Perspective

Joan Thompson worked for forty-one years for Bullseye Distillery in Memphis, Tennessee. When the plant closed down, Joan was offered a position in the Lexington, Kentucky, plant. She refused because she was sixty-three and a half. When she reached age sixty-five, she applied to Bullseye for pension benefits but was turned down because she had left the company before retirement. How would ERISA have addressed this problem? Joan would have been completely vested after either five years or seven years if the graduated method had been used. The retirement benefits lost by leaving the job one and one-half years before her retirement would have been negligible. ◆

Employment Perspective

Dennis Lynch had worked as a blackjack dealer for Shore Road Casino for seventeen years. He left for a job in Crazy Horse Casino when he was fifty-five. At sixty-five, he applied to Shore Road for pension benefits. Dennis was denied because he had worked for Shore Road only ten out of the last twenty years, whereas fifteen years out of twenty years immediately prior to retirement is required. How would this situation work out under ERISA? Dennis would have been completely vested for the contributions made by Shore Road Casino for his seventeen years of service and would have been entitled to collect these upon his retirement. ◆

Employment Perspective

Marjorie Quinn worked as a legal stenographer for Westfield, Morgan, and Kane (WMK) for fifteen years before resigning at age thirty-five after the birth of her son. At age fifty, after her sons had entered high school, she resumed stenographic work with WMK until retirement. When she applied for pension benefits, the law firm denied her because she had not served twenty years consecutively. Under ERISA, what would happen today? Marjorie would have become fully vested during her first service with the firm. Her fifteen-year absence would have had no effect on the situation. On her return, she would have continued to be fully vested in all the contributions made both before and after her absence. Marjorie would have been entitled to all these benefits upon retirement. ◆

Employment Perspective

Matthew Price had worked as a foreman for the Stingray Automobile Company for thirty-five years when he was forced to resign because of kidney failure. He was fifty-three years old at the time. When he reached sixty-five, he applied for pension benefits. Matthew was turned down because only those who worked with the company until age fifty-five were entitled to a pension. How would he be treated under ERISA? Matthew would have been fully vested and entitled to all the employer contributions made during his thirty-five years of service. Under ERISA, mistreatment of an individual who had contributed lengthy service to one employer would have been prevented. ◆

Minimum Funding Requirements

ERISA requires minimum funding requirements. The fiduciaries who administer the plan are required to act prudently when making investments. In addition, ERISA established the Pension Benefit Guarantee Corporation (PBGC) a not-for-profit enterprise administered by the Secretary of Labor to guard against loss of benefits when pension plans are terminated by companies. Employers are required to purchase pension termination insurance. There are maximum limits; retirees are insured up to the full value of their pensions, as long as the value does not exceed the maximum limit. Employees currently working who are vested are insured up to the value of the pension upon termination.

Employment Perspective

Nancy Woodward worked for Z Mart Department Stores for forty years. Upon retirement at age sixty-five, Nancy began to collect her pension two years later. When Z Mart went out of business, her benefits were reduced by 70 percent because the pension plan was underfunded. How would she be treated under ERISA? The likelihood is that Z Mart's pension would be better funded and more prudently invested under ERISA to guard against loss of benefits. But if the plan was still inadequate, PBGC would step in and provide proceeds from its termination insurance fund. The amount that Z Mart was underfunded would be covered up to a maximum amount. ◆

The next case concerns the issue of whether a company can contribute real property to the pension fund and, if so, what the tax consequences are of such a contribution.

Commissioner of Internal Revenue v. Keystone Consolidated Industries, Inc.

CASE

113 S.Ct. 2006 (1993)

JUSTICE BLACKMUN delivered the opinion of the Court.

In this case, we are concerned with the legality of an employer's contributions of unencumbered property to a defined benefit pension plan. Specifically, we must address the question whether such a contribution, when applied to the employer's funding obligation, is a prohibited "sale or exchange" so that the employer thereby incurs the substantial excise taxes imposed by the statute.

I

A "defined benefit pension plan," as its name implies, is one where the employee, upon retirement, is entitled to a fixed periodic payment. The size of that payment usually depends upon prior salary and years of service. The more common "defined contribution pension plan," in contrast, is typically one where the employer contributes a percentage of payroll or profits to individual employee accounts. Upon retirement, the employee is entitled to the funds in his account.

If either type of plan qualifies for favorable tax treatment, the employer, for income tax purposes, may deduct its current contributions to the plan; the retiree, however, is not taxed until he receives payment from the plan.

II

The facts that are pertinent for resolving the present litigation are not in dispute. During its taxable years June 30, 1983, through June 30, 1988, inclusive, respondent *Keystone Consolidated Industries, Inc.,* a Delaware corporation with principal place of business in Dallas, Tex., maintained several tax-qualified defined benefit pension plans. These were subject to the minimum funding requirements prescribed the Employee Retirement Income Security Act of 1974 (ERISA). Respondent funded the plans by contributions to the Keystone Consolidated Master Pension Trust.

On March 8, 1983, respondent contributed to the Pension Trust five truck terminals having a stated fair market value of $9,655,454 at that time. Respondent credited that value against its minimum funding obligation to its defined benefit pension plans for its fiscal years 1982 and 1983. On March 13, 1984, respondent contributed to the Pension Trust certain Key West, Fla., real property having a stated fair market value of $5,336,751 at that time. Respondent credited that value against its minimum funding obligation for its fiscal year 1984. The truck terminals were not encumbered at the times of their transfers. Neither was the Key West property. Their respective stated fair market values are not challenged here.

Respondent claimed deductions on its federal income tax returns for the fair market values of the five truck terminals and the Key West property. It also reported as taxable capital gain, the difference between its income tax basis in each property and that property's stated fair market value. Thus, for income tax purposes, respondent treated the disposal of each property as a "sale or exchange" of a capital asset.

Section 4975 of the Internal Revenue Code, was added by 2003(a) of ERISA. It imposes a two-tier excise tax on specified "prohibited transactions" between a pension plan and a "disqualified person." Among the "disqualified persons" listed in the statute is the employer of employees covered by the pension plan. Among the transactions prohibited is "any direct or indirect . . . sale or exchange . . . of any property between a plan and a disqualified person."

The Commissioner of Internal Revenue, who is the petitioner here, ruled that respondent's transfers to the Pension Trust of the five truck terminals and the Key West property were sales or exchanges prohibited under 4975 (c) (1) (A). This ruling resulted in determined deficiencies in respondent's first-tier excise tax liability of $749,610 for its fiscal year 1984 and of $482,773 for each of its fiscal years 1983 and 1985–1988, inclusive. The Commissioner also determined that respondent incurred second-tier excise tax liability in the amount of $9,655,454 for its fiscal year 1988.

Respondent timely filled a petition for redetermination with the United States Tax Court. That court, with an unreviewed opinion on cross-motions for summary judgment, ruled in respondent's favor.

The Tax Court acknowledged that "there is a potential for abuse by allowing unencumbered property transferred to plans in satisfaction of minimum funding requirements." Nonetheless, it did not agree that the transfers in this case constituted sales or exchanges under 4975. It rejected the Commissioner's attempt to analogize the property transfers to the recognition of income for income tax purposes, for it considered the issue whether a transfer is a prohibited transaction under 4975 to be "separate and distinct from income tax recognition."

A

It is well established for income tax purposes that the transfer of property in satisfaction of a monetary obligation is usually a "sale or exchange" of the property.

Even if this phrase had not possessed a settled meaning, it still would be clear that 4975 (c) (1) (A) prohibits the transfer of property in satisfaction of a debt. Congress barred not merely a "sale or exchange." It prohibited something more, namely, "any direct or indirect . . . sale or exchange." The contribution of property in satisfaction of a funding obligation is at least both an indirect type of sale and a form of exchange, since the property is exchanged for diminution of the employer's funding obligation.

B

We note, too, that this construction of the statute's broad language is necessary to accomplish Congress' goal. Before ERISA's enactment in 1974, the measure that governed a transaction between a pension plan and its sponsor was the customary arm's-length standard of conduct. This provided an open door for abuses such as the sponsor's sale of property to the plan at an inflated price or the sponsor's satisfaction of a funding obligation by contribution of property that was overvalued or nonliquid. Congress' response to these abuses included the enactment of ERISA's 406 (a) (1) (A) and the addition of 4975 to the Internal Revenue Code.

Congress' goal was to bar categorically a transaction that was likely to injure the pension plan. The transfer of encumbered property may jeopardize the ability of the plan to pay promised benefits. Such a transfer imposes upon the trust the primary obligation to pay the encumbrance, and thus frees cash for the employer by restricting the use of cash by the trust. Overvaluation, the burden of disposing of the property, and the employer's substitution of its own judgment as to investment policy, are other obvious considerations. Although the burden of an encumbrance is unique to the contribution of encumbered property, concerns about overvaluation, disposal of property, and the need to maintain an independent investment policy animate any contribution of property that satisfies a funding obligation, regardless of whether or not the property is encumbered. This is because as long as a pension fund is giving up an account receivable in exchange for property, the fund runs the risk of giving up more than it is getting in return if the property is either less valuable or more burdensome than a cash contribution would have been.

These potential harmful effects are illustrated by the facts of the present case, even though the properties at issue were unencumbered and not overvalued at the times of their respective transfers. There were exclusive sales-listing agreements respondent had made with respect to two of the truck terminals; these agreements called for sales commissions. The presence of this requirement demonstrates that it is neither easy nor costless to dispose of such properties. The Chicago truck terminal, for example, was not sold for three and a half years after it was listed for sale by the Pension Trust.

These problems are not solved, as the Court of Appeals suggested, by the mere imposition of excise taxes. It is 4975 that prevents the abuses.

C

We do not agree with the Court of Appeals' conclusion that 4975 (f) (3) limits the meaning of "sale or exchange," as that phrase appears in 4975 (c) (1) (A). Section 4975 (f) (3) states that a transfer of property "by a disqualified person to a plan shall be treated as a sale or exchange if the property is subject to a mortgage or similar lien." The Court of Appeals read this language as implying that unless property "is encumbered by a mortgage or lien, a transfer of property is not to be treated as if it were a sale or exchange." We feel that by this language Congress intended 4975 (f) (3) to expand, not limit, the scope of the prohibited-transaction provision. It extends the reach of "sale or exchange" in 4975 (c) (1) (A) to include contributions of encumbered property that do not satisfy funding obligations. Congress intended by 4975 (f) (3) to provide additional protection, not to limit the protection already provided by 4975 (c) (1) (A).

We feel that the Commissioner's construction of 4975 is a sensible one. A transfer of encumbered property, like the transfer of unencumbered property to satisfy an obligation, has the potential to burden a plan, while a transfer of property that is neither encumbered nor satisfies a debt presents far less potential for causing loss to the plan.

The judgment of the Court of Appeals is reversed. Judgment for Commissioner of Internal Revenue.

FIDUCIARY DUTIES

A fiduciary's duty is one of trust and confidence. The requirement of a pension plan trustee is to exercise prudence in the management of a pension's investments. In a defined contribution plan, the employee usually has discretion to allocate risk by selecting among a number of mutual funds. The range of funds will usually be from conservative to aggressive.

In a defined benefit plan, the employee has no say over the risk of the pension plan's investments. The duty of care owed by the fiduciary is greater in that the total responsibility falls upon him or her to act in a prudent manner. The defined benefit is paid according to a formula such as an average of the three final years of salary times the number of years of service times 2 percent.

Employment Perspective

Ronald Fishburn was employed by Marvelous Muffins, a gourmet bakery chain, where he worked for thirty years until retirement. Ronald's salaries for his final three years were $38,000, $40,000, and $42,000. How much will Ronald's pension be? His average salary was $40,000; $40,000 × 30 years of service = $1,200,000 × 2% = $24,000 per year pension. ◆

The following case addresses the question of whether an actuary who is not a fiduciary but who aids in the fiduciaries' breaching their obligation is liable for the losses suffered by the plan.

William J. Mertens, Alex W. Bandrowski, James A. Clark, and Russell Franz v. Hewitt Associates

CASE

113 S.Ct. 2063 (1993)

Justice SCALIA delivered the opinion of the Court.

The question presented in whether a nonfiduciary who knowingly participates in the breach of a fiduciary duty imposed by the Employee Retirement Income Security Act of 1974 (ERISA), is liable for losses that an employee benefit plan suffers as a result of the breach.

I

According to the complaint, the allegations of which we take as true, petitioners represent a class of former employees of the Kaiser Steel Corporation (Kaiser) who participated in the Kaiser Steel Retirement Plan, a qualified pension plan under ERISA. Respondent was the plan's actuary in 1980, when Kaiser began to phase out its steelmaking operations, prompting early retirement by a large number of plan participants. Respondent did not, however, change the plan's actuarial assumptions to reflect the additional costs imposed by the retirements. As a result, Kaiser did not adequately fund the plan, and eventually the plan's assets became insufficient to satisfy its benefit obligations, causing the Pension Benefit Guaranty Corporation (PBGC) to terminate the plan. Petitioners now receive only the benefits guaranteed by ERISA, which are in general substantially lower than the fully vested pensions due them under the plan.

Petitioners sued the fiduciaries of the failed plan, alleging breach of fiduciary duties. They also commenced this action against respondent, alleging that it had caused the losses by allowing Kaiser to select the plan's actuarial assumptions, by failing to disclose that Kaiser was one of its clients, and by failing to disclose the plan's funding shortfall. Petitioners claimed that these acts and omissions violated ERISA by effecting a breach of respondent's "professional duties" to the plan, for which they sought, monetary relief. In opposing respondent's motion to dismiss, petitioners fleshed out this claim, asserting that respondent was liable (1) as an ERISA fiduciary that committed a breach of its own fiduciary duties, (2) as a nonfiduciary that knowingly participated in the plan fiduciaries' breach of their fiduciary duties, and (3) as a nonfiduciary that committed a breach of nonfiduciary duties imposed on actuaries by ERISA. The District Court for the Northern District of California dismissed the complaint, and the Court of Appeals for the Ninth Circuit affirmed in relevant part.

Petitioners sought certiorari only on the question whether ERISA authorizes suits for money damages against nonfiduciaries who knowingly participate in a fiduciary's breach of fiduciary duty. We agreed to hear the case.

II

ERISA is, we have observed, a "comprehensive and reticulated statute," the product of a decade of congressional study of the Nation's private employee benefit system. The statute provides that not only the persons named as fiduciaries by a benefit plan, but also anyone else who exercises discretionary control or authority over the plan's management, administration, or assets, is an ERISA "fiduciary." Fiduciaries are assigned a number of detailed duties and responsibilities, which include "the proper management, administration, and investment of plan assets, the maintenance of proper records, the disclosure of specified information, and the avoidance of conflicts of interest." Section 409 (a) makes fiduciaries liable for breach of these duties, and specifies the remedies available against them: the fiduciary is personally liable for damages ("to make good to the plan any losses to the plan resulting from each such

breach"), for restitution ("to restore to the plan any profits of such fiduciary which have been made through use of assets of the plan by the fiduciary"), and for "such other equitable or remedial relief as the court may deem appropriate," including removal of the fiduciary. Section 502 (a) (2), "the second of ERISA's 'six carefully integrated civil enforcement provisions,' "allows the Secretary of Labor or any plan beneficiary, participant, or fiduciary to bring a civil action" for appropriate relief.

The above described provisions are, however, limited by their terms to fiduciaries. The Court of Appeals decided that respondent was not a fiduciary, and petitioners do not contest that holding. Lacking equivalent provisions specifying nonfiduciaries as potential defendants, or damages as a remedy available against them, petitioners have turned to 502 (a) (3), which authorizes a plan beneficiary, participant, or fiduciary to bring a civil action: "(A) to enjoin any act or practice which violates any provision of ERISA or the terms of the plan, or (B) to obtain other appropriate equitable relief (i) to redress such violations or (ii) to enforce any provisions of ERISA or the terms of the plan. . . ."

Petitioners contend that requiring respondent to make the Kaiser plan whole for the losses resulting from its alleged knowing participation in the breach of fiduciary duty by the Kaiser plan's fiduciaries would constitute "other appropriate equitable relief" within the meaning of 502 (a) (3).

Petitioners point to ERISA 502 (1), which was added to the statute in 1989, and provides as follows:

> "(1) In the case of—
>
> "(A) any breach of fiduciary responsibility under (or other violation of) part 4 by a fiduciary, or
>
> "(B) any knowing participation in such a breach or violation by any other person,
>
> "the Secretary shall assess a civil penalty against such fiduciary or other person in an amount equal to 20 percent of the applicable recovery amount."

The text that we have described is certainly not nonsensical; it allocates liability for plan-related misdeeds in reasonable proportion to respective actors' power to control and prevent the misdeeds. Under traditional trust law, although a beneficiary could obtain damages from third persons for knowing participation in a trustee's breach of fiduciary duties, only the trustee had fiduciary duties. ERISA, however, defines "fiduciary" not in terms of formal trusteeship, but in functional terms of control and authority over the plan, thus expanding the universe of persons subject to fiduciary duties—and to damages. Professional service providers such as actuaries become liable for damages when they cross the line from advisor to fiduciary; must disgorge assets and profits obtained through participation as parties-in-interest in transactions prohibited by 406, and pay related civil penalties, and (assuming nonfiduciaries can be sued under 502 (a) (3)) may be enjoined from participating in a fiduciary's breaches, compelled to make restitution, and subjected to other equitable decrees. All that ERISA has eliminated, on these assumptions, is the common law's joint and several liability, for all direct and consequential damages suffered by the plan, on the part of persons who had no real power to control what the plan did. Exposure to that sort of liability would impose high insurance costs upon persons who regularly deal with and offer advice to ERISA plans, and hence upon ERISA plans themselves. There is, in other words, a "tension between the primary ERISA goal of benefitting employees and the subsidiary goal of containing pension costs." We will not attempt to adjust the balance between those competing goals that the text adopted by Congress has struck.

*   *   *

The judgment of the Court of Appeals is Affirmed.
Judgment for Hewitt Associates.

INFLATION

In a defined benefit pension, the amount per year is fixed. What may seem to be a generous amount initially will erode over time because of inflation. Defined contribution plans usually offer a choice of graduated payments that will increase as time goes by. If a fixed amount is taken, the retiree must be disciplined enough to save a portion to offset the loss of purchasing power down the road.

Employment Perspective

John Jacobs retired from Bull and Bear Investment Company after forty years of service at age sixty-five. The defined benefit pension plan paid him $7,000, which was a generous amount at the time. He is now ninety-two years old. The pension, which by itself provided for him and his wife at retirement, today provides about one-quarter of their needs. ◆

A multifunded pension plan is one into which several companies contribute. It is usually formed in response to provisions in collective bargaining agreements, which stipulate that employees be given credit for length of service toward a pension when they work for more than one member of the plan.

In the next case, the employer was a member of a multiemployer pension plan. When the employer withdrew from the plan, it was assessed its proportionate share of the plan's unfunded vested benefits. The issue is whether the assessment is appropriate.

CASE

Concrete Pipe and Products of California, Inc. v. Construction Laborers Pension Trust for Southern California

113 S.Ct. 2264 (1993)

JUSTICE SOUTER delivered the opinion of the Court.

Respondent Construction Laborers Pension Trust for Southern California (the Plan) is a multiemployer pension trust fund established under a Trust Agreement executed in 1962. Petitioner Concrete Pipe and Products of California, Inc. (Concrete Pipe), is a employer and former contributor to the Plan that withdrew from it and was assessed "withdrawal liability" under provisions of the Employee Retirement Income Security Act of 1974 (ERISA), added by the Multiemployer Pension Plan Amendments Act of 1980 (MPPAA). Concrete Pipe contends that the MPPAA's assessment and arbitration provisions worked to deny it procedural due process. And, although we have upheld the MPPAA against constitutional challenge under the substantive component of the Due Process Clause and the Takings Clause, Concrete Pipe contends that, as applied to it, the MPPAA violates these provisions as well. We see merit in none of Concrete Pipe's contentions.

A pension plan like the one in issue, to which more than one employer contributes, is characteristically maintained to fulfill the terms of collective-bargaining agreements. The contributions made by employers participating in such a multiemployer plan are pooled in a general fund available to pay any benefit obligation of the plan. To receive benefits, an employee participating in such a plan need not work for one employer for any particular continuous period. Because service credit is portable, employees of an employer participating in the plan may receive such credit for any work done for any participating employer. An employee obtains a vested right to secure benefits upon retirement after accruing a certain length of service for participating employers; benefits vest under the Plan in this case when an employee accumulates 10 essentially continuous years of credit.

Multiemployer plans like the one before us have features that are beneficial in industries where "there is little if any likelihood that individual employers would or could establish single-employer plans for their employees . . . , where there are hundreds and perhaps thousands of small employers, with countless numbers of employers going in and out of business each year, and where the nexus of employment has focused on the relationship of the workers to the union to which they belong, and/or the industry in which they are employed, rather than to any particular employer." Multiemployer plans provide the participating employers with such labor market benefits as the opportunity to offer a pension program (a significant part of the covered employees' compensation package) with cost and risk-sharing mechanisms advantageous to the employer. The plans, in consequence, help ensure that each participating employer will have access to a trained labor force whose members are able to move from one employer and one job to another without losing service credit toward pension benefits.

Since the enactment of ERISA in 1974, the Plan has been subject to the provisions of the statute as a "defined benefit plan." Such a plan is one that does not qualify as an " 'individual account plan' or 'defined contribution plan,'" which provide, among other things, for an individual account for each covered employee and for benefits based solely upon the amount contributed to the covered employee's account. Concrete Pipe has not challenged the determination that the Plan falls within the statutory definition of defined benefit plan, and no issue as to that is before the Court.

We have canvassed the history of ERISA and the MPPAA before. ERISA was designed "to ensure that employees and their beneficiaries would not be deprived of anticipated retirement benefits by the termination of pension plans before sufficient funds have been accumulated in [them]. . . . Congress wanted to guarantee that if a worker has been promised a defined pension benefit upon retirement" and if he has fulfilled whatever conditions are required to obtain a vested benefit "he will actually receive it." As enacted in 1974, ERISA created the Pension Benefit Guarantee Corporation (PBGC) to administer and enforce a pension plan termination insurance program, to which contributors to both single-member and multiemployer plans were required to pay insurance premiums. Under the terms of the statute as originally enacted, the guarantee of basic benefits by multiemployer plans that terminated was not to be mandatory until 1978, and for terminations prior to that time, any guarantee of benefits upon plan termination was discretionary with PBGC. If PBGC did choose to extend a guarantee when a multiemployer plan terminated with insufficient assets to pay promised benefits, an employer that had contributed to the plan in the five preceding years was liable to PBGC for the shortfall in proportion to its share of contributions during that 5-year period, up to 30 percent of the employer's net worth. "In other words, any employer withdrawing from a multiemployer plan was subject to a contingent liability that was dependent upon the plan's termination in the next five years and the PBGC's decision to exercise its discretion and pay guaranteed benefits."

"As the date for mandatory coverage of multiemployer plans approached, Congress became concerned that a significant number of plans were experiencing extreme financial hardship." Indeed, the possibility of liability upon termination of a plan created an incentive for employers to withdraw from weak multiemployer plans. The consequent risk to the insurance system was unacceptable to Congress, which in 1978 postponed the mandatory guarantee pending preparation by the PBGC of a report "analyzing the problems of multiemployer plans and recommending possible solutions." PBGC issued that report on July 1, 1978. "To alleviate the problem of employer withdrawals, the PBGC suggested new rules under which a withdrawing employer would be required to pay whatever share of the plan's unfunded liabilities was attributable to that employer's participation."

Congress ultimately agreed, and passed the MPPAA, which was signed into law by the President on September 26, 1980. Under certain provisions of the MPPAA, if an employer withdraws from a multiemployer plan, it incurs "withdrawal liability" in the form of "a fixed and certain debt to the pension plan." An employer's withdrawal liability is its "proportionate share of the plan's 'unfunded vested benefits,'" that is, "the difference between the present value of vested benefits" (benefits that are currently being paid to retirees and that will be paid in the future to covered employees who have already completed some specified period of service," and the current value of the plan's assets.

The parties to the Trust Agreement creating the Plan in 1962 are the Southern California District Council of Laborers (Laborers) and three associations of contractors, the Building Industry of California, Inc., the Engineering Contractors Association, and the Southern California Contractors Association, Inc.

In 1976, Concrete Pipe, which is a wholly owned subsidiary of Concrete Pipe and Products Co., Inc., purchased certain assets of another company, Cen-Vi-Ro, including a concrete pipe manufacturing plant near Shafter, California, which Concrete Pipe continued to operate much as Cen-Vi-Ro had done. Cen-Vi-Ro had collective-bargaining agreements with several unions including the Laborers, and Concrete Pipe abided by the agreement with the latter by contributing to the Plan at a specified rate for each hour worked by a covered employee. In 1978, Concrete Pipe negotiated a new 3-year contract with the Laborers that called for continuing contributions to be made to the Plan based on hours worked by covered employees in the collective-bargaining unit. The collective-bargaining agreement specified that it would remain in effect until June 30, 1981, and thereafter from year to year unless either Concrete Pipe or the Laborers gave notice of a desire to renegotiate or terminate it. "'Such written notice was to be given at least sixty (60) days prior to June 30 . . . and if no agreement was reached by June 30 . . . the Employer or the Laborers might thereafter give written notice to the other that on a specified date at least fifteen (15) days thereafter the Agreement should be considered terminated.'"

In August 1979, Concrete Pipe stopped production at the Shafter facility. Although the details do not matter here, by October 1979, work by employees covered by the agreement with the Laborers had virtually ceased, and Concrete Pipe eventually stopped making contributions to the Plan. In the spring of 1981, Concrete Pipe and the Laborers each sent the other a timely notice of a desire to renegotiate the collective-bargaining agreement. Concrete Pipe subsequently bargained to an impasse and, on November 30, 1981, sent the Laborers a letter withdrawing recognition of that union as an employee representative, and giving notice of intent to terminate the 1978 collective-bargaining agreement. At about the same time, however, in November 1981, Concrete Pipe reopened the Shafter plant to produce 7,000 tons of concrete pipe needed to fill two orders for which it had successfully bid. It hired employees in classifications covered by its prior agreement with the Laborers, but did not contribute to the Plan for their work.

In January 1982, the Plan notified Concrete Pipe of withdrawal liability claimed to amount to $268,168.81. Although the demand letter did not specify the date on which the Plan contended that "complete withdrawal" from it had taken place, it referred to the failure of Concrete Pipe to make contributions to the plan since February 1981, and stated that "we are further advised that you have not signed a renewal of a collective bargaining agreement obligating you to continue contributions to the Plan on behalf of the Construction laborers currently in your employ."

The Plan filed suit seeking the assessed withdrawal liability; Concrete Pipe countersued to bar collection, contending that "complete withdrawal" had occurred when operations at the Shafter plant ceased in August 1979, a date prior to the effective date of the MPPAA, and challenging the MPPAA on constitutional grounds.

At the time Concrete Pipe purchased Cen-Vi-Ro and began its contributions to the Plan, pension plans had long been subject to federal regulation, and "those who do business in the regulated field cannot object if the legislative scheme is buttressed by subsequent amendments to achieve the legislative end."

"The employer in the present litigation voluntarily negotiated and maintained a pension plan which was determined to be within the strictures of ERISA." In light of the relationship between Concrete Pipe and the Plan, we find no basis to conclude that Concrete Pipe is being forced to bear a burden "which, in all fairness and justice, should be borne by the public as a whole."

Having concluded that the statutory presumptions work no deprivation of procedural due process, and that the statute, as applied to Concrete Pipe, violates no substantive constraint of the Fifth Amendment, we affirm the judgment of the Court of Appeals.

Judgment for Construction Laborers Pension Trust.

In the case that follows, a company sought to withdraw from a multiemployer pension plan. The issue is whether the company must pay a lump sum or amortize its debt over a schedule of payments. The debt is the employer's proportionate share of the plan's unfunded liabilities.

CASE

Milwaukee Brewery Workers' Pension Plan v. Jos. Schlitz Brewing Company and Stroh Brewery Company

115 S.Ct. 981 (1995)

BREYER, Judge.

The Multiemployer Pension Plan Amendments Act of 1980 (MPPAA), provides that an employer who withdraws from an underfunded multiemployer pension plan must pay a charge sufficient to cover that employer's fair share of the plan's unfunded liabilities. The statute permits the employer to pay that charge in lump sum or to "amortize" it, making payments over time. This case focuses upon a withdrawing employer who amortizes the charge, and it asks when, for purposes of calculating the amortization schedule, interest begins to accrue on the amortized charge. The Court of Appeals for the Seventh Circuit held that, for purposes of computation, interest begins to accrue on the first day of the year after withdrawal. We agree and affirm its judgment.

I

We shall briefly describe the general purpose of MPPAA, the basic way MPPAA works, and the relevant interest-related facts of the case before us.

A. MPPAA's General Purpose

MPPAA helps solve a problem that became apparent after Congress enacted the Employee Retirement Income Security Act of 1974 (ERISA). ERISA helped assure private-sector workers that they would receive the pensions that their employers had promised them. To do so, among other things, ERISA required employers to make contributions that would produce pension-plan assets sufficient to meet future vested pension liabilities; it mandated termination insurance to protect workers against a plan's bankruptcy; and, if a plan became insolvent, it held any employer who had withdrawn from the plan during the previous five years liable for a fair share of the plan's underfunding.

Unfortunately, this scheme encouraged an employer to withdraw from a financially shaky plan and risk paying its share if the plan later became insolvent, rather than to remain and (if others withdrew) risk having to bear alone the entire cost of keeping the shaky plan afloat. Consequently, a plan's financial troubles could trigger a stampede for the exit-doors, thereby ensuring the plan's demise. MPPAA helped eliminate this problem by changing the strategic considerations. It transformed what was only a risk (that a withdrawing employer would have to pay a fair share of underfunding) into a certainty. That is to say, it imposed a withdrawal charge on all employers withdrawing from an underfunded plan (whether or not the plan later became insolvent). And, it set forth a detailed set of rules for determining, and collecting, that charge.

B. MPPAA's Basic Approach

The way in which MPPAA calculates interest is related to the way in which that statute answers three more general, and more important, questions: First, how much is the withdrawal charge? MPPAA's lengthy charge-determination section sets forth rules for calculating a withdrawing employer's fair share of a plan's underfunding. It explains (a) how to determine a plan's total underfunding; and (b) how to determine an employer's fair share (based primarily upon the comparative number of that employer's covered workers in each earlier year and the related level of that employer's contributions).

One might expect MPPAA to calculate a withdrawal charge that equals the withdrawing employer's fair share of a plan's underfunding as of the day the employer withdraws. But, instead, MPPAA instructs a plan to make the withdrawal charge calculation, not as of the day of withdrawal, but as of the last day of the plan year preceding the year during which the employer withdrew—a day that could be up to a year earlier. Thus (assuming for illustrative purposes that a plan's bookkeeping year and the calendar year coincide), the withdrawal charge for an employer withdrawing from an underfunded plan in 1981 equals that employer's fair share of the underfunding as calculated on December 31, 1980, whether the employer withdrew the next day (January 1, 1981) or a year later (December 31, 1981). The reason for this calculation date seems one of administrative convenience. Its use permits a plan to base the highly complex calculations upon figures that it must prepare in any event for a report required under ERISA, thereby avoiding the need to generate new figures tied to the date of actual withdrawal.

Second, how may the employer pay the withdrawal charge? The statute sets forth two methods: (a) payment in a lump sum; and (b) payment in installments. The statute's lump-sum method is relatively simple. A withdrawing employer may pay the entire liability when the first payment falls due; pay installments for a while and then discharge its remaining liability; or make a partial balloon payment and afterwards pay installments. The statute's installment method is more complex. The statutory method is unusual in that the statute does not ask the question that a mortgage borrower would normally ask, namely, what is the amount of each of my monthly payments? What size monthly payment will amortize, say, a 7% 30-year loan of $100,000? Rather, the statute fixes the amount of each payment and asks how many such payments there will have to be. To put the matter more precisely, (1) the statute fixes the amount of each annual payment at a level that (roughly speaking) equals the withdrawing employer's typical contribution in earlier years; (2) it sets an interest rate, equal to the rate the plan normally uses for its calculations; and (3) it then asks how many such annual payments it will take to "amortize" the withdrawal charge at that interest rate.

It is as if Brown, who owes Smith $1000, were to ask, not, "How much must I pay each month to pay off the debt (with 7% interest) over two years?" but, rather, "Assuming 7% interest, how many $100 monthly payments must I make to pay off that debt?" To bring the facts closer to those of this case, assume that an employer withdraws from an underfunded plan in mid-1981; that the withdrawal charge (calculated as of the end of 1980) is $23.3 million; that the employer normally contributes about $4 million per year to the plan; and that the plan uses a 7% interest rate. In that

case, the statute asks: "How many annual payments of about $4 million does it take to pay off a debt of $23.3 million if the interest rate is 7%?" The fact that the statute poses the installment-plan question in this way, along with an additional feature of the statute, namely that the statute forgives all debt outstanding after 20 years, suggests that maintaining level funding for the plan is an important goal of the statute. The practical effect of this concern with maintaining level payments is that any amortization interest MPPAA may cause to accrue is added to the end of the payment schedule unless forgiven.

Third, when must the employer pay? The statute could not make the employer pay the calculated sum (or begin to pay that sum) on the date in reference to which one calculates the withdrawal charge, for that date occurs before the employer withdraws. (It is the last day of the preceding plan year, i.e., December 31, 1980, for an employer who withdraws in 1981.) The statute, of course, might make the withdrawing employer pay (or begin payment) on the date the employer actually withdraws. But, it does not do so. Rather, the statute says that a plan must draw up a schedule for payment and "demand payment" as "soon as practicable" after withdrawal. It adds that "withdrawal liability shall be payable . . . no more than 60 days after the date of the demand."

Thus, a plan that calculates quickly might demand payment the day after withdrawal and make the charge "payable" within 60 days thereafter. A plan that calculates slowly might not be able to demand payment for many months after withdrawal. For example, in the case of the employer who withdraws on August 14, 1981, incurring a withdrawal charge of $23.3 million (calculated as of December 31, 1980), the lump sum of $23.3 million, or the first of the installment payments of roughly $4 million, will become "payable" to the plan "no later than 60 days" after the plan sent the withdrawing employer a demand letter. The day of the first payment may thus come as soon as within 60 days after August 15, 1981, or it may not come for many months thereafter, depending upon the plan's calculating speed.

C. This Case

The facts of this case approximate those of our example. Three brewers, Schlitz, Pabst, and Miller, contributed for many years to a multiemployer pension plan (the Plan). On August 14, 1981, Schlitz withdrew from the Plan. By the end of September 1981, the Plan completed its calculations, created a payment schedule, and sent out a demand for payment (thereby making the first installment payment "payable") "on or before November 1, 1981." From the outset, the parties agreed that the annual installment payment amounted to $3,945,481 and that the relevant interest rate was 7% per year. After various controversies led to arbitration and a court proceeding between Schlitz and the Plan, the courts and parties eventually determined that the withdrawal charge (calculated as of the last day of the previous plan-bookkeeping year, December 31, 1980) amounted to $23.3 million.

But, the parties disagreed whether interest accrued during 1981, the year in which Schlitz withdrew. The Plan claimed that, for purposes of calculating the installment schedule, interest started accruing on the last day of the plan year preceding withdrawal (December 31, 1980). Schlitz, on the other hand, argued that accrual began on the first day of the plan year following withdrawal (January 1, 1982). Under either reading, the number of annual payments is eight. But, under the Plan's reading, the final payment would amount to $3,499,361, whereas, in Schlitz's reading, that payment would amount to $880,331.

The arbitrator in this case agreed with Schlitz's reading. The District Court, reviewing the arbitration award, disagreed, but the Court of Appeals for the Seventh Circuit reversed the District Court. Because the Seventh Circuit's decision conflicts with a holding of the Third Circuit, this Court granted certiorari. Our conclusion, like that of the Seventh Circuit, is that, for purposes of computation, interest does not start accruing until the beginning of the plan year after withdrawal.

II

At first glance, the statutory provision that (the parties agree) governs this case says that a withdrawing employer "shall pay the amount determined . . . over the period of years necessary to amortize the amount in level annual payments calculated as if the first payment were made on the first day of the plan year following the plan year in which the withdrawal occurs and as if each subsequent payment were made on the first day of each subsequent plan year."

After considering the parties' arguments, which focus upon the emphasized language, we have become convinced that, for purposes of computation, this provision, although causing interest to accrue over subsequent plan years, does not cause interest to accrue during the withdrawal year itself.

A

The Plan points out, and we agree, that the word "amortize" normally assumes interest charges. After all, the very idea of amortizing, say, a mortgage loan, involves paying the principal of the debt over time along with interest. But the Plan (supported by the Government, which is taking a view of the matter contrary to the view the Pension Benefit Guaranty Corporation took goes on to claim that the word "amortize" indicates that interest accrues during the withdrawal year as well as during subsequent years. We do not agree with that claim. In our view, one generally does not pay interest on a debt until that debt arises-that is to say, until the principal of the debt is outstanding. And, the instruction to calculate payment as if the first payment were made at the beginning of the following year tells us to treat the debt as if it arose at that time (i.e., the first day of the year after withdrawal), not as if it arose one year earlier.

We consequently hold that MPPAA calculates its installment schedule on the assumption that interest begins accruing on the first day of the year following withdrawal. The judgment of the Court of Appeals is therefore

Affirmed.
Judgment for Schlitz.

In the next case, multiemployers withdrew from one fund and became affiliated with another. The second fund acquired some of the original fund's liabilities. The employers on behalf of the second fund sought the transfer of contributions from the original fund to offset the liabilities assumed.

113 S.Ct. 2252 (1993)

Justice SCALIA delivered the opinion of the Court.

This case presents the question whether a federal district court may issue an injunction pursuant to the Labor Management Relations Act, 1947 (LMRA), requiring the trustees of a multiemployer trust fund to transfer assets from that fund to a new multiemployer trust fund established by employers who broke away from the first fund.

Respondents include a group of employers that, until 1981, were members of a multiemployer bargaining association, the Greater New York Health Care Facilities Association, Inc. (Greater Employer Association). Two trust funds—the Local 144 Nursing Home Pension Fund and the New York City Nursing Home-Local 144 Welfare Fund (collectively, Greater Funds)—were established pursuant to collective-bargaining agreements between the Greater Employer Association and the relevant union, Local 144 of the Hotel, Hospital, Nursing Home and Allied Services Employees Union, Service Employees International Union, AFL-CIO (Local 144). Prior to 1981, the respondent employers made contributions to the Greater Funds on behalf of their employees in accordance with the terms of collective-bargaining agreements negotiated between the Greater Employer Association and Local 144.

In 1981, the respondent employers broke away from the Greater Employer Association and executed independent collective-bargaining agreements with Local 144. The initial agreements required continuing employer contributions to the Greater Funds, but those concluded in 1984 when the respondent employers provided for establishment of a new set of trust funds, the Local 144 Southern New York Residential Health Care Facilities Association Pension Fund and the Local 144 Southern New York Residential Health Care Facilities Association Welfare Fund (Southern Funds). At approximately the same time, the respondent employers ended their participation in the Greater Funds.

In negotiating the transfer from the Greater Funds to the Southern Funds, the "primary concern" of Local 144 was to make sure that the shift would not cause its members to lose benefits. To address that concern, the respondent employers guaranteed in their collective-bargaining agreements that the Southern Funds would recognize all credited service time earned under the Greater Funds and, more generally, that employees would not lose any benefits as a result of the withdrawal from the Greater Funds. That guarantee obviously created some peculiar liabilities for the Southern Funds. For example, an employee who had earned nine years credited service time under the Greater Funds would, after just one more year of service, acquire vested rights to pension benefits pursuant to the 10-year vesting requirement of the Southern Funds—even though the Southern Funds had received only one year of employer contributions for that employee. The Southern Funds' assumption of these liabilities, however, did not alter the obligations of the Greater Funds, which were not parties to the collective-bargaining agreements: They remained liable to the departing employees for all vested benefits.

To help cover the Southern Funds' liabilities and in general to help finance the change from the Greater Funds to the Southern Funds, the respondent employers—joined by several of their employees and the trustees of the Southern Funds—brought this action to compel petitioners, the Greater Funds and the Greater Funds' trustees, to transfer an appropriate fractional share of the Greater Funds' assets to the Southern Funds. They asserted right to relief under the Employee Retirement Income Security Act of 1974 (ERISA), and under 302 of the LMRA; only the latter claim is at issue here.

To describe respondent's claim, it is necessary to sketch the structure of that provision. Subsection (a) prohibits an employer (or an association of employers, such as the Greater Employer Association) from making payments to any representative of its employees, including the employees' union and union officials. Paragraph (b) (1) is the "reciprocal" of subsection (a), making it unlawful for employee representatives to receive the payments prohibited by subsection (a). The prohibitions of subsection (a) and paragraph (b) (1) are drawn broadly, and would prevent payments to union employee health and welfare funds such as those at issue here. Subsection 302(c), however, provides exceptions to the prohibitions. Most significantly for our purposes, paragraph (c) (5) excepts payments to an employee trust fund so long as certain conditions are met, including that the trust fund be "established . . . for the sole and exclusive benefit of the employees," and that the payments be "held in trust for the purpose of paying" employee benefits.

Respondents' theory is that the Greater Funds cannot meet those last quoted conditions unless they transfer to the Southern Funds the portion of their reserves that is attributable to the respondents' past contributions. If they fail to do so, according to respondents, they will suffer from a "structural defect" which can be remedied by federal courts pursuant to the power conferred by 302 (e) to "restrain violations of this section."

We hold today that 302 (e) does not provide authority for a federal court to issue injunctions against a trust fund or its trustees requiring the trust funds to be administered in the manner described in 302 (c) (5). By its unmistakable language, 302 (e) provides district courts with jurisdiction "to restrain violations of this section." A "violation" of 302 occurs when the substantive restrictions in 302 (a) and (b) are disobeyed, which happens, not when funds are administered by the trust fund, but when they are "paid, lent, or delivered" to the trust fund, 302(a), or when they are "received or accepted" by the trust fund, or "requested or demanded" for the trust fund. And the exception to violation set forth in paragraph (c) (5) relates, not to the purpose for which the trust fund is in fact used (an unrestricted fund that happens to be used "for the sole and exclusive benefit of the employees" does not qualify); but rather to the purpose for which the trust fund is "established," and for which the payments are "held in trust." The trustees' failure to comply with these latter purposes may be a breach of their contractual or fiduciary obligations and may subject them to suit for such breach; but it is no violation of 302.

Judgment for Local 144 Nursing Home Pension Fund.

TAX INCENTIVES

Although employers are not obligated to offer any benefits, a tax incentive exists for an employer that makes contributions to a qualified plan. A qualified plan is one that meets the requirements of the Internal Revenue Code. The tax incentive is a deduction for all employer contributions to the pension trust fund from which benefits will ultimately be paid to the employees. The monies paid into the trust fund do not have to be reported by the employees until they receive the benefits. This deferral helps the income grow faster because it is tax free. Thus, pension benefits can be paid out with smaller initial investments by the employer. This tax-free deferral plan can be withdrawn if the plan no longer qualifies under the Internal Revenue code because of violations surrounding vesting or other fiduciary responsibilities. Enforcement of ERISA is spread out among various federal departments. The Department of Labor receives ERISA plan reports and initiates civil suits for violations of reporting and disclosing. The employee plans and exempt organizations component of the Internal Revenue Service, deals with tax law violations of the Internal Revenue Code and can authorize removal of qualified plan status for tax deferral of pension contributions. The Pension Benefit Guaranty Corporation actively pursues employers that have underfunded plans, particularly those employers that are in bankruptcy. Finally, the Department of Justice pursues criminal violations of ERISA, such as embezzlement of funds.

REVIEW QUESTIONS

1. Define ERISA.
2. Explain the difference between a defined benefit plan and a defined contribution plan.
3. Define profit-sharing plans.
4. When does an employee become eligible to participate in a company's pension plan?
5. Define vesting.
6. Explain the graduated method of vesting.
7. If an employee is discharged prior to vesting, what happens to the contributions?

8. When can employees access their contributions?
9. Are many pension plans underfunded?
10. Who administers pension plans?
11. A state law requires payment of severance benefits but does not provide for the establishment of an ongoing plan. Is this law preempted by ERISA? *Fort Halifax Packing Co. v. Coyne,* 482 U.S.1 (1987)
12. A collection agency attempted to garnish an ERISA plan participant's salary pursuant to the state's general garnishment statute. The participant claimed that the state law was preempted by ERISA. What was the result? *Mackey v. Lanier Collection Agency & Service, Inc.,* 486 U.S. 825 (1988)
13. Is pension plan regulation exclusively under federal domain? *Allessi v. Raybestos Manhattan, Inc.,* 451 U.S. 504 (1981)
14. McGann sued H&H Music Co., claiming violation of ERISA when H&H severely reduced health benefits for employees with AIDS. What was the result? *McGann v. H&H Music Co.,* 946 F.2d 401 (5th Cir. 1991)
15. Seaman was discharged by Arvida Realty Sales when it learned of Seaman's life-threatening illness. Seaman contended that Arvida violated ERISA by discharging him to avoid paying benefits. What was the result? *Seaman v. Arvida Realty Co.,* 985 F.2d 543 (11th Cir. 1993)
16. In the case on pp. 559 is the company's use of a restrictive covenant with its employees ethical?
17. In the case on pp. 562, was the company's actions ethical?
18. In the case on pp. 567, can a company's contributions to its employees' pension fund be something other than cash?
19. Was the case on pp. 570 decided ethically?
20. In the case on pp. 572, why would a company want to be part of a multifunded pension plan?

Employee Retirement Income Security Act of 1974

Sec. 1001 Congressional Findings and Declaration of Policy.

Subtitle A—General Provisions

(a) Benefit plans as affecting interstate commerce and the Federal taxing power.

The Congress finds that the growth in size, scope, and numbers of employee benefits plans in recent years has been rapid and substantial; that the operational scope and economic impact of such plans is increasingly interstate; that the continued well-being and security of millions of employees and their dependents are directly affected by these plans; that they are affected with a national public interest; that they have become an important factor affecting the stability of employment and the successful development of industrial relations; that they have become an important factor in commerce because of the interstate character of their activities, and of the activities of their participants, and the employers, employee organizations, and other entities by which they are established or maintained; that a large volume of the activities of such plans is carried on by means of the mails and instrumentalities of interstate commerce; that owing to employees lack of information and adequate safeguards concerning their operation, it is desirable in the interests of employees and their beneficiaries, and to provide for the general welfare and the free flow of commerce, that disclosure be made and safeguards be provided with respect to the establishment, operation, and administration of such plans; that they substantially affect the revenues of the United States because they are afforded preferential Federal tax treatment; that despite the enormous growth in such plans many employees with long years of employment are losing anticipated retirement benefits owing to the lack of vesting provisions in such plans; that owing to the inadequacy of current minimum standards, the soundness and stability of plans with respect to adequate funds to pay promised benefits may be endangered; that owing to the termination of plans before requisite funds have been accumulated, employees and their beneficiaries have been deprived of anticipated benefits, and that is therefore desirable in the interests of employees and their beneficiaries, for the protection of the revenue of the United States, and to provide for the free flow of commerce, that minimum standards be provided assuring the equitable character of such plans and their financial soundness.

Sec. 1002 Definitions.

For the purpose of this title:

(1) The terms "employee welfare benefit plan" and "welfare plan" mean any plan, fund, or program which was heretofore or is hereafter established or maintained by an employer or by an employee organization, or by both, to the extent that such plan, fund, or program was established or is maintained for the purpose of providing for its participants or their beneficiaries, through the purchase of insurance or otherwise, (A) medical, surgical, or hospital care or benefits, or benefits in the event of sickness, accident, disability, death or unemployment, or vacation benefits, apprenticeship or other training programs or day care centers, scholarship funds, or prepaid legal services, or (B) any benefit described in section 302(c) of the Labor Management Relations Act, 1947 (other than pensions on retirement or death, and insurance to provide such pensions).

(2) (A) Except as provided in subparagraph (B), the terms "employee pension benefit plan" and "pension plan" mean any plan, fund, or program which was heretofore or is hereafter established or maintained by an employer or by an employee organization, or by both, to the extent that by its express terms or as a result of surrounding circumstances such plan, fund, or program—
(i) provides retirement income to employees, or
(ii) results in a deferral of income by employees for periods extending to the termination of covered employment or beyond, regardless of the method of calculating the contributions made to the plan, the method of calculating the benefits under the plan or the method of distributing benefits from the plan.

(21) (A) Except as otherwise provided in subparagraph (B), a person is a fiduciary with respect to a plan to the extent (i) he exercises any discretionary authority or discretionary control respecting management of such plan or exercises any authority or control respecting management or disposition of its assets, (ii) he renders investment advice for a fee or other compensation, direct or indirect, with respect to any moneys or other property of such plans, or has any authority or responsibility to do so, or (iii) he has any discretionary authority or discretionary responsibility in the administration of such plan.

Sec. 1003 Coverage.

(a) This subchapter shall apply to any employee benefit plan if it is established or maintained—

(1) by an employer engaged in commerce or in any industry or activity affecting commerce; or
(2) by an employee organization or organizations representing employees engaged in commerce or in any industry or activity affecting commerce; or
(3) by both.

(b) The provisions of this subchapter shall not apply to any employee benefit plan if—
(1) such plan is a governmental plan;
(2) such plan is a church plan.

Sec. 1052 Minimum participation standards

(a) (1)(A) No pension plan may require, as a condition of participation in the plan, that an employee complete a period of service with the employer or employers maintaining the plan extending beyond the later of the following dates—
(i) the date on which the employee attains the age of 21; or
(ii) the date on which he completes one year of service.

Sec. 1053 Minimum vesting standards

(a) Nonforfeitability requirements
Each pension plan shall provide that an employee's right to his normal retirement benefit is nonforfeitable upon the attainment of normal retirement age and in addition shall satisfy the requirements of paragraphs (1) and (2) of this subsection.
(1) A plan satisfies the requirements of this paragraph is an employee's rights in his accrued benefit derived from his own contributions are nonforfeitable.
(2) A plan satisfies the requirements of this paragraph if it satisfies the requirements of subparagraph (A), (B), or (C).
(A) A plan satisfies the requirements of this subparagraph if an employee who has completed at least 5 years of service has a nonforfeitable right to 100 percent of the employee's accrued benefit derived from employer contributions.
(B) A plan satisfies the requirements of this subparagraph if an employee has a nonforfeitable right to a percentage of the employee's accrued benefit derived from employer contributions determined under the following table:

Years of service:	*The nonforfeitable percentage is:*
3	20
4	40
5	60
6	80
7 or more	100

(C) A plan satisfies the requirements of this subparagraph if—
(i) the plan is a multiemployer plan and
(ii) under the plan—
(I) an employee who is covered pursuant to a collective bargaining agreement who has completed at least 10 years of service has a nonforfeitable right to 100 percent of the employee's accrued benefit derived from employer contributions.

Sec. 1054 Benefit accrual requirements

(a) Satisfaction of requirements by pension plans
Each pension plan shall satisfy the requirements of this section, and—
(1) in the case of a defined benefit plan, shall satisfy the requirements of subsection (b)(1) of this section; and
(2) in the case of a defined contribution plan, shall satisfy the requirements of subsection (b)(2) of this section.

(b) Enumeration of plan requirements
(1) (A) A defined benefit plan satisfies the requirements of this paragraph if the accrued benefit to which each participant is entitled upon his separation from the service is not less than—
(i) 3 percent of the normal retirement benefit to which he would be entitled at the normal retirement age if he commenced participation at the earliest possible entry age under the plan and served continuously until the earlier of age 65 or the normal retirement age specified under the plan, multiplied by

(ii) the number of years (not in excess of 33 1/3) of his participation in the plan.

In the case of a plan providing retirement benefits based on compensation during any period, the normal retirement benefit to which a participant would be entitled shall be determined as if he continued to earn annually the average rate of compensation which he earned during consecutive years of service, not in excess of 10, for which his compensation was the highest. For purposes of this subparagraph, social security benefits and all other relevant factors used to compute benefits shall be treated as remaining constant as of the current year for all years after such current year.

(2) (A) A defined contribution plan satisfies the requirements of this paragraph if, under the plan, allocates to the employee's account are not ceased, and the rate at which amounts are allocated to the employee's account is not reduced, because of the attainment of any age.

(B) A plan shall not be treated as failing to meet the requirements of subparagraph (A) solely because the subsidized portion of any early retirement benefit is disregarded in determining accruals.

Sec. 1056 Form and payment of benefits

(a) Commencement date for payment of benefits

Each pension plan shall provide that unless the participant otherwise elects, the payment of benefits under the plan to the participant shall begin not later than the 60th day after the latest of the close of the plan year in which—

(1) the date on which the participant attains the earlier age 65 or the normal retirement age specified under the plan,

(2) occurs the 10th anniversary of the year in which the participant commenced participation in the plan, or

(3) the participant terminates his service with the employer.

Sec. 1082 Minimum funding standards

(a) Avoidance of accumulated funding deficiency

(1) Every employee pension benefit plan subject to this part shall satisfy the minimum funding standard for any plan year to which this part applies. A plan to which this part applies shall have satisfied the minimum funding standard for such plan for a plan year if as of the end of such plan year the plan does not have an accumulated funding deficiency.

Case Index

All entries that appear in italic appear in the Review Questions within the chapters.

Abood v. Detriot Board of Ed., 497
Ahearn v. Baker, 53
Allan Dampf, P.C. v. Bloom, 128
Allen v. Dept. of Employment Training, 287
Allessi v. Raybestos Manhattan, Inc., 581
American Friends Service Committee v. Thornburgh, 381
American Hospital Assoc. v. N.L.R.B., 487
Amoroso v. Samuel Friedland Family Ent., 11
Armour & Co. v. Wantock, 513
Asplundh Tree Expert Co. v. Challis, 550
Aucutt v. Six Flags Over Mid America, 438
August v. Offices Unlimited, Inc., 431

Badih v. Myers, 326
Bahadirli v. Domino's Pizza, 388
Barker v. Taft Broadcasting Co., 270
Barrash v. Bowen, 333
Bender Ship Repair, Inc. v. Stevens, 155
Biggs v. Wilson, 502
Bingham Memorial Hosp. v. Special Indemnity Fund, 537
Birmingham Television Corp. v. DeRamus, 35
Blake v. Giarrusso, 222
Blare v. Husky Injection Systems, Inc., 177
Bobcat Enterprises, Inc. v. Duwell, 35
Boyd v. Harding Academy of Memphis, Inc., 318
Brennan v. National Telephone Directory Corp., 135
Brooklyn Savings Bank v. O'Neill, 513
Brown v. Board of Education of Topeka, 161
Bruhn v. Foley, 74
Budget Rent-A-Car Corporation v. Fein, 34
Bunce v. Parkside Lodge of Columbus, 52, 306
Burns v. McGregor Electronic Industries, Inc., 276

California Federal S&L Assn. v. Guerra, 310
Canada v. Boyd Group, Inc., 273
Carl v. Angelone, 268
Caroll v. Talman Fed. S&L, 271
Car Parts Distribution Ctr. v. Auto Wholesaler's Assoc., 457
Carr v. F.W. Woolworth Co., 233
Carreno v. Local Union, 354
Carter v. Caring for the Homeless of Peekskill, 279
Carter v. South Central Bell, 83
Casserly v. State, 508
Central Adjustment Bureau, Inc. v. Ingram, 15
Chalk v. U.S. District Court, 456
Chambers v. Omaha Girls Club, Inc., 320
Chance v. Rice University, 263
Chaney v. Southern Ry. Co., 245
Chaudmuri v. State of Tennessee, 245, 372
Chavero v. Local, 177
Claflin v. Leinheim, 53
Cleghorn v. Hess, 89
Clinchfield Coal Co. v. U.S. Dept. of Labor, 533
Clowes v. Allegheny Valley Hosp., 150
C.M.C. v. A.P.F., 104
Collum v. Argo, 44
Comm. of IRS v. Keystone Industries, 567
Concrete Pipe, Inc. v. Construction Laborers, 572
Conroy v. Anchor Savings Bank, 412
Consolidation Coal Co. v. U.S. Dept. of Labor, 533
Cook v. Chrysler, 356
Corning Glass Works v. Brennan, 271
Coventry v. United States Steel Corp., 426
Cronan v. New England Telephone, 450
Cruz v. Ecolab, 390
Cumpiano v. Banco Santander Puerto Rico, 289
Cuyamoga Valley R.R. Co. v. United Transp. Union, 533

Dallas Fire Fighters v. City of Dallas, 77
Darrell N. Williamson v. A.G. Edwards and Sons, 352
Davis Supermarkets, Inc. v. N.L.R.B., 474
Deaver v. Texas Commerce Bank, 423
Decker, Berta and Co. Ltd. v. Berta, 14
De La Cruz v. N.Y.C. Human Resources Dept., 231
de Parrie v. State, 340
Dept. of Fair Employment and Housing v. Raytheon Co., 452
Dept. of Health & Human Services v. FLRA, 491
Doe, Esq. v. Kohn, Nast & Graft, P.C., 457
Doerter v. Bluffton College, 270
Dombeck v. Milwaukee Valve Co., 304

E.E.O.C. v. ARAMCO, 382
E.E.O.C. v. Borden's Inc., 426
E.E.O.C. v. Ilona of Hungary, Inc., 358
E.E.O.C. v. Local 350 Plumbers, 399
E.E.O.C. v. Lutheran Family Services, 308

Ellis v. Railway Clerks, 479
Employment Div. Dept. of Human Res. of Ore. v. Smith, 372
Equality Foundation v. City of Cincinnati, 338
Espinoza v. Farah Manufacturing Co., 385
Euclid Candy of N.Y. v. Summa, 477
Eyerman v. Mary Kay Cosmetics, Inc., 4, 11
Ezold v. Wolf, Block, Schorr, and Solis-Cohen, 251

Falczynski v. Amoco Oil Co., 386
Farmer v. Heard, 540
Finch v. Hercules, Inc., 137
Flynn v. Gold Kist, Inc., 53
Fort Halifax Packing Co. v. Coyne, 581
Fortune v. National Cash Register, 11
Fox v. Sierra Development Co., 354
Frazier v. Garrison, 85
Frederick v. Dept. of Justice, 122
Frey v. State of Cal., 417
Fullilove v. Klutznick, Sec. of Commerce, 223

Gade, Dir. Ill. EPA v. Nat'l Solid Wastes Mgt. Assoc., 528
Gaither v. Anne Arundel County, 433
Garcia v. San Antonio Metro Transit Auth., 511
Garcia v. Spun Steak Co., 391
Garner v. Arvin Industries, Inc., 419
Garrison v. Dept. of Justice, 96
Gary v. Washington Metro Transit Auth., 153
Gawel v. Two Plus Two, Inc., 92
General Electric Co. v. Gilbert, 333
Gilmer v. Interstate/Johnson Lane Corp., 407, 426
Glover v. Nebraska Comm. Office of Retardation, 457
Golden State Transit Corp. v. City of Los Angeles, 478
Gonzalez v. Dept. of Army, 222
Green v. Walker, 103
Griggs v. Duke Power Co., 168
Gross v. Burggraf Construction Co., 292
Grote v. Meyer Land and Cattle Co., 52, 557

Haley v. Pataki, 151
Hampton v. Rubicon Chemicals, Inc., 46
Hanan v. Corning Glass Works, 34
Handicapped Children's Education Board v. Lukaszewski, 11
Hanlon v. Harrolds, 86
Hannon v. Chater, 215
Hansen v. Dean Witter Reynolds, Inc., 291, 324
Harris v. Forklift Systems, Inc., 306
Harris v. Johnson, 35
Harris v. Saif, 556
Harriston v. Chicago Tribune Co., 240
Hastings v. Saiki, 252
Hayes v. Equine Equities, Inc., 29
Hazen Paper Company v. Walter F. Biggins, 395, 564
Helm v. California, 425
Henley v. Prince George's County, 80
Hennessy v. Commonwealth Edison Co., 41
Hickman Datsun, Inc. v. Foster, 155
Highlands Cty. Schools v. Savage, 545
Hodgson v. Approved Personnel Serv., 63
Hoffman La Roche, Inc. v. Campbell, 155
Holloway v. Arthur Andersen & Co., 354
Hong v. Children's Memorial Hosp., 375
Howard v. Wolff Broadcasting Corp., 140
Hudgins v. Bacon, 52
Huffman v. Ace Elec. Co., Inc., 551
Huisgenga v. Opus Corp., 434

Ingersoll-Rand Co. v. McClendon, 562
Inter-Community Ctr. for Justice v. INS, 391
ISS Intern Services v. Human Rights Comm., 390
In Re Ellis, 34

James v. Ranch Mart Hardware, Inc., 342
Jantz v. Muci, 347
Jean v. Walgreen Co., 379
Jensen v. Eveleth Taconite Co., 306
Jessee v. Amoco Oil Co., 39
Jiminez v. Mary Washington College, 229
Johnson v. Boeing Airplane Co., 127
Jones v. Pepsi Cola Bottling Co., 489
Jones v. UNISYS Corp., 139, 410

Kampen v. Dept. of Transportation, 51
Katz v. United States, 127
Kelley v. Vaughn, 351
Kelsay v. Milwaukee Area Tech. College, 220
Kern v. Kollsman, 421
King v. Board of Regents of Wisconsin, 271
Kunze v. Columbus Police Dept., 556

Lance Roof Inspection Service v. Hardin, 35
Lattanzio v. Security Nat. Bank, 163
Lawson v. Dept. of Health and Hospitals, 202
Leckelt v. Bd. of Commissioners, 457
Lefevre v. Sec. Dept. of Veterans Affairs, 554
Le Gault v. Arrusso, 83
LeGrand v. Trustees of Univ. of Arkansas, 83
Lehnert v. Ferris Faculty Assoc., 485
Lemnitzer v. Philippine Airlines, Inc., 390
Lenzer v. Flaherty, 128
Litton Financial Printing Div. v. N.L.R.B., 494
Livadas v. Bradshaw, Cal. Labor Commissioner, 492
Local Joint Exec. Bd. of Local 226 v. Royal Ctr., 497
Local 144 Nursing Home Pension Fund v. Demisay, 578
Lockhart v. Louisiana-Pacific Corp., 344
Lord v. Kerr-McGee Coal Corp., 300
Lorentz v. Coblentz, 11
Lundberg v. Church Farm, Inc., 6
Lysak v. Seiler Corp., 325

Mackey v. Lanier Collection Agency, 581
Madison Square Garden Corp. v. Carnera, 26
Mancusi v. DeForte, 127
Manuel Tovar v. Community Memorial Hospital, 34
Marie v. City of New Orleans, 507
Martin v. Ryder Distrib. Resources, Inc., 397
Martin, Sec. of Labor v. OSHRC, 520
Martino v. Michigan Window Cleaning Co., 513
Matter of Hens v. Colucci, 82
McAlester v. United Air Lines, Inc., 245
McCann v. Texas City Refining, Inc., 416
McDonald v. Santa Fe Trail Transp. Co., 245
McDonnell Douglas Corp. v. Green, 166

McGann v. H&H Music Co., 581
McMillan v. Mass. Soc. of Cruelty to Animals, 262, 271
Meeks v. Opp. Cotton Mills, Inc., 155
Meiri v. Dacon, 372
Merrill v. Southern Methodist Univ., 257
Mertens v. Hewitt Associates, 570
Milwaukee Brewery Workers Pension v. Schlitz Co., 575
Mochelle v. J. Walker, Inc., 145, 177
Mooney v. Aramco Services Co., 402
Moreau v. Klevenhagen, 504
Morgan v. Hustler Magazine, Inc., 113
Mowat v. Transportation Unlimited, Inc., 430
MTD Products, Inc. v. Robatin, 557
Munchak v. Cunningham, 34

NAACP v. Button, 497
NAAS v. Westinghouse Elec. Corp., 425
Nash v. Fla. Industrial Comm., 478
National League of Cities v. Usery, 513
National Solid Wastes Mgt. Assoc. v. Killian, 533
Nationwide Ins. Co. v. Darden, 559
Newport News Shipbuilding & Dry Dock Co. v. E.E.O.C., 332, 333
N.Y.C. Transit v. State Exec. Dept., 372
New York Times v. Sullivan, 112
N.L.R.B. v. Town & Country Electric, Inc., 472

O'Connor v. Ortega, 117
Ode v. Omtvedt, 404
O'Donnell v. Burlington Coat Factory, 266
Oswalt v. Sara Lee Corp., 438

Paegle v. Dept. of Interior, 438
Palsgraf v. Long Island Railroad Co., 49
Parsons v. Nationwide Mutual Ins. Co., 286
Pauley v. Bethenergy Mines, Inc., 523
Pearlstein v. Staten Island Univ. Hosp., 322
Phillips v. Martin Marrietta Corp., 333
Pierce v. Montgomery Cty. Opportunity Bd., 144
Piersall v. Sportsvision of Chicago, 110
Plouffe v. Burlington Northern, Inc., 9
P.M. Palumbo, Jr., Inc. v. Bennett, 35
Power Equipment v. First Alabama Bank, 52

Radtke v. Everett, 297
Railway Clerks v. Allen, 497
Railway Employees v. Hanson, 479
Respect Inc. v. Committee on the Status of Women, 21
Richardson v. Hotel Corp. of America, 66
Roberts v. U.S. Fidelity and Guaranty Co., 50
Robinson v. Central Brass Mfg. Co., 469
Robinson v. New Jersey, 497
Rosenberg v. Equitable Life Assurance, 52, 104
Rudolph v. Hechinger Co., 315
Rutan v. Republican Party of Ill., 148

Saari v. Smith Barney, 93
Sanchez v. Philip Morris, Inc., 377
School Board of Nassau Cty., Fla. v. Arline, 454
Seaman v. Arvida Realty Co., 581
Sedalia School Dist. v. Com'n on Human Rights, 369
Sheffield v. State of N.Y. Education Dept., 37
Shoenthal v. Bernstein, 53
Showalter v. Allison Reed Group, Inc., 282
Shuttleworth v. Broward County Office, 449
Sims v. Montgomery County Com'n, 243
Sinclair v. Long Island R.R., 531
Sitgraves v. Allied Signal, Inc., 83
Skidmore v. Swift Co., 513
Skinner v. Railway Labor Exec. Assoc., 103
Slagle v. White Castle Systems, Inc., 543
Soderberg v. Gem, 53
Sorenson v. City of Aurora, 248
*Soroka v. Dayton Hudson Corp.,*104
Sparks v. Regional Medical Ctr. Bd., 52, 306
Spence v. Webster Parish School Bd., 53, 155
State v. Century Camera Inc., 90
Steiner v. Showboat Operating Co., 306
Stetson v. NYNEX Services Co., 413
Stinnett v. Buchele, 533
Stock v. Universal Foods Corp., 216
Stoller v. Citizens' Civil Affairs Committee, 476
Stukey v. U.S. Air Force, 58

Taylor v. Kennedy, 557
Tee v. Albertsons, Inc., 546
Texas World Service Co. v. N.L.R.B., 177
Thomas v. Korvette, Inc., 127
Thompson v. Price Broadcasting Co., 236
Torcaso v. Watkins, 479
Trans World Airlines v. Hardison, 372
Tuttle v. Buck, 127
Tyson v. L'Eggs Products, Inc., 111

UAW v. Johnson Controls, Inc., 328, 527
Ulrich v. Exxon Co. U.S.A., 69
U.S. v. Bd. of Educ. of H.S. Dist., 312
United Steelworkers of America v. Weber, 206
University of California Regents v. Bakke, 212
U3S Corp. of America v. Parker, 35

Valentine v. Smith, 222
Vandeventer v. Wabash Nat. Corp., 278
Vernonia School Dist. 475 v. Acton, 99
Vetter v. Farmland Industries, Inc., 366
Vokes v. Arthur Murray, Inc., 30

West v. Marion Merrell Dow, Inc. 255
Wetherall Bros. Co. v. U.S. Steel Corp., 34
Wetzel v. Rixse, 34
Wilson v. Bailey, 245
Wilson v. U.S. West Communications, 364
Wood v. C.G. Studios, Inc., 341
Wood v. Omaha School Dist., 436
Wygant v. Jackson Board of Ed., 223
Wytrwal v. Mowles, 120

Zelewski v. American Fed. Sav. Bank, 250
Zep Mfg. Co. v. Harthcock, 35
Zervas v. District of Columbia, 239
Zimmerman v. North American Signal Co., 177

Subject Index

Affirmative Action, 201–27
Advertisements, 204–10
Career counseling, 210
Civil Service Commission, 209
Commitment of management, 210
Defined, 201
Equal Employment Opportunity Act, 208
Gender neutral language, 211
Guidelines for private sectors, 210
History, 208
Job descriptions, 210
Origins, 203
Plan, 205, 211
Quotas, 205
Recruitment, 210
Reverse discrimination, 211–12
Skills utilization surveys, 209
Title VII violators, 204
Training programs, 209
Uniform guidelines on employment selection procedures, 203
accuracy, 225
adverse impact, 223
bottom line, 224
compliance, 226
cut off scores, 225
definitions, 225–26
documentation, 224–25
options, 223
standards, 224
Voluntary actions, 205
Age Discrimination, 394–428
Age Discrimination In Employment Act, 394, 426–28
limitation, 427
prohibition, 426
purpose, 426
statute, 426–28
Back pay, 401
Comparative treatment of elderly, 420–21
Damages, 401
Downsize, 409–11, 419–20
Early retirement, 413–15
E.E.O.C., 401
Justification, 409
Layoffs, 409–11
Limitation, 427
Mandatory retirement, 394, 398
Minimum age, 398
Protected class, 394, 398
Reinstatement, 401
Requirements, 396
Retirement packages, 409
Statute of Limitations, 401
Age Discrimination in Employment Act, 394, 426–28
Limitation, 427
Prohibition, 426
Purpose, 426
Statute, 426–28
Agency, 3–4
Agents, 3
Employees, 3
Independent contractors, 3–4
Principals, 3
AIDS Discrimination, 446–60
American Council on Life Insurance, 448
Center for Disease Control, 446, 448
Company policy, 455
Contagious diseases, 453–55
Defined, 447
Disclosure, 446–47
Educational program, 446
Insurance, 448
Invasion of privacy, 450
Model AIDS policy, 455–56
Preventative planning, 447–48
Privacy, 447
Protection, 448
Rehabilitation Act, 454–58
definitions, 458
federal contracts, 458
statute, 458
Sources of AIDS, 447
Testing for AIDS, 448
Alcohol use, 444
American's with Disabilities Act, 429, 439–45
Alcohol use, 444
Defenses, 443
Definitions, 441
Discrimination, 441
Drug use, 444
Enforcement, 445
Findings, 439
Medical examinations, 442
Notification, 445
Posting notices, 445
Purpose, 439
Regulations, 445
Statute, 439–45
At Will Employment, 137–42, 144

Benefits, 558–84
Eligibility, 559
Plans, 558–59, 569, 572
Retirement, 558–84
Vesting, 561–64

Civil Rights, 161–200
Act of 1964, 162–72, 175–76, 178–96
Act of 1991, 173–74, 196–200
Advancement of woman and minorities, 199
Advertising, 175, 184
Bona fide occupational qualification, 174
Burden of proof, 182
Business necessity, 173
Compensatory damages, 173, 197
Damages, 173, 196–97
Defined, 162
Discrimination, 162
Disparate impact, 168–171
requirements, 168–71
Disparate treatment, 166–68
requirements, 166–68
EEOC, 171–73, 184–92
affirmative action, 190

civil actions, 191
composition, 171, 184
creation, 171, 184
filing complaint, 171
injunction, 190
powers, 171, 185
statute of limitations, 171
time for filing complaint, 172
EEO Coordinating Council, 194
Effect on state laws, 192
Eighty percent rule, 170–71
Employer, 165
defined, 165
exemptions, 165
Enforcement, 187
Equal opportunity plan, 173
Equal rights, 161
Exemptions, 174–75, 181
BFOQ, 174, 181
communists, 174, 181
drug addicts, 174
location of employment, 175
merit, 175, 181
seniority, 175, 181
quality, 175
quantity, 175
Fourteenth Amendment, 161
Glass Ceiling Act, 198–200
Glass Ceiling Commission, 173–74, 199–200
advancement of minorities, 199–200
Impact, 175–76
Investigation, 171–72, 192–94
Interstate commerce, 162
Penalties, 194
Posting of notices, 194
Protected class, 166
Punitive damages, 173, 197
Record keeping, 171–72
Retaliation, 171
Statutes, 178–200
Test scores, 183
Title VII, 162, 171
violation, 171
Civil Rights Act of 1964, 162–72, 175–76, 178–96
Civil actions, 191
Conduct of hearings, 194
Definitions, 178
EEOC, 184
powers, 185
EEO Coordinating Council, 194
Effect on state laws, 192
Enforcement, 187
Federal employment, 194
Investigations, 192
Penalties, 194
Posting of notices, 194
Religious employment, 179–80
Unlawful practices, 180
Civil Rights Act of 1991, 196–200
Compensatory damages, 197
Damages, 196–97
Glass Ceiling Act, 198–200
Punitive damages, 197
Clayton Act, 465, 467, 479–80
Statute, 479–80
Collective Bargaining, 484–500
Agreement, 484
Defined, 484
National Labor Relations Act, 497
elections, 499
employees rights, 498
policies, 497
representatives, 499
unfair labor practices, 498
National Labor Relations Board, 498
Negotiation process, 484
Purpose, 492
Terms, 484
Unlawful, practices, 494, 498
Color Discrimination, 241–42
Defined, 241
Constitutional Amendments,
1st, 355, 369, 371, 373
4th, 95–97, 117–19, 128
5th, 242
14th, 242–43, 246
15th, 246
Constructive Discharge, 149–54, 240–41

Defamation, 109–10
Libel, 109
Malice, 110
Slander, 109
Truth, 110
Disability Discrimination, 429–45
Accessibility, 429
Accommodations, 429–34
Americans with Disabilities Act, 429, 439–45
alcohol use, 444
defenses, 443
definition, 440
discrimination, 441
drug use, 444
enforcement, 445
findings, 439
medical examinations, 442
notifications, 445
posting notices, 445
purpose, 439
regulations, 445
statute, 439–45
Categories, 429
disease, 429
mental, 429
physical, 429
sensory, 429
Future for disabled workers, 436
Major life activities, 429
Qualifications, 430
Questioning, 434–36
Discharge, 134, 142–54
Constructive, 149–54
Retaliatory, 147–49
Wrongful, 134, 142–47
Discrimination, 159–458
Age, 394–428
AIDS, 446–58
Civil Rights, 161–200
Color, 241
Disability, 429–45
Equal Opportunity Employment Commission, 171–72
Gender, 247–345
National origin, 374–93
Pregnancy, 317–32
Promotion, 73–81
Racial, 228–46
Racial harassment, 239–40
Religious, 355–73
Retaliation, 147–53
Reverse, 211–20
Selection, 57–83
Sex, 247–71
Sexual harassment, 272–306
Sexual orientation, 337–54
Title VII, 161–200
Drug Free Workplace Act, 98
Drug testing, 95–103
Drug use, 444

Electronic Communications Act, 108
Employee Polygraph Protection Act, 91, 104–6
Statutes, 104–6
Employment
At will, 137–42, 144
Authority, 4–6
actual, 4–5
apparent, 5–6
express, 4
implied, 5
Capacity to contract, 12, 16
Contract, 4, 12–35
agreement, 12
assignment, 22–23
breach, 23–24
capacity, 12, 16
compensatory damages, 27
conditions, 31
consideration, 12, 16–17
damages, 27–28
death, 13, 16
defenses, 28–33
duties, 19, 28
form, 17–22
fraud, 28–30
freedom to contract, 19

Employment, contract (*continued*)
impossibility, 32
incompetency, 13
injunction, 25–26
lawful purpose, 12–13
misrepresentation, 28–30
mistake, 32–33
mitigate damages, 28
prior legal obligation, 16–17
promise to perform, 12, 16
promissory estoppel, 17
proper application of laws, 20
punitive damages, 27–28
release, 32
remedies, 24–28
rescission, 27
restitution, 27
restrictive covenants, 13–15, 21
rights, 19
specific performance, 25–26
statute of frauds, 17
validity, 19
writing requirement, 12, 17–22
Creation of, 4
verbal, 4
written, 4
Discrimination, 159–458
Duties, 6–10, 28
accounting, 8
compensation, 8–9
employees, 6–8
employers, 8–10
good faith, 7–8
independent contractors, 6–8
loyalty, 6–7
maintenance of work area, 9–10
mitigate damages, 28
Employees, 4–8, 36–38
authority, 4–6
duties, 6–8
liability, 36–38
Employers, 8–10, 38–51
duties, 8–10
liability, 36–38
Independent contractors, 6–8, 36–38
duties, 6–8
liability, 36–38
Liability, 36–53
contractual, 38–39
employees, 36–38
employers, 38–51
independent contractors, 36–38
negligence, 44–45, 49–50
third parties, 50–51
tort, 40–45
Promotions, 73–81
Ratification, 45, 49
Recruitment, 57
Retirement, 558–84
Selection, 57
Theft, 114–19
company policy, 119
conversion, 114–15
fourth amendment, 116
padded payroll, 115
searches, 117–19
security, 117
surveillance, 116–17
time, 115–16
Third parties liability, 50–51
Whistle-blower Protection Act, 129
corrective action, 129
disciplinary action, 129
investigation, 129
Whistle-blowing, 119–29
statute, 129
Writing requirement, 18–20
Employment Retirement Income Security Act, 558, 581–84
Benefit accrual, 583
Coverage, 582
Definitions, 528
Fiduciary duties, 569–71
Findings, 581
Minimum funding requirements, 565, 584
Participation standards, 583
Payment of benefits, 584
Pension Benefit Guarantee Corp., 566
Pension termination insurance, 566
Policy, 581
Purpose, 565
Statute, 581–84
Vesting standards, 583
Equal Employment Opportunity Act, 208–10
Civil Service Commission, 209
Promotions, 203
Selection, 203, 208
Skill utilization survey, 209
Uniform guidelines on employee selection, 203
Equal Employment Opportunity Commission, 171–73, 184–92
Composition, 171, 184
Eighty percent rule, 170–71
Equal Opportunity Plan, 173
Filing a complaint, 171
Investigation, 171–72, 192–94
Record keeping, 171–73
Responsibility, 171
Violations, 171
Equal Pay Act, 261–64

Fair Credit Reporting Act, 108
Fair Labor Standards Act, 501–5, 510–11, 514–15
Child labor, 515
Findings, 514
Maximum hours, 515
Minimum wage, 515
Statutes, 514–15
Family and Medical Leave Act, 307, 333–36
Benefits protection, 336
Certification, 335
Definitions, 333
Eligible employee, 333
Employment benefits, 333
Leave requirements, 334
Maintenance of health benefits, 336
Family Leave, 307–17
Adoption, 307, 309
Birth, 307, 309
Certification, 317
Eligibility, 307
Family and Medical Leave Act, 307, 333–36
benefits protection, 336
certification, 335
definitions, 333
eligible employee, 333
employment benefits, 333
leave requirements, 334
maintenance of health benefits, 336
second opinion, 335
Intermittent leave, 317
Maintenance of health benefits, 314
Personal days, 311
Pregnancy, 317
Serious health condition, 307
Sick time, 311
Vacation time, 311
Fetal Protection Policies, 321–22, 328–32
Fifteenth Amendment, 246
Fifth Amendment, 242
Files, Right to View, 107
First Amendment, 359, 369, 371, 373
Fourteenth Amendment, 161, 242–43
Fourth Amendment, 95–97, 116–19, 128
Freedom of Information Act, 107

Gender Corrective Surgery, 341–42
Glass Ceiling Act, 173–74, 198–200
Statute, 198–200
Glass Ceiling Commission, 173–74, 199–200
Grooming, 265, 344–45

Hostile Work Environment, 291–96

Immigration Act, 380
Immigration Reform and Control Act, 374, 380–84, 391–93
  Aliens, 391
  Application, 380
  Documentation, 380, 392
  Legal immigration status, 380
  Statute, 391–93
  Unfair immigration, 393
  Unlawful employment, 393
  Verification, 381
Investigations, 68–71, 171–72, 192–94

Labor Law, 461–83
  AFL, 464–66
  Arbitration, 467
  CIO, 466
  Clayton Act, 465, 467, 479–80
    restraining order, 479
    statute, 479–80
  Collective bargaining, 466
  Federal Anti-Injunctive Act, 468, 480
  Federation of Organized Trades, 465
  GATT, 468
  History, 461–64
  Knights of Labor, 463–65
  Labor dispute, 482
  NAFTA, 468
  National Labor Relations Act, 464–65, 497–500
    employee rights, 498
    findings, 497–98
    National Labor Relations Board, 498
    representatives, 499–500
    statutes, 497–500
    unfair labor practices, 498–99
  National Labor Relations Board, 498
  Norris LaGuardia Act, 468, 480–82
    conspiracy, 481
    definitions, 482
    injunction, 480
    public policy, 480
    statute, 480–82
    yellow dog contracts, 480
  Railway Labor Act, 468
  Restraining order, 479–80
  Sherman Act, 465, 467, 483
    statutes, 483
  Socialist Labor Party, 465
  Tammany Hall, 463
  Unfair labor practices, 498–99
  Unions, 462–64, 468
  Wagner Act, 464–65
  Working Woman's Association, 464
  Yellow dog contract, 467–68, 480

Model Employment Termination Act, 143, 156–57
  Agreement, 156
  Awards, 157
  Definitions, 156
  Limitations, 157
  Procedure, 157
  Prohibited termination, 156
  Scope, 156

National Labor Relations Act, 464–65, 497–500
  Employee rights, 498
  Findings, 497–98
  National Labor Relations Board, 498
  Representatives, 499–500
  Statute, 497–500
  Unfair labor practices, 498–99
National Labor Relations Board, 498
National Origin Discrimination, 374–93
  Aliens, 391
  Americans working abroad, 382–84
    for American companies, 382–84
    for foreign companies, 382
  Defined, 374
  Discrimination against, 380
    association, 380
    name, 380
    school, 380
    spouse, 380
  Foreign companies, 382
    employing Americans in U.S., 382
    employing Americans overseas, 382
  Immigration Act, 380
  Immigration Reform and Control Act, 374, 380–84, 391–93
    aliens, 391
    application, 380
    documentation, 380, 392
    legal immigration status, 380
    statute, 391–93
    unlawful employment, 393
    unfair immigration, 393
    verification, 381
  Intent to discriminate, 380
  Kinds of, 380
  National origin of,
    association, 380
    name, 380
    school, 380
    spouse, 380
  Non-citizens, 384
  Requirements, 374
  Unfair immigration, 393
  Unlawful employment, 393
Norris LaGuardia Act, 468, 480–82
  Conspiracy, 481
  Definitions, 482
  Injunction, 480
  Public policy, 480
  Statute, 480–82
  Yellow dog contracts, 480

Occupational Safety and Health, 516–35
  Act, 516–20, 534–35
    statute, 534–35
  Administration, 516–20
  Black Lung Benefits Act, 522–23
  Citations, 518
  Commision, 516, 520–22
  Disability, 519
  Duties, 534
  Employee duties, 534
  Employer
    defenses, 526
    duties, 534
    expenses, 525
  Expenses, 525
  Fatalities, 525
  Federal Register, 525
  Hazard, 526
  Injury, 525
  Inspections, 517–18
  National Institute of, 516
  National Consensus Standard, 518
  National Solid Waste Association, 529
  Notification of hazards, 526, 532
  Partial disability, 522
  Penalties, 518
  Permanent disability, 522
  Permanent standards, 522
  Physical impairment, 522
  Precautions, 517
  Pregnant woman, 526–28
  Safe working environment, 531–32
  Secretary of Labor, 517, 520–22
  Standards, 517–18
  Variance, 517, 526
  Workplace hazards, 526
Occupational Safety and Health Act, 516–20, 534–35
  Commission, 535
  Definitions, 534
  Duties, 534
  Inspections, 535
  Investigations, 535

Occupational Safety and Health Act (*continued*)
- Penalties, 535
- Recordkeeping, 535
- Standards, 534
- Statute, 534–35

Omnibus Crime Control and Safe Streets Act, 108

Pensions, 558–84
- Defined benefit plan, 558, 569, 572
- Defined contribution plan, 558–59, 569, 572
- Eligibility, 559
- Employment Retirement Income Security Act, 558, 581–84
  - benefit accrual, 583
  - coverage, 582
  - definitions, 582
  - findings, 581
  - minimum funding requirements, 565, 584
  - participation standards, 583
  - payment of benefits, 584
  - Pension Benefit Guarantee Corp., 566
  - pension termination insurance, 566
  - policy , 581
  - purpose, 565
  - statute, 581–84
  - vesting standards, 583
- Fiduciary duties, 569–71
- Inflation, 558
- Minimum funding requirements, 565
- Multi-funded pension plan, 572–80
- Pension Benefit Guarantee Corp., 566
- Pension termination insurance, 566
  - maximum limit, 566
- Tax incentives, 580
- Vesting, 561–64

Pregnancy Disability Act, 317

Pregnancy Discrimination, 317–32
- Disclosure of pregnancy, 325–26
- Fetal protection policies, 321–22, 328–32
- Pregnancy Disability Act, 317
- Pre-natal counseling, 332
- Women in the workplace, 317

Privacy, 107–131
- Defamation, 109
- Electronic Communications Act, 108
- Employee Polygraph Protection Act, 91, 104–6
  - definitions, 104
  - exemptions, 105
  - pretest, 106
  - prohibitions, 105
  - rights, 105
- Fair Credit Reporting Act, 108
- Files, 107
- Fourth Amendment, 117–19, 128
- Freedom of Information Act, 107
- Interference with business relations, 112–13
- Invasion of privacy, 111–13
- Omnibus Crime Control and Safe Streets Act, 108
- Polygraph, 88–94
  - act, 91, 104–6
  - administration, 92
  - license, 94
- Privacy Act, 107, 130–31
  - access to records, 131
  - criminal penalties, 131
  - disclosure, 130
  - record keeping, 131
  - statute, 130–31
- Right to view files, 107
- Searches, 117
- Surveillance, 116–17
- Tape recorded conversations, 116
- Testing, 84–106
- Time sheets, 116

Privacy Act, 107, 130–31
- Access to records, 131
- Criminal penalties, 131
- Disclosure, 130
- Record keeping, 131
- Statute, 130–31

Protected Class, 166

Punitive Damages, 173, 197

Quid Pro Quo, 287–89

Quotas, 205

Racial Discrimination, 228–46 (*see also* Civil Rights)
- Burden of proof, 235–39
- Color, 241–42
- Defined, 228
- Disparate treatment, 235–39
- Fourteenth amendment, 242–43
- Harassment, 239–40
- Reconstruction Era Act, 242, 246
- Statute, 246

Racial Harassment, 239–40

Reconstruction Era Act, 242, 246
- Statute, 246

Record keeping, 68–71, 171–72

Religious Discrimination, 355–73
- Accommodation, 356–57, 369–71
- Beliefs, 356, 358–62
- Bona fide occupational qualification, 362
- First amendment, 355, 369, 371, 373
- Government infringement, 355
- Observance, 358–62
- Proximity to religious community, 366–69
- Religious practices, 363–65
  - buttons, 363–65
  - clothing, 363
  - grooming, 363

Retaliation, 233–35

Retaliatory Discharge, 147–49

Retirement (*see* Pensions)

Reverse Discrimination, 211–20

Searches, 117

Selection, 57–83
- Bottom line approach, 72
- Discrimination, 57
- Disparate impact, 68
- Disparate treatment, 68
- Eighty percent rule, 68
- Investigation, 68–71
- Negligent hiring, 79–82
- Nepotism, 76
- Procedures, 66–67
- Process, 62
- Promotion, 73–79
  - criteria, 73
  - from within, 76–79
- Questioning, 72
- Record keeping, 68–71
- Recruitment, 57, 62
- Samples, 72
- Uniform guidelines, 65–68

Sex Discrimination, 247–71 (*see also* Civil Rights)
- Against men, 252
- Against women, 247–51, 254–71
- Bona fide occupational qualification, 247, 260–61, 268–69
- Comparable worth, 264
- Customer preferences, 267–68
- Dress code, 266–67
- Equal pay, 261–64
- Equal Pay Act, 261–64
- Family leave, 307–17
- Gender corrective surgery, 341–42
- Grooming, 265
- Pregnancy, 317–32
- Sex plus, 254–60
- Sexual harassment, 272–306
- Sexual orientation, 337–54
- Stereotypes, 247
- Transsexual, 341–42

Sexual Harassment, 272–306
- After an affair, 279–81
- Against men, 275

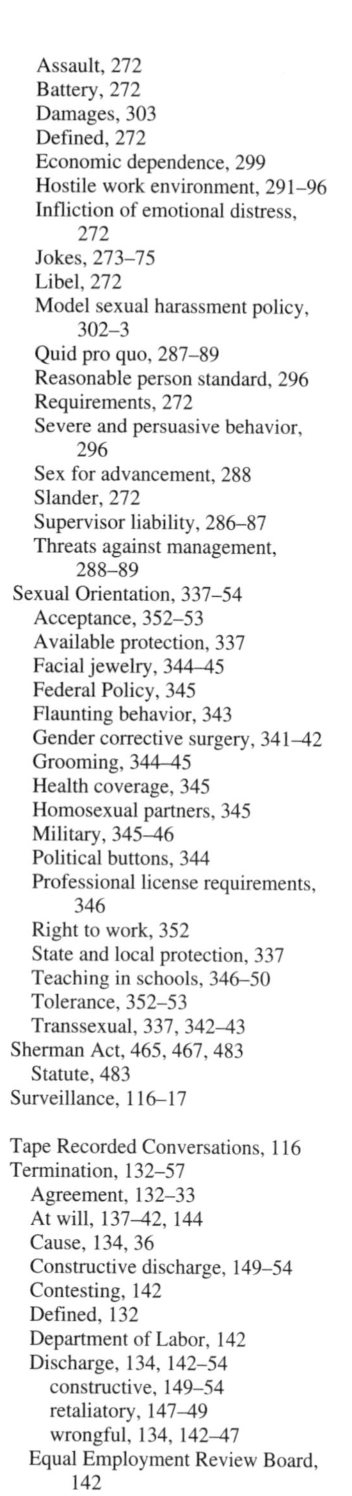

- Assault, 272
- Battery, 272
- Damages, 303
- Defined, 272
- Economic dependence, 299
- Hostile work environment, 291–96
- Infliction of emotional distress, 272
- Jokes, 273–75
- Libel, 272
- Model sexual harassment policy, 302–3
- Quid pro quo, 287–89
- Reasonable person standard, 296
- Requirements, 272
- Severe and persuasive behavior, 296
- Sex for advancement, 288
- Slander, 272
- Supervisor liability, 286–87
- Threats against management, 288–89

Sexual Orientation, 337–54
- Acceptance, 352–53
- Available protection, 337
- Facial jewelry, 344–45
- Federal Policy, 345
- Flaunting behavior, 343
- Gender corrective surgery, 341–42
- Grooming, 344–45
- Health coverage, 345
- Homosexual partners, 345
- Military, 345–46
- Political buttons, 344
- Professional license requirements, 346
- Right to work, 352
- State and local protection, 337
- Teaching in schools, 346–50
- Tolerance, 352–53
- Transsexual, 337, 342–43

Sherman Act, 465, 467, 483
- Statute, 483

Surveillance, 116–17

Tape Recorded Conversations, 116

Termination, 132–57
- Agreement, 132–33
- At will, 137–42, 144
- Cause, 134, 36
- Constructive discharge, 149–54
- Contesting, 142
- Defined, 132
- Department of Labor, 142
- Discharge, 134, 142–54
  - constructive, 149–54
  - retaliatory, 147–49
  - wrongful, 134, 142–47
- Equal Employment Review Board, 142
- For cause, 134–36
- Fulfillment of purpose, 132–34
- Investigation, 142
- Model Employment Termination Act, 143, 156–57
  - agreements, 156
  - awards, 157
  - definitions, 156
  - limitations, 157
  - procedure, 157
  - prohibited terminations, 156
  - scope, 156
- Operation of law, 132, 134
  - bankruptcy, 134
  - death, 134
  - destruction of subject matter, 134
  - insanity, 134
- Political reasons, 144–47
- Retaliatory discharge, 147–49
- Revocation of authority, 132, 134
- Unfulfilled conditions, 134, 134
- Wrongful discharge, 134, 142–47

Tests, 84–106
- Aptitude, 84–6
- Drug, 95–103
  - Drug Free Workplace Act, 98
  - employee acceptance, 103
  - Fourth Amendment, 95–7, 99–102
  - job relatedness, 98
  - lab testing, 98
  - procedure, 103
- Honesty, 88
  - polygraphs, 88–94
  - psychological stress evaluators, 88
  - voice stress analyzers, 88
- Lie detectors, 88
- Polygraph, 88–94
  - administration, 92–4
  - Employee Polygraph Protection Act, 91, 104–6
  - exemptions, 105
  - licensing, 94
  - pretest, 94
  - prohibitions, 105
  - rights, 105
- Psychological, 88
- Residency, 86–88

Theft By Employee, 114–19
- Company policy, 119
- Conversion, 114–15
- Fourth amendment, 116
- Lie detector, 88
- Padded payroll, 115
- Polygraph, 88–94
- Property, 114
- Security, 117
- Surveillance, 116–17

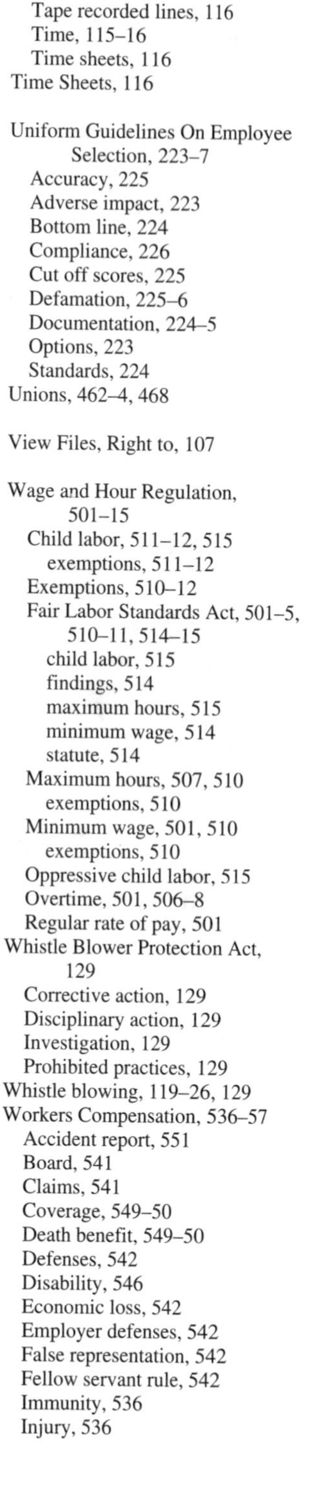

- Tape recorded lines, 116
- Time, 115–16
- Time sheets, 116

Time Sheets, 116

Uniform Guidelines On Employee Selection, 223–7
- Accuracy, 225
- Adverse impact, 223
- Bottom line, 224
- Compliance, 226
- Cut off scores, 225
- Defamation, 225–6
- Documentation, 224–5
- Options, 223
- Standards, 224

Unions, 462–4, 468

View Files, Right to, 107

Wage and Hour Regulation, 501–15
- Child labor, 511–12, 515
  - exemptions, 511–12
- Exemptions, 510–12
- Fair Labor Standards Act, 501–5, 510–11, 514–15
  - child labor, 515
  - findings, 514
  - maximum hours, 515
  - minimum wage, 514
  - statute, 514
- Maximum hours, 507, 510
  - exemptions, 510
- Minimum wage, 501, 510
  - exemptions, 510
- Oppressive child labor, 515
- Overtime, 501, 506–8
- Regular rate of pay, 501

Whistle Blower Protection Act, 129
- Corrective action, 129
- Disciplinary action, 129
- Investigation, 129
- Prohibited practices, 129

Whistle blowing, 119–26, 129

Workers Compensation, 536–57
- Accident report, 551
- Board, 541
- Claims, 541
- Coverage, 549–50
- Death benefit, 549–50
- Defenses, 542
- Disability, 546
- Economic loss, 542
- Employer defenses, 542
- False representation, 542
- Fellow servant rule, 542
- Immunity, 536
- Injury, 536

Workers Compensation (*continued*)
Insurance, 541
Master/Servant, 540
Negligence, 542
No fault insurance, 549
On the job, 544
Origin, 540
Pain and suffering, 551
Permanently disabled, 546–49
Permanently partially disabled, 546–49
Purpose, 536
Reporting a claim, 536
Retaliation, 542
Schedule of benefits, 546
Scope of employment, 544
Skeptical claims, 541
State Workers Compensation Board, 541
Temporary injuries, 546
Working conditions, 542
Workers Compensation Board, 536, 541
Wrongful Discharge, 134, 142–47